Yosef Bronstein

ENGAGING THE ESSENCE

THE TORAH PHILOSOPHY

OF THE

LUBAVITCHER REBBE

Maggid Books

Engaging the Essence
The Torah Philosophy of the Lubavitcher Rebbe

First Edition, 2024

Maggid Books
An imprint of Koren Publishers Jerusalem Ltd.

POB 8531, New Milford, CT 06776-8531, USA
& POB 4044, Jerusalem 9104001, Israel
www.korenpub.com

© Yosef Bronstein, 2024

© Cover photo: Shlomo Vishinsky | Courtesy
Zev Markowitz | All Rights Reserved

The publication of this book was made possible through the generous support of *The Jewish Book Trust*.

All rights reserved. No part of this publication may be reproduced, stored in a retrieval system, or transmitted in any form or by any means, electronic, mechanical, photocopying, or otherwise, without the prior permission of the publisher, except in the case of brief quotations embedded in critical articles or reviews.

ISBN 978-1-59264-550-3, *hardcover*

Printed and bound in the United States

To the Rebbe,
זכותו יגן עלינו

George Rohr
New York City

Contents

Introduction ix
Acknowledgments xv
List of Rebbes of Chabad xxi

Part 1: Setting the Stage
1. Who Was the Lubavitcher Rebbe? 3
2. *Tanya:* The Written Torah of Hasidism 25
3. The Coronation *Maamar* 44

Part 2: The Theology of *Dira BaTahtonim*
4. The Hallway That Is the Palace: The Nature
   of the Material World 71
5. From Sinai to Mitzva Tanks 98
6. The Definition of a Human Being: Body and Soul 120
7. Free Choice and the Disclosure of the Self 149
8. Spreading the Wellsprings 175
9. Talmud Study in the Age of Hasidism 203

Part 3: Aspects of a Godly Life
10. *Hashgaha:* Living with God 233

11. *Bittahon:* Trusting and Jumping.............................. 258

12. *Simha* Breaks Barriers 286

13. Jewish Unity and Love 317

14. Mending the Fragmented Life 350

Part 4: The Demographics of *Dira BaTahtonim*

15. "The Female Will Encircle the Male": The Rise of Women in the Final Generations.................................. 369

16. Between Universalism and Particularism: Non-Jews in the *Dira BaTahtonim* 403

17. The *Nasi* and the People..................................... 456

Part 5: Contemporary Issues

18. The Secularization and Spiritualization of Science........... 507

19. The Land of Israel and the State of Israel 543

Part 6: The True and Complete Redemption

20. "Until When?" The Rebbe's Push for *Mashiah* 585

21. Redemption Is Here?....................................... 616

22. The Rebbe and the *Mashiah* 636

Bibliography of Secondary Literature 665

Introduction

When canons of great Jewish thinkers of the twentieth century are compiled, the Lubavitcher Rebbe is often not on the list. His accomplishments are usually thought of in terms of his innovative initiatives that significantly impacted the face of world Jewry.

However, as Chabad Hasidim always knew and as many academics have come to realize, the notion that the Rebbe's achievements are limited to his social impact is a grave mistake. Rather, the Rebbe rightfully deserves a place in the elite cadre of expositors of a unique and creative Torah philosophy. Moreover, similar to figures such as Rav Kook and Rav Soloveitchik, the Rebbe's philosophy is simultaneously a timeless articulation of Torah and also filled with innovative timely messages geared toward those living in the tumultuous modern world.

This reservoir of intellectual sophistication and potential existential meaning, unfortunately, has largely remained untapped outside of the Chabad community. In many cases, this is simply due to a lack of exposure. But even those who do study the Rebbe's teachings often have difficulty understanding the philosophy as a whole. Instead of writing programmatic and organized monographs, the Rebbe mainly presented his philosophy in individual lectures and essays over the course of the forty years of his leadership. Thus, even after learning a sizable number of *sihot* (literally, "talks") one can still form the mistaken impression that the Rebbe's Torah is a series of intricate, inspirational, but independent ruminations on different aspects of Torah and not appreciate that when integrated they form a total philosophy.

This book seeks to partially remedy the relative obscurity of the Rebbe's philosophy. My goal is to systematically present the key themes of the Rebbe's philosophy in a sophisticated but accessible fashion. For those who are not familiar with the Rebbe's Torah, I hope this book serves as a general introduction. And for those who have studied the Rebbe's Torah, I hope that this book aids in understanding the overall structure of the Rebbe's system of thought.

Methodology

As will be discussed in greater detail in chapter 1, the main body of the Rebbe's voluminous corpus stems from his oral talks and tens of thousands of written letters over the course of his forty years of leadership. Each chapter in this book collates dozens of primary sources to demonstrate a consistent theme that emerges from the teachings as a whole.

Even as each chapter stands on its own as an independent study, the discerning reader will note the recurrence of certain key themes throughout the volume. Ultimately, this book attempts to demonstrate the holistic unity of the Rebbe's thought despite the diverse array of topics and sources that he discussed. Over the course of the book, over one thousand primary sources will be marshaled to demonstrate how each theme of the Rebbe's thought is part of a single but multifaceted project.

While this approach assists in developing an organized broader perspective on the Rebbe's Torah, it inevitably means that much of the Rebbe's textual analysis in individual talks that led to the development of these concepts will be de-emphasized. In effect, I will be focusing on creating a constellation of concepts as opposed to tracking the Rebbe's hermeneutics. I am aware that extracting a concept from its textual web creates a danger of misappropriation and misunderstanding and I tried to carefully militate against such eventualities. The reader, though, should be aware that he or she is not receiving the full picture of any individual talk.

Introduction

A related point that must be noted at the outset is the peril of analyzing the written transcripts of oral lectures. The Rebbe was not an ivory tower philosopher who developed his thought system in the abstract but was constantly communicating to an ever-growing group of living individuals. Scholars of Hasidism have noted the problematics of trying to grasp the full meaning of hasidic Torah when it is translated from a dynamic oral communication between two parties into a static written text. For this reason, I highly encourage the reader of this book to watch recordings of full-length *farbrengens* that are available online to better appreciate the context in which the Rebbe delivered his Torah.

In addition, it is important to state that there was another layer of translation in my understanding and explicating of these talks. Unfortunately, I am not proficient enough in Yiddish to study the Rebbe's Torah in its original language of delivery. Therefore, instead of making use of the original audio recordings of the Rebbe's talks or the majority of the volumes of *Likkutei Sihot* that were first published by the Rebbe in Yiddish, I had to make do with the Hebrew translations of the talks. This is particularly unfortunate due to the Rebbe's meticulous editing of *Likkutei Sihot*. In instances where a precise translation of the original Yiddish was necessary, I consulted with non-Chabad colleagues who are experienced Yiddish-English translators.

Another methodological reservation is that I am not a social scholar or an ethnographer. I have not spent significant time in Crown Heights or interviewed Chabad Hasidim who were close to the Rebbe. This volume is therefore not a study of how the Rebbe's teachings were received and applied by the living and breathing community of Hasidim. Rather, it is a conceptual overview of the teachings themselves.

Beyond the primary sources, my understanding of the Rebbe's philosophy has been much enriched by the two forms of secondary literature: internal Chabad works and academic studies. Each chapter concludes with references to the main secondary sources that I drew from when writing the chapter.

As Elliot Wolfson has noted, the Rebbe can be studied from multiple frames of reference. Already, only twenty-nine years after his passing, the Rebbe's philosophy has been analyzed through the lenses of mystical studies, sociology, and educational theory. While each frame of reference highlights a certain aspect of the Rebbe's thought, I chose to retain the frame that is indigenous to the Rebbe's own talks: the intellectual history of Jewish mystical, philosophical, and halakhic thought. Therefore, most chapters begin with a brief introduction outlining previous Jewish perspectives on the topic at hand which helps highlight the Rebbe's unique contribution.

Continuing with this notion of following the Rebbe's own frame of reference, my goal in this book is to try to objectively and accurately record the Rebbe's teachings without adulation or criticism of the content of his ideas. I do not judge the accuracy of the Rebbe's understanding of talmudic passages, his diagnosis of his generation's needs, or the ethics of specific stances that he took. I tried as much as possible to keep an evenhanded tone regarding the content of the philosophy, preferring to allow the reader to form his or her own perspective.

This is especially true regarding the final chapters of the book which relate directly to the most controversial and sensitive issue discussed in the book: the Rebbe's messianism. My goal was, as much as possible, to present what the Rebbe said and, in some cases also how it was interpreted by leading Chabad Hasidim, in an objective fashion. I do not take the liberty to describe the Rebbe as being prescient or irresponsible, as a courageous leader or a dangerous demagogue. In the final pages of the book, I do make an interpretive suggestion to explain some of the contradictory statements the Rebbe made, but I deliberately avoid a moral judgment. Once again, such evaluations I leave to the reader.

I am familiar enough with modern philosophy and literary theory to realize that a wholly detached and objective viewpoint is impossible. In that vein, let me briefly self-disclose so the reader can be aware of my orientation. I am a proud product of Yeshiva University, beginning as a student in Yeshiva University's high school and currently an instructor of Jewish philosophy in Yeshiva University's Isaac Breuer College of Hebraic Studies. My formal educational training has mainly been in the tomes of the Talmud – traditional *beit midrash* learning under Rabbi Michael Rosensweig and academic talmudic studies under Professor Yaakov Elman *z"l*. I did not grow up with Hasidism and do not self-define as a Hasid.

Introduction

However, I find that many of the ideas of Hasidism, and of the Rebbe in particular, resonate with me deeply, and I have tried to integrate them into my life. Other aspects of Chabad, though, remain foreign to me. My goal in writing was, as much as possible, to hide my personal preferences and present the Rebbe's philosophy on its own terms.

That being said, one motivating factor to write this book was the positive response that I received during my first forays into teaching this material in the Modern Orthodox community. Both in adult education programs and in Yeshiva University classrooms, I saw that many people were intellectually stimulated and, at times, existentially moved by aspects of the Rebbe's Torah. It is my prayer that this book serves as a source of Torah for all and existential meaning for some.

Finally, due to my own limitations and the scope of the project, the discerning reader might find mistakes in the book. While I tried to be careful in my checking and rechecking of the sources, there can be instances where I misunderstood a line in a talk and attributed words to the Rebbe that he never said. If the reader finds such occurrences, please reach out and inform me.

One final note regarding citations and translations. All citations from *Tanya* and primary Chabad sources refer to the standard editions of Kehot Publication Society. Translations of biblical verses are based on the Judaica Press edition, and quotes from *Mishneh Torah* are adapted from the Moznaim editions, both available on Chabad.org. Translations of talmudic passages are adapted from the Koren Talmud Bavli.

Acknowledgments

I always thought that writing a book would be a solitary experience. In truth, however, even as much of the work was done alone, it took a community of collaborators, partners, and supporters to produce the current volume. As such, I would like to acknowledge some of the main members of this community and express a little of the gratitude that they deserve.

My first thank you is to Rabbi Zalman Shmotkin, the director of Chabad.org and spokesperson for the Chabad-Lubavitch movement. How someone who has two more-than-full-time positions still has the time and energy for side projects is beyond me. But I was the beneficiary of his boundless energy and unflappable character. I do not know what drove him to trust a young product of Yeshiva University with a project such as this, but Rabbi Shmotkin was instrumental in securing the resources necessary for the researching and writing of this book. Without his leap of faith in me, this project would not have been launched.

My admiration of Rabbi Shmotkin grew as the project developed. As I began to write chapter drafts, Rabbi Shmotkin became my *havruta*. We spent hundreds of hours discussing the Rebbe's Torah, learning through texts, arguing over their meaning, and debating how to best capture them in English. I was amazed to discover that someone so steeped in the world of organizational work was also a formidable scholar in his own right. The content and presentation of the book is more accurate due to these sessions.

However, as is the way of study partners, we did not always agree. I know that he does not throw his full support behind every sentence or even section of this book. But, more than any other *havruta* that I ever had, I feel that we fulfilled the Talmud's maxim regarding study partners: "They become enemies with each other [due to the intensity of their studies]. But they do not leave there until they love each other." Despite our debates (or perhaps precisely due to them), our friendship grew. I am honored to call this true Hasid of the Rebbe a mentor and a friend.

Early in the process, Rabbi Shmotkin introduced me to Mr. George Rohr. While Mr. Rohr's reputation precedes him, he is among the unique individuals whose sterling public name tells only a fraction of the truth. The more we interacted, the greater his stature grew for me. His generosity, refined character, and partnership were the essential catalysts for me to embark on this project.

In addition to Rabbi Shmotkin himself, I benefited greatly from the editorial comments of several other Chabad scholars. Their insights contributed to the accuracy and clarity of this volume, and I am very grateful to them for the time and energy that they individually and collectively invested into this project.

Rabbi Dovid Olidort is the senior editor of Kehot Publication Society and was a member of the unique group that memorized, transcribed, and edited the Rebbe's talks. His mastery of the entire Chabad corpus is legendary, as is his fine character and critical editorial eye. It was an honor to have Rabbi Olidort review many chapters of the book. His terse but important comments contributed to the accuracy of several key sections.

Rabbi Dr. Eli Rubin is a senior editor at Chabad.org. While he is a generation younger than Rabbi Olidort and did not merit to listen to the Rebbe himself, Rabbi Rubin is nonetheless a respected authority on the philosophy of Chabad. He is esteemed, both within Chabad and in academic circles, for the integration in his writings of the internal discourse of Chabad teachings and the best of academic methodology. The bearer of a hasidic heart, organized mind, and precise pen, Rabbi

Acknowledgments

Rubin's ever-growing collection of books and articles truly illuminates the extensive and at times overwhelming oeuvre of Chabad writings. It was an honor and a pleasure to spend so many hours corresponding over email, phone, and Zoom. Of all content consultants, Rabbi Rubin's insights have most impacted this volume, and I feel truly indebted to him.

Finally, Rabbi Levi Shmotkin was instrumental in helping me think through certain chapters of this volume. His passion for the truth, methodical approach, and impressive command of the relevant material are truly admirable. Several lengthy email correspondences, long phone conversations, and finally several in-person study sessions contributed to more precise formulations in several chapters.

To ensure that the book would be understandable to those who are not already familiar with Chabad ideas and jargon, I sought people who would be willing to read chapter drafts and provide feedback. In this context, I would like to thank Rabbi Marc Eichenbaum, who carefully read through several of the early chapters.

Mostly, though, my gratitude goes to my father, Rabbi Chaim Bronstein. My father read through every chapter with his expert editorial eye and provided invaluable feedback that greatly improved this book's clarity and style. In short, if anyone unfamiliar with Chabad parlance is able to understand this book, it is due to my father. It is needless to say that it was both very meaningful and a pleasure to work with my father, who is the living embodiment of modesty and *mentchlichkeit*.

Much of this book was written in an apartment in Ramat Bet Shemesh that is owned by Mr. and Mrs. Herb and Annette Klaver and is used as an office of Naaleh.com, which is directed by Mrs. Tzippy Klaver. My sincere gratitude goes to the Klavers who literally opened their home for a new *oleh* to Israel lacking a quiet space to work. The room that they provided was the perfect environment in which to sit, study, and write.

I have been privileged to teach aspects of the Lubavitcher Rebbe's thought in several higher education settings. My appreciation goes to the administrations of Yeshiva University, Nishmat, and Michlelet Mevaseret Yerushalayim for trusting me to present this material. But, most of all, my gratitude is extended to those who attended my classes. Their challenging questions and insightful analysis have forced me to revisit texts and rethink ideas.

Engaging the Essence

It was an honor to work together with Koren Publishers on the editing and publishing of this volume. Publisher Matthew Miller gracefully acted as a central organizing force, with a practical and goal-oriented mindset, to see this project through to fruition. Rabbi Reuven Ziegler, editorial director of Koren and Maggid, has been gracious with his time and supportive of the project. Rabbi Dr. Tzvi Hersh Weinreb, the executive vice president emeritus of the OU, in his capacity as Koren's rabbinic advisor, provided counsel and perspective regarding how to structure certain topics to best capture the Rebbe's unique perspective. On the more granular level of editing, working with professional editors the likes of Ita Olesker, Debbie Ismailoff, and Nechama Unterman has been an amazing experience. They had the unenviable task of grappling with a large and unwieldy manuscript. Their attention to every detail while still keeping the global picture in mind was truly unique. Overall, their balance of patience and professionalism greatly enhanced my experience as an author and the quality of this volume.

While my family was less directly involved with the content of this book (with the exception of my father), they have played and play an equally important role in shaping who I am as a person. My parents, Rabbi Chaim and Brenda Bronstein, gave me a home that was warm, protective, and unpressured, but was simultaneously filled with intellectual stimulation and curiosity. My earliest memories include learning sessions with my father and trips to the library with my mother, which nurtured a love for learning and the confidence that with hard work I, too, could accomplish my academic goals. In addition, my parents practice much quiet kindness, the extent of which I did not fully appreciate as a child. Being raised in a home of learning and kindness set the stage for my interest in the Lubavitcher Rebbe.

My Bubby, Mrs. Florence Fleschner *z"l*, was an integral part of my life since childhood. Filled with zest and vitality, she was a constant model for how to take initiative and live every day to its fullest. Her love for and pride in her grandchildren knew no bounds, and I felt her support and confidence in me throughout this process. Unfortunately, she passed away during the final stages of editing this work. I hope and pray that she is looking down now with *naḥat*.

Acknowledgments

Similar to my parents, my in-laws, Rabbi Heshy and Chasida Reichman, are paragons of wisdom and kindness. They embody the Rebbe's idea that one's true self can only emerge through acts of selfless dedication to others. They are living reminders to me and all who know them that scholarship and knowledge must be framed by a life of sensitivity to others: "The Torah begins and ends with acts of kindness."

It sounds trite, but *aharon aharon haviv* is my nuclear family. My children, Talya, Yehuda, Yonatan, and Ella are such blessings and sources of joy. Though they certainly competed with this project in terms of time and attention, I cannot imagine life without them. I am grateful that they are growing up in a home where the "Lubavitcher Rebbe" is a household name.

After fourteen years of marriage I can say with certainty that every aspect of my life is enriched by my wife, Batya, but in the present forum I will highlight an item directly relevant to this volume. The process of writing and editing this book was, overall, an enjoyable and even thrilling experience, but it contained many unexpected twists and turns. Luckily, I am married to a psychologist who was supportive of me and this project every step of the way. In this sense, I wholeheartedly feel that this volume is a joint effort of the two of us.

It is always incumbent upon those of us who merit to live in the Land of Israel to feel and express gratitude to the soldiers and security forces that protect our country from our enemies. This indebtedness has exponentially increased since this cruel war has been thrust upon us on Simhat Torah. May Hashem protect our soldiers, free our captives, and help us gain total victory against those who rise to destroy us.

I conclude with gratitude to *Hashem*, who put all the pieces of this book together. I feel that every step of my journey into studying and writing about the Rebbe's teachings has been guided by providence and geared toward producing the current volume. Ultimately, it is my prayer that this book creates *nahat ruah* for God in this world.

Yosef Bronstein
December 2023 / Tevet 5784

List of Rebbes of Chabad

1745–1812   R. Shneur Zalman of Liadi (The Alter Rebbe)

1773–1827   R. Dovber Schneuri (The Mitteler Rebbe)

1789–1866   R. Menahem Mendel Schneersohn
            (The *Tzemah Tzedek*)

1834–1882   R. Shmuel Schneersohn (The Maharash)

1860–1920   R. Shalom Dovber Schneersohn (The Rashab)

1880–1950   R. Yosef Yitzhak Schneersohn (The Frierdiker Rebbe)

1902–1994   R. Menahem Mendel Schneerson (The Rebbe)

Part 1

Setting the Stage

Chapter 1
Who Was the Lubavitcher Rebbe?

On November 2, 1994, a few months after his passing, the Lubavitcher Rebbe was awarded the Congressional Gold Medal, the highest civilian honor bestowed by the United States Congress. The text of the bill reads as follows:[1]

> The Congress hereby finds the following:
> (1) Rabbi Menachem Mendel Schneerson, the leader of the Lubavitch movement for 40 years, has made outstanding and lasting contributions toward improvements in world education, morality, and acts of charity.
> (2) Rabbi Menachem Mendel Schneerson, as a refugee first from Stalinist Russia and then from Nazi Germany, has made the headquarters of the Chabad-Lubavitch movement in New York City a center of over 2,000 educational, social, and rehabilitative

---
1. www.gpo.gov/fdsys/pkg/BILLS-103hr4497rds/html/BILLS-103hr4497rds.htm.

institutions touching millions of people from all walks of life in every corner of the globe.

(3) Rabbi Menachem Mendel Schneerson, throughout his 92 years of life, has exemplified the highest ideals of scholarship, teaching, ethics, and charity.

(4) Rabbi Menachem Mendel Schneerson has interpreted with keen insight the miraculous events of our time and has inspired people to a renewal of individual values of spirituality, cooperation, and love of learning.

(5) Rabbi Menachem Mendel Schneerson's extraordinary life and work have long been recognized by the Congress through the enactment of joint resolutions designating his birthday in each of the last 16 years as "Education and Sharing Day, U.S.A."

In this ceremony, the Lubavitcher Rebbe achieved a level of national gratitude and recognition merited by only a select few global religious leaders, including Mother Theresa and the Dalai Lama.

This bill is an embodiment of an unlikely life. In 1902, close to a century earlier, no one could have predicted that the little Ukranian-hasidic baby, Menahem Mendel, would revolutionize the Jewish world from his headquarters in Brooklyn, New York, half a world away. And yet, revolutionize he did.

The Rebbe's colossal achievements in the service of world Jewry are well known. Over the course of forty years of leadership (1951–1994) he took a hasidic group that was decimated by the Holocaust and Soviet Communism and shepherded it into one of the most influential movements on the contemporary Jewish scene. From his office in 770 Eastern Parkway, he initiated some of the most successful and innovative programming that the Jewish world has ever seen: a global network of *sheluhim* (emissaries), Chabad Houses, mitzva campaigns, Torah lectures over radio and later satellite television, educational initiatives, and organizations for women, children, the elderly, and the disabled.

In addition, as is evident from his congressional award, he became a national religious figure as public advocate for the integration of biblical values, morality, and spirituality in American society and education.

He corresponded with presidents[2] and was regularly visited by leading politicians and statesmen from all levels of government. His face adorned the cover of an issue of the *New York Times Magazine*[3] and his insight and opinion were often cited in leading news outlets.[4]

His circle of admirers was similarly broad and eclectic. Elie Wiesel and R. Jonathan Sacks refer to private meetings (*yehidut*) with the Rebbe as significantly impacting the course of their lives. Israeli president Zalman Shazar and Prime Minister Menachem Begin closeted themselves with him for hours at a time. Luis Lacelle, president of Uruguay, and Lech Walesa, president of Poland, both carried a dollar received from the Rebbe.[5]

In summary, this was a hasidic man who broke old paradigms. While many Jews in America either isolated themselves from modern society or assimilated into it, the Rebbe charted a unique path. He remained distinctly hasidic, while still engaging the world and trying to change it for the better.

WHAT MOTIVATED THE REBBE?

Care and Concern

What motivated his bold posture and innovative programming? What led the Rebbe to take an insular hasidic group and send them out into the world? In a 1994 eulogy, R. Aharon Lichtenstein, *rosh yeshiva* of Yeshivat Har Etzion and a leading Modern Orthodox thinker, reflected on the Rebbe's achievements:

> The Rebbe's primary quality was caring. Not in the narrow sense of the word, i.e., concern for his own home, movement or *shtibel*, but seeing the big picture. This included the big geographical picture, with a movement with emissaries, men and women, on every continent, as well as the big cultural picture. Not only

---

2. A sampling of these correspondences is available at www.chabad.org/816636.
3. *New York Times Magazine*, March 15, 1992.
4. Samuel Heilman and Menachem Friedman (2010), 204–6.
5. See "The Rebbe and World Leaders," available at www.chabad.org/992475.

in the yeshiva world but in the university world; not only in the religious world but in the secular world, in places from which he should have ostensibly kept his distance. What did he have to do with the IDF? It was his concern that brought this about. He cared enough to see things on a historic and national scale. This is also part of Chabad's admirable tradition – concern for the Kingdom of Heaven in general.[6]

According to R. Lichtenstein, care and concern motivated the Rebbe. He saw Jews losing their way in the world and felt a responsibility to spiritually save them. He saw a general society that was becoming increasingly secularized and wanted to return it to its roots. This sense of care and concern for all aspects of God's world, coupled with tremendous organizational abilities and a willing army of Hasidim to carry out his vision, served as the basis for the Rebbe's grand projects and striking influence.

A Torah Philosophy
While R. Lichtenstein is certainly correct about the centrality of the Rebbe's empathy, his depiction is one facet of the whole picture. In addition to empathy, Chabad's approach and activism in the second half of the twentieth century are also direct applications of the Rebbe's highly sophisticated and nuanced Torah philosophy. While being deeply rooted in classical Chabad teachings, the Rebbe deepened the wells and expanded the frontiers of hasidic thought and developed strikingly innovative formulations and ideas. It was this synthesis of philosophy and passion that served as the substructure of Chabad life in the second half of the twentieth century.

The Rebbe's philosophy is all-encompassing and holistic. There is a single central concept – the nature of God's relationship to the world – which sustains every aspect of theoretical Torah and practical

---

6. For a transcription of the original Hebrew, www.yutorah.org/sidebar/lecturedata/745886/Hesped-for-the-Lubavitcher-Rebbe. The translation above is adapted from www.scribd.com/doc/111005773/Rav-Aharon-Lichtenstein-s-Hesped-for-the-Lubavitcher-Rebbe-English.

life.[7] In the Rebbe's teachings, the *Sheluhim* program was intimately connected with the proper methodology for studying the Talmud's legal passages. His unique brand of hasidic feminism was vivified by the same principles that led him to proactively employ innovative technology in the service of God. Chabad's concern for the general American public was intricately intertwined with his understanding of the relationship between body and soul. And, as he emphasized time and time again, all these ideas and programs were uniquely apt for the sui generis historical moment of the post-World War II world.

THE REBBE'S SCHOLARSHIP
The Rebbe as a Torah Scholar

The Rebbe was first and foremost a towering Torah scholar. While some have questioned the extent of his scholarly prowess,[8] even a cursory glance at the Rebbe's vast output demonstrates an impressive mastery of the entire range of Torah disciplines. Without notes or books, the Rebbe would often speak for hours, weaving together hundreds of sources and citations from a wide array of halakhic, midrashic, philosophical, and mystical texts.[9] In addition, he had complete command of the voluminous corpus of earlier Chabad literature, which included hundreds of extremely dense volumes of hasidic teachings.

In addition to breadth, the Rebbe's teachings also display a methodical, yet stunningly creative mind. The Rebbe would subject each major citation to a rigorous and detailed textual analysis before placing it in conversation with other sources, often across disciplinary lines. This synthesis of micro- and macro-analyses, together with his interdisciplinary approach, frequently led the Rebbe to innovative but well-reasoned readings of many often-used classical texts.

---

7. The fact that the essence of an item permeates its entirety, even to the farthest peripheries, is a central theme in the Rebbe's philosophy. See chapter 8, section "Hasidism and *Mashiah*," and chapter 9, section "The Unifying Essen`zx`ce of Torah."
8. Samuel Heilman and Menachem Friedman (2010), 112–13, 123.
9. For a convincing argument that the Rebbe's charismatic leadership was largely due to his mastery of Torah, see Nehemia Polen (2014): 123–34. For a similar contention, though focusing more on the messages and lessons the Rebbe imparted as opposed to scholarship per se, see Yehiel Harari (2013), 19–21, 176.

As impressive as each talk is on its own, the Rebbe's real genius emerges after widening one's interpretive lens to encompass his entire corpus. Chabad and academic scholars alike have discerned an intricate method to the Rebbe's thought. As noted above, through the multitude of individual teachings he conveyed during his lifetime, the Rebbe presented a systematic philosophy revolving around a single core idea and several supporting themes. Once identified, these principles provide a framework in which to properly understand many of the Rebbe's teachings that might have otherwise appeared to be independent ruminations. A bird's-eye view of the total structure thus aids in understanding and contextualizing any individual talk and, conversely, the individual talks emerge as building blocks of a magnificent edifice.

The Rebbe's Corpus

The primary setting for the Rebbe's scholarly output were his talks at *farbrengens* (hasidic gatherings).[10] Originally roughly a monthly occurrence and then slowly transitioning to a weekly or even more frequent activity, these events featured a traditional hasidic mix of singing, *lehayyims*,[11] and hearing Torah from the Rebbe. Each *farbrengen* had several *sihot* (literally, "talks") that spanned from a few minutes to a few hours. The talks often began with the *parasha* or holiday at hand and moved on to broader topics of Torah, Chabad activities, or current events.

An elite group of Hasidim would transcribe these talks (often from memory, as many *farbrengens* were held on Shabbat or a holiday) and translate them from the original Yiddish into Hebrew. These transcriptions were published as the *Torat Menahem* series, currently reaching 112 volumes (each several hundred pages long), which covers thirty-six years of his talks (5710–5734/1950–1974; 5742–5752/1982–1992). Transcriptions of the remaining years of talks (5735–5741/1974–1981) are

---

10. For the historical development of these *farbrengens*, see Ariel Roth (2017), 158–61.
11. For the restrictions that the Rebbe placed on drinking at a *farbrengen*, see *Torat Menahem* 5723: 2, 351–54. For a comprehensive overview of the Rebbe's repeated emphasis on limiting one's drinking at a *farbrengen* and a discussion about the proper approach to drinking on Purim, see *Kuntres Mashkeh HaMesame'ah: BeInyan Takkanat Shetiyat HaMashkeh* (2003), which collates material from over one hundred distinct occasions when the Rebbe spoke or wrote about this issue.

available in Yiddish under the title *Sihot Kodesh* and are currently being edited and translated into Hebrew. While the transcriptions in the *Torat Menahem* series are important sources, one should be cognizant that they are translations of transcriptions and were mostly unedited by the Rebbe.[12]

Some drafts were presented to the Rebbe for review and editing. The Rebbe reportedly invested many hours in carefully reviewing, editing, and footnoting these transcripts,[13] resulting in the thirty-nine volumes of *Likkutei Sihot*. Each volume contains dozens of tightly organized talks that the Rebbe himself reviewed and sent to be published.

On a less frequent basis, the Rebbe delivered a *maamar*, or an in-depth discourse in Hasidism.[14] These discourses, which often begin with a citation of a *maamar* of one of his predecessors, are the deepest and most esoteric of the Rebbe's talks. As per Chabad tradition, there was a distinct ceremonial aspect to the delivery of a *maamar*. The Rebbe would signal that he wanted to deliver a *maamar* and the Hasidim would sing a preparatory, wordless tune to ready themselves. They would then rise and stand in rapt attention while the Rebbe sat with his eyes closed and spoke in a distinctive melody reserved for such occasions. Historically referred to by the Hasidim as *divrei Elokim hayyim* ("the words of the living God"), it was assumed that the Rebbe delivered a *maamar* from a place of higher consciousness. The Rebbe also edited transcripts of many of these discourses, eventually creating the four volumes of *Sefer HaMaamarim Melukat*.[15]

Another major source of the Rebbe's teachings are his tens of thousands of letters. According to R. Leibel Groner, a member of the Rebbe's secretariat, the Rebbe would receive between 250 and 300 letters

---

12. R. Simon Jacobson describes the history and process of editing and publication of the Rebbe's teachings in an interview available at old2.ih.chabad.info/images/notimage/57211_he_1.pdf.
13. Chaim Miller (2014), 309.
14. According to Chaim Rapoport (2011), 11, the Rebbe delivered 1,558 *maamarim*.
15. For an academic description of the nature of a *maamar* in Chabad history, see Ariel Roth (2017), 68–86. For an internal Chabad description, see "What Is a *Maamar*?" available at www.chabad.org/2905524.

Setting the Stage

a day[16] asking him for blessings, advice, or for clarification of a Torah source, ranging from the simple to the scholarly. In 1987, a group of Hasidim began to gather the Rebbe's responses that contained advice or Torah expositions and published them as the *Iggerot Kodesh* series. This series currently consists of thirty-two volumes, containing 12,226 letters, which span the years 5688–5737/1928–1977. It is also a work in progress.

A conservative estimate of the volume of the Rebbe's talks and letters places his published output at approximately seventy thousand pages. While much of this is routine advice or "lighter" inspirational material, the majority of this corpus are heavily sourced and analytical talks. The sheer volume of this places the Rebbe as one of the greatest generators of published Torah in Jewish history. When one considers that he concurrently headed an ever-growing hasidic movement, personally met with tens of thousands of people from all walks of life, and eventually directed a global network of institutions, this is a truly remarkable feat.

A BIOGRAPHICAL SKETCH

The Early Years

Before launching into the Rebbe's teachings, a brief biographical sketch is in order.[17] On 11 Nisan/April 18, 1902, R. Levi Yitzhak and Chana Schneerson of Nikolayev, Russia, were blessed with their oldest son, Menahem Mendel, named after the baby's great-great-grandfather, the *Tzemah Tzedek*, the third Rebbe of Chabad. (See list of Rebbes of Chabad, p. xxi.) R. Levi Yitzhak, a Hasid of the Rashab (the fifth Rebbe of Chabad), was known for his prodigious mastery of both classical talmudic scholarship (he received rabbinic ordination from R. Hayyim Soloveitchik of Brisk, the famed sage of Lithuanian Jewry) and mystical

---

16. Lecture available at www.torahcafe.com/rabbi-leibel-groner/the-rebbe-cares-for-all-video_873c613b4.html.
17. For more biographical details the reader is encouraged to see any of the biographies listed in the "For Further Research" section. The sketch below is common to all the major biographies and I added references only where a specific fact or statistic would be difficult to locate in the biographies or if it appeared in one biography but not the others.

texts.[18] After living with his father-in-law for several years immersed in his studies, R. Levi Yitzhak and his family moved to Yekatrinoslav, Ukraine, in 1909, where he became the city's rabbi.

Yekatrinoslav was an unusual setting for a hasidic boy to be raised. It was a cosmopolitan city that boasted every type of Jew from hasidic to secular Zionist and socialist. In his role of chief rabbi, R. Levi Yitzhak, while still dressed in traditional hasidic garb, interacted with and won the respect of large swaths of the diverse population. Thus, Menahem Mendel grew up in a home that was distinctly hasidic and yet welcoming to people of all walks of life and ideologies. In fact, the Schneersons' cousins the Shlonskys, who were also both neighbors and good friends, were Zionists and not as observant of halakha. The two families had an open-door policy, and the Schneerson and Shlonsky children and adults were often in each other's homes.[19]

From a young age, Menahem Mendel was known to be introverted, pensive, studious, and blessed with a prodigious intellect. During the tumultuous first part of the twentieth century, which included World War I and the Bolshevik Revolution, Menahem Mendel spent most of his time in private study. His main interests were the traditional topics for a young Hasid – Talmud and Hasidism. He began these studies with his father, transitioned to a small *heder*, but by the time he was a teenager he was mostly studying on his own. In addition, he was interested in mathematics and science, and during his teenage years R. Levi Yitzhak and Hana hired Yisrael Idelson (later Bar-Yehuda), a secular Zionist and later a member of the Israeli Knesset, to be his tutor.[20]

Despite this preoccupation with study and his inner thoughts,[21] there are accounts of Menahem Mendel assisting his father with

---

18. See *Likkutei Sihot* 9, 20 Av, *se'if* 1, where the Rebbe recounted this story.
19. For an extensive documentary survey of the relationship between the Schneerson and Shlonksy families, see Boruch Oberlander and Elkanah Shmotkin (2016), 71–73.
20. Samuel Heilman and Menachem Friedman (2010), 72; Chaim Miller (2014), 18.
21. In a letter to his father-in-law from 1930, Menahem Mendel wrote about himself that although he does not see it as a virtue, he was a person "for whom the central, overwhelming focus of their lives is in the world of thought...focused inwards" and not "the outside world surrounding them" (*Iggerot Kodesh Admor Moharaayatz* 15, 78; translation from Chaim Miller [2014], 99).

communal affairs from time to time. Most notably, as R. Levi Yitzhak's oldest son who was fluent in Russian, he was interrogated several times in his teenage years by the Yevsektsiya (the Jewish section of the Communist Party) about his father's activities. As was their wont, his interrogators ridiculed him, screamed at him, and threatened to send him to Siberia. Menahem Mendel managed to answer their questions satisfactorily, and, for the time being, R. Levi Yitzhak avoided prosecution by the atheist Communist regime.[22]

The Schneersons had two other children: Berel and Leibel. Leibel was Menahem Mendel's peer intellectually but had a very different personality. Precocious, loud, and gregarious, Leibel often challenged his teachers and joined the adults in conversations about Torah, science, or the politics of the day. He and Menahem Mendel were constant childhood companions. Berel, on the other hand, developed a mental disorder and features less in the family history.[23]

Menahem Mendel in the Chabad Court

It is noteworthy that Menahem Mendel's upbringing lacked a direct encounter with a Chabad Rebbe.[24] It was not until 1923, when he was in his early twenties, that Menahem Mendel first met his distant cousin, R. Yosef Yitzhak Schneersohn, the sixth Rebbe of Chabad. Over the

---

22. The Rebbe himself described these incidents in his later talks. See, for example, *Sihot Kodesh* 5739: 3, 566. For a comprehensive survey of the Rebbe's descriptions of his interactions with the Yevsektsiya, see Boruch Oberlander and Elkanah Shmotkin (2016), 109–10.
23. Samuel Heilman and Menachem Friedman (2010), 70.
24. Different theories have been proposed to explain why R. Levi Yitzhak did not send his brilliant children to study in Chabad's central yeshiva, Tomkhei Temimim, as teenagers. Samuel Heilman and Menachem Friedman (2010), 85–86, propose that R. Levi Yitzhak desired that his children would receive a broader education than the traditional one afforded in Tomkhei Temimim. Shaul Deutsch (1995), 134–36, argues that R. Levi Yitzhak, a Hasid of the Rashab (the fifth Rebbe of Chabad), saw himself as an equal and not a subordinate to R. Yosef Yitzhak (the sixth Rebbe of Chabad), and therefore did not see a need to send his son to a yeshiva that was headed by R. Yosef Yitzhak. Nehemia Polen (2014), 128–29, though, simply notes that it was standard at the time for young prodigies of rabbinic families to be educated at home.

course of the next several years, Menahem Mendel would spend significant time with R. Yosef Yitzhak in Leningrad, where he had relocated in 1924. Menahem Mendel had a range of varied yet overlapping activities in Leningrad: experiencing and studying in the Chabad court, university studies, and a courtship leading to engagement with R. Yosef Yitzhak's second daughter, Haya Mushka.

During this period, Menahem Mendel met R. Yosef Rozen, known as the Rogatchover Gaon, who was also living in Leningrad at the time.[25] Their subsequent correspondence displays the young scholar's mastery of the Talmud and its classical commentaries. Menahem Mendel wrote with humility toward the older Torah scholar but nonetheless had enough self-confidence to argue with certain halakhic rulings of the Rogatchover.[26] As we will see, the Rogatchover greatly influenced Menahem Mendel's own path in Torah study.[27]

At this time, R. Yosef Yitzhak was fully immersed in directing an underground Jewish religious network of resistance to the Communist, anti-religious regime. This included an impressive array of Hasidim who, at great personal risk, taught Torah and provided other forms of ritual service in over seven hundred Jewish communities throughout Russia.[28] R. Yosef Yitzhak's leadership and efforts on behalf of the beleaguered Russian Jewish community caught the eye of many international Jewish leaders who were watching the Soviet treatment of Jews with increasing wariness. Soon, the Joint Distribution Committee, an American-Jewish charitable organization, began providing R. Yosef Yitzhak with funds to distribute to Russian Jewish communities and causes.[29] Soviet officials put him under surveillance, and eventually, in the summer of 1927, R. Yosef Yitzhak was arrested by the secret police and sentenced to death.

---

25. Chaim Miller (2014), 41.
26. See, for example, *Iggerot Kodesh* 7, letter 7759. This is a letter from 1925 from Menahem Mendel to the Rogatchover in which Menahem Mendel expresses his great respect for his interlocuter, but, nonetheless, marshals over forty talmudic and halakhic sources to argue against a position that the Rogatchover had taken.
27. See chapter 9, section "The Rogatchover."
28. Chaim Miller (2014), 23.
29. Samuel Heilman and Menachem Friedman (2010), 77–78.

Setting the Stage

In response, a committee of leading Chabad Hasidim, including R. Yosef Yitzhak's son-in-law, R. Shmaryahu Gurary, and future son-in-law, Menahem Mendel, quickly mounted a campaign to pressure Soviet officials to reverse the sentence. Finally, after a month of pressure from the Red Cross, the governments of the United States and several western European countries, and prominent Russian Jews, R. Yosef Yitzhak was released from prison on 12 Tamuz, a date celebrated annually by Chabad Hasidim. A few months later, R. Yosef Yitzhak and his family moved to nearby Latvia, from where he continued assisting Russian Jews. Soon afterward, Menahem Mendel also left Russia to join his future wife and father-in-law in Riga, Latvia.

University Studies

R. Menahem Mendel, however, was not to remain in Riga for long. In the winter of 1927 his life took an unusual turn for a young Hasid and he left eastern Europe for the University of Berlin. He would remain in university settings, funded by R. Yosef Yitzhak, first in Berlin and then, after the Nazis' rise to power, in Paris, for the better part of the next decade. Eventually, in 1938, he received a degree in engineering from ESTP, a Parisian engineering school.[30]

Early in his time at the University of Berlin, R. Menahem Mendel and Haya Mushka married, ending five years of courtship and engagement. Instead of having the wedding in Riga where the Chabad court was at the time, R. Yosef Yitzhak planned a lavish affair in Warsaw, a major Jewish center, and invited Jewish leaders from throughout Europe to join in the celebration. From various accounts it seems that R. Yosef Yitzhak tried to showcase his new son-in-law's brilliance to his scholarly guests, but R. Menahem Mendel evaded these efforts as much as possible.[31] After the week of *sheva berakhot*, the newlyweds moved to an apartment in Berlin, where they lived for the next five years.

30. Ibid., 121; Chaim Miller, (2014), 115.
31. See *Sihot Kodesh* 5731: 2, 43, summarized by Chaim Miller (2014), 79. See there also for Miller's fascinating comparison of R. Yosef Yitzhak's lavish description of the groom as recorded by Mordechai Menashe Laufer (1991), 273, and the abridged and modest version that Menahem Mendel himself recorded in a letter to his father who was not able to be present at the wedding. In a return letter, R. Levi Yitzhak

Who Was the Lubavitcher Rebbe?

What was R. Menahem Mendel's connection to Chabad during this era of his life? The young couple spent significant time in the Chabad court, most notably returning for many of the High Holy Days and other festivals. According to R. Menahem Mendel's diary, R. Yosef Yitzhak used this time to share his private thoughts, nighttime visions, and Torah with his son-in-law.[32] In this diary, R. Menahem Mendel also meticulously noted different aspects of his father-in-law's conduct and customs,[33] as well as anecdotes relayed to him by his father-in-law about earlier Rebbes and Hasidim that had been handed down from his forebears.[34] Importantly, in 1929, R. Yosef Yitzhak was absent for the holiday season and appointed R. Menahem Mendel to lead the congregation in his stead. At least one senior member of the court recorded that the Hasidim were taken with R. Menahem Mendel's intensity, piety, and Torah knowledge.[35]

R. Yosef Yitzhak also entrusted his son-in-law with the editing and publication of his Torah teachings, a matter of prime significance in the Chabad movement,[36] as well as other duties.[37] On a personal level,

---

encouraged his son to elaborate more on R. Yosef Yitzhak's lavish descriptions of his new son-in-law and not hide any of the praise due to a fear of arrogance (*Mikhtevei HaHatuna*, 15). See also Yehiel Harari (2013), 106.

32. Recorded in *Torat Menahem – Reshimat HaYoman*. See, for example, the first entry (pp. 3–4) from 5 Tevet 5689 (1929), where Menahem Mendel records that R. Yosef Yitzhak told him that the Rashab appeared to R. Yosef Yitzhak in a dream and taught him Torah. For more examples, see Chaim Miller (2014), 104–5.
33. See, for example, *Torat Menahem – Reshimat HaYoman*, 343–44, where R. Menahem Mendel details his father-in-law's practices during Elul and Rosh HaShana 5684–5 (1933). For other examples, see Eli Rubin, "Literary Spirit: The Significance of Chassidic Lore."
34. See, for example, *Torat Menahem – Reshimat HaYoman*, 331–32, where R. Menahem Mendel records that his father-in-law told him that the Maharash had a child who was a prodigy and that the *Tzemah Tzedek* possibly referred to this child as containing the soul of the Alter Rebbe.
35. For a summary of these accounts see Chaim Miller (2014), 106; Yehiel Harari (2013), 115–17.
36. See *Iggerot Kodesh Admor Moharaayatz* 3, introduction, 9–12, for evidence that this was part of Menahem Mendel's responsibility in his capacity as an editor of the Chabad journal *HaTamim*.
37. See Telushkin, 464–66. For a description of these activities, see Chaim Miller (2014), 103–6; Adin Even-Israel Steinsaltz (2014), 38–41.

Setting the Stage

R. Menahem Mendel maintained a rigorous regimen of solitary study of Torah in general and Chabad Hasidism in particular, as demonstrated by his complex and intricately source-based entries in his personal journal from that period (later to be published as *Reshimot*). Many of these entries contain the kernels of some of the key themes and ideas that the Rebbe would later develop.[38]

At various points, R. Yosef Yitzhak strongly encouraged his talented son-in-law to take a more active, public role in Jewish service, but as far as we know R. Menahem Mendel mostly refused.[39] One notable exception though is that R. Yosef Yitzhak at times referred people with complicated questions in Talmud and Hasidism to Menahem Mendel who, at times, responded with full treatises.[40] It would seem that at this stage in his life, R. Menahem Mendel's plan was to work as an engineer and continue his practice of solitary Torah study and service.[41]

---

38. For an example, see later on in this book, chapter 6, section "Body and Soul in Exile and Redemption."
39. See *Iggerot Kodesh Admor Moharaayatz* 15, letter 5523, for a letter from R. Yosef Yitzhak to Haya Mushka in which he expresses frustration that her talented husband does not want to enter the public sphere. For more sources and elaboration, see Chaim Miller (2014), 117–18.
40. Two examples of this are: 1) an encyclopedic essay about the placement of the Menora in the *Beit HaMikdash* incorporating halakhic and hasidic texts (published as *Reshimot HaMenora: Seder Hadlakat HaNerot BeVeit HaMikdash*); 2) a letter outlining different approaches to the kabbalistic notion of *Tzimtzum* (published in *Iggerot HaKodesh* 1, letter 11). This letter was a response to a question originally composed by R. Eliyahu Dessler. For the historical background to this letter, see "Pulmus HaTzimtzum bein Gedolei HaMahshava," in *Or VeHiyut* 4 (*Adar* 5776): 16–21, available at toratchabad.com/Content/Images/uploaded/or/or4.pdf.
41. Samuel Heilman and Menachem Friedman (2010), 105–39, suggest that during his years in Berlin and Paris, Menahem Mendel did not lead a hasidic life and even, perhaps, was nominally observant. Their contention was harshly critiqued by Chaim Rapoport (2011), 133–54. While some reviewers such as Yoram Bilu (2011) side with Heilman and Friedman's basic position, many others assert that Rapoport has the upper hand in the argument. For example, Abraham Socher (2010) highlights the fact that Heilman and Friedman's thesis is based on several factual errors, omissions, and a reliance at times on hearsay. Most importantly, Heilman and Friedman do not make use of Menahem Mendel's personal journals which clearly demonstrate that he was fully ensconced in the world of Chabad teachings and service. For a lengthy critical review of Heilman and Rapoport's thesis, see Nehemia Polen (2014).

Coming to America

This quiet life was soon to end. In 1939 Germany invaded Poland, forcing R. Yosef Yitzhak and the family members with him to flee to America. After several months of learning the lay of the land, he established his court at 770 Eastern Parkway in the Crown Heights neighborhood of Brooklyn due to its central location and large Jewish community. Similarly, R. Menahem Mendel and Haya Mushka fled Paris in 1941, just ahead of the Nazi invasion, and eventually made their way to America in that same year, settling as well in Crown Heights, just a few blocks away from R. Yosef Yitzhak. It was here that they began to build the next phase of their lives.

Soon after arriving in America, R. Yosef Yitzhak continued his activism and set out to strengthen American Jewry. He spoke publicly and regularly of World War II as the final birth pangs before the arrival of *Mashiah* and called for a mass return to Torah observance.[42] To this end, he established several new organizations: Mahane Yisrael to encourage the observance of mitzvot, Merkaz LeInyenei Hinnukh to promote educational initiatives such as afternoon Torah classes for Jewish children enrolled in public schools, and Karnei Hod Torah (Kehot), a Jewish publishing house that produces everything from children's stories to sophisticated works of Torah scholarship. R. Menahem Mendel was appointed executive director of all three of these organizations, and also served as Kehot's editor-in-chief. In this capacity, he corresponded with rabbis and community leaders throughout America and across the world, and led a project to publish Chabad texts, some of which had remained in manuscript for 150 years.[43]

In addition, R. Menahem Mendel used his degree and took a job as an electrical engineer at the Brooklyn Navy Yard, working on the electrical wiring of navy warships.[44] At some point he discontinued his work as an engineer and dedicated himself entirely to the wide-ranging

---

42. For more details regarding this depiction of World War II, see chapter 20, section "Positive Phenomena."
43. Chaim Miller (2014), 158–59. For a summary of these activities as they are reflected in the Rebbe's letters during this time period, see *Iggerot Kodesh* 2, introduction, 8–11.
44. Chaim Miller (2014), 144. See ad loc., note 13, for Miller's extensive research into this aspect of the Rebbe's life.

Setting the Stage

work of growing Chabad's central organizations into forces in Jewish life. Under the auspices of Kehot, R. Menahem Mendel published his first original composition – *Haggada im Likkutei Taamim UMinhagim* – a commentary on the Haggada which succinctly summarizes and synthesizes halakhic, liturgical, kabbalistic, and hasidic sources, often adding his own explanations. In addition, R. Menahem Mendel addressed those attending prayers at 770 on a monthly basis.

Becoming the Rebbe

During the 1940s, R. Yosef Yitzhak's health slowly deteriorated until he passed away on Shabbat morning, 10 Shevat 5710 (1950). After searching for and not finding a will, the Hasidim were left with three theoretical candidates: the two sons-in-law and Barukh Dovber Gurary, the twenty-six-year-old son of R. Shmaryahu and Hana Gurary, the only grandchild of R. Yosef Yitzhak. In reality, however, the two middle-aged sons-in-law were the only viable options. While R. Yosef Yitzhak had once expressed hope that his only grandchild would succeed him, Barry, as he was known, was already on his way out of the hasidic world and pursuing graduate studies. Both sons-in-law, though, were known figures in Chabad and had been entrusted with important institutional positions by R. Yosef Yitzhak. As described above, R. Menahem Mendel headed the new organizations that R. Yosef Yitzhak founded in America, while R. Shmaryahu was the executive director of Yeshivat Tomkhei Temimim, Chabad's yeshiva system.

On the day following *shiva*, R. Shmaryahu and R. Menahem Mendel issued a joint letter calling on the Hasidim to rededicate themselves to their deceased Rebbe's teachings and programs. Ambiguity, though, ensued regarding who would become the next Rebbe.

For his part, over the course of the following months, R. Menahem Mendel forcefully and emotionally rejected multiple requests from Hasidim to assume the mantle of leadership. Whenever he spoke in public, he emphasized that the spiritual life of a Rebbe transcends physical life and therefore they were all still Hasidim of his father-in-law.

Eventually, as the year of mourning progressed, it became clear that the majority of Hasidim saw R. Menahem Mendel as R. Yosef Yitzhak's rightful successor. In what he later described as the Hasidim "putting the key into [my] pocket and walking away,"[45] it seemed that R. Menahem Mendel was slowly coming around to the idea of becoming the seventh Rebbe of Chabad. On 10 Shevat 5711 (1951), one year after his father-in-law's death, R. Menahem Mendel spent most of the day immersed in prayer at R. Yosef Yitzhak's graveside. Later that evening, at the *farbrengen* commemorating the first anniversary of R. Yosef Yizhkak's passing, R. Menahem Mendel delivered a *maamar* marking his official acceptance of his position as Rebbe. He held this post until 3 Tamuz 5754 (1994) when he passed away.

AN ALL-CONSUMING ROLE

R. Menahem Mendel's achievements as the Lubavitcher Rebbe are well known and chronicled in great detail elsewhere. What remains relevant for this brief sketch are the major personal events in the Rebbe's life after he assumed the leadership of Chabad. This is not a difficult task as the Rebbe had hardly any relationships or activities outside of his role as the Rebbe.

The Rebbe's Family
The Rebbe's Parents and Siblings

Already at the time of his appointment to the helm of Chabad, the Rebbe did not have many close relatives. R. Levi Yitzhak, the Rebbe's father, was arrested in 1939 and exiled to Kazakhstan where he passed away in 1944, never to see his oldest son's ascendency to the throne of Chabad. The Rebbe's mother, Hana, returned from exile and eventually came to America to live near her son in Crown Heights. Despite his busy schedule, the Rebbe visited her daily and accorded her great honor until she passed away in 1964.

After the passing of his parents, the Rebbe perpetuated their memories through Torah. R. Levi Yitzhak wrote glosses to the Zohar and *Tanya* while in exile and they were later delivered to the Rebbe. For the uninitiated, these glosses are not easy to decipher, and the Rebbe devoted many talks to explaining and expanding on his father's unique

---

45. See Herbert Weiner (1994); this was part of the Rebbe's answer to Herbert Weiner when the latter asked him "How did you become a Rebbe?"

insights. Similarly, when his mother passed away, he launched a new interpretive project focusing on Rashi's commentary on the Torah, to which he devoted a weekly talk for several decades.

As for his siblings: The Rebbe's younger brother Berel, who had remained in Yekatrinoslav, was killed when the Nazis occupied the city. The Rebbe's other brother and childhood companion, Leibel, had first become a socialist and then a Zionist and had left observance as a young man. He was forced to flee Stalinist Russia due to his support of Trotsky and lived for a while with Menahem Mendel and Haya Mushka in Paris. There, Leibel met and fell in love with Regina Milgram, a secular Zionist nurse. He followed her to Tel Aviv in 1935 where they married and led a secular lifestyle. The family later moved to England, where Leibel pursued a degree in science, but he passed away in 1952. The Rebbe arranged for Regina to be employed in a Lubavitch school and kept in contact with their only daughter, Dalya, and later her husband Avner, hosting them and their children during their stays in America.[46]

The Gurarys
After the Rebbe ascended to the helm of Chabad, it was an adjustment for his brother-in-law, R. Shmaryahu, to accept this new reality. However, already by 1953, R. Shmaryahu publicly declared himself to be mystically bound to his brother-in-law as a Hasid to his Rebbe. The Rebbe always treated R. Shmaryahu with respect and accorded him unique honors.[47]

This family reconciliation, however, was not complete. While R. Shmaryahu himself became a loyal Hasid, other members of the family such as Hana, the sixth Rebbe's daughter and R. Shmaryahu's wife, and their son Barry, never recognized the seventh Rebbe of Chabad. For their part, the Rebbe and Haya Mushka never publicly criticized the Gurarys and ate holiday meals together until the passing of Nehama Dina, the wife of R. Yosef Yitzhak.

---

46. Chaim Miller (2014), 312.
47. For a description of these honors and a series of private letters from R. Shmaryahu to the Rebbe in which he relates to his brother-in-law with great deference, see Mendele (5776).

This unresolved tension peaked decades later in a very public court case. R. Yosef Yitzhak had always been very proud and protective of the library he had amassed in Europe, part of which made its way to America and became the centerpiece of the impressive Chabad library in Crown Heights. In 1985, several rare books were discovered missing from the library and a hastily installed surveillance system showed that Barry Gurary, the Rebbe's nephew and R. Yosef Yitzhak's sole grandson, was taking the books. When confronted, Barry argued that R. Yosef Yitzhak was survived by his two daughters, Hana Gurary and Haya Mushka Schneerson, and each one inherited half of the library. Since Barry's mother, Hana Gurary, gave him permission to take books, he was empowered to take up to half of the library's content.

Unable to resolve the issue internally, Agudat Hasidei Chabad, the umbrella Chabad organization, sued Barry in federal court. They contended that R. Yosef Yitzhak procured the library on behalf of Chabad and never intended the books to be his personal property, as a Chabad Rebbe's sole focus is his Hasidim.[48] While the formal court case revolved around ownership of the library, Hana Gurary, the Rebbe's sister-in-law, made it clear during her deposition that she did not recognize her brother-in-law Menahem Mendel as her father's heir. In the end, Judge Charles Slifton decided in favor of Agudat Hasidei Chabad and the books were returned. The breach, however, between the Rebbe and his sister-in-law and nephew was irreparable.

The Rebbetzin

As this sketch demonstrates, for most of his leadership years the Rebbe had few close relations. He was childless, his parents and siblings were no longer among the living, one sister-in-law and niece were secular and out of the country, and his other sister-in-law and nephew became estranged from him. While he was constantly in the public eye, one can

---

48. In addition to the legal question at hand, the Rebbe identified spiritual dimensions to this court case. See Chaim Miller (2014), 364–66; Adin Even-Israel Steinsaltz (2014), 81. For the importance of written Torah works in the thought of the Rebbe, see chapter 17, section "Means of *Hitkashrut*." For an analysis of the extent of the dedication of a Rebbe to the people in Chabad teachings, see chapter 17, section "Complete Dedication to the People."

hardly consider Hasidim and others who sought the Rebbe's counsel to be close companions. In this period of his life, the Rebbe's single close companion was his wife, Haya Mushka.[49]

Haya Mushka was an extremely private person and we have precious little window into her mind. She was well educated, spoke several languages, and seemed to have been satisfied with the life that she and Menahem Mendel established for themselves in Paris away from the limelight. When it was clear, however, that the Hasidim wanted her husband as the Rebbe, she reportedly was instrumental in convincing him that it was necessary for him to accept the mantle of leadership to ensure the continuation of her father's work.[50] While the Rebbe's difficult schedule did not afford him much time at home, he insisted on spending some time with his wife every day, and he referred to their time together being as precious to him as putting on tefillin.[51] When she passed away in 1988, the Rebbe cried bitterly.

R. Yosef Yitzhak

The last relationship of note during the Rebbe's leadership years was with his deceased father-in-law. In accordance with Chabad practice, the Rebbe would receive thousands of *panim* (requests for blessings and prayers). The Rebbe's standard response, penned hundreds of thousands of times[52] over the course of his career, was "I will mention it at the [grave] marker." At first twice a month and eventually increasing to twice a week, the Rebbe would travel from Crown Heights to Old Montefiore Cemetery in Queens to pray at his father-in-law's graveside. He would spend hours at the site reading all the notes and sometimes

---

49. The fact that the Rebbetzin was the Rebbe's only close companion that he met on an equal footing is noted by his biographers. See Adin Even-Israel Steinsaltz (2014), 164–66; Joseph Telushkin (2014), 373.
50. Chaim Miller (2014), 180; Joseph Telushkin (2014), 32.
51. Chaim Miller (2014), 192; Joseph Telushkin (2014), 374. This odd phrase seems to be sourced in a teaching of the Rashab recorded in *HaYom Yom* for 22 Tevet.
52. This number is from "The Ohel: An Overview," retrieved from www.chabad.org/36247.

attributed positive changes in his petitioners' lives to his father-in-law's heavenly intercession.[53]

These trips to the cemetery had a mystical hue. While the Rebbe was extremely circumspect about his own thoughts and feelings, from a few stray comments he made over the years it was clear to the Hasidim that at Old Montefiore Cemetery the Rebbe would communicate with his father-in-law and receive instructions from him.[54] While this was not uncommon in the Chabad tradition (R. Yosef Yitzhak spoke of visitations from his deceased father and predecessor, the Rashab), the frequency of these trips and the appearance of the Rebbe's total dependency on his deceased father-in-law were unique even in the annals of Chabad.[55]

What emerges from this brief outline is that besides his wife and mother, the Rebbe had no deep familial relationships. Similarly, he did not have friends with whom he would speak and confide in about personal matters. His life was enveloped by his public identity and mission as the seventh Rebbe of Chabad.[56]

The Rebbe's Work Ethic

The Rebbe maintained an all-consuming work schedule throughout his career. Arriving at his office at 770 in the morning, he consistently returned home late at night, even then bringing back a stack of letters to respond to. He never took a vacation and deviated from this long workday only when he sat *shiva* and immediately following a heart attack in 1977. With the exception of several visits to Chabad summer camps during the early years of his tenure, the Rebbe never left what he called "Lubavitch," which consisted of Crown Heights and the Old Montefiore

---

53. See the collection of sources and stories cited by Mordechai Menashe Laufer (5758).
54. Samuel Heilman and Menachem Friedman (2014), 75–76.; Chaim Miller (2014), 215; Adin Even-Israel Steinsaltz, (2014), 179–81.
55. For an elaboration on the mystical relationship between the Rebbe and his father-in-law, see chapter 17, section "Who Is the *Nasi* of the Seventh Generation?"
56. The Rebbe nearly explicated the all-consuming nature of his public role. Herbert Weiner once asked the Rebbe about his personal life and feelings. The Rebbe did not respond directly about himself but said that for a person with a communal role, the primary barometer of the existential "Where am I?" is the extent of one's accomplishments in the public domain. See Herbert Weiner (1994).

Setting the Stage

Cemetery in Queens, the places where his father-in-law had lived and was buried. His energies were totally dedicated to the mission that he defined for himself as the leader of Chabad.

CONCLUSION

Even as the introverted and reclusive Menahem Mendel Schneerson did not seem to have ambitions to lead, he eventually ascended to the leadership of Chabad and dedicated himself entirely to his new position. Beyond his piety and humanity, he brought to the table a bold vision and a well-defined philosophy. Teaching and implementing the Torah of the seventh generation of Chabad became his major focus and his life's mission. It is these unique Torah teachings that are the subject of this work.

Secondary Literature Consulted for Chapter 1, "Who Was the Lubavitcher Rebbe?"

Shaul Shimon Deutsch, *Larger than Life: The Life and Times of the Lubavitcher Rebbe Rabbi Menachem Mendel Schneerson*.

Adin Even-Israel Steinsaltz, *My Rebbe*.

Samuel Heilman and Menachem Friedman, *The Rebbe: The Life and Afterlife of Menachem Mendel Schneerson*.

Boruch Oberlander and Elkanah Shmotkin, *Early Years: The Formative Years of the Rebbe, Rabbi Menachem M. Schneerson, as Told by Documents and Archival Data*.

Chaim Miller, *Turning Judaism Outward: A Biography of the Rebbe, Menachem Mendel Schneerson*.

Joseph Telushkin, *Rebbe: The Life and Teachings of Rabbi Menachem Mendel Schneerson, the Most Influential Rabbi in Modern History*.

Chaim Rapoport, *The Afterlife of Scholarship: A Critical Review of "The Rebbe" by Samuel Heilman and Menachem Friedman*.

Eli Rubin, "The Rebbe: An In-Depth Biography of a Scholar, Visionary and Leader."

Chapter 2

Tanya: The Written Torah of Hasidism

As the seventh leader of Chabad, the Rebbe was heir to a rich intellectual legacy that spanned over 150 years of Torah discourses, letters, and published works. From this voluminous corpus, the single book that most influenced the intellectual history of Chabad was *Tanya*, known within Chabad as "The Written Torah of Hasidism."[1] First published by R. Shneur Zalman of Liadi, the founder of Chabad Hasidism, in 1796, it has a sacred status within the Chabad canon and the ideas articulated therein became the building blocks for later Chabad thought.[2] Accordingly, a brief sketch of the key themes in *Tanya* is integral to any attempt to understand the thought and even lexicon of the seventh Rebbe.

---

1. *Iggerot Kodesh Amdor Moharaayatz* 4, letter 1001. The Rebbe identified several meanings latent in this description. See, for example, *Torat Menahem* 5742: 1, 472–75 and *Iggerot Kodesh* 8, letter 2527.
2. See *Torat Menahem* 5742: 1, 472–75, which states that just as all of Torah is encapsulated in Scripture, similarly, all of Hasidism is rooted in *Tanya*.

Setting the Stage

R. SHNEUR ZALMAN AND THE BEGINNINGS OF CHABAD
A Brief Biography

Shneur Zalman (1745–1812), later known as the Alter Rebbe, was born in the village Liozna, which was then part of the Kingdom of Poland and is now in Belarus.[3] He gained fame as a child prodigy and by his early teens a community ledger referred to him with accolades usually reserved for great rabbinical authorities.[4] Searching for more than Torah knowledge, in his late teenage years he traveled to learn from R. Dovber of Mezritch (the Maggid of Mezritch), one of the primary students of the Baal Shem Tov. Despite his relative youth, R. Shneur Zalman was initiated into the Maggid's inner circle and studied mystical and hasidic teachings under the Maggid's guidance.

After the Maggid's passing in 1772, his students spread throughout Eastern Europe and established their own hasidic courts. R. Shneur Zalman eventually settled and taught Torah in his hometown of Liozna, gradually acquiring renown as "the Maggid of Liozna." Until 1777, the regional leader of the hasidic community was R. Shneur Zalman's senior colleague, R. Menahem Mendel of Vitebsk. But when R. Menahem Mendel led a large contingent of Russian Hasidim, to settle the Land of Israel, he appointed R. Shneur Zalman as his emissary to lead the even larger community of Hasidim who remained in Russia.

During this time R. Shneur Zalman slowly grew into a leader on his own merits.[5] His reputation as an eminent Torah scholar and spiritual guide brought tens of thousands of people to Liozna to be with him and learn from him. Eventually overwhelmed by the volume of visitors, he was forced to limit their number in various ways.[6]

---

3. This brief biographical sketch of R. Shneur Zalman's early years is based on the work by Chabad chronicler Hayyim Heilman, *Beit Rebbi* (1902), and the work of Nissan Mindel (1973). For a description of the problems and yet necessity to draw from these sources, which are largely based on internal Chabad traditions, see Roman Foxbrunner (1993), 44–52. An accessible biography and timeline which incorporates primary source material such as letters of R. Shneur Zalman and old community records is available at www.chabad.org/2076432.
4. See *MiBeit HaGenazim*, ed. Shalom Dovber Levin (2009), 13.
5. See Immanuel Etkes (2015), 8, who writes that the Russian government estimated that he had forty thousand followers.
6. For a detailed description of this process, see Immanuel Etkes (2015), 39–45.

Writing *Tanya*

In this setting he wrote and published his magnum opus, *Tanya*. In an introductory letter,[7] R. Shneur Zalman wrote that "since time no longer permits" him to meet with each Hasid individually and provide proper guidance, it was necessary to pen and disseminate a book that would be a comprehensive guide for Hasidim in their service of God.

Tanya is unique in the canon of early Hasidism. Most hasidic masters delivered their teachings as homilies on the weekly *parasha* or the holiday at hand and their published works reflect this calendrical organization. While this approach allowed the hasidic master to focus on ideas and modes of service that were seasonally relevant, it also precluded the presentation of hasidic philosophy in a conceptually systematic manner. In this sense, *Tanya* marks a watershed in the presentation and understanding of Hasidism. For the first time, a major hasidic master authored a systematized presentation of hasidic ideas and modes of service, unfurling the depth and breadth of Hasidism in an organized fashion.

While *Tanya* is an organized and accessible work, it is also erudite and challenging. R. Shneur Zalman called the first and major section of the book *Likkutei Amarim* ("A Collection of Sayings"), as he drew from "books and sages, exalted saints, whose souls are in Eden."[8] This modest statement belies the range of his source material.[9] The reader of *Tanya* will engage sources from the entire scope of the biblical and rabbinic canons, a large quantity of classical Kabbala (mostly Zohar and the writings of Arizal), and hasidic teachings from the Baal Shem Tov and Maggid of Mezritch. These sources are not just cited and elucidated but are also contextualized within R. Shneur Zalman's own unique system of thought and practice. Clearly, R. Shneur Zalman had high expectations of his Hasidim.

---

7. *Tanya*, *Hakdamat HaMelaket*.
8. *Tanya*, title page.
9. See *Iggerot Kodesh* 17, letter 6240, which says that according to Chabad tradition this phrase refers to the writings of the Maharal of Prague.

Setting the Stage

FOR IT IS EXCEEDINGLY NEAR TO YOU

While *Tanya* discusses many themes relating to God and the cosmos, its main thrust and organizing principle is the practical service of God. To this end, the title page of the book informs us:

> Compiled from (sacred) books and from sages, exalted saints, whose souls are in paradise; based on the verse "For it is exceedingly near to you, in your mouth and in your heart, to do" (Deut. 30:14); to explain clearly how it is exceedingly near, in a lengthy and short path, with the aid of the Holy One, may He be blessed.

R. Shneur Zalman's stated goal is to explain to his reader how the service of God is "exceedingly near" to a person. The first section of *Tanya* is loosely organized around this verse. Over the course of fifty-three chapters, R. Shneur Zalman proceeds to explain how the service of God is "near" to every Jew, in two distinct but intertwined manners – the "lengthy and short path."[10]

The Lengthy Path
Types of Souls

Tanya opens with an expedition into the human soul, dividing all people into several distinct categories based on their spiritual aptitude. While in classical rabbinic literature, the terms *Tzaddik* (righteous), *Beinoni* (intermediate), and *Rasha* (evil) usually relate to one's behavior and the number of merits and sins that a person has accrued,[11] *Tanya* explains these categories as reflecting the inner chemistry of the soul. The *Tzaddik* is a person who is completely divested of the evil inclination and, to varying degrees, is constantly and completely in love with God.[12]

---

10. The following structural division of *Likkutei Amarim* into chapters 1–17 and then 18–24 is based on a lecture of Yoel Kahn (Kislev 5768), one of the of the preeminent authorities on Chabad teachings in modern times. For other interpretations of *Tanya's* reference to the lengthy and short paths, see *Likkutei Sihot* 34, *Nitzavim*, no. 2; *Torat Menahem* 5719: 1, 270–74.
11. Rosh HaShana 16b.
12. *Likkutei Amarim*, ch. 10.

R. Shneur Zalman states that this type of unique soul is a divine gift,[13] and it is beyond the capabilities of most people to achieve that state through personal effort.[14] Conversely, a complete *Rasha* is dominated by his evil inclination and is generally overcome by impulses that are at best selfish and bodily and at worst evil.[15]

While *Tanya* discusses these archetypes, its focus is on the average person and his mission to become a *Beinoni*. It is with this group that the internal drama and tension of religious life unfolds. Most Jews are torn between their "divine soul," which is "truly a part of God" (*helek Eloka mimaal mamash*),[16] and their "animal soul," which stems from the "*Sitra Ahra*" (literally, "the Other Side," referring to the forces of evil and impurity).[17] These souls are engaged in a constant battle over dominion of the individual and particularly a person's three faculties that "clothe" and express the soul – thought, speech, and action.[18] The divine soul wants to express itself through holy thoughts, speech, and actions, while the animal soul directs these faculties toward "all the deeds that are done under the sun"[19] that are not related to Torah and mitzvot[20] and eventually to actual sin.

The individual's life mission is to actively favor and express the "divine soul" while controlling the animal soul and hindering its expression. A victory in this regard means that an individual achieves behavioral perfection to the degree that he never sins and punctiliously performs each mitzva. Nonetheless, in terms of the deeper composition of his

---

13. Ibid., ch. 14. It is important to note, though, that while one can be born with the soul of a *Tzaddik*, it is still the individual's responsibility to actualize that potential through the service of God.
14. However, see the end of *Likkutei Amarim* ch. 14 that even a person who is not graced with the soul of a *Tzaddik* might be rewarded by being "impregnated" with the soul of a *Tzaddik* and thus be able to intermittently experience the all-consuming love for God that a *Tzaddik* experiences.
15. *Likkutei Amarim*, ch. 11.
16. Ibid., ch. 2. It is important to note that the phrase *helek Eloka mimaal* stems from a verse in Job (31:2). R. Shneur Zalman added the word *mamash* (literally).
17. Ibid., ch. 1.
18. Ibid., ch. 4.
19. Ibid., ch. 6.
20. Ibid., ch. 7.

inner psyche, even a person with a perfect religious record is still a *Beinoni* and not a *Tzaddik*. The *Beinoni* can never let down his guard. The animal soul forever lurks beneath the surface, causing him to constantly "feel a desire for the lusts of the world and its delights."[21] The animal soul can be controlled but not utterly eradicated; therefore, the *Beinoni* must engage in this inner struggle for his entire lifetime.

The existence of the selfish and evil impulse within the *Beinoni* necessarily limits the full expression of the divine soul and the religious experience of loving and fearing God that is associated with it. While a *Tzaddik* constantly experiences the raging fire of "delight in Godliness,"[22] the *Beinoni* is able to experience such illumination only at specific spiritual moments such as during prayer.[23] Afterward, the animal soul within is stirred again and the battle must be reengaged.

Hokhma, Bina, Daat

What strategy does R. Shneur Zalman recommend to the average person in his quest to become a *Beinoni*? How can the *Beinoni* control his evil inclination and, perhaps, expand those moments of spiritual illumination? *Tanya*'s answer, surprising as this might be for a hasidic work, focuses on training one's intellect and thoughts. Focusing one's mind on God and contemplating His greatness will have a positive effect on the entire human personality.

R. Shneur Zalman bases this contention on his understanding of the kabbalistic structure of the cosmos and its reflection in the human psyche. Kabbala teaches that God sends the flow of divine influence into the world through the medium of ten *sefirot*, or channels. According to Chabad teachings, these *sefirot* serve a dual function, both of which are hinted to in the word *sefira*. On the one hand, a *safir* is a bright jewel, indicating that each *sefira* allows for a specific attribute of God to shine and manifest itself. Simultaneously, however, the word *sefira* is related to *mispar*, or "number," which represents a fixed and limited quantity. This signifies that the manifestation of a single divine attribute necessarily

---

21. Ibid., ch. 12.
22. Ibid., ch. 9.
23. Ibid., ch. 12.

Tanya: The Written Torah of Hasidism

limits the boundless *Ein Sof*, a kabbalistic name for God that highlights His infinity.[24]

The first three of the *sefirot* – *hokhma*, *bina*, and *daat* – are collectively known as the *mohin* (minds).[25] The kabbalists employed different stages of the cognitive process as an extended metaphor for the emergence of the divine flow.[26] *Hokhma* (wisdom) refers to the initial, lightning-like revelation of the divine light. This "seed" is placed into the womb of *bina* (understanding), where the initial kernel is developed into a well-defined form. *Daat* (knowledge) represents the further concretization of this divine light's specific form,[27] which enables it to flow into the seven lower *sefirot*, which are parallel to emotions and then action.

With this background we can now return to *Tanya*'s kabbalistic-psychological advice for the person who strives for greater heights in the divine service. While the earlier kabbalistic texts referred to the *sefirot* as key stations in the flow of the divine light into our world, the hasidic masters taught that every Jew is a microcosm of this cosmic drama. Thus, in addition to *hokhma*, *bina*, and *daat* being stages in the travels of the divine light, they are also specific cognitive levels in the mind of each individual.[28]

Accordingly, when Kabbala teaches that the cognitive *sefirot* "give birth" to the lower *sefirot* regarding the flow of the divine light into our world, this also speaks to a basic psychological truth: cognitions trigger emotions. In this vein, R. Shneur Zalman offered the following formula:

---

24. See Yosef Ives (2010), 97–99. For a clear English explanation sourced in earlier kabbalistic teachings, see Aryeh Kaplan (1990), 40–41.
25. See, for example, *Tikkunei Zohar* 17a. For a translation and explanation of this key passage, see Aryeh Kaplan (1990), 43–45.
26. For an elucidation of these ideas in the Zohar and other kabbalistic texts, see Aryeh Kaplan (1990), 57–60; Moshe Hallamish (1990), 131–33. For Chabad sources on this cosmic process, see Yosef Ives (2010), 117–46.
27. In many earlier kabbalistic texts, *daat* is not mentioned and, instead, *keter* is placed above *hokhma*. For an elaboration on these two schemes in early Kabbala, see Aryeh Kaplan (1990), 52–56; Moshe Hallamish (1990), 153–54. For one place where R. Shnuer Zalman related to the basis for these two schemes, see *Likkutei Torah, Bemidbar*, 49c.
28. For a further elaboration of this point, see chapter 8, section "Early Hasidism."

> For when the intellect...deeply contemplates and immerses itself exceedingly in the greatness of God...there will be born and aroused in his mind and thought the emotion of awe for the Divine Majesty, to fear and be humble before His blessed greatness, which is without end or limit, and to have the dread of God in his heart. Next, his heart will glow with an intense love, like burning coals, with a passion, desire and longing, and a yearning soul, toward the greatness of the blessed *Ein Sof*.[29]

If a person wants to *feel* fear and love for God but, as a *Beinoni*, the evil within prevents these powerful religious emotions from arising naturally, he must *choose* to focus his mind on the greatness of God. It is this *hitbonenut*, or extended contemplation of one's *hokhma, bina,* and *daat* (the initial letters of these words form the acronym Habad),[30] that will ultimately generate proper emotions and actions.[31]

This is the "long path" toward closeness to God, which highlights the existence of an intense inner battle between two equally powerful but diametrically opposed souls. In the context of this struggle, the service of God can be "close" to a person only if he consciously chooses to focus his thoughts on God, which then enables the divine soul to permeate the totality of the human experience, arousing love and awe of God and motivating positive action.

The Short Path

Chapter 18 begins a new segment in *Tanya* by introducing the complementary "short path." While in the first segment, R. Shneur Zalman mostly speaks of a deep connection to God as something that must be generated/created through contemplation, R. Shneur Zalman now shifts his language from generating/creating to revealing/extracting. Thus, we read that even a person "whose understanding in the knowledge of God

---

29. *Likkutei Amarim*, ch. 3.
30. Although the transliteration rules employed in this book would dictate the spelling "Habad" for this acronym, we have employed the spelling "Chabad" in deference to the movement's preferences in its literature and websites.
31. See *Likkutei Amarim*, chs. 15–16 for application of this idea to the *Beinoni*.

is limited"[32] and therefore cannot produce love and fear of God through intellectual focus is still "exceedingly close" to God and His service. This is by virtue of the nature of the Jewish soul, which innately "desires...to unite with its origin and source in God."[33]

While R. Shneur Zalman bases this metaphysical conception of the Jewish soul on kabbalistic sources, he famously offers a tragically not uncommon occurrence in Jewish experience as a proof:

> Even the...transgressors of the Jewish people, in the majority of cases sacrifice their lives for the sanctity of God's name and suffer harsh torture rather than deny the One God, although they be boors and illiterate and ignorant of God's greatness. [For] whatever little knowledge they do possess, they do not delve therein at all, [and so] they do not give up their lives by reason of any knowledge and contemplation of God. Rather [they suffer martyrdom] without any knowledge and reflection, but as if it were absolutely impossible to renounce the One God; and without any reason or hesitation whatever.[34]

Ignoramuses and sinners do not sacrifice their lives due to their intellectual understanding of God's greatness and the love and awe resulting from such cognitions. Rather, there is something embedded within the Jewish psyche, referred to as the *yehida*, or the *pintele Yid* (the Jewish core),[35] that is always inherently bound with God in a manner that transcends reason or ordinary cognition.

Building on this dramatic example of martyrdom, *Tanya* continues by elaborating on the more routine methods of actualizing the *yehida*'s desire to unite with God, namely, studying Torah and performing mitzvot. While these may seem very far from a spiritual connection

---

32. *Likkutei Amarim*, ch. 18.
33. Ibid., ch. 19.
34. Ibid., ch. 18.
35. R. Shneur Zalman himself does not use these terms, but later Chabad literature expresses that the *yehida* is the deepest part of the soul which is associated with the capacity for even a heretic to give up his life for God. See, for example, *Torat Menahem* 5716: 1, 6; ibid., 5745: 2, 820.

Setting the Stage

to transcendence, R. Shneur Zalman argues that a proper understanding of the nature of Torah and mitzvot demonstrates that these are the optimal ways to unite with God. The basis for this is a passage in the Zohar that describes how God contracted Himself into the ideas and text of the Torah. Therefore, occupying one's thoughts, speech, and actions – the three garments of the soul – with Torah and mitzvot creates the most profound bond imaginable with God, fulfilling the ultimate desire of the *yehida*.[36]

After this exposition, *Tanya* transitions to an array of specific aspects in the service of God that aid a person in his battle against the animal soul. These include the importance of joy,[37] humility,[38] and loving fellow Jews.[39]

THE RELATIONSHIP BETWEEN GOD AND THE WORLD

Even as R. Shneur Zalman places the individual and his service of God at the center of *Tanya*, he also engages in lengthy theosophic expositions about the nature of God and His relationship to the world. For R. Shneur Zalman, a proper understanding of the God-world relationship is crucially necessary for a Jew's practical, day-to-day service of God.

Tzimtzum

Jewish thought from Scripture through the medieval period conceived of God and the world as utterly distinct entities. God created the world, guides it, and cares about it, but the world is not God and God is not the world. This picture, though, was problematized in the monumental teachings of the great sixteenth-century kabbalist of Safed, R. Yitzhak Luria, known as Arizal. He taught that before Creation, God, described in Kabbala as *Ein Sof* (Infinity), was everything and everywhere. There was no "space" for the world to be created.

---

36. *Likkutei Amarim*, ch. 23.
37. Ibid., chs. 26–29.
38. Ibid., chs. 30–31.
39. Ibid., ch. 32.

How then did God create the world? Arizal's answer is that He did so through the process of *tzimtzum*, "contraction." As R. Hayyim Vital, the main transcriber and disseminator of Arizal's teachings, wrote:

> Before all things were created...the Supernal light was simple. It filled all existence. There was no empty space which would be space, emptiness, or void. Everything was filled with the simple light of *Ein Sof*. There was no category of beginning and no category of end. All was one simple undifferentiated Infinite Light.
>
> When it arose in His simple will to create all universes, He contracted His Infinite Light distancing it to the sides...leaving a vacated space in the middle...after this contraction took place...there was a place in which all things could be brought into existence.[40]

By contracting and limiting the infinite divine light, God created an "empty space" that allowed for the creation of the world. The complex system of contractions that led to the creation of the spiritual and material worlds is known as *Seder Hishtalshelut*.[41]

The Paradox of a Non-Literal *Tzimtzum*
What is the nature of this "empty space" and our world that is created within it? Is it really bereft of God? Many kabbalists indeed understood Arizal's depiction literally and professed that the "empty space" and our material world that exists within it are truly empty of God. Hasidism, however, followed a different school of kabbalistic interpretation. Early hasidic masters emphatically argued for a metaphorical understanding of *tzimtzum*. In their view, God created an *illusion* of a space and a world bereft of Him, but, in reality, even after Creation nothing exists other than God.[42]

---

40. R. Hayyim Vital, *Etz Hayyim*, 27. Translation is from Aryeh Kaplan (1990), 120.
41. For a clear articulation of the shift from earlier Jewish philosophy to Arizal, see Norman Lamm (1998), 47–51; Feital Levin (2002), 43–49.
42. For a summary of this debate in kabbalistic literature, see Moshe Hallamish (1990), 199–201; Eli Rubin, "Immanent Transcendence."

R. Shneur Zalman forcefully articulates this non-dualistic perspective throughout *Tanya*. Here is one classic formulation:

> As for His blessed Being and Essence, it is written: "I, the Lord, I have not changed" (Mal. 3:6), neither in terms of changes in the development from the uppermost of levels to the nethermost – for just as He, blessed be He, is found in the upper worlds, so He is in precisely that measure in the netherworlds – nor in terms of temporal changes, for just as He was alone, one, and unique, before the six days of Creation, so He is now after the Creation. This is so because everything is absolutely as nothing and naught in relation to His being and essence.[43]

Nothing exists other than God. God has not changed at all from that moment before Creation when Creation was impossible. This is the true meaning of God's unity – not only that He is of a single essence and is not comprised of different elements, but that He is the *only* being in existence.[44]

Why then do we experience a created world teeming with materiality and diversity but not divinity? Similarly, how can Kabbala teach of an infinite number of spiritual worlds? The answer, once again, is *tzimztum* which allows for the world to exist, while simultaneously not removing God from the picture. R. Shneur Zalman explains that in creating the world, God is manifest in both a revealed manner and a concealed manner: God's infinite power is revealed to animate the world, and at the very same time God conceals that infinite power in order to endow the creations with finite and independent form and identity. When R. Shneur Zalman juxtaposes these two contradictory ideas and argues for the truth of both, he assuredly reminds us that "it is not possible for any creature's mind to comprehend his Creator"[45] nor any of His attributes that are expressed in this process of Creation. The human mind cannot negotiate this paradox, but it is nonetheless true.

---

43. *Tanya, Iggeret HaKodesh*, sec. 6.
44. This is the basic thrust of the second section of *Tanya*, entitled *Shaar HaYihud VehaEmuna*.
45. *Tanya, Shaar HaYihud VehaEmuna*, ch. 4.

When the dust of these complex analyses settles, one point is clear: our sensory perception that allows us to see the world but not God is misleading. As R. Shneur Zalman emphatically writes: "There is nothing truly besides Him. Only that the visible worlds appear to be an entity and something separate in itself to our eyes alone because of the concealment and the great number of withdrawals."[46]

Rather, as the Chabad maxim goes, *altz iz Gott* (everything is God) – and, in reality, the world is *batel* (effaced or nullified) before Him.[47]

The Lower Unity and the Upper Unity

The story, however, does not end here. Within the framework of an all-encompassing God and a world that is utterly united with Him, R. Shneur Zalman proposes two distinct perspectives on the God-world relationship that differ regarding the precise standing of the created worlds. Ultimately, despite the fact that these perspectives might ostensibly be seen as mutually exclusive, R. Shneur Zalman once again affirms both.[48]

One perspective begins within the confines of time, space, and human sensory perception. We see the world as existing – trees are trees, rocks are rocks, and people are people. The spiritually astute person, however, realizes that while it seems that he is looking at hard matter, what he is *really* seeing is entirely composed of contracted divine light. This aspect of divinity is described in the Zohar as *Memalei Kol Almin* – God as He contracted Himself and "fills" the created worlds.[49] When one affirms the unity of God by coming to the realization that

---

46. *Likkutei Torah, Shir HaShirim*, 41a. Translation is adapted from Rachel Elior (1993), 50.
47. According to R. Shneur Zalman, this seemingly theoretical debate regarding the literalness of Arizal's doctrine of *tzimtzum* was the major ideological divide between the Hasidim and their opponents (the *mitnagdim*), led by the Vilna Gaon. In a letter sent to his Hasidim (published in *Iggerot Kodesh Admor HaZaken*, letter 52), R. Shneur Zalman explained that the fundamental difference in ideology between the groups was their disagreement regarding the literalness of Arizal's notion of *tzimtzum*. For the historical unfolding of the bans issued against Hasidism and R. Shneur Zalman's role as a defender of the movement, see Immanuel Etkes (2015), 108–22.
48. See *Tanya, Shaar HaYihud VehaEmuna*, ch. 7, and the buildup toward these ideas in the preceding chapters. A clear articulation of these two forms of divine unity can be found in Yoel Kahn (Nisan 5764), 2–8.
49. For a clear explanation of this term, see Nissan Mindel (1974), 124–25.

everything around him is just contracted divine light, one achieves the consciousness of *Yihuda Tataa* – the lower unity.[50]

The second perspective emerges from relating to the divine light *before* it contracts to the degree necessary for the created worlds to exist. This "higher" aspect of divinity, known as *Sovev Kol Almin* – God as He "encircles" the world – is too transcendent to become "clothed" in a created reality. Looking down, so to speak, from *Sovev Kol Almin*, the world is entirely effaced before God, "a complete effacement of the reality."[51] This is known as *Yihuda Ilaa* – the higher unity – in which the whole existence of the world is insignificant.[52] However, in keeping with the non-literal interpretation of *tzimtzum*, R. Shneur Zalman makes it clear that this "surrounding light" is not actually "above" the world, but actually vivifies the world in a "hidden and concealed manner."[53]

---

50. The paradoxical notion of the finite world's divine makeup has deep roots in kabbalistic literature. Chabad sources quote the sixteenth-century kabbalist R. Meir ibn Gabai (*Avodat HaKodesh* 1:8) as asserting that if God would be in some way limited regarding the finite reality, then this itself would be an impossible limitation on God. See, for example, *Maamarei Admor HaZaken* 5567, 22–26. In the thought of the Alter Rebbe this power of God over finitude is associated with the *Reshimu*; in this regard see Nahum Greenwald (5771), 48–60; Yosef Ives (2010), 63–70; Eli Rubin, "Absent Presence"; Eli Rubin, "Covert Luminosity."
51. *Likkutei Torah, Devarim*, 4c.
52. The connection between the terms *Memalei Kol Almin* and *Yihuda Tataa*, and also between *Sovev Kol Almin* and *Yihuda Ilaa*, is not explicit in *Tanya*. However, it is explicit in other sources from R. Shneur Zalman. See, for example, *Likkutei Torah, Devarim* 4a–b; *Maamarei Admor HaZaken al Inyanim*, 443. For the Rebbe's alignment of these aspects of divinity with their respective form of "unity," see *Torat Menahem* 5725: 3, 162; *Torat Menahem* 5743: 1, 78.
53. *Likkutei Amarim*, ch. 48. Later Chabad literature explains this idea by contrasting how a teacher transmits his wisdom to a student with how the sun illuminates a room with its rays. A good teacher contracts his lofty ideas and "enclothes" himself in explanations that are fitted to the student's level of intellect. This, in turn, allows the student to internalize the teacher's wisdom and make it his own. While the student's entire wisdom clearly emanates from the teacher and not his own independent talent, the very fact that the teacher engages with the student in a personalized fashion gives the student significance and "existence." However, the sun does not personalize its rays to the level of the room it illuminates. In fact, the room hardly has significance relative to the sun. Rather, the infinite and powerful rays of the sun, automatically, and without contracting itself, illuminate the room equally with all other locations. As a consequence of this transcendent character, the light of the sun, though it clearly

The dialectic between God as *Memalei Kol Almin* and *Sovev Kol Almin* generates an awareness of God's immanence and transcendence. On the one hand, God is extremely immanent, as He literally fills all of existence. Simultaneously, though, He continues to exist in a fashion that completely transcends created reality.

Contemplating God's Unity

Far from viewing the attempt to understand these truths as an esoteric exercise, *Tanya* argues that every Jew[54] should spend time daily meditating on them. Prayer is the ideal time for such contemplation, but other times are proper as well. For example, *Tanya* teaches that when a person is beset with sadness, he should consider the following:

> Let him then concentrate his mind and envisage in his intelligence and understanding the subject of His blessed true Unity: how He permeates all worlds, both upper and lower, and even the fullness of this earth is His blessed glory; and how everything is of no reality whatever in His presence.... For all things created are effaced (*betelim*) beside Him in their very existence, as are effaced (*kebittul*) the letters of speech and thought within their source and root.... Exactly so, figuratively speaking, is the effacement (*bittul*) of the world and all that fills it in relation to its source, which is the light of the blessed *Ein Sof*.[55]

Tanya then segues to emphasize that the awareness of God's immanence that is implied by *bittul* will engender a feeling of closeness to God and

---

impacts the room, only "encircles" it and does not "fill" and become one with the room's identity. This is the reason that the moment the sun stops shining, the room immediately reverts back to its natural dark state. By contrast, the wisdom of the teacher who has contracted his insights to meet the student's limited capacities remains with the student even after the teacher finishes teaching him, for it has "filled" the student and become one with him the student. For an explanation of these two analogies, see Yoel Kahn (5771).

54. See *Likkutei Sihot 9, Hosafot*, 344, that the Rebbe highlighted the Alter Rebbe's desire for every Jew, and not just Hasidim, to study *Tanya*.

55. *Likkutei Amarim*, ch. 33.

joy in God's presence. More generally, R. Shneur Zalman enjoins his readers to contemplate the *bittul* of the world and of oneself before the one true existence – God.

MITZVOT AND THE MESSIANIC ERA

Complete Revelation in the Lowest Realm

R. Shneur Zalman's conceptualization of the *Seder Hishtalshelut* from *Ein Sof* to our created world establishes the framework for his description of other major issues such as the purpose of Creation, the nature of the Messianic Era, and the role of mitzvot. From the above depictions one might have concluded that the truest perspective to be attained is that of *Yihuda Ilaa* which entails the effacement of the world as we know it. This, however, is not the case. Throughout his writings, R. Shneur Zalman describes the Messianic Era as a time when the higher aspects of divinity will not negate the world but rather will be fully expressed through it.

Here is a key passage in *Tanya*, chapter 36, concerning the purpose of Creation and its realization in the messianic reality:

> It is a well-known rabbinic statement that the purpose of the creation of this world is that the Holy One, blessed be He, desired to have an abode in the lower worlds (*Dira BaTahtonim*)…the ultimate purpose [of Creation] is this lowest world, for such was His blessed will that He shall have satisfaction when the *Sitra Ahra* is subdued and the darkness is turned to light, so that the divine light of the blessed *Ein Sof* shall shine forth in the place of the darkness and *Sitra Ahra* throughout this world, all the more strongly and intensely, with the excellence of light emerging from darkness.

Our material world is the "lowest" plane of reality due to its composition from extremely contracted divine light. This allows for the existence of evil, both globally and within each individual. The goal of Creation, however, is for the light of *Ein Sof* – the highest aspect of divinity – to shine brightly within the confines of our lowly world without the latter "dissolv[ing] out of existence."

The Role of Mitzvot

How is this possible? How can the divine light shine brightly in the lowest world without eradicating it? R. Shneur Zalman's response is that the steady accumulation of mitzvot over the course of human history creates the capacity for this intense divine revelation:

> For this purpose, the Holy One, blessed be He, gave to Israel the Torah, which is called "might" and "strength," as the Sages, of blessed memory, have said, that the Almighty puts strength into the righteous in order that they may receive their reward in the hereafter, without being nullified in their very existence in the divine light that will be revealed to them in the hereafter without any cloak.[56]

In the next chapter, R. Shneur Zalman elaborates on the mechanics of this process.[57] Every mitzva that a person performs draws the infinite light of God into the material world, although its full revelation will not be apparent until the Messianic Era.[58] As such, each mitzva literally builds a miniscule fraction of the messianic reality in a manner that is currently concealed but will be revealed in the end of time.[59]

---

56. Ibid., ch. 36.
57. Ibid., ch. 37.
58. Scholars of early Hasidism note a tension that often exists between a mystical consciousness of an all-encompassing divinity and the resultant loss of a sense of an individual bodily self, and the obligations of the halakhic system. Rivka Schatz-Uffenheimer (1993) notes, however, that the Chabad program outlined by R. Shneur Zalman does not contain such tension, as mitzvot are described as the vehicle of revealing this higher level of divinity within the material realm. Moshe Hallamish (1976), 253–55, however, argues that *Tanya*'s formulations regarding the importance of action were meant for the masses, while R. Shneur Zalman articulated elsewhere that a spiritual cleaving to God was the most elevated experience. A rejoinder and affirmation of the integral importance of physical actions in Tanya can be found in Naftali Loewenthal (1987). This importance of action becomes a theme of the last Rebbe's thought, as will be described in chapter 5. Similarly, the Rebbe himself (*Iggerot Kodesh* 32, letter 12,003) wrote to Hallamish that the Alter Rebbe would never have engaged in such duplicitous writing.
59. See, for example, *Torah Or*, vol. 1, 22c, where R. Shneur Zalman clearly states that this sort of revelation is impossible today, as the divine light is too overbearing for

Current Relationship to the Material World

In this context it must be emphasized that R. Shneur Zalman's focus on the messianic potential of the lowest realm did not lead him to advocate that one should fully interface with the corporeality of our world. Rather, in our current unredeemed reality, he argues for prudently relating to this world with suspicion and apprehension due to the pervasiveness of the *kelippot* (negative forces; literally, "shells"). From the outset, *Tanya* paints a starkly dualistic perspective in which engagement with the world is recommended by the Torah only if it is done with specific intent for the service of God. However, all mundane activities such as eating, drinking, and sexuality, even if sanctioned by the Torah but done for the sake of physical pleasure, envelop an individual within the *kelippot*.[60]

In fact, R. Shneur Zalman consciously quieted some radical ramifications of seeing God everywhere and in everything, which appear in earlier hasidic teachings. One primary example is the strategy of dealing with *mahshavot zarot* – stray thoughts – during prayer. The Baal Shem Tov taught that if a stray sexual thought invades one's mind during prayer, one should elevate it to its ultimate source, which is love of God.[61] The theoretical basis for this approach is that the all-encompassing divinity must include even lustful thoughts. While R. Shneur Zalman clearly affirms the *altz Gott* underpinnings of such an approach, he interpreted this teaching of the Baal Shem Tov as being relevant only to a *Tzaddik*. Even the perfect *Beinoni* cannot risk engaging these thoughts due to the persistent existence of inner evil. Instead, he should attempt to divert his mind and refocus on addressing God in prayer.[62]

In summary, *Tanya* describes a material world that is utterly united with God and is yet a treacherous place to navigate. Only through properly engaging the material world in our current exilic state will we ultimately merit to see its true divine nature in the Messianic Era.

---

our material world. It is only possible when the world will be perfected through the service of the Jewish people. For more sources about this messianic reality and its relationship to our current state of *tzimtzum*, see Dov Shwartz (2010), 277–80.
60. *Tanya, Likkutei Amarim*, ch. 7.
61. See, for example, *Tzavaat Rivash, siman* 87.
62. *Tanya, Likkutei Amarim*, ch. 28. This analysis is from Immanuel Etkes (2015), 91–92. For an elaboration of this topic, see Yehoshua Mundshine (1997).

CONCLUSION

The 150 years following *Tanya*'s publication saw Chabad teachings both deepen and expand. Starting with R. Shneur Zalman himself, the leaders of Chabad plumbed some of the basic themes of *Tanya* while also using the worldview outlined in the book to broach new topics. As is evident from his published personal journal *Reshimot*, from a young age Menahem Mendel Schneerson was fully ensconced within the comprehensive and complex Chabad worldview, and it was the lens through which he saw the spiritual and material realities. As we will see, the Rebbe did not find the legacy and lens of *Tanya* to be stifling constraints, but rather the springboard for an immensely creative but rooted philosophy that he developed and shared over the course of forty years of leadership.

Secondary Literature Consulted for Chapter 2, "*Tanya*: The Written Torah of Hasidism"

Immunel Etkes, *Rabbi Shneur Zalman of Liady: The Origins of Chabad Hasidism.*

Ariel Evan Mayse, "The Sacred Writ of Hasidism: Tanya and the Spiritual Vision of Rabbi Shneur Zalman of Liady," *Books of the People*, 109–56.

Roman Foxbrunner, *Chabad: The Hasidism of R. Shneur Zalman of Lyady.*

Nissan Mindel, *Rabbi Schneur Zalman Volume 2: The Philosophy of Chabad.*

Dov Shwartz, *Mahshevet Chabad: MiReshit VeAd Aharit.*

Rachel Elior, *The Paradoxical Ascent to God: The Kabbalistic Theosophy of Chabad Hasidism*, trans. Jefferey Green.

Yosef Wineberg, *Lessons in Tanya* (available at www.chabad.org/6237).

Chapter 3

The Coronation *Maamar*

The Rebbe's tenure as the leader of Chabad formally began at a *farbrengen* held on the evening after 10 Shevat 5711 (1951), the first anniversary of his father-in-law's passing. By now it had become clear that R. Menahem Mendel's initial refusal to accept the mantle of leadership was eroding. Well before 10 Shevat, R. Menahem Mendel had been seeing Hasidim *biyehidut* (in private audiences) and sending out preholiday letters of blessing and guidance, slowly assuming increasing levels of leadership.

In Chabad, however, the true crowning of the next leader, with all of the associated personal and cosmic ramifications,[1] can be sealed only through the deliverance of "words of the living God" – a hasidic discourse (*maamar*) – that the Hasidim requested and accepted.[2] This

---

1. See chapter 17 for an elaboration.
2. See *Torat Menahem* 5743: 1, 473, where the Rebbe explained that this is modeled on the laws pertaining to the sacred vessels of the *Beit HaMikdash*, which are sanctified through an act of service (Shevuot 15a). Similarly, a person attains the status of a *nasi* of Chabad through teaching a hasidic discourse, which is one of the main "services" of a Rebbe.

crucial final step took place on 11 Shevat 5711 (1951), establishing R. Menahem Mendel as the official seventh Rebbe of Chabad.[3]

The Rebbe used the opportunity of his opening *maamar* to focus on the themes that his father-in-law broached in his final *maamar*, thereby demonstrating the continuity of leadership. However, through his analysis and exploration of these motifs, the Rebbe elaborately developed a unique task for the seventh generation of Chabad. Intertwining Chabad theosophy, cosmology, and eschatology with a clearly defined practical mission, this *maamar* foreshadowed the key themes of the Rebbe's thousands of later talks and created the theoretical structure for the dozens of programs that he would launch over the course of the next four decades. In many ways, this first discourse, *Bati LeGani* 5711, serves as a blueprint for the Torah and activities of Chabad until today.

THE THREE LOVES

The Rebbe began the *farbrengen* by underscoring the enduring relevance of his deceased father-in-law and the need for all of those present to strengthen their connection with their longtime leader. Then, after a song, the Rebbe delivered a brief message before launching into the actual *maamar*:

> When he came to America, the Rebbe [R. Yosef Yitzhak] said: "When one comes to a city one should follow its customs" (Genesis Rabba 48:14). Here in America, they love to hear a "statement," a new idea – and preferably something surprising. I do not know if this is a necessary phenomenon, but one should follow the customs of the [local] city.
>
> The three loves – love of God, love of Torah, and love of one's fellow – are one. One cannot differentiate between them, for they are of a single essence.... And since they are of a single essence, each one embodies all three.[4]

---

3. A detailed internal Chabad account regarding the events of 10–11 Shevat 5711, compiled from firsthand accounts, is available in the book *Yemei Bereshit: Yoman MiTekufat "Kabbalat HaNesiut" shel Kevod Kedushat Admor Menahem Mendel Schneerson*, 369–90.
4. *Torat Menahem* 5711: 1, 210. Translation adapted from Yanki Tauber, "Love According to the Rebbe."

Setting the Stage

The Rebbe elaborated that this interconnection of the three loves has a dual implication. First, one's purported love for any of the items is definitionally incomplete if there are deficiencies in the other elements: "When there is love of God but not love of Torah and love of the Jewish people, this means that the love of God is also lacking. On the other hand, when there is love of a fellow Jew, this will eventually bring also a love of Torah and a love of God"[5] Since God, the Torah, and the Jewish people are all of a single essence, it is impossible to fully love God without loving fellow Jews. Conversely, love of a fellow Jew while alone insufficient, will eventually lead to love of God and love of Torah.[6]

The single essence of this tripartite love also generates a positive formulation. If one truly feels an affinity to either God, the Torah, or the Jewish people, this feeling provides a platform for the cultivation of the other two intertwined loves. While sometimes the missing aspects of this tripartite love develop naturally, at times, some measure of outside assistance is necessary to spark these feelings. As the Rebbe exhorted:

> So if you see a person who has a love of God but lacks a love of Torah and a love of his fellow, you must tell him that his love of God is incomplete. And if you see a person who has only a love for his fellow, you must strive to bring him to a love of Torah and a love of God – that his love toward his fellows should not only be expressed in providing bread for the hungry and water for the thirsty, but also to bring them close to Torah and to God.[7]

Thus, while the unity of the loves is an immutable fact, it is the task of those who understand their interpenetration to ensure their wholeness. The Hasidim must teach themselves and then spread to others the fact that God, the Torah, and the Jewish people are inseparable.

---

5. Ibid., 211.
6. For a longer elaboration on why *ahavat Yisrael* plays such a foundational and central role in cultivating the other prongs of this single love, see chapter 13, section "*Ahavat Yisrael* and Love of God."
7. *Torat Menahem* 5711: 1, 211.

Throughout the talk, the Rebbe's particular emphasis was on the foundational importance of love of fellow Jews. In line with this emphasis, he concluded these introductory remarks by asserting that this proactive stance toward the kindling of love of fellow Jews would lead directly to the ultimate redemption.[8]

Soon afterward, the Rebbe shifted from his normal speaking voice to the distinct chant reserved for a *maamar*. In a rush of astonishment, the Hasidim rose from their chairs and stood for the discourse as per the Chabad custom. In a wide-ranging but tightly structured *maamar* that was punctuated by the Rebbe's tears, several melodies, and the recitation of the blessing of *Sheheheyanu* by a senior Hasid, the Rebbe outlined a theosophy and a mission that would soon reverberate well beyond the confines of Crown Heights.

BATI LEGANI 5711, SECTION 1: THE *SHEKHINA*'S HOME
Song of Songs Rabba 5:1

The Rebbe opened the *maamar*[9] with the midrashic passage that was the focus of his father-in-law's last published *maamar*.[10] This passage relates to the historical journey of the *Shekhina* (Divine Presence):

> "I have come to my garden" (Song. 5:1): R. Menahem the son-in-law of R. Elazar the son of Avuna in the name of R. Shimon ben Yosna said: It doesn't say, "I have come to a garden (*legan*)," but rather, "to my wedding canopy (*leganuni*)," to the place where my main essence was in the beginning, and was the Essence of the *Shekhina* not in the lowest place (*tahtonim*)? That is what the verse states: "And they heard the sound of *Hashem* walking in the garden" (Gen. 3:8).[11]

---

8. Ibid.
9. The *maamar* appears in *Torat Menahem* 5711: 1, 192–203; *Sefer HaMaamarim Melukat*, vol. 2, 263–71. Citations will be adapted from Eli Touger's translation, retrieved from www.chabad.org/115145. This section of the chapter summarizes *se'ifim* 1–3 of the *maamar*.
10. Printed in *Sefer HaMaamarim Bati LeGani*, vol. 1, 1–28.
11. Song of Songs Rabba 5:1.

Setting the Stage

The *Shekhina* originally occupied the lowest levels (*tahtonim*), identified as the primordial garden. However, the midrash continues, this occupancy was short-lived:

> R. Abba said: It doesn't say, "walking," but rather, "walking away" – jumping and ascending, jumping and ascending. Adam sinned and the *Shekhina* left to the first heaven, Cain sinned and it left to the second heaven, Enosh sinned and it left to the third heaven, the generation of the Flood sinned and it left to the fourth heaven, the generation of the Tower of Babel sinned and it left to the fifth heaven, the people of Sedom sinned and it left to the sixth heaven, the Egyptians sinned in the days of Abraham and it left to the seventh heaven.

Human sin caused the *Shekhina* to ascend to the seventh and highest heaven, far from its original terrestrial abode.

But this is not the end of the *Shekhina*'s migrations. The midrash then records the next stage in this epic tale:

> Corresponding to them [the seven sinners] stood seven righteous individuals (*Tzaddikim*) who brought the *Shekhina* down to earth. Abraham merited and he lowered the *Shekhina* from the seventh to sixth [heaven], Isaac stood and lowered it to the fifth, Jacob stood and lowered it to the fourth, Levi stood and lowered it to the third, Kehat stood and lowered it to the second, Amram stood and lowered it to the first, Moses stood and brought it down to the ground.

The seven *Tzaddikim* reversed the effect of the seven sins, bringing the *Shekhina* back down to its terrestrial terrain.

While this intriguing midrash clearly discusses the relationship between God and the world – a primary topic in Chabad literature – it is cryptic. What is meant by the identification of the Garden of Eden as the original abode of the *Shekhina*? What of the subsequent narrative of the *Shekhina*'s trek from the "lowest level" to heaven and then back down to the ground?

The Coronation Maamar

Characteristically, the Rebbe began his exposition of this midrash by dissecting its key phrase – *Ikkar Shekhina batahtonim* (the Essence of the *Shekhina* is in the lowest level) – and offering an itemized analysis of each word. After reaching a specific definition of each component unit, the Rebbe's ultimate understanding of the statement's integrated meaning served as the backbone of the rest of the address.

Ikkar Shekhina

The Rebbe began his analysis by noting that in Kabbala and Hasidism the term *Shekhina* is used to refer to several distinct levels of divinity. As we have seen, the Alter Rebbe, R. Shneur Zalman, expended considerable energy elucidating different levels of divinity and their relationships to the created reality. Most notably, he distinguished between God as He "fills" and vivifies the worlds (*Memalei Kol Almin*), and God as He "encircles" the worlds (*Sovev Kol Almin*) rendering them as nothing relative to His all-encompassing infinitude. Despite the fundamental differences between *Memalei* and *Sovev*, they share a fundamental commonality in that they describe God as part of the *Seder Hishtalshelut*. Both outlooks assert that there are "worlds" that are worthy of discussion and differ only regarding the specific relationship between God and these worlds.

The Rebbe argued, however, that the term *Ikkar Shekhina* implies that of the various levels of *Shekhina* and divine revelations, this midrash refers to the *Ikkar* or most essential aspect of God: the radiance of the Divine Essence. This is the "divine light prior to the *tzimtzum*"[12] that stands above the *Seder Hishtalshelut*, or God as He exists unto Himself prior to His decision to conceal Himself and make space for the world. The radiance of the most elusive and singular Divine Essence is the subject of this midrashic passage.[13]

Ikkar Shekhina BaTahtonim

Next, the Rebbe turned his attention to the definition of *tahtonim*. Here, the midrash itself provides the necessary clues for identifying

---

12. *Bati LeGani* 5711, *se'if* 1.
13. For the precise relationship between the divine light prior to the *tzimtzum* and the Divine Essence itself, see *Sefer HaArakhim: Chabad*, vol. 3, 42–48.

this "location." In the second half of the passage, the midrash describes the descent of the *Ikkar Shekhina* from heaven down to earth with the Giving of the Torah on the physical Mount Sinai, presumably parallel to the initial ascent of the *Ikkar Shekhina* from the *tahtonim*. As such, it would seem that *tahtonim* should be defined as "this physical world."[14]

Now the import of the entire sentence becomes clear. *Ikkar Shekhina BaTahtonim* means that the radiance of the Divine Essence, which transcends the entire *Seder Hishtalshelut*, originally inhabited planet Earth, the lowest plane of reality. Despite the seeming incongruence of this idea, the *Ikkar Shekhina* dwelled specifically in the physical world that conceals divinity, as opposed to the spiritual worlds that are "higher" in the *Seder Hishtalshelut*.

The Rebbe then used this precise definition of the midrash's initial assertion to evaluate the relationship between the seven sins that banished the *Shekhina* from its home. While all the sins were devastating, the most cataclysmic was the original sin of Adam and Eve. It was this sin that drove the *Ikkar Shekhina* from its original abode and forced it to begin its celestial migration. Correspondingly, the most significant stage in the process of return was the final step, accomplished by Moses, who drew the *Shekhina* back from its heavenly exile to its earthly quarters. In the words of the Rebbe:

> Just as the principal stage in its withdrawal and ascent was the departure from this world caused by the sin of the "Tree of Knowledge," so too, the principal stage in the descent and return of the *Shekhina* was accomplished when it was drawn down into this world.[15]

Moses's descent from the heavens with the Torah provides the tools and blueprint for the Jewish people throughout history to draw down the

---

14. *Bati LeGani* 5711, *se'if* 2. See *maamar* "*Bati LeGani* 5729" (*Sefer HaMaamarim Melukat*, vol. 2, 319), where the Rebbe returned to this point and marshaled further proofs that the *tahtonim* and "garden" referred to by the midrash is the physical world and not a higher spiritual world.
15. *Bati LeGani* 5711, *se'if* 2.

Divine Essence. This historical aspiration culminates in the last generation, which completes this mission, beginning the Messianic Era.

The Rebbe then reflected on Moses's unique mission by citing his father-in-law's association of Moses's singular status with the rabbinic statement that "all sevenths are cherished."[16] This saying led the Rebbe to articulate two important ideas regarding the seventh in a series. First, the rabbinic adage emphasizes the nature of the seventh's favored position:

> He is cherished not on account of his choice, desire, or spiritual service, but because he is seventh – and this is something that he is born into. Yet the fact remains that "all those who are seventh are cherished."[17]

Being the beloved seventh is the result of a divine determination, irrespective of worthiness or personal piety. Thus, even though Abraham, from a certain perspective, was greater than Moses,[18] it was still the latter who received the most privileged position simply due to his being the seventh.

The Rebbe then noted that the sequential reference to the "seventh" immediately invokes the six that preceded it: "For the whole meaning of 'seventh' is 'seventh from the first.'"[19] The undeserving seventh is capable of actualizing its great potential only by receiving the spiritual powers accrued by its six predecessors.[20] Moses was able to fulfill his mission of drawing down the *Ikkar Shekhina* only because he was, on his own level, continuing the path originally blazed by Abraham.

The Seventh Generation

At this point in the *maamar* the Rebbe shifted his focus from the past to the present. As those attending the *farbrengen* were well aware, they

---

16. Leviticus Rabba 29:11.
17. *Bati LeGani* 5711, *se'if* 3.
18. As a proof to this assertion, the Rebbe cited a midrash (Deuteronomy Rabba 2:7) that describes God telling Moses: "Do not stand in the place of greats," referring to the patriarchs.
19. *Bati LeGani* 5711, *se'if* 3.
20. For a longer exposition on the complex relationship between Moses and the *Avot*, see *maamar* "Vaydaber Elokim el Moshe 5732" (*Sefer HaMaamarim Melukat*, vol. 2, 238–41).

were experiencing the commencement of the seventh generation of Chabad. Thus, the Rebbe's next statement was particularly powerful:

> This, then, is why the seventh is so cherished: it is he who draws down the *Shekhina*, in fact, the *Ikkar Shekhina*; moreover, he draws it down into this lowly world.
>
> It is this that is demanded of each and every one of us of the seventh generation – and "all those who are seventh are cherished":
>
> Although the fact that we are in the seventh generation is not the result of our own choosing and our own service, and indeed in certain ways is perhaps contrary to our will, nevertheless, "all those who are seventh are cherished."
>
> We are now very near the approaching *ikveta deMeshiha* [literally, "the footsteps of *Mashiah*," referring to the period immediately before the *Mashiah*'s arrival]; indeed, we are at the conclusion of this period, and our spiritual task is to complete the process of drawing down the *Shekhina* – moreover, the *Ikkar Shekhina* – specifically within our lowly world.[21]

While the midrashic narrative of the ascent and descent of the *Shekhina* serves as a general blueprint for human history, in the Rebbe's reading, it had specific resonance for the seventh generation of Chabad.

The Rebbe and the Hasidim were fully cognizant of R. Yosef Yitzhak's (the sixth Rebbe of Chabad) fervent belief in the imminent arrival of *Mashiah* and his interpretation of the calamitous events of World War II in this light. With this historical context in the background, the Rebbe invoked the *Bati LeGani* midrashic passage to argue that the mission of the seventh generation of Chabad was akin to that of Moses.[22] This final generation was charged with executing history's climactic

---

21. *Bati LeGani* 5711, *se'if* 3.
22. The fact that the Rebbe referenced this midrash with regard to the generations of Chabad is not mere homiletics. While the mission applies to the entire generation – men, women, children, Jews, and non-Jews – Chabad still has a unique role to play. Chapters 8 and 17 discuss the significance of the Chabad movement in the Rebbe's historiography.

finale: the final descent of the *Ikkar Shekhina* into this lowly world and the creation of a *Dira BaTahtonim* (a home for God in the lowest realm).[23]

THE CONCEPTUAL EXPLANATION FOR *IKKAR SHEKHINA BATAHTONIM*

The Divine Essence and the Lowest Realm

After defining the mission of the seventh generation, the Rebbe returned to his earlier exposition to further refine the relationship between the Divine Essence and the lowest level.[24] Intuitively, one might have thought that the physical world is the realm farthest from the Divine Essence and while "there is no place bereft of [God]," this maxim is hardest to justify regarding our material world. The Rebbe, however, argued that the midrash clearly indicates that a special bond exists between the "highest" and the "lowest." As we will see throughout this book, the Rebbe's explanation of this connection, despite its abstractness, led him to concretize a specific set of strategies for the generation to adopt to fulfill its mission of drawing the *Ikkar Shekhina* back into the world.

In addition to the language of the midrash, as a further proof of the affinity between the Divine Essence and this lowly world the Rebbe cited chapter 36 of *Likkutei Amarim*. There, the Alter Rebbe declared that the entire purpose of Creation was God's desire to dwell in the lowest realm. While this habitation will occur only in the Messianic Era, this goal justifies God's initiation of Creation as a whole. Once again, we see the Alter Rebbe asserting a unique connection between the highest level of divinity that will be disclosed in the Messianic Era and our lowly world.

But what is the meaning of this seemingly paradoxical bonding? One can understand that God desired to be "at home" *even* in the lowest realm, but why would such a coarse and corporeal world be the original and eschatological home for the Divine Essence?

---

23. It is important to note that the Rebbe very carefully transitioned from the earlier six *Tzaddikim* to the seventh generation as a whole. This shift in the Rebbe's formulation and its connection with the verse "And your nation are all righteous; they will eternally merit the land" will be discussed in chapter 20, "Personal Redemption."
24. *Bati LeGani* 5711, *se'ifim* 4–5.

Atzmut Cannot Be for the Sake of Giluyim

The Rebbe's response to this question builds upon the distinction made in earlier Chabad philosophy between the Divine Essence (*Atzmut*) and the Divine Revelations (*Giluyim*).[25] A *Gilui* refers to any aspect of God that is *revealed* through the process of contraction and devolution. Each of the myriads of worlds that are described in Kabbala and Hasidism are characterized by a distinct spiritual quality that is tangible to those occupying that level of reality. In fact, *Tanya* discusses a variety of spiritual realms and delineates the aspect of divinity that is revealed and experienced by the angels and souls that occupy that spiritual world.[26] In short, a *Gilui* bears a specific spiritual quality that can be experienced by other entities.

These descriptions are not true regarding the Divine Essence. Figuratively situated above the *Seder Hishtalshelut*, the Divine Essence transcends the very notions of contraction and revelation that define the created worlds. It is beyond any human conceptualization; the only statement that can be made about the Divine Essence is that it exists. However, even in this regard, there is a fundamental difference between the existence of the Divine Essence and the existence of other created entities.[27]

Generally, beings assert their existence in a variety of ways that are perceptible to other entities. The sun shines, rocks are hard, and angels sing. The Divine Essence, however, is non-contingent, self-referential, and self-sufficient – it is totally indifferent to other beings. Compared to a luminary that does not necessarily illuminate,[28] the Divine Essence simply exists; it *is*, without expressing its existence in any manner that

---

25. For the general difference between *Azmut* and *Giluyim* in Chabad literature, see Yosef Ives (2010) 33–39; Eli Rubin, "Everywhere Revealed"; Yaakov Gottlieb (2009), 112–18, and Yoel Kahn (5772).
26. *Tanya, Likkutei Amarim*, ch. 52.
27. See *Torat Menahem: Hadranim al HaRambam*, 15, where the Rebbe approvingly cited Rambam's formulation (*Guide for the Perplexed*, I:57) that God "exists but is not in reality" (*matzui lo bemetziut*). See also *Sefer HaMaamarim 5666* (*Hemshekh Samekh-Vav*), 464, of Rebbe Rashab that "*Atzmut* exists in a form that is not real but existent" (*Atzmut hu nimtza bebehinat bilti metziut nimtza*).
28. See, *Sefer HaArakhim: Chabad*, vol. 3, 78–79.

is meaningful to others. Despite its being the singular substance of all reality, even referring to the Divine Essence as "creator" is an affront to its total transcendence over created categories.

As such, in contrast to the *Giluyim* which are spiritually perceptible, the Divine Essence itself cannot be felt or sensed. It would be impossible for a person or angel formed through the *Seder Hishtalshelut* to experience or understand the Divine Essence that transcends the limitations that are inherent to created beings. In the words of the Rebbe Rashab (the fifth Rebbe of Chabad): "God exists. In what way He exists we do not know, but He exists."[29]

Armed with these categories, the Rebbe returned to the Alter Rebbe's declaration that the entire purpose of Creation was God's desire to dwell in the lowest realm. As the Alter Rebbe explained, it is impossible to argue that the higher, spiritual realms were God's central objective when initiating Creation: "The purpose of the *hishtalshelut* of the worlds, and of their descent from level to level, is not for the sake of the higher worlds, since for them this constitutes a descent from the light of His countenance."[30]

As mere *revelations* of God, the "higher" worlds are in fact a descent and a concealment of the Divine Essence. Thus, they cannot be the goal of Creation. Rather, as the Alter Rebbe continued, the Divine Essence, which transcends the contractions of the *Seder Hishtalshelut* responsible for the spiritual realms, is uniquely suited for residing in the lowest realm.

This, however, creates a more perplexing problem. If the celestial worlds are a descent from the Divine Essence and therefore cannot be the objective of Creation, the same reasoning is surely true regarding our lowly physical world. How, then, can the *tahtonim*, which results from the greatest descent of all, be the ultimate dwelling place for the Divine Essence that transcends Creation?

---

29. Cited from an oral tradition in Eli Rubin, "Everywhere Revealed," note 46.
30. *Tanya, Likkutei Amarim*, ch. 36.

Setting the Stage

Atzmut and the Lowest Realm

The Rebbe responded to this perplexity by invoking a principle that the Alter Rebbe discussed in a letter published in the last section of *Tanya*.[31] This letter is considered in Chabad as being simultaneously one of the most fundamental and yet cryptic passages in the Alter Rebbe's canon.[32] Throughout his career, the Rebbe often cited,[33] developed, and applied this principle to practice, even referring to it as one of the major innovations of the Alter Rebbe, and hence of Chabad Hasidism.[34]

In this letter, the Alter Rebbe explains that while all the infinite worlds of the *Seder Hishtalshelut* were constructed through a contraction of the Infinite Light that enabled a specific *Gilui* to emerge, the lowest physical world had a different point of origin. The process of Creation via contraction indicates that the resultant world is not an entirely new entity, but is merely a devolved manifestation of the world above it. The *Seder Hishtalshelut* is depicted as a long chain, each new link being a lower manifestation of what is included in the higher elements of the chain.

To use a crude analogy, let us assert that a certain world of the *Seder Hishtalshelut* can be signified by the number five, indicating the "amount" of divine light that is revealed therein. Then, the world below it, while seemingly a new creation, is, in fact, simply the number four. It is composed of the same element as the higher world, just further contracted and devolved.

While this process of contraction and devolution explains the construction of the heavenly realms, it would never result in a physical world. As the Alter Rebbe explained:

---

31. *Tanya, Iggeret HaKodesh*, ch. 20.
32. See, for example, the introduction to this letter in *Lessons in Tanya*, available at www.chabad.org/7965.
33. See, for example, *Torat Menahem* 5716: 1, 125; ibid., 5718: 1, 29; ibid., 5720: 1, 317; ibid., 5746: 1, 183; *Likkutei Sihot* 7, *Tazria*, no. 1, *se'if* 6; ibid., 12, *Tazria*, no. 2, *se'ifim* 6–7; ibid., 20, *Motza'ei Shabbat Parashat Lekh Lekha*, *se'ifim* 17–18; *Sefer HaMaamarim Melukat*, vol. 2, 409; vol. 4, 288. This is a small sampling.
34. *Torat Menahem* 5745: 2, 1341. The Rebbe noted that while it is unclear what sources the Alter Rebbe relied on when formulating this idea, still, "the Alter Rebbe does not need proofs," meaning that he himself is a primary source of Torah ideas.

The Coronation Maamar

Through the *Seder Hishtalshelut* alone, even myriads of contractions would not be able to create physicality from spirituality, and therefore this level [physicality] is referred to as "something from nothing" (*yesh me'ayin*). This is what the philosophers wrote: "There is no greater creation of something from nothing than the creation of physicality from spirituality,"[35] as an infinite number of devolutions and contractions would not help to create physicality from spirituality.[36]

Physicality is so qualitatively different from spirituality that even an infinite number of contractions would not form a material world.[37] Accordingly, as opposed to each of the spiritual worlds that are devolved forms of the worlds that stand above them and therefore not truly "new" creations, the material world needed to be created from nothing. It is the only true creation of *yesh me'ayin*.[38]

The Alter Rebbe continued in his letter that only the Divine Essence, as opposed to the lower *Giluyim*, has the ability to create *yesh me'ayin*. Therefore, the only possible explanation for the existence of physicality is a direct act of creation of the Divine Essence that stands above the *Seder Hishtalshelut*. In a word, the radiance of the Divine Essence "skipped over" the *Seder Hishtalshelut* and directly created the physical world; the beginning and the end – the highest and the lowest – both stand apart from the infinite number of worlds that stand in between.[39]

With this background, the Rebbe explained that we can understand the unique bond between the Divine Essence and the lowest

---

35. This is a reference to Yosef Albo, *Sefer HaIkkarim*, maamar 1, ch. 23.
36. *Likkutei Torah, Re'eh* 20d.
37. See also *Torah Or, Megillat Ester*, 92b. For a clear articulation of this idea from the Rebbe, see *Torat Menahem* 5722: 3, 373.
38. For an elaboration of this unique approach to the concept of *yesh me'ayin*, see Yosef Ives (2010), 455–71; Yaakov Leib Altein (2003), 405–6; and Yaakov Gottlieb (2009), 63–65.
39. See *Sefer HaArakhim: Chabad*, vol. 3, 91–92, and the sources cited therein. For more sources regarding this "jumping" over the *Seder Hishtalshelut*, see chapter 11, note 32. For analysis, see Elliot Wolfson (2016) 45–86; Shneur Zalman Gopin (5772).

realm and justify the Alter Rebbe's declaration that the whole purpose of Creation was for God to dwell in the lowest realms:

> It is thus understandable that the intent of Creation is not the higher worlds, whose purpose is revelation, but this lowly world – that imagines itself to be not a [mere] revelation (*Gilui*) but a self-sufficient entity (*atzmi*) whose being derives from its own self. Through man's spiritual service in this world, subduing and transforming [the physical into holiness], the Divine Essence is revealed [in this world], for the sake of which the worlds at large were created and for the sake of which they progressively descended.[40]

The *tahtonim* is the part of creation that is rooted in the Divine Essence – the *Ikkar Shekhina* – and hence a fitting abode for the Divine Essence. Throughout history, human sin severed God from His home, forcing Him to proverbially wander in the celestial, spiritual realms, far from His terrestrial garden. Now, however, with the imminent arrival of the Messianic Era, it was finally time to reveal the divinity of the *tahtonim* and to reunite the Divine Essence with its original home.

The Concealment of the Divine Essence

The Rebbe explained that this direct link between the Divine Essence and the physical world accounts for God's terrestrial concealment. The spiritual planes of the *Seder Hishtalshelut* represent the various levels of *Giluyim*, and hence God's presence there is revealed and discernible. The materiality of our world, however, circumvents this entire process and is instead rooted in the Divine Essence itself. Since the Divine Essence exists because He exists and is not there to reveal anything but itself (as opposed to *Giluyim*), our material world, which is rooted in the Divine Essence, exudes a sense of existing from and for itself, concealing its divine source. In the words of the Rebbe:

---

40. *Bati LeGani* 5711, *se'if* 4.

[Physical] created beings not only fail to reveal [their] Creator; they actually hide and conceal their source. Moreover, they feel that their being derives from themselves (and only reason dictates that this cannot possibly be so). Although this [perception of a physical creation whose existence derives from its own self] is but its own [false] impression, nevertheless, the very fact that it is able to imagine that it derives from its own self results from its being rooted in the Divine Essence [of whom it could alone be said that] His Being derives from His Essence.[41]

The seeming independent and mundane nature of the material world accounts for its description as *tahtonim*. Simultaneously, though, this banality indicates its deeper divine root that is beyond discernment.[42]

A Focus on the *Tahtonim*

Based on this analysis, the fundamental identity of the *tahtonim* is wherever God seems to be absent.[43] The charge of the seventh generation is to finish transforming this world's mundanity and indifference to God into a *Dira BaTahtonim*.

Accordingly, though the Rebbe did not fully explicate this in this *maamar*, it presumably follows that the seventh generation will need to transform the lowly passions of one's own heart, seemingly secular people, mundane items, and pedestrian places of this lowly world into fertile arenas for accessing and drawing out the imperceptible Divine Essence. As we will see in the subsequent chapters, this mission engenders a shifting of generally assumed religious hierarchies. In previous generations, when God was high in His heavenly exile, there was more of a religious push to focus solely on the spiritual and the intangible.

Slowly, however, due to the intense service of hundreds of generations, God had finally descended toward this world and was approaching His original terrestrial abode. For the final generation to fulfill its

---

41. Ibid.
42. See *Sefer HaArakhim: Chabad*, vol. 3, 94–95, and the sources cited therein.
43. Later in the *maamar* (*Bati LeGani* 5711, *se'if* 8), the Rebbe exhorted people to go to places where people do not even know the Hebrew alphabet in order to teach Torah.

Setting the Stage

mission of bringing the Divine Essence home, it would need to focus on the *tahtonim*, i.e., the areas perhaps not focused on by its predecessors, and demonstrate that every aspect of our material world is a fitting home for the Divine Essence.[44]

THE HOLY FOLLY OF SELF-SACRIFICE

This focus on the *tahtonim* may not be intuitive for the average religious person who might instinctively want to stay in a spiritually suffused environment and not engage with people or places that seem distant from spirituality and God. As such, the Rebbe emphasized that the service of the seventh generation would need to be permeated with counterintuitive self-sacrifice.[45] While Jews were always enjoined to sacrifice themselves for the sake of God, this final generation, to succeed in its task, needs to be totally mission-focused, ready to sacrifice personal desires for the sake of the mission.

One acute manifestation of this form of self-sacrifice is the need, at times, to sacrifice not only one's physical life, but even one's perceived spirituality and *feelings* of closeness to God for the sake of the mission. Many will have to leave their safe, spiritual, and familiar environments in order to engage the broad *tahtonim* and transform it into a dwelling place for God. Only such a mission-based approach of self-sacrifice would be able to disclose the divine core of reality.

Homiletically, the Rebbe connected this form of self-transcendent service with the items that formed the structure of the *Mishkan*, God's original home on earth. R. Yosef Yitzhak had already noted that the Torah describes the boards that formed the perimeter of the *Mishkan* as *atzei shittim*, acacia wood. The word *shittim* contains identical letters as the root of *shetut*, or folly. While folly is usually associated with a sub-rational state of mind that leads one toward sin, the same abandonment of regular rationality can be transformed to the super-rational "folly of holiness" that is implemented when one sacrifices his

---

44. The Rebbe's focus on revealing *Atzmut* stands in contrast to much of the Lithuanian kabbalistic tradition, which was reticent to speak about *Atzmut* at all. In this regard, see Tamar Ross (1982), 115–20.
45. *Bati LeGani* 5711, *se'ifim* 6–7.

personal spiritual aspirations for the sake of the mission. Similar to the *Mishkan*, the creation of a *Dira BaTahtonim* requires the implementation of a "folly of holiness" that transcends the calculated cognitive faculties of a human being.

The Rebbe identified models and inspirations for this pervasive form of self-transcendent service in the work of earlier generations which began this process of drawing the *Shekhina* back into this world. In particular, the previous six leaders of Chabad led the way by embodying the self-sacrifice for other Jews that was necessary to become the purview of all in the last generation:

> Whatever was demanded of us by the Rebbe [R. Yosef Yitzhak], of blessed memory, and by all the Rebbes, they demanded of themselves.... The reason that they revealed to us that they too performed these things was in order to make it easier for us to perform them.[46]

The Rebbe continued to recount a specific story regarding each of the Rebbes of Chabad that exemplifies the self-sacrifice necessary to help other Jews:

> Accordingly, there are many stories regarding the love of a fellow Jew involving each of the Rebbes. The Alter Rebbe, for example, once interrupted his prayers in order to go and chop wood, cook a soup, and feed it to a woman who had just given birth, because there was nobody else to do it.[47]

Elsewhere, the Rebbe elaborated that this story actually occurred on Yom Kippur.[48] While the Alter Rebbe would have *felt* closer to God by staying in the synagogue and praying, he sacrificed this experience and vitiated his experience of the day's sanctity to feed a poor woman. This

---

46. Ibid., *se'if* 6.
47. Ibid.
48. *Torat Menahem* 5744: 2, 627–31. In this talk the Rebbe also provided a halakhic justification for such an act.

form of self-sacrifice must become the model of service for the entire seventh generation.

This form of service harks back to the first *Tzaddik* who began the process of drawing the *Shekhina* back to its home. Abraham is the paradigm of a person who took his spiritual status very seriously and yet dedicated his life to demonstrating the divinity of the most secular people. To illustrate this aspect of Abraham's service, the Rebbe cited a midrash that he used as a model for the mission of his generation. Following Abraham's treaty with Abimelech, the Torah describes Abraham as settling in Be'er Sheva, where "he called (*vayikra*) there in the name of the Lord, the God of the world (*El Olam*)."[49] Using a midrashic hermeneutical tool, the Talmud comments: "Do not read it as 'he proclaimed' (*vayikra*), but rather 'he made others proclaim' (*vayakri*). This teaches us that Abraham caused every passerby to proclaim the name of God."[50] Abraham not only proclaimed God for himself, but self-effacingly engaged the passersby of the world to act in kind.

According to the Rebbe, the first *Tzaddik* is the model for the seventh generation:

> This is demanded of each of us: To know that we find ourselves in the seventh generation, the quality of the seventh of a series merely being that he is seventh to the first. The conduct of the first was that he sought nothing for himself.... This kind of divine service resembles that of Abraham: arriving in places where nothing was known of Godliness, nothing was known of Judaism, nothing was even known of the *alef-beit,* and while there setting oneself completely aside [and proclaiming God's name] in the spirit of the teaching of the Sages, "Do not read 'he proclaimed,' but 'he made others proclaim.'"[51]

Teaching about God to people and places that seem "lowly" and unaware of Him through *tremendous* self-sacrifice is what brings the Divine

---

49. Gen. 21:33.
50. Sota 10a.
51. *Bati LeGani* 5711, *se'if* 6.

Essence into the world. This is what reveals the true nature of reality as *El Olam*, in which God and the world are wholly one (*she'olam veElokut hu kulo had*).[52] The mission of the seventh generation is clearly defined: to engage the *tahtonim* with self-sacrificial service in order to reveal the Divine Essence that heretofore remained concealed.

SOURCES OF STRENGTH

The Rebbe admitted that the seventh generation was charged with a most difficult task. As God is fair, he provided the people of the final generation with sources of strength that would aid them in their work. In line with the notion that the seventh in a sequence builds upon the earlier six, the Rebbe outlined various ways in which the previous six Rebbes of Chabad, and particularly his father-in-law, provided the seventh generation with the resources necessary to complete its task.

The Power of the Six

In addition to serving as role models for a *tahtonim*-focused and self-sacrificial service, the Rebbe felt that his six predecessors also metaphysically provided the seventh generation with their strength and vitality:

> The power to do so has been granted to us through the conduct of the first [of the Rebbes], and from thence onward, up to and including the conduct displayed by the Rebbe [R. Yosef Yitzhak], of blessed memory. They have paved the way and granted us the necessary powers [that we may follow in their footsteps]. This in itself indicates the dearness of the seventh generation: so much strength has been given and revealed for our sakes.[53]

The seventh must be beholden to its predecessors as it can fulfill its mission only due to the accomplishments of the service of the previous generations.

---

52. Ibid., *se'if* 8.
53. Ibid., *se'if* 9.

Setting the Stage

The Death of a *Tzaddik*

In addition to the service of the previous six Rebbes, the Rebbe focused on the metaphysical significance of a recent event that was on the minds of all those present: the passing of the sixth Rebbe.

The background to the Rebbe's conceptualization of the meaning of his father-in-law's passing is seen in two letters of consolation penned by the Alter Rebbe. One was addressed to his colleague R. Levi Yitzhak of Berditchev upon the death of the latter's son, in which the Alter Rebbe described the great effect of a *Tzaddik*'s death.[54] Citing a midrash that compares the death of a *Tzaddik* to the rite of the red heifer, the *para aduma*, the Alter Rebbe explained that even as the passing of a *Tzaddik* seems to constitute a concealment of the *Shekhina*, in truth, it engenders a greater and deeper revelation of divinity in this world. Thus, the death of a *Tzaddik* atones even for egregious sins, like the red heifer that creates purity even beyond the pristine confines of the *Beit HaMikdash*.

Similarly, the Rebbe continued, the death of the sixth Rebbe, while disturbing and leaving a void, actually indicated the disclosure of an even higher element of divinity:

> This, then, is the significance of the "departure of a *Tzaddik*." Although there has already been considerable concealment and cloaking [of holiness], and there have also been many questions and inexplicable occurrences, nevertheless, all this did not suffice; in order for there to be the tremendous degree of revelation of the glory of God throughout all the worlds, there was also the departure of *Tzaddikim*.[55]

This ultimate revelation in the face of apparent tragedy and concealment would propel the Hasidim to complete their final mission.

R. Yosef Yitzhak's Continued Leadership

Beyond the divine revelation engendered by the departure of their leader, the Rebbe underscored a related theme that he had been

---

54. *Tanya, Iggeret HaKodesh*, ch. 28.
55. *Bati LeGani* 5711, *se'if* 7.

The Coronation Maamar

consistently reiterating since his predecessor's passing a year before. The Rebbe once again declared that despite the fact that R. Yosef Yitzhak no longer walked among them, he was still ever-present and leading his Hasidim.

The Rebbe sourced this assertion in another letter of consolation from the Alter Rebbe addressed to the hasidic public upon the death of his older colleague R. Mendel of Vitebsk.[56] In this letter, the Alter Rebbe stressed that a true *Tzaddik* does not truly depart from this world upon his physical demise. Rather, as the Zohar states, "*Tzaddikim* shield the world, and after their death even more than during their life," and "when a *Tzaddik* departs he is to be found in all the worlds more than during his lifetime," highlighting the continued terrestrial, if not physical, presence of a *Tzaddik*. This is especially relevant for the *Tzaddik's* Hasidim, who, from a certain angle, can connect with the *Tzaddik* (and absorb his faith and love of God)[57] to an even greater degree after the disappearance of corporeal restraints. In the words of the Rebbe:

> All the Rebbes – the Alter Rebbe, the Mitteler Rebbe, the *Tzemah Tzedek*, the Rebbe Maharash, the Rebbe Rashab, and the Rebbe [R. Yosef Yitzhak], of blessed memory – have explained that [the passing of a *Tzaddik*] does not mean (God forbid) ascending on high, but rather that he is still found [with us] below, though in a transcendentally lofty manner.[58]

Aspirations for Redemption

This concept is crucially significant for understanding the leadership structure of Chabad in the seventh generation. While for all practical purposes the Rebbe acted like a Rebbe, he was insistent that his father-in-law was still the true leader of the generation.[59] Therefore, the messianic aspirations of the seventh generation included the leadership of

---

56. *Iggeret HaKodesh*, ch. 27.
57. See chapter 17 for a more thorough discussion of this concept.
58. *Bati LeGani* 5711, *se'if* 7.
59. For elaboration on the ramifications and metaphysics of this idea, see chapter 17, section "Who Is the *Nasi* of the Seventh Generation?"

Setting the Stage

R. Yosef Yitzhak. Applying prophetic descriptions of *Mashiah* to his father-in-law, the Rebbe said the following:

> And my revered father-in-law, the Rebbe, of blessed memory, who "bore the ailments and carried our pains" (Is. 53:4), who was "anguished by our sins and ground down by our transgressions" (Is. 53:5) – just as he saw us in our affliction, so will he speedily in our days and rapidly in our times, redeem the sheep of his flock simultaneously both from the spiritual and physical exile, and uplift us to [a state where we shall be suffused with] rays of light. The above, however, is the enjoyment of [mere] *revelations* of Godliness. Beyond this, the Rebbe [R. Yosef Yitzhak] will bind and unite us with the infinite *Essence* of God.[60]

R. Yosef Yitzhak, the true leader of the generation, will bind the people with the Divine Essence, which is the true mission of the seventh generation and the key element of redemption.

The Rebbe concluded the *maamar* with the following prayer:

> Since we have already experienced all these [troubles], everything now depends only on us, the seventh generation. May we be privileged to see and meet with the Rebbe [R. Yosef Yitzhak] here is this world, in a physical body, in this earthy domain – and he will redeem us.[61]

In a footnote, the Rebbe referred to a midrashic passage which describes that in the time of redemption, each community will enter the Land of Israel together with its leader.[62]

---

60. *Bati LeGani* 5711, *se'if* 9.
61. Ibid.
62. The precise meaning of the final words of *Bati LeGani* 5711 – "and he will redeem us" – has been the subject of internal Chabad debate. One author, Ish HaYarei (anonymous) (5757), 8–10, contended that this line must be understood in light of the midrash cited in the footnote in the sense that the Rebbe felt that R. Yosef Yitzhak would lead his community to redemption. However, Yoel Kahn (5757), 14–16, vociferously argued that the Rebbe knew that the average person would

The Coronation Maamar

THE WORK BEGINS

With the conclusion of the *maamar*, the Rebbe reverted from the distinctive chant associated with a *maamar* to his regular speaking voice. He surveyed the room and underscored the extent of hard work that lay before them. In the first of many such statements, the Rebbe emphasized that while in other hasidic sects the Hasidim heavily relied on the Rebbe to "do the work for them," this was never the approach of Chabad and would certainly not be his approach. Rather, each and every Hasid would have to move mountains in order to fulfill his or her generational task:

> The leaders of Chabad always demanded that the Hasidim must achieve things themselves and not rely on the Rebbe. All the more so when we are dealing with only the son-in-law of the Rebbe...do not be complacent to think that you can pass the work onto me and you will be free...to have a good time with a serene life.... Make no mistake! No one is relieving you of your missions...no one is relieving you of any work.[63]

The Rebbe emphasized that he would be able to be a guide and helping hand, but each person would need to fulfill his own individual mission:

> I do not, Heaven forbid, recuse myself from doing whatever I possibly can to help.... It is obvious that the fashioning of a *Dira BaTahtonim* requires the participation of all of us, of every Jew. Each person needs to work in order to fulfill his mission.[64]

---

not look up the reference in the footnote and would interpret the line to mean that R. Yosef Yitzhak himself will be *Mashiah*. He asserted that this line should be understood in light of *Likkutei Sihot* 2, *Hosafot* 10 Shevat, *se'ifim* 9–10, that the Resurrection of the Dead will occur for the righteous before the coming of *Mashi'ah*, allowing R. Yosef Yitzhak himself to be the actual *Mashiah*. For more on this topic, see chapter 22.

63. *Yemei Bereshit: Yoman MiTekufat "Kabbalat HaNesiut" shel Kevod Kedushat Admor Menahem Mendel Schneerson*, 386–87.
64. *Torat Menahem* 5711: 1, 213.

Setting the Stage

And so the work began.[65]

CONCLUSION

While the themes of *Bati LeGani* 5711 require more explication and development, this *maamar* can serve as the basis for understanding the Rebbe's unique philosophy. The mission of disclosing the physical world as the true home for the Divine Essence, and a particular emphasis on sacrificing for the sake of the other, are integral components of the Rebbe's Torah output and activities. As will be discussed over the next several chapters, the Rebbe's innovative approaches to the nature of mundane space, the physical body, the performance of mitzvot, and a host of other issues, all stem from the nature of the Divine Essence and its being "wholly one" with the physical world.

While many of the ideas the Rebbe discussed have their roots in earlier Chabad thought, the Rebbe's philosophy stands out in two interrelated ways. First, he intensely developed the themes of Chabad that pertain to the nature of the Divine Essence and physicality, demonstrating that they form a unified and holistic philosophy. Second, he sought to apply these principles practically on a heretofore unprecedented scale. As we will see in subsequent chapters, each of these innovative elements can be traced to the mission for the generation as outlined in *Bati LeGani* 5711.

Secondary Literature Consulted for Chapter 3, "The Coronation *Maamar*"

Alon Dahan, *Goel Aharon: Mishnato HaMeshihit shel R. Menahem Mendel Schneerson*, 395–403.

Faitel Levin, *Heaven on Earth: Reflections on the Theology of Rabbi Menachem Mendel Schneerson, the Lubavitcher Rebbe*, 6–24, 91–103, 145–49.

Yitzhak Kraus, *HaShevi'i: Meshihiyut BaDor HaShevi'i shel Chabad*, 25–33.

---

65. See *Likkutei Sihot* 12, *Tazria*, no.2, *se'if* 5, that a true *Dira BaTahtonim* can be created only through the service of the *tahtonim* themselves. Hence, it is up to humans in general and Jews in particular to create the *Dira BaTahtonim*.

Part 2
The Theology of *Dira BaTahtonim*

Chapter 4

The Hallway That Is the Palace: The Nature of the Material World

One of the mainstays of rabbinic Judaism is a belief in the existence of a world beyond the material one that we inhabit. While a literal reading of Scripture might leave one with the impression that our world is the sole reality, the Sages took for granted that in addition to "this world" (*Olam HaZeh*), there exists "the World to Come" (*Olam HaBa*).[1] Such a division immediately gives rise to the question of the relationship between these planes of existence. Is there a hierarchical relationship between the worlds? Should we consider one of the worlds to be primary and the other secondary?

The thrust of classical Jewish thought asserts the primacy of *Olam HaBa*. Armed with an array of rabbinic sources and logical arguments, many philosophers and kabbalists alike affirmed that our material world

---

1. See, for example, Sanhedrin 90a.

The Theology of Dira BaTahtonim

is of mere functional importance. *Olam HaBa* is the true site of one's connection to God, presumably the goal of Creation. This world, however, filled with spiritual and physical trials and tribulations, is at most a painful necessity that must be traversed on the path to the world beyond.

The Rebbe, however, orchestrated a paradigm shift regarding the proper outlook toward *Olam HaZeh*. While from one perspective this world is "lowly" and limits the scope of our spiritual vision, the very identification of the material world as *tahtonim* indicates that this world is inherently God's home. Throughout his four decades of leadership, the Rebbe cultivated a realistic and yet idealistic attitude toward *Olam HaZeh* in all of its expanse, contending that the here and now is the true arena for religious drama.

EARLIER JEWISH PHILOSOPHY

One central rabbinic passage regarding the proper perspective on this world appears in a mishna: "R. Yaakov says: This world is like a hallway before the World to Come. Fix yourself in the hallway so you may enter the palace."[2] This straightforward metaphor accentuates the primacy of *Olam HaBa* and relegates our material world to a functional and secondary role.

Rambam

Rambam, in his *Commentary to the Mishna*, explains the parable of the hallway as follows:

> The parable is simple and the intention known. [It means] that in this world a person should acquire the levels through which one can merit the World to Come, as this world is a path and a road to that world.[3]

The Mishna teaches that we should view our lives in this world as a means of acquiring that which we will need in the next world.

---

2. Mishna Avot 4:16.
3. Rambam, *Commentary to the Mishna*, Avot 4:16.

As Rambam describes elsewhere, the wise and righteous realize the transient and functional nature of our current lives and therefore set their sights on the World to Come. They are always cognizant that the goods of this world "are vain and empty things, without any purpose,"[4] and like King David they "desire the life of the World to Come."[5]

This functional perspective regarding our world is in consonance with Rambam's notion of divine transcendence. In his view, God is so transcendent and so beyond the created worlds that no "correlation"[6] can exist between God and any created being. This distance from God is most accentuated for corporeal beings in our material world. God is infinite and transcendent, while materiality is definitionally finite and imperfect. God is one, and our world teems with diversity. Clearly, then, the "location" of our ultimate connection with God is not the here and now but the World to Come. In this vein, Rambam portrayed the death of the righteous as an ecstatic and positive experience, as their souls are finally able to transcend the confinements of materiality and connect with God in a manner that was previously impossible.[7]

Early Hasidism

As noted in chapter 2, Hasidism introduced a new model for conceptualizing the God-world relationship. As opposed to seeing God and the world as two distinct entities, the Baal Shem Tov taught that God is the only true reality, leading to the conclusion that the entire material world is in some way a manifestation of the singular Divine Essence.

What sort of attitude toward this world does this mindset engender? One popular portal into the thought of the Baal Shem Tov on this topic is a parable that he relayed to his students on Rosh HaShana prior to the blowing of the shofar:

---

4. *Mishneh Torah, Hilkhot Teshuva* 8:6.
5. Ibid. 8:7.
6. *Guide for the Perplexed*, I:52 (Pines, 117).
7. Ibid., III:51. For more sources and analysis of this idea in Rambam's thought, see Kenneth Seeskin (2000), 23–36, 95–123. For an even sharper preference for the World to Come, see R. Bahya ibn Pakuda, *Hovot HaLevavot, Shaar Heshbon HaNefesh*, ch. 3, *Shaar HaBittahon*, ch. 4, *Shaar HaPerishut*, ch. 7.

The Theology of Dira BaTahtonim

> There was a great and wise king, and he made walls and towers and gates by means of illusion (*ahizat einayim*). And he commanded that people will come to him through these gates and towers, and he commanded that the treasures of the king be spread out in each of the gates. And there was one person who went until the first gate and took the money and returned. And there were others...until his son, his beloved one, made a great effort to go to his father the king. Then he saw that there was no screen separating him and his father and everything was an illusion.[8]

In this parable, the king is obviously God and the undeterred son is a Jew. But what is the meaning of the illusory walls and towers? What does the son realize upon reaching the king?

While scholars and possibly early hasidic leaders have struggled to answer this question, one prominent approach identifies the illusion with the entire material world.[9] Once the son reaches the king and is privy to the divine and true perspective on reality, he apprehends that the entire world is an illusion. Instead of seeing the walls, towers, money, or any other physical entity, all he sees is pure divinity.

Though the Baal Shem Tov's parable certainly affirms an extreme degree of divine immanence, it seems to simultaneously deepen a negative association with this world. Not only is our world a transient and treacherous path toward the World to Come as earlier authorities taught, its very existence is somehow illusory. Accordingly, our goal in this world is to gain access to the King's inner chamber and cultivate the capability of seeing beyond the veil of physicality and see the world as He does – simple divinity.

The Alter Rebbe

Of all hasidic leaders, some scholars argue that the Alter Rebbe most exemplifies this approach. As noted in chapter 2, the existence/non-existence of the world is one of the great paradoxes upon which *Tanya*

---

8. *Keter Shem Tov*, siman 51b, p. 31; *Ben Porat Yosef* 70c. Translation is from Moshe Idel (2007), 91–92.
9. See Moshe Idel, ibid.; Norman Lamm (1999), 21, note 47.

turns. God as He "fills" the worlds affirms the existence of reality and permeates every corner of it. However, the seemingly higher and truer perspective of God as He "encircles" the world seems to negate the realness of reality. As the Alter Rebbe wrote:

> For just as He was all alone, single, and unique before they were created, so is He all alone, single, and unique after they were created, since, besides Him, everything is as nothing, verily as null and void.[10]

Even after Creation, "everything is as nothing."

This perspective seems to be ensconced in Chabad lore as well. The story is told that close to the Alter Rebbe's death, he asked his grandson, "Do you see the beams [of the ceiling]?" The grandson was dumbfounded by the question and did not know how to respond. The Alter Rebbe continued: "Believe me, now I only see the divine *ayin* [literally, "nothingness," i.e., divine vitality that transcends ordinary characteristics of empirical existence] that vivifies it." With one foot in the next world, the Alter Rebbe saw our world as it truly is.[11]

This favoring of *ayin* (divine nothingness) over *yesh* (our ordinary notion of "being") is not a small detail in the Alter Rebbe's system. Rather, he seems to characterize it as the whole goal of one's service of God:

> And this is the basis of the entire Torah, that there be the effacement of existence into divine nothingness (*bittul hayesh le'ayin*), and each of the three things on which the world stands – Torah, *avoda*, and charity – are all aspects of the effacement of being into nothingness.[12]

---

10. *Tanya, Likktuei Amarim*, ch. 20.
11. Hayyim Heilman, *Beit Rebbi*, vol.1, 46a, note 1.
12. *Torah Or, Noah*, 11a. Translation adapted from Rachel Elior (1992), 144. See there for a broader analysis of this contemplative process.

The Theology of Dira BaTahtonim

Thus, several statements of the Alter Rebbe seem to present a philosophy and a way of life that is predicated on the ontological non-existence of the material world.

As we have seen,[13] however, the Alter Rebbe simultaneously speaks of the existence and importance of this world. In Tanya, he clearly states that the transcendent light actually pervades the entire world and is the vitalizing power that brings it out of nothing into existence.[14] Similarly, he highlights the ability to draw divinity down into the material world through our spiritual service. Notably, his description of the messianic reality, which is built through our work during the era of exile, consists of a revelation of the deepest core of divinity in the material realm.[15]

---

13. Chapter 2, section "The Upper Unity and the Lower Unity."
14. Tanya, Likkutei Amarim, ch. 48.
15. Scholars struggle to precisely define the Alter Rebbe's perspective on this world. Rachel Elior (1993), 49–57, characterizes early Chabad as being "acosmic." This description is shared by Norman Lamm (1998), 4, and Rivka Schatz-Uffenheimer (1963), 516–20. However, Moshe Hallamish (1976), 121–32, and Yaakov Yaakovson (5736) argue against characterizing Chabad philosophy as acosmic. More recently, Elliot Wolfson (2009), 96, favors the term "apophatic panentheism."

Internal Chabad sources also underscore the ontological realness of the material world. See, for example, *Derekh Mitzvotekha* 54b, where the *Tzemah Tzedek* argues against the stance that this world "is not real at all." A central source on this topic in Chabad literature is a *maamar* of the Rebbe Maharash (*Sefer HaMaamarim* 5629, 143–51). There, the Maharash explicitly raises the question – is the world an illusion or an actual existence? – and concludes that it actually exists. His two main proofs are: (1) the existence of the entire halakhic system that seems to relate to our world as a reality, and (2) the fact that halakha (Sanhedrin 67a) differentiates between using magic to pluck real grain and using magic to pluck grain that was created only via magic. If the world itself was only an illusion, then no such difference would exist. The Rebbe cited this *maamar* as background for his description of our world as the true *yesh*. See, for example, *Torat Menahem* 5743: 1, 288–92.

For a recent summary of the scholarship on the realness or illusory nature of the material world in Hasidism more broadly, and particularly the debate between Gershom Scholem and Martin Buber on this topic, see James Jacobson-Maisels (2016), 186, note 8.

The Nature of the Material World

THE MATERIAL WORLD IN THE THOUGHT OF THE REBBE
The Hallway That Is the Palace

One portal into the Rebbe's perspective toward the material world is his interpretation of the aforementioned rabbinic imagery of this world as a hallway. While affirming the earlier and intuitive reading of the ephemeral nature of this world, the Rebbe added a twist that upends the simple import of the passage.

On Simhat Torah 5715, the Rebbe elaborated on the theme that the sukka represents the fleeting nature of the material world.[16] The Rebbe began by reflecting on the fact that Jacob made booths for his cattle[17] (*ulemiknehu asa sukkot*):

> *Miknehu* refers to all the acquired items, meaning all of the material items to which the soul on its own has no connection, but are "acquired" and appended to the soul due to its descent into the body. And the verse tells us: "And for his cattle (*miknehu*) he made booths (*sukkot*)" – that all things material should be regarded as *sukkot*, i.e., as merely transient. As our Sages said, "This world is like a hallway," meaning that the entirety of this world is only a "hallway."[18]

Thus far, the Rebbe's homily is a direct continuation of the classical rabbinic approach of downplaying the significance of this world.

Then, however, the Rebbe veered sharply in a different direction:

> [The Mishna's] phrase, "So that you can enter the palace," does not necessarily mean only after 120 years, but [can be interpreted] based on what our Sages say: "You should see your world in your lifetime" (Berakhot 17a). Meaning, when a person is here below [in this world], he should regard material matters as transient

---

16. For a large selection of sources on this interpretation of the mitzva of sukka that ends with a negative attitude toward this world, see Shalom Pilma (5766), 20–22.
17. Gen. 33:17.
18. *Torat Menahem* 5715: 1, 67.

The Theology of Dira BaTahtonim

(*ara'i*) in order to make them into something permanent (*keva*) through Torah and mitzvot.[19]

Accordingly, the goal of life is not to traverse and exit the hallway to arrive at the palace. Rather, the hallway itself, despite its seeming transience and insignificance, should be transformed into the permanent palace. Somehow, the material world itself is the location of ultimate meaning. Aware of the incongruence of this statement, the Rebbe explained:

> "God desired that He should have a *Dira BaTahtonim*,"[20] meaning a dwelling place for the Divine Essence, which is the true and constant reality and the ultimate and true "permanence" (*keva*). Through connecting the world with God, which means transforming this world into a dwelling place for God via our Torah and mitzvot, the world itself becomes "permanent."[21]

Independently, the material world bears little value, not worth our time and attention. Through Torah and mitzvot, however, one has the capacity to transform this world itself into a dwelling place for the Divine Essence, the one true and permanent being. As the Rebbe concluded: "Materiality *on its own* should be regarded as transient (*ara'i*), as only then one has the ability to connect it to God and to transform it thereby into something permanent (*keva*)."[22]

---

19. Ibid., 68. In its original context, "You should see your world in your lifetime" is a blessing to a student that he should not have any unfulfilled needs during his life (Rashi, s.v. *olamkha*). See, however, Hanna Kasher (5767), 415–54, who traces the long interpretive history that this blessing refers to the ability to tap into the World to Come even while living in the present. In line with this meaning, the Rebbe often cited this talmudic blessing as expressing the potential permanent and final nature of the material world. See, for example, *Likkutei Sihot* 30, *Vayeshev, se'if* 6; *Torat Menahem* 5711: 2, 192; ibid., 5717: 2, 333. It is significant and telling that the Alter Rebbe (*Tanya, Likkutei Amarim*, ch. 14) interprets the line as referring to the tremendous love that the *Tzaddik* experiences for God.
20. *Tanya, Likkutei Amarim*, ch. 36.
21. Ibid.
22. On several occasions, the Rebbe returned to these interpretations of the nature of our world as a "hallway" and the nature of Sukkot. See, for example, *Torat Menahem*

The Nature of the Material World

This radical reinterpretation of such a foundational mishna is not an aberration in the Rebbe's thought. Rather, it reflects the Rebbe's overall understanding of the relationship between God and the world. Let us now turn to some of the Rebbe's more general reflections about the nature of the material world.

"The Humble Soul" and "This World of Falsehood"

As noted above, the notion of *ayin* – divine "nothingness" – has a prominent place in early Hasidism in general and Chabad in particular. The import of many passages is that this *ayin* is the single true reality and religious persons should strive to see through the illusion of materiality to the *ayin* within.

The Rebbe noted, however, that the Alter Rebbe seemed to strike the opposite chord at the very end of his life. Instead of extolling the virtues of this spiritual perspective, the final writings of the Alter Rebbe focused on the inherent superiority of the material world and physical actions. Most notably, shortly before his passing, the Alter Rebbe penned a particularly strong and yet cryptic formulation of this idea:

> The essential service of the truly humble soul lies in the material dimension of Torah (*Torah gashmit*), both in studying it for himself and explaining it to others, and in doing acts of material kindness (*gemilut hesed gashmiyim*) in lending an empathizing mind and counsel regarding household concerns – even if the majority, if not all, of these concerns are matters of falsehood (*divrei sheker*).[23]

Despite the "falsehood" of people's "household concerns," focusing on these concerns is the primary objective of the truly humble soul.

5713: 1, 24–29, 112–13; ibid., 5714: 1, 253–54; ibid., 5720: 2, 185–89; *Likkutei Sihot* 9, 20 Av, no. 2, *se'if* 4.

23. "*Nefesh HaShefela*," cited in *Likkutei Dibburim*, vol. 4, 597. Translation is adapted from "The Physical World According to Rabbi Schneur Zalman of Liadi," retrieved from www.chabad.org/2734.
See *Torat Menahem* 5715: 1, 184–85, for the Rebbe's description of this letter's origins based on earlier Chabad tradition.

The Theology of Dira BaTahtonim

Thus, it was "material" matters that preoccupied the Alter Rebbe on his deathbed.

The Rebbe aptly articulated the discord in this new chord:

> Throughout his lifetime, a *Tzaddik*'s life is not one of physicality, but spirituality... certainly at the very end of a *Tzaddik*'s life, when he is preparing to leave this physical world, materiality is not at all significant for him. And yet, just before his passing, the Alter Rebbe teaches that people should pay attention to and act with "material kindness" toward the material concerns of household members. And not just as a means for the fulfillment of "the true Torah" but simply material advice for the benefit of the material matter itself (which appears to be "matters of falsehood")?[24]

How should this final teaching be synthesized with the primacy granted to the divine *ayin*?

The Rebbe explained that the background to the Alter Rebbe's perplexing parting message is section 20 of the *Iggeret HaKodesh* section of *Tanya*, also penned in the final days of the Alter Rebbe's life. This letter, which the Rebbe had already referenced and identified as central to Chabad philosophy in his inaugural address,[25] differentiates between the spiritual worlds of the *Seder Hishtalshelut* that each express a specific aspect of Godliness (*Gilui*), and our material world that was created *yesh me'ayin* as a direct act of creation from the Divine Essence (*Atzmut*). The Rebbe argued that these variegated levels of divinity account for the differing attitudes toward this world.

From the perspective of the various rungs of the *Seder Hishtalshelut*, the materiality of our world and all its mundane matters are an impossible falsehood in the face of a transcendent and spiritual God. To express this point, the Rebbe reiterated his predecessor's citation of a midrash which describes the anthropomorphized value of "Truth" as advising God against creating the world.[26] As the Rebbe explained:

---

24. *Likkutei Sihot* 16, 24 Tevet, *se'if* 2.
25. Chapter 3, section "*Atzmut* and the Lowest Realm."
26. Genesis Rabba 8:5.

The Nature of the Material World

> The divine Truth within the *Seder Hishtalshelut*… only reaches to the levels that Truth is discernible. However, since this world is "the world of falsehood" where God's Truth is not discernible, therefore "Truth said, 'Do not create.'"[27]

The materiality of our world conceals the single true reality of God. Therefore, Truth argued that there is no justification for the material world to exist.

Ultimately, God decided against Truth and created our world. The reason for this rejection is that Truth's argument stemmed from the limited perspective of the spiritual worlds and thus failed to recognize the utter transcendence and limitlessness of the Divine Essence. As the Rebbe continued:

> But the truth of the Divine Essence has no limit. It is not limited to [only] the levels in which its truth is recognized. Rather, even in a place of concealment and veiling, even a concealment that appears as a falsehood… still the true essence of this world's existence is "from the truth of His existence,"[28] the truth of the Divine Essence.[29]

The Divine Essence transcends the human categories of revelation and concealment, of spirituality and materiality. Saying that God can be accessed only through the abstract, pristine, and spiritual is an affront to the utter limitlessness of God. Rather, *ayin* and *yesh* are both meaningless terms when it comes to the Divine Essence. Despite the seeming association of *ayin* with divine spirituality and *yesh* with the material world, in truth, both can be equally transparent to the Divine Essence. What appears to our spiritual sense as devoid of God is really permeated with divinity.

---

27. *Likkutei Sihot* 16, 24 Tevet, *se'if* 5.
28. This phrase is taken from Rambam's *Mishneh Torah* (*Hilkhot Yesodei HaTorah* 1:1). For an elaboration of the Rebbe's understanding of Rambam's opening statements in *Mishneh Torah* and how they relate to the nature of the material world, see Yoel Kahn (5772).
29. *Likkutei Sihot* 16, 24 Tevet, *se'if* 5.

In summary, even though our world presents as a falsehood that conceals the true *ayin* of God, there is, in fact, a strong ontological basis for all the mundane matters of the material world: the Divine Essence itself. Returning to the original point, the Rebbe explained that this notion justifies the Alter Rebbe's final exhortation. The founder of Chabad wanted his followers to be engaged with mundane materiality in order to reveal that "even this materiality, which appears as a falsehood, is connected with the truth of God's existence."[30]

The "True *Yesh*"

The above formulation stresses that *even* materiality is connected to the Divine Essence, indicating that *ayin* and *yesh* are equally transparent to the Divine Essence. This, however, does not capture the true extent of the Rebbe's perspective on the material world. On other occasions the Rebbe went further and argued that it is *specifically* the material world that allows us access to the Divine Essence.

We have already seen the Rebbe's underlying explanation for this phenomenon in his inaugural address.[31] From all of the created worlds, only material matter does not serve or reflect anything but itself and seems to be independent of any source. Thus, it is only the physical world that is rooted in the Divine Essence, which also is there for Itself and for nothing else. The seeming banality of the world is, in fact, indicative of a higher root.

Accordingly, in several talks the Rebbe emphasized that the contemplative process of effacing reality in one's mind (*bittul*) is a necessary but penultimate step in the advancement of human consciousness. Thinking of the materiality of our world as an illusory veil that conceals the *ayin* of God properly conditions us to recognize that God is the one true reality. The final messianic paradigm shift, however, is to understand that the notion of all-inclusive divinity *affirms* specifically the material world as inherent expression of the divine. Borrowing a phrase from the Mitteler Rebbe, according to which the "created existence" is ultimately

---

30. Ibid.
31. See chapter 3, section "*Atzmut* and the Lowest Realm." See also *Likkutei Sihot* 16, 24 Tevet, *se'if* 4.

The Nature of the Material World

identified with God's single "true existence" (*yesh haamiti*),[32] this world is reconceived as the greatest expression of "the truth of His existence" (*amitat himatzo*).[33]

One clear articulation of this sequence appears in a *maamar* delivered on the first day of Hanukka 5713 (1953). After reviewing some themes from his first *maamar*, the Rebbe said:

> The ultimate goal of the *hishtalshelut* of the worlds is not the upper worlds, but rather this lowest world.... The sequence of service is as follows: First there must be the effacement of existence into the nothingness (*bittul hayesh el haayin*), but this is still insufficient. Rather, afterward, there must be the drawing of the true existence (*yesh haamiti*) into the *ayin*... which is the drawing of the Divine Essence.[34]

The first step in the service of God is to overcome one's intuitive perception of the created world (*yesh hanivra*) in order to see the divine *ayin* that underlies it. But, then, the ultimate goal is to apply one's appreciation for the oneness of God to the material world itself. One must look anew at this world and realize that its materiality is really the ultimate expression of the *yesh haamiti*, i.e., the Divine Essence.[35]

The Rebbe highlighted this two-stage process by distinguishing between two similar verses that earlier Chabad literature frequently employed to convey the hasidic notion of divine unity. In one verse, Moses tells the people that at Mount Sinai they saw that God was the

---

32. *Biurei HaZohar* 43c.
33. Paraphrase of *Mishneh Torah, Hilkhot Yesodei HaTorah* 1:1.
34. *Torat Menahem* 5713: 1, 235–36. See there that the Rebbe associated the first step of transforming the *yesh hanivra* into *ayin* with the recitation of *Keriat Shema* and the second step of finding the *yesh haamiti* with *Shemoneh Esreh*. For other clear expressions of this two-stage process, see *Torat Menahem* 5749: 1, 291–98 (in particular, note 20); ibid., 5750: 4, 174–75.
35. The Rebbe frequently returned to this characterization of this world as the *yesh haamiti*. See, for example, *Likkutei Sihot* 1, *Vayishlah*, *se'if* 11; *Torat Menahem* 5711: 2, 114–15; ibid., 5713: 1, 235–36; ibid., 5716: 1, 9; ibid., 5746: 3, 403–4. The Rebbe used this formulation so frequently that he eventually referred to it as "the known formulation" (*lashon hayadua*). See *Torat Menahem* 5746: 3, 245; *Sefer HaSihot* 5751, 604.

The Theology of Dira BaTahtonim

sole power in the heavens and earth: "And you shall know this day and consider it in your heart, that the Lord He is God in heaven above, and upon the earth below; there is none else (*ein od*)" (Deut. 4:39). A few verses earlier, Moses similarly exhorts: "You have been shown, in order to know that the Lord He is God; there is none else besides Him (*ein od milvado*)" (Deut. 4:35).

Read simply, both verses affirm God's omnipotence by negating the existence of other opposing powers. Characteristically, the Alter Rebbe asserted that these verses not only negate other powers but also any existence other than God. This usage is apparent in the following two quotes from the Alter Rebbe:

> You will consequently know that "in heaven above, and upon the earth below, there is none else (*ein od*)".... Therefore, even the earth and that which is below it are naught and utter nothingness in relation to the Holy One, blessed be He.[36]

> The second level of effacement is the "Upper Unity," that there is none else besides him (*ein od milvado*), and this is true effacement (*bittul*).[37]

On Simhat Torah 5743 (1982), the Rebbe introduced an admittedly new interpretation of these verses that highlighted a shift in consciousness regarding the material reality.[38] After asserting that the subject of the verse "There is none else besides Him (*ein od milvado*)" is the Divine Essence as opposed to other levels of divinity, the Rebbe explained:

> The difference between "there is none else" (*ein od*) and "there is none else besides Him" (*ein od milvado*) is that [the phrase] "there is none else" entirely negates the existence of the world, but [the phrase] "there is none else besides Him" means that "besides Him" there is no reality, but together with Him the world is real,

---

36. *Tanya, Shaar HaYihud VehaEmuna*, ch. 6.
37. *Likkutei Torah, Shir HaShirim*, 31c.
38. *Torat Menahem* 5743: 1, 288.

The Nature of the Material World

meaning that the reality of the world and all therein is "the truth of His existence" (*amitat himatzo*).[39]

"There is none else" nullifies the existence of the world before an all-encompassing God – the transformation of *yesh* into *ayin*. "There is none else besides Him" is the next and final stage that affirms the reality of our world by demonstrating that the created existence is, in fact, nothing other than the *yesh haamiti* (the true being) encompassed within and permeated by the Divine Essence.[40]

The Rebbe further elucidated that such an affirmation of the divine composition of the material realm is indeed incomprehensible. As such, it must be rooted in the Divine Essence, which transcends all limitations of logic:

> There is a synthesis of opposites in the concept of "there is none else besides Him": On the one hand there is the actual existence of the world (and not just the apparent existence), and on the other hand there is the fact that its existence is God. This means... that the existence of the world is felt, and yet, "there is none else besides Him," for the existence of the world is "the truth of His existence".... For there to be a synthesis of opposites – this is the sole purview of the Divine Essence, which has no limitations and therefore can combine two opposites in the same matter.[41]

This paradoxical approach to materiality is impenetrable to the logical human mind, that cannot tolerate such a synthesis of opposites. And yet, this precisely should be expected of the Divine Essence that transcends all created categories.

To summarize, earlier hasidic sources are ambiguous on how the relationship between God and the world should be understood. But

---

39. Ibid., 292.
40. The Rebbe frequently referenced this interpretation of "there is none else besides Him." See, for example, *Torat Menahem* 5744: 1, 330 (where the Rebbe connected this interpretation with a non-ascetic approach to this world); ibid., 5746: 1, 357; ibid., 5746: 3, 220–21, 556; ibid., 5749: 1, 237–38.
41. *Torat Menahem* 5743: 1, 292–93.

The Theology of Dira BaTahtonim

the Rebbe was crystal clear: Rather than negating the world, identifying materiality itself as the ultimate expression of the Divine Essence affirms the significance of this world as being part of God.[42]

AN OUTWARD FOCUS
God, Person, and World

This perspective on the material world can also radically shift one's religious orientation and practice. While a religious person might intuitively gravitate toward a life of isolation and seclusion in pursuit of spirituality and transcendence, such a path is not appropriate for a generation responsible to transform the world. Rather, the creation of a *Dira BaTahtonim* and the disclosure of the essential divinity of materiality requires an active engagement with the world at large, albeit with the proper mindset.

The Rebbe powerfully expressed this outward-focused orientation in a talk he delivered toward the end of his life. He cited a mishna that exhorts its reader to ponder three items to avoid sin: "Akavya b. Mahalalel says: 'Keep your eye on three things, and you will not come to sin: Know from where you came, and to where you are going, and before whom you are destined to give an account and a reckoning.'"[43] The Rebbe noted that the mishna first mentions the need to look at three items and then delineates them. The splitting of these clauses provides the interpretive space to inject additional meanings in the first statement by identifying other threesomes that can save a person from sin. In this

---

42. The Alter Rebbe's relationship with this material world of falsehood seems to have developed over the course of his life. Even internal Chabad sources understand the letter "*Nefesh HaShefela*" that is cited above as indicating a shift in the Alter Rebbe's perspective. In a letter published in *Tanya, Iggeret HaKodesh*, sec. 22, the Alter Rebbe writes that he does not want to discuss "earthly matters" with his Hasidim during their private meetings. For the historical background to this letter, see Immanuel Etkes (2005), 28–31. Later in life, though, the Alter Rebbe changed his practice and discussed both spiritual and earthly matters with Hasidim. See *Torat Menahem* 5713: 3, 127–28; ibid., 5751: 4, 200, note 101, where the Rebbe relayed that he heard from older Hasidim that the Alter Rebbe's affirmation of the false matters of this world in "*Nefesh HaShefela*" was a retraction from that original position. Regarding this shift in the Alter Rebbe's policy and perspective, see Elhanan Nir (5774), 190–205.
43. Mishna Avot 3:1.

spirit, the Rebbe offered a novel interpretation to the mishna's opening exhortation to "keep your eye on three things":

> A person can think that there need to be only two items: himself and God, whom he serves...but the mishna says...there is a third item. In addition to the existence of God and one's own existence, there needs to be a third item: the existence of the world that was created by God, through which a person serves his Creator.[44]

Instead of just isolating oneself with God, to truly avoid sin one needs to also meditate on the existence of the world. The world is integral to a productive religious life.

The Rebbe elaborated that this is the deeper meaning of the old Chabad adage that notes an affinity between the Hebrew words for exile (*gola*) and redemption (*geula*). The two words have identical spellings apart from the *alef* that appears only in the word *geula*. The Alter Rebbe noted that this orthographic fact is a metaphor for the relationship between these two states of existence. One can transform exile (*gola*) into redemption (*geula*) by injecting an *alef*, which has the numerical value of one, representative of the One God, into the equation.[45]

At first glance this statement is rather surprising. As the Rebbe asked: "Is not redemption the absolute opposite of exile? If so, how can it be that *geula* includes within it the word for exile?"[46]

The answer, argued the Rebbe, stems from a proper understanding of the relationship between our current reality and the utopian messianic world:

> Redemption (does not nullify the exile, rather it includes the exile) within it. Moreover [redemption] elevates the exile through inserting into it and revealing in it the "Master [*Alufo*, a play on the added letter *alef*] of the world." The goal is to create a *Dira BaTahtonim* for God, even as the *tahtonim* exist in

---

44. *Torat Menahem* 5751: 3, 179–80.
45. *Likkutei Torah, Behaalotekha*, 35c.
46. *Torat Menahem* 5751: 3, 178.

exile...to reveal in the *tahtonim* themselves the Master of the World...this is the essence of redemption: "The revelation of Infinite light, blessed be He, in this physical world" (*Tanya, Likkutei Amarim*, ch. 36).[47]

There is nothing fundamentally wrong with our material world; we simply need to reveal its divine core. This is perfectly represented by the affinity between the words *gola* and *geula*.

A Realistic Yet Optimistic Outlook

The fact that *gola* and *geula* are both opposite and closely related categories sheds light on the Rebbe's dual perspective on the world at large. On the one hand, the Rebbe was a realist who did not gloss over the harshness and decadence of our current exilic reality and the challenges it places before so many. However, a leitmotif in his talks is that even as one cannot be naive about evil and the hiddenness of God, one must always be cognizant of the Godly core of our material world and all therein. This "inner" perspective generates a positive attitude toward this world and confidence in the inexorable success of the mission of disclosing the divinity of the *tahtonim*.

When reflecting on the lowliness of this world, the Rebbe would often cite the Alter Rebbe's description:

> [This world] is the lowest in degree; there is none lower than it in terms of concealment of His light, and no world compares with it for doubled and redoubled darkness; nowhere is God's light hidden as in this world. So much so, that it is filled with *kelippot* and the *Sitra Ahra*, which actually oppose God, saying: "I am, and there is nothing else besides me."[48]

---

47. Ibid., 181.
48. *Tanya, Likkutei Amarim*, ch. 36. See *Torat Menahem* 5712: 2, 92; ibid., 5719: 1, 163; ibid., 5721: 1, 296; ibid., 5721: 2, 323; *Likkutei Sihot* 6, *Shemot*, no. 2, *se'if* 10; ibid., 12, *Tazria*, no. 2, *se'if* 6; ibid., 38, *Hukkat*, no. 1, *se'if* 3.

According to the Rebbe, in this passage the Alter Rebbe pointed to two distinct degradations of our world.[49] First, as discussed above, the materiality of this world conceals God's presence and expresses a seeming autonomy from God. On this level, our world is the only plane of reality that seems to be *indifferent* to God.

In addition to this banality, the Alter Rebbe highlighted the existence of the *kelippot* (literally, "shells"), which express *open hostility* toward God. While the materiality of this world simply conceals God, our world is also brimming with brazenly evil elements that blatantly taunt God. Elements of this world constantly seduce humans to defy God and to sin. These pervasive negative forces allow such insolent behavior to be rewarded, causing the wicked to prosper. As the Alter Rebbe described our world: "This world with all it contains is called the world of *kelippot* and *Sitra Ahra*.... This is also why all affairs of this world are difficult and evil, and the wicked prevail in it."[50]

Based on these two forms of darkness, the Rebbe at times painted a starkly negative picture of this world. In one talk, delivered during the height of the Cold War, the Rebbe spoke about the "wicked prevailing in [this world]" such that "each day a new destructive weapon is added, and a new fear: How will the world look in another day from now, in another hour?"[51] In a different talk, the Rebbe reflected more generally on the darkness of this world, going so far as to refer to the birth of a baby as an entry into a place that is spiritually contaminated by "death," as the new baby will have to endure this world's sinister concealment of God's presence and the associated vicissitudes of life.[52]

However, the Rebbe did not allow this realism to obfuscate the true divine nature of the material world. Instead, he carefully differentiated between the two sources of this worldly darkness. The *kelippot*, or the aspects of reality that oppose Godliness, are a later and non-essential addition to the world. As the midrash the Rebbe quoted in his first discourse, *Bati LeGani* 5711, describes, it was human sin that caused God

---

49. See *Likkutei Sihot* 6, 10 Shevat, *se'if* 3; ibid., 25, *Miketz*, note 52.
50. *Tanya, Likkutei Amarim*, ch. 6.
51. *Torat Menahem* 5719: 2, 40–41.
52. *Likkutei Sihot* 38, *Hukkat*, no. 1, *se'if* 3.

to "leave this world," creating the space for the forces of the *Sitra Ahra* to enter and inhabit the terrestrial realm. However, underneath these "shells" lies the essential material world, which, while seemingly mundane, in truth contains a divine core that can be disclosed via human service.

In a talk on 10 Shevat 5731, exactly twenty years after ascending to the leadership of Chabad, the Rebbe reflected on this realistic yet optimistic perspective. The Rebbe rhetorically admitted that there is ample reason to be pessimistic about the prospect of creating a *Dira BaTahtonim*:

> When a Jew contemplates this world, which (as the Alter Rebbe cites) is "filled with *kelippot* and *Sitra Ahra*," i.e., every part of it is filled with *kelippot*, to the extent that it is referred to as "the world of *kelippot*," he might think to himself: Since the Holy One, blessed be He, created the world this way, it is impossible for me to change it. Therefore, I will separate myself entirely from the world, isolate myself in "the four cubits of" Torah and prayer, and have nothing at all to do with the world!"[53]

This is a natural and understandable religious reaction. God's concealment leads many toward isolationism and disdain for the world at large. How can one transform a hostile world into a home for God?

In response to this pressing question, the Rebbe invoked the strategic differentiation described above. First, the *kelippot* and antagonistic forces are not deeply interwoven into the fabric of this world but are temporary additions, destined to be removed: "The fact that this world is a world of *kelippot* is not a necessary element of the essence of this world. Rather, this is an element that was added after Creation through the sin of the Tree of Knowledge."[54]

Once freed from hostile *kelippot*, the essential material world, despite its seeming indifference to God, is His most fitting home:

---

53. Ibid., 6, 10 Shevat, *se'if* 3.
54. Ibid.

Focusing on the essence of this world, this world is advantageous over the upper worlds, because the Essence of the *Shekhina* was specifically in the lowest realm....

So even now, the inner essence of [this world's] every component, even those that appear to be oppositional to God, is to be "an abode for Him." One must therefore spread Torah everywhere in order to *reveal* the essential good that already exists in every place.[55]

The inner divinity and goodness of the world is an ontological fact waiting to be revealed. In this sense, the Jew's responsibility is not to revolutionize and create, but rather to demonstrate and disclose. He must peel away the final veil of indifference and uncover the divinity of the material world and its inhabitants.

This realistic yet positive approach toward the world and all therein is a primary theme in the Rebbe's talks. Time and time again he emphasized that on completing Creation God declared this world to be "very good" (Gen. 1:31), and nothing has fundamentally changed since that moment.[56] While the inner divinity of the world does not obscure the reality of evil, the inner goodness should be one's compass when interacting with any element of the terrestrial plane. The inner *alef* of God is already present in the indifferent *gola*, and the mission of the Jewish people is simply to reveal it.

---

55. Ibid.
56. For the Rebbe's usage of God's positive description of reality, see, for example, *Torat Menahem* 5722: 1, 135; ibid., 5746: 2, 446–50; ibid., 5749: 1, 259. For more general formulations regarding the inner goodness of the world, see *Likkutei Sihot* 17, *Shemini*, no. 1, *se'if* 7; *Torat Menahem* 5725: 1, 183. The Rebbe also connected this goodness of the world with the language of the original *Bati LeGani* midrash which describes the world as a "garden" which is a beautiful and pleasurable location. In this regard, see *Torat Menahem* 5743: 2, 886–91; ibid., 5746: 2, 450; and the video excerpt from 10 Shevat 5732 available at www.chabad.org/253998.

Conquering the Mundane Spaces of the World

This perspective on the relationship between God, the world, and human service undergirded the Rebbe's push to continuously "conquer"[57] mundane spaces. While sanctified space still has a crucial role, the Rebbe sought to break aspects of the binary between sanctified and secular spaces, as such sharp divisions are philosophically untenable in the face of the all-encompassing Divine Essence. The final mission is to reveal the entire world, and not just the spiritual oases, as the divine and "true *yesh*."

This unification is apparent in several talks that focus on the status of the *Mishkan* and *Beit HaMikdash*, the apex of spatial sanctity. The Rebbe's multilayered treatment of the uniqueness of these locations and their relationship with the outside world is intertwined with his understanding of the relationship between the Divine Essence and the material world more generally. Characteristically, he first developed these ideas in the textual and theoretical world of Torah, and then applied them as a model for practical living.

On one level, the very existence of sanctified space expresses the utter transcendence of the Divine Essence over created categories. To paraphrase King Solomon's statement of astonishment, the God whose presence nullifies the world surely cannot be housed in a finite home of wood and stone.[58] Rather, the incomprehensible confluence of opposites of an infinite God dwelling in a finite structure is a hallmark feature of the unbounded Divine Essence. As the Rebbe once said:

> God is truly limitless, meaning that He is not bound, Heaven forbid, with any limitations – not the limitations of space, nor the limitations of transcending space. Just as we cannot define God through the limitations of space, so too, it is impossible to define Him through the "limitations" of transcending space ... for God is

---

57. The Rebbe often referred to the disclosure of divinity in seemingly secular space as *kibbush*, "conquering." See, for example, *Likkutei Sihot* 30, Vayehi, *se'if* 4; *Torat Menahem* 5716: 2, 150–54. This language is rooted in God's initial blessing and command to the first man and woman: "Be fruitful and multiply and fill the earth and conquer it" (Gen. 1:28).
58. I Kings 8:27.

above all limiting descriptions. Rather, only when space and transcendence of space come together, finitude and infinity [come] together, this combination of opposites teaches of the power of the Essence which is "the impossible of impossibilities" (*nimna hanimnaot*) and combines two opposing things. Only here can there be the dwelling of God.[59]

The unity of antinomies expresses the Divine Essence's boundless freedom from even boundlessness. This is the meaning of the talmudic statement that the finite and physical Holy Ark took up no space in the Holy of Holies where it was situated.[60] The Divine Essence is able to unify space and the transcendence of space.

Despite the fact that the paradoxical existence of sanctified space seems to perfectly express the limitlessness of the Divine Essence, this is not the case. The Rebbe consistently contended that the same logic that identifies a physical structure as a fitting home for God is even more apt regarding the mundane space of the world at large. The argument goes as follows. If the Divine Essence is expressed through the paradox of God dwelling in a finite structure, then the more the paradox is sharpened and the logical incongruity accented, the more truly the Divine Essence is revealed.

Accordingly, the Rebbe contended that the ultimate impossibility lies not in God's dwelling in sanctified space, but in His revelation within the previously mundane space of the world:

> It is understandable that the "lowness" of the inanimate materials and "space" used to build the *Mishkan*...does not compare to the "lowness" of the inanimate materials and "space" in the broader world. Therefore, when a person brings sanctity to the inanimate materials and "space" of the broader world he completes the true

---

59. *Likkutei Sihot* 3, *Teruma, se'if* 3. The phrase *nimna hanimnaot* in this quotation is taken from *Shu"t Rashba, siman* 418. For the precise meaning of this description, see chapter 18, section "An Unnecessary Order."
60. *Megilla* 10b.

The Theology of Dira BaTahtonim

intention a *Dira BaTahtonim*, namely, that from the lowest of the low he makes an abode for the Divine Essence.⁶¹

The revelation of God specifically within the lowest elements of the world – a *Dira BaTahtonim* – is the ultimate expression of the Divine Essence's transcendence over all created categories. Part of the goal of sanctified space is that it ultimately transcends itself and spills over to the outside world, on one level blurring distinctions between sanctified and mundane.⁶²

Ramifications of the Sanctification of Mundane Space

Characteristically, the Rebbe took this expansion of the sanctified into the mundane as a model for individual and communal living. While the manifest spirituality of the world's *Mishkan*s are important way-stations for training and rejuvenation, much of the work lies beyond the walls of these havens.

For example, on the individual level, the Rebbe applied this fundamental denial of secular space in his teachings regarding the proper perspective toward one's workspace. In the fall of 5747 (1986), the Rebbe discussed the relationship between the holiday-packed and spiritually charged month of Tishrei and the next several months, where most people would be engaged primarily in "ordinary matters" (*uvdin dehol*).⁶³ Many Hasidim would leave their homes to spend the holidays with the Rebbe in Crown Heights. This custom follows the talmudic teaching that just as one is obligated to make a pilgrimage to the *Beit HaMikdash* for the three festivals, so one must visit their Torah teacher

---

61. *Likkutei Sihot* 3, *Teruma*, *se'if* 5.
62. For other places where the Rebbe spoke of the transformation of the outside world as the ultimate goal of the *Mishkan*, see *Likkutei Sihot* 16, *Pekudei*; ibid., 6, *Shemot*, no. 2, *se'if* 9; ibid., 4, *Hukkat*, *se'if* 3; ibid., 17, *Aharei Mot*, no. 2, *se'if* 8; *Torat Menahem* 5749: 2, 324–25; ibid., 5750: 2, 327–38; *Likkutei Sihot* 6, *Shemot*, no. 2, *se'if* 9. For a detailed explanation for the differing expressions but ultimate unity of the third *Beit HaMikdash* and the rest of the world that is couched in kabbalistic and hasidic language, see *maamar* "*Gadol Yihye Kevod* 5722" (*Sefer HaMaamarim Melukat*, vol. 4, 111–20).
63. *Torat Menahem* 5747: 1, 466.

at these times.⁶⁴ Before they returned home, the Rebbe exhorted them that instead of growing despondent in their ordinary engagements with the outside world in the form of working for a livelihood, they should consider their leaving an opportunity to "extend the light and sanctity of the *Beit HaMikdash* to the entire world."⁶⁵

On another occasion⁶⁶ the Rebbe noted that the halakhic system legitimizes and even mandates the average person to spend the majority of his life engaged in "the work of the field." Shabbat and the *Shemitta* year, the temporal equivalents of the *Beit HaMikdash*, represent a mere one-seventh of one's time, while the Torah prescribes that the average person should spend the preponderance of his time in the field. This lopsided proportion is not problematic or happenstance, but rather reflects God's purpose for Creation:

> The explanation of this is based on the known notion that the goal of Creation is that God desired a *Dira BaTahtonim* reaching until the lowest level that has nothing lower, and therefore the primary focus and majority of one's service is not in matters of inherent sanctity... but rather in the matters of this world – "Six years you shall sow your field" (Lev. 25:3) – that God should be revealed even in the field, which is the lowest place.⁶⁷

The pure and pristine spirituality of the *Beit HaMikdash* and Shabbat exists in part to facilitate an equal revelation of God in the outer field, representing one's mundane place of work. The Rebbe continued that this requires those who work in the field to have set times to study Torah as then the sanctity of Torah will also permeate their work in the "field."⁶⁸

On the communal level, the imperative to reveal the divine within the mundane is manifest in the Rebbe's continued emphasis on "conquering" the entire globe. Throughout history, Jewish communities

---

64. Rosh HaShana 16b.
65. *Torat Menahem* 5747: 1, 468.
66. Ibid., 5750: 4, 194–96. See also *Likkutei Sihot* 1, Vayak'hel, se'ifim 9–10.
67. *Torat Menahem* 5750: 4, 196.
68. Ibid., 198.

were limited to the Middle East, Europe, and parts of Asia and Africa, but the tumultuous events of the twentieth century brought Jews to new shores. According to the Rebbe, the existence of the relatively young Jewish communities of North and South America, Australia, and South Africa indicates that the time has arrived to reveal God in "all corners of the world, even abandoned corners."[69] This dispersion facilitates the revelation of the divinity of each new country through the service of the local Jewish community:

> From this is understood the advantage in the fact that Jews are dispersed and are dwelling in multifold and diverse countries, in the manner of the verse "And you shall spread forth" (Gen. 28:14). As only through the service of the Jewish people in all the countries of the world through settling there and acting in accordance with the permissible customs of the country, can a Jew accomplish the purification of each place, in accordance with its nature, such that a *Dira BaTahtonim* is made.[70]

The entire world is the home of the Divine Essence and hence divinity must be revealed in every corner of it.[71]

CONCLUSION

While the majority of classical Jewish philosophical sources see the material world as bearing mere functional importance at best, and being non-existent at worst, the Rebbe, building from strands found in earlier rabbinic and hasidic sources, offered a different perspective. Combining these classical sources with a redemption-oriented consciousness, the Rebbe consistently and systematically taught that this material world is an instantiation of God's "true existence" and harbors the ultimate goal of Creation, as it is the most perfect home for the revelation of the

---

69. Ibid., 5749: 1, 298, note 64.
70. Ibid., 5752: 1, 400.
71. For how this idea is reflected in the Rebbe's approach to the relationship between the Land of Israel and the Diaspora, see chapter 19.

Divine Essence. The following chapters will outline the methods that the Rebbe advocated to effect this disclosure.

Secondary Literature Consulted for Chapter 4, "The Hallway That Is the Palace: The Nature of the Material World"

Shneur Zalman Gopin, "Mitzvat Ahdut Hashem."

Faitel Levin, *Heaven on Earth*, 43–54, 91–103.

Yitzhak Kraus, *HaShevi'i*, 56–71.

Eli Rubin, "Beyond Borders: International Jewish Renaissance."

Elliot Wolfson, *Open Secret*, 66–129.

Chapter 5

From Sinai to Mitzva Tanks

The *Dira BaTahtonim* theology that is reflected in the Rebbe's perspective on the physical world also permeates his discussions of the essential nature of Torah, mitzvot, and the Sinaitic revelation. As we have seen, the Sinaitic revelation is described in the midrash the Rebbe quoted in *Bati LeGani* 5711 as the moment in which the *Shekhina* returned to the *tahtonim*. This reestablishment of the connection between the upper and lower realms was hailed by the Rebbe as the essential breakthrough of the Giving of the Torah.

The transformative impact of this event in the Rebbe's thought can be best understood through a historical analysis which compares and contrasts the nature of the Torah and mitzvot in the pre-Sinai and post-Sinai periods. This will help us see the Rebbe's understanding of the Sinaitic fulcrum as part of the conceptual basis for several of his flagship programs. Most notably, the mitzva campaigns, in which the Rebbe sent his followers to the streets to encourage and enable their non-observant brethren to perform mitzvot, can be seen as a direct application of his unique outlook regarding the nature of mitzvot in the post-Sinai period.

BACKGROUND
The Patriarchs Kept the Entire Torah
The Talmud teaches that the forefathers observed all of the mitzvot, even prior to the Giving of the Torah at Sinai: "Abraham our father performed the entire Torah [even] before it was given, as it says, 'Because Abraham listened to My voice, and he observed My statutes, commandments, laws, and teachings'" (Gen. 26:5).[1] Even bereft of a divine command, the patriarchs intuited the Torah through their own superlative spiritual sense.[2] While this teaching underscores the greatness of the *Avot*, it simultaneously poses a challenge for the significance of the Giving of the Torah at Sinai. If people of great spiritual stature are able to discern the mitzvot without an explicit divine imperative, was Sinai then only necessary for the uncouth masses? Why is the Giving of the Torah at Sinai such a pivotal historical event?

The Significance of Sinai in Early Jewish Thought
Jewish thought has grappled with precisely defining the significance of Sinai since at least the time of "the first speaker in all issues,"[3] Saadia Gaon. He was particularly troubled by God's revelation of the rational mitzvot that could have been reached through independent human thought. While Saadia Gaon offered several solutions to this vexing question, one of his arguments simply concedes to the premise of the question. Really human beings could have discerned many of these precepts independently, but only after engaging in an arduous and multigenerational saga of inquiry. God, in His kindness, expedited the process through giving the Jewish people the Torah.[4]

According to Saadia Gaon, the Revelation at Sinai did not fundamentally revise the value of the mitzvot but was rather an act of divine grace. Most

---

1. Mishna Kiddushin 4:14.
2. See Genesis Rabba 61:1 that Avraham's "kidneys" counseled him the content of the Torah.
3. Avraham ibn Ezra, *Mozenei Lashon HaKodesh*, 1b.
4. Saadia Gaon, *The Book of Doctrines and Beliefs*, abridged edition translated from the Arabic by Alexander Altmann (Oxford: East and West Library, 1946), 95. For a longer analysis of Saadia Gaon's approach to this topic, see Alexander Altmann (1944), 320–29.

subsequent thinkers, however, perceive a unique advantage in performing mitzvot specifically because they are commanded by God, even those that have a rational basis. These approaches are often linked to the talmudic dictum "Greater is one who is commanded to do a mitzva and performs it than one who is not commanded to do a mitzva and performs it."[5]

Tosafot, for example, proposed that the very fact that a person is obligated to perform a specific action engenders a greater resistance from the evil inclination.[6] Overcoming this inner tension grants one more reward, as "the reward is correspondent to the pain."[7] Taking another approach, Ritva[8] notes that mitzvot are for our benefit as opposed to God's. Therefore, even though mitzvot are inherently positive actions, the reward that naturally flows from an inherently good action pales in comparison to the reward for the fact that we are obeying God's command. Thus, Ritva sees the command as a means of increasing the reward of a mitzva by allowing us to simply obey the law commanded by God.

The Significance of Sinai in the Thought of the Alter Rebbe

In contrast to *Tosafot* and Ritva, the Alter Rebbe taught that the Giving of the Torah at Sinai significantly changed the cosmic landscape. As we have seen,[9] *Tanya* describes how God contracted and expressed Himself through the words and commands of the Torah that were given at Sinai.[10] Building from these ideas, the Alter Rebbe taught that even as the patriarchs intuited and performed all of the mitzvot, they were able to access only a certain level of divine light.[11] By contrast, at Sinai, God revealed His "inner will,"[12] which emerges from a place "higher than the *Seder Hishtalshelut*"[13] and gave each Jewish person the ability to interface with God through the study of Torah and the performance of mitzvot.

---

5. Kiddushin 31a.
6. *Tosafot* on Kiddushin 31a, s.v. *gadol*.
7. Mishna Avot 5:23.
8. Ritva on Kiddushin 31a, s.v. *de'amar Rebbi Hanina*.
9. See chapter 2, section "The Short Path."
10. *Tanya, Likkutei Amarim*, chs. 22–23.
11. *Torah Or, Yitro*, 67a, 68a–b.
12. Ibid., 68b.
13. Ibid.

THE REBBE ON THE SIGNIFICANCE OF SINAI
The Fragrances of the *Avot*
Building on the Alter Rebbe's depiction of the Giving of the Torah, the Rebbe would frequently cite an enigmatic midrash that directly contrasts the mitzvot of the patriarchs with the mitzvot of the post-Sinai reality:

> "Because of the fragrance of Your goodly oils, Your name is an oil poured forth" (Song. 1:3). R. Yannai the son of R. Shimon said: "All the songs that the patriarchs sang before You were merely fragrances, but for us 'Your name is an oil poured forth,' as a person who pours from a vessel to a vessel. All of the mitzvot that the patriarchs performed before You were mere fragrances, but for us, 'Your name is an oil poured forth' – 248 positive commandments and 365 negative commandments."[14]

R. Yannai clearly differentiates between the mitzvot of the *Avot*, which are symbolically represented as the fragrances of oil, and "our" mitzvot, which are the actual oil. Why does the midrash use these particular metaphors? What do these cryptic formulations mean?

The Rebbe explained that R. Yannai pointed to a fundamental difference in the very nature of these two sets of mitzvot. The fragrance of oil is beautiful and purifying, but it is ultimately an ephemeral emission that emerges from the oil, in contrast to the more permanent oil itself. While the service of the patriarchs was indeed very lofty, it was lacking insofar as it was similar to a fragrance:

> The mitzvot of the patriarchs are compared to fragrances for these reasons:
>
> (1) The mitzvot that they fulfilled drew forth a mere emission of Divine Revelation rather than the Divine Essence. (This is due to the fact that their fulfillment of the mitzvot was through their own abilities, and it is known that a creation cannot with its own abilities reach beyond its own source and root.)

---
14. Song of Songs Rabba 1:3.

(2) The mitzvot that the patriarchs fulfilled did not have the power to permanently and overtly infuse the sanctity of the mitzva within the physical item used to fulfill the mitzva, in such a manner to ensure that the sanctity would remain revealed in it even after the mitzva's fulfillment. (This is analogous to a fragrance that evaporates.)[15]

As great as the patriarchs were, their service stemmed from their finite human intuition and was perforce inherently limited. They were able to access only the "fragrant" spiritual revelations of God, as opposed to the Divine Essence itself.[16] This, in turn, severely restricted the impact of their service, as, similar to a fragrance, their spiritual service purified the "air" while not having a lasting impression on materiality itself.[17]

As the Rebbe elaborated in many talks, the goal of the patriarchs' service was distinctly spiritual: "To reveal the spiritual light of God." These *revelations* of God fundamentally transcend the lowest physical realm and ordinarily cannot be absorbed therein.[18] Accordingly, even when the patriarchs employed a physical item for a mitzva, their intention was to channel the spiritual light of God through the object, as opposed to engendering a permanent and transformative effect on the physical item itself. This otherworldly objective afforded the patriarchs flexibility regarding the items they used for the mitzva, and hence, according to the Zohar, Jacob performed the mitzva of tefillin with the sticks that he placed in front of Lavan's sheep. In more halakhic terms, the concept of a *heftza demitzva*, a physical object that becomes sacrosanct through its usage in a mitzva, simply did not exist in the pre-Sinai era.[19]

---

15. *Likkutei Sihot* 8, Naso, no. 3, *se'if* 11.
16. See also *Likkutei Sihot* 5, 20 Heshvan, *se'if* 4.
17. See also *Likkutei Sihot* 1, Hayei Sara, *se'if* 16.
18. *Likkutei Sihot* 3, Yitro, *se'if* 1.
19. Ibid., 5, 20 Heshvan, *se'if* 3. In the continuation of this talk, the Rebbe noted that the mitzva of *mila* is unique insofar as it did have a partial impact on the sanctity of Abraham's body. Therefore, *mila* should be considered a transition mitzva that links the service of the patriarchs with our service of the post-Sinai era.

In addition to citing R. Yannai's comparison of the patriarchs' service to fragrances, the Rebbe also often rooted his characterization of the pre-Sinaitic mitzvot in a different midrash:

> "And God said to Moses, 'Stretch forth your hand heavenward'" (Ex. 9:22).... God decreed, "The heavens are heavens of the Lord, but the earth He gave to the children of men" (Ps. 115:16). It is analogous to a king who decreed and said that Romans should not descend to Syria and Syrians should not ascend to Rome. Thus, when God created the world He decreed, "The heavens are heavens of the Lord, but the earth He gave to the children of men."[20]

God is likened to a king who creates a categorical chasm between heaven and earth. Even while the patriarchs performed mitzvot, they did not succeed in breaking the barrier that existed between the spiritual stratosphere and mundane materiality.[21]

The Unification of the Upper and Lower Realms

All of this changed with the Giving of the Torah. Here is the continuation of the above midrash:

> When God desired to give the Torah, He nullified His original decree and declared: "The lower realms shall rise to the higher realms and the higher realms shall descend to the lower realms, and I will be the initiator," as the verse states, "And God descended on Mount Sinai" (Ex. 19:20), and later it is written, "And to Moses [God] said, 'Ascend to God'" (Ex. 24:1). We see that "all that the Lord wished, He did in the heavens and on the earth" (Ps. 130:6).

---

20. Exodus Rabba 12:3.
21. It is important to note that despite the limitations of the patriarchs' service, it was a still a crucial preparatory step toward the events at Sinai (*Likkutei Sihot* 15, *Lekh Lekha*, no. 2, *se'if* 2). This process of transitioning from the service of the patriarchs to the service of the post-Sinai era serves as a model for each individual Jew throughout history (ibid., *se'ifim* 5–6).

The Theology of Dira BaTahtonim

At Sinai, God nullified His earlier decree and created a bridge between the upper and lower realms in the form of the Torah.

The mechanism for this unification of the celestial and terrestrial realms is the emergence of the all-inclusive Divine Essence that was inaccessible to the *Avot*.[22] The divine revelations that account for ordinary spirituality transcend the physical world and therefore cannot truly affect it. However, as we discussed, the definition-less Divine Essence is beyond the categories of physical and spiritual and therefore has the ability to unite the two. Thus, the result of Sinai is a system of physical actions in the form of mitzvot that are empowered by the Divine Essence to fundamentally and permanently sacralize even the most terrestrial and physical of objects.[23]

Characteristic of his approach of perceiving the macro in the micro, the Rebbe saw this idea reflected in the first three words uttered by God at Sinai – *Anokhi Hashem Elokekha* (I am the Lord your God). The name *Elokim* refers to God who both controls the natural world and is expressed through it. The tetragrammaton (*Hashem*) refers to a level of Godliness which transcends the natural order of time and space. In contrast to these levels of divinity, it is the indescribable *Anokhi* – "I" – that refers to the Divine Essence:

> *Anokhi* is His Essence, may He be blessed, that cannot be signified by any letter or hint … meaning that it is higher not only than the revelation of *Elokim*, which has the numerical value of [the term] *teva* (nature), but it is also higher than the revelation of *Hashem*, which transcends nature; it is not limited by any limitation, not

---

22. See *maamar* "*VaYedabber Elokim* 5729," *se'if* 8 (*Sefer HaMaamarim Melukat*, vol. 3, 334), that this revelation of the Divine Essence was the main instigator of all the changes that occurred at the Giving of the Torah.
23. As a source for the uniqueness of mitzvot in the post-Sinai world, the Rebbe cited Rambam's comments (*Perush HaMishnayot*, Hullin 7:6) that we perform mitzvot due to God's command to Moses, even in the case of a command that predates the Giving of the Torah (such as not eating the *gid hanasheh*). In *Likkutei Sihot* 5, 20 Heshvan, notes 23–25; ibid., 10, *Lekh Lekha*, no. 3, *se'if* 2, the Rebbe intertwined these words of Rambam with the midrash that the mitzvot of the patriarchs were "fragrances."

the limitations of nature nor the limitations of being above nature. It is therefore able to unite them....

This is the meaning of *Anokhi Hashem Elokekha*, that at the Giving of the Torah, God gave the boundless power of *Anokhi* and from this force comes the fusion of *Hashem*, which transcends nature, with ... *Elokekha*.[24]

It is only through a revelation of the *Anokhi*, the Divine Essence, that the antinomies of heaven and earth can be unified.[25]

Mitzvot and the Divine Essence

The Sinaitic revelation of the Divine Essence was not a transient event, but eternally stamped all the mitzvot that were commanded at Sinai with the power to combine transcendent spirituality with earthly nature. This is reflected in the three different terms that the Torah uses to refer to all its commandments: *mishpatim, hukkim,* and *edot*.[26] The *mishpat* level of a mitzva corresponds to the name *Elokim*, the aspect of divinity that "fills" the world. This refers to the fact that the performance of a mitzva benefits the person in a specific, understandable, and demonstrable fashion. For example, the average human can grasp the moral elegance of giving charity and the spiritual benefits of Shabbat observance.

Despite the existence of these reasons, all mitzvot are simultaneously described as *hukkim* which stem from the transcendent name *Hashem* – the aspect of divinity that "encircles" the world and leaves no room for human comprehension or benefit. On this level, the performer simply admits that his finite mind is insignificant in the face of the supernal

---

24. *Likkutei Sihot* 3, *Yitro, se'if* 4.
25. See *Likkutei Sihot* 3, *Yitro, se'if* 3, that this is the reason the last five commandments of the Decalogue are intuitive moral precepts such as the prohibition against killing and kidnapping. God was emphasizing that even such mitzvot that we can understand with our finite human mind should be performed not just due to our understanding of and identification with the mitzva, but mainly due to the divine command which stems from the Divine Essence. See Yoel Kahn (1994), 38–43, for an elaboration of this point.
26. See *maamar* "Ki Yishalkha Binkha 5738" (*Sefer HaMaamarim Melukat*, vol. 3, 138–46).

The Theology of Dira BaTahtonim

divine will. The mitzva is performed, not due to a sense of identification or meaning, but rather like a servant obeying his master's inscrutable will.[27]

The third and deepest level of mitzvot, however, is that they are *edot*. This dimension corresponds to the *Anokhi*-Divine Essence that emerged at Sinai, which is not only beyond human comprehension (*mishpatim*) but is also so beyond the confined categories of our limited world that it cannot even be described as negating our human comprehension (*hukkim*). Rather, mitzvot as edot "testify" to the Divine Essence, regarding which previously dichotomous categories of physicality/spirituality or self-motivation/blind obedience have no bearing whatsoever. As an expression of the Divine Essence's will, the performance of a mitzva testifies to the connection between the Divine Essence and all aspects of reality, or in the language of the midrash, the unification of the upper and lower realms.

Thus, in contrast to the fragrant mitzvot of the patriarchs that accessed only the revealed spirituality of the lower aspects of divinity, each post-Sinai performance of a mitzva engages the actual oil, or the Divine Essence itself. Therefore, while the service of the patriarchs might have been more ecstatic, intention filled, and spiritually uplifting than the service of subsequent generations, it is only the post-Sinai mitzvot that can have the ultimate impact of uniting the upper and lower realms.

The Historical Role of Mitzvot

Within this system, the breakthrough of Sinai should not be conceived as a onetime event, but rather as the beginning of a long historical process. The Rebbe noted a subtle textual tension in the previously cited midrash that describes the events at Sinai. In God's initial command to shatter the barriers between the upper and lower levels, He first declared that the lower levels should rise and only then commanded the upper levels to descend: "The lower realms shall rise to the higher realms and the higher realms shall descend to the lower realms." However, at the end of the sentence the sequence is reversed, and God Himself begins the process by descending onto Mount Sinai: "I will be the initiator." Only after God's descent does Moses then ascend the mountain to meet

---

27. *Likkutei Sihot* 3, *Yitro, se'if* 3.

God. The midrash, then, seems to present a contradiction regarding the chronological order of the ascent and descent.

The Rebbe explained that the first half of the midrash describes the ultimate purpose of the Sinaitic revelation, while the second half describes the chronological sequence of the events. Chronologically, God descended first because only God's descent could trigger the initial breakthrough between the upper and lower realms and empower our subsequent service with the ability to raise the lower realms. However, the midrash begins with the raising of the lower realms because that is the ultimate method of overcoming the barrier between spirituality and physicality.

How so? When God initiated the descent from on high, the saturation of the lower realm with spirituality was superimposed on the inherent physicality of the created world. On its own terms, the world remained unchanged, and thus the barrier between higher and lower was still subtly present. But the ultimate purpose is that we, embodied inhabitants of the lower realm, should use Torah and mitzvot to transform the very nature of the world itself, incrementally refining it and raising it up from below. This gradual and arduous process of transforming the lower realm can be accomplished only through the aggregate of generations of Jews performing mitzvot and is thus the historical mission of the Jewish people.[28]

As noted earlier, the ultimate purpose of Creation is not the revelation of God in a manner that will negate the existence of the world, rather "specifically where there is a reality of a world, and yet the fact that there is no reality other than God is felt *in the world*."[29] However, as the Rebbe said, this goal seems impossible: "But, how can the world, which ... hides and conceals Godliness, become a 'vessel' to receive and reveal the Master of the world?"[30] The Rebbe responded that this impossible feat is accomplished through human service, which is empowered by the Divine Essence's Revelation at Sinai: "For this purpose, Torah and mitzvot were given to the Jewish people at the Giving of the Torah – so

28. *Likkutei Sihot* 8, *Hag HaShavuot, se'if* 3.
29. Ibid., 11, *Shemot*, no. 2, *se'if* 5.
30. Ibid., *se'if* 6. The Rebbe noted that the Hebrew word for "world" (*olam*) is similar to the word for "hidden" (*he'elem*), meaning that the world conceals God. This word association is cited by the Baal Shem Tov (*Keter Shem Tov, siman* 24) and has deep roots in kabbalistic literature (*Sefer HaBahir, siman* 10).

that they will purify the world and create 'a dwelling for Him, blessed be He, in the lowest realm.'"[31]

As the Alter Rebbe writes in *Tanya*, it is our mitzvot that actively create the messianic reality.[32] At Sinai, God made the initial cracks in the barrier that separates heaven from earth, but it is ultimately our work in the post-Sinai period that completely erases the barrier by permanently revealing the Divine Essence within the lowest realm.[33]

MAASEH GADOL
Torah Study versus Actional Mitzvot

This definition of the Jewish people's mission in the post-Sinai era has practical ramifications for the nature and focus of our service of God as we approach the completion of the mission. We already mentioned that *Tanya* divides human activity into three realms: thought, speech, and action. What is the role that each one plays in our service of God? While the Torah certainly mandates submersion of the entire self in the service of God, is there a particular human faculty that should be emphasized in our quest to connect with God? In Chabad thought in general, and for the Rebbe in particular, the answer to these questions is very much informed by the above perspective on the role of mitzvot in uniting the upper and lower realms.

Arguably, this fundamental question of the relationship between our different faculties in the service of God is first explicitly addressed in the Talmud:

---

31. See *Likkutei Sihot* 11, *Shemot*, no. 2, *se'if* 6, where the Rebbe also described the impact of the Giving of the Torah on the world itself. It was the intense divine revelation at Sinai that elevated the world to such a state that it would be able to become a *dira* for God through the subsequent mitzvot of the Jewish people.
32. *Tanya, Likkutei Amarim*, ch. 37.
33. The Rebbe (*Likkutei Sihot*, 11, *Shemot*, no. 2, *se'if* 7) explained that this is the conceptual basis for the linkage of Moses to *Mashiah* in many midrashic passages. They are parallel personalities in the sense that Moses represents the potential and beginning of the purification process which will only be completed with the arrival of *Mashiah*.

> And there already was an incident in which R. Tarfon and the Elders were reclining in the loft of the house of Nit'za in Lod, when this question was asked of them: Is study greater or is action greater?[34]

The *Tanna'im* debated the relative importance of intellectual study (*talmud*) and actional mitzvot (*maaseh*). This is the Talmud's cryptic conclusion:

> R. Tarfon answered and said: Action is greater. R. Akiva answered and said: Study is greater. Everyone answered and said: Study is greater, as study leads to action.

What is meant by this final pronouncement? The conclusion seems self-contradictory. If *talmud* is greater, what is the meaning of the rationale that *talmud* leads to *maaseh*, which grants primacy to the realm of action?

In order to understand the Rebbe's approach to this perplexing issue, it is useful to broaden the scope of our discussion and see how classical Jewish thinkers related to the relative importance of intellectual and actional service. As foils to the Rebbe's perspective, I will briefly outline the views of Rambam and R. Hayyim of Volozhin.

The Approach of Rambam

Throughout his works, Rambam refers to the intellectual service of God as the pinnacle of a religious life. In the last chapter of the *Guide for the Perplexed*, Rambam lists the various levels of attainable human perfection. The fourth and ultimate level, the "true perfection of man," is

> the acquisition of the rational virtues – I refer to the conception of intelligibles, which teach true opinions concerning the divine things. This is in true reality the ultimate end; this is what gives the individual true perfection, a perfection belonging to him alone; and it gives him permanent perdurance; through it man is man.[35]

---

34. Kiddushin 40b.
35. *Guide for the Perplexed*, III:54 (Pines, 635).

The Theology of Dira BaTahtonim

Despite Judaism's intricate halakhic system, Rambam sets the sights of the religious questor on intellectual perfection. In fact, Rambam describes the entire system of actional mitzvot with all of its breadth and depth as a divine lesson plan to enable and engender greater intellectual meditation of God.[36]

The Approach of R. Hayyim of Volozhin

R. Hayyim of Volozhin fundamentally adopts Rambam's espousal of the cognitive faculty as the ideal method of connecting with God. However, instead of using one's intellect to philosophically contemplate God, R. Hayyim of Volozhin advocates filling one's mind with Torah. It is the study of Torah per se that creates the greatest of all possible bonds with God, as "He and His Torah are one." While God certainly demands the fulfillment of actional mitzvot, their performance cannot compare with the level of connection to God that is engendered by the study of Torah. This is the meaning of the famous mishnaic dictum "The study of Torah is the equivalent of all of them."[37]

The Approach of the Alter Rebbe

With this background from Rambam and R. Hayyim of Volozhin in mind, let us begin our analysis of Chabad's perspective on this central issue. We will begin with outlining key passages from the Alter Rebbe's thought and then transition to the additional elements emphasized by the Rebbe.

The Alter Rebbe developed a complex relationship between the study of Torah and the fulfillment of actional mitzvot. A cursory reading of certain passages would indicate that he is in full agreement with

---

36. Marvin Fox (1990), 316–17; Norman Lamm (1989), 143; Menahem Kellner (2009), 63–80. See *Guide for the Perplexed*, III:27, where Rambam explicates this point. However, Lamm (1989), 174, notes that the assertion that Rambam unequivocally favors intellectual enlightenment to observance of the halakhic system is challenged by Dr. Isadore Twersky in his *Introduction to the Code of Maimonides*.

37. *Nefesh HaHayyim*, shaar 4, is dedicated to the nature and significance of Torah study. For R. Hayyim's understanding of the relationship between Torah study and the fulfillment of actional mitzvot, see 4:29–30. For analysis and contextualization, see Lamm (1989), 153–54.

the approach supporting intellectual Torah study's supremacy over the performance of mitzvot.

For example, in an early chapter of *Tanya*, the Alter Rebbe posits a unity between God and His wisdom (the Torah) and a unity between the knower of knowledge and the knowledge itself. Employing a form of the transitive property, the Alter Rebbe teaches that when a person understands the Torah he becomes unified with God's wisdom which, in essence, translates into cognitively uniting with God Himself. The result is "a wonderful union, like which there is none other, and which has no parallel anywhere in the material world."[38] By contrast, one who fulfills an actional mitzva is only "enveloped" by the divine light but does not become unified with it. The Alter Rebbe writes that this is the meaning of the aforementioned rabbinic statement: "The study of Torah is the equivalent of all of them."

However, three interrelated points mitigate this lopsided superiority of *talmud* over *maaseh*.[39] First, elsewhere in *Tanya* the Alter Rebbe describes an advantage of actional mitzvot over the study of Torah. While Torah study draws divinity into one's faculties of cognition and speech, the ultimate mission is to have one's entire being enveloped in the divine light. Only the bodily performance of actional mitzvot allows for Godliness to extend even to the body, which is generally associated with man's baser desires and animalistic soul.[40] In the words of the Alter Rebbe:

> Therefore, when a person occupies himself in the Torah, his *neshama*, which is his divine soul, with her two innermost garments only, namely, the power of speech and thought, are absorbed in the divine light of the blessed *Ein Sof*, and are merged within it in perfect unity.... *However, in order to draw the light and radiance of the Shekhina upon his body and animal soul as well, i.e., upon the vitalizing soul actually clothed in the physical body, one must fulfill the actional commandments that are performed with the body itself....* Then the energy of the vitalizing soul actually clothed within the body... is

---

38. *Tanya, Likkutei Amarim*, ch. 5.
39. Moshe Hallamish (1976), 244–72, elaborates on many of these themes.
40. *Tanya, Likkutei Amarim*, ch. 1.

The Theology of Dira BaTahtonim

> transformed from evil to good, and is actually absorbed into holiness like the divine soul itself.[41] [Emphasis added.]

It is the physical action of a mitzva that transforms the lowly body and animal soul into a sanctified entity.[42]

A second element of the Alter Rebbe's approach to the relationship between *talmud* and *maaseh* is that the relationship shifts as history progresses. Each generation has its own unique spiritual character and challenges, which cause the people in different generations to place greater emphasis on one or another aspect of the divine service. Accordingly, the Alter Rebbe posits that in the times of the *Tanna'im* and *Amora'im* the primary divine service was through Torah study. In the post-rabbinic era, the focus shifted from Torah study to prayer. Then, as history marched forward and the nineteenth century arrived, the Alter Rebbe saw another major alteration: "In these generations, the main revelation of God is in the performance of acts of loving-kindness."[43]

This concept is further elucidated in a fundraising letter the Alter Rebbe wrote to Hasidim on behalf of their brethren in the Land of Israel:

> Therefore, my beloved, my brethren: Set your hearts to these words expressed in great brevity…how in these times, when the approaching footsteps of *Mashiah* are close upon us (*ikveta deMeshiha*), the principal service of God is the service of charity, as our Sages, of blessed memory, said: "Israel will be redeemed only through charity." *Our Sages, of blessed memory, did not say that the study of Torah is equivalent to the performance of loving-kindness except in their own days.* For with them the principal service was the study of Torah and, therefore, there were great scholars: *Tanna'im* and *Amora'im*. However, when the approaching footsteps of *Mashiah* are close upon us (*ikveta deMeshiha*)…there is no way of truly cleaving unto it and to convert the darkness into its

---

41. Ibid., ch. 35. See also ibid., ch. 37.
42. See also *Tanya, Iggeret HaKodesh*, letter 5.
43. *Torah Or, Megillat Ester*, 120b.

light, except through a corresponding category of action (*maaseh*), namely, the act of charity.⁴⁴ [Emphasis added.]

The rabbinic statements regarding the ultimate primacy of Torah study over actional mitzvot were primarily directed toward earlier generations. As we approach the Messianic Era, the focus of our service needs to shift toward sanctifying the lower elements of the world and "converting darkness to light," which requires a new focus on bodily involvement in mitzvot.

It is not random that actional mitzvot intended to purify the lower elements of the world become the primary form of service in the pre-messianic era. In several passages, the Alter Rebbe develops an inverted hierarchy of spirituality. Whatever is revealed to us as "lower," i.e., more physical and less spiritual, is, in fact, rooted in a higher aspect of divinity. This radical idea is often expressed with the phrase *sof maaseh bemahshava tehila*, meaning the final action was first in thought. This indicates that what comes at the end of the cosmic hierarchy ("the final action") is the primary intention of God from the start ("first in thought"), very fittingly reflecting the Alter Rebbe's conceptualization of physical actions' significance.⁴⁵

It is natural to assume that Torah study, which absorbs one's "higher" cognitive faculties, is the ideal path to connecting with God. The Alter Rebbe posits, however, that while from a certain perspective this remains true, the seemingly contradictory, but in reality, complementary perspective of *sof maaseh bemahshava tehila* teaches that it is bodily involvement with actional mitzvot that bind a person with the most essential aspect of divinity.⁴⁶ Using kabbalistic terminology, the Alter Rebbe elsewhere argues that understanding the Torah connects one

---

44. *Tanya, Iggeret HaKodesh*, letter 9. See ibid., letter 5, for the explanation of why charity in particular is the paradigmatic actional mitzva.
45. Jerome Gellman (1995), 288, lists fourteen distinct places where this idea appears in the thought of the Alter Rebbe.
46. See *Seder Tefillot MiKol HaShana*, vol. 1, 23a, where the Alter Rebbe connects the unique relevance of action for the later generations with the fact that action is rooted in the highest level of divinity. For other sources, see *Maamarei Admor HaZaken* 5564, 165–66; ibid., 5568: 1, 338–39.

The Theology of Dira BaTahtonim

with God's *hokhma* (wisdom), while physical, actional mitzvot involving material items embody the higher element of God's *ratzon* (will).[47]

In summary, while Rambam and R. Hayyim of Volozhin assumed a constant hierarchy between intellectual and actional service that is weighted toward the former, the Alter Rebbe developed a multitiered approach.[48] From one perspective Torah study has primacy over the fulfillment of actional mitzvot. However, an equally valid and complementary viewpoint creates a system in which actional mitzvot are seen to have an advantage that study does not. It is this latter form of worship that has the ability to purify even the lower aspects of the world in anticipation of the coming of *Mashiah*.

The Approach of the Rebbe

The Rebbe took his predecessor's idea, expanded it, and applied it. He would often end his talks with a citation from a mishna in Avot: *Hamaaseh hu ha'ikkar*.[49] This was not just a rallying cry to galvanize people to take action, but reflected an acute implementation of the Alter Rebbe's emphasis on the increasing importance of *maaseh* as the world readies for redemption. As noted above, the ultimate mission of the Jewish people's service in the post-Sinai era is to transform the physical, "lowest," realm into a vessel that best expresses the Divine Essence. Therefore, as we approach the Messianic Era and edge toward the completion of the exilic mission, it is imperative to place a unique focus on

---

47. *Torah Or, Noah*, 9bc. For an explanation of the terms *hokhma* and *ratzon*, see Nissan Dubov, "The *Sefirot*," available at www.chabad.org/361885. It is important to note that the performance of mitzvot in this system is an end unto itself and not a means toward a higher goal, as there can be no further regression beyond God's will. In this regard, see *Likkutei Sihot 6, Shemot*, no. 2, *se'if* 9, and notes 69–70.

48. This presentation, namely that the Alter Rebbe did not categorically favor actions over learning, reflects the internal tradition of Chabad Hasidim. Similarly, see Moshe Hallamish (1976), 269–71, who marshals many conflicting statements regarding the hierarchy of Torah study and actional mitzvot and therefore concludes that in the Alter Rebbe's final estimation one cannot speak of a true hierarchy but of complementary perspectives. However, see Norman Lamm (1989), 147–51, and Rivka Schatz-Uffenheimer (1963), 513–28, who assert that ultimately the Alter Rebbe gave action a higher place in the spiritual hierarchy than Torah study.

49. Based on Mishna Avot 1:17.

maaseh. This is due to the fact that *maaseh* expresses the otherwise hidden Divine Essence in the lowest realm, thereby uniting the two seemingly contradictory poles of spirituality and physicality.

It was within this framework that the Rebbe once interpreted the Talmud's enigmatic conclusion that "study is greater, as study leads to action":

> *Talmud* is greater only now, but in the future, *maaseh* will be greater (Alter Rebbe, *Sefer Maamarim* 5567, 309). And even now, when *talmud* is preeminent, the reason for this is that "*talmud* leads to *maaseh*," and from this it is proven that *maaseh* is the primary end goal.[50]

According to the Rebbe, the Talmud's conclusion encodes a subtle message, namely that the answer to the question shifts over the course of history. Initially, *talmud* is greater, because without the initial revelation from above transformative action is not even possible. Ultimately, though, it is really *maaseh* that is greater. This perspective will be fully revealed only in the Messianic Era, when the Divine Essence will once again inhabit the *tahtonim*.[51]

While one might think that this eschatological prediction has little bearing on those living in the pre-Messianic Era, the Rebbe argued that the notion of *maaseh gadol* is urgently relevant:

> The notion that in the future *maaseh* will be greater was revealed (as with all the teachings of Hasidism) specifically in the later generations. The reason this was revealed to us (even though now the halakha is that *talmud* is greater) is because all the revelations of the future time are "dependent on our current actions and service" (*Likkutei Amarim* ch. 37). That *maaseh* will be greater in the future will come about through our effort and alacrity in the realm of *maaseh* now. Therefore, in the generation of *ikveta deMeshiha* it was revealed to us that in the future *maaseh* will be

---

50. Maamar "BaYom HaShemini 5746," *se'if* 5 (*Sefer HaMaamarim Melukat*, vol. 2, 195).
51. See also *maamar* "VeAvdi David Melekh 5746," *se'if* 5 (*Sefer HaMaamarim Melukat*, vol. 3, 211); *Torat Menahem* 5750: 2, 108.

greater, in order to arouse even greater effort and alacrity in the realm of *maaseh* now, and through this it will cause to be in the future that *maaseh* is greater.[52]

As we reach the final stages of the process initiated at Sinai, we need to increase our engagement with the physical and terrestrial *maaseh* in order to complete the historical mission of the Jewish people.

It is important to note, though, that this focus on *maaseh* did not signify an abdication of *talmud*. In fact, the opposite is the case. The Rebbe dedicated many lengthy discourses to the importance of *talmud*, the unique spiritual heights that can be attained only through learning Torah, and in fact constantly exhorted everyone to quantitatively and qualitatively intensify their study of Torah. He often insisted that scholar and layman alike can and must study in the loftiest manner of R. Shimon and his cohort of whom it was said, "Torah is their occupation,"[53] meaning to put aside all worldly concerns to concentrate solely on Torah study as if they have no other occupation.[54] However, alongside his constant call for increased Torah study, the Rebbe highlighted the increased significance of *maaseh* in the later generations.[55]

---

52. Maamar "BaYom HaShemini 5746," se'if 7 (*Sefer HaMaamarim Melukat*, vol. 2, 197). For a similar idea, see *Torat Menahem* 5719: 2, 256.
53. Shabbat 11a.
54. See, for example, *Likkutei Sihot* 12, Hosafot – Lag BaOmer, 229; *Torat Menahem* 5748:3, 270.
55. The Rebbe dedicated several talks to the interrelation of *talmud* and *maaseh*. He explained that *maaseh* draws down the Divine Essence into the material world, but in a concealed fashion. It is *talmud* that allows for the Divine Essence to be "revealed" and "bright" in the lowest realms and perceptible to human beings. See, for example, *Likkutei Sihot* 8, *Matot*, no. 2. In other talks, the Rebbe went further regarding the future role of *talmud* by contending that the superiority of *maaseh* will spread to and elevate *talmud*, ultimately blurring the differences between *maaseh* and *talmud* as distinct forms of service. See, for example, maamar "VaYigash Eilav Yehuda 5736," se'if 7 (*Sefer HaMaamarim Melukat*, vol. 2, 218–19); *Torat Menahem* 5750: 2, 107–8. In particular this interpenetration of *maaseh* and *talmud* occurs in the posture of the worshipper. In classic Chabad thought, *talmud* is associated with the Jew as God's child (*ben*), meaning that a person uses his own intellectual faculties to understand and innovate in Torah. By contrast, the performance of actional mitzvot is associated with the Jew as God's slave (*eved*), meaning that a person nullifies himself (*bittul*) and simply performs the

Practical Consequences of the *Maaseh* Era

This *maaseh*-centric and *Mashiah*-oriented ethos has several practical ramifications. For the Alter Rebbe, the primary meaning of *maaseh* was the simple performance of mitzvot. The Rebbe, though, emphasized that after spending one's formative years immersed in Torah study one should leave the sanctified study halls in order to engage the broader outside world. It is only through the service of *maaseh* in the "lowest" realms that the true power of *maaseh* can be realized.

One model for this form of service was the biblical Jacob, who spent his younger years in the tents of Torah study but then left to engage the outside world:

> The obvious directive for our generation that results from [a study of Jacob's life] is: We must carry out the order of divine service [related to *Parashat*] *Vayetzeh* – of going out to the world and illuminating it. Before this, one must prepare by studying Torah in the tents of Shem and Ever. But to attain [the peak of] "And the man became exceedingly prosperous" (Gen. 30:43), i.e., "fill[ing] up the land and conquer[ing] it" (Gen. 1:28), one must go out to the world and occupy himself with illuminating it.

The Rebbe felt that this model was particularly apt for modern times in which the increased importance of *maaseh* intersected with a dire need for this form of illumination:

> More than that, "in this era of *ikveta deMeshiha*, the primary dimension of our divine service is *maaseh*" (*Iggeret HaKodesh* ch. 9). This differs from the talmudic period, when Torah study

---

will of God. Future *talmud* and *maaseh* will both stem from a deeper point of complete identification with God, which allows these two distinct perspectives to be viewed as unified and complementary as opposed to dichotomous and distinct. See, for example, *maamar* "*Margela BeFumei DeRava* 5740" (*Sefer HaMaamarim Melukat*, vol. 2, 86–94). See also *maamar* "*BaYom HaShemini* 5746," *se'ifim* 3–4 (*Sefer HaMaamarim Melukat*, vol. 2, 194–95) where the Rebbe argued that *maaseh*'s unique connection with the Divine Essence will impact the totality of a person: "Through *maaseh* all of the faculties (including intellect) are brought to their most complete state."

The Theology of Dira BaTahtonim

was the primary element of divine service. This is reflected in the ruling of the *Shulhan Arukh* (*Orah Hayyim*, *siman* 146), that there is no one in the present age of whom it can be said: "His Torah is his occupation" (as was the level of R. Shimon bar Yohai and his colleagues). Not even a small percentage of the Jewish people are on that level, because the fundamental divine service of the present era is action [such as] the act of giving charity. And in particular, in our generation this involvement of searching for Jews who are lost in the darkness of exile... is a matter of literal saving of lives![56]

The increasing significance of *maaseh* is intertwined with notion of "conquering" the outside world. The "lowest" human faculty of *maaseh* done in the "lowest" places has the power to truly engage and reveal the Divine Essence and illuminate the world.

This outlook provides part of the philosophical background for the initiation of the mitzva campaigns in which the Rebbe urged Jews to go out to the streets with the mission of encouraging and enabling their brethren to perform mitzvot.[57] While the ideal result would be for this single mitzva to initiate a trajectory of ever-increasing engagement in mitzvot, the Rebbe constantly emphasized the importance of every single mitzva action not as a means to a greater result but as a goal in itself. As he once put it when describing the "tefillin campaign":

> The involvement with another Jew to perform an actional mitzva is not in order that through this he will become closer to learning the secrets of the Torah, *Maaseh Merkava*, the Torah of Hasidism.... *Rather, the involvement with another Jew to enable him to perform actional mitzvot is not a means to attain some other more elevated goal, but it is the goal itself*, as there is a special emphasis

---

56. *Likkutei Sihot* 15, *Vayetzeh* no. 4, *se'if* 9. Translation of both paragraphs is adapted from www.chabad.org/2295019.
57. See also chapter 13, section "A Proactive Approach."

on matters of maaseh, and there is even an advantage to *maaseh* over learning, as in the future *maaseh gadol*.[58] [Emphasis added.]

Very clearly, the Rebbe connected the newfound significance of *maaseh* with the need to increase mitzva actions in the world, no matter the spiritual level of the person. Each *maaseh mitzva* is cosmically significant, particularly as the world approaches the era of *maaseh gadol*.

Thus, the enterprise of going into the world at large and enabling other Jews to perform mitzvot is directly related to the Rebbe's unique perspective regarding the significance of Sinai. The emergence of the Divine Essence at Sinai began the process of uniting the upper and lower realms that can be completed only through our mitzvot. In this sense, the mitzva campaigns represent a final surge toward the finish line of creating a *Dira BaTahtonim* and ushering in the Messianic Era.

Secondary Literature Consulted for Chapter 5, "From Sinai to Mitzva Tanks"

Alon Dahan, *Goel Aharon*, 140–70.

Yoel Kahn, "HaHiddush HaMahapkhani SheNit'hollel BeMatan Torah."

Yoel Kahn, "Moshe Rabbenu, David HaMelekh VehaBaal Shem Tov."

Yoel Kahn, "She'eilat HaBen HeHakham."

Yoel Kahn, *Gidran shel Mitzvot: Hukkim UMishpatim BeMishnato shel HaRebbe*.

Yitzhak Kraus, *HaShevi'i*, 137–43.

Faitel Levin, *Heaven on Earth*, 114–22.

Eli Rubin, "A Bridge Across Infinity: How the Revelation at Sinai Changed the Cosmic Map."

Elliot Wolfson, *Open Secret*, 189–99.

---

58. *Torat Menahem* 5743: 3, 1554. The importance of even a single mitzva as the subtext for the mitzva campaigns is highlighted in "The Rebbe's 10-Point Mitzva Campaign for Jewish Awareness and Observance," available at www.chabad.org/62228.

Chapter 6

The Definition of a Human Being: Body and Soul

We have seen that the goal of revealing the Divine Essence and creating a *Dira BaTahtonim* plays a central role in the Rebbe's conception of the material world and of Torah and mitzvot. These same themes are reflected in his vision of the nature and mission of each individual. We now turn to the Rebbe's teachings regarding the nature of a human being.

The fact that human beings consist of a body and a soul is a basic axiom of Jewish philosophy. While expressed in a multiplicity of manners, Jewish philosophers throughout the ages have generally agreed upon two central assumptions regarding the relationship between these two elements of a person: (1) the body and soul are radically disparate from each other, and (2) the soul is naturally more connected to God than is the body.

Building on earlier hasidic teachings, however, the Rebbe challenged both of these assumptions. The perceived chasm between the deficient body and sanctified soul that is perceived in earlier Jewish sources results from an incomplete vision of reality's true nature. As the world marches toward redemption and the Divine Essence slowly becomes

The Definition of a Human Being: Body and Soul

more manifest in the *tahtonim*, these earlier sources are illuminated in a new light that reveals a more holistic philosophy of body and soul. Characteristically, the Rebbe developed this aspect of his philosophy both as an intricate conceptual edifice and as a practical guide to life.

THE BODY AND SOUL IN EARLIER JEWISH PHILOSOPHY

Body and Soul in Rabbinic Literature

The division between body and soul has deep roots in rabbinic literature.[1] A sampling of statements on this topic reveals that the Sages differentiated between body and soul regarding their basic composition and source. The soul is a vivifying[2] and pure[3] entity which is "God's portion" of the person,[4] while the body on its own is impure,[5] dead matter,[6] and stems from one's human parents as opposed to God.[7]

This bifurcated characterization, however, does not imply that the Sages completely downgraded the body.[8] For example, Hillel, an early *Tanna*, applies the elusive term "image of God" to the human body as a support for the virtue of proper hygiene and self-care.[9] This indicates that the human body itself, and not just the soul, is somehow associated with divinity.

Rambam

Rambam develops the body-soul binary even further. He identifies the soul with one's cognitive capabilities, and describes this faculty as "the image of God" that elevates humans above animals.[10] It is the soul

---

1. Ephraim Urbach (1975), 197–98.
2. Ecclesiastes Rabba 5:10.
3. *Mekhilta DeRabbi Yishmael, Masekhta DeShira*, sec. 2.
4. Nidda 31b.
5. *Mekhilta DeRabbi Yishmael, Masekhta DeShira*, sec. 2.
6. Ecclesiastes Rabba 5:10.
7. Nidda 31b.
8. See Ephraim Urbach (1975), 190–93, who notes that the Sages were less extreme regarding their division between body and soul than parallel Hellenistic philosophies.
9. Leviticus Rabba 34:3. Yair Lorberbaum (2004) traces this idea in tannaitic literature and demonstrates that it is a principle associated with R. Akiva and his students.
10. *Mishneh Torah, Hilkhot Yesodei HaTorah* 4:8–9.

that can acquire knowledge of God, which is the spiritually pleasurable reward for a life of Torah and mitzvot.[11] The body, however, is composed of the four basic material elements that are common to all terrestrial matter.[12] As such, the body can appreciate only corporal pleasures and is as distant from the spiritual reward of the soul as a fish is from fire.[13]

For Rambam, these characterizations of body and soul have moral implications. While Rambam is adamant that the body's needs are not to be ignored,[14] he is equally forceful in regarding the body as the source of man's shortcomings and lusts.[15] This conception of the body led Rambam to encourage an austere lifestyle, at the very least for the spiritual elite.[16]

However, despite these inherent deficiencies of the body, Rambam does paint an expansive picture in which necessary bodily functions can become integrated into the service of God. Working with the verse "Know Him in all of your ways"[17] and the rabbinic injunction "And all of your actions should be for the sake of Heaven,"[18] Rambam describes a religious life that incorporates bodily activities:

> A person should direct his heart and the totality of his behavior to one goal, becoming aware of God, blessed be He. The [way] he rests, rises, and speaks should all be directed to this end....
>
> When he eats, drinks, and engages in intimate relations, he should not intend to do these things solely for pleasure to the point where he will eat and drink only that which is sweet to the palate and engage in intercourse for pleasure. Rather, he should

---

11. Ibid., *Hilkhot Teshuva* 8:1–2.
12. Ibid., *Hilkhot Yesodei HaTorah* 4:1.
13. Rambam, *Perush HaMishna*, introduction to *Perek Helek*, s.v. *veAta Aheil*.
14. *Mishneh Torah, Hilkhot Deot* 4:1; *Shemona Perakim*, sec. 4.
15. *Guide for the Perplexed*, III:8.
16. See, for example, *Guide for the Perplexed*, III:48, where Rambam praises the Nazirite for his abstention from all wine. For a collection of Maimonidean sources and analysis of this topic, see Howard Kreisel (1988), 13–22.
17. Proverbs 3:6.
18. Mishna Avot 2:12.

take care to eat and drink only in order to be healthy in body and limb.

> He should have the intent that his body be whole and strong, in order for his inner soul to be upright so that [it will be able] to know God. For it is impossible to understand and become knowledgeable in the wisdoms when one is starving or sick, or when one of his limbs pains him.[19] [Emphasis added.]

For Rambam, eating, drinking, and the array of bodily activities are not worthless enterprises, but neither are they granted a primary role in one's religious life. Rather, through a disciplined and directed lifestyle, they can attain secondary significance as a necessary support for the spiritual service that is the true end of the religious life.

With this in mind, it is no surprise that Rambam views the ideal "human being" in the utopian Messianic Era as a disembodied soul basking in the glory of the *Shekhina*, finally unfettered by the constraints of the body. Accordingly, Rambam relegates the physical resurrection of the dead to a relatively minor place in the eschatological hierarchy. He posits that after souls are returned to their bodies, they will live for a period of time, only to once again die and exist eternally as independent souls.[20]

Ramban

Ramban certainly affirms the superiority of the soul over the body[21] and in certain ways even expands on Rambam's ascetic approach.[22] Simultaneously, though, he indicates that there is an inherent bond between the body and soul and that the body can be redeemed through the soul. Ramban's most extended discussion on this topic appears in his *Shaar*

---

19. *Mishneh Torah, Hilkhot Deot* 3:2.
20. *Iggeret Tehiyat HaMetim*, s.v. *vekhen nireh lanu*. For a summary and analysis of the relevant Maimonidean sources, see Baruch Brody (2016–17), 100–107.
21. See, for example, Ramban on Gen. 6:3: "Man is also flesh like the other animals and he is not fitting to have the divine spirit within him" (translation from Jonathan Feldman [1999], 50).
22. See, for example, Ramban's treatment of the Nazirite in his commentary to Num. 6:14 and Lev. 19:1. For a summary and analysis of many relevant sources in Ramban's corpus, see Jonathan Feldman (1999), 106–22, and Daniel Schreiber (2011), 36–43.

HaGemul, in which he takes issue with Rambam's description of a bodiless soul in the end of days. While Rambam's negative view of the body condemns it to oblivion in the utopian reality, Ramban argues for the enduring existence of a purified body in the end of time.[23]

Ramban teaches that through an ascetic lifestyle which allows the soul to dominate the body and nullify its desires, the body becomes weakened and spiritualized. In this state, even the physical body will be nourished from spiritual substances, similar to the experience of Moses on Mount Sinai and the generation that ate the manna. The bodily form will be maintained, but normal bodily functions will cease.[24]

Early Hasidism
From its nascency, Hasidism had a more positive attitude toward the body and its activities than that of earlier Jewish philosophers and mystics. The Baal Shem Tov consciously diverged from earlier kabbalistic practices of self-mortification and asceticism, instead advocating a deeper integration of bodily necessities and pleasures into the service of God.[25] Based on this practical reorientation of service and several of the Baal Shem Tov's teachings, some scholars have characterized the Baal Shem Tov's approach as an outright embrace of the corporeal body and a leveling of the hierarchy between body and soul.[26]

However, a more careful reading of the Baal Shem Tov's corpus indicates that he too emphasized the radical supremacy of the soul over the body.[27] His affirmation of human corporeality stemmed not from an abolishment of the previously established hierarchy, but from a conviction that the body and soul were intertwined and inevitably shared an identical fate. For the human being as a whole to ascend toward God,

---

23. *Torat HaAdam, Shaar HaGemul* (Mossad HaRav Kook, 304). Translation from Feldman (1999), 229.
24. Jonathan Feldman (1999), 320–30.
25. Immanuel Etkes (2005), 116–21.
26. Martin Buber (1960), 124–27.
27. For the first major critique of Buber's portrayal of this aspect of Hasidism, see Gershom Scholem (1971), 228–50. See also Feital Levin (2002), 104–13. For a more nuanced perspective on this issue, see Ron Margoliyot (2004) and Tsippi Kauffman (2009).

the soul, which is still the main subject of the divine command, needs to harness the body's forces in an attempt to purify it. [28]

One such teaching of the Baal Shem Tov speaks of the soul as an understanding teacher that needs to gently and patiently guide the body in the proper direction. Commenting on the verse "If you see your enemy's donkey lying under its burden, would you refrain from helping it? You shall surely help along with him,"[29] the Baal Shem Tov is recorded as teaching:

> *If you see "a donkey" [hamor]:* When you carefully examine your materiality [*homer*], your body, you will see...
>
> *"your enemy"*: meaning, that your materiality [*homer*] hates your divine soul that longs for Godliness and the spiritual, and furthermore, you will see that it is...
>
> *"lying under its burden"*: placed upon the body by God, namely, that it should become refined through Torah and mitzvot, but the body is lazy in fulfilling them. It may then occur to you that...
>
> *"would you refrain from helping it"*: to enable it to fulfill its mission, and instead you will follow the path of mortification of the flesh to break down the body's crass materiality. However, not in this approach will the light of Torah reside. Rather...
>
> *"you must aid it"*: purify the body, refine it, but do not break it by mortification.[30]

While this is certainly a shift in how the soul should relate to the body, the simple import of the teaching retains the body-soul binary and the superiority of the soul over the body.

---

28. See, for example, *Toledot Yaakov Yosef*, 23a.
29. Ex. 23:5.
30. *Keter Shem Tov, Hosafot, siman* 21. Translation is adapted from www.chabad.org/6078.

A similar line of reasoning can be gleaned from the writings of the Alter Rebbe. Several central passages from his corpus indicate that the Alter Rebbe retained the traditional assumptions regarding the nature of the body and the soul. For example, *Tanya* opens with a description of how the body is vivified by the animalistic and not the divine soul.[31] Also, one of the most celebrated lines in *Tanya* states that the foundation of the entire Torah "is to raise up and elevate the soul over the body, higher and higher."[32] Scholars have even noted that the Alter Rebbe's teachings lean toward asceticism more than do those of other early hasidic leaders.[33]

At the same time, however, it is significant that the Alter Rebbe did identify a path for the elevation of the body into the embrace of God. Through the performance of mitzvot, one can transform the lowly physical body into a vehicle (*merkava*) that is completely surrendered to the will of God and through which God can be manifest.[34]

THE REBBE: "THE SOUL WILL BE NOURISHED FROM THE BODY"

Further developing deeply rooted strands of earlier Chabad teachings, the Rebbe issued a two-pronged challenge to the traditional assumptions of the body-soul relationship. On one level, the Rebbe argued that from a certain perspective the body is in fact more deeply rooted in the essence of God than is the soul. Second, on a more fundamental level, the Rebbe asserted that the whole mindset of conceptualizing the body and soul in stark binary terms is mistaken, as ultimately they are different expressions of the same singular substance.

The Soul's Hearkening to the Body

One method of highlighting the Rebbe's sharply different orientation toward the body is by analyzing his understanding of the aforementioned teaching of the Baal Shem Tov regarding the need for the soul to assist

---

31. *Tanya, Likkutei Amarim*, ch. 1.
32. Ibid., ch. 32.
33. Immanuel Etkes (2015), 103; Roman Foxbrunner (1993), 114 and 132–33.
34. *Tanya, Likkutei Amarim*, ch. 23; *Likkutei Torah, Behar*, 42b–c.

The Definition of a Human Being: Body and Soul

the "enemy donkey" of the body. In isolation, the passage describes the body as "lazy," "crass," and in need of purification. The Rebbe, however, built a framework in which this very passage demonstrates the advantage of the body over the soul.

Still in the first year of his leadership, the Rebbe opened a talk[35] by noting a Zoharic passage that interprets a Scriptural reference to Abraham and Sarah as referring to the soul and the body, respectively. Despite the seemingly limited purview of the Zohar's approach, the Rebbe characteristically applied this symbolism to each mention of Abraham and Sarah in the Torah and accordingly asked how we should understand the verse in which God commands Abraham to listen to Sarah regarding the expulsion of Ishmael: "Whatever Sarah tells you, hearken to her voice."[36] According to the Zoharic definition, this verse reads as a divine command to the soul (Abraham) to listen to the body (Sarah), an imperative that seems to negate millennia of ethical teachings. What is the meaning of this command?

The Rebbe answered this by citing the aforementioned teaching of the Baal Shem Tov that one needs to "help" his "enemy" body as opposed to breaking it. While the Baal Shem Tov seems to have cast this "help" as a kindness that the superior soul should bestow upon the deficient body, the Rebbe contextualized this passage within a more radical shift in perspective that situates the body at the center of religious life. Mitzvot are generally performed by the body, and even mitzvot of emotions should ideally be somatically felt.[37] All of this indicates that God's ultimate plan involves the body more than the soul. As the Rebbe summarized his view:

> Based on this we can explain the verse "All that Sarah says to you listen to her voice" according to the interpretation of the Zohar that Sarah alludes to the body. *The main intent [of God] is for*

---

35. *Torat Menahem* 5711: 1, 87–92.
36. Gen. 21:12.
37. In this context, the Rebbe often cited from the Alter Rebbe (*Tanya, Likkutei Amarim*, ch. 37), who cites from Eitz Hayyim: "The [divine] soul itself does not need perfecting at all."

> the body, but this is now hidden. In the future, the advantage of the body will be revealed to the extent that "the soul will be nourished from the body."[38] Since the patriarchs tasted the World to Come in the present world (Bava Batra 16b), they felt the advantage of the body even over the soul. [Emphasis added.]

Thus, according to the Rebbe's reading of the Zohar, God's directive to Abraham will be the norm in the Messianic Era, when the true nature of the body will be disclosed to all. Until then, the soul needs to assist the body in its current concealed state as emphasized in the Baal Shem Tov's teaching. In the Messianic Era, however, the roles will be reversed and the body will be revealed as the provider of Godly sustenance to the soul.

The Creation of the Body

What is the theoretical background of this radical inversion? The answer, once again, relates to the Rebbe's conception of God's relationship with the created worlds. For the Rebbe, the soul, an overtly spiritual entity, is rooted in the *Giluyim*, or the perceptible external revelation of God. In contrast, the material body, with its seeming mundanity, is in fact covertly rooted in the ineffable Divine Essence. The Rebbe developed this association of the soul with *Giluyim* and the body with the Divine Essence through the lens of different key stages in the timeline of a body's existence: its point of creation, the duration of its life, and the end of days.

The earliest point of differentiation between body and soul is the moment of Creation. As discussed in chapter 2, the Alter Rebbe describes the process of Creation as a series of gradual descents and contractions of the infinite divine light.[39] Each subsequent level of contraction in the *Seder Hishtalshelut* produces a world that discloses less of the divine light than the worlds above it. The end of the chain is our lowly physical world, which completely conceals its underlying divinity.

---

38. This phrase originated with the Rebbe Maharash, *Hemshekh VeKakha* 5637, *siman* 88, and appears frequently in the Rebbe's talks. See, for example, *Torat Menahem* 5712: 2, 135–36; ibid., 5715: 1, 186; ibid., 5716: 2, 226; maamar "*Bati LeGani* 5731" (*Sefer HaMaamarim Melukat*, vol. 2, 365).
39. See, for example, *Tanya, Likkutei Amarim*, ch. 21.

The Definition of a Human Being: Body and Soul

This general description of Creation holds true regarding the soul. In order for the soul to travel from on high to inhabit a human body in this lowly world, it needs to undergo this process of descent, contraction, and devolution.[40] But as we have seen, the material substance of the physical world, and likewise the body itself, is an exception to this principle.[41] Being corporeal and so distant from the spiritual worlds, even an infinite number of contractions would never be able to produce the physical body. Instead, the body is produced through a direct act of the Divine Essence that stands above this entire system of *hishtalshelut*. The Rebbe crisply articulated this idea regarding the human body:

> The creation of the bodies of creatures and of the human could not have occurred through the means of *hishtalshelut*, for even if there were tens of thousands of levels of descent, physicality cannot be formed from spirituality. Like the saying of the rational philosophers (cited in Hasidism),[42] that the creation of physicality from spirituality is the greatest expression of "something from nothing." Instead, the source of the creation of "something from nothing" is the simple will ... of His Essence.[43]

Only the Divine Essence, which surpasses the binary categories of spirituality and physicality, can directly create the body "from nothing." While it might seem that the coarse body is the lowest link in the chain that begins with the highest recesses of God and descends through all of the worlds, it is in fact a product of the Divine Essence "skipping over" the regular *Seder Hishtalshelut*.

This teaching of the Rebbe dovetails with the line of thinking that we have previously encountered regarding the nature of mundane space and actional mitzvot. Counterintuitively, it is the "lowest" level, bereft of manifest spirituality, that is most rooted within the Divine Essence. As we will presently see, the difference between the body and soul at the

---

40. *Tanya, Likkutei Amarim*, ch. 2.
41. Chapter 3, section "*Atzmut* and the Lowest Realm."
42. This is a reference to Yosef Albo, *Sefer HaIkkarim*, maamar 1, ch. 23.
43. Maamar "*VeNigleh Kevod Hashem* 5722," *se'if* 4 (*Torat Menahem* 5722: 2, 368–78).

The Theology of Dira BaTahtonim

point of their creation defines their respective missions for the duration of human history and determines their ultimate status in the eschaton.

The Soul's Embodied Mission

The state of exile conceals the true nature of the body and prevents its lofty potential from being realized. Prior to the redemption, the supremacy of the soul over the body that is elucidated in earlier Jewish philosophy remains in place. As the Rebbe expounded in many places, to the extent that it distracts a person from serving God, the body is "lowly and degrading."[44] The soul, by contrast, is the pinnacle of spirituality that must be granted primacy in the life of a servant of God.[45] The descent of the soul into the body in order to create human life is described by the Rebbe as miraculous, due to the contradictory characters of the body and soul.[46] In fact, as the Alter Rebbe describes, the spiritual soul does not desire its descent into this world, and would rather remain as a disembodied spiritual entity.[47]

Why then does God banish the soul to corporeal captivity? As the Rebbe related, Chabad teachings contain two answers to this question:

> (1) The service of God performed by the soul as it exists within [this material realm], enclothed in a body and an animal soul, reveals the intensity of the soul's bond with God; that it is so powerful that the concealment and hiddenness caused by the body and the animal soul cannot negate, or even weaken, this connection.

> (2) By serving God in this material world, the soul purifies and refines the body, the animal soul, and its surrounding environment.[48]

---

44. *Torat Menahem* 5712: 1, 167.
45. See, for example, *Iggerot Kodesh* 14, letter 5175, where the Rebbe encourages someone to strengthen "form over matter, spirit over materiality, the soul over the body."
46. *Torat Menahem* 5716: 2, 304.
47. *Tanya, Likkutei Amarim*, ch. 37. The Rebbe cited this passage on many occasions. For example, see *maamar* "Bati LeGani 5730," se'if 6 (*Sefer HaMaamarim Melukat*, vol. 2, 337).
48. *Maamar* "Tziyon BeMishpat Tippadeh 5741," se'if 5 (*Sefer HaMaamarim Melukat*, vol. 4, 149). English translation is from www.chabad.org/145196. For a longer analysis

The Definition of a Human Being: Body and Soul

In the Rebbe's analysis, these two complementary reasons represent fundamentally different rationales for the soul's descent. The first reason is to benefit the soul itself – the soul needs to inhabit a body so that it can actualize its inherent connection to God by serving Him even while being banished to a foreign, corporeal world. The second reason, however, veers from seeing the soul's descent in terms of the soul itself, and instead underscores the mission of the soul vis-à-vis the body.

The Rebbe argued that the second rationale is the primary reason for the soul's descent.[49] In line with the general purpose of Creation being the fashioning of a *Dira BaTahtonim*, the main mission of the soul is to purify the body through influencing it to perform mitzvot. The result of the soul's arduous labor is that after a lifetime spent observing the mitzvot, the body is readied to be a home for God.

Crucially, while the process of purifying the body might appear as a revolutionary *transformation* of the material flesh, this really constitutes a *revelation* of the body's true essence:

> [When the soul purifies the body] the additional measure of light comes from the darkness itself – the darkness (of the body, the animal soul, and our material world) is transformed into light ... the *transformation* of darkness into light *reveals* the Divine Essence.[50] [Emphasis added.]

Hence, the soul's mission is to reveal the true nature of the body as a direct expression of the Divine Essence, transforming darkness into light.[51]

The Rebbe explained that even though this advantage of the body is currently hidden, it is nevertheless sensed on some level by the soul. It is precisely this advantage of the body that motivates the soul to descend from its heavenly abode to inhabit a body: "The fact that the soul is drawn to vivify the body is due to the advantage of the body due

---

of these two reasons, also see *Likkutei Sihot* 15, *Vayetzeh*, no. 3.
49. Maamar "*Tziyon BeMishpat Tippadeh* 5741," *se'if* 5, based on *Tanya, Likkutei Amarim*, ch. 37.
50. Ibid.
51. See also *Torat Menahem* 5750: 2, 117–19.

to its root [in the Divine Essence]."[52] Sensing that, covertly, the body is more elevated, the soul is motivated to be the vehicle through which the body's true essence is revealed.

Body and Soul in the Eschaton

This connection between the Divine Essence and the physical body is also integrated into the Rebbe's eschatological perspective. Chabad Hasidism had long supported Ramban over Rambam regarding the existence of the purified physical body in the ultimate utopian era.[53] But Chabad teachings, sharpened by the Rebbe, provide a framework that further develops Ramban's orientation of the body's role in the post-resurrection world.

The existence of the body in the ultimate eschaton is not a foregone conclusion for Ramban. Even while Ramban argues for the body's existence, he is troubled by how such a lowly thing can exist in such an acutely spiritual age. In response, he relies on the aforementioned notion of the body's purification through its being overpowered by the soul, which will *allow* the body to exist even in a time when it seems to have lost its relevance.[54] By contrast, according to the Rebbe there is a much deeper divine plan at work. It is specifically when embodied, that one can fully appreciate the ultimate revelation of God in the end of history due to the body's fundamental rootedness in the Divine Essence.

In one *maamar*,[55] the Rebbe directly addressed the nature of the future existence of the body in light of the above ideas. The Rebbe began by comparing the reward that the righteous will receive upon their death as disembodied souls in the Garden of Eden, and the reward in the final stage of redemption – the period following the resurrection of

---

52. Maamar "Kol Yisrael Yesh Lahem Helek 5733," *se'if* 3 (*Sefer HaMaamarim Melukat*, vol. 3, 219).
53. *Derekh Mitzvotekha, mitzvat tzitzit*, 14b. For the Rebbe's description of the known details of the revival of the dead, see *Iggerot Kodesh* 2, letter 200.
54. *Torat HaAdam, Shaar HaGemul*, 305.
55. Maamar "Kol Yisrael Yesh Lahem Helek 5733" (*Sefer HaMaamarim Melukat*, vol. 3, 217–20).

The Definition of a Human Being: Body and Soul

the dead.[56] After establishing that the revelation of God will be greater in the latter than in former, the Rebbe posed the following question:

> The revelation [of God] in the Era of Resurrection is much greater than the revelation [of God] in the Garden of Eden [where souls go after death]. But seemingly, since the Garden of Eden is the world of disembodied souls, and in the Era of Resurrection the souls will be within bodies, what is the explanation [of the fact] that the revelation [of God] will be greater in the Era of Resurrection... if the limitations of a material item are greater than the limitations of a spiritual item?[57]

The Rebbe's answer hinges on comparing the relationship between the body and soul with the relationship between Torah and mitzvot. As described earlier, there are two complementary perspectives on the relationship between Torah and mitzvot.[58] In terms of their manifest nature, the transcendent and boundless Torah is more elevated than the concrete mitzvot that are bounded by time and space. Within the confines of our limited reality, it is the Torah that vivifies and lends importance to the mitzvot.

However, based on the Chabad principle of "Whatever is lower [perforce] has a higher root,"[59] the opposite is true. The "lower" manifestation of mitzvot belies their rootedness in the Divine Essence, whose all-inclusive nature transcends the bounds of transcendence. It is specifically the bounded and concrete actional mitzvot, more than the infinite Torah, that more directly engage the Divine Essence.

A parallel relationship, the Rebbe explained, exists between the body and soul:

> In a similar manner one can understand the relationship between a person's soul and the body (which are analogous to the Torah

---

56. This is the time period referred to in Mishna Sanhedrin 10:1, which teaches that all Jews have a portion in the World to Come.
57. Maamar "*Kol Yisrael Yesh Lahem Helek* 5733," *se'if* 2.
58. See chapter 5, section "The Approach of the Alter Rebbe."
59. *Likkutei Torah, Shir HaShirim* 9d.

and mitzvot). Even as the vitality of the body stems from the soul, the root of the body is higher than the root of the soul.[60]

Studying the spiritual Torah is associated with the soul, the root of cognition and spirituality. Only the body, however, is able to perform actional mitzvot, and, like them, is manifestly a meaningless shell[61] yet covertly rooted in the Divine Essence.

The Rebbe employed this parallelism to explain the two stages of reward for our service of God. Upon death, the transcendent soul is no longer restrained by concrete corporeality and ascends to the Garden of Eden to receive spiritual reward in the form of understanding the truth of God.[62] The level of pleasure that the soul receives from this experience is proportionate to and a direct result of the Torah that it cognitively studied while the person whose body housed that soul was alive.

The image of an independent soul gaining spiritual pleasure through understanding God is the pinnacle of a reality that is governed by the overtly spiritual *Giluyim*. However, the resurrection of the dead in their purified bodies will be accompanied with the revelation of the Divine Essence itself. Then, the body, which was created directly from the Divine Essence, will be able to receive reward for the physical performance of actional mitzvot, which also stem from the Divine Essence.

The Rebbe's affirmation of the body's existence in the eschaton is not a position he finds logically troubling but was forced into due to the rabbinic sources, as seems to have been the case for Ramban. Rather, due to the association of actional mitzvot and the body, and their joint rootedness in the Divine Essence, it is natural that in the utopian era the body will receive the ultimate reward with the final disclosure of its essential nature.

In summary, the Rebbe described the body as being more elevated than the soul. This rootedness of the body in the Divine Essence is apparent from analyzing the beginning and end of history. In the interim, however, the loftiness of the body is concealed. The spiritual soul is sent into this lowly world with the mission of revealing the true nature of the body.

---

60. Maamar "*Kol Yisrael Yesh Lahem Helek* 5733," *se'if* 3.
61. See chapter 5, section "The Approach of the Alter Rebbe."
62. *Mishneh Torah, Hilkhot Yesodei HaTorah* 4:8–9.

The Definition of a Human Being: Body and Soul

A HOLISTIC PERSPECTIVE

Until this point we have discussed body and soul in a binary fashion, as two distinct entities with different inceptions and different roles. Within this framework, the Rebbe's main innovative idea is the surprising advantage of the body over the soul. In truth, though, the Rebbe's ultimate message was to overturn the whole conception of relating to body and soul as a dichotomous pair. Rather, body and soul should be perceived as different manifestations of the same essence, utterly unified both conceptually and practically. This perspective will be developed stage by stage in the ensuing sections.

The Unity of the Divine Essence

The Divine Essence is the singular substance of which all of reality is constituted. As such, the revelation of the Divine Essence in the utopian era will generate the dissipation of all essential differences, disclosing, instead, an existence that is harmonious, holistic, and unified. As we have seen, this basic idea undergirds the Rebbe's understanding of the potential union of seemingly dichotomous pairs such as sacred and mundane space. Similarly, in that era, body and soul will also be revealed to be fundamentally united.

The Rebbe explained in numerous places that the elevation of the body in the eschaton will not leave the soul unaffected. Rather, as noted above, "the soul will be nourished from the body." In other words, the soul, too, will be raised up and transformed via the more essential revelation that is vested in the body. This is the reason that the ultimate utopian era will be comprised of bodies and souls together:

> The revelation of the Era of Resurrection will relate primarily to our bodies, for the observance of the mitzvot is mainly associated with the body, as above. And we can [nevertheless] suggest that the revelation of the Era of Resurrection will be appreciated by the souls as well (which will then be vested within bodies.)[63]

---

63. *Maamar "Kol Yisrael Yesh Lahem Helek 5733," se'if* 5. Translation adapted from www.chabad.org/145233.

The Theology of Dira BaTahtonim

Since bodies can achieve their destiny only via the agency of the soul, the soul will share in the body's reward. Ultimately, body and soul act in concert, as a single entity, and therefore they will receive the reward of the post-resurrection world together.[64]

The Divine Essence, the *Yehida*, and the Body

The assertion that body and soul will ultimately be unified relates to the Rebbe's understanding of the various aspects of the soul. Following earlier midrashic[65] and kabbalistic[66] sources, hasidic teaching differentiates between five levels of the soul: *nefesh, ruah, neshama, haya*, and *yehida*.[67] These levels can be described in two different ways: (1) as representing different human faculties and (2) as corresponding to different aspects of divinity.

Nefesh, ruah, and *neshama*, the lowest three levels, are found within a person and are associated with the faculties of action, speech, and thought, respectively. In terms of their correspondence to God, these three parts of the soul collectively represent the aspect of divinity that "fills the worlds" and provides them with vitality.

The next level, *haya*, is more transcendent than *nefesh, ruah*, and *neshama*. With regard to a person, *haya* is expressed in a person's supraconscious "will" that transcends the routine faculties of action, speech, and thought. In divine terms, *haya* is associated with God as He "encircles the worlds," meaning the aspect of divinity that transcends and effaces created reality.

The commonality between these four aspects of *nefesh, ruah, neshama*, and *haya* is that they emerge through the process of descent, contraction, and devolution, i.e., the *Seder Hishtalshelut* as described

---

64. See also maamar "VaYomer Lo Yehonatan 5728," se'ifim 10–11 (*Sefer HaMaamarim Melukat*, vol. 3, 235–36), for another description of the ultimate elevation of the soul due to the influence of the elevated body.
65. Genesis Rabba 14:9.
66. Etz Hayyim, shaar 42.
67. For a clear summary of the different levels of the soul, see Moshe Miller, "Levels of Soul Consciousness," available at www.chabad.org/380651.
    For a detailed explanation from the Rebbe, see maamar "VeHaya KaAsher Yarim 5730" (*Torat Menahem* 5730: 2, 323–34).

above. However, at the core of the soul is *yehida*, which is categorically different from the other four levels.⁶⁸ The mysterious and often inaccessible *yehida* of a person is "the essence of the soul that is connected with the Divine Essence,"⁶⁹ never having experienced the contractions that govern the rest of creation. From the perspective of *yehida*, a person is not defined by his own limited faculties of action, speech, and thought (*nefesh, ruah,* and *neshama*). Nor is the human being simply effaced before the all-encompassing God, as expressed by *haya*. Rather, the revelation of *yehida* unveils the complete oneness of the person with the Divine Essence, eliminating the notion of the person as a separate entity from God.⁷⁰

Just as the ultimate revelation of the Divine Essence/*yehida* overcomes the false dualism of the God-person duality by disclosing the complete union of the person with God, the same holds true for the duality of body and soul. While intuitively we conceive of the body and soul as being fundamentally different entities, and much of earlier Jewish philosophy seems to emphasize this point, the disclosure of the Divine Essence will illuminate the underlying unity between these seemingly incongruous parts of a person. In the end of days, it will no longer be possible to say that the body is connected with the Divine Essence while the soul exists as a mere lower spiritual revelation. Rather, the elevated level of the body will inevitably impact the soul as well, unveiling an integrated being that is completely enfolded in the quintessence of all of reality – the Divine Essence.⁷¹

---

68. The Rebbe developed this idea at length in a seminal treatise entitled *Inyana shel Torat HaHasidut, se'ifim* 4–5. For more on the relationship between *yehida* and the other aspects of the soul, see *Likkutei Sihot* 4, *Pinhas*.
69. *Likkutei Sihot* 24, *Hag HaSukkot, se'if* 5.
70. See also *Torat Menahem* 5715: 1, 285–98, and ibid., 5730: 2, 329–30, that the other aspects of the soul are paralleled by opposing and negative forces that result from the *Seder Hishtalshelut*. It is only at the level of *yehida*, which is enmeshed in the Divine Essence, that opposing forces cease to exist and the entirety of a person is effaced (*batel*) before God.
71. The Rebbe often articulated the unification of body and the *yehida* and their shared rootedness in the Divine Essence in the context of analyzing the nature of Yom Kippur and Purim. See, for example, *Torat Menahem* 5746: 1, 107–9; ibid., 5747: 1,

The Theology of Dira BaTahtonim

"Know Him in All of Your Ways"

These theoretical principles serve as the background to one of the most notable charges of the Rebbe: to expand the scope of a religious life. If body and soul essentially form an integrated entity that is connected to God, it follows that all of a person's engagements can potentially be effective vehicles to the singular Divine Essence. To this end, the Rebbe developed an all-inclusive religious outlook from which no activity is relegated to a secondary or supportive role. If executed in proper accordance with the dictates of halakha (which limit these activities in various ways[72]) and with correct intentions, every human action could be elevated to the highest of all ends: the disclosure of the Divine Essence.[73]

The Rebbe often developed this idea through a close reading of Rambam's description of the role of bodily activities in one's religious life. As noted above, a cursory reading of *Mishneh Torah* indicates that eating is a means toward achieving a healthy body, which will then allow one to focus on the true spiritual ends of the religious life. The Rebbe, however, honed in on Rambam's concluding lines:

> Even when he sleeps, if he retires with the intention that his mind and body rest, lest he take ill and be unable to serve God because he is sick, then his sleep is service to the Omnipresent, blessed be He.
>
> On this matter, our Sages have directed and said: "And all your deeds should be for the sake of Heaven" (Avot 2:12). This is what

---

113–20; ibid., 5748: 2, 403–6; *Sefer HaMaamarim* 5732–33, "Ish Yehudi Haya 5733," 355–61. See also *Torat Menahem* 5749: 2, 150–51.

72. It is important to note that from a practical standpoint, the Rebbe at times recommended limiting the time and passion that one dedicates to physical matters. See, for example, *Likkutei Sihot* 6, *Tetzaveh*, no. 2, *se'if* 10, where the Rebbe reiterated his understanding of "Know Him in all of your ways" but still advised that one only "half-heartedly" engage in activities other than pure Torah and mitzvot. For a similar construct, see chapter 12, section "*Simha* Breaks Barriers."

73. See, however, maamar "*HaSam Nafsheinu* 5718," *se'ifim* 3–4 (*Sefer HaMaamarim Melukat*, vol. 4, 3–4), where the Rebbe explained that the full actualization of this idea is a messianic desideratum. For a similar formulation, see *Likkutei Sihot* 1, *Kedoshim*, *se'ifim* 11–13.

> Solomon declared in his wisdom: "Know Him in all your ways and He will straighten your paths" (Prov. 3:6).[74]

Why, asked the Rebbe, does Rambam need to cite two proof texts to support his thesis? In addition, the order of these sources seems awry. Why would Rambam cite the rabbinic statement "All your deeds should be for the sake of Heaven" prior to a biblical verse from Proverbs? Certainly, primacy should be granted to Scripture over a mishna.[75]

The Rebbe responded that rather than being superfluous, each source refers to a distinct mode of service:

> "And all your deeds should be for the sake of Heaven" means that the intent of all of one's activities is not a personal matter but is for the sake of Heaven. However, the actions themselves remain mundane matters (*inyenei hol*). But the service of "Know Him in all your ways" is such that the "know Him" is inherent in all of one's ways. Not that they are *for the sake of* knowing Him, but through the actions themselves one knows God.[76]

The mishna refers to the utilitarian model of bodily activities in which one eats and drinks in order to have strength to serve God through spiritual pursuits. While such a level is certainly laudable, it does not reflect the true zenith of service, which is represented by the second source, "Know Him in all your ways." This verse teaches that seemingly mundane activities can become holy, transformed from a mere means into an elevated end:

> One might think that the only path toward "knowing Him" is through holy activities such as learning God's Torah and performing His mitzvot. Therefore, comes the teaching "Know Him in all of your ways" – meaning that the eating itself should be holy and a mitzva, similar to the eating on Shabbat at a meal which is

---

74. *Mishneh Torah, Hilkhot Deot* 3:3.
75. *Likkutei Sihot* 3, *Teruma*, note 37.
76. Ibid., 10, *Vayishlah*, Yod-Tet Kislev, *se'if* 6.

The Theology of Dira BaTahtonim

a mitzva, or the eating of sacrificial meat, which are themselves mitzvot.[77]

Elsewhere, the Rebbe related to business activities in the same vein:

> It is not enough that a Jew's responsibility in business matters should be expressed only in refraining from the prohibitions of overcharging (*onaa*) and illegitimate encroachment (*hasagat gevul*)...*but the highest level of service is that in the midst of the business, Godliness is perceived and felt; not just that the business is done for the sake of Heaven, that a person uses materiality for the sake of holiness, but rather that the materiality itself should be holy*... and this is the meaning of "Know Him in all your ways," not just that your "ways" should be for the sake of "knowing Him," but in [your ways] themselves you "know Him."[78] [Emphasis added.]

Bodily activities, whether eating, drinking, or conducting business, can be elevated to the point that they are akin to formal mitzvot as moments of ultimate God-consciousness.

What generates this radical approach? As the Rebbe explained elsewhere, this is an outgrowth of Chabad's notion of the all-encompassing unity of God:

> As the Alter Rebbe emphasized, "There is no other" (*ein od*); the entire world is literally nothing, and is not even described as *od*, which refers to a secondary thing.... This feeling inspires a person to the service of "Know Him in all of your ways...." Not

---

77. Ibid. It is important to note that even as the Rebbe emphasized the importance inherent in eating, it is less clear if he thought it was ideal to actually enjoy one's food. For example, see *Likkutei Sihot* 10, *Vayishlah*, Yod-Tet Kislev, *se'if* 8, where the Rebbe approvingly cites the Alter Rebbe's declaration that from his youth he never felt the taste of the food that he was eating. However, other sources seem to indicate that the Rebbe allowed some form of physical pleasure; see *Torat Menahem* 5717: 3, 56 and ibid., 5750: 2, 117–18. Regarding more general Jewish perspectives on pleasure, see Moshe Sokol (2013), 83–111.
78. *Likkutei Sihot* 3, *Teruma, se'if* 6.

The Definition of a Human Being: Body and Soul

only that his actions should be [merely] for the sake of Heaven, *dedicated to* God...but that the mundane matters should themselves become holiness.[79]

Contemplating this conception of divine unity will lead to the conclusion that bodily activities can become permeated with Godliness just like spiritual pursuits, as God is the only true reality.[80]

HISTORICAL DEVELOPMENT
Body and Soul in Exile and Redemption

As we have seen regarding other issues, the Rebbe took a historical approach to the proper perspective regarding the body and its activities. While previous generations generally favored a more austere stance toward the body and its activities, as redemption approaches and divinity becomes revealed, we are enjoined to slowly re-engage the full breadth of corporeality and imbue it with Godliness.

This developmental model is already apparent in the Rebbe's *Reshimot* from his pre-leadership years. In an entry dated Passover 1941,[81] the Rebbe noted that we are biblically enjoined to eat three foods at the Seder: the meat of the *Pesah* sacrifice, matza, and *maror*. After the destruction of the *Beit HaMikdash*, however, the fate of these mitzvot varies. Matza retains the full force of a biblical command, *maror* currently constitutes only a rabbinic mitzva, and the *Pesah* sacrifice disappeared entirely. In addition to the technical halakhic reasons for this,[82] the Rebbe read these foods homiletically as symbolizing three different models of our engagement with food and other bodily activities.

Matza, the simplest food of the human's diet, represents the bare minimum of necessary engagement with the body and the material world as a whole. On the opposite side stands the *Pesah* sacrifice, which consists of meat, representing desire, extravagance, and full-fledged engagement

---

79. Ibid., 3, *Vayak'hel, se'if* 3.
80. See also *Torat Menahem* 5748: 3, 305, note 47, that "Know *Him* in all of your ways" refers specifically to the Divine Essence.
81. *Reshimot, Hoveret* 10, 301–11.
82. See Pesahim 120a.

The Theology of Dira BaTahtonim

with corporeality. Between these two extremes are the vegetables of *maror*, which are not a necessity for human sustenance but do not connote the same level of opulence as meat.

The Rebbe posited that the halakhic status of these commandments teaches us about the proper level of engagement with corporeality across the historical timeline. As we saw above, the Rebbe saw physicality and spirituality as being intertwined and fundamentally unified in their core essence. Therefore, during the time of the *Beit HaMikdash*, when the soul reveled in the bounty of revealed spirituality, the body was fully engaged in the service of God. and therefore sacrificial meat was a biblically mandated element of the Seder.

The destruction of the *Beit HaMikdash* caused a waning of spirituality and a concurrent necessary recalibration of this high measure of bodily engagement. The vanishing of the sacrificial meat from the Seder and the demoting of the status of *maror* to a rabbinic commandment represent the exilic adjustment to a lifestyle that is more impoverished, both spiritually and physically. While the body must be healthily sustained with basic nutrients in order to support one's spiritual pursuits, anything that surpasses this bare, "matza-like" minimum is discouraged.

In short, for the Rebbe, when spirituality is at its peak there is a corresponding expansion of corporeal engagement. Conversely, the limitation of spiritual revelation generates a parallel limitation in the bodily realm.

While in this early *Reshimot* entry the Rebbe only hinted at the epic culmination of the body and soul's joint destiny, in several later talks he built on these ideas and developed their trajectory from the present into the future. On Purim 5718, the Rebbe began a talk[83] by noting that his predecessor, the Rebbe Rashab, encouraged the students of Yeshivat Tomkhei Temimim, the central Chabad yeshiva, to emulate the soldiers in King David's army. The Sages teach that before going to battle, David's soldiers would issue a divorce document to their wives, lest they get lost in battle and leave their wives in a state of marriage limbo, unable to remarry.[84] So too, taught the Rashab, a young man who enters the hal-

---

83. *Torat Menahem* 5718: 2, 150–56.
84. Ketubot 9b.

The Definition of a Human Being: Body and Soul

lowed halls of the yeshiva needs to have his soul (the male, or husband) divorce itself of bodily matters (the female, or wife) and be exclusively focused on spiritual pursuits. Only this form of abnegation of the physical will allow a student to be successful in his spiritual battles.

The Rashab's analogy clearly does not place a premium on being fully engaged in bodily pursuits, but rather idealizes a "matza-like" existence. The Rebbe, however, while never distancing himself from the Rashab's rhetoric and message, shifted the ultimate orientation toward the body by extending the analogy to its logical end. While during active military engagement the soldiers need to disengage from their wives to be singly focused on the task at hand, once victory is achieved the soldiers can return home and reinitiate their marital lives. In fact, he noted, the love of the husband and wife after their period of separation will be greater than before the temporary period of separation.

The same holds true, argued the Rebbe, for the soul's relationship with the body. While the exilic battlefield requires the soul to divorce itself from the body, the ultimate messianic victory will entail a reunification of these seemingly opposite poles. The previously "divorced" body will regain its significance and be revealed to be one with the Divine Essence.[85]

Between the exilic notion of divorce and the messianic remarriage of body and soul, the Rebbe placed the post-World War II era – that of *ikveta deMeshiha*. Since the time of the Baal Shem Tov and the revelation of Hasidism onward, the true nature of the relationship between body and soul was slowly becoming increasingly revealed in both theory and practice.[86] This movement came to a head in the Rebbe's time period, standing at the cusp of redemption. While not yet fully living the messianic reality, no longer could the paradigms of the previous generations apply to the people of this era.

---

85. Another illustration of the sharp shift that will take place in the Messianic Era is the nature of the Nazirite. See *Likkutei Sihot* 38, *Naso*, no. 2 *se'if* 6, where the Rebbe described the ultimate messianic Nazirite as one who is able to fully engage in the food of this world in a sanctified manner. See also *Likkutei Sihot* 31, *Shemot*, no. 3; *Torat Menahem* 5717: 3, 56–57.
86. *Likkutei Sihot* 10, *Vayishlah*, Yod-Tet Kislev, *se'ifim* 4–10.

The Theology of Dira BaTahtonim

This idea was once expressed by the Rebbe regarding the distinction between using the body as an instrument for the *sake* of Heaven and the body itself becoming connected with God. While elaborating on the level of "Know Him in all of your ways," the Rebbe emphasized that this idea, though lofty and messianic, is nevertheless extremely relevant at the cusp of redemption: "A Jew's activities in all matters of his daily life, even nowadays in the time immediately prior to the redemption, should be modeled upon and similar to the life and behavior of Jews in the times of *Mashiah*."[87]

It is specifically "nowadays," in "the time immediately prior to the redemption," that we should aspire to fuller engagement between the spiritual and mundane realms, thereby making our own lives more fully transparent to the Divine Essence.

Healthy in Body and Spirit

The Rebbe taught that the notion of a unified body and soul manifests practically in the realm of physical and mental health. In dozens of letters to those suffering from somatic and super-somatic ailments, the Rebbe emphasized the critical importance of a holistic approach to health, underscoring the intertwinement of the spiritual and physical sides of a person. A myopic focus on a single side is doomed to subpar efficacy, as such an approach is based on the mistaken presumption of the independence of the somatic and super-somatic aspects of the person.

For example, the Rebbe once sharply admonished a person who was seriously invested in his spiritual development yet took a laissez-faire approach to physical health:

> Based on the information that I received...it seems that you are not at all organized regarding your body's health, which will invariably negatively influence the health of your soul. This is in accordance with the letter of the Maggid of Mezritch...: "A small hole in the body will cause a large hole in the soul." This is also the strict halakha, as Rambam records (*Mishneh Torah, Hilkhot Deot* 4:1)....

---

87. *Torat Menahem* 5752: 1, 147.

The Definition of a Human Being: Body and Soul

> It would be a pity to spend time debating such an obvious point. If you listen to me and maintain your physical health through a proper diet and sleep schedule, it will benefit your spirituality as well. And the statement of the Baal Shem Tov on the verse "When you see the donkey of your enemy…you shall surely help it" is already well known.[88]

As is clear from the letter, the Rebbe saw the maintenance of proper health habits as crucial for a person's spiritual development. In another letter, the Rebbe implored his interlocutor to take care of her body due to its inherent preciousness:

> I believe I have already written to you that you need to be more careful in guarding your physical health. Thus, you are to be strict in following the doctor's orders and not take them lightly, for [guarding one's health] is also part of our holy Torah and is a mitzva similar to all other mitzvot.
>
> [Moreover] there is the well-known saying of the Alter Rebbe: "We have absolutely no conception of how precious a Jew's body is to God"[89] – and that which is stated many times in Hasidism needs no further proof [of its veracity].[90]

These practical directives reflect the ideas that the Rebbe developed in his Torah talks as described above. The rootedness of the body in the Divine Essence and the intertwinement of spirituality and physicality should motivate a person to meticulously care for his or her physical health.

The Rebbe also applied his historical scheme to the issue of maintaining healthy habits. In an early talk[91] he elaborated on the innovative nature of the hasidic doctrine of the body. At the end of the talk, the

---

88. *Iggerot Kodesh* 7, letter 2055. The Rebbe cited the letter of the Maggid of Mezritch on other occasions as well. See, for example, *Iggerot Kodesh* 5, letter 1275; ibid., 6, letter 1755.
89. *HaYom Yom*, *Erev Rosh HaShana*.
90. *Iggerot Kodesh* 7, letter 2209. Translation is from R. Shalom Wineburg (2005), 9–10, retrieved from www.chabad.org/2306895.
91. *Likkutei Sihot* 2, *Hosafot*, *Mishpatim*, *se'ifim* 5–9.

Rebbe stated: "This is the reason that in the later generations there is a particular emphasis on the body's health."[92] The hasidic-messianic perspective on the body impels us to leave behind the older model of ascetic piety and take the preservation of our body's health as a serious religious duty.

This interconnection of body and soul also works in the opposite direction. Just as the health of the body is integral to the health of the soul, so, too, the health of the soul is integral to the health of the body. To this end, the Rebbe counseled many a sick patient to take on an additional mitzva as well as strictly following the doctor's regimen. In one letter, the Rebbe described the underpinnings of this approach:

> Surely, I need not draw your attention to the deeper meaning of the concept that the Jewish people are "the one nation on earth" – not only the simple meaning that Jews believe in one God and in one Torah, but that they draw down oneness into all aspects of this world.
>
> This is to say that there is no disunity and plurality within this world at all: Just as God is one with an utter and simple unity, so, too, is unity and singularity found within all worldly aspects, particularly since the physical and the spiritual are not separate entities, but are truly one....
>
> The same holds true with regard to one's health: *When one needs to improve and increase his physical health and well-being, he should do so in conjunction with and with a concurrent and corresponding increase in his spiritual health and well-being* – in the words of our Sages: "Whoever will increase, will see an increase" (Taanit 31a).
>
> In light of the above, I am taking the liberty to bring to your awareness that it would be beneficial for your father, *shlita*, to increase his study sessions in our Torah, the Torah of life.[93] [Emphasis added.]

---

92. Ibid., *se'if* 8.
93. *Iggerot Kodesh* 7, letter 2001.

The Definition of a Human Being: Body and Soul

According to the Rebbe, the extra Torah study will benefit not just the soul, but the body as well.

Under the same rubric of the soul affecting the body, the Rebbe also emphasized the importance of patients developing an optimistic attitude to aid the healing process. The effect of this sort of positive thinking, which the Rebbe noted was becoming increasingly clear to the medical community, is an outgrowth of the intertwinement of body and soul:

> If in the past, emphasis was placed on "a healthy spirit in a healthy body," in our days it is an accepted principle that even a small spiritual defect causes grievous physical harm. The healthier the spirit and the greater its influence over the physical body, the greater its ability to correct or overcome physical shortcomings.
>
> *This is to the extent that even in many instances which involve physical healing, prescriptions and drugs are considerably more effective if they are accompanied by the patient's strong will and determination to cooperate* [and become well]....[94] [Emphasis added.]

The health of body and soul are inherently inseparable and cannot be treated in isolation from one another.[95]

CONCLUSION

The Rebbe's reconceptualization of the status and role of the human body was part of his larger project of reorienting people to elevate the "mundane." Even the simple aspects of life such as eating, sleeping, conducting business, and taking care of one's body can and should be vehicles of connection with God. This form of service helps transform the world at large into a dwelling place for God, the ultimate state of redemption.

---

94. Ibid., 11, letter 3594. Translation adapted from R. Shalom Wineburg (2005), 113, retrieved from www.chabad.org/2306901. In this regard, also see chapter 11, section "The Rebbe's Definition of *Bittahon*."
95. The Rebbe also applied his model of an integrated body and soul to areas beyond the realm of health. For example, his understanding of physical hunger (*Likkutei Sihot* 19, 6 Tishrei, *se'if* 8) and of certain aspects of neuroscience (*Iggerot Kodesh* 13, letter 4501) is based on viewing the body and soul as a single unit.

Secondary Literature Consulted for Chapter 6,
"The Definition of a Human Being: Body and Soul"

Alon Dahan, *Goel Aharon*, 420–25.

Yaakov Gottlieb, *Sekhaltanut BiLevush Hasidi,* 106–9, 141–46.

Yekutiel Green, "Derishot HaRebbe BeAvodat Hashem Gedolot mishel Admor HaZaken."

Faitel Levin, *Heaven on Earth*, 104–13.

Eli Rubin and Max Ariel Abugov, "Do Chabad Teachings Say Anything About the Mind-Body Problem?"

Elliot Wolfson, *Open Secret*, 130–60.

Chapter 7

Free Choice and the Disclosure of the Self

A cursory sampling of classic Jewish sources demonstrates that free choice is a fundamental tenet of Jewish faith. Rambam posits that the ability of an individual to make moral choices undergirds the entire system of Torah, mitzvot, and reward and punishment.[1] Characteristic of such a central topic, Jewish philosophers and kabbalists have spilled much ink debating the precise definition and nature of human moral agency.

Integrating earlier Chabad teachings, an expansive role for divine providence, and a seemingly incompatible conviction in human moral agency, the Rebbe developed an innovative approach to the meaning and significance of free choice. He built from the themes developed in the previous chapters and enmeshed free choice with the already familiar concepts of the Divine Essence, *yehida*, and the role of our physical bodies, and actions, adding another layer to his holistic philosophy. For

---

1. *Mishneh Torah, Hilkhot Teshuva* 5:3; *Iggerot HaRambam*, ed. Yitzhak Sheilat, vol. 2 (1988), 486.

the Rebbe, free choice is not only an essential subtext for the system of mitzvot but is also definitional to what it means to be human.

FREE CHOICE IN EARLIER JEWISH PHILOSOPHY

The Eternality of Free Choice

Rambam categorizes free choice as an eternal aspect of the human condition. Humans always had and always will have the agency to choose among moral options.[2] The eternality of free choice, however, was debated by proponents of another strand in Jewish thought, which affirmed the centrality of free choice in our current reality but contended that this was subject to change.

Most notably, Ramban argues that our current degree of moral agency is a negative consequence of Adam and Eve's sin in the Garden of Eden. Prior to that time, humans were programmed to fulfill the will of God much like the rest of the natural world, rendering sin a remote possibility.[3] Similarly, Ramban asserts that in the days of *Mashiah* the evil inclination will be neutralized and humans will once again be solely inclined to fulfill God's will.[4] This overpowering magnetic pull of good and the instinctual aversion to evil will render human choice essentially meaningless. Therefore, the Talmud surprisingly describes the Messianic Era as an "undesirable" time due to the fact that "there is neither merit nor liability."[5]

Divine Omniscience and Free Choice

Another primary issue discussed in classical Jewish philosophy is the seeming incompatibility of free choice with the nature of God. In the medieval period, this issue was discussed mainly regarding divine

---

2. *Guide for the Perplexed*, I:2. A minority of scholars, however, challenge this approach and assert that even Rambam thought that free choice did not fully exist prior to the sin of Adam and Eve in the Garden of Eden. For sources and analysis, see Warren Harvey (1984), 15–22; Moshe Sokol (1998); Netanel Wiederblank (2018), 40–49.
3. Ramban on Gen. 2:9. For a longer analysis of Ramban's approach, see Neryah Gutel (2002); Netanel Wiederblank (2018), 26–40.
4. Ramban on Deut. 30:6.
5. Shabbat 151b.

omniscience. God's foreknowledge of what an individual will choose seemingly renders the "choice" predetermined and mitigates the autonomy of the chooser. While this line of reasoning caused some Jewish philosophers to limit either divine foreknowledge[6] or the extent of human agency,[7] the majority of Jewish authorities found a variety of ways to navigate this tension and affirm both principles.[8]

For example, one approach,[9] which the Rebbe echoed,[10] asserts that God relates to time in a fundamentally different manner than does the human chooser. God's atemporality and transcendence above time allows Him to simultaneously enfold the past, present, and future and "experience" all three categories as one. Therefore, God's "present" knowledge of an individual's future "choice" in no way impedes the agency of the said individual who is faced with a moral choice.

Divine All-Inclusivity and Free Choice

The rise of hasidic philosophy generated a similar but more radical challenge to free choice. As described in chapter 2, Hasidism, and Chabad in particular, espoused a doctrine of divine all-inclusivity, according to which all of reality is a manifestation of God. If the world and all of its inhabitants are not ontologically distinct from God, but are rather "completely nullified"[11] before Him, from whence comes the human agency to make an independent choice?[12]

In fact, Chabad teachings use this very argument to demonstrate God's categorical control over all elements of the natural world. For example, in response to a query whether anything occurs in the world due to coincidence or natural forces, the Rebbe responded with an emphatic negative:

---

6. Ralbag, *Milhamot Hashem, helek* 3, chs. 2–3.
7. Hasdai Crescas, *Or Hashem, maamar* 2, *kelal* 2, chs. 1–2.
8. For a comprehensive summary of the various approaches, see Netanel Wiederblank (2018), 67–126.
9. R. Moshe Almoshninu, cited in *Tosefot Yom Tov* to Mishna Avot 3:7.
10. *Torat Menahem* 5746: 2, 649–50, note 14. See also *Iggerot Kodesh* 3, letter 439.
11. *Tanya, Shaar HaYihud VehaEmuna*, ch. 3.
12. See Jerome Gellman (1997), 111–13, who notes that it is the particularly sharp formulations of the Alter Rebbe that create an acute problem.

> It is obvious to a believer in the Torah of God with even a small amount of contemplation [that] all of the Jews believe [in God's direct involvement in the world], based on what it says: "The heavens and earth I fill" (Jer. 23:24), as a verse does not deviate from its simple interpretation. And in the language of the master, Rashbi, in *Tikkunei Zohar, Tikkun* 57, "There is no place bereft of Him." And since God is present and fills every point in space and time, it is impossible that any event should occur without His providence. This is obvious. Also see the Alter Rebbe's *Tanya, Shaar HaYihud VehaEmuna*, chapter 2, and the end of chapter 7.[13]

The presence of God throughout the world leads to God's complete and comprehensive control over every occurrence.

It is readily apparent that this reasoning is not limited to inanimate items, but rather logically extends to human actions as well. In fact, the Rebbe himself expanded God's direct supervision into the realm of human activity, thereby limiting the extent of true human agency. For example, the Rebbe argued that any "ordinary" matter, i.e., any matter that has no moral or religious implication, is directly ordained by God:

> "From the Lord, a mighty man's steps are established" (Ps. 37:23):[14] Wherever a person may come and go – despite it appearing that he does so of his own volition – [his steps] are guided by the will of God Who wanted him to come and go there (which, in turn, causes the person's will, for... the Supernal Will is felt inside the person's will).
>
> However, this is true only regarding the ordinary matters of this world. But regarding Torah and mitzvot, free choice is granted to a person to act in accordance with his own will.[15]

---

13. *Iggerot Kodesh* 10, letter 3713. The verse quoted from Jeremiah is used several times in *Tanya* to illustrate the Chabad notion of divine all-inclusivity. See, for example, *Likkutei Amarim*, chs. 41, 48; *Iggeret HaTeshuva*, ch. 5.
14. See *Tanya, Iggeret HaKodesh*, sec. 11.
15. *Likkutei Sihot* 5, *Lekh Lekha*, no. 1, *se'if* 8. See also *HaYom Yom* for 10 Tamuz and 14 Heshvan.

Free Choice and the Disclosure of the Self

Admittedly, the Rebbe had a particularly broad definition of actions with potential religious and moral implications,[16] relegating this exclusion of free choice from "ordinary matters of the world" to a negligible percentage of human endeavors. Conceptually, though, the Rebbe's statement is important, as it represents the encroachment of divine all-inclusivity into the realm of human choice. It seems that a worldview which affirms that God is the only true being leaves little conceptual space for the human actor's autonomous agency.

This logical intrusion of God into the realm of human choice obligates us to analyze the exceptions to this rule. The Rebbe repeatedly argued that human beings have full agency over their moral lives and underscored the significance of our choices in this arena. This exception, however, begs for a philosophical justification. How can free choice exist at all if there is no such thing as an independent moral agent?

Free Choice and Rational Thought

To understand the parameters of and justification for free choice in the Rebbe's thought, we must first turn to defining the term. In much of traditional Jewish philosophy, free choice is associated with rational thought. Humans are capable of considering two options that face them and then acting in accordance with the option that they deem to be optimal. For example, both Rambam[17] and Ramban[18] associate human free choice with the following verse: "Now the Lord God said, 'Behold, man has become like one of us, *having the ability of knowing good and evil*, and now, lest he stretch forth his hand and take also from the Tree of Life and eat and live forever'" (Gen. 3:22). Man's freedom to choose is intertwined with his knowledge of good and evil.[19]

---

16. See chapter 6, section "Know Him in All of Your Ways."
17. *Mishneh Torah, Hilkhot Teshuva* 5:1.
18. Ramban on Gen. 3:22. As noted above, Ramban sees this verse as God's declaration of the newfound existence of free choice.
19. See, for example, Herman Cohen's formulation regarding Rambam: "Freedom of will always presupposes freedom of reason as its vital ground and premise" (Herman Cohen, *Ethics of Maimonides*, translated with commentary by Almut Sh. Bruckstein [Madison, WI: University of Wisconsin Press, 2004], 31).

Rambam, in particular, develops the connection between rational thought and free choice. He emphasizes that training oneself to rationally analyze and weigh one's options is integral to executing a proper choice:

> Man is the only being in the world who possesses a characteristic which no other being has in common with him. What is this characteristic? It is that by and of himself man *can distinguish between good and evil, and do that which he pleases*, with absolutely no restraint....
>
> Since it is an essential characteristic of man's makeup that he should of his own free choice act morally or immorally, doing just as he chooses, *it becomes necessary to teach him the ways of righteousness*, to command and exhort him.[20] [Emphasis added.]

Considering the nature of good and evil and understanding the chasm that separates them is a key element in properly exercising free choice. The intellect both allows for free choice and is the vehicle through which one chooses correctly.

A Compelled Choice?

The Rebbe noted, however, that Chabad tradition taught that such a process of contemplation, analysis, weighing of the options, and then choosing the optimal avenue cannot be described as truly free of coercion. He contended that if a person is drawn to a certain path due to its superior qualities, then those qualities themselves are compelling a person to make the rational choice:

> True choice means that there is no coercion involved, both coercion that stems from a "superior" entity that directs him and forces him to choose, and coercion that stems from one's

---

20. *Shemona Perakim*, ch. 8. Translation is from *A Maimonides Reader*, edited and translated with introductions and notes by Isadore Twersky (New York: Berhman House, 1972), 383. See also *A Maimonides Reader*, 381, where Rambam emphasizes the need to study in order to make the proper choices. For more sources and analysis, see Netanel Wiederblank (2018), 11–14.

Free Choice and the Disclosure of the Self

desire for the superior qualities of the item that is being chosen (as then one's desire for this superior quality itself forces one to choose the item that contains this quality). Rather, true choice is completely free.[21]

If one chooses a path based on the results of a cost-benefit analysis, then the choice is not truly free, as the person is compelled by the results of his logical analysis.

The same logic applies to choices that are not traceable to a rational weighing of the options. Any attraction that one feels toward a certain item that triggers the choice can also be defined as a coercive force. As the Rebbe once said:

> The true form of choice is when there are no reasons for the choice (for when there are reasons for the choice then one is coerced into the choice). This means that [free choice occurs when] the chooser has no attraction to the item that he is choosing; rather he chooses it due to his free choice.[22]

One might think that if a person is faced with a wide spread of scrumptious food at a buffet then he is executing his autonomous agency in choosing certain dishes over the others. In truth, though, it is the attraction of certain foods that "coerces" the individual to choose those foods. Therefore, a choice that is based on an irrational taste is, in a sense, similar to a choice that is reached through contemplative analysis. Both are compelled by an identifiable factor and hence are not truly "free."

This more subtle and expansive definition of compulsion contains yet another challenge to the notion of human agency. If the presence of any rational or instinctual reason dilutes our ability to choose freely, then what sort of choice can be defined as truly "free"? Seemingly every choice that a person makes can be traced to some rational quality or non-rational attraction that determines the path of action.

---

21. *Torat Menahem* 5743: 3, 1547. See also *Likkutei Sihot* 11, *Shemot*, no. 1, *se'if* 6; ibid., 31, *Shemot*, no. 2, *se'if* 5.
22. *Likkutei Sihot* 4, *Hosafot*, Shavuot, 1309.

The Theology of Dira BaTahtonim

THE FREE CHOICES OF THE DIVINE ESSENCE

Choices Without a Reason

It is for this reason that Chabad teachings, sharpened by the Rebbe, teach that the truest form of free choice is the sole purview of the Divine Essence. Every other being, whether angelic or human, is – to a greater or lesser degree – coerced into certain choices by various cognitive, spiritual, or physical attractions. Only the Divine Essence transcends the influence of all possible extraneous attractions.

> True choice can only come from the Divine Essence, which has no preceding cause. When we speak of all the levels of...the *Giluyim* – since they have a starting point, source, and root, all of their facets (including the matter of will)...are forced into a certain mold. Therefore, only God's Essence that has no preceding cause can have true free choice.[23] [Emphasis added.]

It is only the singular Divine Essence, which is definitionally independent and utterly uninfluenced by anything external to itself, that truly has the agency to choose freely.

The Framework for a Free Choice: Two Identical Paths

According to this definition of free choice, the agency of the Divine Essence is highlighted by the fact that all possible options are equally uncompelling. The utter equality of the alternate avenues precludes the possibility that the choice is based on any attraction to the superior qualities of one option or the other. Thus, bereft of any possible rational or irrational reason, God's choice is truly free.

One such choice, to which the Rebbe frequently returned in his talks, is God's choice of the Jewish people. The Alter Rebbe describes in the opening chapters of *Tanya* that Jews contain an additional transcendent soul fundamentally different from all other nations of the world, a distinction which manifests in a myriad of matters.[24] Ultimately, however,

---

23. *Torat Menahem* 5743: 3, 1547. See also *Iggerot Kodesh* 4, letter 1089.
24. See Yoel Kahn (2001).

God's selection of the Jewish people was not based on the nature of the Jewish soul or their inherent superior qualities.

In *Tanya*, the Alter Rebbe elucidated the blessing recited immediately prior to the recitation of *Keriat Shema* in the morning prayers. On the line "And You have chosen us (*uvanu vaharta*) from among all nations and tongues," the Alter Rebbe glossed: "This refers to the material body which, in its corporeal aspects, is similar to the bodies of the gentiles of the world." [25]

God *chose* the Jewish body as opposed to the Jewish soul. The Rebbe explained that the Alter Rebbe's surprising explanation is predicated on the basic definition of a free choice:

> "Choice" is applicable only regarding two things that have equal value and are identical. Therefore, it is untenable that "And You have chosen us (*uvanu vaharta*) from among all nations and tongues" refers to the soul, as only the Jewish people have the "divine soul" (as is explained in *Tanya*).[26]

The *choosing* of the Jewish people could never relate to the soul, as there exists an inherent, pre-existent difference between Jewish and non-Jewish souls that would stand as the basis for the choice. Rather, God's election of Israel occurs in the realm of the body. Physically, there is no apparent difference between the body of a Jew and that of a non-Jew. Thus, God freely chose the physical bodies of the Jewish people, completely irrespective of the transcendence of the Jewish soul or any other value consideration.

The Rebbe explained that this is the import of the midrashic narrative of God offering the Torah to all of the world's nations before delivering it to the Jewish people at Sinai.[27] God's entreatments to the non-Jewish nations highlights the fact that from the perspective of the singular Divine Essence there is no essential distinction between Jews and non-Jews and the Torah could have equally been given to either.

---

25. *Tanya, Likkutei Amarim*, ch. 49.
26. *Torat Menahem* 5717: 1, 41–42.
27. *Mekhilta DeRabbi Yishmael, BaHodesh parasha* 5; *Sifrei Devarim, piska* 343.

The Theology of Dira BaTahtonim

And yet, despite this fundamental equality of Jews and non-Jews, the Divine Essence freely chose the Jewish people.[28]

According to the Rebbe, the following statement of Malachi expresses the nature of God's choice of the Jewish people: "'I loved you,' said the Lord, and you said, 'How have You loved us?' 'Was not Esau a brother to Jacob?' says the Lord. 'And I loved Jacob, and I hated Esau'" (Mal. 1:2).

As the Rebbe commented:

> The verse states, "Was not Esau a brother to Jacob," meaning to say that they are equal. And, nevertheless, "And I loved Jacob." The Torah was given from the Divine Essence, and from its perspective, "Esau was a brother to Jacob." Therefore, God traveled to all of the nations...but nevertheless, He chose and gave the Torah to the Jewish people.[29]

Despite the initial equality of the options, God freely chose the Jewish people over the other nations of the world. Hence, despite the sameness of the twins, the verse concludes: "I loved Jacob...."[30]

The Basis for the Divine Essence's Choices

The Rebbe's definition of a free choice generates yet another question. If God does not choose based on reasons or attractions, then what motivated His choices? If there is no difference between Jews and non-Jews, as "Esau was a brother to Jacob," why did God ultimately choose the Jewish people? While as finite humans we are definitionally precluded from understanding the mechanisms of such a choice, the Rebbe still described some essential characteristics of the Divine Essence's seemingly arbitrary choices.

---

28. *Likkutei Sihot* 4, *Hosafot*, Shavuot, 1308–9. The fact that from the perspective of the Divine Essence all choices seem to be equal is in line with the Rebbe's notion of the essential equality of sacred and secular space (ch. 4) and body and soul (ch. 6).
29. Ibid. Also, ibid., 36, *Bo*, no. 1, *se'if* 6; *Torat Menahem* 5719: 1, 11–12; ibid., 5718: 3, 291–92.
30. See, for example, *Torat Menahem* 5747: 4, 258–59; ibid., 5752: 1 325–27.

Free Choice and the Disclosure of the Self

Unlike most human "choices" that have their basis in a non-essential element of an individual's identity, such as one's rational thought or neural wiring, the Divine Essence contains nothing other than its own singular self. Hence, God's choices are pure, essential expressions of His Essence, nothing more and nothing less.

One would think that if all of reality is equally permeated with the Divine Essence, then a meaningful choice between two aspects of reality is impossible. Surprisingly, this is not the case. The Divine Essence transcends all limitations, including the very limitations established by its oneness, and can, counterintuitively, be identified with certain aspects of reality more than others.[31]

It is this paradox that creates a framework both for free choice on the one hand and for God's execution of a meaningful choice on the other. From one perspective, "darkness is as light" and "Esau was a brother to Jacob," meaning that no specific quality of the Jewish people compelled God to choose them over the nations of the world. However, this lack of attraction to a specific quality of the Jewish people demonstrates that God's choosing of the Jewish people is entirely a free expression of the Essence of His own identity. This means that the Jewish people have an intrinsic and essential bond with God, rather than an extraneous and contingent one that depends on any particular quality that they might be perceived to possess. In the words of the Rebbe:

> True choice (*behira*) is not based on a reason (as then it is not true choice), but rather is completely free. This means that even on the level of "Esau was a brother to Jacob," i.e., they are both equal, for the virtuosity of Jacob is not discernible, nevertheless: "I loved Jacob," not based on a reason, *but rather with free choice, since God and the Jewish people are in essence the same entity*.[32] [Emphasis added.]

---

31. Elliot Wolfson (2009), 102–3, notes the difficulty in parsing the fact that the Divine Essence on one level is the ultimate equalizer but simultaneously favors certain elements of creation over others.
32. *Torat Menahem* 5718: 3, 291–92. See also *Likkutei Sihot* 4, *Nitzavim*, *se'if* 5; *Torat Menahem* 5747: 4, 379; *Likkutei Sihot* 4, *Rosh HaShana*, *se'if* 5.

God's free choice of the Jewish people derives from their essential oneness with Him. This choice is entirely a subjective expression of God's most basic essence.

The fact that certain elements of reality are more engrained in the Divine Essence than others is truly beyond human comprehension. The tenability of this logical incongruity is based on the fact that the Divine Essence transcends all human logic and categories. We have seen that the Divine Essence's power is best expressed through its paradoxical revelation in the lowest and finite realm.[33] Similarly, the incongruence of God choosing the Jewish people over the seemingly equal nations of the world indicates that such a choice is rooted in the utterly transcendent and boundless Divine Essence which is one with the Jewish people.[34]

God's Choice of Mitzvot

The Rebbe outlined a similar system regarding the Torah's commandments. He cited the following midrash as a key to decoding the essence of the mitzvot:

> "And God said, 'Let there be light'" (Gen. 1:3): These are the actions of the righteous. But I do not know which one of them He desired, the actions of these or the actions of those. Since it is written, "And God saw the light that it was good" (Gen. 1:4), He desires the actions of the righteous and not the actions of the wicked.[35]

While on the level of *Giluyim,* mitzvot are identified with goodness and sins with the opposite, this is not the core basis for God's choice of mitzvot. The midrashic statement "I do not know which of them God desired" indicates that from the perspective of the Divine Essence there appears to be no difference between the actions of the righteous and those of the wicked.

---

33. See chapter 4, section "Conquering the Mundane Spaces of the World."
34. See *Torat Menahem* 5720: 2, 306, where the Rebbe connected the Divine Essence's choice with its ability to unite finitude with infinity.
35. Genesis Rabba 2:5. Translation is adapted from www.sefaria.org.

Free Choice and the Disclosure of the Self

The choice of "the actions of the righteous," accordingly, is not defined by any external measure of goodness or moral virtue, but is entirely based on the fact that the mitzvot are part of God's essential being. As the Rebbe once said: "From the perspective of the Divine Essence, 'I do not know which ones I desire....' But God *chose* with *free choice* to 'desire the actions of the righteous.'"[36] This indicates that the desire for "the actions of the righteous" is a choice embedded in the very core of the Divine Essence.[37] The rationality and morality of the mitzvot are built upon this foundational choice.[38]

In summary, God's choices are free of any reason and external interference. But this does not mean they are generated by an arbitrary roll of the divine dice. While one could delineate various logical superior qualities of Jews over non-Jews and of mitzvot over sins, it is inconceivable that God was "coerced" into His choices due to these external considerations. Instead, we recognize (1) that all distinctions dissolve before the transcendent singularity of the Divine Essence, allowing God to choose freely between two equally uncompelling options, and (2) when a choice is made it is a free expression of the innermost identity of the Divine Essence.[39] Hence, God's choice of the Jewish people

---

36. *Likkutei Sihot* 7, *Vayikra*, no. 3, *se'if* 5.
37. See also in this regard, *Torat Menahem* 5712: 1, 338–39; ibid., 5718: 2, 107–9. In contrast to the Rebbe's approach, other hasidic thinkers understood that divine all-inclusivity leads to a deterministic philosophy in which sins, at least retrospectively, can also be seen as the will of God. This notion is most identified with the Ishbitz school of Hasidism. See *Mei HaShilo'ah*, vol. 1 (4b); Yosef Weiss (1960), 447–53; Shaul Magid (2003), 113–36, 201–48; Jerome Gellman (1997), 111–31; Allan Brill (2002), 169–234. See also *Orot HaTeshuva* 12:1. It is important to note that even as the Rebbe did not embrace the partial antinomian formulations of the Ishbitz school, he still describes ramifications of the fact that at on one level mitzvot and sins are indistinguishable: see *Likkutei Sihot* 5, *Lekh Lekha* no. 1, *se'ifim* 8–13; ibid., 7, *Vayikra* no. 3, *se'ifim* 4–7.
38. For an elaboration on this point, see chapter 5, section "Mitzvot and the Divine Essence."
39. The Rebbe often spoke of these free choices as occurring in the context of a seemingly arbitrary lottery (*goral*). For this theme in the Rebbe's talks about Purim and Yom Kippur, which both feature a lottery and then the emergence of the Divine Essence, see *Likkutei Sihot* 4, *Hosafot LePurim*, *se'if* 2; ibid., 6, *Purim*, *se'if* 1; *maamar*

The Theology of Dira BaTahtonim

and of mitzvot reflects the fact that both are innate expressions of the Divine Essence.[40]

The Choice of *Dira BaTahtonim*

This understanding of the Divine Essence's free choice means that these choices are essential and not functional. Since the Divine Essence is the ultimate essence of reality, its self-expression in the form of a free choice cannot be construed as a means toward some other end. Rather, every choice of God is entirely self-contained and is a goal in and of itself.[41]

This notion of the essentialness of God's choices was discussed by the Rebbe regarding the reason for God's choice to create the world. Earlier kabbalistic works developed the idea that God had various goals in mind when initiating the Creation process. For example, R. Hayyim Vital records that God wanted to create the world in order that He have creations recognize His greatness[42]

As we have discussed, starting with the Alter Rebbe, Chabad teachings emphasized the centrality of the midrashic statement that "the purpose for which this world was created is that the Holy One, blessed be He, desired to have an abode in the lower realms."[43] On the surface, one might assume that this line in *Tanya* is just one explanation among many in classical Jewish thought as to why God created the world. The Rebbe, however, followed the Rashab in arguing that the import of the Alter Rebbe's statement is fundamentally different.

Chabad tradition records that when the Alter Rebbe was asked to identify what motivated God to have this desire for a *Dira BaTahtonim*, he responded, "On a *taava* (desire) there are no questions." The Rebbe

---

"Al Ken Karu LaYamim HaEleh Purim," *se'if* 9 (*Sefer HaMaamarim Melukat*, vol. 3, 72); *Torat Menahem* 5750: 2, 364–65.

40. At times, the Rebbe would add an element of inexorability to God's choices, as He chooses based on His own identity. In this regard, the Rebbe cited a passage from Ruth Rabba, *petihta* 3: "I am unable to trade them with another nation." See, for example, maamar "Al Ken Karu LaYamim HaEleh Purim," note 69 (*Sefer HaMaamarim Melukat*, vol. 3, 71); *Torat Menahem* 5715: 2, 173–74; ibid., 5720: 1, 303–4.
41. *Likkutei Sihot* 6, *Shemot*, no. 1, note 71.
42. *Etz Hayyim, Shaar HaKelalim*. Cited by the Rebbe, *Likkutei Sihot* 6, *Shemot*, no. 1, note 55.
43. *Midrash Tanhuma, Naso, siman* 16; *Tanya, Likkutei Amarim*, ch. 36.

Free Choice and the Disclosure of the Self

unpacked this terse statement through contextualizing this inscrutable *taava* in the framework of God's free choice:

> [The Alter Rebbe meant] that God's will for a *Dira BaTahtonim* is not due to any reason, but rather as a *taava* that is above reason. From this it is understandable that [the creation of a] *Dira BaTahtonim* as the object of "God's desiring" does not mean that through this some elevated level or perfection is attained. If this were the case then this elevated level would be the reason for God's desire to have a dwelling place. Rather, the creation of a *Dira BaTahtonim*... is not considered an elevated level or perfection.[44]

There is nothing extraneous about the *Dira BaTahtonim* that attracts God and compelled Him to create the world. Rather, just as God's choice of the Jewish people and mitzvot is an expression of His innermost essence, the same is true for God's choice to have a *Dira BaTahtonim*. It is futile to probe for the sources of such a choice or some divine need that this can fulfill, as no further regression beyond the innermost essence of God is possible.[45]

As creating a *Dira BaTahtonim* is the historical mission of the Jewish people, reaching its culmination in the modern era, this understanding of God's choice of a *Dira BaTahtonim* has far-reaching ramifications for human service. With this in mind, let us now transition from divine free choice to that of a human.

HUMAN CHOICES

Human Choice and the Divine Essence

As noted above, true free choice is only the provenance of the Divine Essence, as it alone is not compelled by any external factors. This fact poses a considerable challenge for the existence of human free choice. As finite beings created with preprogrammed neural pathways and predilections toward qualities external to themselves, free choice should

---

44. *Likkutei Sihot* 6, *Shemot*, no. 1, *se'if* 9.
45. See *Likkutei Sihot* 6, *Shemot*, no. 1, note 71. However, it is important to note that this essential choice does not negate those reasons that can be articulated.

The Theology of Dira BaTahtonim

not exist for human beings. And yet, Jewish tradition has hailed human free choice as an axiomatic principle of faith.

The Rebbe was cognizant of this difficulty and argued that human free choice must also be rooted in the Divine Essence. This connection between a human's free choice and that of the Divine Essence means that the latter is a model for the former. Therefore, the same two-tiered system of the Divine Essence's free choice has its parallel in free choice of the human. First, the external qualities of the two options facing a person must be stripped away, creating two seemingly indistinguishable paths. Then, similar to the process God employs when choosing, this framework of indifference sets the stage for the emergence of a person's core self in a choice. Let us outline these stages.

The Framework for a Jew's Free Choice

Earlier in the chapter we noted that the Chabad notion of divine unity should preclude any form of human free choice. If God permeates all of existence, how can a person choose to sin? The Rebbe's answer is simply that God willed it to be so:

> A person can act against God's will because the Divine Essence is not bound by anything... and even though the Infinite Light permeates everything and there is nothing that is external to it, nevertheless, because God is omnipotent, He created the human being in such a way that he should be able to serve God from his own abilities.[46]

Part and parcel of God's inscrutable "desire" for a *Dira BaTahtonim* is that humans take an active part in the process of renewing creation through their choice of mitzvot. As such, God hid Himself and created a framework in which mitzvot and sins can sometimes seem to be of equal merit or value, granting a person the capacity to act in a manner that is "the opposite of [God's] will."[47] This leveling of the options

---

46. *Maamar "Bati LeGani 5731," se'if 7 (Sefer HaMaamarim Melukat*, vol. 2, 358).
47. See *Likkutei Sihot* 5, *Lekh Lekaha*, *siha* 1, *se'ifim* 8–13, and *Likkutei Sihot* 7, *Vayikra*, no. 3, *se'ifim* 4–7, for the Rebbe's discussion of sin as a partial manifestation of God's will.

Free Choice and the Disclosure of the Self

facilitates a person's ability to actively choose good and help create a Dira BaTahtonim through one's own service.[48]

This ability to choose between two seemingly equal options also highlights the fact that choice is rooted in the Divine Essence:

> We see that a person ("You are called *adam*") is different from all creations. God created all of them in such a way that they do not have any [independent] ability, but rather act only in accordance with His command and will. The exception is the human... who can act in whatever way he desires, similar to the Divine Essence, which can do whatever it wants.... Accordingly, it is clear that a person, by his very nature, is connected to... the Divine Essence.[49]

The lack of clarity experienced in this world regarding God's true will and the connected ability to choose is due to an affinity between the human being and God.

Interestingly, in this passage, the talmudic phrase "You are called *adam*"[50] indicates that this level of essential choice and rootedness in the Divine Essence is limited to Jews as opposed to gentiles.[51] Elsewhere, however, the Rebbe expressed uncertainty about this issue[52] and in other instances even assuredly asserted that non-Jews have agency regarding all moral issues.[53] This issue should be contextualized within the Rebbe's general approach to the status of non-Jews which will be discussed more fully in chapter 16.

---

48. *Tanya, Likkutei Amarim*, chs. 29 and 36. *Likkutei Sihot* 4, *Hosafot, Re'eh*, 324.
49. *Torat Menahem* 5746: 2, 827. See also *Likkutei Sihot* 11, *Shemot*, no. 1, note 56.
50. Bava Metzia 114b.
51. Also see *Likkutei Sihot* 7, *Hosafot, Shemini*, 299, where the Rebbe states categorically that non-Jews do not have "true" free choice.
52. See ibid., *Hosafot, Avot*, 365–66, where the Rebbe seems unsure about this issue. Similarly, in *Likkutei Sihot* 16, *Hosafot*, 574, the Rebbe raised the possibility that non-Jews have true agency for the Noahide laws.
53. *Torat Menahem* 5747: 3, 176.

The Theology of Dira BaTahtonim

A Jew's Choice

Just as the Rebbe explained regarding the Divine Essence that free choice is occasioned by the fact that all possible options are equally uncompelling, the same applies for a Jew: The fact mitzvot and sins may appear to be equally attractive options allows for the innermost core of a Jew to express itself in a truly free and subjective choice. As we have seen, the basic core of a Jew is the *yehida*, the innermost part of the soul, which is inextricably bound with the Divine Essence. Therefore, when a Jew's *yehida* expresses itself, it will recognize its oneness with the Divine Essence and perforce freely choose to perform mitzvot, which are also one with the Divine Essence.

In one talk, the Rebbe elaborated on this theme in light of God's message to the Jewish people at the end of the Torah: "I have set before you life and death, the blessing and the curse. You shall choose life."[54] What does it mean to choose life? The Rebbe explained:

> The source of a Jew's choice of God stems from the fact that the essence of a Jew's soul is united, so to speak, with the Divine Essence. The meaning of freedom [of choice] on this level – despite the fact that it is impossible for the essence of one's soul to choose anything other than God – is that a Jew's choice and connection to God do not flow from any reason.[55]

Bereft of any external compulsions or reasons that can be articulated, a Jew's core essence will consistently express itself in a choice of God. Similar to God's choice of the Jewish people, this choice is both an inexorable conclusion while simultaneously being truly free in the sense that it is not driven by any external factor.

Just as the Divine Essence itself is currently concealed behind the causality of nature, so too the Jewish soul. In our current reality, the constant influence of the *yehida* is often hidden and imperceptible, making the full revelation of the *yehida* in a true free choice a rare occurrence. According to Chabad tradition, however, there are choices that are so

---

54. Deut. 30:19.
55. *Likkutei Sihot* 19, *Nitzavim*, no. 3, *se'if* 11.

Free Choice and the Disclosure of the Self

irrational that they can only be explained as a revelation of a person's most inner essence. One example is *Tanya*'s assertion that even Jewish heretics and sinners are willing to die rather than apostatize. As the Alter Rebbe writes:

> *They are prepared to sacrifice their lives* without any knowledge or reflection, but as though it were absolutely impossible to renounce the One God, without any reason or rational argument whatsoever. This is so because the One God illuminates and animates the entire soul.[56] [Emphasis added.]

The pressure and pain pierces through the external concealments and reveals the *yehida* that is one with the Divine Essence. As such, the choice of these "sinners" to die for the sake of God is essential expression of their innermost identity.

The Rebbe explained that the same principle undergirds the halakha that a court can corporeally beat a recalcitrant husband to encourage a "volitional" divorce. While the applied pressure seems to negate the possibility of willful delivery of the divorce document, the Rebbe argued that the external pressure enables the revelation of the husband's core identity. As Rambam writes:

> [The husband] wants to be part of the Jewish people, and he wants to perform all the mitzvot and eschew all the transgressions; it is only his evil inclination that presses him. Therefore, when he is beaten until his [evil] inclination has been weakened, and he consents [to the divorce], he is considered to have performed the divorce willfully.[57]

The Rebbe understood that this passage contains an ontological assertion about the nature of a Jewish soul.[58] A Jew's *yehida* is bound with the Divine Essence and therefore always "wants" to choose the path of

---

56. *Tanya, Likkutei Amarim*, ch. 18.
57. Rambam, *Mishneh Torah, Hilkhot Geirushin* 2:20.
58. *Likkutei Sihot* 11, *Shemot*, no. 1, note 59.

mitzvot. In this case, the court's pressure is merely a means of facilitating the ultimate free choice of the *yehida*.⁵⁹

Choice in the Messianic Era

The concealment of the *yehida* is the result of our exilic state. This will change in the Messianic Era when the Divine Essence will be revealed and its connection to the *yehida* of each Jew will be apparent. Then each Jew will be "free" to fully follow the essential "desire" of his own *yehida* and always choose God. This will negate our current lower level of free choice and will reveal a deeper reality of entirely free choices:

> [In] the Messianic Era, when "I will remove the spirit of impurity from the land"…there will no longer be two paths…but rather through a Jew's free choice he will be connected with the Divine Essence, as that is the "place" of free choice and the source of free choice.⁶⁰

Following Ramban, the Rebbe asserted that sin will not be an option in the Messianic Era. However, for the Rebbe, this is not the *abolition* of free choice, but rather its ultimate expression. The ability to follow one's core identity leads to a choice that is inexorable, but also completely subjective and therefore free.

RAMIFICATIONS OF THE NATURE OF FREE CHOICE

For the Rebbe, these ideas had several specific ramifications. Two key assertions that are derivatives of the above understanding of free choice are: (1) all Jews subconsciously want to perform mitzvot, and (2) there

---

59. Even though the Rebbe felt that true free choice emanates from the *yehida*, these choices must also affect the "revealed" faculties of a person. Therefore, one must also understand and identify with the mitzvot, while knowing full well that one's true connection to them stems from the *yehida*. In this regard, see *maamar* "BeYom Ashtei Asar Yom 5731" (*Sefer HaMaamarim Melukat*, vol. 3, 127–37); *Likkutei Sihot* 19, Nitzavim, no. 3, *se'if* 10; *Torat Menahem* 5718: 3, 199; ibid., 5742: 4, 1934. For the general notion that the *yehida* needs to affect the other levels, see *Kuntres LeInyana shel Torat HaHasidut*, *se'if* 18.

60. *Torat Menahem* 5718: 3, 137.

Free Choice and the Disclosure of the Self

is a unique significance to service in the form of *mesirut nefesh* (self-sacrificial service).

Jews of the Street and Mitzvot

As noted above, the Rebbe thought that regarding free choice, there is no essential difference between our exilic state and the Messianic Era. The *yehida* is already present in the deep substratum of a Jew's unconscious and it is capable of expressing itself in a free choice at certain moments of illumination and extreme pressure. The Messianic Era will simply allow for the complete revelation of this latent core.

As such, helping each Jew reveal his inner essence through freely choosing to perform mitzvot is a key element in accelerating the messianic process.[61] This is a formidable task, especially in the final and darkest moments of exile, when many Jews are distant from their inner essence and desires. However, it is essential that particularly such Jews should begin to perform mitzvot as a method of revealing their *yehida* and their rootedness within the Divine Essence.

In one talk, the Rebbe outlined this process and its significance. Drawing a lesson from Abraham, who fed all the passersby and then pressed them to thank God for the food, the Rebbe called for each Jew to "go out to the streets and interact with the Jewish passersby[62] and motivate them to perform a mitzva,"[63] even if this necessitates offering them food and drink or even a mild form of pressuring.

The Rebbe then addressed those who might construe the entire enterprise as essentially meaningless:

> Let us suppose that one argues: What is the purpose of this? A person who is pressured to make a blessing over food, to recite *Keriat Shema*, to pray – he does this without a will, without a desire. This person puts on tefillin once in order to free himself from the "pressure," but who knows what will happen tomorrow?[64]

---

61. See chapter 20, section "Revealing the Inner *Tzaddik*."
62. The Rebbe paraphrased the language of Rashi on Gen. 18:1.
63. *Likkutei Sihot* 15, *Vayera*, no. 3, *se'if* 10.
64. Ibid.

The Theology of Dira BaTahtonim

The Rebbe's response draws from the nature of free choice and the basic identity of a Jew:

> Since the Giving of the Torah [when God chose the Jewish people], each Jew "wants to be part of the Jewish people, and he wants to perform all the mitzvot"[65] and the performance of mitzvot is his inner will. Even more so, the pressure and coercion will cause this to become his revealed will up until the point of "one mitzva brings another mitzva" (Avot 4:2) and he will perform all of the mitzvot in a complete fashion.

The one who acquiesces and dons tefillin might consciously think that he is simply freeing himself from the annoyance of being accosted by a young, bearded man. On a deeper level, however, this mitzva is extremely significant. Using Rambam's formulation regarding the recalcitrant husband, the Rebbe asserted that when a seemingly non-observant Jew "randomly" performs a mitzva without any conscious spiritual intention, it is actually a subconscious expression of the core identity of this Jew as being one with God. This is the Jew's inner will even if the individual is as yet unaware of it.

The aggregate effect of such choices is that eventually the "inner will" will be increasingly revealed on the conscious level as well, culminating in nothing less than the revelation of everyone's inner *yehida* and the coming of *Mashiah*, who Rambam describes will "force all Jews to follow [the Torah]" by bringing their essence to the fore of consciousness.[66]

The Rebbe's perspective on the nature of a Jew's free choice also provided him with complete confidence in the success of this mission. No matter how unlikely it might seem that unobservant Jews would agree to perform mitzvot, the Rebbe was certain that if given the right opportunities, at some point such an act was inevitable. Mitzvot are simply part of a Jew's inner core:

---

65. *Mishneh Torah, Hilkhot Geirushin* 3:20.
66. *Likkutei Sihot* 15, *Vayera*, no. 3, *se'if* 10.

Free Choice and the Disclosure of the Self

> When God *chose* the Jewish people (at the time of the Giving of the Torah), forging a connection that stemmed from His very Essence, it caused the Jewish people, too, to connect with God from their very essence.... It is understood that it is henceforth impossible for a Jew to negate this connection, for at his essence and core he is choosing God. As to his external unwillingness to leave exile – it is the opposite of his essential true choice. *Therefore, it is clear that, eventually, a Jew's essential choice will be revealed and he will also openly choose God as his portion.*[67] [Emphasis added.]

It is impossible for a Jew to forever deny God, as God is his own essence. Therefore, the mitzva missions were bound to succeed.

Mesirut Nefesh and the *Yehida*

The notion that true free choice is the pure revelation of a person's *yehida* also impacts the proper frame of service for those who are already overtly observant. Generally, people engage in religious pursuits due to a discernible motivation, be it to satiate a spiritual desire, to find meaning in a connection to God, or to be part of a certain social group. These motivations can be articulated and are definable, and therefore, while important, are rooted in the revealed, lower elements of the soul.

There is a form of service, though, that is not only bereft of a goal that can be articulated but even seems to detract from the above stated benefits of observance. This form of utter dedication even to the point of self-sacrifice (*mesirut nefesh*) so transcends rational bounds that it can only be rooted in the fact that a person's *yehida* is simply one with God. As the Rebbe once explained:

> The aspect of *yehida*, which transcends the revealed faculties, expresses itself in the service of *mesirut nefesh*, since *mesirut nefesh* is also above all of the revealed faculties, reasons, and thought. From the perspective of one's rational thought there is no reason

---

67. These final words are a paraphrase of *Mishneh Torah, Hilkhot Shemitta VeYovel* 13:13. The citation as a whole appears in *Likkutei Sihot* 11, *Shemot*, no. 1, *se'if* 7.

for true *mesirut nefesh*, a service not for the sake of a reward. The power of *mesirut nefesh* stems from the *yehida*.[68]

Such suprarational dedication must stem from the essence of the soul, which is accessible only after transcending one's external ego leading to a sense of being enveloped by God who is the only entity that truly permeates all of existence (*bittul*).[69]

Accordingly, *mesirut nefesh* is the ultimate expression of an essential choice that reveals the true core of the soul as being one with God. As the Rebbe once put it: "*Mesirut nefesh* comes from the essence of the soul, meaning that the essence of a soul *chooses* the Divine Essence."[70] In short, it is selflessness and self-effacement that lead to the ultimate revelation of the "self." The *bittul* leads to the revelation of the *yesh haamiti* – the true nature of a person in which he is shown to be utterly united with God.[71]

Creating Redemption

The Rebbe felt that these interrelated concepts of free choice, Jewish identity, and *mesirut nefesh* rose to an increasing level of practical urgency as the responsibility to complete the creation of a *Dira BaTahtonim* intensified. The revelation of the *yehida*'s oneness with God's Essence is a key component of creating a *Dira BaTahtonim*, and an essential element of the generational mission. The generation, then, has a dual mission: for each person to reveal his own inner core while simultaneously helping others access their *yehida*.

Based on the above constellation of ideas, the Rebbe explained that observant Jews acting with *mesirut nefesh* to enable other Jews to perform a mitzva helps accomplish the creation of a *Dira BaTahtonim*.

---

68. *Torat Menahem* 5718: 3, 194.
69. Ibid., 5711: 2, 184.
70. Maamar "*Al Ken Karu LaYamim HaEleh Purim*," *se'if* 9 (*Sefer HaMaamarim Melukat*, vol. 3, 71–72). See also maamar "*VeAta Tetzaveh* 5741," *se'ifim* 4–7 (*Sefer HaMaamarim Melukat*, vol. 3, 35–38); maamar "*Pada BeShalom* 5731," *se'if* 8 (*Sefer HaMaamarim Melukat*, vol. 2, 470–71).
71. See chapter 4, section "The 'True *Yesh*.'"

Free Choice and the Disclosure of the Self

The *mesirut nefesh* of the first group in prioritizing the physical and spiritual needs of others over their own, together with the mitzvot voluntarily performed by the second group, even if they do not consciously understand their meaning, are means of revealing the identity of the *yehida* with the Divine Essence. These free choices, which reveal this identity, will ultimately help bring the complete redemption.

An example of this reasoning appears in a talk the Rebbe delivered on Shavuot of 5743/1983. After discussing the importance of *maaseh* in general, the Rebbe encouraged his listeners that "tomorrow morning each person should try to influence another Jew to don tefillin." He then concluded his exhortation with the following statement:

> Through the involvement in matters of *maaseh* at the end of the exile...we will soon merit the future redemption.... In particular when the involvement in *maaseh* is in the form of choice (*behira*) – "And you shall *choose* life" (Deut. 30:19) – meaning that this service is conducted...not for the sake of a reward, including the World to Come, but rather a service for its own sake – through this, the matter of "He shall choose us as His portion" (Ps. 47:5) should be revealed.[72]

The joint action of one Jew assisting another Jew to perform a mitzva represents the epitome of free choice and is therefore of crucial importance at the end of the exile.[73]

---

72. *Torat Menahem* 5743: 3, 1554. Berakhot 61b associates the phrase from Deuteronomy 6:5 with sacrificing one's life for God. In subsequently stating that this service should be for its own sake, the Rebbe referenced *Mishneh Torah, Hilkhot Teshuva*, ch. 10, where Rambam describes the ideal form of service.
73. It is important to note that the Rebbe felt that contemporary Western free societies provide a unique opportunity for a higher form of *mesirut nefesh* that was not attainable in countries that persecuted Jews. See *maamar* "*VeAta Tetzaveh* 5741," *se'if* 9 (*Sefer HaMaamarim Melukat*, vol. 3, 39–40); Eli Rubin, "Emancipation, Multiculturalism, and the Perpetual Passover: Rabbi Menachem M. Schneerson's Vision of Modern Progress as Religious Opportunity."

CONCLUSION

While building from classical sources, the Rebbe's unique conception of free choice extends beyond the traditional boundaries of the topic. For the Rebbe, the nature of a Jew's moral agency traverses from the heights of the Divine Essence directly down to the Jew on the street. The Rebbe's mixture of a very specific and objective understanding of the nature of the Jewish soul and a valuing of a deeply subjective, or essential, expression of identity, served as part of the background for his signature programs.

Secondary Literature Consulted for Chapter 7, "Free Choice and the Disclosure of the Self"

Alon Dahan, *Goel Aharon*, 425–41.

Yoel Kahn, "Ad Delo Yada: LeMaala MehaYedia," *Maayanotekha* 6 (2003): 2–12.

Yoel Kahn, *Mahutan shel Yisrael*, 101–10.

Nissan Mindel, *The Philosophy of Chabad*, ch. 1.

J. Immanuel Schochet, "The Philosophy of Lubavitch Activism," 27–29.

Elliot Wolfson, *Open Secret*, 40–58, 167–99.

Chabad.org Staff, "On the Essence of Choice," retrieved from www.chabad.org/54491.

Chapter 8
Spreading the Wellsprings

The matrix of concepts discussed in the previous chapters leads directly toward another notable initiative of the Rebbe – the spreading of hasidic teachings to the masses. The Rebbe strongly encouraged all Jews, irrespective of their level of observance and knowledge, to engage with the deepest secrets of the Torah. While in earlier generations there was a doctrine of esotericism surrounding these teachings, the Rebbe argued that the time was now ripe for the full disclosure of the secrets. This chapter will trace the Rebbe's conception of spreading hasidic teachings and how this enterprise plays an integral part in the revelation of the Divine Essence/*yehida* and the creation of a *Dira BaTahtonim*.

A BRIEF HISTORY OF ESOTERICISM
Esotericism in Rabbinic Literature
The notion that certain sections of the Torah are esoteric secrets and thus intended for only an elite few has its roots in rabbinic literature. The Mishna teaches:

> One may not expound the laws of forbidden sexual relations before three people, nor the account of Creation before two, nor

The Theology of Dira BaTahtonim

the Divine Chariot (*Maaseh HaMerkava*) before one, unless he is wise and understanding from his own knowledge.[1]

The explanation of the opening chapter in the book of Ezekiel that describes God's chariot must be reserved for the elite. It can be taught only one-on-one to a student who demonstrates prodigious Torah knowledge and understanding.

In addition to intellectual acuity, other sources record that personal piety is also a key requirement for becoming worthy of the secrets. *Heikhalot*, an early mystical text, records that in order to engage in mystical learning and experiences, one needs to be "clean and free of idolatry and incest and bloodshed and evil talk and false oaths and rudeness and gratuitous hatred and observe all positive and negative commandments."[2] Only the greatest sages with the highest standards of conduct were initiated into the secrets of the Torah.

The divulgence of these secrets to the average person was considered a dangerous endeavor. The Talmud records several stories of people running the gamut from children[3] to great sages[4] who were damaged through exposure to the secret knowledge and the experiences that it induces. The practice of esotericism is not only proper, but also prudent.[5]

Medieval Philosophers and Kabbalists

Many of Judaism's most authoritative medieval thinkers continued this doctrine of esotericism. Though concerned with the preservation of their secret knowledge through turbulent times, they still maintained the value of secrecy. As such, they developed strategies to enable the formation of written records while simultaneously arguing against spreading the secrets to the masses.

---

1. Mishna Hagiga 2:1.
2. *Heikhalot*, Peter Schafer, *Synopse zur Hekhalot-Literatur* (Tübingen, Germany: J. C. B. Mohr, 1981), sec. 199, p. 86. Translation is from Moshe Halbertal (2007), 26.
3. Hagiga 13a.
4. Ibid. 15a.
5. This secrecy is particularly noteworthy due to the rabbinic zeal for spreading Torah to the masses. See, for example, Bava Batra 21a; Shaye Cohen (2014), 119–21.

Spreading the Wellsprings

Rambam provides a primary example for navigating esotericism in this manner. In his *Guide for the Perplexed*, Rambam explicitly set out to explain the philosophical truths that he saw as the secrets of the divine chariot in seeming contravention of the Mishna's ruling. Cognizant of this issue, Rambam justified his endeavor in the introduction to his work:

> God, may He be exalted, knows that I have never ceased to be exceedingly apprehensive about setting down those things that I wish to set down in this Treatise. For they are concealed things; none of them has been set down in any book…. How then can I now innovate and set them down? However, I have relied on two premises, the one being [the Sages'] saying in a similar case, "It is time to do something for the Lord [they have broken your Torah]" (Ps. 119:126); the second being their saying, "Let all your acts be for the sake of Heaven" (Avot 2:12). Upon these two premises have I relied when setting down what I have composed in some of the chapters of this Treatise.[6]

Rambam modeled himself upon R. Yehuda HaNasi, who, due to dire necessity, "broke the Torah" with his written codification of the Mishna.[7]

In the introduction to his commentary on the divine chariot itself, Rambam further elaborates on the pressing need to record the secrets:

> If I had omitted setting down something of that which has appeared to me as clear, so that that knowledge would perish when I perish, as is inevitable, I should have considered that conduct as extremely cowardly with regard to you and everyone who is perplexed.[8]

Rambam was fearful that he would take his knowledge with him to the grave and the secrets would be lost.

---

6. *Guide for the Perplexed*, introduction (Pines, 16).
7. See Temura 14b and Rambam's introduction to *Mishneh Torah*.
8. *Guide for the Perplexed*, introduction to sec. 3 (Pines, 415–16).

The Theology of Dira BaTahtonim

Even as Rambam's hand was forced into recording the secrets, he explains that he deliberately wrote the *Guide* in a confusing, convoluted, and self-contradictory fashion to preserve the esoteric nature of the knowledge. Only one with sufficient background knowledge and a keen mind would be able to unlock the secrets encoded in the book.[9] It is clear that Rambam only begrudgingly broke from the doctrine of esotericism and did so in a manner that most preserved the secretive nature of the wisdom.

On the other side of the esoteric ledger stands Ramban. A dedicated adherent to the kabbalistic tradition, Ramban felt that that the secret of the divine chariot mentioned in the Mishna was Kabbala and not the rational philosophy that Rambam described in the *Guide*. Despite this major difference, he was caught in a similar bind as was Rambam, feeling a need to record his secret knowledge while not wanting to compromise its esoteric nature, and he navigated it in a similar manner. He did record kabbalistic teachings in his commentary to the Torah, but his introduction contains a stern warning about the dangers for the average person to study that part of his commentary.[10]

Early Hasidism

One of the innovations of the Baal Shem Tov was the demystification of Kabbala. While earlier kabbalistic literature is occupied with theosophy, cosmology, and the structure of the celestial realms, the Baal Shem Tov channeled these concepts into a model of a human's psyche and a guide for the practical service of God.[11]

The transformation of kabbalistic teachings into relatable human terms impacted the extent of their secrecy. A story regarding the Maggid of Mezritch succinctly expresses this dual shift:

---

9. Ibid., introduction (Pines, 18–20).
10. Ramban, introduction to the Commentary on the Torah, translation by Charles Ber Chavel, in *Ramban: Commentary on the Torah*, 7–9. For an elaboration of Ramban's conservatism regarding divulging or even innovating kabbalistic teachings, see Moshe Idel (1983), 31–81; Elliot Wolfson (1989), 103–78; Moshe Halbertal (2007), 81–89.
11. See Moshe Idel (1988), 150–53; Idel (1995), 227–38.

> Once the rabbi [the Maggid] admonished someone because he was discussing Kabbala in public. That person answered him: "Why do you discuss Kabbala in public too?" He [the Maggid] answered him: "I teach the world to understand that everything written in the book *Etz Hayyim* [by R. Hayyim Vital, student of Arizal] also exists in this world and in man. However, I do not explain the spiritual concepts of *Etz Hayyim*. But you explain everything which is written in *Etz Hayyim* literally, and thus you transform the spiritual into corporeal; but the sublime spiritual world is [indeed] ineffable."[12]

Once hasidic masters used kabbalistic terminology to frame the contours of an accessible path in the service of God as opposed to just abstract discussion about the celestial spheres, the secrets became increasingly relevant to the general public.

Despite this opening of the doors to the secrets, it is likely that the Baal Shem Tov did not define his mission as spreading his deep and innovative teachings to the entirety of the Jewish people. His most profound teachings were transmitted to only a small, close-knit group of elite students.[13] Similarly, despite the above anecdote of the Maggid, an examination of his teachings and social involvement indicates that his core esoteric doctrine was primarily transmitted to a cohort of elite, spiritually capable students, while he sent more general and basic ethical teachings to the masses.[14]

The Alter Rebbe

One of the unique aspects of the Alter Rebbe's leadership was his insistence on teaching the esoteric aspects of the Torah to all of his followers. While his peers continued the Maggid's method of a split regimen of instruction, the Alter Rebbe's general curriculum for all his Hasidim

---

12. *Or HaEmet* 36b. Translation adapted from Moshe Idel (1988), 151.
13. Immanuel Etkes (2005), 127–66; 208–9.
14. Naftali Loewenthal (1990), 33–40.

included a heavy dosage of kabbalistic content.[15] This pedagogical philosophy is apparent in *Tanya*, which is intended for the average Hasid yet includes an organized and accessible presentation of many teachings of the Zohar and Arizal.

The uniqueness of the Alter Rebbe's approach to esotericism is brought into sharp relief through a strongly worded letter of critique penned by his older colleague, R. Avraham of Kalisk. In this letter, he accused the Alter Rebbe of deviating from the approach of their shared teacher, the Maggid of Mezritch, who taught the majority of his followers "only the paths of ethics...and faith in the Sages." R. Avraham was particularly troubled by the publication of *Tanya* in 1796:

> I have seen the book of the Intermediate Man [*Tanya*] that you had printed. I do not consider it useful for helping people.... For this kind of person, it is sufficient to have one spark which will have many meanings for him – this is the path of Torah. Too much oil in the lamp could, Heaven forfend, cause the flame to be extinguished.[16]

R. Avraham of Kalisk felt that the Alter Rebbe's disclosure of the secrets was unwise and even harmful. This critique was dismissed by the Alter Rebbe, who contended that a solid understanding of kabbalistic doctrine was necessary for the transformative work of contemplative practice. Without it one could not hope to cultivate a true and abiding relationship with God.[17]

THE HISTORY OF ESOTERICISM ACCORDING TO THE REBBE

This brief historical outline leaves many unanswered questions. Most pressingly for our purposes: What justified the Alter Rebbe's shift regarding esotericism? In light of the strong esoteric doctrine stemming from

---

15. Immanuel Etkes (2015), 45–48, 105–7; Naftali Loewenthal (1990), 45–54; Rachel Elior (1992), 20–21.
16. Translation adapted from Loewenthal (1990), 51.
17. Rachel Elior (1992), 168–72.

Spreading the Wellsprings

the earliest strata of rabbinic literature, what motivated the Alter Rebbe to disclose the secrets systematically and accessibly?

Later Chabad teachings, most developed by the Rebbe himself, directly tackle this issue. In fact, it was the Rebbe's historiographical understanding of esotericism that was part of the basis for his unprecedented efforts to spread the secrets.

A Temporary Restriction

When discussing the Rebbe's perspective on the secrets of the Torah, it is crucial to highlight that he did not perceive the doctrine of esotericism as an eternal mitzva or a formal halakha. Rather, the need for concealment recorded in rabbinic literature was due to a set of specific circumstances and hence malleable if those circumstances were to change. The Rebbe employed halakhic terminology to describe the nature of the initial restrictions against studying the secrets:

> It is clear that the prerequisites and limitations regarding the study of the "wisdom of truth" [a reference to the secrets of the Torah] are not prohibitions that stem from the *heftza* (object) of the Torah [meaning that this part of the Torah needs inherently to be concealed], but rather from deficiencies of the *gavra* (the person), i.e., since most people cannot properly understand these concepts, therefore studying them can generate damage.[18]

This relativistic perspective on the mishna's ban[19] flowed from the Rebbe's conviction that these secrets are an inherent part of the Torah. As such, it is inconceivable that a part of the Torah, which is described as an inheritance for all of the Jewish people, should be eternally restricted to an elite few.[20]

Moreover, the Rebbe noted that both halakhic and kabbalistic literature predicted that the Messianic Era will include the complete disclosure of the secrets. The same Rambam who codified the need for

---

18. *Likkutei Sihot* 30, Yod-Tet Kislev, *se'if* 2.
19. Mishna Hagiga 2:1.
20. *Likkutei Sihot* 30, Yod-Tet Kislev, *se'if* 2.

secrecy regarding the divine chariot concludes his *Mishneh Torah* with the following description of the utopian era:

> In that era, there will be neither famine nor war...the occupation of the entire world will be solely to know God. *Therefore, the Jews will be great sages and know the hidden matters,* grasping the knowledge of their Creator according to the full extent of human potential, as it states: "The world will be filled with the knowledge of God as the waters cover the ocean bed" (Is. 11:9). [Emphasis added.]

This expansive vision of an entire nation privy to "the hidden matters" indicates that these restrictions are not just theoretically malleable but are destined to fade away.[21] Similarly, the Zohar predicts that in the end of time the secrets will be revealed for all, underscoring the existence of a consensus regarding the finite nature of these restrictions.[22]

Gradual Revelation and Dissemination

Between these poles of the strict restrictions recorded in the Mishna and the complete revelation that will characterize the Messianic Era, the Rebbe saw a gradual and incremental increase in the disclosure of the secrets. As opposed to viewing the secrets of the Torah as a fixed amount of information to be faithfully transmitted from generation to generation, the Rebbe developed a dynamic perspective: namely, that the secrets were being increasingly revealed and developed over the course of history.[23]

In this regard, the continuous unfolding of the secrets of the Torah runs parallel to the notion of an ever-increasing corpus that we find regarding the revealed Torah:

---

21. Ibid., 31, *Va'era, siha* no. 1, *se'if* 7; ibid., 5, 9 Kislev, *se'if* 3, note 16.
22. *Torat Menahem* 5744: 1, 451–52.
23. However, see *Torat Menahem* 5715: 1, 134–35, that even though the secrets of the Torah should be analyzed and developed, the goal of one's investigation should simply be to better understand one's teacher. This is in contrast to the revealed aspects of the Torah, where there is a role for more expansive personal innovation.

> We find a similar form of development [as the continuously evolving revelation of the secrets of the Torah] regarding the general Torah, which in each and every generation is increasingly revealed, until in recent generations... the Torah is more revealed than in all of the previous generations...this is particularly true regarding the secrets of the Torah.[24]

The Torah becomes increasingly unfurled with the passing of time as each generation excavates and explicates new meanings in the classical corpus of Torah texts.[25]

In consonance with the continuously increasing depth of revelation came a parallel increase in the scope of the intended audience.[26] This process of revelation and dissemination will culminate with *Mashiah*, who will teach the deepest aspects of the secrets to everyone.

In the Rebbe's historiography the crucial personalities in this development are R. Shimon bar Yohai, Arizal, the Baal Shem Tov, and the Alter Rebbe. Let us now turn to the unique role played by each of these figures.

The Zohar

According to Chabad tradition, the *Tanna'im* were masters of the secret doctrine of the divine chariot.[27] However, among this elite cohort, the Zohar singles out R. Shimon bar Yohai as the first to reveal these secrets in a setting that was beyond the parameters established by the Mishna.[28] Despite the fact that the Zohar generally advocates a high level of secrecy regarding these teachings, R. Shimon bar Yohai nevertheless was willing to disclose them to gatherings of his closest students, and

---

24. *Torat Menahem* 5747: 4, 343. For a similar idea, see *Likkutei Sihot* 7, Hosafot, 2 Nisan, *se'if* 1.
25. *Likkutei Sihot* 19, 18 Elul, *se'ifim* 4–5.
26. See for examples the Rebbe's statement regarding the Baal Shem Tov (*Torat Menahem* 5745: 3, 2006): "Through him, this wisdom began to be revealed and to be disseminated widely (*lehitgalot ulehitpashet*) among all of the Jews."
27. *Likkutei Sihot* 5, 9 Kislev, *se'if* 2.
28. See the Alter Rebbe's *Seder Tefillot MiKol HaShana*, vol. 2, 304 b–c; *Likkutei Sihot* 5, 9 Kislev, *se'if* 2.

The Theology of Dira BaTahtonim

even commanded that they be written down. Henceforth, the protective "wall" around the secrets of the Torah was rendered more permeable than initially assumed.[29]

Since the Messianic Era is characterized by the disclosure of the secrets, R. Shimon's initial step in the revelatory process represents a cosmic fulcrum that tilted the world toward *Mashiah*.[30] This move toward the utopian era through the revelation of the secrets is the primary cause for celebration on Lag BaOmer, the day on which R. Shimon disclosed his most esoteric teachings and then left this world.[31] However, despite the Zohar's significance, the restrictions against learning the secrets still remained in full force for the majority of the population for many generations to come.

Arizal

The next major figure in the Rebbe's historical narrative is Arizal.[32] The emergence of Lurianic Kabbala in the sixteenth century allowed for an even deeper understanding of and insight into the inner workings of the divine chariot. It is especially noteworthy that Arizal is cited by his chief student and stenographer, R. Hayyim Vital, as declaring: "In these later generations, it is permitted and a mitzva to reveal this wisdom."[33]

This does not mean that Arizal launched a campaign to spread the secrets without limitations. The Rebbe noted that a careful reading of the kabbalistic and historical materials demonstrates that Arizal and

---

29. *Likkutei Sihot* 5, 9 Kislev, *se'if* 2. The Rebbe explained that this is the significance of the fact that the Alter Rebbe (*Seder Tefillot*, vol. 2, 304 b–c) associated Lag BaOmer with the verse "This pile (*hagal hazeh*) is a witness" (Gen. 31:51). A pile of rocks creates a barrier but still allows for a much greater level of access than a cemented wall and is therefore an apt analogy for the nature of the secrets in the post-R. Shimon world. See also *Iggerot Kodesh* 3, letter 601.
30. *Iggerot Kodesh* 3, letter 601; *Likkutei Sihot* 1, Lag BaOmer, *se'ifim* 13–18. This point is already explicit in the Zohar itself. See *Raaya Mehemna, Vayikra* (Jerusalem: Mossad HaRav Kook, 1978), 124b, that "through the book of the Zohar they will go out of exile."
31. *Iggerot Kodesh*, vol. 4, letter 1002; ibid., vol. 20, letter 7639.
32. *Torat Menahem* 5714: 1, 271; *Likkutei Sihot* 3, 10 Shevat, *se'ifim* 1–2.
33. *Tanya, Iggeret HaKodesh*, sec. 26. See, there, for sources and an explanation that ground and justify this shift.

his students were still highly selective regarding the recipients of these secrets.[34] Arizal revealed another layer to a larger audience but did not fully break the bonds of esotericism.

The Baal Shem Tov

In the Rebbe's view the next watershed moment in the history of esotericism was the emergence of the Baal Shem Tov and the hasidic movement. The Rebbe saw Hasidism as an even deeper layer of the esoteric doctrines than Zoharic and Lurianic Kabbala. Together with the disclosure of this deeper layer came a mandate to spread these teachings to the greatest extent possible.

The impetus for this dissemination is located in one of the oldest hasidic documents referenced hundreds of times by the Rebbe and central to his teachings and programs.[35] In a letter to his brother-in-law, R. Gershon, the Baal Shem Tov described an ascent of his soul to heaven that occurred on Rosh HaShana 1746.[36] The key passage for our purposes reads as follows:

> I ascended from level to level until I entered the chamber of *Mashiah*, where *Mashiah* learns Torah with all the sages and *Tzaddikim*....
>
> I saw great joy there, but I did not know the reason for it. At first I thought that the reason for this joy was that I had passed away from the physical world, Heaven forbid. Later, they told me that my time had not yet come to die, since they have great pleasure on high when I bring about unifications through the holy Torah down below. To this very day, I do not know the reason for that joy.
>
> I asked the Mashiah: "When will the master come?" and he answered: "By this you shall know: In the time when your teaching will become public and revealed in the world, and your wellsprings spread outward (*yafutzu maayanotekha hutza*) – that which I have taught you and you have comprehended – and they also shall be able

---

34. *Torat Menahem* 5714: 1, 271.
35. See, for example, *Likkutei Sihot* 3, 10 Shevat, *se'ifim* 1–2.
36. For critical studies of the manuscript history of this letter, see Jonathan Dauber (2009), 226–34, and Immanuel Etkes (2005), 222–33.

The Theology of Dira BaTahtonim

to perform unifications and elevations as you, and then all of the *kelippot* will cease to exist, and there shall be a time of goodwill and salvation."³⁷ [Emphasis added.]

According to the Rebbe, the import of the Baal Shem Tov's conversation with *Mashiah* is that redemption is dependent on the dissemination of Hasidism, i.e., "when your wellsprings spread outward." This echoes the Zoharic passages that link redemption with the study of the secrets of the Zohar but places a focus on the new teachings of the Baal Shem Tov.

The Alter Rebbe

The Rebbe noted that despite this mandate from *Mashiah*, the Baal Shem Tov did not immediately create a system that allowed the average Jew to study his esoteric teachings. As the revolutionary initiator of a new movement, the Baal Shem Tov's mission was to reveal hasidic light into the world from above.³⁸ It took two more generations for this mission to be fully engaged by a hasidic leader who consciously set out to empower everyone to undertake the work of studying, understanding, and internalizing these teachings and toiling to raise themselves upward from below. That leader was the Alter Rebbe of Chabad, who worked tirelessly to actualize *Mashiah*'s mandate to "spread the wellsprings."³⁹

Looking retrospectively, the Rebbe identified two primary unique aspects of the Alter Rebbe's leadership and argued that these innovations were conscious choices of the Alter Rebbe to spread the secrets:

> (1) The Alter Rebbe instructed all of his followers to study the secrets of the Torah. As noted earlier, this learning regimen sparked the ire of several of his older colleagues, who saw this as a deviation from accepted practice. While the Alter Rebbe himself attributed his shift to the simple fact that the secrets of

---

37. Originally published in *Ben Porat Yosef*, 128a. Translation adapted from www.chabad.org/380401.
38. *Torat Menahem* 5747: 4, 337.
39. As we will see in chapter 17, this point has implications for the Rebbe's perception of the significance of Chabad and its leaders.

the Torah are necessary for attaining true love and fear of God, the fifth leader of Chabad, the Rashab, contended that his predecessor's activities were an intentional fulfillment of *Mashiah*'s response to the Baal Shem Tov.[40]

(2) The Alter Rebbe's systematic and clear approach, along with his usage of analogies from human experience, allowed doctrines that were previously abstract and vague to be readily assimilated into and analyzed by the finite human mind. The Rebbe emphasized that in the post-*Tanya* world it is possible to learn a topic from the secret dimensions of the Torah with the same intellectual rigor and analytical methods normally reserved for a legal section of the Talmud.[41]

This ability to understand the secrets with one's cognitive capabilities fundamentally changed the effect that they have on the person. Previously, the Baal Shem Tov had used the newly revealed light of Hasidism to inspire even the simplest Jews. However, for this new light to move beyond inspiration and become a fully transformative force, the ideas and values of Hasidism needed to be capable of being fully integrated into a person through his own intellectual effort.

This crucial stage in the development of Hasidism was accomplished by the Alter Rebbe, who transformed the secrets of the Torah into an accessible corpus that can be rationally grasped and practically applied using the human faculties of thought, speech, and action.[42] As the Rebbe quoted his father-in-law: "The Baal Shem Tov showed *that* each and every Jew could serve *Hashem*, and the Alter Rebbe showed the path of *how* each and every Jew could serve *Hashem*."[43] The move from the inspirational to the intellectual also brings the idealistic vision of the Baal Shem Tov into the realm of personal practice.

---

40. *Torat Menahem* 5711: 1, 97, 114; ibid., 5715: 1, 130; *Likkutei Sihot* 25, *Vayeshev*, Yod-Tet Kislev, *se'if* 11; ibid., 30, Yod-Tet Kislev, *se'if* 2; *Iggerot Melekh* 1, letter 74.
41. *Torat Menahem* 5711: 1, 114; *Likkutei Sihot* 29, 18 Elul, *se'ifim* 5–9; ibid., 30, Yod-Tet Kislev, *se'if* 3.
42. *Torat Menahem* 5747: 4, 337; *Likkutei Sihot* 29, 18 Elul, *se'ifim* 5–9.
43. *Torat Menahem* 5713: 1, 205.

Yod-Tet Kislev

In Chabad lore, these innovations of the Alter Rebbe are enmeshed with the episode of his imprisonment by the Russian government in 1798 and his subsequent release on Yod-Tet Kislev (19 Kislev). While the overt issue at hand was the Alter Rebbe's loyalty to Russia and his alleged encouragement of lawlessness among his followers, Chabad tradition records that the long-deceased Baal Shem Tov and Maggid of Mezritch visited him in prison and revealed that the terrestrial charges were a reflection of a heavenly accusation. As the Rebbe once put it:

> When the Alter Rebbe began to reveal the inner parts of the Torah – concepts of Kabbala and even higher than Kabbala, the secrets of the secrets of the Torah... and he revealed them and disseminated them in a manner that each and every Jew could "grasp" – this generated the accusations in heaven and from this devolved the incarceration below.[44]

It was the Alter Rebbe's educational philosophy of spreading the secrets in an accessible fashion that caused the ire of the angels, who rose up against him to protect the secrets.

The story continues that, understandably, the Alter Rebbe asked his teachers if he should cease his activities upon his release: "They responded to him that not only should he not stop, but just the opposite; he should continue to spread the Torah of Hasidism with greater strength."[45] Based on the nature of the imprisonment and the answer that he received from his teachers, the Alter Rebbe's release from prison on Yod-Tet Kislev was understood as divine endorsement of his new approach. The celestial court case had been won, and God Himself decided that a new epoch was beginning which would be defined by the spread of accessible Hasidism.

Once secure in his approach, in the time period known as "after Petersburg," the Alter Rebbe intensified his efforts to disseminate his

---

44. Ibid.
45. Ibid., 206. See also *Torat Menahem* 5715: 1, 129; *Likkutei Sihot* 30, Yod-Tet Kislev, *se'if* 1.

systematic and accessible hasidic philosophy. The discourses related by the Alter Rebbe in the years subsequent to his imprisonment and release were particularly lucid and expansive, a change that the Rashab ascribed to the heavenly vindication of the Alter Rebbe's approach represented by Yod-Tet Kislev.[46]

For this reason, Yod-Tet Kislev is a highly significant date on the Chabad calendar. Referred to by the Rashab as "Rosh HaShana for Hasidisim,"[47] this holiday publicly celebrates the new approach to the secrets together with its messianic potential. As the Rebbe once put it:

> This is the content of the holiday (*yom tov*) of Yod-Tet Kislev: We won (*didan natzah*), in that the approach of the Alter Rebbe was accepted, that Hasidism is relevant for each and every Jew, and that each and every Jew can learn and understand the concepts of Hasidism with his own mind. This is the preparation for the coming of *Mashiah*, as *Mashiah* told the Baal Shem Tov in response to his question, "When will the master come?"[48]

The Rebbe attributed immense significance to Yod-Tet Kislev, referring to it as "the holiday of holidays,"[49] and drew parallels between it and an assortment of Torah holidays.[50] In the long history of the continuous unfolding of the Torah throughout history, Yod-Tet Kislev marks the watershed moment that affirmed the Alter Rebbe's bold new path

---

46. This demarcation of the Alter Rebbe's imprisonment as a watershed moment in the Alter Rebbe's mode of teaching was most prominently articulated by the Rebbe Rashab. For a sampling of the Rebbe's citing this idea, see *Torat Menahem* 5711: 1, 97, 114–15; ibid., 5712: 1, 159; ibid., 5719: 1, 253; *Iggerot Kodesh* 5, letter 1263; ibid., 6, letter 1708.
47. This phrase is from a letter of the Rashab and is printed in the introduction to *HaYom Yom* (Hebrew edition, 1990), 34.
48. *Torat Menahem* 5711: 1, 115.
49. Ibid., 5720: 1, 171. See *Likkutei Sihot* 35, *Hosafot*, 279, for an explanation of this description.
50. See *Likkutei Sihot* 5, Yod-Tet Kislev, *se'if* 2, where the Rebbe developed parallels between Yod-Tet Kislev and Passover; *Torat Menahem* 5713: 1, 206–7 for Rosh HaShana.

The Theology of Dira BaTahtonim

of explaining and disseminating the deepest parts of the Torah – "the secret of secrets" – in preparation for the coming of *Mashiah*.[51]

The Rashab

Even after the Alter Rebbe's development and revelation of the Chabad system, more still needed to be revealed. According to the Rebbe, as the world accelerates toward the Messianic Era, each subsequent generation has the sacred task of building on the Alter Rebbe's efforts through intensifying the dissemination of Hasidism:

> Just as there is a difference between the later generations and the earlier generations, the same is true within the later generations. With each generation that moves closer to the coming of *Mashiah*, just as the responsibility increases, so too there is an increase in the revelation of the supernal concepts of the Torah in relation to the earlier generations.[52]

The Rebbe outlined how each of the leaders of Chabad further this mission of explanation and dissemination.[53] For example, on multiple occasions the Rebbe highlighted several aspects of the multifaceted career of the fifth Lubavitcher Rebbe, the Rashab, demonstrating how the latter fulfilled this mission.[54]

The Rashab is most known for being "the Rambam of Hasidism" due to his lengthy *hemshekhim*, or series of connected discourses that analyze a constellation of hasidic ideas from manifold perspectives and in an organized, comprehensive fashion. These monographic expositions brim with explanatory analogies from human experience and psychology and greatly advanced his audience's ability to cognitively understand and apply hasidic teachings. In addition, as a leader, the Rashab defined

---

51. See *Torat Menahem* 5742: 1, 419–24, where the Rebbe notes several parallels between the Giving of the Torah on Mount Sinai and the events of Yod-Tet Kislev.
52. *Likkutei Sihot* 7, *Hosafot*, 2 Nisan, *se'if* 2.
53. See, for example, *Torat Menahem* 5714: 1, 271–72.
54. *Likkutei Sihot* 7, *Hosafot*, 2 Nisan.

each Hasid as a "lamplighter,"[55] charging his followers to spread the fire of Torah and Hasidism to all whom they encounter. This confluence of a deeper revelation of hasidic ideas and the charge to "light up" those not yet exposed to Hasidism was identified by the Rashab as a further realization of *Mashiah*'s mandate to spread the wellsprings and "bring the master,"[56] i.e., to bring *Mashiah*.

R. Yosef Yitzhak Schneersohn

According to the Rebbe, this intense focus on spreading the wellsprings in depth and breadth was intensified by the Rashab's son, R. Yosef Yitzhak. He was known for teaching Hasidism to all types of people, no matter their background or level of religious observance, in a fashion that was understandable to the listener.[57] In addition, he was the first to see that hasidic teachings were translated into the vernacular, thereby expanding the audience beyond Yiddish and Hebrew speakers.[58]

Perhaps most significantly for the Rebbe, his father-in-law was charged with the sacred task of bringing Hasidism to America,[59] described in Chabad literature as "the lower half of the world."[60] This was a difficult task, as according to Chabad tradition these new shores had not yet manifestly felt the effects of the Sinaitic revelation.[61]

---

55. Related by his son, R. Yosef Yitzhak, *Sefer HaSihot* 5701, 136. See *Torat Menahem* 5722: 3, 129–40, where the Rebbe analyzed this definition of a Hasid at great length. It is also significant that the Rashab was the first Rebbe to formally send *sheluhim* to teach Torah and Hasidism to the remote communities of the Caucasian Mountains. See Shalom DovBer Levine (2010), 304–5; Andrew Koss (2010), 231–63, and www.chabad.org/109629.
56. *Torat Menahem* 5747: 1, 494–95.
57. *Likkutei Sihot* 3, 10 Shevat, *se'ifim* 3–5. In this talk, the Rebbe portrayed R. Yosef Yitzhak as continuing and intensifying the work begun by R. Shimon bar Yohai, Arizal, the Baal Shem Tov, and the Alter Rebbe. See also *Torat Menahem* 5714: 1, 272.
58. *Likkutei Sihot* 3, 10 Shevat, *se'if* 4; *Torat Menahem* 5747: 1, 495.
59. *Likkutei Sihot* 33, *Hosafot*, 28 Sivan, *se'if* 1; *Torat Menahem* 5713: 3, 125; ibid., 5718: 2, 147–50.
60. For the origins of this phrase see *Iggerot Kodesh Amdor Moharaayatz* 2, letter 617 (pp. 492, 497–98).
61. *Iggerot Kodesh Admor Moharaayatz* 2, letter 617.

The Theology of Dira BaTahtonim

R. Yosef Yitzhak saw his exile to America as part of a divine mission to help complete the process that began with the Giving of the Torah. In this regard, R. Yosef Yitzhak was similar to Jacob, who was begrudgingly compelled to descend to Egypt but realized the divine mission embedded in his descent.[62] Bringing Torah and Hasidism to America, the "lowest of the low," was the ultimate spreading of the wellsprings and hence the final task before the coming of *Mashiah*.[63]

THE END OF ESOTERICISM

The Rebbe saw the mission of the next generation as cultivating the seeds sown by his father-in-law. The generation before *Mashiah* needed to spread Torah in general and hasidic teachings in particular to the utmost degree. On several occasions the Rebbe defined these goals based on an itemized but integrated interpretation of *Mashiah*'s response to the Baal Shem Tov: *Yafutzu maayanotekha hutza*, "Your wellsprings should spread outward."

Yafutzu

According to the Rebbe, *Mashiah* selected his words with great precision. Here is the Rebbe's definition of *yafutzu*, "they should spread":

> In the language of the Torah, there are many words and phrases regarding influence and dissemination.... The word *yafutzu* indicates influence and dissemination in the manner of complete dispersion (*pizzur*). The emphasis in the language *yafutzu* is that the learning of Hasidism should be... executed with the ultimate degree of dispersion, without any limitation or restriction. If there are any restrictions or limitations (even in the slightest form), then it is not a true dissemination (*hafatza*).[64]

---

62. *Torat Menahem* 5710, 61.
63. Ibid., 5751: 3, 376–85, and particularly 380–83.
64. *Likkutei Sihot* 33, *Hosafot*, 28 Sivan, *se'if* 3.

The Rebbe further specified that *yafutzu* means that the dissemination must be total, entailing the complete dispersion of even the most esoteric hasidic teachings to everyone throughout the entire world.[65]

Maayanotekha

The Rebbe noted that a *maayan* (wellspring) has a unique halakhic status vis-à-vis other bodies of water. While there are other bodies of water that remove ritual impurity through immersion, most require a certain quantity of water to be potent. Only the water of a wellspring can purify with even a single drop.[66]

The Rebbe explained that the uniqueness of a wellspring stems from its being the water's source. When water is gathered in a pool it is severed from its source and therefore has a weakened ability to purify. Accordingly, a larger quantity of water is needed to compensate for this deterioration in quality. Water in a wellspring, by contrast, is located at its source; therefore, each drop is entirely identified with its source and acquires the limitless potency of the entire wellspring.[67]

As water is often a metaphor for Torah, the imagery of water that is identical with its source has ramifications for the nature of the teachings that need to be disseminated: "*Maayanotekha* of the Torah refers to the most supernal aspects of the Torah...the essence of the Torah... which is connected to the Essence of God."[68] The deepest aspects of the Torah, which are bound to the Divine Essence itself, need to experience the highest level of dissemination.

Hutza

Last, the Rebbe noted that the final word in this phrase, *hutza* (outward), signifies the farthest distance from the wellspring. It refers to "*hutza* that has nothing farther than it."[69] This indicates not only the farthest

---

65. Ibid.
66. *Mishneh Torah, Hilkhot Mikvaot* 9:4.
67. *Torat Menahem* 5715: 1, 133–36; *Likkutei Sihot* 33, *Hosafot*, 28 Sivan, *se'if* 4; *Torat Menahem* 5715: 1, 40–42; ibid., 5717: 2, 182.
68. This connection to the Essence of God will be explained in the next section "The Rationale for Spreading the Secrets."
69. *Likkutei Sihot* 33, *Hosafot*, 28 Sivan, *se'if* 5.

geographic periphery, but also the farthest reaches within each person, and it also refers to those people who are the most spiritually distant from the teachings of Hasidism.[70]

The Integrated Meaning

The Rebbe emphasized that the three criteria marked by the words *yafutzu maayanotekha hutza* are interdependent. It is not enough that the water from the wellspring shall reach the *hutza* as a trickle. Rather, the true and integrated meaning of *Mashiah*'s mandate is that the wellspring (*maayanotekha*) must be disseminated (*yafutzu*) to such an extent that the farthest periphery (*hutza*) itself is transformed into a wellspring. What was the outer edge must become the source itself.[71]

On a global level, during his tenure the Rebbe felt that this transformation of the periphery into the wellspring was occurring in America. What began as "the lower half of the world" and the farthest periphery from the wellsprings was being transformed into the largest producer and exporter of Hasidism that the world had ever seen – the wellspring itself. Characteristically, the Rebbe attributed this process of transformation to his father-in-law:

> In the setting of the "outside," where nothing is farther than it, my father-in-law worked to strengthen and disseminate Torah and Judaism, spreading the wellsprings outward, until the lower half of the world became the source of disseminating Torah and Judaism and the wellsprings [of Hasidism] to the entire world.[72]

The Rebbe described this transformation of America into a wellspring of Hasidism as a key preparation for *Mashiah*.[73]

---

70. Ibid., 15, *Vayishlah*, no. 3, *se'if* 5.
71. *Likkutei Sihot* 33, *Hosafot*, 28 Sivan, *se'if* 6; ibid., 15, *Vayishlah*, no. 3, *se'if* 3; ibid., 10, Yod-Tet Kislev, *se'if* 9.
72. *Likkutei Sihot* 33, *Hosafot*, 28 Sivan, *se'if* 7.
73. *Torat Menahem* 5751: 3, 376–85 and particularly 380–83. See also *Likkutei Sihot* 13, 302–3, where the Rebbe called for every community to be as permeated with Torah and Hasidism as the town of Lubavitch, the center of Chabad Hasidism for

THE RATIONALE FOR SPREADING THE SECRETS
Why Now?

Having outlined the Rebbe's historiography regarding the gradual movement away from esotericism, we can now turn our attention to the conceptual justification for this trend. Why did God program history such that the veil around the secrets would slowly be removed as the world marches toward *Mashiah*?

The Rebbe sharpened this question by highlighting the rabbinic notion of *yeridat hadorot*, which teaches that each generation in the post-Sinai world functions on a lower spiritual level than the generation prior to it. This doctrine would lead us to conclude that the final generations leading to the coming of *Mashiah* are characterized by a deep darkness and spiritual deficiencies. If, so, asked the Rebbe, "How is it possible that specifically these generations merit such elevated revelations that the previous generations, including those of the *Tanna'im, Amora'im, Geonim,* and *Rishonim,* did not merit?"[74]

In several talks the Rebbe provided two distinct but intertwined responses to this fundamental question. Both answers are predicated on his understanding of how divine providence directs intellectual history. According to the Rebbe, just as God orchestrates worldly events to fulfill His specific plans, God also determines when certain ideas should be introduced into the world. The introduction or proliferation of an idea at a specific historical moment indicates that the idea is necessary for the people of that time to fulfill their roles in God's plans.[75]

This being the case, the Rebbe highlighted two complementary aspects of the later generations that necessitated the revelation and proliferation of the deepest secrets of the Torah: (1) their lowliness and (2) their proximity to *Mashiah*.

---

several generations. For an analysis of the Rebbe's conceptualization of America, see Philip Wexler and Eli Rubin (2020).
74. *Likkutei Sihot* 7, *Hosafot*, 2 Nisan, *se'if* 1; ibid., 30, Yod-Tet Kislev, *se'if* 2.
75. Ibid., 7, *Hosafot*, 2 Nisan, *se'if* 2.

The Theology of Dira BaTahtonim

The King's Jewel

The Rebbe often spoke of the period of the later generations as a particularly challenging time to be a Jew. Due to the steady decline of the generations and the increasing darkness of the exile, those living later in history do not have the internal reservoir of spiritual and moral fiber of the earlier generations.

It is for this reason that the secrets must be revealed specifically in the later generations. As the Rebbe explained:

> It was crucial to reveal the wisdom of the inner parts of the Torah, which inspires the powers that are hidden in the human soul and helps a person overcome the external darkness of exile and the internal impediments to arousing himself with love and fear of God.[76]

Elsewhere, the Rebbe connected this idea to a parable told by the Alter Rebbe to defend the spreading of Hasidism to the masses:

> It is analogous to a prince who became deathly ill and they found him only a single cure – to take the precious jewel embedded in the king's crown that gave the whole crown its preciousness, to grind it into dust and mix it with water, and to pour from this mixture between the lips of the prince, with the hope that perhaps one drop will enter his mouth and save his life.[77]

Similarly, when Jews are "deathly ill" due to the severe hazards of the end of time, it is critical that they receive the necessary treatment, no matter the cost. God is willing to squander His most precious Torah for the sake of the Jewish people's survival.

However, the Rebbe noted that this parable justifies only a minimalistic spreading of the secrets. If it is fundamentally improper for the masses to know the secrets and God allowed it only to save the spiritual

---

76. Ibid., 30, Yod-Tet Kislev, se'if 2. See also *Likkutei Sihot* 15, Vayishlah, no. 3, se'if 2; *Torat Menahem* 5713: 1, 332–33; *Iggerot Kodesh* 22, letter 8290.
77. *Likkutei Sihot* 30, Yod-Tet Kislev, se'if 1.

lives of His children, one would expect that necessity would be the ultimate barometer of permissible proliferation. This would not justify the elaborate detail and clarity provided in the teachings of Chabad. Therefore, the Rebbe argued, there must be another, more positive rationale for the spreading of the secrets that undergirds the comprehensive style of his predecessors' teachings.[78]

Hasidism and *Mashiah*

If the first reason for revealing Hasidism focuses on the lowliness of the later generations, the second focuses on their unique mission and looks toward a brighter future. The Rebbe often noted that the primary responsibility of the final generations is to complete the service of the exile and usher in the Messianic Era. As we have seen, the Baal Shem Tov's letter makes the coming of *Mashiah* dependent on the dissemination of Hasidism. Therefore, it is incumbent upon the later generations to spread Hasidism without limit.

While the mandate of the letter is clear, *Mashiah*'s response leaves a gaping conceptual hole: What is the link between the spreading of Hasidism and the coming of *Mashiah*? Why should universal redemption be dependent on the dissemination of this specific form of Torah?

The Rebbe addressed this question in his seminal treatise "On the Essence of Hasidism,"[79] which interweaves the spreading of Hasidism with the concepts discussed in the previous chapters regarding the importance of action, the human body, and the disclosure of the *yehida*.

The Rebbe opened the treatise with various opinions regarding the defining contribution of Hasidism, ranging from its ability to arouse a sleeping public from spiritual slumber to its ability to teach people how to channel all of their faculties toward the service of God.[80] While the Rebbe affirmed these earlier definitions as accurately describing different aspects of Hasidism, he argued that they all fail to identify its

---

78. Ibid., *se'if* 3.
79. *Kuntres Inyana shel Torat HaHasidut*. Translations will be adapted from *On the Essence of Chasidus*, translated by Rabbi Y. H. Greenberg and Dr. Susan Handelman (Brooklyn, NY: Kehot, 1986).
80. Ibid., *se'if* 1.

The Theology of Dira BaTahtonim

essence. Rather, the core of Hasidism consists of a single essential point (*nekuda atzmit*) from which all of the particular facets and advantages of Hasidism flow.

What is the nature of this quintessential point? Is it graspable in any form or fashion? In this context, the Rebbe cited the following definition from his predecessor, the Rashab:

> This quintessential point of Hasidism... is the effusion of a new light from the innermost level of *keter* – and from even higher: it is an effusion from the innermost level of *atik* itself, which is the level of the *Ein Sof* [the Infinite] that is found in *Reisha DeLo Ityada* (the beginning that is not known).[81]

In other words, the essence of Hasidism is the innermost point of divinity, otherwise referred to as the Divine Essence.

This point can best be understood when comparing Hasidism with four other aspects of Torah known as *peshat, remez, derush,* and *sod*.[82] Each of these aspects of Torah is a particular genre with its own distinctive mode of expression and analysis. As such, if a person focuses on any of these layers of the Torah, he will manifestly engage with a certain aspect of divinity, a powerful but limited experience.

Hasidism, however, is the quintessential expression of the Divine Essence itself, transcending all the limited layers while simultaneously demonstrating their utter unity. It reveals the essential soul – the *yehida* – of the Torah, which expresses the inexpressible Divine Essence. Therefore, engagement with Hasidism makes one transparent to the Divine Essence itself as opposed to a particular manifestation of divinity.

We can now begin to understand the association of Hasidism with *Mashiah*. Chabad tradition teaches that *Mashiah* will reveal the *yehida* of the world:

---

81. Ibid., *se'if* 2.
82. For early sources regarding this interpretive scheme, see Gershom Scholem (1965), 56–62.

Spreading the Wellsprings

The essential idea of the *Mashiah* is – *yehida*. As it is known, David possessed the level of *nefesh,* Elijah the level of *ruah,* Moses the level of *neshama,* Adam the level of *haya,* and the *Mashiah* will possess the level of *yehida*.

The superior quality of the *yehida* in relation to the other four levels [of *nefesh, ruah, neshama,* and *haya*] ... is that these four categories are each particular individual levels – *and the category of yehida is the essence of the soul, and it transcends particulars, as indicated by its name ("the only one").*

Now in the same way that the *yehida* of every individual soul is that soul's quintessential point, so also is the level of *yehida* the quintessence of the (life force and) soul of the *Seder Hishtalshelut. The yehida of the world (which is the level of Mashiah) is the essential life force of the world that transcends any limitation.*[83] [Emphasis added.]

Throughout history different aspects of God are disclosed. Each of these aspects is a specific manifestation of God, one of the manifold *Giluyim*. The coming of *Mashiah* signifies the revelation of the single divine core of all of reality, the *yehida* of the world.

As we have noted, the revelation of the Divine Essence/*yehida* banishes the binaries that create the basic structure of our current consciousness and reveals the single, true identity of everything. From the perspective of the *Giluyim* there are items, persons, or places that are devoid of divinity and hence seemingly unredeemable. However, the all-pervasive Divine Essence transforms even the most apparent darkness into light. In the words of the Rebbe:

> All of the Revelations (*Giluyim*), even the most elevated, since they are defined in the forms of "light" and "revelation," are opposed by the opposite of light, and they cannot transform [this darkness] to good.... Only the Divine Essence, which is "simple" with an absolute "simplicity" and transcends all forms,

---

83. *Kuntres Inyana shel Torat HaHasidut, se'if* 5.

has nothing that opposes it, and therefore [the Divine Essence] alone can change [the darkness] to good.[84]

Consequently, the most powerful expression of the Divine Essence is its ability to be revealed in the "lowest [point], such that there is no point lower."

The Rebbe argued that this transformative power of the Divine Essence binds Hasidism and *Mashiah*. Hasidism, as the revelation of the Divine Essence, is best expressed when it reaches the farthest peripheries and demonstrates their inclusion in the Divine Essence. This is the true import of the mission to "spread the wellsprings outward," thereby transforming the "outside" into a "wellspring." The revelation of the Divine Essence will demonstrate that there really is no essential difference between "outside" and "inside." The essence of everything is God.

As the Rebbe once formulated this idea elsewhere:

> The ultimate effect of "spreading the wellsprings outward"... only occurs when the wellsprings themselves go to the "outside." The wellsprings can only reach such a place of "outside"... through the revelation of the essence of the wellsprings. *Since the essence of the wellsprings is the Divine Essence [which is the only] true reality... it is able to pierce even the "outside."*[85] [Emphasis added.]

The ultimate teaching of Hasidism is that the Divine Essence is the essence of all things and that all things can be made transparent to the Divine Essence. When Hasidism is disseminated and this idea permeates all people, places, and items, the Divine Essence will be revealed as the basic core of every aspect of our material world.

This transformative/revelatory process which is engendered by the dissemination of the essence of Hasidism is identical with the ultimate essence of the Messianic Era. As the Rebbe concluded his treatise:

---

84. Ibid., *se'if* 19.
85. *Likkutei Sihot* 15, *Vayishlah*, no. 3, *se'if* 12.

Spreading the Wellsprings

Considering all we have discussed, it is most fitting that the preparation and vessel for the "coming of the master" is precisely the "spreading of the fountains abroad."...

Indeed, for as long as the wellsprings are found only inside, their true nature is not yet expressed. And since it is the *essence* of Hasidim which is the vessel for the coming of the *Mashiah*, it is therefore imperative to spread the wellsprings specifically outward, until the "outside," too, will be transformed into wellsprings, for through this, the essential nature of the wellsprings is manifested, and then "the master comes," which is the king *Mashiah*.

And in the words of the Alter Rebbe:[86] "Then the dross of the body will be purified (indicating that there will be physicality, but it will be purified) and the dross of the world will be purified (and the light of God will shine forth to the Jewish people without any garment), and from the overflow of the illumination on the Jewish people, the darkness of the nations will also be illuminated, as it is written: 'And all flesh shall see together… and all the inhabitants of the world.'"[87]

All of the changes in perspective that we have discussed regarding the nature of mundane space, actions, and the body – in short, the creation of a *Dira BaTahtonim*[88] – will be effected through the spread of Hasidism, which at its core reveals the divinity inherent in every aspect of reality.

It follows that the dissemination of Hasidism is not merely a preliminary step that prepares the ground for the coming of *Mashiah*. Rather, the Rebbe argued that at their core, the Messianic Era and Hasidism have a unified identity. Therefore, the spread of Hasidism itself discloses the Divine Essence, which itself is the essence of the Messianic Era.[89] This

---

86. *Tanya, Likkutei Amarim*, chs. 36–37.
87. *Kuntres Inyana shel Torat HaHasidut, se'if* 21.
88. See *Torat Menahem* 5750: 1, 471, where the Rebbe discussed these same themes using the term *Dira BaTahtonim*.
89. The Rebbe's understanding of the significance of studying and spreading Hasidism led him to attribute cosmic significance to the publication of hasidic texts and of *Tanya* in particular. See *Likkutei Sihot* 15, Noah, no. 2, *se'if* 1, which says that the *Tzemah Tzedek* associated the publication of *Likkutei Torah* in 5608 with the

The Theology of Dira BaTahtonim

is the true import of *Mashiah*'s mandate to the Baal Shem Tov that is being brought to completion in the last generation.

CONCLUSION

The Rebbe's unprecedented effort at "spreading the wellsprings" has deep roots in his interpretation of Chabad philosophy and its application to the modern era. The Rebbe considered the secrets of the Torah to be essential for the spiritual life of a Jew in the darkest moments of exile, and ultimately, vital for creating the bright messianic reality.

Secondary Literature Consulted for Chapter 8, Spreading the Wellsprings"

Alon Dahan, *Goel Aharon*, 237–310.

Yoel Kahn, "Hasidut UMashiah Hainu Hakh," 3–21.

Yitzhak Kraus, *HaShevi'i*, 34–91.

Naftali Loewenthal, "The Baal Shem Tov's *Iggeret HaKodesh* and Contemporary Chabad Outreach," 69–101.

Eli Rubin, "Making Chasidism Accessible."

Eli Rubin, "The Essence of Chasidism: A Message Beyond the Medium."

J. Immanuel Schochet, "The Philosophy of Lubavitch Activism," 18–35.

Elliot Wolfson, *Open Secret*, 28–65.

---

messianic predictions regarding that year. In *Torat Menahem* 5742: 1, 472–80, the Rebbe compared the effect of the publication of *Tanya*, the "Written Torah of Hasidism," on the world of Hasidism, to the effect that the Giving of the Torah at Sinai had on Torah in general. In this vein, the Rebbe encouraged the printing of *Tanya* in every Jewish community around the globe; see *Likkutei Sihot* 26, 320–27. For an elaboration on this campaign, see "Tanya to the World," *A Chasidisher Derher*, Issue 42 (Adar II, 5776), 47–61. For a story regarding the Rebbe's insistence that *Tanya* be published and studied in Beirut during the First Lebanon War, see www.chabad.org/2081442.

Chapter 9

Talmud Study in the Age of Hasidism

The Rebbe's talks are strikingly multidisciplinary. While most hasidic texts focus on mysticism, philosophy, and practical strategies for the service of God, even a quick perusal of *Likkutei Sihot* or *Torat Menahem* exposes the reader to many thousands of pages dedicated to what is traditionally referred to as the "revealed" aspects of the Torah (*nigleh*).

Most notably, the Rebbe often ventured into two areas of Torah study usually not associated with Hasidism: in-depth analysis of intricate talmudic legal discussions, and the world of biblical commentary, with a particular focus on Rashi. More than mere aberrations in the sea of Hasidism, the sheer volume of these detailed and painstaking studies demonstrates the significance that the Rebbe attributed to these undertakings and the seriousness with which he approached them.

This chapter will outline the Rebbe's detailed, multilayered, and multidisciplinary approach to Talmud study and illustrate how his

The Theology of Dira BaTahtonim

methodology and execution were an application of his general philosophy.[1]

BACKGROUND AND BASICS

Traditional Distinction Between Halakha and Aggada

The relationship between the legal and non-legal aspects of the Torah is an immense topic and the subject of many long studies. However, it is fair to say that, generally, rabbis and scholars have treated halakha and *aggada* (the non-legal aspects of the rabbinic corpus) as two distinct disciplines.[2] This distinction has deep roots in rabbinic literature itself, which often presents halakha and *aggada* as related but discrete, and at times even competing, fields of study.[3]

For example, the Talmud records the following story:

> R. Abbahu and R. Hiyya bar Abba happened to come to a certain place. R. Abbahu taught matters of *aggada*, and at the same time R. Hiyya bar Abba taught halakha. Everyone left R. Hiyya bar Abba and went to R. Abbahu, and R. Hiyya was offended. R. Abbahu said to him to appease him: I will tell you a parable: To what is this comparable? It is comparable to two people, one who sells precious stones and one who sells small items. Upon whom do the customers spring? Don't they spring upon the one who sells small items? Similarly, you teach lofty and important concepts that do not attract many people. Everyone comes to me because I teach minor matters.[4]

---

1. Unfortunately, space does not allow for a similar outlining of the Rebbe's unique approach to Rashi's commentary to the Torah.
2. For a brief overview of this phenomenon in both traditional and academic Torah study, see Yair Lorberbaum (2007), 29–48. For a more extensive summary of traditional post-talmudic sources, see Moshe Tzuriel (5738).
3. See, for example, Bava Kamma 60b; *Sifrei Devarim, piska* 49; ibid., *piska* 317; *Avot DeRabbi Natan* (*nus'ha alef*), ch. 29.
4. Sota 40a.

Talmud Study in the Age of Hasidism

While commentators offer a range of interpretations to this story,[5] one essential point emerges clearly: the legal and non-legal aspects of the Torah were taught in separate lectures to disparate audiences. This bifurcation continues to animate many contemporary institutions and groups. In particular, the yeshiva movement, beginning with the Volozhin Yeshiva, isolates the study of talmudic law from all other Torah disciplines and favors the former over the latter in terms of curriculum and focus.[6] This approach is adopted by authorities as great and varied as R. Eliezer Shach[7] and R. Joseph B. Soloveitchik,[8] who affirm the special and singular nature of in-depth study of the halakhic parts of the Torah.

The Unified Torah

The Rebbe, however, took a different approach. He emphasized that it is axiological that the Torah is an expression of God, and thus, similar to God, Torah must be a single and singular entity. The Rebbe frequently sourced this notion in midrashic or other rabbinic statements that assert that Torah, in essence, contains only a single word or idea. For example, in one talk, he traced this fundamental unity of the entire Torah to the midrashic statement that the entirety of the Torah is encapsulated in the Ten Commandments, which were originally articulated by God in a single utterance.[9] Elsewhere, the Rebbe affirmingly cited the Ramban's characterization of the entire Torah as a single name of God and connected it with a statement of the Rogatchover Gaon that the entire Torah is a single word.[10]

How then do we account for the myriads of component details that make up the Torah? We already noted above that the Sages themselves differentiated between the legal and non-legal aspects of Torah.

---

5. See Yitzchak Blau (2009), 3–4.
6. See Yair Lorberbaum (2007), 37–38.
7. See his introduction to *Avi Ezri*, where he posits that the learning of *aggada* and esoteric matters is not included in the standard mitzva of learning Torah, but rather is an independent mitzva.
8. See Chaim Saiman (2006), 75–94.
9. *Likkutei Sihot* 18, Naso, no. 5, se'if 10; ibid., 31, Yitro, no. 1, se'if 3.
10. *Reshimot*, Hoveret 155, 474–75; *Torat Menahem* 5719: 3, 113.

The Theology of Dira BaTahtonim

In addition, the Rebbe himself at times outlined the dizzying level of categoric diversity in Torah study. Each mitzva is unique, replete with its own laws, parameters, and meaning.[11] Rabbinic literature is prone to deconstructing "the Torah" into its component parts: the Written Torah and the Oral Torah,[12] positive and negative commandments,[13] mitzvot with different forms of punishments, monetary law, ritual law, etc.[14] If we consider the post-talmudic literature, then dozens of different orientations, methodologies, and opinions exist to analyze each of these rabbinic categories. How, then, can one assert the fundamental unity of the Torah?

The Unifying Essence of Torah

The Rebbe addressed this issue directly in the seminal treatise "On the Essence of Hasidism" cited at the end of the previous chapter. There, he noted that traditional commentators affirm the multifarious meanings of any Torah text, and, in particular, refer to four layers of interpretation: *peshat, remez, derush,* and *sod*.[15] Each of these layers possesses a unique hermeneutic, analytic methodology, and mode of expression. Therefore, if one properly employs the four methodologies, he will emerge with four discrete and seemingly disconnected meanings to the passage at hand. Given that the Torah is an expression of God, each Torah genre allows the learner to engage a particular sort of divine revelation, a powerful but still limited experience.

For the Rebbe, however, Hasidism made possible a new and groundbreaking level of Torah study. Traditionally, commentators primarily dealt with specific expressions of divinity that are rooted in a specific genre and methodology of Torah study. Hasidism, though, is the revealed expression of the Divine Essence which transcends all the

---

11. *Torat Menahem* 5751: 2, 251; ibid., 5751: 3, 269–70.
12. Sifra, *Behukkotai, parasha* 2; *Likkutei Sihot* 4, *Devarim*; ibid., 30, *Bereshit*, no. 2, *se'ifim* 4–8.
13. Yevamot 3b; *Torat Menahem* 5711: 1, 278–82; *Torat Menahem* 5714: 3, 25–26; *Torat Menahem* 5751:2, 249–50.
14. Berakhot 19b; *Torat Menahem* 5745: 1, 126; *Sihot Kodesh* 5736: 2, 295.
15. *Kuntres Inyana shel Torat HaHasidut, se'if* 8.

limited expressions. The advent of Hasidism thus allowed for this deeper dimension of Torah to be studied.[16]

Intuitively, one might have thought that Hasidism would supersede the more limited genres of Torah and render them obsolete. The Rebbe, however, argued that this would be a fundamental misunderstanding of the nature of the Divine Essence. Instead, Hasidism breathes new life into the earlier interpretations and injects them with "new vitality, clarity, and depth."[17] This new form of essential illumination allows one to see the underlying unity of what seemed to be discrete interpretations. As the Rebbe expressed it:

> As the *yehida* is the quintessential point, it does not negate the *nefesh, ruah, neshama, haya,* but on the contrary, it is the essence of all of the specific levels.... Therefore, one of the main emphases of Hasidism is the unification of the details with the essence.[18]

The quintessential point is by definition the essence of everything. The revelation of the Divine Essence, therefore, brings to light the substratum of oneness that undergirds the apparent discreteness and diversity. In the realm of Torah study this translates into Hasidism disclosing how the interpretations stemming from the other modalities all interrelate and ultimately express an identical idea in a multiplicity of manners.[19]

We can now return to the Rebbe's insistence that the Torah be perceived as a unified entity despite the dizzying diversity that has characterized Torah study for millennia. The parsing of this puzzle is possible only through the unveiling of Hasidism, which serves as the essential glue that binds the discrete passages, interpretations, and genres

---

16. *Kuntres Inyana shel Torat HaHasidut, se'ifim* 8–9.
17. Ibid., *se'if* 8.
18. Ibid., *se'if* 17. See also *Torat Menahem* 5752: 1, 443–44.
19. See *Kuntres Inyana shel Torat HaHasidut, se'ifim* 8–17, where the Rebbe carefully and rigorously applied this approach to the text of *Modeh Ani*. He first outlined the discrete meanings of the passage according to the four levels of *peshat, remez, derush,* and *sod*. Afterward, he introduced the hasidic interpretation of the passage and then demonstrated that this sheds new light on each of the earlier meanings and reveals their underlying unity.

The Theology of Dira BaTahtonim

together.[20] Thus, without sacrificing the integrity of the details and specifics,[21] Hasidism creates the broader framework that allows us to see Torah in the way that God sees Torah: as a single entity expressing the Divine Essence.[22]

For the Rebbe, a direct outgrowth of the oneness of the Torah is its practicality. While the Torah in general, and Hasidism in particular, thrives on abstract thought and philosophical speculation, these ideas definitionally always have an application for the practical daily life of a Jew. As the Rebbe said, citing R. Yosef Yitzhak: "My father-in-law the Rebbe emphasized in so many of his talks that every topic learned in Hasidism must be brought to actuality, as specifically through actional service one grasps the essence of Hasidism."[23]

As we saw in the last chapter, the power of the Divine Essence is best expressed when it permeates even the farthest peripheries, illustrating the unity of all of existence. Similarly, the synthesis of abstruse

---

20. In each of the above instances cited in notes, after outlining the differences between the dichotomous categories, the Rebbe continued to demonstrate that each contains aspects of the others and together reflect a broader unity.
21. See, for example, *Torat Menahem* 5719: 3, 113–20, where the Rebbe described the unity of the Torah as a "single point" that is spread out over a large expanse. The Rebbe pointed to various passages from the Rogatchover Gaon as models for this notion of a single point that comprises a multitude of details or moments.
22. For the notion that from God's perspective (*mitzad HaNoten*) the Torah always remains unified, see *Torat Menahem* 5751: 2. In general, the Rebbe advocated analyzing the nature of Torah from two perspectives: that of the divine giver and that of the human recipients. From the divine perspective, all of Torah is one, fixed in stone, and above human understanding. From the human perspective, however, Torah is characterized by multiplicity, details, malleability, and understandable principles. For a development of these two tracks, see, for example, *Likkutei Sihot* 30, Bereshit, no. 2, se'ifim 4–8; *Torat Menahem: Hadranim al HaRambam*, 146–56. These categories broadly map onto the Written and Oral Torahs. For many more sources and analyses of these models, see Chaim Miller (2007), 131–42, and Yanki Tauber, "The Divine and the Human in Torah." Ultimately these competing perspectives of Torah are to be unified. See, for example, *Likkutei Sihot* 4, Devarim; ibid., 19, Devarim, no. 2; ibid., 36, Rosh Hodesh Shevat, se'ifim 4–5; and *Torat Menahem* 5752: 2, 242–49. For more sources and analysis, see Chaim Miller (2007), 43–44; Elliot Wolfson (2009), 22–24; Eli Rubin, "On the Eternal Unfolding of the Transcendent Torah: Torah Hermeneutics in the Thought of R. Menachem M. Schneerson."
23. *Kuntres Inyana shel Torat HaHasidut*, se'if 18.

Talmud Study in the Age of Hasidism

concepts with practical action demonstrates the all-encompassing nature of Torah/the Divine Essence. Therefore, as the Rebbe would often say, the etymology of the word "Torah" is *horaa*, or teachings, as every concept in the Torah teaches us how to act.[24]

THE REBBE'S METHODOLOGY

A General Overview of the Rebbe's Talmudic Methodology

Following his own understanding of the Torah's applicability, the Rebbe used this theoretical structure of the Torah as a model for his own learning methodology. While this methodology can be seen in the Rebbe's engagement with several Torah disciplines, one of the most prominent in which his contributions can be highlighted is Talmud study.

The Rebbe began his talks regarding talmudic legal passages with a meticulous textual[25] and conceptual analysis of a specific passage, which led him to a specific understanding of the topic. After explaining the narrow topic on its own terms, the Rebbe then proceeded to demonstrate that a deeper meaning could be disclosed by broadening one's interpretive horizons.

The Rebbe expanded from the specific passage at hand in two ways, both of which he explicitly identified as important hermeneutical tools that derived from his understanding of the unified nature of Torah. First, remaining firmly within the traditional bounds of Talmud study, the Rebbe sought to identify a conceptual link between the topic at hand and an expansive array of other halakhic topics. He argued that each topic, when properly understood, can be shown to hinge upon an

---

24. *Likkutei Sihot* 2, *Hukkat, se'if* 1; ibid., 9, *Haazinu, se'if* 1; ibid., 32, *Emor*, no. 2, *se'if* 2. In this latter source the Rebbe argued that even minority opinions that are not followed practically still contain a lesson regarding how to practically live life. For the importance of practical halakhic rulings in the thought of the Rebbe, see *Likkutei Sihot* 16, 10 Shevat, *se'ifim* 5–8; *Torat Menahem* 5748: 3, 425; ibid., 5749: 1, 15; ibid., 5751: 1, 169–70. See also *Torat Menahem* 5745: 3, 1481, where the Rebbe quotes from the Rashab that *pesak halakha* "reaches until the hidden essential aspect of *Ein Sof*." However, see Alon Dahan (2014), 391–95, who notes that the Rebbe himself was reticent to rule on halakhic matters, but would rather refer people to leading rabbinc authorities.
25. See *Torat Menahem* 5710, 152–53, where the Rebbe emphasized that even in Talmud each word is precise and must be carefully weighed.

The Theology of Dira BaTahtonim

abstract conceptual issue that is also at the bottom of many other seemingly unrelated talmudic discussions.

Second, the Rebbe sought to deconstruct the traditional boundaries of Talmud study by putting the halakhic texts in conversation with parallel, non-halakhic material. His goal was to demonstrate that despite the various modes of expression, there are general conceptual issues that unify the different parts of the Torah. As the final stage in this interdisciplinary analysis the Rebbe would introduce the teachings of Hasidism, which create a more general framework that encompasses all facets of the topic and displays their interrelationship. Finally, the Rebbe would proceed to translate these abstract ideas into a practical lesson for one's daily service of God

As we shall see, the Rebbe attributed both of these techniques to the influence of one of the talmudic giants of the previous generation: R. Yosef Rozen, known as the Rogatchover Gaon. As a young man, the Rebbe periodically corresponded and met with the Rogatchover and considered him to be one of his teachers in the area of Talmud study.[26] This influence is apparent both in terms of the hundreds of times that the Rebbe cited the Rogatchover's writings, by far the highest quantity of any post-medieval, non-hasidic master quoted in his talks,[27] and in the Rebbe's adoption of the Rogatchover's learning methodology. The Rebbe related these methodological tools to the advent of Hasidism and characterized them as precursors of the Torah of *Mashiah*.

Stage 1: Intra-Halakhic Broadening

With some notable exceptions, the Rebbe was very circumspect about his own inner life and very rarely spoke or wrote in the first person. One such exception is a letter the Rebbe wrote regarding his methodology in talmudic study. After affirming the validity of different styles and methodologies, the Rebbe wrote as follows:

---

26. Chaim Miller (2014), 40–41; Yisrael Meitles (1993), 28–29.
27. This is apparent from a glance at the indexes to *Likkutei Sihot*. See Menahem Bronfman, "Te'ima MiTorato shel HaRebbe," who makes this claim.

> Perhaps you know about my approach in this regard... in consonance with what the Rogatchover emphasized and demonstrated – to find the commonality between this particular detail with many other details, [meaning to say,] the principle and concept that unifies them. And it is understandable that depth and breadth emerge in this way.[28]

Invoking the Rogatchover, the Rebbe encouraged his interlocutor to find a single principle that connects seemingly disparate talmudic topics. What motivates this approach? Why not suffice with treating each legal topic as an entirely discrete entity and plumb its depth only within its own parameters? Elsewhere, the Rebbe explained that the unified nature of the Torah leads us to try to find common threads that connect disparate topics:

> It has already been explained several times that there are topics and laws in the Torah which, despite giving a first impression of being disparate and unrelated, can be found to share a common point or a common underlying premise. This can be discovered through proper analysis; and it is due to the fact that the Torah is one. This is found in the books of a number of great [Torah scholars] of the Jewish people, and, in particular, in the works of the Rogatchover Gaon.[29]

The fact that the Torah is a single expression of the single God necessitates the existence of unifying themes.

Stage 1 Case Study: From the Law of the Abutter to the General Nature of Proximity

After making the above statement, the Rebbe demonstrated this principle with a representative example of this methodology. The Talmud in Tractate Bava Metzia records a law that if a person wants to sell his field, he must first offer the owner of the adjacent field the opportunity

---

28. *Likkutei Sihot* 16, *Hosafot*, 572.
29. Ibid., 19, *Va'et'hanan*, no. 3, *se'if* 5.

The Theology of Dira BaTahtonim

to buy the property.[30] This law of the abutter (*dina debar metzra*) extends so far that if someone purchases the field without it being first offered to the abutter, the purchaser is obligated to sell the field to the abutter upon request. As the Talmud records:

> The Sages of Neharde'a say: Even if the claim [to the field] was due to the law of the abutter (*dina debar metzra*), we still remove him [the one who bought the field], as it is stated: "And you shall do that which is right and good in the eyes of the Lord" (Deut. 6:18).[31]

Based on the verse "And you shall do that which is right and good," the halakha forces the outside buyer to resell it to the abutter.

Following the style of modern talmudic commentators, the Rebbe raised two possible conceptual formulations for the buyer's obligation to resell his purchase to the abutter. In his words:

> (1) This is merely a matter of proper behavior. Meaning to say, the potency of the buyer's acquisition is not hurt, but still the Sages required him to act in a fashion that is "right and good."
> (2) The obligation to "do that which is right and good" causes the abutter to gain a certain amount of ownership rights to the field. Therefore, the buyer is obligated to give the field to the abutter not just due to his obligation of proper behavior but also because the field is connected to the abutter. This is what the *Nimmukei Yosef* says: "As if he has ownership rights in the field itself"' (*Nimmukei Yosef*, Bava Metzia 64a in the pagination of R. Alfasi).[32]

The first option situates the entire law in the realm of proper interpersonal interactions, as is implied by the talmudic proof text "And you shall do that which is right and good." The second option, however, posits that interpersonal obligation creates a legal reality of the abutter's rights to the field.

---

30. Bava Metzia 108a.
31. Ibid.
32. *Likkutei Sihot* 19, *Va'et'hanan*, no. 3, *se'if* 2.

The Rebbe noted that Rashi and Rambam seem to debate this issue. When explaining the buyer's obligation toward the abutter, Rashi speaks directly to the buyer: "'And you should do that which is right and good': Regarding something that will not cause you too much of a loss, since you can find a field elsewhere, you should not cause trouble to the abutter and have his properties divided."[33] The fact that Rashi emphasizes the obligation of the buyer indicates that the whole law stems solely from the buyer's need to act properly.

Rambam, however, articulates the law in more objective terms:

> The neighbor receives priority and may remove the purchaser. This practice stems from the charge: "And you shall do what is right and good." Our Sages said: "Since the sale is fundamentally the same, it is 'right and good' that the property should be acquired by the neighbor instead of the person living farther away."[34]

Rambam does not address the purchaser per se, but rather simply states that the abutter's purchase of the field is the objective "right and good" path in this scenario. This formulation signals that the law of the abutter is not limited to the buyer's personal obligation to act benevolently, but rather creates an objective legal reality of the abutter's rights to the field.

Thus far, the Rebbe's analysis of this talmudic law demonstrates his knowledge of the relevant texts and acuity in talmudic reasoning. Fundamentally, though, it fits well within the standard model for modern talmudic interpreters.[35] The Rebbe's unique contribution based on his theoretical model of Torah and Hasidism emerges from the next stage of the talk.

Based on the conviction that all parts of Torah are inherently united with one another through core conceptual principles that undergird and unite them, the Rebbe broadened the issue from geographic

---

33. Rashi on Bava Metzia 108a, s.v. *ve'asita*.
34. *Mishneh Torah, Hilkhot Shekhenim* 12:5.
35. See *Hiddushei HaGrah HaShalem: Bava Metzia*, siman 104, that R. Hayyim of Brisk raised the same basic conceptual issue.

The Theology of Dira BaTahtonim

neighbors to a more general interpretation of proximity. Perhaps the medieval debate regarding the standing of the abutter hinges not just on a local issue of the interplay between proper supererogatory behavior and legal rights, but on the broader issue of the nature of proximity. Namely, does the proximity of two items simply mean that they are close to each other, or does their proximity have the power to change the nature and legal status of the items by creating a partially shared identity? The latter option would justify the approach of *Nimmukei Yosef* and Rambam that the abutter acquires some rights to the field simply by being a neighbor.

This broader conceptualization allowed the Rebbe to connect the debate regarding the law of the abutter with a seemingly unrelated dispute regarding the nature of the time added onto Shabbat and the holidays (*tosefet Shabbat*). In line with the Jewish circadian cycle, Shabbat and the holidays begin at sunset and continue until the next nightfall. In addition to this set duration, the Talmud records an obligation to "add" onto these special days by beginning their observance a few minutes before sunset and concluding a few minutes after dark.[36]

While the Talmud is clear that the restrictions of Shabbat commence during this additional time prior to nightfall, medieval and modern commentators debate the effectiveness of performing positive, Shabbat-oriented mitzvot before nightfall. For example, R. Yitzhak of Corbeil permits one to recite Kiddush and partake of the Shabbat meal during the appended time,[37] while R. Shlomo ben Aderet records that the *Geonim* required a person to wait until actual nightfall. Neither authority explicitly provides a reason for their opinion.[38]

The Rebbe contended that their debate revolves around the fundamental status of this additional time. If halakha can accommodate two logical possibilities regarding the nature of geographic proximity, then two parallel possibilities can be raised regarding temporal proximity. In the words of the Rebbe:

---

36. Yoma 81b; *Mekhilta DeRabbi Yishmael, Masekhta DevaHodesh, parasha 7*.
37. *Tosafot* on Pesahim 99b, s.v. *ad shetehshakh*.
38. Rashba, Berakhot 27b, s.v. *ha de'amar*.

(1) "Proximity" creates an inner connection, so that the time before and after Shabbat changes due to its proximity to Shabbat and receives the essential sanctity of Shabbat.

(2) The time itself does not become sanctified with the sanctity of Shabbat, but due to its proximity to Shabbat, an obligation to prepare for Shabbat comes to rest on the person.[39]

The Rebbe argued that the medieval debate regarding the ability to fulfill the positive commandments of Shabbat during the additional time hinges upon these two options. The adoption of the first option, that the temporal proximity to Shabbat bestows the additional time with some level of sanctity, would lead to the opinion of R. Yitzhak of Corbeil that one may fulfill the positive mitzvot of Shabbat during this time as well. The second option, however, which conceptualizes proximity as a mere technical phenomenon, would lead to the opinion of the *Geonim* and naturally limit the scope of *tosefet Shabbat* to the restriction from work on the part of the individual without assigning the sanctity of Shabbat to the time itself. The *person* must refrain from forbidden labor, but Shabbat itself as a unit of sanctified time commences only at nightfall. Therefore, no license exists to recite Kiddush prior to that time.

Thus, while the laws of the abutter and the additional time for Shabbat seem to be discrete and disconnected, the Rebbe's analysis intended to disclose a unifying conceptual principle. As noted above, he explicitly rooted this methodology and its execution in the theory of Torah's underlying oneness.

Stage 2: The Theory of Interdisciplinary Broadening

Over and above the identification of overarching conceptual categories that link disparate legal issues, the Rebbe focused on the interpenetration of halakhic and non-halakhic parts of the Torah, with, of course, a particular focus on the "inner Torah" of Hasidism. As noted above, the notion of viewing Torah as a single entity with many manifestations is fully apparent with the advent of Hasidism.

---

39. *Likkutei Sihot* 19, *Va'et'hanan*, no. 3, *se'if* 6.

The Theology of Dira BaTahtonim

Once again, the Rebbe pointed to the Rogatchover Gaon as an antecedent for this approach. One of the most unique aspects of the Rogatchover's writings is the integration of philosophical concepts and terms from Rambam's *Guide for the Perplexed* into the heart of his legalistic talmudic analysis.[40] One example is his description of a Torah scroll. While generally, a man can execute a marriage by giving a woman an object of monetary value, the Talmud Yerushalmi teaches that a Torah scroll cannot be used to create a marriage.[41] The Rogatchover explains that even though the man can deliver the "matter" (*homer*) of the Torah scroll to his intended wife, he is incapable of legally transferring the "form" (*tzura*) of the Torah.[42] The terms *homer* and *tzura* are not indigenous to talmudic legal parlance, but were rather explicitly transplanted from Rambam's *Guide for the Perplexed*.

While many students of the Rogatchover have reflected on his unique synthesis of philosophy and Talmud study, the Rebbe noted that the Rogatchover's integrationist tendencies extended also to the realm of Kabbala.[43] The Rebbe admitted that the quantity of explicit kabbalistic references in the Rogatchover's talmudic writings is much lower than that of references to the *Guide for the Perplexed*, yet he insisted that the spilling over of Talmud study into other realms was a fundamental thrust of the Rogatchover's approach. It was not just that the Rogatchover Gaon saw fit to explain talmudic law in philosophical terms, but rather that he saw and wanted to express the general unity of all parts of the Torah.

The Rebbe made this point explicitly in a letter to R. Moshe Grosberg, a Hasid who was set to publish a book elucidating various innovative interpretations of the Rogatchover.[44] Sensing that the author

---

40. See Menahem Kasher (1976), 32–38; Yisrael Meitles (2013) 11–16.
41. Y. Nedarim 5:5.
42. Shu"t *Tzafenat Paane'ah* (Dvinsk), 2:24.
43. See, for example, *Iggerot Kodesh* 18, letter 6903. In this letter to R. Menahem Kasher, another student of the Rogatchover Gaon who was involved with organizing and publishing his Torah teachings, the Rebbe noted that those who were close to the Rogatchover were aware of his knowledge of Kabbala. In addition, he includes one explicit and one implicit reference to kabbalistic works in the Rogatchover's published writings.
44. R. Moshe Grosberg, *Tzefunot HaRogotchivi* (Jerusalem: 1958).

was hesitant to embrace the full extent of the Rogatchover's inclusivist tendencies, the Rebbe wrote to him as follows:[45]

> A unique point [of the Rogatchover] is that he nullified the dividing walls that were established within our one Torah between halakhic matters and other aspects of the Torah, [and in particular] between the revealed aspects of the Torah and the "inner" aspects of the Torah....
>
> May it be God's will that since he [the author of this work] touched the edge of the stick, he should continue and diminish the hesitation that is found in this work to transcend the shackles of those who want to constrict the halakhic matters only to halakha, as this is the opposite of the approach of the Rogatchover, and certainly contrary to the outlook of Kabbala and Hasidism, which sees absolute unity in the entire world and in a revealed manner in the Torah as well, as "God looked into the Torah and created the world."[46]

The Rebbe perceived the Rogatchover's interpenetration of the various disciplines of Torah as a manifestation of the hasidic perspective on the nature of Torah's unity.

It is therefore no surprise that this interdisciplinary approach is a hallmark of the Rebbe's own Talmud study. From a methodological perspective he frequently returned to the theme that the revealed and inner aspects of the Torah need to be studied together and ultimately united. For example, in another rare first-person statement, in the midst of a letter regarding a kabbalistic concept, the Rebbe wrote:

> As a parenthetical statement, one should note that this topic of the double *yod* is also hinted to in the revealed parts of the Torah. And this is in accordance with my longtime approach that whatever is discussed in the exoteric parts of the Torah has its parallel in the esoteric aspects of the Torah, and that which is stated in

---

45. Published in Yisrael Meitles (2013), 35.
46. Genesis Rabba 1:1.

The Theology of Dira BaTahtonim

the esoteric aspects of the Torah has its parallel in the exoteric parts of the Torah.[47]

In other methodological remarks, the Rebbe analogized the relationship between the exoteric and esoteric aspects of the Torah with the relationship between the body and the soul.[48] Just as body and soul are apparently distinct but share an underlying unity and therefore create a holistic single entity, the same is true regarding the Torah. Each discipline contains its own rules and demarcations, and this does not lead to discreteness, but rather to interpenetration and the revelation of Torah as a single holistic entity.

Stage 2 Case Study: From Legal Proximity to Ethical Proximity

With this methodological background in mind, let us return to the Rebbe's talk on the nature of proximity. After finding a common thread connecting the halakhic issues of geographic and temporal proximity, the Rebbe then ventured into the realms of *aggada* and Hasidism.[49]

The end of Tractate Sukka discusses the division of the priests into twenty-four family groups which worked on a rotating basis in the *Beit HaMikdash*. For all intents and purposes, the families were all treated as equals, receiving the same materials and performing the same services. However, the Talmud records that one family was punished by the Sages in the wake of a harrowing incident:

> The Sages taught in a *baraita*: There was an incident involving Miriam, the daughter of a member of the Bilga watch, who apostatized and went and married a soldier [*sardeyot*] serving in the army of the Greek kings. When the Greeks entered the Sanctuary, she entered

---

47. *Iggerot Kodesh* 19, letter 7232. In this regard, see also *Iggerot Kodesh* 7, letter 1919, to R. Yitzhak Hutner.
48. *Likkutei Sihot* 30, *Hosafot* 314; ibid., 32, *Vayikra*, no. 3, *se'if* 3; ibid., 33, *Shelah*, no. 2, *se'if* 1; *Torat Menahem* 5713: 1, 43–45; ibid., 5751: 3, 420–21. See also *Torat Menahem* 5721: 2, 117.
49. See *Torat Menahem* 5752: 1, 438, that *aggada* is the *nistar* section of the Talmud in relation to the halakhic material.

with them and was kicking with her sandal on the altar and said: Wolf, wolf [*lokos*], until when will you consume the property of the Jewish people, and yet you do not stand with them when they face exigent circumstances? And after the victory of the Hasmoneans over the Greeks, when the Sages heard about this matter and how she denigrated the altar, they fixed the ring of the Bilga watch in place, rendering it nonfunctional, and sealed its niche.[50]

While the commentators debate the precise meaning of this cryptic punishment, the basic import of this story is clear: the family was punished due to Miriam's impudent behavior.

The Talmud proceeds to question the justice of such an extreme measure. Miriam herself was the sole perpetrator and, at most, the guilt can be extended to her nuclear family, from whom she imbibed this attitude. What then motivated the Rabbis to punish the entire clan? The Talmud responds:

And due to Miriam's father and mother, do we penalize an entire watch? Abaye said: Woe unto the wicked, woe unto his neighbor.

The punishment's extension to the broader clan is rooted in their familial and geographic proximity to the guilty party.

The Rebbe cited this passage in full and noted that the medieval commentators debate the identity of the ring and niche that the Sages rendered unusable. Rashi explains that these were items that aided in the slaughtering of the sacrifice: the ring was used to hold the neck of the animal in place,[51] and the niche was used to store the ritual knives.[52] Rambam, however, posits that the ring was meant to assist in the skinning of the animal and the niche was for storing the priestly garments.[53]

While the debate seems to revolve around an insignificant detail in the story, the Rebbe argued that these two interpretations differ

---

50. Sukka 56b.
51. Rashi on Sukka 56a, s.v. *vetaabatah*.
52. Ibid., s.v. *halonah*.
53. Rambam, *Commentary to the Mishna*, Sukka 5:6.

The Theology of Dira BaTahtonim

on a fundamental point. According to Rashi, even while the sanction extended to the entire clan, it focused specifically on items or activities that were relevant to Miriam herself. As a woman, she was excluded from most aspects of the Temple service.[54] One exception, however, is the slaughtering of the sacrifice, which women can perform.[55] Therefore, Rashi maintained that the punishment was limited to items pertaining to the slaughtering, which can be seen as having direct proximity to the perpetrator. Rambam did not agree with this limitation and contended that the sanctions extended to items and activities that were anyway barred from Miriam, such as the priestly garments, which suggests that proximity imposes a broader responsibility.

Rashi and Rambam debate the fairness of having the sanctions extend beyond the purview relevant to the original, guilty party. As the Talmud justifies the sanctions to the entire clan with the principle "Woe unto the wicked, woe unto his neighbor," it seems that Rashi and Rambam are debating the parameters of this principle. Does the proximity of the broader family to Miriam justify a sanction that transcends the actual perpetrator?

The Rebbe explained that, once again, this debate turns on the general nature of proximity and can even be related to the specific positions that Rashi and Rambam staked regarding the law of the abutter. The Rebbe had inferred from Rashi's commentary to the law of the abutter that geographic proximity is limited to a technical connection that obligates the buyers to act in a specific manner. Similarly, Rashi assumed that the proximity of the clan to Miriam does not completely implicate them in her wrongdoings. The sanctions do not primarily target the clan, but rather Miriam herself; the clan are impacted only due to their proximity to her and the impact extends only to the slaughtering equipment, which she could use.

Rambam, however, asserted that geographic proximity grants the abutter legal rights to the adjacent property based on the notion that proximity fundamentally impacts the neighbors. When that model of proximity is applied to the relationship of Miriam's sin to the rest of the

---

54. Zevahim 32a.
55. Ibid. 31b.

Bilga clan, all of her extended relatives become complicit in the actual crime. As the Rebbe posited:

> However, according to Rambam, who holds that proximity creates an essential bond, regarding our topic of "Woe unto the wicked, woe unto his neighbor," the intention is not merely an external matter regarding the *punishment* of the neighbor, but even regarding the *wrongdoing itself*, that the proximity influences the nature of the neighbor.[56]

This construct of proximity and the extension of guilt that it implies explains why Rambam applied the sanctions to aspects of the priestly service that had never been permitted for Miriam. The entire clan is complicit and therefore can be directly punished.

The Rebbe once again explicitly noted that connecting the story of Bilga with the laws of the abutter would provoke protest from certain circles. As the Talmud itself consciously self-divides into halakhic and aggadic sections, what right do we have to synthesize the two? The Rebbe retorted that these potential protesters have not properly internalized the notion of an all-encompassing God:

> These who lack an understanding of the unity of God are also lacking in their understanding of the unity of the Torah (for just as God is one, so too, His Torah is one). Therefore, they divide between different sections of the Torah.[57]

While it takes strenuous mental effort to understand the unity of God and His Torah, this is the path that leads to the deepest understanding of Torah.[58]

---

56. *Likkutei Sihot* 19, *Va'et'hanan*, no. 3, *se'if* 10.
57. *Torat Menahem* 5714: 3, 148. This line was omitted from the published talk in *Likkutei Sihot* but reflects what the Rebbe said immediately following his analysis of Miriam of the Bilga family.
58. Ibid.

The Theology of Dira BaTahtonim

The Creative Contributions of Hasidism

After demonstrating the existence of these general conceptualizations of proximity, the Rebbe concluded his talk with a hasidic approach to the issue. Hasidism adds two interrelated layers to the discussion: (1) the creation of a more encompassing model that accounts for both competing notions of proximity, and (2) the application of these abstract models to the practical life of a Jew.

The Rebbe began by arguing that Rashi's model of the limited nature of proximity cannot be applied universally. After citing the principle "Woe unto the wicked, woe unto his neighbor," Tractate Sukka concludes on a positive note: "Good for the righteous, good for his neighbor." As a source for this idea Rashi comments: "The positive aspect is greater than the negative aspect."[59] Thus, if punishment can spread to a neighbor, certainly the goodness of the righteous should have a contagious effect.

The Rebbe highlighted Rashi's seemingly gratuitous emphasis that the positive aspect is *greater* than the negative. Presumably, even if the two aspects were equal, we should be able to extrapolate that the goodness of the righteous spreads to those in their proximity in the parallel fashion that the negativity of the wicked spreads. Rather, the Rebbe argued, Rashi's choice of language hints to a fundamental difference between proximity to evil and proximity to good.

In general, the notions of evil, wickedness, sin, and punishment cannot touch the inner nature of a Jew. As we saw in our discussion of free choice, the Rebbe consistently affirmed the essential good and divine core of every Jew. The sins of a wicked person remain external to his own identity, and surely then they can only superficially affect one's neighbor. In the story of Miriam and her Bilga clan, the superficiality of "Woe unto the wicked, woe unto his neighbor" is expressed in the shallowness of the punishment. The closing of the family's ring and niche served as a public denigration but did not in fact prevent the members of Bilga from performing the actual service of the *Beit HaMikdash*, which is the core of their priestly identity. Evil, and therefore proximity to evil, are definitionally external phenomena.

---

59. Rashi, Sukka 56b, s.v. *oy lerasha*.

When we shift to the other side of the ledger and focus on righteousness, we touch upon traits that are essential aspects of a Jew's identity. Therefore, even Rashi, who generally asserted a limited model of proximity, concedes to Rambam's notion that being close to to the righteous has a fundamental effect on the identity of the neighbor. As the Rebbe contended, this is the secret encoded in Rashi's insistence that the positive aspect be "greater" than the reverse:[60]

> It is not sufficient that "Good for the righteous, good for his neighbor" should be identical to its opposite.... A technical proximity to the wicked affects one only externally. However, even if one has merely a technical connection to the righteous person, the latter effects his Jewish neighbors internally and essentially and brings them inner goodness.

A righteous person can access and nourish the present, if latent, inner core of his neighbors and thereby create a shared identity. The wickedness of a sinner, however, remains external to the perpetrator himself and certainly cannot essentially affect those associated with the sinner. Thus, proximity to the righteous and the wicked both affect a person, but the former creates a shared identity while the latter does not.[61]

This difference between "Good for the righteous, good for his neighbor" and "Woe unto the wicked, woe unto his neighbor" has several very practical ramifications. First, it teaches of the importance of associating oneself with righteous people, as this very proximity can actualize one's basic positive identity. Second, as we have seen, viewing Jews as fundamentally righteous and their sins as external to their inner identities was a key element in the way the Rebbe taught how one should perceive and interact with all Jews.

Hasidism thus creates a broad framework that demonstrates the coexistence and interrelationship of the two models of proximity that the Rebbe teased out from the legal and non-legal sections of the Talmud.

---

60. *Likkutei Sihot* 19, *Va'et'hanan*, no. 3, *se'if* 12.
61. For a similar distinction between the positive and negative formulations of the proximity principle, see *Likkutei Sihot* 33, *Bemidbar*, no. 2, *se'if* 7.

The Theology of Dira BaTahtonim

In addition, the hasidic interpretation of the notions of proximity spans from essential ontology – the inner nature of a Jew – to providing practical guidance in the daily life of a Jew in encouraging him to strengthen his own positive identity through proximity to a righteous person.

This concludes the case study of the Rebbe's talmudic methodology. Beginning with a single obscure legal passage, the Rebbe first engaged in a thorough textual and conceptual analysis to arrive at the core issue upon which the halakha hinges. He then broadened the scope of this core issue to include other legal topics and eventually non-legal passages. Finally, he employed Hasidism to illustrate the interconnection of the previously dichotomous ideas and to teach a practical lesson. The Rebbe applied this method to hundreds of talmudic passages, and this discussion should be seen as characteristic of his broader project to demonstrate the unity of the Torah.

THE HISTORY OF A UNIFYING TALMUDIC METHODOLOGY

Once again, the Rebbe's own methodology can be understood as the latest stage in a gradually developing process. As noted above, medieval Torah authorities tended to divide the Torah into discrete genres and relate to them separately. According to the Rebbe, it was the advent of Hasidism that revealed the potential for the dismantling of these barriers, triggering a gradual process that will culminate in the full disclosure of the unified Torah of *Mashiah*.[62]

Alter Rebbe

Kabbalistic and hasidic tradition emphasize that the name of an item represents its essence. Accordingly, it is God who guides the parents to choose a name for their baby that signifies that child's essence.[63] If this is true regarding the names of average people, there is certainly significance to the fact that the Alter Rebbe's name was Shneur Zalman.

---

62. The Rebbe also highlighted R. Shimon bar Yohai as an early initiator of this process. See *maamar "Lehavin Inyan DeRashbi 5745," se'if* 2 (*Sefer HaMaamarim Melukat*, vol. 3, 278).
63. *Likkutei Sihot* 6, 24 *Tevet, se'if* 2; ibid., 30, *Vayetzeh*, no. 2, *se'if* 1.

The Rebbe noted that the name Shneur is a composite of the words *shenei or*, or "two lights." As light is often a metaphor for Torah, these two lights refer to the two areas of Torah that the Alter Rebbe illuminated: the revealed aspects of the Torah through his writing of a new legal code called *Shulhan Arukh HaRav*, and the inner aspects of the Torah through his founding of the Chabad system of thought.[64] While there were certainly authorities before the eighteenth century with expertise in both of these fields, the Rebbe contended that the unification of these "two lights" into a single word that is the name/essence of the Alter Rebbe is highly significant.[65]

While the Alter Rebbe himself did not overtly or systematically integrate his halakhic teachings with the inner aspects of the Torah, the Rebbe argued that he did bring the two aspects of Torah closer together by allowing for a methodological interpenetration. The Alter Rebbe's legal code does not simply contain a list of final rulings but attempts to broaden the reader's understanding of the halakha by explaining the reasons behind each ruling.[66] Similarly and more significantly, the Alter Rebbe brought the secrets of the Torah closer to full revelation through explaining them in a fashion that is understandable to the human mind.[67]

According to the Rebbe, these methodological crossovers indicate Chabad Hasidism's engagement with the *yehida* of Torah, which demonstrates the unity of the seemingly discrete elements of the system. As the full revelation of the Torah is a messianic desideratum, the Alter Rebbe's Torah is a precursor (a "taste") of the messianic Torah.[68]

Tzemah Tzedek

According to the Rebbe, it was the third leader of Chabad, known as the *Tzemah Tzedek*, who built on the Alter Rebbe's foundation and significantly advanced the agenda of unifying disparate aspects of Torah. A prolific halakhic decisor and a creative hasidic thinker, the *Tzemah*

---

64. Ibid., 6; ibid., *se'if* 3; *Torat Menahem* 5712: 1, 241–43; ibid., 5752: 1, 443–44; *Iggerot Kodesh* 19, letter 7164; ibid., 22, letter 8653.
65. *Likkutei Sihot* 6, *se'if* 3.
66. Ibid., note 38.
67. Ibid., *se'ifim*, 7–8.
68. *Torat Menahem* 5752: 1, 443.

Tzedek's writings brim with a synthesis of halakhic and hasidic sources and ideas. The Rebbe noted that this writing style was unique in the annals of hasidic history:

> Among all hasidic leaders we find many teachings of both exoteric and esoteric aspects of the Torah.... However, the esoteric aspects of the Torah stand alone and the exoteric aspects of the Torah stand alone. In the teachings of the *Tzemah Tzedek*, however...we find a unique contribution: the connection and unification of the exoteric and esoteric aspects of the Torah.[69]

For the Rebbe, it was not inconsequential that the *Tzemah Tzedek* was the third leader of Chabad. In hasidic thought, the number three represents the synthesis of two disparate elements to create a total that is greater than the sum of its parts.[70] The *Tzemah Tzedek* began to actually reveal the interconnections between the two parts of the Torah, which allows for a deeper understanding of the Torah's totality than ever before. Once again, the Rebbe explicitly identified this approach of the *Tzemah Tzedek* as "similar to the innovation of *Mashiah*."[71]

The Rogatchover

We already noted that the Rebbe attributed immense significance to the Rogatchover Gaon's integrationist approach to learning and used it as a model for his own. What remains to be noted is the Rebbe's contextualization of the Rogatchover's methodology in this progressive disclosure of the Torah's unity.

On Purim 5747, the Rebbe dedicated a section of his talk to listing some of the "astounding" events of recent history and interpreting them as indications of *Mashiah*'s imminent arrival.[72] One item that he

---

69. Ibid., 5747: 1, 270. See also *Torat Menahem* 5747: 3, 82; *Iggerot Kodesh* 26, letter 9596. For a brief history regarding the significance that the Rebbe attached to publishing the manuscripts of the *Tzemah Tzedek*, see R. Mordechai Menashe Laufer (5774), 7–10. For an explanation of the term *nesi'im*, see chapter 17.
70. *Torat Menahem* 5747: 3, 82.
71. Ibid. See also *Torat Menahem* 5750: 1, 181–82.
72. *Torat Menahem* 5747: 2, 626–30.

focused upon was the explosion of "new" Torah ideas and methodologies in learning. Within this general framework, the Rebbe singled out the Rogatchover as being particularly noteworthy:[73]

> This also seems to be the explanation for the existence of the [methodology of] the Rogatchover, which is entirely *sui generis*.... The intention is not to minimize, Heaven forbid, the value of a different methodology in learning...but all concede that the Rogatchover's methodology in learning was wondrous.

While in this talk the Rebbe did not describe the contours of the Rogatchover Gaon's methodology and what made it so wondrous, the citations earlier in this chapter should suffice. Through his interdisciplinary approach, the Rogatchover further disclosed the unity of the Torah, bringing us yet closer to the emergence of the messianic Torah.

The Rebbe

As we have seen, the Rebbe identified the Messianic Era with the complete revelation of Hasidism, often referring to the "Torah of *Mashiah*" as a new level of disclosure of the inner aspects of the Torah.[74] This revelation will engender new clarity in all aspects of the Torah and hence, the "Torah of *Mashiah*" really includes all aspects of the Torah.[75] As an heir to and practitioner of the unifying interdisciplinary methodology of Torah study, the Rebbe can be seen as presenting the next stage in the unfurling of the "Torah of *Mashiah*."

In addition to the revelation of the deepest aspects of the Torah, the Rebbe saw the dissemination of these ideas as integral to the messianic process. As such, the Rebbe did not want his learning methodology to be idiosyncratically his, but rather encouraged everyone to likewise combine all aspects of Torah in their own studies as a means of hastening the coming of *Mashiah*.

---

73. Ibid., 627–28.
74. *Likkutei Sihot* 20, Yod-Tet Kislev, no. 2, *se'if* 6; *Torat Menahem* 5719: 1, 259; ibid., 5721: 2, 117–18; ibid., 5746: 3, 137.
75. See, for example, *Likkutei Sihot* 16, *Shemot*, 24 Tevet, note 45.

The Theology of Dira BaTahtonim

For example, once, while speaking of the importance of Torah study generally, the Rebbe emphasized that there is a specific methodology that is crucial to employ nowadays:

"Uncover my eyes and I shall look at hidden things from Your Torah" (Ps. 119:18); [this refers to] the light and revelation of the learning of Torah, both the exoteric parts of the Torah and the inner aspects of the Torah, as they are both a single Torah – "Your Torah." This is the ideal preparation for the studying of the Torah of *Mashiah*.[76]

Studying all aspects of the Torah in a manner that elicits the "single Torah" paves the way for the ultimate revelation of the Torah's singular essence, which itself is the essence of the Messianic Era.

CONCLUSION

We have seen that the revelation of the Divine Essence was an overarching goal for the Rebbe. It not only influenced the programs he initiated and the Hasidism he taught, but it even directly impacted his talmudic methodology. Thus, the Rebbe's studying and teaching of Talmud was transformed into a key element in his holistic philosophy and a crucial means of accelerating the coming of *Mashiah*.

Secondary Literature Consulted for Chapter 9, "Talmud Study in the Age of Hasidism"

Menahem Bronfman, "Hamisha Me'afyenim LeDarko HaToranit HaYihudit shel HaRebbe MiLubavitch."

Menahem Bronfman, "Madua HaRebbe MiLubavitch Koh Hibbev et Torat HaGaon HaRogatchover?"

Menahem Bronfman, "Te'ima MiTorato shel Rabbenu."

Eliyahu Meir Elituv, *Mishnato shel HaRebbe MiLubavitch.*

---

76. *Torat Menahem* 5743: 2, 917. See also *Likkutei Sihot* 20, *Vayishlah*, no. 2, *se'if* 14; ibid., 25, *Hayei Sara*, 5746, *se'if* 2; *Torat Menahem* 5743: 1, 252–53.

Yisrael Meitles, *HaLamdanut HaFilosophit shel Rebbe Yosef Rozen BiDerashotav shel Rebbe Menahem Mendel Schneerson.*

Yisrael Meitles, *Hakirot VeHitbonenut Hasidiyot BaHiddushim shel HaGaon HaRogotchivi.*

Menahem Mendel Reitzes, "LeShitateih BeMishnato," *HaShevi'i*, 243–60.

Yehudah Leib Shapira, "BaDerekh el HaTamtzit," *HaShevi'i*, 221–42.

Part 3
Aspects of a Godly Life

Chapter 10

Hashgaha: Living with God

One of the Rebbe's most central and ubiquitous teachings was that each individual should live with a constant God-consciousness. Irrespective of one's location, current occupation, or station in life, God is ever-present, ever-caring, and ever-accessible. One theme developed by the Rebbe that enabled and empowered Jews to live with such a consciousness was the notion of divine providence (*hashgaha*). The Rebbe's teachings on this topic begin with defining the nature of *hashgaha* from a theoretical perspective and then develop into outlining the immense practical ramifications of this theory. Once again, both the theoretical and practical aspects of the Rebbe's understanding of *hashgaha* are fully intertwined with the other prominent themes in his thought.

HASHGAHA IN EARLIER JEWISH PHILOSOPHY
Hashgaha According to Rambam
While various statements in biblical and rabbinic literature affirm God's active involvement in worldly affairs, these sources do not

lend themselves to a precise philosophical theory of *hashgaha*.[1] The situation changes with medieval Jewish philosophers, who expended considerable energies developing precise theories and parameters of *hashgaha*.

The *locus classicus* for the issue of *hashgaha* in medieval Jewish philosophy is Rambam's systematic treatment of the subject in his *Guide for the Perplexed*.[2] Over the course of a long chapter, Rambam outlined four different approaches to *hashgaha*, rejected all of them, and then developed what he considered the correct approach of "the Law of Moses our master." As many, including the Rebbe,[3] have noted, Rambam seems to greatly limit the provenance of *hashgaha* in two related ways.[4]

One limitation relates to a distinction between different types of creations. In the course of his discussion, Rambam cited the Ash'ariyya school of Islam, which professed that direct divine providence extends even to inanimate objects. Rambam, however, rejected this expansive approach and instead contended that God's providence

> watches over only the individuals belonging to the human species.... But regarding all the other animals and, all the more, the plants and other things, my opinion is that of Aristotle. For I do not by any means believe that this particular leaf has fallen because of a providence watching over it, nor that this spider has devoured this fly because God has now decreed and willed something concerning individuals.... For all this is in my opinion due to pure chance, just as Aristotle holds.[5]

---

1. For a collection of sources from biblical and rabbinic literature, see Ephraim Urbach (1975), 227–53. For general treatments of *hashgaha* in Jewish thought from the rabbinic period to the modern era, see Aryeh Leibowitz (2009); Shmuel Ariel (5767), 33–50.
2. *Guide for the Perplexed*, III:17.
3. *Likkutei Sihot* 8, *Hosafot*, 280.
4. Rambam's actual opinion on *hashgaha* has been the subject of dozens of studies. For a bibliography of ninety-eight distinct treatments of this subject, see Israel J. Dienstag (1988), 17–28.
5. *Guide for the Perplexed*, III:17 (Pines, 471).

Hashgaha: Living with God

Rambam's opinion is that only the affairs of human beings are subject to direct *hashgaha*. All other occurrences in this world are the result of "pure chance."

A second limitation occurs within the human species. In the next chapter, Rambam argues that God does not apply *hashgaha* uniformly across humanity, but instead bestows it in a fashion that is proportional to a person's spiritual stature: "Divine providence does not watch in an equal manner over all the individuals of the human species, but providence is graded as their human perfection is graded."[6]

In summary, while Rambam affirms God's omniscience, he seems to still seriously limit His direct involvement in the world and even in human affairs.[7]

Hashgaha According to the Kabbalists

In an encyclopedic letter on medieval and early modern approaches to *hashgaha*,[8] the Rebbe noted that several pre-hasidic kabbalists presented a complex view regarding the scope of *hashgaha*. While these kabbalists did not embrace the extreme of the Ash'ariyya group cited by Rambam above, the Rebbe concluded that they still affirmed a more active role for God in all terrestrial affairs.

As an example, the Rebbe cited conflicting passages discussing *hashgaha* in the work *Shomer Emunim* by R. Yosef Ergaz (1685–1730).[9] In one passage, R. Ergaz appears to adopt the Maimonidean approach to *hashgaha* over subhuman creations:

> All animals, and definitely all plants and inanimate objects, are not governed [with specific individual divine providence], for their

---

6. Ibid., III:18 (Pines, 475).
7. The limitations of Rambam are echoed by other medieval authorities. For example, see *Sefer HaHinnukh* (mitzva 169, 545); *Sefer HaIkkarim* 4:7. Ramban, however, seems to present conflicting approaches to the scope of *hashgaha*. See, for example, his comments to Gen. 18:19; Ex. 13:16; Lev. 26:11; Job 36:7. For an approach to navigating these passages, see David Berger (1983), 1–16.
8. Printed in *Likkutei Sihot* 8, *Hosafot*, 277–84, and *Iggerot Kodesh* 1, letter 94.
9. *Likkutei Sihot* 8, *Hosafot*, 278–79. In the letter itself, the Rebbe briefly treats close to a dozen medieval and early modern approaches to *hashgaha*.

aim is achieved only through their species, and there is no need for the individuals to have [specific individual] divine providence. Therefore, everything that relates to the individuals is completely left to chance, and not decreed by God.[10]

However, a few paragraphs earlier, R. Ergaz presents a more expansive role for God in worldly occurrences:

> You should know that there is nothing that occurs by chance, be it an insignificant or significant [event], and even the system of "nature" is directly from God – for [nature's] secret is [God's] name *Elokim*, which is the numerical value of *teva* (nature). There is no creation [that was created] by chance, without direct intent and divine providence.[11]

At first blush, this statement contradicts the first passage, which eschewed *hashgaha* from sub-human creations.

After noting this apparent tension, the Rebbe claimed that R. Ergaz himself already hinted at the resolution. In the words of the Rebbe:

> To resolve the contradiction between the *Shomer Emunim*'s earlier words that there is no such thing as chance, and the end of his words, that matters relating to individual animals are completely up to chance; it is perhaps to address this question the *Shomer Emunim* wrote that even the level of "chance" relates back to God for everything is from Him with detailed providence.[12]

While the Rebbe's terse formulation is difficult to parse precisely, the general contours of his interpretation of the *Shomer Emunim* are clear. Ultimately, all events relate back to God and nothing is truly by chance. God's providence, however, operates along different channels, and while

---

10. *Shomer Emunim*, sec. 2, argument 21. Translation is from Aryeh Leibowitz (2009), 95.
11. Ibid.
12. *Likkutei Sihot* 8, *Hosafot*, 278–79. See also *Torat Menahem* 5745: 3, 1836–37.

Hashgaha: Living with God

some entities are privileged to receive direct *hashgaha*, other beings are guided by God through more concealed and circuitous mediums.

Hashgaha According to the Baal Shem Tov

Early hasidic leaders cite their teacher, the Baal Shem Tov, as consciously promulgating a different approach to this topic. For example, R. Pinhas of Koretz, a close student of the Baal Shem Tov, writes that "a person must believe that even the straw resting on the ground [is there] due to a heavenly decree. He decreed [that the straw should lie] there [specifically], with this end here and that [end] there."[13] A Chabad tradition recorded by R. Yosef Yitzhak elaborates on this theme:

> This is what we learn from the teachings of the Baal Shem Tov, that all of the creations of *detza"h* [an acronym that refers to inanimate objects, flora and fauna] are all under His providence in each and every detail of their existence, each according to its level.... Everything is due to a detailed providence that is discernible. [For example], in the middle of the summer on a clear day with a shining sun, suddenly a strong wind comes and blows and shakes the leaves of a tree and several of the leaves are detached...the intent of the strong wind was an event by God to cause the falling of the leaf from the tree.[14]

This passage is particularly powerful, as a leaf falling from a tree was the precise example that Rambam used to describe as an event that stems from pure chance. Hasidism took Rambam's *reductio ad absurdum* and emphatically adopted the diametrically opposed approach by maintaining that there is direct *hashgaha* in this very case.[15]

---

13. *Imrei Pinhas*, 179 (Mishor, 1988). Translation is from Aryeh Leibowitz (2009), 86. See there, 85–91, for more references to hasidic thinkers citing the Baal Shem Tov regarding his view of *hashgaha*.
14. *Sefer HaMaamarim: Kuntresim*, vol. 2, *hateh Elokai*, 279, cited in *Keter Shem Tov, Hosafot, siman* 180. The Rebbe cited this statement in *Likkutei Sihot* 30, *Vayishlah*, no. 1, *se'if* 6 (see there, note 46).
15. The leaders of Chabad emphasized that there were earlier sources that support and prefigure the "revelation" of the Baal Shem Tov regarding *hashgaha*. See, for example, *Yahel Or, Tehillim*, 132 (from the *Tzemah Tzedek*); *Likkutei Sihot* 7, *Shemini*,

The Basis for an All-Pervasive *Hashgaha*

As noted in our discussion of free choice,[16] this comprehensive approach to *hashgaha* is a direct outgrowth of the hasidic notion of the God-world relationship. Many hasidic thinkers, including the Rebbe, argued that if the entire world is enveloped within God, then perforce God is intimately involved in all its happenings..[17]

In Chabad thought, this thesis is sharpened through the distinction between Divine Revelations (*Giluyim*) and the Divine Essence (*Atzmut*). As we have seen, the *Seder Hishtalshelut* consists of an infinite number of contractions that produce a myriad of specific revelations of God, each with its own character and hue. This system allows for differentiation and distinctions. The Divine Essence, however, while transcending all of these revelations, also indescribably encompasses them all in a single point.

The Alter Rebbe argued that this definition of the Divine Essence leads to God's intimate and direct *hashgaha* over every one of the revealed entities:

> This will help explain the mistake of the heretics, who deny *hashgaha peratit* (providence over details), as they think that all the divine influence over *detza"h* travels incrementally from level to level based on the *Seder HaHishtalshelut*.... But the light of the Divine Essence that is prior to the contractions [actually] shines equally... to the extent that the Infinite Light shines even in the inanimate objects of the world of action just as it shines above....[18]

---

no. 1, *se'ifim* 13–14. For a wide array of sources see Dovid Shraga Polter (2015), "A Historical Analysis of Learning Something from Everything."

16. See chapter 7, section "Divine All-Inclusivity and Free Choice."
17. *Tanya, Shaar HaYihud VehaEmuna*, ch. 2; *Iggerot Kodesh* 2, letter 405; ibid., 10, letter 3713; *Likkutei Sihot* 4, *Hosafot*, 1254; ibid., 13, *Hosafot*, 170–71; *Torat Menahem* 5745: 3, 1835. The interpenetration of the hasidic notions of the God-world relationship and of *hashgaha* is deftly described by Norman Lamm (1999), 1–53 and especially p. 52, note 5. It is also important to note that the Alter Rebbe in *Tanya, Shaar HaYihud VehaEmuna*, ch. 2, connects God's intimate involvement with all matters of this world to the fact that God is continuously recreating the world.
18. *Maamarei Admor HaZaken* 5568: 1, 123.

Hashgaha: Living with God

Chabad teachings, then, draw a direct line between the singular nature of the Divine Essence and God's direct involvement in every aspect of creation.[19]

THE REBBE'S THEORETICAL MAPPING OF *HASHGAHA*

The Rebbe contributed to both the theory and practice of *hashgaha*. On the theoretical plane, the Rebbe placed a wide variety of conflicting sources in dialogue and constructed a unified but multitiered theory of *hashgaha*. The Rebbe then applied these constructs to specific types of occurrences and situations, thereby developing cognitive tools for people to properly respond to a range of encounters. As we will see, the Rebbe interwove both his conceptualization and applications of *hashgaha* with broader themes in his thought.

Over the course of many talks, the Rebbe mapped out several modalities of *hashgaha*, all situated within the framework of the Baal Shem Tov's expansive notion of direct divine providence. In general, the Rebbe differentiated between various types of *hashgaha* along two axes: inner versus outer, and functional versus inherent. Within both distinctions, the inherent connection between a Jew and God is a keystone of his system.

Inner *Hashgaha* versus Outer *Hashgaha*

In several talks, the Rebbe argued that, in fact, Rambam would not dispute the Baal Shem Tov's expansive theory of *hashgaha*. Using a well-worn Chabad methodological tool, the Rebbe asserted that Rambam's consignment of *hashgaha* to elite humans was only regarding a specific and unique form of *hashgaha*.[20] All people, animals, and

---

19. The Rebbe also reiterated this idea on several occasions. See *Torat Menahem* 5744: 2, 1148; ibid., 5745: 3, 1834. See also *maamar* "Pada BaShalom 5731," *se'if* 5 (*Sefer HaMaamarim Melukat*, vol. 2, 468).
20. Chabad thinkers' adoption and interpretation of Rambam regarding *hashgaha* began with the Mitteler Rebbe, *Derekh Hayyim, Shaar HaTeshuva*, 25. It is interesting that in the Rebbe's early letter he wrote about the Mitteler Rebbe's interpretation of Rambam that "further study is needed for someone on my [limited] level to understand how to explain this in the words of the Rambam" (*Likkutei Sihot* 8, 280). However, as noted in the chapter, already in 1973 (*Likkutei Sihot* 18, *Korah*, no. 2) the Rebbe quoted the Mittler Rebbe's understanding of Rambam without any reservations. In a later talk from 1985 (*Torat Menahem* 5745: 3, 1836), the Rebbe

objects, however, are subject to the basic level of *hashgaha* described by the Baal Shem Tov.[21]

Here is the Rebbe's description of the two forms of *hashgaha*:[22]

(1) Inner *hashgaha*: *Hashgaha* that is revealed, meaning to say that it is not hidden and concealed in nature. It is regarding this form of *hashgaha* that Rambam said that it is in proportion to [the individual level of] each mind's cleaving to Godliness. Thus, *detza"h* and the wicked are not under the purview of individual *hashgaha*.

(2) Outer *hashgaha*: *Hashgaha* that is enclothed in a concealed manner in natural mediums. This form of *hashgaha* exists regarding all creations, in accordance with the Baal Shem Tov's approach.

All aspects of this world are under the direct control of God, albeit with differing degrees of concealment and revelation.

Who merits the revealed form of *hashgaha*? The Rebbe noted that a cursory reading of Rambam indicates that only the righteous receive this overt *hashgaha*. The wicked, however, are, in the language of Rambam, *mufkar lemikreh*,"[23] which, according to the Rebbe's interpretation, means that their direct *hashgaha* is concealed in natural means. The Rebbe noted that over and above Rambam's formulation, the Torah

---

argued that Rambam's formulations in *Mishneh Torah* indicate that he prefigured the Baal Shem Tov's expansive view of *hashgaha*. The Rebbe interpreted lines in *Mishneh Torah* as affirming a notion of an all-inclusive divine unity, akin to that developed by Chabad, This logic leads to an expansive view of *hashgaha* as well. Similarly, see *Torat Menahem* 5728: 3, 47, where, regarding the topic of *hashgaha*, the Rebbe noted that at times the words of *Guide for the Perplexed* cannot be understood according to their simple meaning (*einam kifshutam*). Yaakov Gottlieb (2009), 88–110, argues that this is representative of a broader phenomenon that with the passage of years the Rebbe became more apt to interpret Rambam as being consistent with Chabad teachings.

21. See *Likkutei Sihot* 18, *Korah*, no. 2, *se'if* 5; ibid., 9, *Nitzavim*, no. 1, *se'if* 8; *Torat Menahem* 5745: 3, 1836; ibid., 5750: 1, 232–33.
22. *Likkutei Sihot* 18, *Korah*, no. 2, *se'if* 5.
23. *Guide for the Perplexed*, III:51; *Likkutei Sihot* 18, *se'if* 5.

Hashgaha: Living with God

itself warns that sin will cause God to "hide My face from them,"[24] seemingly referring to a withdrawal of *hashgaha*. As the Rebbe summarized the evidence:

> When a Jew does not fulfill God's will, *hashgaha* controls his fate in an external manner (*hashgaha hitzonit*), and it is thus enclothed in the garments of nature, like the *hashgaha* which controls the fate of the gentiles.[25]

It appears that a Jewish sinner does not merit the inner, discernible *hashgaha* but rather is relegated to being governed by the *hashgaha* hidden in nature that governs the rest of the world.

The Rebbe, however, went on to argue that this is an impossible conclusion. Within Rambam's scheme, only the righteous are considered close to God and thus deserving of His overt involvement in their life. As we have seen, though, from the Rebbe's read of other texts, he deduced that all Jews, no matter what their current spiritual state is, are always essentially bound to God.[26] How then are we to understand the above sources, which indicate that Jewish sinners merit only *hashgaha* that is hidden in natural channels?

The Rebbe deduced from this question that there must be two forms of this inner *hashgaha*. While to the average observer the *hashgaha* over a Jew who sins might be identical to the *hashgaha* over the natural world, including gentiles, a deeper level of scrutiny will demonstrate that all Jews are privy to this inner *hashgaha*. To explain this structure, the Rebbe connected the various levels of *hasghaha* with different names and aspects of God.[27]

The name *Elokim* refers to God as He is enclothed and concealed within nature. This aspect of God is responsible for the *hashgaha* over non-Jews and the rest of the natural order. While still being under the

---

24. Deut. 31:17.
25. *Likkutei Sihot* 18, Korah, no. 2, *se'if* 7.
26. See chapter 7, section "Ramifications of the Nature of Free Choice."
27. See also *Likkutei Sihot* 15, Vayishlah, no. 3, *se'ifim* 7–8. Also see chapter 16, section "An Essential and Transcendent Connection to God."

direct control of God, His involvement is not evident as it is hidden behind the mask of the natural order.

By contrast, the name *Hashem* (the tetragrammaton) denotes God as He transcends nature. This aspect of Godliness bestows providence over the Jewish people, whose essence transcends the natural order. As God's involvement stems from a point that transcends the existence of the natural order, God's involvement in a Jew's life should be apparent and not camouflaged in nature.

Herein lies the distinction between the two groups of Jews. Righteous Jews merit direct involvement from the tetragrammaton and therefore experience fully revealed *hashgaha* that is immediately apparent. The providence over Jewish sinners, however, while also stemming from the tetragammaton, is channeled through the name *Elokim* and the natural forces. The result is that God's *hashgaha* over Jewish sinners is hidden in nature and difficult to detect, but is still discernible on some level after thought and contemplation (unlike the *hashgaha* over the natural world and non-Jews, which stems from *Elokim* and is thus fully concealed).

As the Rebbe said:

> Although the *hashgaha* that controls the fate of Jews who do not carry out God's will is concealed and enclothed in nature, this does not mean that the *hashgaha* from the name *Hashem* departs from them, God forbid. [On the contrary,] in whatever situation a Jew is found, he is [part of] "the people to whom *Hashem* is close" ([as our Sages quote God as saying:] "Regardless, they are My children" [Kiddushin 36a]). [In this instance, however,] the *hashgaha* which stems from the name *Hashem* is enclothed in the name *Elokim*.[28]

According to the Rebbe, this is the deeper meaning of the verse "And I will conceal My face from them":[29] God's face, or His inner dimension, will be *concealed* but not removed. God's presence and discernible involvement in the life of a Jew is a constant reality.

---

28. *Likkutei Sihot* 18, Korah, no. 2, *se'if* 7.
29. Deut. 31:18.

Counterintuitively, this concealment of God's overt involvement in the life of the Jewish sinner paves the way for the revelation of a more fundamental connection between the Jew and God. In the Rebbe's words:

> Since [this] providence of *Hashem* is present (not in relation to the revealed aspects of the Jewish people, from whom it is concealed…but) in connection with their quintessential essence [*lemahuto ha'atzmi*], therefore it touches his essence. As is known, repentance that comes from [a sense of] colossal distance from Godliness affects the very essence of the soul, and therefore involves and brings about a change in the *entirety* of the person's divine service.[30]

As we have discussed, the elusive essence of a Jewish soul – the *yehida* – is one with the Divine Essence. When all perceptible connections to God are absent, the masked *hashgaha* will lay bare the essential transcendent nature of a Jewish soul and generate a turnabout in the person's life.

In summary, through a rigorous textual and conceptual analysis, the Rebbe arrived at a construct of *hashgaha* that seems very far from that of Rambam's initial presentation. According to the Rebbe, all terrestrial items are subject to direct *hashgaha*, while all Jews, including sinners, experience this direct *hashgaha* in a manner that is fully or somewhat revealed. A crucial part of the Rebbe's argument rests on the oneness of the essence of the Jewish soul with the Divine Essence. This is an ontological fact, irrespective of a Jew's actual behavior. The revelation of this truth, though, will transform a Jew's actual behavior for the better.

Functional *Hashgaha* versus Inherent *Hashgaha*

The notion of a constant direct *hashgaha* in the life of a Jew leads directly to a second distinction that the Rebbe made within his conception of an all-pervasive *hashgaha*. The background to this division is a further novelty of the Baal Shem Tov that relates to God's purpose in orchestrating the events of this world in the way that He does. Instead

---

30. *Likkutei Sihot* 18, *Korah*, no. 2, *se'if* 8.

of attributing God's motivation to local circumstances, the Baal Shem Tov argued for a broader and more cosmic perspective. As R. Yosef Yitzhak recorded:

> As is well known regarding the topic of *hashgaha peratit* that our master the Baal Shem Tov elucidated: It is not merely that all of the details of the movements of all creations stem from direct *hashgaha* from God.... Rather, even more than this: the specific movement of a specific creation has a relationship to the general purpose of all of creation.[31]

In other words, each event is an integral piece in God's larger plan for the entirety of the cosmos; every event helps all of creation advance on its trajectory toward perfection.[32]

The Rebbe elucidated this concept by analogizing God to an industrious homemaker:

> This concept can be illustrated by a simple example from our everyday life. The nature of a woman of valor and proficient mainstay of the home is to meticulously oversee all the many details of her home, making sure that everything is in its proper place and functions in a particular order. Moreover, she makes certain that all the possessions within the home are aligned with the general mission to which her household is directed. Everything is carefully planned out....
>
> If this is the manner in which an individual woman runs her home, how much more so does this apply with regard to Him who creates the world and oversees its functioning. All the particular events which occur to each created being in God's world

---

31. *Sefer HaMaamarim: Kuntresim*, vol. 2, 370b. Cited in *Keter Shem Tov, Hosafot, siman* 179.
32. In *Likkutei Sihot* 23, 12–13 Tamuz, *se'if* 11, the Rebbe added that this formulation of the Baal Shem Tov teaches that every movement of every inanimate object is inherently significant on its own (*mitzad atzmo*) as opposed to *just* serving the needs of humans. For a similar formulation, see *Likkutei Sihot* 13, *Hosafot*, 164–65.

are overseen by His *hashgaha* and have an effect on the realization of the divine intent for creation.[33]

Every event in this world is necessary to fulfill God's purpose for the world.

The assertion that God orchestrates events to facilitate a specific goal leads to the conclusion that His *hashgaha* is more focused on certain items and events than others.[34] This is true since nothing guarantees that every moment of existence of every creation is equally significant in furthering God's plans for the cosmos. The Rebbe noted that for this reason R. Yosef Yitzhak emphasized that God's providence extends over everything, "each according to its level. "[35] Despite the comprehensiveness of *hashgaha*, God's involvement is stratified in proportion to the functional importance of the particular item in the general advancement of the world.

As we have seen, however, the Jewish people cannot be conceived of in mere functional terms.[36] Rather, they have a unique status as God's *chosen* due to their oneness with the innermost recesses of the Divine Essence, or, in the words of the Rebbe, "He and the Jewish people are the same essence, as it were."[37] As such, when the *yehida* of a Jew is manifest and this level of identification with the Divine Essence is revealed, the *hashgaha* over a Jew cannot be measured *merely* in relation to his or her function in advancing the world. Rather, the presence of each Jew in the world, which is God's presence in the world, is inherently itself the goal of creation.

The Rebbe articulated this idea as follows:

> This concept is also reflected in our Sages' statement that the world was created "for the sake of the Torah and for the sake of the Jewish people" (Rashi on Gen. 1:1). The Torah and the Jewish

---

33. *Likkutei Sihot* 30, Vayishlah, no. 1, *se'if* 2. For a slightly different rendition of this analogy, see *Torat Menahem* 5744: 4, 2646 and ibid., 5745: 4, 2088.
34. *Likkutei Sihot* 30, Vayishlah, no. 1, *se'if* 5.
35. See above, note 14.
36. See chapter 7, section "The Basis for the Divine Essence's Choices."
37. *Likkutei Sihot* 30, Vayishlah, no. 1, *se'if* 7.

people are the ultimate intent of the creation...God's will and His choice are focused on them themselves.[38]

With regard to the creation as a whole, He manifests His *hashgaha* on each detail according to its individual virtue. Regarding the Jewish people, however, "the nation close to Him," the providence which He manifests over them is a result of His desire and choice of them.[39]

It follows that this form of *hashgaha* does not vary according to the merits of the individual, but rests on all Jews equally. From this vantage point, even Jewish sinners who are not overtly advancing the general mission of the cosmos at the moment are still inherently bound to God.[40] It is needless to state, though, that this inherent connection to God does not absolve a Jew from his mission to further reveal divinity within oneself and the world at large.[41]

Summary of the Rebbe's Theoretical Mapping of *Hashgaha*

Even while affirming the hasidic notion of God's direct *hashgaha* over all things, the Rebbe reserved a unique space for Jews. For most creations, the direct *hashgaha* is veiled in the natural world and exists in proportion to the extent that it advances the cosmic mission. By contrast, each Jew, irrespective of personal piety or overt contribution to the cosmic mission, receives overt and discernible *hashgaha*, as the identity of each Jew is one with the innermost recesses of the Divine Essence.

LIVING WITH *HASHGAHA*

In conjunction with his theoretical exposition of *hashgaha*, the Rebbe developed a specific set of implications for its application to daily life. While firmly rooted in earlier hasidic thinking, the Rebbe, perhaps uniquely, transformed the abstract principle of providence into a

---

38. For a lengthier exposition of the Rebbe's perspective on the ultimate role of Jews and non-Jews in God's creation, see chapter 16, section "The Particular, the Universal, and the Coming of *Mashiah*."
39. *Likkutei Sihot* 30, *Vayishlah*, no. 1, *se'if* 4.
40. See also *Torat Menahem* 5745: 3, 1837.
41. *Torat Menahem* 5744: 4, 2646–47.

Hashgaha: Living with God

comprehensive lens through which to perceive everything that happens in the world. In his view, the fact that each Jew is subject to discernible and direct *hashgaha* both compels and empowers him to constantly live in the presence of God, attentive to the messages that God is constantly sending.

Guided by Stimuli

According to an oral tradition recorded in later hasidic writings, the Baal Shem Tov himself already articulated the key practical application of an all-pervasive *hashgaha*. Most crucial for our topic is the Rebbe's succinct summary of this teaching:

> Our master, the Baal Shem Tov, taught: "Whatever a person sees or hears is a directive for his service of God. This is what divine service consists of – understanding and deducing a way to serve God from everything [one sees or hears]."[42]

Based on the above analysis, the metaphysical basis for this statement is readily understandable. God directs all worldly affairs for the sake of the "general purpose" of creation. Thus, the very fact that *hashgaha* orchestrated that a person encounter a particular phenomenon means that that experience must have a unique lesson to teach him that will further this mission.

More than a pithy statement, the Rebbe understood the Baal Shem Tov's teaching as a comprehensive and transformative mindset for life. Even in his early, pre-leadership writings, the Rebbe underscored the magnitude of this idea. In a passage that foreshadows a central theme of his later talks and letters, the Rebbe wrote the following about the Baal Shem Tov's conception of *hashgaha*:

> The creation of the world took place because God desired a *Dira BaTahtonim*... through the mitzvot of the Jewish people. "Everything else was created to serve me, and I was created to serve my Creator" (Kiddushin 82b). If so, all of a person's actions and what

---

42. *HaYom Yom*, 9 Iyar. Translation is from www.sie.org/3354609.

occurs to him must all be to fulfill a mitzva... and if so, when a person sees or hears something or he gains knowledge about a matter, we must conclude that (1) it was not for nought, (2) there is one correct path to follow [in the wake of this event], and (3) it is to use [this event] to do a mitzva.... As a result of this [perspective], there is nothing in the world – in the world of each individual – except God and himself. Everything else is merely a means through which a person can fulfill his service to God.[43]

In this passage, the Rebbe underscored the far-reaching personal ramifications of the Baal Shem Tov's approach to *hashgaha*. God's cosmic goal of creation and the individual's life-mission are one and the same: the creation of a *Dira BaTahtonim*. Accordingly, God constantly orchestrates the daily events in each individual's life to grant him the situations and tools necessary to fulfill his own part of the cosmic mission. Each phenomenon one encounters entails a charge from God; each event presents a divine mission.

The notion that everything that occurs in one's life should be understood as an individualized mission from God is a major theme in the Rebbe's talks. Accordingly, knowledge of Torah alone is not sufficient to properly serve God as one must also pay careful attention to the guidance that God provides through the worldly phenomenons that one encounters. The Rebbe once spoke about this need to learn lessons from everything in the context of analyzing a conversation between Moses and Pharaoh. In the wake of the plague of locusts, Pharaoh offered that Moses and the entire Jewish people should depart but leave their cattle behind. Moses responded that not only would the Jewish people take their own animals, but the Egyptians would even provide them with extra animals to sacrifice to God.[44]

The Rebbe explained that the imagery of Jews not only serving God through their own means but even incorporating non-Jewish contributions was pregnant with meaning:

---

43. *Reshimot, Hoveret* 44, 419–20.
44. Ex. 10:25–26; Rashi, s.v. *gam*.

Hashgaha: Living with God

> There are aspects of the service of God that one learns from the [broader] world…. So when a Jew hears about an event that took place in the world, even regarding other nations, even something negative such as strife or a war or something similar – embedded in this [hearing about the event is] a teaching and a lesson for one's service of God…. These imperatives in the service of God that one learns from what occurs in the world regarding and which concern between non-Jews – cannot be found in the actual Torah.[45]

In a similar fashion to how the sacrificial animals owned by the Jews were insufficient, the Torah alone is not the sole source of practical guidance. Rather, due to the all-pervasive *hashgaha*, one must also look to derive lessons from whatever one encounters – even the Pharaohs of the world – as God is constantly teaching lessons of how to act through what occurs around us.[46]

Learning from the News

One concrete illustration of this mindset was the Rebbe's reaction to American astronauts landing on the moon. In a wide-ranging talk dedicated to the theological implications of this event,[47] the Rebbe framed his discussion with the Baal Shem Tov's principle of *hashgaha*:[48]

> It is clear, according to the Baal Shem Tov, that whatever a person sees or hears, he should learn from it regarding his service of God, and this principle is true regarding even surprising and unusual events, such as the journey of the astronauts.

---

45. *Torat Menahem* 5746: 2, 427–30.
46. The Rebbe applied this idea to one's encounter with non-kosher animals (*Likkutei Sihot* 21, 24 Tevet, *se'if* 21), Rashi's commentary (Ex. 28:4) on seeing a non-Jewish woman riding a horse in an immodest fashion (*Likkutei Sihot* 26, Tetzaveh, no. 1, *se'if* 10), and the Baal Shem Tov's sighting of a cross (*Torat Menahem* 5723: 1, 126–30).
47. See *Torat Menahem* 5729: 2, 113–30. For more references and elaboration, see Yirmiyahu Branover and Yosef Ginsburg, (2000), 195–214; Yizhak Rozen (5764), 230–44; and Mordechai Menashe Laufer (22 Adar 5758).
48. *Torat Menahem* 5729: 2, 115–16.

Aspects of a Godly Life

Among other things, the Rebbe focused on the necessary discipline that astronauts must exhibit due to the catastrophic negative ramifications of even slight deviations:

> Astronauts on a space shuttle flight are instructed in advance exactly how they must eat, sleep, dress, and behave in all areas of their life. They are told that any deviation can cause the waste of all that has been invested in the process, billions of dollars....
>
> This is true whether or not or how much he understands the benefits of these specific directions, or the damage caused by refusing to follow them. Only the experts on the ground, who spent years researching the issues, know all the specific details. Similarly, an astronaut does not make the mistake of thinking, "I'm just one of three, so what difference does it make if I don't do everything I should do? I'm just the minority." He is certain of the fact that any deviation from his instructions puts his colleagues at risk as well.[49]

After underscoring the critical importance of self-discipline and the acceptance of responsibility for one's own life and the lives of others, the Rebbe used this as a model for the halakhic system.

> On this basis, we may respond to a question that has caused much unjustified confusion and equivocation among those whose job it is to clarify such matters:
>
> According to Jewish law, if a person eats an amount of non-kosher food equal to the size of an olive, a Jewish court would be obligated to punish him with thirty-nine lashes. The question then is: How can we meddle in someone's private life? What about personal privilege and the right to privacy?
>
> The Mishna states: "Man was created alone, for every person must say: For me the world was created." This world, as well as

---

49. Ibid., 123.

Hashgaha: Living with God

all of the spiritual realms leading to it, was created for each and every person individually.[50]

Just as astronauts need to abrogate some level of personal autonomy and embrace a detailed regimen, the same holds true for a Jew's fealty to the Torah. The Rebbe used the historic moon landing as a springboard to remind his listeners of the immense significance of every single person's actions, especially his or her observance of mitzvot.

Learning from One's Job

In addition to learning lessons from the unusual news events that one hears, the Rebbe consistently emphasized the need to apply the same model to the daily and mundane. More particularly, the Rebbe often emphasized that aspects of one's professional career should be perceived as divinely ordained stimuli to inspire greater service.

One example of this *hashgaha*-oriented framework for one's career is the Rebbe's comments about the legal profession. We have already seen that the Rebbe understood the verse "Know Him in all of your ways"[51] as teaching that even when involved in physical pursuits one should still be conscious of the divinity inherent in such activities. In an early talk, the Rebbe recommended that contemplating God's all-pervasive *hashgaha* is one method of achieving this God-consciousness:

> As mentioned above, all the material matters that a Jew is involved with are due to *hashgaha peratit,* and the intent is that a person be trained in that profession such that he can use those very things for holiness. For example, when a person's livelihood is sent to him through the means of his being a lawyer, he needs to use this very profession for holiness: the essence of a lawyer is to find ways to exonerate the other, and he should use this very trait for the sake of loving other Jews, to find the good in every

---

50. Ibid., 121–22.
51. Prov. 3:6.

Jew... through this method one truly executes the goal of "God desired to have a *Dira BaTahtonim*."⁵²

A defense lawyer who is trained to prove the innocence of his client, at times against a preponderance of evidence, should perceive this skill as a divinely ordained mission to cultivate a sense of appreciation and love toward other Jews. Over the course of his tenure, the Rebbe employed this model to dozens of other professions.⁵³

Transforming Challenges into Opportunities

The Rebbe was very aware of the unique challenges of modern times. Responding to the difficulties in fulfilling individual and communal missions, the Rebbe employed the principle of *hashgaha* to arm people with a method of reframing difficult situations. When viewed from the perspective of *hashgaha*, challenging circumstances can be transformed into unique opportunities for personal and cosmic growth.

The Rebbe once underscored the efficacy of perceiving desperate situations through the lens of *hashgaha* in a talk marking the anniversary of his father-in-law's release from Russian prison.⁵⁴ R. Yosef Yitzhak attributed his ability to bear the torture of his interrogators to a firm belief in the Baal Shem Tov's conception of *hashgaha*. After a painstaking analysis of the precise innovation of the Baal Shem Tov and its relationship to difficult times, the Rebbe concluded:

> The innovation of the Baal Shem Tov regarding *hashgaha* led to the feeling that... the very imprisonment and torture "fulfills the ultimate goal of Creation": to reveal God.... [This was accomplished] through the very strong stand the Rebbe [R. Yosef Yitzhak] took in his behavior there, that he did not become frightened from or emotional before the enemies... and even more so, he did not even consider them to be real and perceived them as

---

52. *Torat Menahem* 5714: 2, 223–24.
53. See Dovid Shraga Polter (1997) and (2015).
54. *Likkutei Sihot* 23, 12–13, Tamuz.

Hashgaha: Living with God

if "they were literally nothing".... All of this revealed in the very imprisonment that "there is none other than Him."[55]

Similar to the biblical Joseph (Yosef), R. Yosef Yitzhak managed to see his dire straits as a divinely orchestrated opportunity to reveal divinity in a heretofore "lowly" space. The Rebbe continued that this form of reframing is a model for each person in his own service:

> In every situation that a Jew finds himself, even if he does not see any possibility for him to be active in spreading Judaism or the wellsprings [of Hasidism], it is forbidden to give up hope, Heaven forbid, and one must remember that this situation was also caused by *hashgaha peratit*, and when one puts in the effort...one will find a circumstance that will cause the revelation of God – a real revelation – even in this situation. [56]

Implicit in the Rebbe's formulation is an admission that this perspective is non-intuitive and requires effort, as it is more natural to see impediments as negatives. Nonetheless, the capacity to perceive obstructions as opportunities flows directly from the concept of the Baal Shem Tov. Otherwise, an opportunity to move the world forward will be lost.

The Strength to Complete the Mission

In addition to reframing difficult situations as divinely ordained opportunities, the Rebbe underscored that these opportunities are individually customized. As such, he taught that God places a person in a predicament only after endowing him with the latent strength to succeed. In line with this reasoning, the Rebbe often tried to motivate individuals by reminding them that the very fact that God placed this challenge before them indicates that they have the talents and capacity to succeed despite adverse conditions.

For example, in one talk the Rebbe emphasized God's individual *hashgaha* and His fair expectations:

---

55. Ibid., *se'if* 12.
56. Ibid., *se'if* 13.

> Each Jew, in any place that he finds himself – and every place where a Jew reaches is "from the Lord, a mighty man's steps are established" (Ps. 37:23) – he is a *shaliah* [emissary] of God...and since a Jew knows that "the Holy One, blessed be He, does not deal tyrannically with His creations"... he should believe that he also has the ability to transform his surroundings to the [spiritual equivalent of the] Land of Israel....[57]
>
> Even if the difficulties are so great that it seems that the fulfillment of the mission is an impossibility, the Holy One, blessed be He, always provides the strength to overcome all of the difficulties and to execute the mission (*shelihut*).[58]

As the Rebbe deemed a person's connection to a specific locale as an act of *hashgaha*, he must have the capability to succeed in his local mission.[59]

The Rebbe poignantly articulated this theme in a letter sent to a Jew who had a homosexual orientation and asked the Rebbe to pray for him.[60] While expressing sympathy for the person's predicament, the Rebbe rejected the notion that one's inborn tendencies and character traits are always inherently good. A person must try, with the help of professionals, "to improve, indeed even to change, their 'natural' (i.e., innate) traits."

Once again, the Rebbe acknowledged the difficulty of the path he was charting for his interlocutor:

---

57. See chapter 19, section "Make, Here, the Land of Israel: Transforming the World into the Land of Israel."
58. *Likkutei Sihot* 8, *Shelah*, no. 1, *se'if* 14. The phrase the Rebbe employs in this talk, that "the Holy One, blessed be He, does not deal tyrannically with His creations," is from Avoda Zara 3b. The Rebbe often cited this talmudic passage when reiterating the notion that God orchestrates tests for a person based on the strength that he possesses. See, for example, *Iggerot Kodesh* 9, letters 2819, 2953; ibid., 13, letter 4468; ibid., 22, letter 8576; *Torat Menahem* 5711: 1, 161; ibid., 5713: 1, 314; ibid., 5720: 2, 200.
59. For a practical application of this idea regarding the relationship between the Diaspora and the Land of Israel, see chapter 19, section "Exile as Hashgaha."
60. Letter dated 25 Shevat 5746, available at www.chabad.org/1872939.

Needless to say, the person who is afflicted with this or other neurological problems may well ask, "Why has God created such a compulsive drive, which is in direct contradiction to His moral code? Why has He afflicted me, who desires to comply fully with His commandments?"

The Rebbe's responded to this hypothetical question with a mixture of humility before God and an assurance of God's fairness:

> No human being can answer such questions, which only God, the Creator, can answer. One observation can be suggested in relation to the question, Why me? If an individual experiences a particularly difficult, or trying, situation, it may be assumed that God has given him extraordinary powers to overcome the extraordinary difficulty. The individual concerned is probably unaware of his real inner strength; the trial may therefore be designed for the sole purpose of bringing out in the individual his hidden strength, which, after overcoming his problem, can be added henceforth to the arsenal of his revealed capacities, in order to utilize both for infinitely greater achievements for the benefit of himself, and others.[61]

The perfectly calibrated system of *hashgaha* would not allow for a person to be placed in a situation where he cannot succeed. Rather, challenging situations are an opportunity to dig within and access hidden strength. As we have seen in previous chapters, this process is akin to that of *mesirut nefesh*, whereby specifically dark and trying times reveal the inner *yehida* of a person.

Hashgaha in the Era of Hasidism

While the Rebbe believed that the Baal Shem Tov's understanding of *hashgaha* is an eternal truth, he emphasized that its adoption and application has heightened significance for the later generations. As we have seen, the Rebbe firmly believed that all worldly events are orchestrated

---

61. Ibid.

Aspects of a Godly Life

by God for the sake of creating a *Dira BaTahtonim*. It follows that this consciousness is crucial for the generation that is charged with finishing the construction of the utopian reality.

In addition, the Rebbe interwove the Baal Shem Tov's conception of an all-pervasive divine providence with the revelation and dissemination of Hasidism. As we have seen, the quintessential point of Hasidism is the revelation of the Divine Essence which is the singular substance that comprises all the cosmos. Studying Hasidism allows one to internalize the idea of the divinity of the world and perceive God everywhere. One ramification of this perception is the ability to understand the divine messages in worldly phenomena.

The Rebbe articulated this point in an early talk dedicated to the differences between the "inner" secrets of the Torah and its "revealed" parts. Studying Talmud is analogized to a distant auditory perception of God, while immersing oneself in the Torah's inner secrets generates an immediate visual experience, creating a much closer bond between the student and God.[62] One expression of this ability to "see" God is the comprehension of constant *hashgaha*:

> Only through learning the inner layer of Torah does the awareness of God's presence in worldly matters become "visual," meaning that even in the matters of this world one sees God tangibly through seeing *hashgaha peratit* at every step, [both] in the world in general and in one's personal lot in particular....[63]

Seeing God's hand and living with *hashgaha* is a direct outgrowth of studying Hasidism, both of which are intertwined with the culmination of the cosmic mission.

---

62. For the preference of the visual over the auditory, see *Likkutei Sihot* 6, *Yitro*, no. 2, *se'if* 4; *Torat Menahem* 5750: 1, 133–36.
63. *Torat Menahem* 5711: 2, 74. See also *Likkutei Sihot* 10, *Hosafot*, 219; *Torat Menahem* 5715: 2, 205.

CONCLUSION

The Rebbe's perspective on *hashgaha* is fully in line with the classic hasidic approach. In his own inimitable way, however, the Rebbe expanded both the conceptual and practical frontiers of this well-established concept. On both levels, he fully integrated *hashgaha* into his holistic broader philosophy and the mission of creating a *Dira BaTahtonim*.

Secondary Literature Consulted for Chapter 10, "*Hashgaha*: Living with God"

Yaakov Gottlieb, *Sekhaltanut BiLevush Hasidi*, 26–27, 98–101.

Nahum Greenwald, "Hashgaha Peratit al pi Shittat HaBesht."

Dovid Shraga Polter, *Listening to Life's Messages: Adapted from the works of the Lubavitcher Rebbe*.

Dovid Shraga Polter, *Learning Something From Everything*.

Yonah Avtzon, ed., *Led by G-d's Hand: The Ba'al Shem Tov's Conception of Hashgachah Peratis – Based on the Works of the Lubavitcher Rebbe, Rabbi Menachem M. Schneerson*, translated by Eliyahu Touger.

Chapter 11

Bittahon: Trusting and Jumping

God's constant *hashgaha* forms part of the basis for another mindset that the Rebbe emphasized: reliance upon God (*bittahon*). Building upon classical analyses of the nature and justification of *bittahon*, the Rebbe recast *bittahon* as an integral element of his philosophy. Characteristically, the Rebbe's discussions of *bittahon* run the gamut from highly abstract discourses that relate to different aspects of divinity to specific guidance for how to mentally and practically relate to real-life situations.

BITTAHON IN EARLIER SOURCES

While many biblical verses and rabbinic statements affirm the need to "trust" God, these sources do not define the precise parameters of this obligation. As a result of this ambiguity, Jewish philosophers developed two general approaches to the meaning of *bittahon*.[1] A brief outline of

---

1. For surveys of the rabbinic passages and classical approaches to *bittahon*, see Avraham Goldberg (2002) and Daniel Stein (2010), 31–48.

these perspectives will provide crucial context for accurately locating the Rebbe's contribution.

The Hazon Ish and the "Mistake"

One conception of *bittahon*, while rooted in classical sources, was forcefully and famously articulated by R. Avraham Karelitz, the *Hazon Ish*. He writes as follows:

> An old mistake has become rooted in the hearts of many concerning the concept of *bittahon*. *Bittahon*... has come to mean that a person is obligated to believe that whenever he is presented with two possible outcomes, one good and one not, then certainly it will turn out for the good. And if he has doubts and fears the worst, that constitutes a lack of trust.... This view of *bittahon* is incorrect, for as long as the future outcome has not been clarified through prophecy, that outcome has not been decided, for who can truly know God's judgments and providence? Rather, *bittahon* means realizing that there are no coincidences in the world, and that whatever happens under the sun is a function of God's decree.[2]

According to the *Hazon Ish*, *bittahon* is not predictive of a specific outcome, but rather refers to an emotional state of calmness that stems from a belief that as difficult as a predicament may be, God controls all terrestrial events and does not act capriciously.

In line with his definition, the *Hazon Ish* contends that *bittahon* should be perceived not as an independent mitzva or perspective, but as the practical outgrowth of one's basic belief (*emuna*) in God. Included in *emuna* is a belief in God's control of every worldly event. *Bittahon* is simply the name of the cognitive and emotional state of a person who is a true believer.

---

2. *Emuna UVittahon* 3:1.

Aspects of a Godly Life

R. Yosef Albo

As many have noted,[3] the approach which the *Hazon Ish* refers to as a "mistake" has adherents in medieval Jewish thought. For example, in a chapter extolling the virtue of *bittahon*, R. Yosef Albo writes the following regarding a person who does not receive a desired kindness from God:

> He does not trust completely that he will be given what is in his heart ... or he does not view himself as being on the spiritual level that God should do him the kindness; he thinks God does not want to grant his request, and because of this he does not hope properly. However, if he had hoped properly, the kindness would not have been withheld by God.[4]

Clearly, R. Albo asserts that proper *bittahon* is predictive in nature. Even if a person is undeserving of divine kindness, *bittahon* teaches that in a moment of crisis one should have complete confidence that God will orchestrate a positive outcome.

THE REBBE'S DEFINITION OF *BITTAHON*

Predictive *Bittahon*

Cognizant of these different definitions of *bittahon*, the Rebbe began one extensive treatment of this topic by noting that many classical sources describe one who has *bittahon* as embodying extreme equanimity.[5] This obligatory serenity extends so far that the Sages criticized biblical figures as great as Moses and Jacob for feeling fear when faced with desperate situations.[6]

After establishing the proper emotional state of a person with *bittahon*, the Rebbe probed the basis for such emotional equanimity:

---

3. Aharon Lichtenstein (2003), 142, and (1976), 352–55; Daniel Stein (2010), 33–39; Avraham Goldberg (2002), 5–12, 70–96.
4. *Sefer HaIkkarim* 4:47. Translation is adapted from Daniel Stein (2010), 36.
5. *Likkutei Sihot* 36, *Shemot*, no. 1, *se'if* 2.
6. Genesis Rabba, *siman* 76:2. The Rebbe noted that the commentators dispute whether or not the midrash is actually criticizing Jacob and Moses, but he developed the rest of the talk within the approach that their fear constituted a sin.

Bittahon: Trusting and Jumping

Now, the grounds for such certainty are problematic. Even when a person has an explicit divine promise, it is possible that "sin would cause" the promise not to be fulfilled. This certainly applies when there is no explicit promise.[7]

What allows a person to be so calm if he is undeserving? Should not the ubiquity of sin justify the emotions of fear and worry?

The Rebbe first raised the possibility of a *Hazon Ish*-esque conception of *bittahon*:

> Everything comes from above. A person with that awareness is therefore utterly serene.... Even if he is not worthy of God's kindness (but instead deserves punishment), his mind is still completely at ease because he knows that his misfortune does not result from any side factor, but from God alone. Since he did not fulfill his responsibilities to his Creator, He brought him to this distressing situation.[8]

The Rebbe, however, proceeded to reject the notion that *bittahon* is limited to emotional equanimity. Assuming that the Sages chose the terms they used with a high level of precision, he noted that the "simple" meaning of *bittahon*, which has the connotation of security and certainty, is that a person trusts in God "that he will receive visible and manifest good, i.e., that God will rescue him from his difficulties."[9] When this definition is combined with the assertion of medieval Jewish philosophers that *bittahon* is obligatory upon each Jew,[10] the emerging picture is that all Jews should always firmly believe that the "visible and manifest good" will occur. According to the *Hazon Ish*, however, such predictive

---

7. *Likkutei Sihot* 36, *Shemot*, no. 1, *se'if* 2. Regarding the statement that "sin would cause" the promise not to come to fruition, see Berakhot 4a, which says that this is the reason for Jacob's fear despite the reinforcement of a divine promise. For a discussion about the interplay between this talmudic passage and the trait of *bittahon*, see Avraham Goldberg (2002), 93–94, 105–25.
8. *Likkutei Sihot* 36, *Shemot*, no. 1, *se'if* 3.
9. Ibid., *se'if* 4.
10. Ibid. The Rebbe cited *Hovot HaLevavot, Shaar HaBittahon*, ch. 2.

Aspects of a Godly Life

capabilities should be the purview of only a select few righteous individuals who have not sinned and therefore for them there is nothing obstructing God's kindness.

Bittahon as an Independent Value

Having drawn the conclusion that *bittahon* contains predictive qualities for the masses, the Rebbe was now faced with a most perplexing proposition. As he put it:

> Even though God's mercy extends also to someone who is not deserving, is it not possible that a person may be deserving of punishment for his undesirable deeds? What is the conceptual foundation for a person's trust that God will act benevolently toward him, even though he is undeserving of this?[11]

In response, the Rebbe cited an array of sources which indicate that an individual's absolute confidence that God will actualize the "visible and manifest good" actually causes God to generate the desired outcome.[12] Most prominently, the Rebbe highlighted a pithy quote from the *Tzemah Tzedek* that expresses this idea: "Think good, and it will be good." The Rebbe explained that "thinking positively (having *bittahon* in God) will in itself give rise to results that are visibly and manifestly good."[13]

Based on his definition of *bittahon*, the Rebbe sharply distinguished between the categories of *emuna* and *bittahon*:

> The obligation of *bittahon* which we are commanded to cultivate is not merely a component and a corollary of one's faith (*emuna*), that everything is in the hands of God and that He is compassionate and merciful. Such an obligation would not need

---

11. *Likkutei Sihot* 36, *Shemot*, no. 1, *se'if* 4.
12. Ibid., note 40. The Rebbe cited *Sefer HaIkkarim* (4:46); *Kad HaKemah*, "Bittahon"; *Netivot Olam, Netiv HaBittahon*, ch. 1; *Keter Shem Tov*, *siman* 382.
13. For other statements regarding the creative capacity of *bittahon*, see *Likkutei Sihot* 26, *Beshallah*, no. 2, *se'if* 2; *Torat Menahem* 5745: 5, 2719–20; *Iggerot Kodesh* 9, letter 2843.

to be stated separately. Rather, the obligation of *bittahon* is a service of its own, the essence of which is that a person should rely and depend on God alone, to the extent that he casts his lot entirely upon Him, as it is written, "Cast your burden upon God," i.e., the person depends on no other support in the world apart from God.[14]

This description of *bittahon* as a distinct and independent trait, once again, stands as a counter-point to the *Hazon Ish*'s collapsing of *emuna* and *bittahon* into a single category.

The Extent of *Bittahon*

It is important to emphasize that this assuredness in an outcome of "visible and manifest good" extends to even the most desperate situations. In fact, the Rebbe cited from his father-in-law that the most hopeless circumstances are, in fact, the most fertile grounds for engaging in *bittahon*:

> Complete trust in God is when there is no shadow of an indication as to where help will come from, nor is there any physical source for it.... When there *is* a shadow of an indication, what one has is hope (*tikva*).... For the term "hope" is appropriate in relation to something that tangibly exists.... By contrast, *trust (bittahon)* in God is what one has when he has not even a shadow of an indication that he will be saved. He does not even have a straw to clutch at. He has only his trust in God.[15]

True *bittahon* is complete confidence that God will generate the "visible and manifest good" even in the face of a hopeless situation.

---

14. *Likkutei Sihot* 36, *Shemot*, no. 1, *se'if* 5. For a longer discussion regarding the precise parameters of *emuna* and *bittahon*, see *Likkutei Sihot* 26, *Beshallah*, no. 2.
15. *Likkutei Sihot* 3, *Beshallah*, note 30. Translation is adapted from www.chabad.org/2313742. For similar formulations, see *Likkutei Sihot* 16, *Beshallah*, no. 3, *se'if* 6; ibid., 26, *Beshallah*, no. 2, *se'if* 2; *Torat Menahem* 5745: 5, 2719; *Iggerot Kodesh* 5, letter 1515.

Aspects of a Godly Life

BITTAHON AND HISHTADLUT

Bittahon and Human Passivity in Hasidic Thought

The doctrine of *bittahon*'s efficacy would seemingly engender a posture of passivity toward human initiative. After all, if trust in God always generates the desired outcome, what space could there be for human endeavor? Indeed, some early hasidic thinkers followed this line of reasoning and argued that, to some degree, human planning and action is an affront to proper *bittahon* and impedes its inner workings.[16] For example, R. Yaakov Yosef of Ostrog (1738–1791) saw this quietist approach to problems as the principle undergirding the Talmud's enigmatic[17] line that redemption comes only "when one's attention is diverted":

> The reason why redemption comes at a time of diversion of one's attention is that when a person is conscious, he thinks of various actions by which he may be saved from his trouble, and he has not complete trust in God... therefore he does not receive assistance from God, for God says, "As you wish to save yourself by means of your actions, I do not wish to save you. ..." But when a person removes his attention from his troubles, and says, "Why do I need to perform any actions?" then God, may He be blessed, will do what he wishes and... help him.[18]

Natural Channels According to the Rebbe

The Rebbe, however, limited this form of passivity to a select cadre of completely righteous individuals. These *Tzaddikim* transcend this world to such a degree that it is unnecessary for them to engage in "natural" activities, as their *bittahon* causes God to care for all of their needs. In one talk, the Rebbe identified the biblical Joseph as being such a person. The Sages record that Joseph was punished with additional years in prison for taking the initiative and asking the butler to entreat Pharaoh

---

16. For an analysis of this trend, see Rivka Schatz-Uffenheimer (1993), 83–92. See, however, Jerome Gellman (2006), 343–49, for a critique of Schatz-Uffenheimer's analysis.
17. Sanhedrin 97a.
18. *Sefer R. Yeivi* 29c. Translation is from Rivka Schatz-Uffenheimer (1993), 85–86.

Bittahon: Trusting and Jumping

on his behalf. As the paradigmatic *Tzaddik*, Joseph should have adopted a passive posture toward his imprisonment and trusted that God would set him free.[19]

In contrast to the completely righteous, the Rebbe challenged the vast majority of people to have as much *bittahon* as Joseph did while simultaneously being fully active and engaged on the plane of regular human initiatives. For example, in response to a question about the propriety of investing effort in "making a vessel" to receive God's blessings versus sufficing "with prayer and *bittahon* alone," the Rebbe wrote:

> It is obvious that apart from having *bittahon*, one must also create a "vessel." Indeed, Scripture and rabbinic midrashim are filled with this concept. Endeavors to create a medium within the natural order do not contradict the concept of *bittahon*, since [every Jew] has been told by God, the Lord in whom he trusts, that "He will bless him in all that he does,"[20] and not when he sits idle.[21]

Despite the logical attractiveness of a passive approach, the Rebbe argued that the Torah itself affirms and makes obligatory the need for human initiative to solve problems. As such, *bittahon* cannot bleed into quietist passivity.

---

19. *Likkutei Sihot* 15, *Hosafot*, 486–87. See also *Likkutei Sihot* 3, *Vayehi*, *se'if* 8; ibid., 26, *Beshallah*, no. 2, *se'if* 4. Similarly, in *Likkutei Sihot* 16, *Beshallah*, no. 3, *se'if* 11, the Rebbe associated Shabbat as a time of utterly passive *bittahon* which disallows any form of human initiative.
20. Paraphrase of Deuteronomy 15:18. This verse is often cited in Chabad literature as teaching the importance of creating a "vessel" in which to receive the divine bounty. See, for example, *Likkutei Torah*, *Devarim* 37b; *Derekh Mitzvotekha*, *Sefer HaMitzvot*, *Mitzvat Tiglahat Metzora* 107b. The Rebbe also cited this verse dozens of times. See, for example, *Likkutei Sihot* 1, *Vayak'hel*, *se'if* 2; *Torat Menahem* 5716: 2, 140–41. The following words "and not when he sits idle" are from *Sifrei Devarim*, *piska* 123. The Rebbe also cited this midrash in *Likkutei Sihot* 18, *Balak*, no. 4, *se'if* 3.
21. *Likkutei Sihot* 15, *Hosafot*, 486. The Rebbe repeated the need to combine *bittahon* with human initiative in several contexts; see, for example, *Likkutei Sihot* 36, *Shemot*, *se'if* 5 (especially note 17); *Iggerot Kodesh* 6, letter 1612, regarding the need to follow a doctor's orders.

The Relationship Between *Bittahon* and Natural Channels

This affirmation of human initiative, however, does not weaken one's complete trust in God. In the continuation of his letter and elsewhere, the Rebbe outlined two basic rules for the interplay between *bittahon* and human initiative (*hishtadlut*). One rule relates to a person's mindset and attitude, while the second to practical caps on the level of one's engagement in natural pathways.

The Proper Mindset

Even as the Rebbe encouraged the pursuit of natural pathways, he established a clear hierarchy between these human initiatives and *bittahon*:

> The vessel and the means must be employed only because we were thus commanded. If, however, one considers [the vessel and the means] to be beneficial or harmful on their own, he debases the attribute of *bittahon*.[22]

Despite an individual's investment in natural pathways, he must realize that such efforts have no independent standing and do not generate the desired result. For example, when working for a living, one must be cognizant that it is God who is providing his livelihood and therefore place his trust in Him. The sole legitimate motivation for the actual labor is that God commanded human beings to be engaged in these pursuits. As such, in one talk the Rebbe described the attitude of a Jew toward pursuit of a livelihood as "with half a heart...due to necessity alone... forced by the word of God."[23]

Practical Limitations on Human Initiative

Viewing God and not human initiative as the ultimate source of goodness generates limits on the extent of a person's worldly efforts. For example, if a conflict were to arise between one's service of God and the natural

---

22. *Likkutei Sihot* 15, *Hosafot*, 486. See also *Likkutei Sihot* 10, *Hosafot*, 289; ibid., 16, *se'if* 6; ibid., 18, *Balak*, no. 4, *se'if* 3; ibid., 31, *Purim* no. 1, *se'if* 4.
23. *Torat Menahem* 5725: 3, 207–8.

means with which one is engaged, the former must be favored over the latter. In one talk, the Rebbe concretely demonstrated this point by arguing that a person should not think that his livelihood will suffer if he spends extra time in prayer or donates generously to charity. Rather, within reason, a person should "give up on involvements in the natural order, as he knows 'the blessing of God bestows wealth' (Prov. 10:22)."[24] Limiting one's divine service in the face of financial concerns would be an affront to proper *bittahon*.

Similarly, one's *bittahon* must be comprehensive and constant. Natural efforts, by contrast, are not absolutely and perpetually obligatory. If a person tried to achieve the desired results through natural means but failed, then he has fulfilled his obligation and does not need to persist in his worldly efforts. As the Rebbe wrote:[25]

> A person is commanded to do only what he is capable of doing, for "the Holy One, blessed be He, does not confront His created beings with unfair demands" (Avoda Zara 3a). Accordingly, if [at some point] one is incapable of making a vessel [to receive God's blessings], that itself is a sign that the Merciful One has exempted him from [the responsibility in this instance]. And this [should] not weaken his *bittahon* that his request will be fulfilled.

As the only true source of blessing, *bittahon* transcends the obligation of human effort.

In summary, the Rebbe's system of *bittahon* consists of two key elements. On the one hand, *bittahon* requires a person to completely rely on God that a specific positive outcome will occur, and it is this absolute reliance that will result in God generating the "visible and manifest good." On the other hand, despite *bittahon*'s efficacy, there is a divine imperative to simultaneously be active along natural pathways.

---

24. *Likkutei Sihot* 18, Balak, no. 4, *se'if* 5. See also *Likkutei Sihot* 10, Hosafot, 289.
25. *Likkutei Sihot* 15, Hosafot, 486.

Aspects of a Godly Life

BITTAHON AND THE DIVINE ESSENCE
Standing, Walking, and Jumping

While the Rebbe textually justified both of these assertions, the system as a whole seems to be riddled with inconsistencies. First, why does complete reliance on God generate a good result irrespective of the person's other merits? Why should trust in God be independently effective? Second, in a system that fundamentally sees *bittahon* as the source of blessings, why would God command that we concurrently work through ineffective natural channels? To put the question in terms of the sources cited above, what is the Rebbe's conceptual break with R. Yaakov Yosef of Ostrog, who associated effective *bittahon* with a posture of passivity?

The Rebbe's responses to these questions interwove *bittahon* with several other prominent themes of his holistic philosophy. One central source for the underlying basis of *bittahon* is a rich *maamar* from the summer of 5712/1952,[26] which contextualizes *bittahon* within a matrix of various levels of divine service and the aspects of divinity to which they correspond.

Basing himself on earlier Chabad sources, the Rebbe analogized modalities of serving God with states of motion. "Standing" consists of having both feet firmly planted on the ground. Correspondingly, a "stander" is a person who serves God in an organized fashion and uses his logic to progress procedurally from one level to the next.[27] This form of service, which remains bounded by finite human logic, reaches God as He "fills" the worlds and is manifest within them. By contrast, "walking" characterizes a higher form of service, in which a person rises to a level where he serves God in a manner that is "above reason and logic."[28] Such a person reaches God as He "encircles" the worlds.[29]

The Rebbe emphasized that even the "walker" is still somewhat associated with the boundedness of a finite human being. He serves God in a fashion that is above logic, but only due to the fact that logic

---

26. Maamar "Mi Mana 5712" (*Torat Menahem* 5712: 3, 26–36).
27. *Torat Menahem* 5712: 3, 29.
28. Ibid., 31.
29. See chapter 2, section "The Lower Unity and the Upper Unity," for an elaboration of the different aspects of divinity signified by these terms.

dictates that God, who surpasses human logic, should be served in such a manner. Similarly, while the aspect of God who "encircles" the world transcends creation, it is still associated with creation, if only to describe God's transcendence.[30]

The Rebbe argued that these limitations in the types of service and their corresponding manifestations of Godliness impact the level of *bittahon* of which such people are capable. Whenever we speak of God as He "fills" the worlds or even as He transcends but still relates to the worlds, we are identifying God and the world as distinct entities. This gap between God and the world allows for the possibility that a person's trust that God will orchestrate events in a very specific way will go unfulfilled.[31]

There is a form of service and corresponding level of divinity, however, that simultaneously transcends and encompasses these two lower levels. Above the "stander" and the "walker" is the person who "jumps" or "leaps" in the service of God. This person, who has both feet off the ground, completely transcends finite human limitations and thus has the ability to access the Divine Essence itself, which similarly exists beyond all bounds.[32]

It is at this level that one's *bittahon* will surely elicit a divine response. As the Rebbe explained:

> The primary form of *bittahon*...is from the Divine Essence, as on this level the *bittahon* is absolute, since there is no place for the existence of *hitzonim* (outside forces) and a person can be certain that the divine influence will be drawn downward (into this world).[33]

---

30. *Torat Menahem* 5712: 3, 32–33.
31. Ibid., 26–28; 34–35.
32. In addition to the concept of *bittahon*, Chabad literature associates the service of "jumping" with the holiday of Passover (see *Likkutei Torah, Tzav*, 16a; *Likkutei Sihot* 17, *Pesah*, no. 1, *se'if* 6; ibid., *Tazria*, no. 1, *se'ifim* 6–9) and with proper repentance (see *Likkutei Torah, Derashot LeShabbat Shuva*, 65a; *Likkutei Sihot* 37, *Erev Pesah* 5751, *se'if* 5; ibid., 39, *Beurim BeLikkutei Levi Yitzhak al Iggeret HaTeshuva, Iggeret* 6, *se'ifim* 4–5; *Torat Menahem* 5711: 2, 349; ibid., 5712: 3, 33; ibid., 5727: 3, 219–24; *maamar* "Lehavin Inyan Simhat Torah 5742" (*Sefer Maamarim Melukat*, vol. 1, 372–78).
33. *Torat Menahem* 5712: 3, 35.

As we have seen, when a person reaches a level of complete self-sacrifice and self-transcendence he reveals his own *yehida*, which is utterly united with the Divine Essence, the only true substance of reality. As such, there is no gap between the person, the world, and the Divine Essence, and consequently there is no possibility that a person's wish for the manifest good will be unrequited.[34]

The Rebbe succinctly summarized this theme in a later talk. After reiterating that *bittahon* means absolute trust that the manifest good will materialize, the Rebbe said, "One might well ask: Why is such an individual certain that God will provide him with all his requirements? Does God owe him anything?"[35] In response, the Rebbe offered an unequivocal formulation: "The answer is simple: he and God are one." It is the identity of the person with God, revealed through self-transcendence, that is the ultimate basis for trust in the Divine Essence.

Natural Channels and the Divine Essence

Armed with this background for the efficacy of *bittahon*, we can now turn to the Rebbe's perspective on the importance of working through natural channels despite their seeming inconsequence. In one talk the Rebbe directly addressed the interplay between human activity and *bittahon* within the framework of the God-world relationship.[36]

The Rebbe began the talk with a verse from the book of Micah which characterizes the end of the exile as a time of heightened *bittahon* in which the remnant of the Jewish people will "not place hope in man, nor look forward to help from a mortal" (Mic. 5:6). While a simple understanding of this verse might have led one to adopt a passive approach to human problems, the Rebbe noted that this posture is contradicted by large swaths of traditional sources.[37] Therefore, he reiterated his opinion that even while working within natural channels, one should trust in God as the only true source of sustenance and help.

---

34. See also *Torat Menahem* 5744: 2, 1140–41, where the Rebbe associated the highest level of *bittahon* with the revelation of the Divine Essence.
35. *Sihot Kodesh* 5734: 2, 398. Translation is adapted from www.chabad.org/2313704.
36. *Likkutei Sihot* 18, *Balak*, no. 4.
37. Ibid., *se'if* 3.

Bittahon: Trusting and Jumping

At this stage of his analysis, the Rebbe raised two possible formulations according to which natural means and efforts are considered to be at once fundamentally required and fundamentally ineffective:

> The requirement to *do*, i.e., to create a natural conduit through which one's living is to be earned, may be approached in one of two ways:
> (1) One knows that nature per se has no self-sufficient existence and is no more than "an ax in the hand of the woodchopper"; nevertheless, since God commanded that one should do, i.e., one should create a natural medium for one's livelihood, nature acquires a certain standing in one's mind, even though this status does not derive from nature in its own right but only by virtue of God's command.
> (2) One engages in natural ways and means only because God so commanded. The natural order is of no account in one's eyes because one perceives it as nothing more than a means of fulfilling God's will.[38]

The first approach posits that God's command to work through natural channels grants these channels an independent, albeit ineffectual, status. The Rebbe argued against this perspective since it incorrectly severs the natural order from God, creating a duality where none should exist.

Instead, the Rebbe concluded that the ultimate synthesis of *bittahon* and human activity is the realization that the natural order itself is itself infused with Godliness:

> The ultimate divine intent is not that the natural order should cease to exist, but that it should be refined and elevated to the extent that it is apparent to every eye that nature is one with God. With regard to the concept at hand – not to place one's hope in

---

38. Ibid., *se'if* 4. The verse the Rebbe quotes is a paraphrase of Is. 10:15. Regarding the first of these two approaches that the Rebbe enumerated, see *Likkutei Sihot* 4, *Shelah*, *se'if* 3, where the Rebbe described the spies Moses sent to the Land of Israel as having this perspective.

man – the divine intent is not that help via mortals will cease to exist. Rather, the natural order will then be so utterly fused with Godliness that we will perceive this help not as help from man, but only as help from God.[39]

Thus, the concept of "not placing hope in man" strikes a middle ground between the incorrect extremes of either abandoning natural channels or granting them an independent identity. Rather, the ideal level is for one to receive one's help "from man," representing the natural order, all the while being clearly conscious of the essential divinity of the natural order itself. As we have seen, this fusion of the natural world with God occurs with the disclosure of the Divine Essence.

Using a similar line of reasoning, the Rebbe once noted that his call for a complete reliance on God while still being actively engaged in natural channels requires the combination of contradictory poles. The only possible justification for this seemingly impossible task is a Jew's rootedness in the Divine Essence, which transcends and encompasses all conflicting categories. As the Rebbe once articulated this theme:

> Both things are expected of a Jew. This is possible because every Jew is connected with God, who can simultaneously accommodate two opposite thrusts...together with our trust in God, individual effort and initiative are required. And since both trust and initiative stem from the Godly soul, which is "an actual part of God" (*Tanya, Likkutei Amarim,* ch. 2) that can embrace opposites, these two thrusts are in fact not contradictory. Rather, one complements the other.[40]

As we have seen many times over, the disclosure of the Divine Essence allows for the coexistence and even unification of opposing poles. The connection of a Jew to the Divine Essence allows him to combine complete reliance on God with human initiative.

---

39. *Likkutei Sihot* 18, *Balak,* no. 4, *se'if* 4.
40. Ibid., 3, *Beshallah, se'if* 6.

Bittahon: Trusting and Jumping

In summary, we can now properly understand and contextualize the Rebbe's approach to *bittahon*. Ultimately, the root of *bittahon* is the identity of a Jew with the Divine Essence. As such, there is no room for any other forces to disrupt the flow of "visible and manifest good" to the Jew who is firmly united with the Divine Essence. The disclosure of the Divine Essence leads to the realization that the natural world is itself utterly one with God, and hence there is no conflict between engagement with natural channels and complete reliance on God. Working through nature is a form of engagement with the Divine Essence itself.

LIVING WITH *BITTAHON*

The Rebbe translated his construct of *bittahon* into clear and practical guidance for living, both for the individual and for the community. In his view, *bittahon* comes to the fore practically following the inculcation of a firm belief in divine providence. After *hashgaha* teaches a person to see every difficult situation as a divine mission for personal and cosmic advancement, *bittahon* then provides the necessary tools and confidence to succeed in this mission.

"Jump First!"

The Rebbe would often quote a statement of the Maharash, the fourth Lubavitcher Rebbe: "The world thinks that when it is impossible to crawl under [an obstacle] then one should jump over it. I, however, say that one should jump first."[41] According to the Rebbe, this teaching encodes a most crucial lesson regarding obstacles that impede divine missions:

> In all matters of Godly service one should not be fazed by impediments, obstacles, and limitations. Rather, one should not reckon with limitations when engaging in divine service: "Jump first!"[42]

---

41. This phrase was first publicized by R. Yosef Yitzhak. See *Iggerot Kodesh Admor Moharaayatz* 1, letter 617. For the importance of the fact that the statement was originally concealed and only disclosed as a later date, see *Torat Menahem* 5749: 1, 82–83.
42. *Torat Menahem* 5746: 1, 145.

Aspects of a Godly Life

Instead of adopting a posture of emotional fear and practical hesitance, one should rather confidently jump headfirst and assume that the positive outcome will occur.[43] As the Rebbe explained, the very *bittahon* expressed by remaining unfazed by practical limitations will guarantee success.

To illustrate the Rebbe's manifold applications of the Maharash's teaching and its interconnection with the trait of *bittahon*, let us look at the Rebbe's practical guidance regarding two seemingly unrelated issues: family planning and institutional finances.

"Jump First!" and Family Planning

The Rebbe emphatically opposed family planning. In cases of medical concern, he emphasized that halakhic authorities allow certain forms of birth control and advised people to consult rabbinic authorities. Absent of medical concerns, though, he exhorted couples to not delay having children, or to "space" their children.

While there are several layers to the Rebbe's arguments against family planning,[44] one recurring theme in his many talks on this matter is *bittahon*. The Rebbe acknowledged that the blessing of children, and especially many children, is often accompanied with a variety of spiritual, educational, and financial challenges. The Rebbe argued, however, that these needs will be more than adequately met by God, who has blessed and provided the parents with the unique opportunity and obligation to procreate.

For example, in a talk to the Lubavitch Women's Organization, the Rebbe highlighted the extensive efforts that biblical Hanna invested to merit a child. After characteristically noting that every story in the Torah teaches a contemporary lesson, the Rebbe commented:

---

43. As noted above, the Rebbe tied in "jumping" with connecting oneself with the Divine Essence, which precipitates the highest level of *bittahon*. Similarly, the Rebbe spoke of following the Maharash's teaching of "jumping first" as a means of connection with the Divine Essence. See, for example, *Torat Menahem* 5743: 1, 288–92.
44. See, for example, *Likkutei Sihot* 25, *Noah*, no. 3, *se'ifim* 8–12; *Iggerot Kodesh* 4, letter 828. For a broad compilation of sources and perspectives from the Rebbe on this topic, see Yosef Yitzhak Halevi Segel (5775).

Bittahon: Trusting and Jumping

> This story emphasizes the extent to which we should negate the whole idea of "family planning." Rather, we need to fulfill the mitzva of "be fruitful and multiply" without any calculations, from a place of faith and trust (*emuna uvittahon*) in God. It has already been noted many times how the calculation that another child will lead to additional expenses regarding livelihood... [is refuted], as livelihood is granted by God, since He created the whole world and sustains it... and it is obvious that God can provide for another child! However, God wants one's livelihood to come through the making of a "vessel" in a natural fashion, as the Torah commands: "One cannot rely on a miracle" (Pesahim 64b).[45]

The confidence endowed by proper *bittahon* neutralizes any hesitation that might stem from the desire to be financially prudent.

The Rebbe similarly allayed the self-doubt of potential parents regarding their capabilities to properly raise their children. As he once said:

> When one approaches a Jew and tells him that he is obligated to fulfill the mitzva of "be fruitful and multiply..." he might ask: "Is this possible? First, I need to become a Torah scholar (*lamdan*) and one who fears Heaven... and we must act properly in all our affairs in order to ensure that we educate our children properly!" *Regarding this, the response is: Jump first!* We know all of the rationalizations... and therefore despite the fact that this person is certainly correct in his claim that he needs to grow in his learning of Torah and his fear of Heaven – still, "if a *mitzva* comes into your hands do not let it go sour!" (Rashi on Ex. 12:17).[46] [Emphasis added.]

The Rebbe's application of his proactive concept of *bittahon* to family planning is clear. When presented with an opportunity to do a mitzva, and especially a mitzva as precious as bringing more Jewish souls into

---

45. *Torat Menahem* 5743: 3, 1481.
46. Ibid., 5744: 1, 160.

the world, one should act without hesitation or calculation, fully confident that God will orchestrate the proper outcome.

"Jump First!" and the Finances of Torah Institutions

The Rebbe felt that this *bittahon*-based jumping was particularly relevant for people involved in spreading Torah and mitzvot to others. One practical expression of this *bittahon* relates to the financial structure of Torah institutions. The Rebbe enjoined the leaders of such institutions to "jump first" and to not limit the institutions' expenditures to their predicted revenue. Rather, within reason, *bittahon* in the desired outcome should be the guiding financial principle.

Just a few months into his leadership, the Rebbe underscored this point.[47] After describing the need to spread Torah beyond the sanctified space of the *beit midrash*, he directly addressed the administrators of educational institutions "both in this city and in the periphery." He noted that managers usually first calculate an institution's income and then create programming that is circumscribed by that sum. The Rebbe, however, argued that this was not the proper way to run a Torah institution. After citing the Maharash's teaching to jump first, the Rebbe asserted:

> Regarding matters that concern fulfilling God's mission, matters of Torah and mitzvot...the aforementioned sequence of calculating expenditure in proportion to revenue is considered an "upside-down world".... [Rather,] we must begin with the primary issue, which is to...properly fulfill the goal and mission of God, and then, after calculating what the expenditures will be, one should search for methods to attain the income necessary to cover the costs.[48]

Similarly, less than two years after these remarks, the Rebbe chastised a Chabad organization for curtailing their expenses based on their financial means:

---

47. Ibid., 5711: 2, 204–13.
48. Ibid., 205. See also *Torat Menahem* 5747: 1, 497–98.

Bittahon: Trusting and Jumping

> It is amazing that an organization connected with my revered father-in-law, the Rebbe, should limit its outlay to such an extent, so that it should not exceed its income. It seems to me that this is the only organization within the precincts of Lubavitch that is conducted in this way. I would not intervene in this matter if not for my concern that due to [this] policy, you limit your activity even where it is very much needed. There is surely no need for me to remind you of the attribute of *bittahon* in general.[49]

Once again, we see that this proactive stance of jumping first is a direct outgrowth of proper *bittahon*. While fundraising and other natural means are integral aspects of managing an organization and must be tirelessly engaged, the manager's limited expectations for the revenue of such avenues should not create an artificial ceiling.

"Jump First!" and the World of Chaos

Despite the categoric nature of his formulations, the Rebbe did place limits on what should be considered possible. Employing kabbalistic imagery, he differentiated between reckless and unrealistic behavior stemming from the "world of chaos," and a more grounded optimism that stemmed from the "world of order." Even when jumping above the natural order, one's expectations must have some rootedness in the realities of this world.

In one talk, for example, the Rebbe said that some people were taking "Jump first!" too literally and were behaving rashly:

> There are those who caught on [to "Jump first!"] and began to behave in a manner befitting the "world of chaos," meaning that they are jumping without any limit at all! For example, they borrow huge sums of money – for holy purposes, of course – in a manner that even with a miracle they will not be able to repay.... Therefore, we need to clarify that the proclamation of "Jump first!" needs to be in a manner that befits the "world of order."[50]

---

49. *Iggerot Kodesh* 7, letter 2090. Translation is adapted from. www.chabad.org/2313507.
50. *Torat Menahem* 5743: 3, 1285–87.

It seems, though, that even this circumspection was established begrudgingly. In the continuation of this talk, the Rebbe expressed understanding for those who tried to completely transcend reasonable limitations and assured them that due to their proper intentions God would help them repay their accrued debts. On a different occasion, the Rebbe expressed this limitation as follows:

> A person came to me with a question of why do I limit him with the limitations of "the world of order"? What difference does it make if "Jump first!" is [executed] from the "world of chaos"; the main point is that it should be "Jump first!"
>
> But I cannot do anything in this regard. We live based on the Torah in the "world of order" and therefore, we are obligated that all our affairs, even "Jump first!" should be in the "world of order."[51]

The Torah itself forces us to maintain a tense balance between jumping first and not completely ignoring the realities of this world. As the Rebbe once put it, one must jump over the mountains, while still keeping the mountains in sight.[52]

Optimism

Another central application of the Rebbe's approach to *bittahon* is constant optimism. As discussed, no matter how dire the situation, a person has the ability to generate a positive outcome through a *bittahon*-based vision of the desired resolution. Thus, the Rebbe would frequently counsel people in desperate situations to think positively, thereby empowering them to create a positive reality for themselves.[53]

---

51. Ibid., 5744: 1, 160.
52. Ibid., 5743: 3, 1286.
53. The Rebbe's perspective on the power of positive thinking should be contextualized within the more general framework of the hasidic notion of the creative capacity of speech. *Tanya, Shaar HaYihud VehaEmuna*, ch. 1, describes how God creates the world through speech. Similarly, the Alter Rebbe (cited in *Me'a She'arim*, 28a–b) says that human speech has a similar creative capacity. For this idea in the thought of the Rebbe, see Alon Dahan (2014), 82–96. While this idea is common to kabbalistic and hasidic texts as outlined by Moshe Idel (1995), 215–18, the Rebbe in

Bittahon: Trusting and Jumping

The Rebbe articulated this principle in dozens of letters to those suffering from sicknesses.[54] Though he consistently recommended that patients punctiliously follow the treatment plans of the most up-to-date specialists,[55] he constantly reminded his interlocutors that a doctor's negative prognosis should have no bearing on their mood and mindset. He tried to empower patients and their families to place their trust in God, cultivating a sense of security and good-spiritedness even in the most difficult of situations, and thereby transform the situation for the better.

For example, the Rebbe wrote the following to a man whose wife received a terminal prognosis:

> This is in reply to your letter...in which you write about what you heard from the doctor [i.e., a negative prognosis about your wife's health] and how disheartening this was to both you and your wife, may she live. I am astonished, for the saying of the *Tzemah Tzedek* in commenting on the expression of our Sages that "permission was granted the healer to heal"[56] seems to have escaped your memory. The *Tzemah Tzedek* noted: "He has permission to heal, but not – Heaven forbid – to bring about a crestfallen spirit...."
>
> Particularly now, in our present era, when new methods of treatment and new medications are discovered daily, it flies in the face of logic to foretell future events as your doctor did.... If only you and your wife would be strong in your *bittahon* in the Creator and Conductor of the world, who oversees each and every person with individual *hashgaha*, then in the very near future it will be clearly demonstrated to you that the doctor's prognosis is false.[57]

Iggerot Kodesh 6, letter 1593, indicates that an innovation of later Chabad leaders is that even unspoken thoughts have a creative capacity.

54. See *Likkutei Sihot* 36, 281–88, and Shalom Wineburg (2005), 57–111, for a sampling of such letters.
55. See, for example, the letters collected in *Likkutei Sihot* 36, *Hosafot*, 276–78.
56. Bava Kama 85a.
57. *Iggerot Kodesh* 15, letter 5499. Translation is adapted from www.chabad.org/2306900. For similar letters, in which the Rebbe counseled people to follow the advice of doctors practically but to mentally disavow their negative prognosis, see *Likkutei Sihot* 36, *Hosafot*, 286–88.

Aspects of a Godly Life

The negative prognosis of the specialist is medical overreach. At the same time the patient's own *bittahon* has the power to bring about healing and recovery. As noted above, this approach is not meant to "break nature" but rather to infuse miraculous success into natural processes, including medical research, diagnosis, and prescriptions.

In another letter, the Rebbe took a harsher tone and reprimanded a hasid who he felt was perseverating on the medical conditions of his wife and granddaughter. After responding that he would pray for them, the Rebbe continued:

> I am not pleased with the behavior of *anshei shelomeinu* [a common term used in Chabad circles to refer to fellow Hasidim] who exaggerate, and overly intensify any hint of a health issue in their speech and writing. This runs contrary to the desire of our leaders (*nesi'im*, literally, "princes"), who often taught, "Think positive, and it will be positive."[58]

The Rebbe consistently emphasized that an attitude of worry and fear runs counter to the thrust of Chabad teachings.

BITTAHON, "JUMP FIRST!" AND DIRA BATAHTONIM

Similar to many other hasidic concepts, the Rebbe felt that *bittahon* was acutely relevant for the people tasked to finish transforming the world into a home for God. First, the people living in the end of exile need to deeply inculcate a proper sense of *bittahon* to garner the strength to fulfill their difficult mission. A sense of assurance in the coming success of the mission will propel them to jump over any apparent impediment. Also, this form of human service will elicit the parallel and ultimate jump by God back into His original abode of this lowly world.

Bittahon to Fulfill the Mission

In a 1974 Rosh HaShana letter, the Rebbe returned to the theme of creating a *Dira BaTahtonim* and highlighted the difficulty of this task. After

---

58. *Iggerot Kodesh* 4, letter 937. See chapter 17 for the precise definition of the term *nesi'im*. In context, it refers to the first six leaders of Chabad.

Bittahon: Trusting and Jumping

describing the need to acknowledge God's sovereignty and to create a home for Him, the Rebbe continued:

> The question arises: How can every Jew be expected to attain such a level, and to do so not only truthfully but happily as well? This question is accentuated when one realizes that on the one hand, the *Dira BaTahtonim* is to be built in a world that is spiritually lowly and that is physical and materialistic, in a world in which Jews are – physically – "the least among the nations"; and on the other hand, this task is demanded of every Jew, placed as he is in a predicament in which his indispensable needs (such as eating, drinking, sleeping, and working) occupy a great part of his time and exertion, leaving little time for holy and spiritual matters. How, then, can a Jew be expected to attain such a level?[59]

The Rebbe's response honed in on the importance of internalizing the attribute of *bittahon* and living according to its precepts. Complete reliance on God encompasses not only one's spiritual and physical needs, but, perhaps most importantly, also relates to the success of this cosmic mission:

> Having trust in God means that one feels a certainty and a conviction that God will help overcome all of life's difficulties, whether material or spiritual, since He is "my light and my salvation." Every man and woman will certainly be able to fulfill their mission in this world – and with joy, great joy – when they consider that it is God Himself who chose them to be His emissary in the world, to build Him a *Dira BaTahtonim*. Moreover, they have God's assurance that as they carry out His mission, He is their light, help, and strength.[60]

---

59. *Likkutei Sihot 9, Hosafot*, 492. Translation adapted from www.chabad.org/2313668.
60. Ibid.

Proper *bittahon* allows the individual and collective to confront their mission of creating a *Dira BaTahtonim* without being paralyzed by the immensity of the task.[61]

Jumping and *Dira BaTahtonim*

On other occasions the Rebbe emphasized that when the Jewish people serve God in the manner of "Jump first!" and transcend normal human limitations, it will elicit a parallel response from God. He, too, will jump over all of the barriers and once again reveal Himself in the lowest realm. On Hoshana Rabba 5743/1982 he explained that this is hinted at in the verses that conclude Moses's final blessing to the Jewish people:

> Yeshurun, there is none like God; He who rides the heavens is at your assistance, and with His majesty, [He rides] the skies, which are the abode for the God who precedes all, and below, are the mighty ones of the world. He expelled the enemy from before you, and said, "Destroy!" (Deut. 33:26–27).

Moses begins by highlighting God's utter transcendence, and then turns to His dominion over the "mighty ones of the world." This sequence, understood symbolically, is integral to one's perspective:

> The verse does not begin with the fact that there are "the mighty ones of the world" and [as a response] also "the God who precedes all" [who stand in opposition to each other]. Rather, in the fashion of jumping first, Moses first says to a Jew: "[There is a] God who precedes all" and everything else is beneath Him... therefore a Jew should never be troubled by the concealments of this world.[62]

A Jew must first realize that he is bound to God, who exists entirely above all the possible impediments to divine service. This connection

---

61. See also *Torat Menahem* 5729: 2, 189; ibid., 5747: 1, 403–4, where the Rebbe similarly emphasized that one must have *bittahon* that God will facilitate the completion of the mission of creating a *Dira BaTahtonim*.
62. *Torat Menahem* 5743: 1, 254.

Bittahon: Trusting and Jumping

allows a Jew to not be fazed by any worldly matter, but rather to jump over all obstacles.

This leads to God's reciprocal leap over the *Seder Hishtalshelut* to become manifest within the confines of this lowly world:

> The notion of "Jump first!" is also expressed in the connection between the "God who precedes all," whose abode is in the skies, and the Jew who lives in this lowest of all the worlds, ... as was explained above, through the fulfillment of Torah and mitzvot in this physical world, one can break all of the barriers of the world and make a *Dira BaTahtonim* for God, meaning to say that this lowest of the worlds can become a dwelling which reveals the Divine Essence.[63]

The ultimate expression of jumping is the reunification of the Divine Essence with its original abode. This divine jump directly follows an initial human leap: a service permeated with *bittahon*.[64]

Natural Channels and a *Dira BaTahtonim*

The Rebbe also underscored the connection between *bittahon* and the Messianic Era when discussing the proper balance between *bittahon* and working through natural channels. As noted above, the Rebbe described the highest level of *bittahon* as attainable by perceiving the Divine Essence within the natural channels.

Once, after outlining this perspective, the Rebbe concluded with a direct message to his generation:

> This lesson is also appropriate in these last days of exile ... all the revelations of the future redemption "depend on our actions and

---

63. *Torat Menahem* 5743: 1, 254–55. See, there, that "the mighty ones of the world" will themselves be transformed from adversaries to people to proclaim and reveal the existence of God.
64. For other instances where the Rebbe associated the service of "Jump first!" with the creation of a *Dira BaTahtonim* and the ultimate redemption, see *Torat Menahem* 5743: 1, 589; ibid., 5749: 3, 87–101 (here the Rebbe also mentioned *shetut dikedusha*); ibid., 5750: 3, 120–27 (especially page 127).

divine service throughout the era of exile" (*Tanya, Likkutei Amarim*, ch. 37). In particular, this applies in the present generation, when we are making the final preparations for the redemption to be led by *Mashiah*.... At this time, therefore, every individual's divine service should have at least a foretaste of the level where we will "not place our hope in man" (Mic. 5:6).

One should not prize the worldly mediums of the natural order at all, but should place his trust in God alone. Through this, every individual will be redeemed from the worries and problems that disturb him.... And this individual redemption which will be experienced by each person will also serve as the preparation and the medium for the all-encompassing redemption led by *Mashiah*, and to "the day that will be entirely Shabbat and rest for life everlasting" (Tamid 33b).[65]

The fact that the Messianic Era is characterized by the unification of transcendent Godliness and the natural world creates a special opportunity and obligation on the generation before *Mashiah* to live in accordance with this reality. Living with this heightened level of *bittahon* brings redemption to the individual and to the world as a whole.

CONCLUSION

The Rebbe's construct and application of *bittahon* are integral elements of his teaching. On the theoretical level, he defined *bittahon* as an independent and creative force and interwove its efficacy with the nature of a Jew's connection to the Divine Essence. On the practical plane, the Rebbe enjoined his students to have *bittahon*, which would provide them with the confidence and optimism to tirelessly work on all planes to transform the world into a home for God.

---

65. *Likkutei Sihot* 18, Balak, no. 4, *se'if* 9. Translation is adapted from www.chabad.org/2296508. The connection between the Messianic Era and a *bittahon*-based perspective that allows a person to see the Divine Essence disclosed in the natural world also seems to be the import of *Likkutei Sihot* 16, Beshallah, no. 3, *se'ifim* 6–7, where the Rebbe argued that the Jewish people needed to be trained toward this perspective before entering the Land of Israel.

Secondary Literature Consulted for Chapter 11, "*Bittahon*: Trusting and Jumping."

Mendel Kalmenson, *A Time to Heal: The Lubavitcher Rebbe's Response to Loss and Tragedy.*

Uri Kaploun and Eliyahu Touger, *As a Father Loves His Only Son: Talks of the Lubavitcher Rebbe on Bitachon.*

Uri Kaploun, *In Good Hands: 100 Letters and Talks of the Lubavitcher Rebbe, Rabbi Menachem M. Schneerson, On Bitachon, Trusting G-d.*

Joseph Telushkin, *Rebbe*, 109–17.

Chapter 12

Simha Breaks Barriers

Simha (joy) is one of the defining features of hasidic life. Characteristically, Chabad teachings probe the source and role of this sublime emotion. The Rebbe extended these teachings to their logical conclusions by constructing a theory and practice of *simha* that places it at the center of the quest to engage the Divine Essence.

SIMHA IN EARLIER JEWISH PHILOSOPHY

Simha in Rabbinic Literature

Rabbinic literature discusses *simha* in, at least, two distinct contexts. The first relates to the holidays, when there is an unequivocal biblical command to be joyful. The Sages understand this mandate as potentially including a wide array of actions, such as eating the meat of the holiday sacrifices,[1] drinking wine,[2] wearing new clothing, singing,[3] and distributing candy to children.[4] Though it is not explicit in the Talmud, many

---

1. Pesahim 109a.
2. Ibid.
3. Arakhin 11a as elucidated by *Emek Berakha, Simhat Yom Tov siman* 1.
4. Y. Pesahim 10:1.

traditional commentators understood that these actions are intended to foster the emotion of joy.[5]

A related but discrete form of *simha* relates to non-holiday periods when there is no explicit biblical mandate for *simha*. Should *simha* be part of a Jew's daily life-experience? One category discussed in rabbinic literature is *simha shel mitzva*, or the *simha* associated with the performance of a mitzva. The Talmud lauds *simha shel mitzva* and asserts that both prayer and prophecy can be properly engaged only in the context of such joy.[6]

One central talmudic passage seems to identify *simha shel mitzva* as the only legitimate expression of *simha*. The Talmud implicitly notes a contradiction between two verses in Ecclesiastes regarding *simha* and resolves them in the following manner: "'So I commended *simha*' (8:15); that is the *simha shel mitzva*. 'And of *simha*: What does it accomplish?' (2:2); that is *simha* that is not *simha shel mitzva*."[7] This passage considers any *simha* not associated with a mitzva as gratuitous and spiritually meaningless.

Definition of *Simha shel Mitzva*

Several medieval authorities accept and amplify the distinction between the admirable *simha shel mitzva* and other forms of *simha*. For example, R. Bahya b. Asher in his book of sermons, *Kad HaKemah*, sharply differentiates between proper and improper *simha*. He begins his entry on *simha* as follows:

> "Serve God with joy, come before Him with song…"(Ps. 100:2). The only proper form of *simha* in this world is in the service of God, and you will not find any holy book praise *simha* except when it is in the context of serving God and understanding God…. Eating, drinking, and the joy of this world do not accompany a person to the World to Come.[8]

---

5. R. Moshe Sternbuch, *Mo'adim UZemanim*, siman 112; R. Joseph B. Soloveitchik, *Shiurim LeZekher Abba Mari*, vol. 2, *Aveilut*.
6. Berakhot 31a.
7. Shabbat 30b.
8. *Kad HaKemah*, "Simha."

Based on his stern outlook toward *simha* that is not *simha shel mitzva*, R. Bahya cautions his readers against expecting a joyful life: "*Simha* does not await a person in this world, and one who is joyful today will not be joyful tomorrow...this is what Solomon said: 'And of *simha*: What does it accomplish?'" According to R. Bahya, the Talmud's favoring of *simha shel mitzva* has tremendous ramifications for the emotional texture of life. As all other forms of joy are meaningless and ephemeral, one cannot expect *simha* to be a constant companion. [9]

Simha According to Rambam

A different tenor regarding the centrality and constancy of *simha* emerges from Rambam's writings. First, following the talmudic paradigm, he lavishly extols the virtues of *simha shel mitzva*, even casting it as a paramount principle in the service of God. After describing the joyous celebrations that occurred in the *Beit HaMikdash* during Sukkot, Rambam pivots to use this *simha* as a model for *simha shel mitzva* more generally:

> The joy with which a person should rejoice in the fulfillment of the mitzvot and in the love of God who commanded them is a great service. Whoever holds himself back from this rejoicing is worthy of retribution, as it states: "Because you did not serve God, your Lord, with happiness and a glad heart" (Deut. 28:47).[10]

Rambam elevates *simha shel mitzva* to a "great service" whose omission is a punishable offense.

Importantly, Rambam does not feel that *simha shel mitzva* exhausts religiously meaningful joy. Earlier in *Mishneh Torah*, when discussing proper character traits, Rambam speaks of cultivating a consistent joyful disposition:

---

9. See *Tzavaat R. Yaakov MiLisa, siman* 8 (printed in *Derekh HaHayyim HaShalem* [Bnei Brak, 5747], 300), where R. Yaakov of Lisa contends that any joy outside of *simha shel mitzva* is reprehensible, as it mitigates the obligatory anxiety that Jews must feel due to the ubiquity of sin.
10. *Mishneh Torah, Hilkhot Shofar VeSukka VeLulav* 8:15.

The straight path: This [involves discovering] the midpoint temperament of each and every trait that man possesses [within his personality]. This refers to the trait which is equidistant from either of the extremes, without being close to either of them.... He should not be overly elated and laugh [excessively], nor be sad and depressed in spirit. Rather, he should be quietly happy at all times, with a friendly countenance.[11]

It is not any particular mitzva that engenders this milder *simha*, but the general exhortation to follow the golden mean. The quality of this generic *simha* is less intense than *simha* when performing a mitzva.[12]

Simha in Early Hasidism

One of the hallmarks of early Hasidism was an emphasis on *simha*, as epitomized by the statement of the Baal Shem Tov: "Always be joyful!"[13] Accordingly, the Baal Shem Tov describes sadness as an impediment to spiritual growth rooted in the influence of the evil inclination.[14] In his worldview, the only exception to comprehensive *simha* is a short bout of sadness in the wake of a sin. However, even then, the Baal Shem Tov underscores that this is a mere bump in the joyful path of serving God.[15]

Theoretical Justification for Simha in Tanya

While the Baal Shem Tov pithily hints at the theoretical justifications and practical techniques for constant *simha*, the Alter Rebbe expands both of these fronts.[16] In *Tanya*, he offers a two-pronged justification

---

11. Ibid., *Hilkhot Deot* 1:4. See also ibid., 2:7.
12. For more sources and an enlightening analysis of these forms of *simha* in Rambam's thought, see Ya'akov Blidstein (1980), 145–63.
13. *Tzavaat HaRivash*, *siman* 137. See Ezriel Shochat (1951), 30–43, who identifies the constancy of *simha* as the main innovation of Hasidism. See also *Iggerot Kodesh* 5, letter 1380, and *Torat Menahem* 5746: 1, 600–602, where the Rebbe has a similar analysis of the hasidic contribution to this topic.
14. *Tzavaat HaRivash*, *simanim* 44–45.
15. Ibid., *siman* 46.
16. For an analysis of the Alter Rebbe's approach to *simha*, see Roman A. Foxbrunner (1993), 110–28; Nissan Mindel (1974), 139–48.

for perpetual *simha*. On one level, *simha* is functionally important, as it aids an individual in his epic battle against the evil inclination:

> Truly this should be made known as a cardinal principle, that as with a victory over a physical obstacle, such as in the case of two individuals who are wrestling with each other, each striving to throw the other – *if one is lazy and sluggish he will easily be defeated and thrown, even though he be stronger than the other, exactly so is it in the conquest of one's evil nature.*
>
> It is impossible to conquer [the evil inclination] with laziness and heaviness, *which originate in sadness and in a heart that is dulled like a stone, but rather with alacrity which derives from simha and from a heart that is free and cleansed from any trace of worry and sadness in the world.*[17] [Emphasis added.]

Enthusiasm and dedication are integral ingredients for success in the internal battle that *Tanya* describes. These traits can be cultivated only through a constant sense of *simha*.

More crucially, the Alter Rebbe also casts *simha* in terms that transcend functionality. He taught that the internalization of the hasidic perspective on the God-world relationship will directly generate *simha*. The Alter Rebbe starkly expresses this point in a letter in which he exhorts his hasidim that their material state regarding "food or children" should not negatively affect their disposition:

> And this is the essence of the faith for which man was created: to believe that "there is no place void of Him" (*Tikkunei Zohar, tikkun* 57) and "in the light of the King's countenance there is life" (Prov. 16:15), and, conclusively, "strength and gladness are in His place" (I Chr. 16:27), because He is only good all the time.
>
> Therefore, first of all, man ought to be happy and joyful at all times, and truly live by his faith in God who animates him and is benignant with him every moment. But he who is grieved and laments makes himself appear as if he has it somewhat bad, and

---

17. *Tanya, Likkutei Amarim*, ch. 26.

(is) suffering and lacking some goodness; he is like a heretic, Heaven forfend. That is why the kabbalists strongly rejected the trait of sadness.[18]

In this passage, the Alter Rebbe describes *simha* as the result of understanding God's all-inclusiveness, omnipresence, caring, and goodness. How can a person be dejected if every aspect of his life is directly guided by the Source of all Good?

Techniques Toward Eliciting Simha in Tanya
In line with the Alter Rebbe's general theory that cognitions spark emotions, he advises his readers to set aside time to contemplate these themes as a means of acquiring *simha*.

> This also will be the true *simha* of the soul, especially when one recognizes, at appropriate times, that one needs to purify and illuminate one's soul with gladness of the heart. Let him then concentrate his mind and envisage in his intelligence and understanding the subject of His blessed true unity: how He permeates all worlds, both upper and lower....
> When one will deeply contemplate this, his heart will be gladdened and his soul will rejoice even with *simha* and singing, with all his heart and soul and might, in [the intensity of] this faith, which is tremendous, since this is the [experience of the] very proximity of God, and it is the whole [purpose] of man and the goal of his creation, as well as the creation of all the worlds, both upper and lower, that He may have an abode here below, as will later be explained at length.[19]

Contemplating the hasidic notion of God's oneness will generate a feeling of divine immanence. Being mindful of God's closeness and caring will then lead to perpetual joy.

---

18. *Tanya, Iggeret HaKodesh*, sec. 11.
19. *Tanya, Likkutei Amarim*, ch. 33.

Aspects of a Godly Life

THE REBBE ON THE CONSTANCY AND TECHNIQUE OF *SIMHA*

Introduction

When analyzed in the above context, the Rebbe's contributions to this topic can be divided into two parts. On one level, the Rebbe's discussions of *simha* often remain within the rubric of the ideas delineated above, and his contribution was to expand, sharpen, and apply these themes. In addition, the Rebbe built upon more esoteric Chabad characterizations of *simha* and expanded the theoretical basis and positive effects of *simha* with a particular emphasis on its crucial significance for the time before *Mashiah*.

The Halakhic Obligation for Constant *Simha*

The Rebbe admitted that the significance attributed to constant joy was historically a hasidic innovation, but he nevertheless underscored that the textual roots of hasidic joy are as ancient as halakha itself. In addition to the Alter Rebbe's functional and philosophical arguments for constant *simha*, the Rebbe contended that an implicit imperative for constant *simha* emerges from Rambam's halakhic writings.

As cited above, Rambam refers to *simha shel mitzva* as a "great" and integral element in a Jew's service of God. A cursory reading of the passage indicates that these comments are limited to the time when one is actively fulfilling a formal mitzva. The Rebbe argued, however, that such a limiting understanding of Rambam is unjustifiable in light of the omnipresence of normative obligations and spiritual opportunities in the life of a Jew.

The Rebbe placed great emphasis on the principle expressed in the verse "Know Him in all of your ways,"[20] which Rambam interprets to mean that even a person's mundane activities must be done for the sake of God.[21] As the Rebbe often reiterated, every moment of a person's day presents him with religious obligations and opportunities.[22] If so, every human action can register as an act of divine service that is worthy of

---

20. Prov. 3:6.
21. *Mishneh Torah, Hilkhot Deot* 3:2.
22. See chapter 6, section "Know Him in All of Your Ways."

simha shel mitzva. When one combines the principles of "Know Him in all of your ways" and *simha shel mitzva*, one realizes that the Baal Shem Tov's revelation of the concept of constant *simha* is really the fulfillment of "these two halakhic rulings [of Rambam]."[23]

Techniques for *Simha*

Having identified a halakhic basis for constant *simha*, the Rebbe frequently discussed methods of eliciting and maintaining this joyful disposition. Following his predecessors, he recommended a two-pronged strategy that balanced contemplation with action.

Contemplation

As noted above, the Alter Rebbe recommended contemplating God's unity as a means of generating *simha*. The Rebbe built upon this strategy by contextualizing it within the broader interplay between cognition and emotion in Chabad thought and by elucidating several related themes for contemplation.

In one talk, after emphasizing the importance of omnipresent *simha*, the Rebbe directly asked how the Torah could command a person to be happy:

> Seemingly, a person could take issue with this: Granted, regarding actions, a person can force himself to act in a certain way, but regarding *simha* – since this is an emotion of the heart – how can there be a command to have an emotion?[24]

The Rebbe's response reiterated the Chabad principle that cognitions affect emotions:

> The response to this question – similar to the response regarding the command "And you shall love, *Hashem* your God" – is that through proper contemplation of matters that inspire love, one

---

23. *Torat Menahem* 5717: 2, 309. See also *Torat Menahem* 5715: 1, 45; *Iggerot Kodesh* 11, letter 3493; ibid., 15, letter 5551.
24. *Torat Menahem* 5746: 2, 664. See also *Torat Menahem* 5713: 1, 95–96.

will certainly come to the emotion of love...the command is not on the emotion itself but rather on the contemplation.[25]

The normative element of perpetual *simha* is largely located in the cognitive realm: one must contemplate a specific set of ideas which will naturally evoke the desired emotional response.

What, then, must be contemplated in order to arouse and maintain *simha*? The Rebbe primarily emphasized the themes of divine immanence and caring that are already explicated in *Tanya*. In fact, at times, the Rebbe advised people who were battling sadness to review the relevant sections of *Tanya* and to think deeply about their content.[26] In addition, the Rebbe often emphasized that cultivating a sense of being endowed with a divine mission and reflecting on the great fortune that, despite one's shortcomings, one has the merit of being an emissary of God Himself to illuminate the world, could help fill a person with *simha*.[27]

Similarly, the Rebbe taught cognitive responses to intrusive thoughts that tempt a person to believe that he is distant from God.[28] For example, people may think that as a finite being trapped in coarse physicality they must be far from the transcendent and infinite God. The Rebbe directed such people to respond with an alternative line of reasoning: "Nonetheless, God gave him the possibility through Torah and mitzvot to connect with the Creator, which is the greatest possible ascent."[29]

Even one who sinned should not let himself grow despondent, as this closeness to God ultimately transcends a Jew's behavior. In order to remain joyful, the person should consider the nature of the Jewish soul, which remains unsullied by sin, or in the words of the Rebbe: "The *pintele Yid* (the Jewish core) that exists in every Jew in every situation

---

25. Ibid.
26. *Iggerot Kodesh* 9, letter 2952; ibid., 11, letter 3455.
27. Ibid., 6, letter 1726.
28. See *Iggerot Kodesh* 17, letter 6238, where the Rebbe noted that many people are misled by their cognitions toward sadness. See also *Torat Menahem* 5742: 2, 846.
29. *Torat Menahem* 5716: 1, 203. See also *Torat Menahem* 5752: 2, 293–94.

that connects him to [God]."³⁰ This form of contemplation will help one reassume one's true identity and successfully repent.³¹

Action

Beyond positive thinking, the Rebbe advised that physical activity plays an important role in avoiding sadness and engendering *simha*. This connection exists along two main pathways.

On one level, excessive rumination can lead a person toward depressing thoughts. In addition to providing alternative templates for thought patterns, the Rebbe also advised keeping active as an antidote to such overthinking. On various occasions, the Rebbe would attempt to take people out of this mindset by expressing astonishment that they had the leisure to engage in saddening internal dialogues when there was work to be done. For example, the Rebbe once wrote to a person who mentioned that he struggled with sadness:

> Concerning that which you wrote regarding sadness: *Tanya* has already stated that sadness comes from an impure source. What is your connection to sadness? I am amazed that a member of our community (*anshei shelomeinu*) has free time for such matters!"³²

When a Jew is constantly actively engaged with God's commands there is little time for excessive preoccupation with saddening thoughts.³³

The Rebbe further pointed to a specific subset of joyful activities that have the capacity to positively engender *simha*. On several occasions, the Rebbe recommended attending a *farbrengen* (hasidic gathering) as a vehicle to attain *simha*. Simply joining this upbeat gathering that includes

---

30. Ibid., 5752: 2, 294.
31. Ibid., 5716: 1, 203; ibid., 5752: 2, 293–94; *Likkutei Sihot* 4, *Avot, perek* 3, mishna 1, *se'if katan* 4.
32. *Iggerot Kodesh* 14, letter 5287. See also *Iggerot Kodesh* 5, letter 1284; *Torat Menahem* 5742: 3, 1521–23.
33. Similarly, the Rebbe often advised being active for those who were experiencing despondency past the time period that halakha allocates for mourning. For sources, see Mendel Kalmenson (2015), ch. 12, "Consolation Through Activity," available at www.chabad.org/3240793.

Aspects of a Godly Life

festive elements for body and soul, and sociability, can raise the spirits of even the most dejected.[34] Similarly, the Rebbe noted that even if one is not feeling exuberant about a mitzva, the halakha still obligates a Jew to nevertheless run to perform it. Acting as if one is joyful through running will itself engender "unlimited joy and vitality in the service of God."[35]

In summary, the Rebbe, following classic Chabad doctrine, contended that every person has the capacity to engender the emotions the Torah mandates.[36] While emotions themselves are elusive and cannot be directly triggered, one should target the faculties that are more directly within a person's control. Regarding *simha*, the Rebbe translated this into a practice of uplifting cognitions and joyous activities, which can consequently elicit real joy.[37]

THE METAPHYSICS OF *SIMHA*

Introduction

Our discussion has focused on the functional, philosophical, and halakhic rationales for perpetual *simha*. The Rebbe, however, argued that these characterizations of *simha* do not seem to justify the lofty significance attributed to it in kabbalistic and hasidic sources. For example, Arizal reported that he merited all of his exalted levels due to his tremendous *simha shel mitzva*.[38] What is it about *simha* that can propel a person to such spiritual heights?

In the same vein, the Rebbe often pointed to Rambam's ruling regarding *simha shel mitzva* for an even more surprising statement about

---

34. *Torat Menahem* 5742: 2, 846–47; ibid., 5747: 4, 57.
35. *Likkutei Sihot* 17, *Avot*, *perek* 4, *se'if* 8. For an elaboration and analysis of this theme in Chabad literature, see Yisachar Dovid Klausner (Elul 5764), 9–15.
36. See *Iggerot Kodesh* 9, letter 2952, where the Rebbe wrote the following to a person who felt himself incapable of ever attaining happiness: "Since the Torah commanded *simha* for every person it is clear that everyone has the ability [to engender joy], and the matter is solely dependent on willpower."
37. For a direct antecedent in Chabad literature regarding *simha*, see the pithy letter of the *Tzemah Tzedek* (cited in *Ozar Pitgamei Chabad*, vol. 1, 184) that if a person thinks, speaks, and behaves in a happy fashion, then "in the end it will actually be true."
38. From *Sefer Haredim, Tena'ei HaMitzvot, HaTenai HaRevi'i*, cited by the Rebbe in *Torat Menahem* 5712: 1, 119–20.

the centrality of *simha*.³⁹ Toward the end of his life, Moses warned the Jewish people that excruciating punishments await them due to their improper behavior. According to Rambam, Moses justified these punishments with the following statement: "Because you did not serve the Lord, your God, with happiness and with gladness of heart, when [you had an] abundance of everything" (Deut. 28:47). The Rebbe highlighted the import of this passage:⁴⁰ Even if the Jewish people scrupulously observe all the commandments, the lack of *simha* still justifies their exile. Why is *simha* such a crucial element in the service of God?

Simha and the Divine Essence

The Rebbe responded to these questions by first pointing to a feature of *simha* that was identified by the Rebbe Rashab.⁴¹ As part of a long *maamar*, the Rashab depicted *simha*'s discernible effect on the human personality:

> We see that in general it is the nature of *simha* to break barriers, meaning to say that regarding every barrier or limitation in the soul, it is the nature of *simha* to break the barrier or limitation and transform [a person] from extreme to extreme.⁴²

The Rashab portrayed this feature with the following imagery:

> When a person is exceedingly joyful at the wedding of his child or a similar event, then his hidden powers are disclosed. For example, a shy and sensitive person who is embarrassed to stand before people or to speak before them... when he is happy he becomes like a person who is strong and bold by nature and he can speak without embarrassment before many people, even people who are greater than he.⁴³

---

39. *Torat Menahem* 5714: 2, 164; ibid., 5715: 1, 16–17; ibid., 5717: 2, 93–94; ibid., 5719: 1, 73; ibid., 5744: 3, 1801.
40. See *Tanya, Likkutei Amarim*, ch. 26.
41. The Rashab himself seems to be building from the Alter Rebbe's succinct formulation in *Likkutei Torah, Derushim LeSukkot*, 82a.
42. *Sefer HaMaamarim* 5657, 223.
43. Ibid., 224.

Rashab associated *simha* with the breaking down of barriers and the disclosure of hidden capacities that are otherwise concealed.

After detecting this characteristic of joy in daily life, Rashab deepened his discussion and described *simha*'s effect on the soul. Using the midrashic five-part division of the soul that was adopted by Hasidism,[44] the Rashab explained that the revelation of concealed capabilities is, in truth, a reflection of *simha*'s ability to access and reveal the ultimate hidden core of a person – the "essence of the soul," or the *yehida*. Since the *yehida* transcends definitions and categories, which by their very nature are limited, its disclosure through the medium of *simha* allows a person to transcend the limitations imposed by the other aspects of the soul and behave in a way that is the opposite of his usual nature.[45]

The Rebbe further developed this aspect of *simha* in his explanation of its central significance. In two long *maamarim*[46] dedicated to the interplay between the performance of a mitzva and *simha*, the Rebbe highlighted a passage from the Zohar that defines the goal of mitzvot as "to fix the secret of the name."[47] After suggesting various interpretations of this cryptic line, the Rebbe identified "the secret of the name" as the Divine Essence that transcends the *Seder Hishtalshelut* and does not undergo the dual process of contraction and revelation. The "fixing" of the Divine Essence refers to the capacity of mitzvot to "access"[48] and "draw"[49] God into the lowest realms.[50]

---

44. See chapter 6, section "The Divine Essence, the *Yehida*, and the Body."
45. *Sefer HaMaamarim*, 5657, 223. For the connection between *simha* and *yehida* in the thought of the Rebbe, see *Likkutei Sihot* 6, *Yitro*, no. 1 (especially *se'if* 13); ibid., 22, *Vayikra*, no. 2, *se'if* 8; *Torat Menahem* 5747: 2, 322. See *Torat Menahem* 5724: 1, 8–9, where the Rebbe explained that *simha* is associated with pleasure (*oneg*), which is seated at the core of a person's *yehida*.
46. *Torat Menahem* 5714: 2, 163–72; ibid., 5719: 2, 173–80.
47. Cited in *Torah Or, Shemot*, 49d.
48. See *Torat Menahem* 5719: 2, 178, where the Rebbe said: "*Avodat nishmot Yisrael magaat behaatzmut*."
49. *Torat Menahem* 5714: 2, 169.
50. This capacity of mitzvot is due to the fact that the desire for mitzvot is a primal desire of the Divine Essence itself. See chapter 5, section "Mitzvot and the Divine Essence," and chapter 7, section "God's Choice of Mitzvot."

Simha Breaks Barriers

This process of "drawing in" the Divine Essence and revealing it in the lowest realm is difficult to understand. How can the undefinable Divine Essence be "drawn" through the entire *Seder Hishtalshelut*, which is characterized by limitation and defined categories? How can the imperceptible Divine Essence be revealed in the lowest realm, as is implied by the term *Dira BaTahtonim*?

According to the Rebbe, a key to resolving these difficulties is the unique quality of *simha*. Based on the above statement of the Rashab, the Rebbe explained that *simha* has the power to break seemingly insurmountable barriers:

> The necessity for *simha* is readily understandable, as according to this explanation [of "fixing the secret of the name"] we need to neutralize... all of the limitations of the *Seder Hishtalshelut* beginning with the first contraction (*tzimtzum*), and this can happen only via *simha*, as "*simha* breaks barriers," and therefore through the fulfillment of mitzvot with *simha* we perform the "fixing of the secret of the name," meaning that the Essence of the light will shine... until the lowest levels.[51]

Simha's metaphysical prowess is analogous to its effect on the human psyche.[52] Just as *simha* breaks through internal barriers and allows for the concealed essence of the soul to be revealed, *simha* also metaphysically allows for the revelation of the ultimate concealed entity – the Divine Essence. While the mitzva itself "touches" the Divine Essence, only *simha* can break through the barriers imposed by creation and disclose the undisclosable.

---

51. *Torat Menahem* 5714: 2, 168. See also *Torat Menahem* 5719: 2, 178.
52. See *Likkutei Sihot* 2, *Hag HaSukkot*, *se'if* 9, where the Rebbe also highlighted the parallelism between the effect of *simha* on the human soul and on the Divine Essence. He associated this parallelism with a teaching of the Baal Shem Tov on the verse that "God is your shade (*tzilkha*)" (Ps. 121:5). While the simple meaning is that God guards a person like a protective shade, the Baal Shem Tov noted that the verse can only be understood as "God is your shadow," meaning that similar to a shadow, God mimics human actions.

Aspects of a Godly Life

Suprarational *Simha*

This exalted role of *simha* impacts its content and technique. While human contemplation and action are admirable methods of achieving *simha*, they restrict the resultant emotion within the natural constraints of human beings.[53] To reveal the *yehida* and correspondingly break the barriers of creation, *simha* needs to transcend a person's natural faculties and become a *simha* that is "above logic and reasoning" (*lemaala mitaam vedaat*).

The Rebbe illustrated the difference between a rational and suprarational *simha* through the episode of King David transporting the Holy Ark to Jerusalem.[54] Originally, when the entourage was traveling toward the city, the verse describes: "And David danced with all his might before the Lord; and David was girded with a linen ephod."[55] However, when the company reached the city, David's dancing intensified: "And [as] the ark of the Lord came [into] the City of David, Michal the daughter of Saul peered through the window, and she saw the king David *hopping and dancing* before the Lord; and she loathed him in her heart."[56] What is the significance of the fact that when traveling toward the city, David simply "danced" while upon entering the city he intensified his dancing by also "hopping"?

The Rebbe posited that a clue to deciphering this transition is the initial mention of David's wearing a linen ephod. In his *Mishneh Torah*, Rambam identified the ephod as the unofficial uniform of "students of the prophets and those who were fit to have the Holy Spirit rest upon them."[57] The Rebbe contended that David recognized the significance of the journey and wanted to use the opportunity to attain prophecy. As *simha* is a prerequisite for a prophetic experience, David danced and sang hymns in an attempt to generate this lofty spiritual experience.

---

53. *Likkutei Sihot* 2, *Hag HaSukkot*, *se'if* 9.
54. *Likkutei Sihot* 1, *Shemini*, *se'ifim* 11–15. Significantly, Rambam (*Hilkhot Shofar VeSukka VeLulav* 8:15) points to David in this episode as the epitome of *simha shel mitzva*.
55. II Sam. 6:14.
56. Ibid. 16.
57. *Mishneh Torah*, *Hilkhot Kelei HaMikdash* 10:13.

Simha Breaks Barriers

Despite the admirability of desiring prophecy, since this *simha* was generated through a cognitive focus on a specific goal it was limited in scope and lacking in its passion, being merely instrumental and not essential. When David entered the city, his intensified dancing reflected a more elevated *simha* that pierced every fiber of his being. This new *simha* transcended the ceiling imposed by cognitively construed objectives and was not bound by natural human limitation. In the words of the Rebbe: "The *simha* was bereft of a goal and therefore limitless."[58] Only this form of *yehida*-revelatory *simha* contains the power to break the barriers of the order of creation and bring God back to His home.

Simha and *Bittul*

The need for a *simha* that transcends natural human limitation raises the following question: How is one to attain and experience a *simha* that surpasses ordinary human cognition and emotion? As explained above, extended contemplation of specific ideas and a particular set of activities have the capacity to stimulate *simha*. But what technique can bring a person to an emotion that definitionally transcends his own ordinary faculties?

The Rebbe repeatedly responded to this central question by considering the major Chabad theme of *bittul* (effacement). As we have seen in several contexts, the Rebbe taught that the path toward accessing and revealing one's essence (*yehida*) is through self-transcending service rooted in a sense of effacement (*bittul*) in relation to God. In other words, the path toward true *simha* lies not in self-indulgence and focusing on one's own needs and wants, but in transcending the self and seeing oneself as part of a greater whole. Ultimately, when one self-defines as a "part" of the one true entity – God – the *simha* of the *yehida* will be expressed.

In one of his discourses, the Rebbe said:

> The vessel for having *simha* in God is effacement (*bittul*), since in the place where there is effacement there is the revelation of the supernal *simha*. However, when there is a feeling of existence

---

58. *Likkutei Sihot* 1, *Shemini*, *se'if* 13.

Aspects of a Godly Life

(*yesh*), there is no *simha*. This is the meaning of the verse "And those who are humble shall increase their *simha* in the Lord" (Is. 29:19), that specifically the *humble* increase their *simha* in God.[59]

Elsewhere, the Rebbe explained that the dissolution of one's external identity affirms the true core of a person as being, in essence, one with God:

> It is specifically through self-effacement and self-sacrifice from the essence of one's soul that one can "take" the Divine Essence.... Self-effacement and self-sacrifice...do not mean that a person breaks himself, but rather that he achieves this [effacement] with *simha*, as we find regarding the *Akeda* that the self-sacrifice was with alacrity and *simha*...and through this the Divine Essence is drawn into the person's essence.[60]

The Divine Essence's disclosure generates a *simha* which transcends even the holiest of cognitions.[61]

Returning to the narrative of David dancing before the Holy Ark, the Rebbe explained that it was precisely David's effacement-inspired *simha* that irked his wife Michal.[62] She understood that even a king, at times, needs to degrade himself and remove his dignified demeanor for the sake of "calculated *simha*." However, in the words of the Rebbe: "'Hopping and dancing' in the city itself, which transcends logic and reason, this she could not understand."[63]

David responded as follows: "Before the Lord, who chose me above your father, and above all his house, to appoint me (*letzavot oti*) prince over the people of the Lord, over the Jewish people; therefore

---

59. *Torat Menahem* 5712: 1, 120–21.
60. Ibid., 5718: 2, 258–59.
61. For a series of proofs that the revelation of the Divine Essence is associated with *simha*, see *Torat Menahem* 5746: 1, 337–41.
62. See *Likkutei Sihot* 1, *Shemini*, *se'ifim* 14–15; *Torat Menahem* 5719: 1, 83; ibid., 5745: 4, 2189–92; ibid., 5746: 4, 302–4.
63. *Likkutei Sihot* 1, *Shemini*, *se'if* 14.

I have made merry before the Lord."[64] According to the Rebbe, this response highlights David's superiority over Saul. While Saul followed his own logic rather than the divine command and refrained from killing captured Amalekite women and children, David's service was characterized by submission and self-effacement:

> Saul followed [his own] reasoning, and therefore the kingship was wrested from him and given to David, "to appoint me prince," meaning that his service was with submission, as it is stated, "And David My servant..." (Ezek. 37:25).[65]

David's sense of effacement enabled him to dance with self-transcending abandonment, experiencing a *simha* that accessed his true core – the *yehida*/Divine Essence.[66]

The Comprehensiveness of True *Simha*

This perspective on the inner workings of *simha* has several ramifications.[67] One, which was alluded to above, is the manner in which the *simha* is expressed. The Rebbe noted that David expressed the highest level of *simha* through passionately dancing before the ark. Similarly, we celebrate Simhat Torah through dancing with the Torah scrolls.

Characteristic of a worldview that eschews coincidence or shallow associations, the Rebbe imparted great significance to the connection between *simha* and dancing. In one talk he began by pointing to an irony inherent in our Simhat Torah festivities:

---

64. II Sam. 6:21.
65. *Likkutei Sihot* 1, *Shemini, se'if* 15.
66. It is important to note that David's *simha* took place in the context of song and dance. For the significance of song in transcending the intellect, see *Torat Menahem* 5720: 1, 458–59; ibid., 5717: 1, 30–31; ibid., 5721: 3, 45–47; ibid., 5745: 1, 445. For analysis of the role of music in Chabad thought and life, see Shmuel Zalmanoff's introduction to his classic book *Sefer HaNiggunim* (originally compiled in 5709); Ellen Koskoff (2001).
67. The Rebbe discussed these elements in a wide variety of contexts. However, for the sake of clarity this chapter will focus on their application to Simhat Torah.

> Seemingly, the main essence of Torah is to study it with one's head and cognition. As such, the *simha* of Simhat Torah should be expressed through more learning of Torah... and the understanding of the Torah will lead to *simha*. Why is the custom to express the *simha* of the Torah through dancing with one's feet? In addition, [why do] we dance with the Torah when it is rolled and covered, such that no one can see it?[68]

The Rebbe responded that while studying and deeply understanding Torah is crucially significant, such an enterprise does not define the true gift of the Torah. The "essence of Torah" is God Himself, who transcends any level of understanding. At the conclusion of a year of study we celebrate our connection with the essence of Torah/the Divine Essence:

> Therefore, we dance on Simhat Torah with a rolled and covered Torah scroll in a fashion that makes it impossible to read it. This signifies the aspect of Torah that transcends understanding, and with that we are joyful. The *simha* is not due to an understanding of the Torah, but rather due to the fact that through (the study and reading of Torah) we grasp the Divine Essence.[69]

Simhat Torah revolves around the deepest form of *simha*, which is associated with the revelation of the Divine Essence.

The Rebbe then related to the relevance of dancing for this form of *simha*: "This is also the reason that the expression of *simha* is dancing with one's feet – as specifically through the feet... the Essence is expressed."[70] As we have seen, the Rebbe argued that the Divine Essence is best expressed when it permeates all of creation and reaches even the lowest places and farthest peripheries. Accordingly, the *simha* associated with the revelation of the Divine Essence is exhibited through

---

68. *Likkutei Sihot* 4, Simhat Torah, *se'if* 3.
69. Ibid.
70. Ibid. The Rebbe cited *Likkutei Torah, Devarim*, 63d, where the Alter Rebbe associates "feet" with "faith," which is one's primal connection to God.

movement of the feet – the lowest extremity of the body.⁷¹ As the Rebbe once similarly put it:

> The *simha* of Simhat Torah is not connected with a specific practice, be it the fulfillment of a mitzva, or even "the study of Torah which is the equal of all other mitzvot," but it is an *essential simha* that is above revelations. This *simha* is expressed not through learning and understanding or similar things, but rather through dancing with one's feet, the simplest of matters.⁷²

The Divine Essence permeates everything equally, and thus, when it is revealed, every aspect of the body and creation equally express this essential *simha*.

The pervasive nature of this *simha* is apparent not only in its bodily expression but also in its demographic inclusiveness. One of the hallmarks of Simhat Torah is that everyone dances together; from the scholars and saints who are the "head" of the Jewish people to the simple Jews allegorized as the "feet." As the Rebbe continued:

> The *simha* of Simhat Torah applies to all Jews equally, Torah scholars and simple Jews as one.... Since this *simha* is not connected to the service of Torah and mitzvot (regarding which we find distinctions in the levels of service), but is rather an essential *simha* that is connected with the very essence of a Jew – regarding this we are all equal, without any distinctions.⁷³

---

71. In this regard, see *Likkutei Sihot* 14, *Vezot Haberakha*, no. 2, *se'if* 5; ibid., 19, *Vezot Haberakha*-Simhat Torah, *se'if* 8; *Torat Menahem* 5750: 1, 206. See also *Torat Menahem* 5715: 1, 206–7, where the Rebbe associated dancing with jumping above the *Seder Hishtalshelut* to reach the Divine Essence, which is discussed in chapter 11, section "Jumping and *Dira BaTahtonim*."
72. *Torat Menahem* 5745: 1, 367.
73. Ibid. See also *Likkutei Sihot* 9, *Vezot Haberakha*, *se'ifim* 12–14; ibid., 14, *Vezot Haberakha*, no. 2, *se'ifim* 5–6; ibid., 19, *Berakha*-Simhat Torah, *se'if* 6; ibid., 20, 2 Heshvan 5740, *se'if* 7.

Aspects of a Godly Life

The *simha* of the Divine Essence's disclosure breaks the barriers that seem to differentiate Jews and highlights their elemental shared essence.[74] The practical expression of this is a joyous dance circle that includes all Jews.[75]

NEGATIVE EVENTS AND "THIS TOO IS FOR THE BEST"

Introduction

Despite all of the textual and conceptual support for the hasidic notion of perpetual *simha*, a serious objection can still be raised: How does one perceive and respond to tragedy? Does the obligation and significance of *simha* imply that one should react to the death of loved ones or lesser negative occurrences with a smile and a dance? The Rebbe's response to this question touches on the seam between the real and the ideal and will lead directly into a discussion of the nature of *simha* in the Messianic Era.

"It Is All for the Best"

The Rebbe emphasized that one must cognitively understand that every event is inherently positive. This perspective emerges directly from two premises: that God is good and that He directly causes every event. As the Rebbe once put it:

> Every [event] in the world is, in truth, good. Since everything comes from the Holy One, blessed be He, and the nature of good is to do good for others, it is readily understandable that even things that appear to mortal eyes as the opposite of good are, in truth, good.[76]

The Rebbe sharpened this point through distinguishing between two similar sounding statements attributed to a rabbinic sage and his student.[77] In one passage, R. Akiva responds to personal setbacks with the phrase "All that God does is for the best."[78] In a different story, Nahum

---

74. See *Torat Menahem* 5748: 2, 426, where the Rebbe associated *simha poretzet geder* with the feelings of connection and unity engendered by joy.
75. See *Likkutei Sihot* 2, Shemini Atzeret-Simhat Torah, *se'if* 2.
76. *Torat Menahem* 5748: 4, 52.
77. *Likkutei Sihot* 2, Tavo, *se'ifim* 4–7.
78. Berakhot 60b.

Ish Gamzu, R. Akiva's teacher, experienced his own set of misfortunes and articulated the principle "*This too* is for the best."[79] After a close reading of the statements in their context, the Rebbe noted that despite their similarity, they represent two different methods of locating concealed goodness in seemingly negative events.

The statement "All that God does is for the best," does not focus on the negative event per se but on the result and purpose of the event. A hardship is a hardship, and no amount of cognitive gymnastics can circumvent this basic truth. However, R. Akiva understood that while he might experience an event as a setback, in God's ultimate plan it is surely a stepping stone toward a greater good. As the Rebbe expressed this perspective:[80] "[The event] was for *the sake of* good, but the event itself was painful."

Nahum Ish Gamzu, however, went one step further:

> The meaning of "This too is for the best" is that this very event is for the best. It is not merely for the sake of goodness, but it itself is good. At the outset there was concealment, the eyes were closed, and it appeared as if there was damage and pain, but when the concealment is removed it becomes clear that from the outset it was good.[81]

Similar to reality as a whole, the essential divinity of negative events becomes apparent after the veil of concealment is removed. Negative events are not merely instrumentally positive in the sense that they lead toward a greater good, but they are themselves essentially good, irrespective of appearances. Nahum Ish Gamzu experienced reality in this manner.[82]

---

79. Taanit 21a.
80. *Likkutei Sihot* 2, Tavo, se'if 6.
81. Ibid., se'if 7.
82. For other places where the Rebbe distinguished between these two levels, see *Torat Menahem* 5711: 2, 267–75; ibid., 5712: 3, 126–31; ibid., 5721: 2, 231; ibid., 5726: 3, 290; ibid., 5745: 5, 2719–22; *Iggerot Kodesh* 6, letter 1744; ibid., 9, letter 2683; ibid., 14, letter 5220; ibid., 17, letter 6412; ibid., 22, letter 8301.

Aspects of a Godly Life

Cognitions and Emotions Regarding Negative Experiences

What caused this experiential difference between Nahum Ish Gamzu and R. Akiva? Surely, R. Akiva also affirmed the hasidic notions of *hashgaha* and divine unity that led to Nahum Ish Gamzu's perspective of total goodness? While the Rebbe pointed to several factors to explain R. Akiva's more limited perspective,[83] his main argument relates to the generation in which they lived:[84]

> Nahum Ish Gamzu was the teacher of R. Akiva. This means that R. Akiva was a generation later than Nahum Ish Gamzu, a generation in which the darkness of exile was greater (as in every generation the darkness grows). In [R. Akiva's] generation, there was no longer the possibility to see every event as essentially good. Even though it was a cognitive truism that every event is essentially good – nonetheless, in our world this is not revealed.

Despite an intellectual understanding that all events are inherently positive, the concealments of exile rendered R. Akiva unable to experience the apparent bad as good. Rather, he had to suffice with the cognitive recognition that misfortunes were vehicles that lead toward a greater good.[85]

This tension, between intellectual truths on the one hand and the emotions engendered by our current, firsthand experiences on the other, was the topic of an impassioned and personal talk that the Rebbe delivered on completing the thirty-day mourning period for his wife's passing.[86] The Torah reading that week involved the ritual of the red heifer, which purifies those rendered impure by contact with a corpse. The Rebbe noted that according to hasidic teachings this cleansing is complete, "such that there is no longer any remnant of the effect of the undesirable matter [impurity of death]."[87] As such, the Rebbe under-

---

83. See *Torat Menahem* 5711: 2, 271–72.
84. *Likkutei Sihot* 2, *Tavo, se'if* 7.
85. See also *Torat Menahem* 5726: 2, 202–5, where the Rebbe said that nowadays only singular individuals (*yehidei segula*) can experience the world as Nahum Ish Gamzu did, while the average Jew and even most great *Tzaddikim* cannot.
86. *Torat Menahem* 5748: 2, 419–31.
87. Ibid., 423.

stood the confluence of the Torah portion with his emergence from intense mourning as imparting a personal message:

> This is the lesson to be learned from the fact that the end of the *sheloshim* occurred on the Friday of [reading] *Parashat Para* – that even today, when we do not have the ashes of the red heifer… it gives us strength, encouragement, and empowerment to change the situation that resulted from the lack of life, so that [we] can return to our original state, that not even a remnant remains.[88]

After this seemingly categorical statement regarding the complete erasure of death's negativity from his consciousness, the Rebbe changed the tenor of his talk. He noted that despite the above argument's simple elegance, both Moses and Solomon expressed astonishment at the effectiveness of the rite of the red heifer. This reflects a tragic but understandable disconnect between what we understand to be true and our emotional reality. In the Rebbe's words:

> One of the main principles of the Torah [is that we do not suffice with] logical understanding alone, but rather that logical understanding should be such that it penetrates the entirety of a person until it impacts even the emotions of the heart. And from the perspective of the heart, after all of the explanations and rationales it is still extremely difficult to… nullify the effect and impact of "the lack of life" on the emotions of the heart, such that there should not remain any doubt.[89]

The capacity for cognition to effect emotions is an axiom in Chabad doctrine. However, our current exilic reality places limits on the extent to which we can dictate a script to the heart.[90]

---

88. Ibid., 5748: 2, 422–23.
89. Ibid., 423–24.
90. See *Torat Menahem* 5748: 2, 424, where the Rebbe also emphasized that the time periods of mourning delineated by halakha should be upheld despite the difficulty. As such, one must work to experience less sadness in the period after *sheloshim* than during *sheloshim*.

SIMHA AND MASHIAH

"This Too Is for the Best" and *Mashiah*

Notwithstanding the realness of grief, sadness, and pain, the Rebbe underscored that they are ultimately temporary phenomena. The coming of *Mashiah* will usher in an era of disclosed divinity that will allow for the essential goodness of all past events to become "visible and manifest." Even the past deaths of loved ones will be understood and experienced as sources of *simha* upon their resurrection.[91]

As we have seen, the Rebbe felt that the final generations before *Mashiah* should align their modes of service with the forthcoming messianic reality. As such, a cognitive appreciation for the principle of "this too is for the best" takes on new significance. For example, in one talk, the Rebbe contended that after the coming of *Mashiah* even the destruction of the *Beit HaMikdash* will be perceived as an essentially positive event. He, then, concluded as follows:

> Even though the transformation of undesirable events into goodness... will occur in the future [redemption]... still we need to prepare in a manner akin to it even now. This is accomplished through a firm *awareness* that "this too is for the best," even if not yet understandable.[92]

This cognitive affirmation, even when lacking full understanding and parallel emotions, lays the groundwork for *Mashiah*.

In addition, the Rebbe taught that even if we are not able to fully experience all events as sources of *simha*, we are still obligated to exert effort to deepen this cognitive understanding, as much as possible, into an emotional reality. In one *maamar*, he identified this practice as a preparation for and generator of the redemption:

---

91. *Torat Menahem* 5748: 2, 419. The Rebbe returned to this comforting theme several times during the mourning period for his wife. See *Torat Menahem: Menahem Tziyon* 1, 167, 183, 230.
92. *Torat Menahem* 5712: 3, 129. See also ibid., 5711: 2, 273–75.

And since all matters of the future are dependent on our actions and service during the time period of the exile, it is understandable that the preparation for the fulfillment of the goal...that everything will be good...is through conducting our actions and service [now] in a similar fashion, to accept [all that happens] with *simha* through contemplating that the source of evil is good.... Through this we will merit to the future reality that everything will be good...in a manner that is visible and manifest to human eyes.[93]

Identifying the silver lining in all events and remaining as happy as humanly possible under all situations is a key element of the transition from exile to redemption.

Simha and *Teshuva* on the Cusp of Redemption

In addition to seeing goodness in apparently negative situations, the Rebbe applied this unique connection between the end of exile and *simha* to several other contexts. One topic impacted by the significance of *simha* at the end of the exilic era is the process of *teshuva* (repentance). Traditional Jewish literature often describes *teshuva* as a heart-wrenching and painful enterprise.[94]

This characterization continues even in early Hasidism. For example, the Alter Rebbe in *Iggeret Teshuva* described two distinct forms of *teshuva*. The "lower *teshuva*" (*teshuva tataa*) purifies a person from the sin that was committed, allowing the sinner to return to his prior state.[95] This process entails reflecting deeply on how sin damages the soul, resulting in the person becoming "extremely grieved" which "crushes" one's negative traits.[96] Only after engaging in this "bitter" form of *teshuva* can

---

93. Ibid., 5726: 2, 204.
94. See, for example, *Shaarei Teshuva, shaar* 1, *simanim* 13–16.
95. *Tanya, Iggeret HaTeshuva*, chs. 6–7.
96. See also *Tanya, Likkutei Amarim*, chs. 26, 31, for the role of *merirut* in the life of a Jew. However, see there that the Alter Rebbe takes great pains to differentiate the positive, albeit limited, role of *merirut*, from the entirely negative emotion of *atzvut* (sadness).

Aspects of a Godly Life

one proceed to the "higher *teshuva*" (*teshuva ilaa*), characterized by a joyous unification of one's soul with God.[97]

In the early years of his tenure, the Rebbe embraced this model of *teshuva*.[98] In 5746 (1985), however, the Rebbe delivered a striking *maamar*[99] in which he argued that aspects of the Alter Rebbe's model were no longer applicable: "The bitterness (*merirut*) associated with *teshuva* is not relevant in our current generation, the generation of *ikveta deMeshiha*."[100] The Rebbe offered two distinct but related rationales for this startling assertion, flowing from the paradoxical identity of the generation. On the one hand, the generation farthest from the Jewish people's glorious past is the most impacted by the long exile. As the spiritually weakest generation, the Rebbe contended: "In our generation, we do not have the strength for [the service of] bitterness."[101]

However, the Rebbe almost immediately transitioned to a second argument focused on the proximity of the generation to the Messianic Era. In *Iggeret HaTeshuva*, the Alter Rebbe associated the two forms of *teshuva* with two parts of the week. The six workdays are an appropriate period for lower *teshuva*, while Shabbat is reserved for higher *teshuva*.[102] Using the standard rabbinic idea that each day of the week represents a one thousand-year period,[103] the Rebbe argued that the contemporary period, close to the end of the sixth millennium, is symbolically situated at the seam between Friday and Shabbat:

> We are situated at the end of the sixth day, not just on the night of the sixth day, but near the end of the day itself, close to Shabbat.

---

97. For summaries and analyses of these forms of *teshuva*, see Yoel Kahn (Elul 5765), 6–15; Norman Lamm (2002), 45–49; Roman A. Foxbrunner (1993), 133–36.
98. See, for example, *Torat Menahem* 5712: 3, 158–64; ibid., 5715: 2, 302–4; ibid., 5719: 1, 15. It is important to note that in all of the above talks, the Rebbe emphasized the need for *simha* to coexist with the bitterness.
99. *Torat Menahem* 5746: 1, 667–70.
100. Ibid., 667. Similarly, see *Iggerot Kodesh* 15, letter 5564, where the Rebbe describes the crucial need for *simha* in "our" generation due to the fact that it is an "orphaned generation."
101. *Torat Menahem* 5746: 1, 667.
102. *Iggeret HaTeshuva*, ch. 10.
103. Rashi on Ps. 90:4.

Accordingly, it is obvious that the service of this era must be with the *simha* of higher *teshuva* ... which is accomplished through the service of prayer and primarily the study of Torah – "The orders of the Lord are upright, causing the heart to rejoice" – as Torah brings one to joy....[104]

Proximity to the Messianic Era necessitates shifting toward the messianic modes of service. Hence, this generation should avoid the bitterness of *teshuva* in favor of putting one's energy into prayer and Torah study which elicits the *simha* of returning to the Source and connecting with God.[105]

Simha to Bring *Mashiah*

One of the Rebbe's starkest formulations of the generation's need for *simha* was an emphatic talk he delivered in the summer of 5748 (1988).[106] The Rebbe noted that throughout the long exile, Jews always yearned to bring *Mashiah* and attempted to facilitate his coming through various means. As history progressed these efforts gained steam, most notably through the spreading of Hasidism in the later generations. The movement to bring *Mashiah* attained a new sense of urgency when R. Yosef Yitzhak identified "bringing redemption" as the "unique mission of this generation."

The Rebbe said that the Hasidim treated the charge of R. Yosef Yitzhak with the utmost seriousness and tirelessly dedicated themselves to this mission. They repented, studied and spread Hasidism, recited Psalms, held *farbrengens,* and thus fulfilled the mission thrust upon them. However, as the Rebbe noted, *Mashiah* had not yet arrived. This fact was a cause of deep vexation and begged the question: "Since the ... storm to bring *Mashiah,* several decades have already passed and *Mashiah* has not yet come ... what more is there to do?"[107]

---

104. *Torat Menahem* 5746: 1, 668.
105. See also *Torat Menahem* 5746: 2, 186–90, where the Rebbe reiterated these two reasons for the unique need for *simha* in his generation.
106. *Torat Menahem* 5748: 4, 263–86.
107. Ibid., 268.

The Rebbe's response was direct: "The answer is that what has yet to be done in order to bring *Mashiah* is the service of proper *simha* for the sake of bringing *Mashiah*."[108] Why is achieving proper *simha* the linchpin of the Jewish people's efforts to bring *Mashiah*? The Rebbe explained:

> *Simha* breaks through barriers, including the barriers of exile. Moreover, *simha* has a unique potential to bring about the redemption.... It is only in the *Beit HaMikdash* to be built in the era of the redemption that there will be perfect happiness. "Then the happiness will be associated with the Divine Essence, the essence of *simha* (*simha atzmit mamash*)."[109]

Only *simha*, with its capacity to break barriers, can unite the Divine Essence with the lowest realm, putting an eternal end to the exilic notion of a concealed God.

The Rebbe continued by carefully analyzing the unique nature of this redemption-oriented *simha* and its relevance for the generation that is to bring about redemption. Throughout history, and especially with the advent of Hasidism, *simha* permeated a Jew's service of God. However, this *simha* was mainly associated with and considered secondary to the actual performance of mitzvot. By contrast, the calling of this generation is to attain a pure and essential *simha*: "The suggestion to use *simha* as a catalyst to bring *Mashiah*... puts the emphasis on the *simha* itself, *simha* in its pure and consummate state."[110]

Earlier generations were not able to achieve this pure and essential *simha* due to the suffering of exile. However, despite the depravity of the final, darkest moments of exile, the Rebbe felt that this generation had no choice but to attempt the impossible:

---

108. Ibid.
109. Ibid., citing the Rebbe Rashab in *Sefer HaMaamarim* 5656, 252. The Rebbe often characterized the Messianic Era as the time of ultimate *simha*. See, for example, *Torat Menahem* 5745: 1, 362; ibid., 5748: 4, 62; ibid., 5751: 2, 54.
110. *Torat Menahem* 5748: 4, 269.

> But nevertheless [despite the suffering of exile], since it is ultimately necessary for us to bring *Mashiah*, we have no choice but to bring *Mashiah* via *simha, simha* in its pure state. And regarding the practical difficulty of achieving the emotion of pure *simha* in the darkness of exile, since we are obligated to bring *Mashiah*... God grants us unique capabilities to be able to achieve pure *simha*...through contemplation that immediately *Mashiah* will arrive.[111]

As with every other challenge that his generation faced, the Rebbe expressed full conviction that as long as people were properly invested in the mission, God would reciprocate by granting them the necessary assistance.

Characteristically, the Rebbe concluded this section of his talk by underscoring the importance of the practical:

> Most importantly: Instead of lengthy speeches and analyses, etc., [people] should begin the practical application: to go out in public and call for a special increase of *simha* in order to bring *Mashiah*, and then certainly through this they will bring *Mashiah* in actuality with the greatest haste.[112]

After several more exhortations, the Rebbe led the Hasidim in an intense and joyful dance "for the sake of bringing *Mashiah*."[113]

CONCLUSION

The Rebbe's understanding of *simha* intertwines practical psychological advice with the most epic of cosmic processes. Breathing new meaning into ancient sources, the Rebbe saw the people living at the cusp

---

111. Ibid.
112. Ibid., 270.
113. Ibid., 271. For other articulations of the connection between *simha* and the bringing of *Mashiah*, see *Torat Menahem* 5714: 1, 81–82; ibid., 5716: 2, 97–100; ibid., 5743, 1641–42.

of redemption as being uniquely equipped for and charged with the service of *simha*.

Secondary Literature Consulted for Chapter 12, "*Simha* Breaks Barriers"

Yoel Kahn, "Bein Yada LeLo Yada."

Mendel Kalmenson, *A Time to Heal: The Lubavitcher Rebbe's Response to Loss and Tragedy*.

Shlomo Majesky, *The Chasidic Approach to Joy*.

Jacob Immanuel Schochet, *Chasidic Dimensions*, 125–50.

Chapter 13
Jewish Unity and Love

The precept of *ahavat Yisrael* (to love one's fellow Jew) has been a central axiom of hasidic thought and life from its beginnings. Following the pattern that we have seen with other issues, the Rebbe made conceptual strides in understanding *ahavat Yisrael*'s underpinnings, its relationship to other elements of hasidic philosophy, and its fundamental centrality to them all. More visibly, he uniquely practicalized these teachings by imbuing his followers with a burning desire to help other Jews, both spiritually and materially. This chapter will track both of these contributions and analyze their interconnection.

EARLIER JEWISH THOUGHT
Introduction
The Torah's command "You shall love your fellow as yourself"[1] presents several serious challenges. On the most basic level, as a legal precept, the phrase requires a precise legal definition. How is "love" normatively defined? Who is "your fellow" that is the object of this love? And what parameters are intended by the comparative "as yourself?"

---
1. Lev. 19:18.

In addition, rabbinic literature celebrates the centrality of this mitzva. R. Akiva refers to loving one's fellow as "the great principle of the Torah,"[2] while Hillel equates it with "the entirety of the Torah."[3] Neither passage, however, offers an explanation for the exalted status of *ahavat Yisrael*. What is the rationale or telos of this love? Why is it so essential to the Torah's system?

With these questions in mind, let us survey several approaches to the definition and rationale of the mitzva in earlier Jewish thought.[4]

Ramban

In his commentary to the Torah, Ramban highlights the difficulties of a literal rendering of the verse:

> The phrase "Love your fellow as yourself" cannot be meant literally, since man cannot be expected to love his fellow as himself. Moreover, R. Akiva has ruled that "your life comes first." The Torah here enjoins us that we should wish upon our neighbor the same benefits that we wish upon ourselves.[5]

Ramban posits that it is impossible for one to love one's fellow with as much depth and passion as himself, and, hence, this cannot be the intention of the verse. Rather, the mitzva must be understood in attitudinal and behavioral terms, namely, that each person is obligated to wish for and invest optimally in the betterment of other Jews, but not actually to love them to the same degree as one's own self.[6]

---

2. Y. Nedarim 9:4.
3. Shabbat 31a.
4. Much of the subsequent analysis is indebted to several surveys of the halakhic and philosophical aspects of this mitzva: Daniel Feldman (2005), 169–77; Avraham Aharon Preiss (5762), 43–140.
5. Ramban to Lev. 19:18.
6. See *Torat Menahem* 5745: 1, 192, where the Rebbe identified the limits that result from Ramban's limiting interpretation of the mitzva. See also *Likkutei Sihot* 17, Kedoshim, no. 2, *se'if* 3 (and particularly, footnote 19) for a succinct summary of other commentators whose interpretation generally aligns with that of Ramban.

Rambam

In contrast to Ramban's behavioral understanding of the mitzva, Rambam defines the core obligation in emotional terms:

> Each man is commanded to love each and every single Jew as himself, as [the verse] states: "Love your fellow as yourself." Therefore, one should speak the praises of [others] and show concern for their money just as he is concerned with his own money and seeks his own honor.[7]

Rambam interprets the verse literally: Each Jew must love his fellow Jew as himself. This love will then engender the positive social interactions and behaviors that Ramban described.

It is important to note that Rambam does not explicitly relate to Ramban's puzzlement. How is a person supposed to generate such intense positive feelings for a fellow Jew? Is it really possible to love another person to the same degree that one loves one's own self?

Who Is "Your Fellow"?

The above-cited formulation of Rambam indicates that this love is to be directed toward all Jews. R. Meir of Rothenberg, though, argues in his comments on *Mishneh Torah* that the Talmud explicitly limits the scope of this love: "And only if he is 'your fellow' regarding Torah and mitzvot. But a wicked person who does not accept rebuke, there is a mitzva to hate him."[8] This limitation is cited by various halakhic decisors and as well as in the later codes of Jewish law.[9]

Reasons for the Mitzva

The author of *Sefer HaHinnukh* highlights *ahavat Yisrael*'s sociological effect when discussing the underlying rationale for the mitzva: "The root of this mitzva is apparent. For in the same manner that one acts toward his fellow, his friend will act similarly toward him. Through this

---

7. *Mishneh Torah, Hilkhot Deot* 6:3.
8. *Haggahot Maimoniyot, Hilkhot Deot* 6:1.
9. *Magen Avraham* 156:2; *Mishna Berura* 156:4.

Aspects of a Godly Life

there will be peace among people."[10] According to this approach, the ultimate telos of *ahavat Yisrael* is the creation of a unified and peaceful society. Mass fulfillment of the emotional and actional components of this mitzva will engender the ideal social reality.

Similarly, when relating to the central significance attributed to this mitzva, *Sefer HaHinnukh* does not focus on love *qua* love. Rather, he attributes *ahavat Yisrael*'s prominence to the fact that many other interpersonal mitzvot flow from this intense love:

> R. Akiva said: "This is a great principle of the Torah," meaning to say that many mitzvot of the Torah are dependent on it, as one who loves his fellow as himself will not steal his money or commit adultery with his wife... and similarly, many other mitzvot are dependent on this [love].[11]

In summary, despite his allegiance to Rambam's emotional definition of the mitzva, *Sefer HaHinnukh* points to factors that lie outside the love itself when describing the telos and centrality of *ahavat Yisrael*.

Ahavat Yisrael in *Tanya*

In a celebrated chapter in the "heart"[12] of *Tanya*, the Alter Rebbe draws from kabbalistic and hasidic sources to relate to these issues from a different perspective. Siding with Rambam, the Alter Rebbe asserts that the command of *ahavat Yisrael* obligates each Jew to love every other Jew as fiercely as oneself. However, in contrast to *Sefer HaHinnukh* who emphasized that Jewish unity is the intended result of the mitzva to love other Jews, the Alter Rebbe highlights that a deep metaphysical oneness is actually a cause of this love.

In the previous section of *Tanya*, the Alter Rebbe recommends that a person primarily self-identify as a soul as opposed to a body. The succeeding chapter of *Tanya* focuses on how this perspective leads to true *ahavat Yisrael*:

---

10. *Sefer HaHinnukh*, mitzva 243.
11. Ibid.
12. Ch. 32, which has the numerical value of *lev* (heart).

> [Identifying one's true self as one's soul and not one's body] is a direct and easy way to attain the fulfillment of the commandment "You shall love your fellow as yourself" toward every Jew, both great and small.
>
> For [regarding]...the soul and spirit [of others], who can know their greatness and excellence in their root and source in the Living God? Moreover, being all of an equal kind and all having one Father, all Jews are called brothers in the literal sense of the word by virtue of the source of their souls in the One God; only their bodies are separated. Therefore, there can be no true love and fraternity between those who regard their bodies as primary and their souls secondary but only a love based on an external factor.[13]

When a person identifies himself as a corporeal being it is impossible to love another as oneself. A paradigm shift occurs, however, when the soul becomes the basis of one's identity. First, this enables a person to see the soulful spark of God deeply embedded in each person, which generates positive feelings toward the other. Second, since the very same divine root is the source of all Jewish souls, they are all essentially the same entity. The Alter Rebbe argues that embracing this essential oneness will generate feelings of love.

The intertwinement of *ahavat Yisrael* with the elevation of the soul over the body impacts the Alter Rebbe's understanding of this mitzva's central significance. What can be more fundamental than internalizing the inner divine nature of oneself and all Jews? In the words of the Alter Rebbe:

> This is what Hillel the Elder meant when he said in regard to the fulfillment of this commandment, "This is the whole Torah; the rest is but commentary." For the basis and root of the entire Torah is to raise and exalt the soul high above the body, to the source and root of all the worlds....[14]

---

13. *Tanya, Likkutei Amarim*, ch. 32.
14. Ibid.

Similarly, as the Alter Rebbe explains in the continuation of the chapter, focusing on the unifying divinity in other people as the basis of *ahavat Yisrael* leads to the broadest of possible scopes for the mitzva. All Jews, no matter their level of observance, are blessed with a divine soul which renders them all as one and demands that they must be loved.

THE REBBE ON *AHDUT YISRAEL* AND *AHAVAT YISRAEL*

Building upon *Tanya*'s description of *ahdut Yisrael* (Jewish unity) and *ahavat Yisrael*, the Rebbe deepened the theoretical rationale for these concepts in addition to accentuating their practical aspects.

Ahdut Yisrael

Following the model outlined in *Tanya*, the Rebbe emphasized the conceptual primacy of *ahdut Yisrael* over *ahavat Yisrael*. He began one paradigmatic talk by raising the following question:

> When we speak of *ahdut Yisrael* and *ahavat Yisrael*, there are those who "seek to complain,"[15] and they ask: What is the meaning of the addition of *ahdut Yisrael*? The verse says only, "And you should love your fellow."[16]

The Rebbe responded by citing a passage from the Talmud Yerushalmi that compares the relationship between all Jews to that of different limbs of the same body. Therefore, taking revenge against another Jew would be just as foolish as one limb retaliating against another limb that caused it pain.[17] Reprisals are nonsensical when relating to different parts of the same organism.

This notion of *ahdut Yisrael*, argued the Rebbe, is the conceptual underpinning of *ahavat Yisrael*:

> This parable explains the rationale and the cause for the mitzva "And you shall love your fellow as yourself," as all Jews are

---

15. Paraphrase of Rashi on Num. 11:1.
16. *Torat Menahem* 5744: 2, 663.
17. Y. Nedarim 9:4.

analogized to limbs of one body.... *Ahdut Yisrael* is the underlying cause that leads toward actual behavior characterized by *ahavat Yisrael*.[18]

As such, inculcating a proper sense of *ahdut Yisrael* is integral to a proper fulfillment of the mitzva of *ahavat Yisrael*.[19]

This being the case, we will first turn to the Rebbe's multi-tiered description of *ahdut Yisrael*. Over the course of dozens of talks, the Rebbe outlined two distinct models of *ahdut Yisrael* and demonstrated their independence and even mutual exclusivity. Characteristically, though, he argued that, ultimately, only synthesizing these two seemingly unsynthesizable models can lead to the deepest perspective on *ahdut Yisrael*.

Ahdut Yisrael Perspective No. 1: Indivisible Unity

The Rebbe taught that, on a primal level, *ahdut Yisrael* refers to the fact that all Jews are at their core a completely indivisible entity. In one talk, the Rebbe discussed this essential oneness through highlighting the difference between the above-cited talmudic parable of each Jew to limbs of a body and the *Tanya*'s formulation that "all Israelites are called brothers in the literal sense of the word by virtue of the source of their souls in the One God":

> Even the level of *ahdut* of a single body is not complete *ahdut*, for even in a body there are divisions between the various limbs.... But the manner in which the Jewish people are encompassed in their root of "a single Father" is above any division.... [And even higher,] just as "the One God" is simple in the greatest degree of simplicity and transcends any division, similarly, the souls of the Jewish people... are akin to a single point that completely transcends any division.[20]

---

18. *Torat Menahem* 5744: 2, 664.
19. The Rebbe then explained that the Torah focuses on *ahavat Yisrael* as opposed to *ahdut Yisrael*, since the former is more readily applied on a practical level. For more articulations of the conceptual primacy of *ahdut Yisrael* over *ahavat Yisrael*, see *Likkutei Sihot* 31, Beshallah, no. 1, *se'if* 4; *Torat Menahem* 5743: 1, 263–66.
20. *Likkutei Sihot* 31, Beshallah, no. 1, *se'if* 5.

While limbs of the body are interconnected and interdependent, each limb serves a different function. By contrast, the single Jewish soul that is rooted in God transcends even such distinctions.

Ahavat Yisrael and Love of God

As alluded to above, the indivisible nature of the Jewish people is not an arbitrary belief but rather conceptually flows from Chabad's definition of the Jewish soul. As the Alter Rebbe wrote in the beginning of *Tanya*, each Jewish soul is "literally a part of God," an idea that the Rebbe developed at great length by associating the *yehida* of a person with the Divine Essence.[21] Thus, the utter simplicity of the Divine Essence leads to the utter unity of the single Jewish soul.

This association helps illuminate how the Rebbe related the categories of *ahavat Yisrael* and *ahavat Hashem* to one another. He construed loving another Jew as a form of loving the One God, who permeates every Jew and unites the two seemingly distinct individuals. In his ethical calendar, *HaYom Yom*, the Rebbe succinctly summarized the manner in which *ahavat Yisrael* and *ahavat Hashem* are intertwined:

> The Alter Rebbe repeated what the Maggid of Mezritch said quoting the Baal Shem Tov: "Love your fellow as yourself" is an interpretation of and commentary on "Love the Lord your God." He who loves his fellow Jew loves God, because the Jew has within himself a "part of God above." Therefore, when one loves a Jew – [the Jew's] inner self – one loves God.[22]

This idea was so central to the Rebbe's thought that he underscored its significance as part of his mission statement in 1951, emphatically stating: "The three loves – love of God, love of Torah, and love of one's fellow – are one. One cannot differentiate between them, for they are of a single essence."[23]

---

21. See chapter 6, section "The Divine Essence, the *Yehida*, and the Body."
22. *HaYom Yom*, 12 Av.
23. *Torat Menahem* 5711: 1, 210. See also *Likkutei Sihot* 2, *Hosafot*, 10 Shevat, *se'ifim* 9–10; ibid., *Bemidbar*, *se'if* 17. For the social ramifications of the integration of the love of one's fellow Jew and the love of God, see Philip Wexler, Eli Rubin, and Michael Wexler (2019), 115–20.

In fact, the Rebbe then went on to even prioritize *ahavat Yisrael* over the other two by asserting that a person who begins by loving his fellow Jews will eventually come to love God and the Torah as well.

Ahavat Yisrael and Self-Love

In addition to casting *ahavat Yisrael* as a form of loving God, the Rebbe employed this perspective on *ahdut Yisrael* to resolve Ramban's skepticism regarding a person's ability to love another person "as oneself." On several occasions, the Rebbe echoed Ramban's question:

> [The mitzva is to love others] "as yourself"; literally, just as your love for yourself does not stem from a specific reason but is rather an essential love (*ahava atzmit*),[24] so too, the love for another Jew must be an essential love. But seemingly, how is this possible? The other person and myself are two distinct people?[25]

The Rebbe's response flows directly from his understanding of *ahdut Yisrael*: "This is not love toward 'another.' It is love of oneself."[26] One is not enjoined to love another person as oneself, but rather to broaden one's definition of "self" to include all other Jews. From this perspective, love of oneself, love of one's fellow, and love of God are all a "single essence."[27]

Ahdut Yisrael as an Equalizer

The Rebbe emphasized that this perspective on *ahdut Yisrael* transcends all possible distinctions between individuals. At their core, all Jews contain the same *yehida* which is inextricably linked with the single Divine Essence, making it possible to overlook differences between them. One this basis, *ahdut Yisrael* and *ahavat Yisrael* are understood to include subgroups of the population that might otherwise have been excluded.

---

24. This love is characterized as being inherent and unbreakable, similar to that of a parent to a child. See, for example, *maamar* "Ata Ehad 5729," *se'if* 4 (*Sefer HaMaamarim Melukat* vol.2, 12–13)
25. *Likkutei Sihot* 2, Shemini Atzeret, *se'if* 4. See also *Likkutei Sihot* 2, Bemidbar, *se'if* 17; *Iggerot Kodesh* 23, letter 8867.
26. *Likkutei Sihot* 2, Shemini Atzeret, *se'if* 4.
27. See *Likkutei Sihot, Bemidbar, se'if* 17.

One demographic that features prominently in the Rebbe's talks is "simple people" (*anashim peshutim*). While intuitively it might be easier to love a righteous Torah scholar due to his superlative traits, the Rebbe argued that perceiving all Jews on their *yehida* level enables equally loving all Jews.

In one teaching, the Rebbe developed this idea through dissecting the midrash which correlates the four species taken on Sukkot with four types of Jews of varying levels of observance.[28] The midrash notes that even the bland *arava*, which represents Jews who neither study Torah nor do mitzvot, needs to be taken in a single bundle with the other species that represent Jews who study Torah and/or perform mitzvot. While it is possible to admire, love, and unite with the latter groups due to their righteousness, the inclusion of the *arava* has a different rationale: "We unite with them simply because they are Jews, which is an inner quality that exists in anyone who is descended from Abraham, Isaac, and Jacob."[29]

The Rebbe further argued that this exhibits the purest and deepest form of unity: "Specifically because simple people are connected with the simplicity of the Divine Essence, through connecting with them one can connect with the Divine Essence."[30] While the outstanding qualities of a Torah scholar or righteous person might overshadow their essential divine nature, no such concern exists regarding a simple person. One loves him due to the Divine Essence that lies at his core which unites all Jews into a single entity.[31]

The Rebbe even extended this essential oneness of all Jews to sinners. Despite sources in Jewish law and thought which exclude sinners from the category of *ahavat Yisrael*, Hasidism embraced a more encompassing and inclusive love. In fact, the Maggid of Mezritch taught his students this lesson from the heavenly academy: "*Ahavat Yisrael* means loving the absolutely wicked as much as the completely righteous."[32]

---

28. Leviticus Rabba 30:12.
29. *Likkutei Sihot* 22, Emor, no. 3, *se'if* 3.
30. Ibid., *se'if* 4.
31. See also *Likkutei Sihot* 29, Hoshana Rabba, *se'if* 4, where the Rebbe traced this idea to the Baal Shem Tov; ibid., 2, Bemidbar, *se'if* 15; *Torat Menahem* 5714: 3, 28–32; ibid., 5718: 1, 259–60; ibid., 5720: 1, 305–7; ibid., 5720: 2, 131–32.
32. Cited in *Likkutei Sihot* 2, Bemidbar, *se'if* 2.

On the halakhic plane, the Alter Rebbe already deftly explained that the talmudic injunction to hate sinners refers only to their sins but not to the sinner, who still must be the object of love.[33] But what is the philosophical justification for this love of the wantonly wicked? Once again, building on *Tanya*, the Rebbe explained that recognizing the pure and shared core of all Jews, including sinners, will lead to a broadening of one's love of self to include all Jews.[34] Violating the Torah cannot sully the *yehida* of the Jewish soul, which "is more elevated than even the Torah" due to its root in the Divine Essence and which binds all Jews together.[35]

Ahdut Yisrael Perspective No. 2: Composite Unity

While the above perspective on *ahdut Yisrael* is certainly necessary and valid, the Rebbe argued that it is insufficient. Perceiving all Jews as a single entity highlights the root of their souls but simultaneously discounts the real-life, significant qualities that differentiate each Jew. Therefore, the Rebbe also developed another tier of *ahdut Yisrael* and *ahavat Yisrael* that is based on accenting the singular nature of each individual.

In one talk, the Rebbe developed this dual perspective from two juxtaposed statements of Hillel in *Pirkei Avot*.[36] As the Rebbe explained:

> We demand two forms of service from the individual: (1) "If I am not for myself, then what am I?" and (2) "When I am for myself, what am I?" A Jew exists as an individual – "I am for myself" – but he is simultaneously part of the Jewish people, and without this he is nothing – "And when I am for myself, what am I?"[37]

---

33. *Tanya, Likkutei Amarim*, ch. 32. For a succinct but dense discussion of the relevant halakhic sources, see *Likkutei Sihot* 17, *Kedoshim*, notes 17 and 38.
34. *Likkutei Sihot* 2, *Bemidbar, se'if* 18.
35. Ibid., 17, *Kedoshim, se'if* 9, based on Genesis Rabba 1:4 and *Likkutei Torah, Shir HaShirim*, 16d. Another category of people included in this perspective of *ahavat Yisrael* is even Jews whom one has never met. See *Likkutei Sihot* 2, Shemini Azeret-Simhat Torah, *se'if* 4; ibid., 1, *Pekudei, se'if* 10; ibid., 23, 424. See also *Likkutei Sihot* 2, *Bemidbar, se'if* 14; *Torat Menahem* 5717: 3, 20, that this form of unity was engendered by the Divine Essence's Revelation at Sinai.
36. Mishna Avot 1:14.
37. *Likkutei Sihot* 18, *Behaalotekha*, no. 2, *se'if* 13.

The second perspective of "When I am for myself, what am I?" reflects the concept described above. There is no individual "I" that is worth perceiving, just the indivisible, national "I" of the Jewish people. Concurrently, though, each Jew needs to maintain an identity as an individual person with unique qualities to nurture and manifest.

Ahavat Yisrael Due to Each Person's Uniqueness
These two poles of self-identification create two different modes of *ahavat Yisrael*. As we have seen, on the root level, a Jew's love for his fellow is a form of loving oneself based on the merging of all individuals into a single entity. Simultaneously, though, in our revealed reality, each person must also view himself and others as unique and harness the uniqueness of the other as a basis for *ahavat Yisrael*. For example, in one talk, after the Rebbe reviewed the perspective of all Jews being a "single entity," he then continued:

> When the Alter Rebbe explains the concept of *ahavat Yisrael*, he does not suffice with saying, "Since they are all of a kind and all have one Father, therefore, all Jews are called real brothers by virtue of the source of their souls in the One God." Instead, he prefaces it with: "[Regarding] the soul and spirit, who can know [each of] their greatness...and source in the living God." This means that one needs to love each Jew [also] due to each one's superlativeness as an individual.[38]

All Jews contain unique "individual capacities" and should be loved not only because of the essence of their souls that is one and the same with all Jews, but also due to their unique virtues as individuals.

Elsewhere, the Rebbe identified the sin of Korah as neglecting to appreciate the unique talents and roles of each individual. In his initial contentious encounter with Moses, Korah argued: "You take too much upon yourselves, for the entire congregation are all holy, and the Lord is in their midst. So why do you raise yourselves above the Lord's

---

38. Ibid., *se'if* 14.

assembly?"³⁹ The Midrash identifies Korah as wise and righteous, and therefore the Rebbe sought to identify a deep, albeit flawed, basis for his rebellion. The Rebbe explained:

> Korah's claim that "the entire congregation is holy" – meaning that there is no possibility of different levels among the Jewish people – stems from his wisdom, since he saw the peace and unity at the root of the Jewish people, where there are no differences in levels, but rather simple oneness.⁴⁰

Korah saw only the inner core of the Jewish people that was revealed at Sinai. He therefore considered the leadership positions of Moses and Aaron to be an outrageous contravention of the fundamental oneness and equality of all Jews.

Ultimately, however, Korah made a fatal error. As Rashi explains, Moses retorted to Korah that "God set up boundaries in this world."⁴¹ While at the root of existence everything is the same "simple oneness," created reality teems with divinely ordained diversity. In a detailed fashion, the Rebbe outlined the heterogeneity that exists in the realms of space (*olam*), time (*shana*), and finally concluding with the realm of people (*nefesh*):

> Similarly, we find different levels... among the souls of the Jewish people. For example, we have the threefold division... into priests, Levites, and Yisrael... and there are ten levels among the Jewish people, from "the heads of your tribes" to the "wood hewers" and "water carriers" (Deut. 29:9).⁴²

Each of these groups is unique, with its own divinely ordained qualities and role. The same is true for each individual within these groups. Korah's attempt to view the Jewish people only in terms of their core

---

39. Num. 16:3.
40. *Likkutei Sihot* 18, *Korah*, no. 3, *se'if* 10.
41. Rashi on Num. 16:5.
42. *Likkutei Sihot* 18, *Korah*, no. 3, *se'if* 6.

identity while discounting the heterogenous reality led to strife and divisiveness, the exact opposite of the unity for which he strived.

A Unity Derived from Diversity

This second perspective highlights the uniqueness of each person and sees this particularity as the source of love. A remaining question, however, is how this perspective conceptualizes *ahdut Yisrael*. How can accenting uniqueness and diversity lead to unity?

The Rebbe often constructed his answer around the metaphor that each Jew is a limb of a body. Each limb has its own unique capacities and yet can optimally perform its function only with the assistance of every other limb. Even the head, while outshining the other limbs in many ways, still requires the collaboration of the feet to achieve its goals.

In line with this analogy, the Rebbe explained that a Jew should appreciate his own uniqueness and the uniqueness of every other Jew. Like limbs of a body, each individual Jew has a unique virtue that only they contain and can contribute, and every member of the "body" of the Jewish people is inherently dependent on the other to access the unique attributes they carry. Thus, as a body, the Jewish people comprises parts that interconnect and are interdependent but still retain their distinctiveness:

> In *this* form of unity [the unity is accomplished] specifically due to the differences [of the parts] and not due to their commonalities. Just as with a body, specifically through the differences between the head, the torso, and the feet...can it be called a complete body.[43]

While from the perspective of the *yehida* part of the soul all Jews are a single, indivisible entity, on the worldly level, unity is modeled after the human body, a single organism that consists of distinct parts that are reliant on each other for each member's unique and individual contribution.[44]

---

43. Ibid., *se'if* 8.
44. See, for example, *Likkutei Sihot* 4, *Nitzavim*, *se'ifim* 3–5; ibid., 30, *Vayigash*, no. 1, *se'if* 4; ibid., 31, *Beshallah*, no. 1, *se'ifim* 4–5.

The Advantages of Each Form of Ahdut

The Rebbe argued that each form of *ahdut* has an advantage over the other. At first blush, seeing all Jews as merged within a singular and indivisible entity expresses a stronger bond.[45] However, a composite unity has a quality that surpasses even this oneness. As the Rebbe said:

> [In indivisible unity,] it is not felt how all Jews are connected even in their external forms (which remain distinct from each other). However, the [advantageous] quality of a composite unity is that even the externalities, the individual capacities of each unit, which differentiate each Jew from the other, are still interrelated and complement each other.[46]

While an indivisible unity posits an unbreakable single entity, it relates only to the core essence of the person. A composite unity, by contrast, does not entirely overcome difference. But it has the advantage of harmoniously incorporating even the external differences that separate one person from another. From this perspective a composite unity is superior to the indivisible unity.

A Synthesized Unity

In summary, the Rebbe described two distinct tracks of *ahdut Yisrael* and *ahavat Yisrael*, with the relative advantages of each one. Characteristically, however, he was not satisfied with allowing each perspective to stand alone. Rather, using the conceptual framework that he developed for the relationship between the one Divine Essence and our diverse world, the Rebbe similarly sought to unify the two modes of *ahdut Yisrael*.

We have seen that the Rebbe conceived of a counterintuitive relationship between the Divine Essence and the material world.[47] While certain hasidic sources regarding the illusory nature of the material world

---

45. See, for example, *Likkutei Sihot* 30, *Vayigash*, no. 1, *se'if* 4, where the Rebbe outlined these levels of *ahdut Yisrael* and concluded that an essential unity is the highest level.
46. *Likkutei Sihot* 4, *Nitzavim*, *se'if* 5.
47. See chapter 4, section "The Material World in the Thought of the Rebbe."

might have led us to believe that the disclosure of the Divine Essence would negate the existence of a material world, the Rebbe contended that just the opposite was the case. The ultimate Divine Revelation will demonstrate that this world itself is in fact the truest expression of the Divine Essence, the *yesh haamiti* (true being). All the diverse elements of this world will retain their disparate features, and yet will, paradoxically, all be equally transparent to the singular Divine Essence.

The Rebbe modeled *ahdut Yisrael* upon this perspective. In one talk, the Rebbe discussed this idea of "drawing the Infinite (*Ein Sof*) ... into the creation as it stands divided into myriads of specifics."[48] This, he argued, could be accomplished by a parallel process occurring within the Jewish people. Generally, when two distinct people feel close to each other, "it is still not absolute unity,"[49] as they ultimately remain separate entities. By contrast, the unique nature of *ahdut Yisrael* is that even as distinct entities serving different functions (the composite model of *ahdut*), the utter essential oneness of all Jewish souls (the indivisible model of *ahdut*) shines clearly. As the Rebbe expressed it:

> Love for another Jew that is literally like self-love flows from the fact that all the Jewish people from the perspective of the root of their souls are a single entity. Nevertheless, the true unity of the Jewish people is expressed when even from the perspective of their individual realities, in which they seem to be different from each other, they are still a single entity.[50]

Just as each aspect of the material world ideally expresses the singular Divine Essence, so too, each distinct Jew can individually express the same inner *yehida*. A true fusion of indivisible and composite *ahdut* can be achieved since the Jewish people contain a single core essence that expresses itself in myriads of distinct ways.[51]

---

48. *Likkutei Sihot* 9, *Ki Tavo*, no. 1, *se'if* 12.
49. Ibid.
50. Ibid.
51. See also *Likkutei Sihot* 4, *Nitzavim*, *se'if* 6; ibid., 18, *Behaalotekha*, no. 2, *se'ifim* 12–14; ibid., 23, *Naso*, no. 2, *se'ifim* 6–14; ibid., 36, *Tetzaveh*, no. 1, *se'ifim* 4–5. For related

The conceptual underpinning for this explanation is an idea that the Rebbe developed at length in his seminal treatise "On the Essence of Hasidism." There, he explained that the quintessential core of an entity, by its very nature, must permeate the entire entity and demonstrate the entity's oneness while not annihilating the differing expressions of the oneness. As we have seen, the Rebbe argued that Hasidism, the core of Torah, demonstrates that each of the other genres of Torah are distinct expressions of the same core essence.[52]

Similarly, the Rebbe applied the quintessential core's pervasiveness to the nature of the Jewish soul:

> Even the distinct forms of each Jew, even their physicality, express the essence of the soul. Therefore, they can be completely one even from the perspective of their distinct realities. Contrariwise, if the unity of the Jewish people did not extend to their distinct realities, this would prove that their unity does not stem from their quintessential core, for the essence is present in all of the details.[53]

Since *ahdut Yisrael* begins with seeing all Jews as a single indivisible entity rooted in the Divine Essence, it follows that even on their "outermost" level of distinct physical beings, they retain this essential oneness.[54]

Similar to the full revelation of the Divine Essence in the material world or the full revelation of Hasidism, the Rebbe noted that this perspective of synthesized unity can only be fully revealed with the coming of *Mashiah*. Nonetheless, it is a perspective that we must currently inculcate and actualize to the best of our ability even within the current framework where the essence is often hidden.[55]

---

ideas, see *Likkutei Sihot* 11, Teruma, no. 1, *se'ifim* 4–8; ibid., 31, Vayak'hel, no. 3, *se'if* 6.
52. See chapter 9, section "The Unifying Essence of Torah."
53. *Likkutei Sihot* 9, Ki Tavo, *se'if* 12.
54. See also *Torat Menahem* 5718: 1, 98; ibid., 5745: 3, 1413.
55. See, for example, *Torat Menahem* 5751: 4, 78

BITTUL: THE METHOD OF ACHIEVING *AHDUT YISRAEL*

How is this exalted form of *ahdut* to be achieved and maintained? In line with the conceptual framework he developed in other areas, the Rebbe argued that effacing the egoistic externals of one's personality (*bittul*) is a key step on the path toward *ahdut*.

In one letter the Rebbe explicitly noted the difficulty in attaining this level of *ahdut*:

> The Creator created people with different minds and opinions, and also the entire world that He created has so much diversity, from extreme to extreme. [If so,] seemingly, how is it possible to achieve this unity?[56]

The Rebbe located the seed of his response in the Torah's narrative of the Sinaitic revelation:

> The answer is hinted to in the verse "And they stood at the bottom of the mountain" (Ex. 19:17), meaning that all 600,000 men, their wives, sons, and daughters strongly placed themselves "underneath the mountain" – [in a state] of complete *bittul* and great joy.[57]

Thus, being "underneath" the mountain without an ego is a prerequisite for *ahdut Yisrael*.

Bittul as Removing Ego

The Rebbe explained the connection between *bittul* and *ahdut Yisrael* along two different planes, the first practical and the second metaphysical. On a basic level, a person's ego leads to a sense of dissonance with other people:

> Divisiveness and separation are a result of *yeshut* (egoism) and arrogance. When a person feels that he exists as an important

---

56. *Likkutei Sihot* 11, *Hosafot*, 250.
57. Ibid.

Jewish Unity and Love

entity, he cannot be unified with his fellow, for the other person decreases his own existence.[58]

A delusional sense of self-importance causes one to think only in terms of oneself, to the point that other people are perceived as threats.[59] This feeling is clearly not in line with *ahdut Yisrael.*

The antidote to this mindset is the process of *bittul.* As the Rebbe continued:

> This is not the case regarding the Jewish people, about whom it is said "You are the smallest of the nations," in that you make yourself small, meaning that you are in the state of *bittul* (the opposite of *yeshut*). Therefore, each person makes space for the other, until they are unified.[60]

Removing the external sense of self allows one to create space for the other and see the interdependence of all Jews.

Bittul as Eliciting the *Yehida*

While there are deeper motifs latent in the above formulation, the Rebbe's words can be understood in very practical and concrete terms. Clearly, arrogance leads to divisiveness while humility allows for a person to appreciate other people. Elsewhere, though, the Rebbe explicated a deeper process that undergirds the association of *bittul* with *ahdut.*

According to the Rebbe, true *ahdut Yisrael* rests upon the disclosure of the *yehida.* As we have seen in several contexts, the Rebbe felt that a self-transcendent *bittul* is a key element in accessing and disclosing the inner *yehida.* Here as well, the path toward unveiling one's *yehida* and achieving true unity is to transcend one's ego.

The Rebbe once developed this idea in the context of Purim. He noted that one of the key themes of Purim is *ahdut Yisrael,* literarily

---

58. Ibid., 31, *Shemot,* no. 2, *se'if* 8.
59. For an interesting psychological description of this phenomenon, see *Torat Menahem* 5714: 1, 187.
60. *Likkutei Sihot* 31, *Shemot,* no. 2, *se'if* 8.

expressed in Queen Esther's plea to "go gather all of the Jews"[61] and concretized in the mitzvot of sending *mishloah manot* to friends and charity to the poor. The Rebbe explained that the precipitant for this unity was the *bittul* and self-sacrifice that Esther, Mordechai, and the Jewish people displayed during the Purim story:

> In order that the Jews be "entirely as one," despite their differences, each person needs to stand with *bittul* and *mesirut nefesh* before the Holy One, blessed be He. [This] *bittul* stems from the simple will of the *yehida* of the soul, which is above reason and logic and which all Jews possess equally.... It is only through the *mesirut nefesh* of Purim...that we can draw from a level that transcends all differences and limitations (of reason and logic), to the Divine Essence itself.[62]

The effacement of the external ego unveils the true essence of a person, which manifests itself in a complete oneness with the Divine Essence and other Jews.

In fact, the Rebbe argued that the *bittul* and *ahdut* of Purim exists on an even deeper level than that of other days that focus on the same themes, such as Yom Kippur and Shavuot. Purim represents the day of God's ultimate hiddenness, as the Book of Esther contains no overt miracles or even mentions of God's name. Bereft of inspiration from above or revelations of God to grasp onto, the Jewish people's connection to God must stem from the deepest recesses of their own being. For this reason, the *ahdut* of Purim includes all aspects of a person – soul and body:

> But on Purim there is another level...as the *bittul* and *mesirut nefesh* which comes from the person himself penetrates the entire existence of the person, even his physicality. Therefore, on Purim there is an obligation for feasting and joy...this means that the *mesirut nefesh* of Purim is connected with drinking

---

61. Est. 4:16.
62. *Torat Menahem* 5748: 2, 401–2.

wine and eating a physical meal.... The *ahdut* of Purim is likewise accomplished not through the dissolution of the body but specifically through physical items: "sending packages to one's friend and gifts to the poor," which unites all Jews that are physically dispersed.[63]

In summary, through the ultimate *bittul* to God, the Jewish people's oneness with God and with each other are revealed. This deepest level of *ahdut* allows for the oneness to permeate even the physicality of the Jewish people, which at first seems to be the ultimate dividing force. Thus, each Jew, in his own distinct physical body, can still be perceived as a single entity with every other Jew.[64]

PRACTICAL *AHAVAT YISRAEL*

Beyond developing the conceptual contours of *ahavat Yisrael*, the Rebbe saw these ideas as having immense practical ramifications. While from one perspective the Rebbe saw *ahavat Yisrael* as permeating every aspect of a Jew's life and undergirding all the various programs that he initiated,[65] he also outlined specific applications of *ahavat Yisrael* itself. These directives flow directly from the framework outlined above and are intertwined with the mission of bringing *Mashiah*.

A Proactive Approach

The Rebbe emphasized that the Baal Shem Tov taught his followers to develop a proactive orientation toward *ahavat Yisrael*. The Mishna in Avot teaches: "Any Torah that is not accompanied with work (*melakha*) will in the end cease."[66] While on a simple level the term "work" refers to gainful employment, the Baal Shem Tov disclosed another layer of meaning: "The meaning of 'work' is preoccupation (*hitaskut*) with

---

63. Ibid., 404.
64. For similar connections between *bittul* and the ultimate level of *ahdut Yisrael*, see *Likkutei Sihot* 36, *Tetzaveh*, no. 2, *se'if* 5; *Torat Menahem* 5750: 2, 106–8; ibid., 5748: 4, 48.
65. *Sihot Kodesh* 5736: 2, 685.
66. Mishna Avot 2:2.

Aspects of a Godly Life

ahavat Yisrael. For Torah to be sustained it must be combined with a preoccupation with *ahavat Yisrael*."[67]

R. Yosef Yitzhak explained that the word "preoccupation" connotes a proactive spirit:

> The meaning of "preoccupation" [can be understood] from the model of a merchant. A merchant does not stay at home with his wares and wait for someone to recognize the value of his wares and come to purchase them. Rather, he opens a store in a busy area and hangs up a sign so all of the passersby can see that there are wares inside. But does he suffice with this? He goes and publicizes the quality of his wares and attempts to convince people to buy from him. He invests much energy to bring people to buy his goods.[68]

The Rebbe identified the Baal Shem Tov's proactive stance in this area as one of his major innovations regarding the mitzva of *ahavat Yisrael*.[69]

The Rebbe taught that this activism is required in both the material and spiritual realms, as we will now describe.

Ahavat Yisrael in the Spiritual Realm

Perhaps the most ubiquitous aspects of the Rebbe's call to practically apply *ahavat Yisrael* was that observant Jews must work to bring their less observant brethren closer to Torah and mitzvot. In his explication of the merchant analogy, the Rebbe said: "One should excessively invest to benefit another Jew, to influence him ... to explain to him the preciousness of Torah and the *mitzvot* and to increase one's efforts that another Jew hear words of Hasidism."[70]

Based on his theory of an all-encompassing and detail-oriented *hashgaha*, the Rebbe argued that the very fact that a Jew received any

---

67. *Likkutei Sihot* 1, *Kedoshim*, *se'if* 14.
68. Ibid., *se'if* 17.
69. *Iggerot Kodesh* 17, letter 6313.
70. *Likkutei Sihot* 1, *Kedoshim*, *se'if* 17.

sort of Jewish education obligates him to share his knowledge with others.[71] When this is combined with a proactive perspective toward *ahavat Yisrael*, the resulting picture is that every Jew who has some knowledge of Torah is obligated to actively seek out ways to share Torah and mitzvot with others.[72]

A Connection Between Outreach and Ahavat Yisrael
Why is helping a person learn Torah or perform mitzvot a primary expression of *ahavat Yisrael*? In one talk, the Rebbe discussed this issue in relation to the statement of Hillel in *Pirkei Avot*: "Be of the disciples of Aaron – a lover of peace, a pursuer of peace, one who loves the created and draws them close to Torah."[73] While the connection between being a lover of people and drawing them close to Torah might be intuitive to most, the Rebbe probed further:

> What is the connection between "loves other people" and "draws them close to Torah"? Should not *ahavat Yisrael* bring every Jew to try to benefit his fellow Jew, not just spiritually, but in all matters: physical and spiritual?[74]

The Rebbe then deepened the question by noting that the connection Hillel makes between *ahavat Yisrael* and spiritually benefiting other Jews seems antithetical to the hasidic rationale for the mitzva. In the words of the Rebbe: "Since the love [for the other] is an essential love from the soul (and not based on the level of the other person in their service of God), why is the love connected with 'draw[ing] them close to Torah'?"[75] *Ahavat Yisrael* flows from the essential nature of the other's Jewish soul, which transcends specific behaviors and mitzva observance. Why, then, did Hillel connect Aaron's love for others with his work in bringing them closer to Torah?

---

71. Ibid., *se'ifim* 16, 19.
72. The Rebbe clearly articulated that this obligation of outreach applied to each and every Jew. See, for example, *Likkutei Sihot* 30, *Vayishlah*, no. 3, *se'if* 9.
73. Mishna Avot 1:12.
74. *Likkutei Sihot* 17, *Kedoshim*, no. 2, *se'if* 8.
75. Ibid.

Aspects of a Godly Life

The Rebbe's response drew upon the notion of the indivisible, tripartite unity of God, the Jewish people, and Torah. While it is true that a Jew remains inherently connected to God irrespective of his level of observance, Torah itself still remains an inexorable part of the equation. Each Jew's deepest desire, if given the space and opportunity to access his inner self to make a real "choice," would be to be one with God by following the path of Torah and mitzvot, as this desire is embedded in the most foundational core of his identity.[76]

Accordingly, one Jew's attempt to bring another Jew closer to Torah does not run counter to the concept that each Jew's essential oneness with God transcends personal behavior. Rather, the attempt to draw a person closer to Torah is fundamentally bound up with the work of nurturing the soul and enabling it to properly express itself:

> In their root, the souls of Jews are above the level of Torah... but here below [in this world], the essential level of "he is a Jew" cannot remain disembodied from observance of Torah and mitzvot; rather, it must lead to the fulfillment of Torah and mitzvot, and through this the essential nature of the soul will be revealed.[77]

A deep consciousness of and love for another Jew's unbreakable connection to God irrespective of observance is precisely what must motivate one's efforts to help other Jews come closer to Torah and greater engagement in the practice of mitzvot.

Ahavat Yisrael as Motivation and Mode of Outreach

The fact that the work of sharing Torah and mitzvot with others is motivated by love for the essential soul of all Jews impacts the method and texture of these activities. In one impassioned talk, the Rebbe harshly critiqued the approach of outreach via fear and threats:

> There is no truth to the approach that in order to bring a Jew close one needs to become angry with him.... It is obvious; Heaven

---

76. See chapter 7, section "A Jew's Choice."
77. *Likkutei Sihot* 17, *Kedoshim*, no. 2, *se'if* 9.

forbid that a person should say words that are the opposite of blessings. Let this not be heard among the Jewish people!... This approach lacks the trait of the students of Abraham, to look at every Jew with a "good eye" (Avot 5:19).[78]

Rather, the Rebbe argued, such activities must be pervaded with unconditional love:

> The proper method... is to approach men, women, and children with a glowing smile, with love and closeness, to speak to them genuinely and to model a personal example, including *an utter negation of arrogance and superiority over the other*. [Emphasis added.][79]

Love, warmth, and humility are fundamental to the work of bringing people close to Torah.

As the Rebbe explicated, unconditional love and a deep understanding of its basis should dispel any feelings of superiority or condescension. All Jews are inherently connected to God, and the goal is to "reveal [the] true greatness,"[80] which is shared equally by all Jews.[81]

Rebutting Challenges to Activism
Textual Support for Activism
The Rebbe sought to rebut opposition from some quarters to his proactive charge. On several occasions he noted that observant people in general, and Torah scholars in particular, might be concerned that investing time in helping others learn more Torah or do more mitzvot will negatively affect their own religious growth. The Rebbe responded to these concerns on several levels.

---

78. *Torat Menahem* 5748: 1, 247–48.
79. Ibid., 248.
80. Ibid., 5751: 2, 115.
81. See also *Likkutei Sihot, Kedoshim, se'if* 21. This point also leads to the Rebbe's assertion that every time one "gives" to another person he must also realize that he "receives" something from them. For an insightful analysis of this dynamic, see Philip Wexler, Eli Rubin, and Michael Wexler (2019), 111–15.

First, on a textual level, the Rebbe associated this self-protective perspective with Pharaoh. After Moses and Aaron initially present God's command to Pharaoh, he responds: "Why, Moses and Aaron, do you disturb the people from their work? Go to your own labors" (Ex. 5:4).

Ramban notes that as Levites, Moses and Aaron were not subject to physical servitude. Rather, Pharaoh was telling them to return to their studies and spiritual pursuits, including their role as teachers of the Jewish people. Here is the Rebbe's reformulation of Ramban's idea:

> Pharaoh was claiming to Moses and Aaron: It should be enough that you are free and able to learn Torah yourselves and even with your fellow Jews. Why should you get involved in communal work and the lives of other Jews and cause them to not live in accordance with the laws and customs of the country?[82]

Pharaoh did not oppose the fact of Moses and Aaron's occasional teaching of Torah to their fellow Jews. However, he wanted the people to continue to live within "the customs of the country." In other words, Pharaoh did not want Moses and Aaron to take responsibility for the spiritual lives of other Jews which would lead them to try to impact the actual lifestyle and mindset of his Jewish slaves.

The Rebbe noted that Pharaoh's appeal to Moses and Aaron's own spiritual pursuits and societal normalcy is intuitively attractive. At the end of the day, however, it is Pharaoh's recommendation. Ultimately, Moses and Aaron rejected this suggestion and threw themselves into their new mission of moving their brethren to an entirely different mindset and lifestyle.[83] The mitzva of *ahavat Yisrael* requires each Jew to care about others and help them live in a way that reflects their true inner essence.[84]

---

82. *Likkutei Sihot* 16, *Shemot*, no. 4, *se'if* 1.
83. Ibid., *se'if* 3.
84. The Rebbe also faulted Noah for adopting a similar approach to that of Pharaoh. See, for example, *Iggerot Kodesh* 18, letter 6542.

The Conceptual Imperative for Activism

In addition to rejecting a passive approach toward the spiritual welfare of other Jews, the Rebbe articulated three intertwined reasons as to why this imperative should outweigh any counter-considerations. First, the Rebbe emphasized the direness of the current situation in which so many Jews were at risk of being spiritually lost. When lives are at risk, one does not have the right to engage in cost-benefit analyses:

> Regarding his claim that it is preferable for a person to protect himself... in consonance with "And I have saved my own life,"[85] he should know that we are faced with a situation of mortal danger (*pikuah nefesh*), and regarding mortal danger it is forbidden to entertain such calculations.[86]

Just as if one sees a person trapped in a burning building he will immediately act to save the person and not first engage in calculations or consultation, the same applies for the spiritual fires that abound.[87]

A second aspect of the Rebbe's rejection of focusing on self-preservation flows directly from his concept of *ahdut Yisrael*. A worldview that sees all Jews as inherently one renders the claim for self-protection at the expense of others to be nonsensical:

> When one sees that the spiritual state of a Jew is not as it should be, not yet fully lit, a person should not delude himself that "I will save my own soul." All Jews are a "single and complete structure,"[88] and therefore when there is a blemish in the perfection of one Jew in Torah and mitzvot, this lack is felt by every Jew.[89]

The hasidic perspective of *ahdut Yisrael* breaks the false conflict between one's own spiritual development and the spiritual development of others,

---

85. Paraphrase of Ezek. 3:21.
86. *Likkutei Sihot* 1, *Kedoshim*, *se'if* 19.
87. Ibid., 16, *Shemot*, no. 4, *se'if* 3.
88. Quotation from Alter Rebbe's *Likkutei Torah*, *Nitzavim*, 44a.
89. *Likkutei Sihot* 16, *Shemot*, no. 4, *se'if* 5.

for, being all part of one body, all Jews are personally affected by the other's spiritual state.

A third, and perhaps the deepest, aspect of the Rebbe's rejection of a self-protective stance was an appeal to the notion of *bittul* and *mesirut nefesh*, which, as noted, are key elements in the quest toward *ahdut Yisrael* and *ahavat Yisrael*. Already in his coronation discourse, the Rebbe outlined the necessity of acting with *shetut dikedusha* (holy folly), in which a person prioritizes aiding others' spiritual development over his own advancement in Torah and the practice of mitzvot. The Rebbe cast this self-transcendence as a central method of revealing the Divine Essence within the lowest realm.

In a later address the Rebbe pointed to the priest who performs the rite of the red heifer as a model for outreach. In order to assist other Jews who are ritually impure, the priest must leave the sanctified space of the camp and even contract impurity. Characteristically, the Rebbe noted that such behavior is counterintuitive for a priest, who spends his days in the sanctity and purity of the *Beit HaMikdash*. This teaches us the extent to which a person must go to assist another Jew.

Then the Rebbe elaborated on the cosmic effects of such an act:

> In order to draw from above the *hishtalshelut* from the "Singular One of the world" (*yehido shel olam*), one's service needs to be from the *yehida* of the soul, a self-effacement (*hitbatlut*) that transcends logic. He needs to efface himself, to leave the camp, and to take a cow, an animal...become involved with it with full knowledge that he will become impure, just in order to purify another Jew.[90]

The ability to sacrifice one's spiritual ambitions for the sake of another Jew is "the entirety of the Torah," as it reveals the *yehida* of one's soul as utterly united with the Divine Essence.

---

90. Ibid., 4, *Hukkat*, *se'if* 4. See also *Torat Menahem* 5746: 2, 412, where the Rebbe elaborated on the need to spiritually endanger oneself for the sake of another Jew.

Materially Benefiting Other Jews

The Mitzva to Materially Benefit Others

While the Rebbe spent considerable time focusing on the need to actively express *ahavat Yisrael* through spiritually impacting other Jews, he consistently emphasized that this does not exhaust the mitzva. Rather, one's dedication to other Jews must be comprehensive – spiritual and material.

The Rebbe emphasized that even though materially benefiting other Jews can open doors toward their spiritual improvement, this should not be the main goal of providing such assistance to another Jew. Instead, the Rebbe quoted a teaching of the Baal Shem Tov: "One should not wait to make the material favor conditional on a spiritual [matter]…but rather materially assist the other person without any form of stipulation."[91]

Another layer of the Rebbe's call to materially help other Jews irrespective of their spiritual level and trajectory relates to the inherent significance of each Jew in God's eyes. In a conversation with the Israeli chief Rabbi Mordechai Eliyahu, the Rebbe once explained that Chabad Hasidim take care of the physical and material needs of other Jews as an end in and of itself. This is related to the midrashic idea[92] that the Jewish people "preceded" even the Torah itself:

> Therefore, in Chabad there is an effort to be involved in helping Jews, to supply their needs, including simple material needs. Not only with a condition that they should study Torah, but because we are speaking about Jewish men, women, and children, whose existence preceded the entire world, including the existence of Torah.[93]

The inherent importance of every Jew, which transcends even the importance of Torah, explains why materially helping other Jews is an end unto itself.

---

91. *Likkutei Sihot* 1, *Kedoshim*, *se'if* 18.
92. Tanna DeVei Eliyahu Rabba, ch. 14.
93. *Torat Menahem* 5752: 1, 231.

Aspects of a Godly Life

Material Favors and the Yehida

Once again, the Rebbe characterized these material favors as integral expressions of true *ahdut Yisrael* and *ahavat Yisrael*. The highest form of *ahdut Yisrael* is when one accesses his *yehida* and realizes that all Jews are but differing expressions of the same core essence. As we have seen, from the perspective of the *yehida*/Divine Essence, there is no essential difference between spirituality and physicality. Therefore, the *ahdut* that is created via the revelation of the *yehida* must permeate even the physical realm.

The Rebbe once elicited this idea from the halakhic concept of being a guarantor (*arev*) for the debt of another Jew. While one might categorize this as a purely monetary affair, the Rebbe demonstrated textually that being a guarantor for a loan is linked with the broader concept of "all Jews are guarantors for one another,"[94] which expresses the general notion of *ahdut Yisrael*. When explaining the link between *ahdut Yisrael* and being a guarantor for a loan, the Rebbe explained:

> The basis for *ahdut Yisrael* to the extent that "all Jews are guarantors for each other" is due to the fact that their soul is rooted in the One God.... Since the goal of the Jewish people is to be "one nation in the land" (II Sam. 7:23), as the Alter Rebbe explained that even in physical matters (i.e., land), they reveal the unity of God, therefore, it is possible for their unity to be revealed even in monetary matters.[95]

Even the monetary aspects of a Jew's life are permeated by the Divine Essence and are an integral part of *ahdut Yisrael*.[96]

AHAVAT YISRAEL TO BRING MASHIAH

In addition to the eternal relevance of *ahdut Yisrael* and *ahavat Yisrael*, the Rebbe characteristically underscored their urgency for the people

---

94. Sanhedrin 27b.
95. *Likkutei Sihot* 30, *Vayigash*, no. 1, *se'if* 3.
96. Similarly, see *Torat Menahem* 5749: 2, 380–81, where the Rebbe used this idea to explain the focus that the Torah places on the Jewish people's material donations to the *Mishkan*.

living in close proximity to *Mashiah*. Understanding and implementing *ahavat Yisrael* is key to usher in the era of ultimate fraternity.[97]

An Antidote for Baseless Hatred

On one level, the Rebbe noted that *ahavat Yisrael* is an excellent antidote for one of the main causes of the exile. In a famous passage, the Talmud identifies "baseless hatred" as the reason for the exile.[98] Therefore, the Rebbe argued, the redemption will be generated by an increase of "baseless love":

> In every generation the value of *ahavat Yisrael* increases, and certainly so in the end of the exile. As the Rabbis explained, the exile is due to baseless hatred, and our generation is the heel of the heel of *Mashiah*[99] ... the value of *ahavat Yisrael* is great, as it repairs the main sinful cause of our exile.[100]

Ahavat Yisrael and Revealing the Divine Essence

While the textual connection between baseless hatred and *ahavat Yisrael* is clear, the Rebbe's understanding of the inner dynamics of *ahdut Yisrael* and *ahavat Yisrael* lends greater conceptual significance to this linkage. The Rebbe characterized both the messianic process and the highest level

---

97. For the Rebbe, this emphasis on *ahavat Yisrael* includes the need to always speak the praises of the Jewish people and defend them from attacks. In this regard the Rebbe implicitly rebuked other Torah leaders for their poor assessment of the Jewish masses.
    For example, *Torat Menahem* 5751: 2, 112–32, was a rebuttal to a speech delivered by R. Eliezer Shach, who spoke publicly about how the sins of Israeli Jewry could bring about another Holocaust. For more details about this episode, see Chaim Miller (2014), 390–94. To a lesser degree, see *Likkutei Sihot* 6, 271–78, where the Rebbe responded to halakhic challenges that emerged from the Satmar community regarding the permissibility of putting tefillin on non-observant Jews. See Yitzhak Kraus (2007), 167–76, for more details.
98. Yoma 9b.
99. The Rebbe employed this double formulation to signal a high level of proximity to the coming of *Mashiah*. For an explanation, see *Torat Menahem* 5711: 2, 181.
100. *Iggerot Kodesh* 5, letter 1527. See also *Likkutei Sihot* 29, *Devarim*, *se'if* 9. The Rebbe also cited other rabbinic statements linking *ahavat Yisrael* to the future redemption. See, for example, *Likkutei Sihot* 34, *Devarim*, *se'if* 8.

of *ahdut Yisrael* as the complete revelation of the *yehida*/Divine Essence. As such, achieving the epitome of an *ahdut Yisrael* consciousness and lifestyle is an integral part of bringing *Mashiah*, the *yehida* of the world.

In one talk, the Rebbe directly linked *ahdut Yisrael* to the foundational midrashic passage he quoted in the *Bati LeGani* discourse with which he began his tenure. After citing the midrash's description of the inexorable descent of the Essence of the *Shekhina* back to ground level, the Rebbe continued:

> The main point is that of *ahdut*. In order to create the reality of "He will dwell forevermore" (Ps. 37:29) and "I will dwell among you" (Ex. 25:8), *ahdut* is necessary. The vessel to draw down the One above is to have unity here below – the unity of the Jewish people.[101]

The highest level of *ahdut Yisrael*, the Rebbe continued, works in a parallel fashion to the revelation of the Divine Essence in the material world. Each individual, in his own unique way, expresses the same divine core, exhibiting the utter unity within diversity. When the Jewish people live with this unity, God can descend into the material world and generate the messianic reality.

This is particularly true regarding the practical manifestations of *ahavat Yisrael*. The Rebbe once characterized the essential task of his *sheluhim* (emissaries) as revealing the *yehida* of each person they encounter.[102] This discloses the Divine Essence in the world and helps create the messianic reality. Similarly, on another occasion the Rebbe quoted from earlier Hasidim that caring for another person's material needs should be seen as a spiritual pursuit. He explained that providing such care with this perspective helps "prepare for the Messianic Era," when "the difference between physicality and spirituality will dissipate."[103]

---

101. *Torat Menahem* 5746: 2, 410. See also *Torat Menahem* 5745: 1, 296–97; ibid., 5751: 3, 360–66; ibid., 5751: 4, 77–78.
102. *Torat Menahem* 5746: 1, 344; ibid., 5743: 3, 1316–19.
103. Ibid., 5712: 3, 148.

Jewish Unity and Love

In short, a consciousness of *ahdut Yisrael* as expressed in a life dedicated to spiritually and materially benefiting other Jews plays a key role in revealing the *yehida* of the world and creating the messianic reality.

CONCLUSION

Ahdut Yisrael and *ahavat Yisrael* are central axioms of the Rebbe's holistic thought system. The Rebbe built upon earlier Chabad teaching to construct an expansive theory of *ahavat Yisrael*, and constantly urged its practical application: to proactively care for the material and spiritual needs of every individual Jew.

Secondary Literature Consulted for Chapter 13, "Jewish Unity and Love"

Nissan Dovid Dubov, *To Love a Fellow Jew: The Mitzva of Ahavas Yisrael in Chasidic Thought*.

Yoel Kahn, *Sugyot BaHasidut*, 51–68.

Yitzhak Kraus, *HaShevi'i: Meshihiyut BaDor HaShevi'i shel Chabad*, 167–76.

Jacob Immanuel Schochet, *Chasidic Dimensions*, 17–81, 179–216.

Chapter 14

Mending the Fragmented Life

The Rebbe guided his followers toward a diverse array of activities. Just as their work was to span the entire globe, their range of enterprises was to be similarly broad. The Hasidim were galvanized to manage institutions, lead communities, invest in the mitzva campaigns, sacrifice their comfort for even a lone Jew, and generally be involved in the broader world, while simultaneously raising large families and intensely engaging in the traditional religious regimen of Torah study, contemplative prayer, and spirited performance of mitzvot. In one form or another, this sort of multitasking is a prevalent feature of modern life that the Rebbe embraced.

While we have outlined the Rebbe's rationale for requiring active engagement in a broad range of activities, what remains to be explored is the correlative inner experience. What effect should juggling such diverse activities have on the inner mental, emotional, and religious life of a Jew?

RAV SOLOVEITCHIK
One model to consider is that of R. Joseph B. Soloveitchik. Similar to the Rebbe, R. Soloveitchik aptly described the rich breadth of a religious life.

Mending the Fragmented Life

Even a cursory reading of R. Soloveitchik's canon reveals the religious value of mundane corporal activities,[1] "conquering" the physical world through science, technology, and proper legislation,[2] while still placing a premium on intense Torah study and emotional prayer. In addition to sourcing the meaningfulness of these diverse activities, R. Soloveitchik, as a religious phenomenologist,[3] had a particular interest in describing the impact of this lifestyle on the human psyche.

While each of R. Soloveitchik's essays has its own unique flavor, the conceptual constellation of dialectic, oscillation, and tension are major themes in his thought. He described the various poles of religious life as drawing from different inner drives and as constituting opposing forces.[4] These contradictory inner forces and halakhic imperatives simultaneously pull a person in different directions and create inner tension. While the halakhic system helps guide a person in this constant oscillation between opposing modalities, it can at best navigate the dialectic without ever fully resolving the unresolvable.[5] The Torah, in effect, demands a broad life, but one that is saturated with dialectical tensions.

THE REBBE: STATEMENT OF THE PROBLEM

In contrast to R. Soloveitchik, the Rebbe taught that a diet of diverse pursuits stemming from disparate human faculties does not necessarily create inner tension. Based on his understanding of the nature of the soul, the material world, and the gamut of human activity, the Rebbe strongly felt that inner serenity should be the lot of even the busiest Hasidim with the most diverse portfolios of activities and concerns.

It is first important to note that the Rebbe realized that constant engagement in diverse enterprises is a recipe for internal feelings of

---

1. *And from There You Shall Seek* (2008), 110–21.
2. *The Lonely Man of Faith* (2012), 12–20, 92–98.
3. See David Shatz (2007), 174–85.
4. See, for example, the essays "Majesty and Humility" and "Catharsis" published in *Tradition*, 1978.
5. For the role of halakha in navigating these tensions, see *The Lonely Man of Faith*, 81–84, and the essay "Catharsis." See also *The Lonely Man of Faith*, endnote to ch. 8; "Majesty and Humilty," 25, that R. Soloveitchik relegates the easing of these inner tensions to the Messianic Era.

Aspects of a Godly Life

scatteredness and anchorlessness. For example, he once addressed the challenges of being a religious businessman:

> When one makes the calculation, one sees that the majority of their time is spent on matters of this world, matters of business and similar things, and only a small amount of time remains for studying Torah. And, furthermore, even in that small amount of time it is difficult to concentrate on the study of Torah – due to internal scatteredness (*pizzur hanefesh*), Heaven forbid, such that even if a person's body is in one place, his thoughts are located in the other end of the world... and he is never in a state of serenity (*menuha*).[6]

As is apparent from the quote, the Rebbe contrasted *menuha* with a mental state of "scatteredness," a state of mind which merited the disapproving comment of "Heaven forbid."[7] In seeming contradiction to his concern for inner scatteredness, the diversity of activities that the Rebbe proposed for his Hasidim seems to lead directly to such a mental state. How did the Rebbe recommend reaching the sought-after state of inner *menuha*?[8]

THE STRATEGY

Unified Goal

One portal into the Rebbe's approach to this topic is a talk from Shavuot 5751.[9] Since that Shavuot began on Motza'ei Shabbat, the Rebbe took the opportunity to elaborate on the common denominators that bind Shabbat and Shavuot. He began by carefully tracing the importance of

---

6. *Torat Menahem* 5722: 3, 50.
7. For similar disapproval of a state of mental scatteredness, see *Torat Menahem* 5710: 1, 14–15; ibid., 5723: 1, 163–64. See also *Iggerot Kodesh* 1, letter 159, where the Rebbe identified finding a sense of unity in all of one's activities as a main principle of Judaism.
8. It is important to emphasize that the Rebbe did speak out against people becoming mentally and emotionally overtaken by their worldly affairs. For example, see *Torat Menahem* 5722: 3, 50; *Torat Menahem* 5724: 3, 46, where he spoke against businessmen becoming too immersed in their businesses and unnecessarily swamping their mind with their business engagements.
9. *Torat Menahem* 5751: 3, 266–77.

Mending the Fragmented Life

"rest" (*menuha*) to both of these days. Shabbat is explicitly rooted in God's resting from His creative activities and is observed by our parallel cessation of the thirty-nine forbidden labors. Similarly, the Talmud records that prior to Shavuot, the world was in a state of existential anxiety, as it knew that it would cease to exist if the Jewish people would not accept the Torah. It was only after the first Shavuot that the world became "quiet" and serene.[10]

Having established the connection between Shabbat, Shavuot, and *menuha*, the Rebbe launched into this grouping's conceptual underpinnings. First, he located "the opposite of *menuha*" as an integral part of the regular order of creation:

> The world on its own was created in a manner of flux and movement (the opposite of *menuha*). [This manifests itself] primarily in the flux of time (Sunday, Monday, etc.), which is all about the change and movement of the past, present, and future. And all creations in this world ... are subservient to the changes of time.... Similarly, the divisions of space ... and the changes from place to place are connected with the opposite of *menuha*.[11]

Reality itself is filled with constant change and flux, seemingly the opposite of the desired *menuha*.

How, then, do Shabbat and Shavuot provide the basis for *menuha*? The Rebbe began by explaining that Shabbat transcends the regular order of reality and brings to the fore a sense of the unifying goal that lies at the root of reality's dynamism:

> Shabbat brought *menuha* into the world ... once creation was completed ... it was felt in the entire world and in all the details of the world – in all of the fluctuations and levels of time and place – that everything was created from the One God. God has a *single* goal for all the details of creation.[12]

---

10. Shabbat 88a.
11. *Torat Menahem* 5751: 3, 267.
12. Ibid., 268.

Similarly, the Giving of the Torah on Shavuot publicly revealed that God's goal for creation was bound with the Jewish people's observance of Torah and mitzvot. Thus, Shabbat and the Torah form a grounding framework in which the single and unifying goal of everything – creating a *Dira BaTahtonim* – becomes apparent. Instead of seeing the fluctuations of time and space as a dizzying array of disconnected details, these vacillations all take place within a structure of unwavering and steady *menuha*, created by the single, all-encompassing goal of creating a *Dira BaTahtonim*.

The Rebbe then took this notion of achieving *menuha* through identifying a unifying goal and applied it to the human psyche:[13]

> When a person does not feel the purpose and goal of his life – "I was created to serve my Creator" (Kiddushin 82b) – he cannot be in a state of *menuha* and true serenity, as the fluctuations of time and place and all of the myriads of details of one's life cause constant noise that fragment him. Only when a person feels the purpose and goal that is latent in all the details – this brings him *menuha*, as [the goal] transcends the movement and fluctuations of time and space. This *menuha* automatically leads a person in the direction of self-perfection, as it is apparent that a person is closer to perfection when he has *menuha* – *menuha* of the soul and *menuha* of the body.

As was noted above, the myriads of diverse details will naturally create constant "noise" and cause a person to feel unmoored. The way to remain fully engaged in all of life's meaningful details while still cultivating inner serenity is to consciously create a framework that encompasses all of the details and highlights their unified purpose. Then, instead of simply living life as a series of unrelated, albeit meaningful activities, the clear sense of purpose can function as the true and single substratum for the gamut of life's details. In this talk, the Rebbe unambiguously identified the single purpose of life: "I was created to serve my Creator."

---

13. Ibid.

Mending the Fragmented Life

Detailed Simplicity
In this talk, the Rebbe mainly focused on the positive psychological ramifications of having a clearly identifiable goal for all of one's diverse activities. Elsewhere, the Rebbe developed the same notion but contextualized it within Chabad's soul-psychology. As we have seen in many contexts, the Rebbe taught that the revelation of the Divine Essence breaks absolute binaries and allows us to see the multiplicity around us as different expressions of the same core entity. Here, as well, the Rebbe construed inner harmony amid all the diversity of one's commitments as the psychological parallel to the disclosure of the Divine Essence. Therefore, true inner serenity is a messianic consciousness, manifestation of the Divine Essence's inner parallel: the *yehida*.

The Rebbe employed these terms in Elul 5715/1955, early in his leadership. He opened the talk with a verse from the chapter of Psalms that is recited during the month of Elul: "One [thing] I ask of the Lord, that I seek – that I may dwell in the House of the Lord all the days of my life, to see the pleasantness of the Lord and to visit His Temple every morning."[14] In a long *maamar*, the Rebbe noted the tension between David's opening declaration that he will ask for "one thing" and the litany of requests that follows. Through a characteristic textual and conceptual analysis, the Rebbe demonstrated that the subsequent specifics are details which naturally flow from David's one central desire: to dwell in the House of the Lord.[15]

After concluding the *maamar*, the Rebbe raised the following question regarding David's phraseology: "Why was it necessary for David to request one thing from which all the subsequent details flowed? He could have independently and explicitly asked for each detail that he needed."[16]

The Rebbe's response was paradigmatic of how he viewed the relationship between diverse religious enterprises: "To a Jew, one thing should be important: 'to dwell in the House of the Lord' – the

---

14. Ps. 27:4
15. *Torat Menahem* 5715: 2, 290–301.
16. Ibid., 304.

Aspects of a Godly Life

connection with God. Nothing else should matter at all."[17] While such an approach would seem limiting, the Rebbe immediately continued: "When one cares about this single goal, then he will automatically ask for all other things, since all the others are part of 'dwelling in the House of the Lord.'"[18]

The one true desire of a Jew is to connect with God. All other aspects of one's life are a dizzying array of diverse ways to achieve this single goal; they are all manifestations of a single inner core.

It is important to emphasize that in this talk, the Rebbe spoke not only of identifying a single goal that encompasses and unifies the details of one's life. Rather, on a deeper level, he described all the diverse details as naturally flowing from a single point within the person. As one might expect, he identified the single indivisible entity that begets this unified diversity as the *yehida*:

> This is the meaning of "One thing I ask..."; the "one" refers to the *yehida*, as the quality of the *yehida* is that it receives from the One (God), and therefore, nothing matters to the *yehida* other than its connection to the One (God).[19]

Tapping into the *yehida* allows for a unified life despite the tug and pull of existence:

> When one fulfills "One thing I ask," then it can be "all the days of my life," meaning in a constant fashion without fluctuation. From the perspective of specific human qualities there are fluctuations, as a certain quality is needed for one thing, while a different quality is needed for another. At times a person is aroused to perform a certain task, and then, "should you blink your eyes at it, it is not here" (Prov. 23:5). But from the perspective of the *yehida*, there is no room for fluctuations or divisions at all.[20]

---

17. Ibid.
18. Ibid., 305.
19. Ibid.
20. Ibid.

Tending to a large family with small children requires a very different skill set than running a communal institution – each draws from its own "specific quality" within the person. However, instead of a person viewing himself as oscillating between two meaningful but clashing poles, he should perceive these activities as different manifestations of the same fundamental drive: the *yehida*'s desire to connect with God. As the Rebbe put it later in the talk, the activities and drives become the many "details of 'simplicity'" (*peratim mitzad hapeshitut*)[21] – the exact type of explanation that is characteristic of his thought.[22]

METHOD OF ACHIEVING INNER UNITY

Bittul

Once again, the Rebbe emphasized that the path toward achieving internal equanimity is self-effacement (*bittul*). It is only through transcending the specific egoistic elements of one's personality that the *yehida* can be accessed and revealed, allowing a person to experience his diverse days as consisting of a single goal. For example, in the above talk from 5751, after the Rebbe explained that mental serenity is dependent on identifying the unifying goal of one's diverse activities, he then launched into a long discussion of *bittul*:

> This [*menuha*] is caused through the *bittul* of a person to the Holy One, blessed be He. Then he feels that his entire existence is just as a servant of God, "to serve my Creator." And specifically via *bittul* to be a servant of God will he achieve the level of "the servant of the king is as the king," meaning that he becomes as if a single entity with the existence of the King.[23]

---

21. Ibid.
22. See also *Torat Menahem* 5717: 2, 296–97. It seems that the Rebbe took pride in the internal serenity of many of his Hasidim. See Herbert Weiner, "Alone with Moses," where R. Weiner, a Reform rabbi with mystical leanings, relates that he told the Rebbe of his impression that the Hasidim did not properly understand the complex nature of the world. In response, the Rebbe spoke of a lack of *kera*, or a split that comes from trying to live in two different worlds.
23. *Torat Menahem* 5751: 3, 271.

This consciousness of self-effacement and transparency to the will of God instantiates the disclosure of the *yehida* wherein the Jew is one with the Divine Essence. Then, just as God's essence is unchanging despite the fluctuations of reality, the same inner stability will permeate the person.[24]

Prayer as *Bittul*

The Rebbe taught that the service of prayer is an opportune time to develop this unified consciousness. In Chabad thought, prayer is ideally a contemplative service that gradually develops and climaxes with the *bittul* embodied in the bowing of *Shemoneh Esreh*.[25] In line with this perspective on the role of prayer, the Rebbe felt that it was highly significant that Jewish law requires that morning prayers precede one's daily activities.[26] Before engaging in any mitzva or mundane activity, one first needs to establish his basic identity as being one with God.

The Rebbe once expressed this idea as follows:

> The first service of the day is the service of prayer. Since each day we are a "new creation" and [must say to ourselves], "I was created only to serve my Creator," it is readily understandable that one's essential connection to the Creator needs to precede everything. This connection to God is prayer... and only afterward can come the specific services for his Creator.[27]

As the Rebbe went on to explain, Chabad doctrine, borrowing a phrase from the Talmud, teaches that when one arises in the morning, one's soul is "in one's nose,"[28] meaning to say that it does not yet permeate the whole body.[29] *Bittul* through prayer engenders the spreading of the

---

24. Ibid., 272.
25. See, for example, *Tanya, Likkutei Amarim*, ch. 39; *Likkutei Torah, Vayikra* 44a; *Likkutei Torah, Devarim*, 20a; *Kuntres HaTefilla, siman* 11, p. 26. The Rebbe also spoke in these terms; see, for example, *Likkutei Sihot* 35, *Vayigash*, no. 1; *Torat Menahem* 5744: 3, 1777.
26. See *Berakhot* 14a, *Shulhan Arukh, Orah Hayyim* 89:3.
27. *Torat Menahem* 5747: 3, 410.
28. See *Berakhot* 14a.
29. *Likkutei Torah, Bemidbar*, 79d.

soul through the entirety of the body, preparing the holistic body/soul entity for a unified engagement with the day's diverse activities.

Tefilla BeTzibbur

In this regard, the Rebbe cited a Chabad teaching about the deeper meaning behind *tefilla betzibbur* (praying with the community). While the halakhic meaning of this phrase is to pray with a quorum of ten men, one of the *Tzemah Tzedek*'s children, R. Yosef Yitzhak, taught an additional layer of meaning:

> The story is told about the son of the *Tzemah Tzedek*...that he would go to the synagogue to hear *Barekhu, Kedusha,* and *Hazarat HaShatz,* and afterward he would pray alone. When they asked him about *tefilla betzibbur*, he responded that he tries to assemble the ten forces of his soul and to pray "with the community."[30]

In other words, R. Yosef Yitzhak felt that *tefilla betzibbur* referred not only to prayer with a quorum, but also to the inner "community" of the human psyche. Unifying the disparate faculties of the psyche and dedicating them all to God is thus a central aspect of prayer.

As expected, the Rebbe argued that this internal ingathering and unification occurs with the revelation of the *yehida*. The innermost core of a person can demonstrate the utter unity of a person's distinct and often oppositional inner drives. As he once related:

> The epitome of service with the *yehida* is when the *yehida* is drawn throughout the soul's forces.... This is the inner meaning of *tefilla betzibbur*, that the prayer is with all of the ten forces of the soul as they are gathered together and united with the *yehida* of the soul, as in the well-known story [cited above regarding R. Yosef Yitzhak].[31]

---

30. *Torat Menahem* 5710, 15.
31. Ibid., 5717: 2, 225.

Aspects of a Godly Life

Thus, the above descriptions of prayer are intertwined. Prayer is a contemplative process of *bittul* which, as we have seen, reveals the true essence of a person – the *yehida*. Once revealed, the *yehida* does not nullify all other aspects of a person, but rather demonstrates the utter unity of its manifold expressions.

This perspective on prayer has relevance for one's entire day. In a different talk, the Rebbe focused on the lingering effect of this ingathering of the soul's disparate qualities. After referring to the above story about *tefilla betzibbur*, he continued, "In prayer, a person needs to elevate all his thoughts, feelings, and actions throughout the day to God. This is the meaning of *tefilla betzibbur*."[32] This internal process of praying with all aspects of oneself markedly impacts one's daily activities. Instead of seeing all of one's disparate engagements as conflicting responsibilities, a proper morning prayer elicits the *yehida* and allows a person to see all his activities as flowing from and working toward a single entity: God.

SERENITY AND *MASHIAH*

Tasting Serenity

The Rebbe saw this inner serenity as a defining feature of the messianic reality. Therefore, as that time approached, he emphasized the need to shift toward this messianic consciousness and realize the inner unity of all our seemingly disparate roles and activities. This connection between inner serenity and the ultimate redemption appears in one of the Rebbe's frequent prayers for the arrival of *Mashiah*. The Rebbe referred to the talmudic tradition[33] that the current order of the world would last for six thousand years and the seventh millennium would be the time of *Mashiah*, comparable to Shabbat,[34] which arrives after the six days of labor. For the Rebbe, the fact that his generation stood toward the end of the sixth millennium increases the potential of achieving inner serenity:

---

32. Ibid., 5719: 1, 276–77.
33. Sanhedrin 97b.
34. For the Rebbe's association of Shabbat with the form of serenity discussed in this chapter, see *Likkutei Sihot* 15, *Vayetzeh*, no. 1; ibid., 31, *Ki Tissa*, no. 2.

> We now stand on Friday – the sixth millennium – after midday, when the preparations begin for the "seventh day" (the seventh millennium), "the day which is entirely a Shabbat of rest (*Shabbat menuha*) for all of eternity." Now we have the status of "the tasters,"[35] meaning that we can already taste the *menuha* of the seventh millennium – rest for the soul and rest for the body.[36]

Being on the cusp of the Messianic Era, we can already "taste" the serenity of the utopian reality, similar to the tasting of Shabbat's delectable delicacies on Friday afternoon.[37]

The National and Personal Ingathering

In the Rebbe's last public talk before his debilitating stroke in 1992, he correlated the inner serenity caused by uniting the diverse aspects of one's personal life to the national ingathering of the exiles that he saw unfolding before his eyes. In his speech, the Rebbe focused on the significance of the fact that *Modeh Ani Lefanekha* ("I thank you [God]") is the waking statement of a Jew. The Rebbe depicted *Modeh Ani* as quickly expressing the inner integration and focus that is the role of prayer more generally:

> The saying of *Modeh Ani Lefanekha* does not occur after thought and contemplation.... Rather, [it is recited] "immediately when one arises from sleep" (*Shulkhan Arukh HaRav, Orah Hayyim* 1:5), because the recognition that "the entire world is filled with His glory" (Is. 6:3) is elemental (even in sleep) to each Jew due to the essence of his soul.... Therefore, when he is made into a "new creation," and gains a renewed sense of existence (a feeling

---

35. The Rebbe frequently spoke of the notion that just as there is a mitzva to taste from the Shabbat meal on Friday afternoon, there is a similar notion of tapping into the spiritual realities of the Messianic Era in the time immediately prior to redemption. For sources and an elaboration, see *Torat Menahem 5717*: 1, 104–5; *Likkutei Sihot* 20, Yod-Tet Kislev, *se'if* 2.
36. *Torat Menahem* 5743: 3, 1216.
37. See also *Torat Menahem* 5743: 2, 765; ibid., 5743: 4, 2018, that the ideal manner in which to prepare for *Mashiah* is with *menuha* of the body and soul.

of *ani*), he immediately says *Modeh Ani Lefanekha*, thereby placing *modeh* before *ani*, and the existence of *ani* is only *lefanekha*, meaning that a person commits his entire life to the Holy One, blessed be He … as the Jewish people and the Holy One, blessed be He, are entirely one.[38]

Thus, *Modeh Ani* is a declaration that a person entirely commits his own identity to God. Afterward, the morning services continue with prayers that relate to specific activities or human attributes, but it is all within the framework of a person's subordination of his identity to and union with God that is established in *Modeh Ani*.

The Rebbe argued that a parallel process needs to occur regarding one's perspective on *ahdut Yisrael*.[39] Arizal taught that before praying one should state: "I accept upon myself the mitzva of *ahavat Yisrael*." One reason for this, explained the Rebbe, is that just as it is crucial to establish the unity of one's inner life and activities at the day's commencement, it is similarly essential that one's day begins with the internalizing that all Jews are a single entity. Through such a framework one can properly interact with the many specific individuals in the course of one's daily encounters.

The Rebbe then argued that this perspective of seeing all Jews as different expressions of a single entity was becoming increasingly actualized in real time through the ingathering of the exiles. Jews from all corners of the globe who seem very distinct from one another were being gathered in a single location – the Land of Israel – giving material meaning to this spiritual consciousness. Also, the Rebbe emphasized that the most recent migration from the former Soviet Union was occurring in a state of calmness and serenity (*menuhat hanefesh*), unlike many earlier waves of migration that occurred under a cloud of peril and fear.[40]

For the Rebbe, this peaceful realization of national unity amid diversity creates a renewed obligation to achieve a parallel serenity in the ingathering of our own individual worlds. The creation of *menuha*

---

38. *Torat Menahem* 5752: 2, 368–69.
39. Ibid.
40. Ibid., 371.

through seeing every aspect of one's inner life and external activities as being expressions of our core identity – the *yehida* – is the personal correlative to the national ingathering of the exiles. Both are essential aspects of the messianic process.

CONCLUSION

Despite the proclivity toward scatteredness among people with full schedules, the Rebbe taught how to live a life of inner serenity and equilibrium. By seeing the unified divine purpose in all of life's diverse activities, one can live holistically in world that often pulls a person in multiple directions. In addition to the advantage of such a lifestyle for mental health and productivity, the Rebbe contextualized this mindset within the general Chabad approach of seeing diversity as different expressions of the same divine essence. In this sense, developing this mental framework is associated with the disclosure of the *yehida* and ultimately, with the coming of *Mashiah*.

Part 4

The Demographics of *Dira BaTahtonim*

Introduction

Just as the Rebbe's vision of a *Dira BaTahtonim* included every aspect of the material world and human activity, it was also demographically inclusive. Everyone in the world would have to work together to create the global redemption. This unity of purpose, however, does not imply uniform missions. The Rebbe taught that each person has a unique role to play in this global movement in consonance with his own divinely endowed unique traits, talents, and life situation.[1]

Between the global and the individual strata, the Rebbe focused on demographic-based missions. Instead of focusing mainly on adult Jewish males, who were often the "privileged" population in traditional Jewish communities and Torah teachings, the Rebbe's broad vision highlighted the uniqueness of an array of diverse groups. In his teachings, he carved out a unique and non-relational role for these somewhat neglected demographics based on his understanding of Torah, the nature of these groups, and the call of the moment.

In the ensuing section, we will explore the Rebbe's traditional yet innovative perspective on the role of women and non-Jews.

---

1. See, for example, *Torat Menahem* 5751: 4, 62; ibid., 5714: 2, 219.

The Demographics of Dira BaTahtonim

Similar chapters could be written about the Rebbe's teachings regarding children,[2] the elderly,[3] and the disabled.[4] Ultimately, according to the Rebbe, the mission of redeeming the world highlights the uniqueness of each person and group and requires the participation of all.

---

2. For a source-based analysis, see Yitzhak Kraus (2007), 183–223. For a summary of the Rebbe's approach, see Simon Jacobson (2002), 21–29.
3. Simon Jacobson (2002), 108–116.
4. See, for example, the Rebbe's correspondence with Dr. Robert Wilkes, the director of the Child Development Center at Coney Island Hospital, available at www.chabad.org/1275.

Chapter 15

"The Female Will Encircle the Male": The Rise of Women in the Final Generations

The role of women in Chabad, Judaism, and the world at large was a topic that occupied a significant place in the Rebbe's thought and talks.[1] As modernity and the feminist movement wreaked havoc on traditional gender roles, religious thinkers were forced to confront and navigate these potentially perilous social changes. In this context, the Rebbe developed a unique approach to these issues: firmly embracing certain aspects of classical Jewish femininity while simultaneously endorsing innovative understanding of ancient sources that opened new vistas for women. Characteristically, his reformulation of a woman's

---

1. See Joseph Telushkin (2014), 221, who records that the Rebbe told R. Shlomo Riskin in the 1960s that the greatest challenge facing Orthodoxy is the role of women.

role is contextualized within his understanding of history and its march toward redemption.

EARLIER JEWISH LAW, THOUGHT, AND LIFE
Halakhic Differences Between Men and Women

The halakhic system sharply differentiates between the genders on a host of issues. While all Jews are bound by the Torah's restrictions, women are exempt from fulfilling time-bound, positive commandments[2] and from engaging in various rituals of Jewish public life such as leading a prayer service or being called up to the Torah.[3] Also, notably, women are exempt from arguably the central mitzva in the rabbinic canon: studying Torah.[4]

In addition, the Talmud cites the verse "All honor [awaits] the King's daughter who is within"[5] as imparting a value of privacy and modesty and discouraging engagement in the public sphere.[6] Rambam, for example, formulates this principle as follows:

> It is uncouth for a woman always to leave home – this time to go out and another time to go on the street. Indeed, a husband should prevent a wife from doing this and not allow her to go out more than once or twice a month, as is necessary. For there is nothing more attractive for a woman than to sit in the corner of her home, as [implied by the verse]: "All honor [awaits] the King's daughter who is within."[7]

While modern decisors argue that Rambam's precise application is societally specific and not a categorically binding doctrine, they still affirm the value statement behind these words.[8] This perspective is affirmed

2. Kiddushin 34a.
3. Megilla 23a.
4. Kiddushin 29a.
5. Ps. 45:13.
6. See the sources cited in *Encyclopedia Talmudit, erekh "isha"* between notes 533 and 541b.
7. *Mishneh Torah, Hilkhot Ishut* 13:11.
8. See, for example, *Tzitz Eliezer* 9:50.

by the fact that rabbinic literature identifies women with the home[9] and homemaking.[10]

Halakhic Spousal Hierarchy

In line with identifying the home as a woman's primary space, rabbinic literature grants a husband decision-making authority for all issues not directly relating to the home.[11] This seems to be the import of the following midrash: "Who is a worthy woman? She who performs the will of her husband (*osah retzon baalah*)."[12] While not citing this precise phrase, Rambam codifies this sentiment:

> Our Sages commanded that a man honor his wife more than his own person, and love her as he loves his own person.... And similarly, they commanded a woman to honor her husband exceedingly and to be in awe of him. She should carry out all her deeds according to his directives, considering him to be an officer or a king. She should follow the desires of his heart and shun everything that he disdains.[13]

Rambam thus affirms a clear power hierarchy within the ideal Jewish marriage.

The Kabbala of Men and Women

The kabbalistic tradition complements the values and sociology of classic rabbinic literature. Early kabbalists taught that the world is composed of a series of active, male "influencers" (*mashpi'im*) that bestow the divine light unto the passive, female "receivers" (*mekablim*). Accordingly, the role of the feminine *sefirot* is to receive the divine influence from the male counterpart, nurture and nourish this influence, and then birth it

---

9. Shabbat 118a.
10. See, for example, *Shulhan Arukh, Orah Hayyim* 263:2, which states that women are the preferred lighters of Shabbat candles, as "they are found in the home and are occupied with the needs of the home."
11. Bava Metzia 59a.
12. *Tanna DeVei Eliyahu Rabba*, par. 10.
13. *Mishneh Torah, Hilkhot Ishut* 15:19–20.

forward to the next stage. In this gendered system, the male partner of each pair is spiritually "above" the female aspect, closer to the source of being – God Himself who is "situated" above the *sefirot*.[14]

The Role of Women in Early Hasidism

As one might expect from the above outline and the social context of the times, scholars have demonstrated that in the early years of Hasidism most women did not participate in several of the spiritual and social aspects of hasidic life that seem to be most central.[15] They generally did not hear Torah from their community's rebbe, and many Hasidic rebbes did not receive women visitors. Many hasidic *shtieblakh* (synagogues), like many other European synagogues at the time, did not even contain a women's section, thus excluding women from engaging in communal prayer, another key element of hasidic life. Due to these clear differences between men and women in hasidic communities, scholars debate the extent to which women of hasidic communities identified as *"hasidot"* (female Hasidim) with their own unique method of service of God.

This perception seems to have been shared by the women themselves. For example, Rebbetzin Rivka Schneerson, the wife of the Maharash and the mother of the Rashab, once said: "Whether or not I am a hasidic Jewess I do not know, but that I am of hasidic stock is certain."[16]

CHANGES IN TWENTIETH-CENTURY CHABAD

Outlining the Changes

In Chabad, the role and place of women began to change under the guidance of the sixth Rebbe, R. Yosef Yitzhak Schneersohn, in the first half

---

14. Aryeh Kaplan (1990), 130–41; Elliot Wolfson (1995), 19–20.
15. Marcin Wodziński (2013), 399–434; Ada Rapoport-Albert (2018), 321–26. Wodziński in particular is extreme in his formulations and argues that women were excluded from the hasidic identity which was essentially a male fraternity. Tsippi Kauffman (2019), 223–57, however, agrees that women did not participate in the public aspects of hasidic life, but argues that they still self-identified and were treated as full members of a hasidic group. In addition, she notes that there were specifically feminine expressions of hasidic service of God.
16. For sources tracing this quote and an analysis, see Ada Rapoport-Albert (2018), 381–82.

of the twentieth century. He encouraged women to create organizations that would actively strengthen mitzva observance among one another as well as among non-observant women. More radically, he created an educational track within the community that for the first time accorded young women systematic access to Chabad teachings. He even named this group "Temimim Sisters" relating them to the central men's yeshiva, Tomkhei Temimim, founded by his father.

In the second half of the twentieth century this nascent sociological and educational shift was considerably broadened by the Rebbe.[17] An early signal of this trajectory occurred within the first year of his leadership when he called for the establishment of a central Chabad women's organization. In doing so, he notably tweaked an appellation invoked by his father-in-law – *neshei uvnot haHasidim* (the wives and daughters of the Hasidim), which highlighted the women's relationship to their male counterparts, and named the organization Neshei UVnot Chabad (Women and Girls of Chabad). It was clear that the Rebbe was carving an independent space for women within the Chabad movement.[18]

This carving of an independent role for women was a hallmark of the Rebbe's leadership. On the one hand he eschewed the women's liberation movement, whose agenda he saw as erasing all differences between the genders, which would diminish the exceptional qualities unique to women. Accordingly, he affirmed many aspects of traditional gender characteristics and roles.[19] Simultaneously, though, he revolutionized the role of women in other ways. He institutionalized high-level Torah studies in Chabad girls' schools, encouraged women's scholarship and literary output, and enjoined women to become leaders and activists with the same urgency as their male counterparts. Several times a year he directly addressed large female-only audiences. On these occasions the main *beit midrash* at 770 Eastern Parkway was vacated of the men and the large space was filled with women.

---

17. For an overview of these activities, see Ada Rapoport-Albert (2018), 447–56.
18. See Ada Rapoport-Albert (2018), 448; Chaim Miller (2014), 241.
19. See, for example, *Torat Menahem* 5745: 1, 127–38.

The Demographics of Dira BaTahtonim

Philosophical Background: The Paradox of *Malkhut*

Similar to other practical programs initiated by the Rebbe, this social shift can be seen as an implementation of his understanding of hasidic philosophy. More particularly, the Rebbe saw the whole feminist movement against the backdrop of an ancient kabbalistic prediction regarding the realignment of the masculine and feminine *sefirot* in the end of times with a particular focus on the *sefira* of *malkhut*. The social manifestations of this new/old cosmic order required the opening of new vistas for women and the recharacterization of many of their traditional tasks within this emerging messianic framework.

At the bottom of the hierarchical order of *sefirot* is *malkhut*.[20] Identified by the Zohar as a "cup"[21] and also the "ocean,"[22] *malkhut* receives the divine light from the higher *sefirot*, most notably from the *sefira* of *yesod*, which is located immediately above it. Accordingly, *malkhut* is described as "having nothing of its own,"[23] as its role is to collect all of the unique revelations of the divine light that are expressed by each of the other *sefirot*. As the passive receiver of the divine light, *malkhut* is unsurprisingly gendered as feminine, and is associated with the *Shekhina* – the feminine aspect of divinity. In consonance with its receiving and dependent nature, Chabad literature affiliates *malkhut* with the service of *bittul* – self-effacement and transparency to divine revelation.[24]

It is important to emphasize that even as *malkhut* passively amalgamates the divine light from the *sefirot* above it, it serves as the active transmitter of this light into the world below it. This process continues until the lowest of all realms – our material world – comes into being. Thus, *malkhut* plays a dual role in the cosmic order: as the lowest *sefira* it

---

20. For longer summaries of the nature and associations of *malkhut*, with a particular focus on Chabad sources, see Yosef Ives (2010), 213–37; Nahum Greenwald (Kislev 5758), 40–48; Greenwald (5763), 33–50.
21. Zohar, *Vayehi*, 250a. For a Chabad analysis of this and other similar sources, see *Sefer HaMaamarim 5659*, 2.
22. Moshe Hallamish (1990), 137.
23. Zohar, *Hayei Sara*, 125a.
24. Here is a brief selection of sources where this connection is highlighted: *Maamarei Admor HaZaken: Inyanim*, 51; *Sefer HaLikkutim Daah Tzemah Tzedek*, vol. 1, 130; *Likkutei Sihot* 17, *Behar*, no. 2, *se'if* 11.

passively receives whatever divine light is bestowed on it, but due to its relatively "low" stature of close proximity to the realms below it, *malkhut* alone has the capacity to reveal some of this light to the realms below.

While this kabbalistic depiction of *malkhut* locates it at the lowest point of the *sefirot* "map" and thus the furthest from the divine light's source, characteristically, Chabad doctrine teaches a complementary opposing perspective. In line with the theme of inverting intuitive hierarchies,[25] Chabad literature explains that even as, manifestly, *malkhut* is the lowest of the *sefirot*, its root is in "the Essence of the Infinite,"[26] a point higher than the entire *Seder Hishtalshelut*. This leads to an emphasis of the essential, generative, and creative quality of *malkhut* and the feminine, which comes to supersede more conventional notions of receptive passivity.

The Eschatological Ascent of *Malkhut*

This lofty, albeit currently concealed, root of *malkhut* will be revealed in the end of time. The Alter Rebbe described this process as the ascent of *malkhut* to the top of the hierarchy of the *sefirot*, culminating with the unification of *malkhut* with *keter*, which transcends even the highest *sefira* of *hokhma*. Concurrently, *malkhut* will be transformed from a passive recipient of the divine light to the active influencer, bestowing the core of the Divine Essence to the other *sefirot*.

Working within the kabbalistic gendering of *malkhut* as feminine, the Alter Rebbe expressed this idea through verses and phrases that speak of the female rising and actively influencing males. For example, in one instance, he launched into this eschatological realignment of the cosmos by noting that the Torah describes the matriarchs in surprisingly active terms:[27]

> Regarding Sarah it is said, "All that Sarah says to you [Abraham], listen to her voice" (Gen. 21:12), meaning that Abraham needed to receive (*lekabel*) from Sarah...to understand this we need to cite the rabbinic statement "God allowed three people a foretaste

---

25. See chapter 3, section "*Atzmut* and the Lowest Realm"; chapter 5, section "Mitzvot and the Divine Essence"; and chapter 6, section "The Creation of the Body."
26. *Sefer HaMaamarim* 5679, 67.
27. *Likkutei Torah, Shir HaShirim*, 15c.

of the World to Come – Abraham, Isaac, and Jacob" (Bava Batra 17a).... In the future, the verse states, "The female will encircle the male" (Jer. 31:21), meaning that the spiritual force of the receiver will ascend and be more elevated than the spiritual force of the masculine influencer; "The woman of valor is a crown of her husband" (Prov. 12:4); and "The final action was first in thought" (*Lekha Dodi*)... and because the patriarchs had a taste of the World to Come, therefore they had this spiritual quality of receiving from the matriarchs.

Let us briefly unpack the Alter Rebbe's allusions. In its original prophetic context, the verse "The female will encircle the male" is a metaphor for the return of the Jewish people (God's wife) to the Land of Israel and to God in the end of time.

The Alter Rebbe, though, consistently added another layer of meaning: that the *sefira* of *malkhut*, the most passive and in this sense the most feminine of the *sefirot*, will be revealed as an active influencer, "encircling or transcending the masculine aspect of the Divine." Similarly, the verse "The woman of valor is a crown of her husband," while seemingly defining the wife in relation to her husband, actually locates her at a "higher" point, as she rests atop his head. This refers to the rise of *malkhut* and its reunification with *keter* – the crown that sits atop the scheme of the *sefirot*.[28]

The above motifs regarding the gender of *malkhut*, its nature, and its final ascent are ubiquitous within Chabad literature. These discussions, however, remain in the spiritual, cosmic realm and did not have noticeable terrestrial, social applications. The Rebbe uniquely drew on these esoteric discussions as a blueprint for the changing role of women in the time preceding redemption.[29] As noted above, this contributed to the Rebbe's recontextualization of traditional female roles and in the encouragement of new ones.

---

28. For several parallel passages, see *Maamarei Admor HaZaken* 5569, 64, 82, 84; *Torah Or*, 44d. For more sources and analysis, see Elliot Wolfson (2009), 209–17.
29. For hasidic sources relating to a change in gender roles *after* the coming of *Mashiah*, see Nathan Polen (1992), 1–21.

"The Female Will Encircle the Male"

RECHARACTERIZING TRADITIONAL FEMALE ATTRIBUTES AND ROLES

Female Passivity and Self-Effacement

Connection Between the Feminine and Bittul

As we have seen, kabbalistic sources describe feminine forces as passive receptacles for masculine forces. At times, the Rebbe drew on this model to describe the service of God represented by femininity. As opposed to a "masculine" form of service, which is characterized by a sense of understanding and personal identification, a "feminine" form of service is infused with a superrational self-effacement (*bittul*) and acceptance of the yoke of Heaven.

In an early talk, for example, the Rebbe contrasted the modes of service represented by the birth of a boy and the birth of a girl:

> The difference between them with regard to our service of God: The birth of a male – "A man's manner is to conquer" (Yevamot 65b) – teaches of the service of conquest and purifying one's space in the world, a service that is connected with logic and rational thought (*taam vesekhel*). However, the birth of a female – "A worthy woman performs the will of her husband" – teaches of the service of accepting the yoke of Heaven.[30]

The Rebbe concluded by affirming the need for every Jew to synthesize the "feminine" form of service into their service of God.

In addition to signifying a form of service, in other contexts the Rebbe employed the rabbinic statement "A worthy woman performs the will of her husband" in a practical sense as well. For example, on one occasion he told husbands that they cannot travel to Crown Heights for the Tishrei holidays without their wives' consent. He then continued: "And all the more so, a woman's travel [to Crown Heights] cannot be

---

30. *Torat Menahem* 5711: 1, 77; ibid., 5718: 2, 172–73. See also *Torat Menahem* 5711:1, 153–54, where the Rebbe reviewed this distinction and used both the terms *bittul* and *kabbalat ol*..

without her husband's consent, 'A worthy woman performs the will of her husband,'"[31] supporting this side of the ledger with this rabbinic dictum.

Women, Bittul, and the Divine Essence

While these statements can be construed as belittling women, the Rebbe consistently contextualized this aspect of femininity in the opposite fashion. As we have seen, it is specifically the service of *bittul* that can access the *yehida* of the soul and the corresponding Divine Essence, which is the very definition of the redemptive process. As such, it is specifically women, who are better suited for *bittul*, who have the capacity to accelerate the coming of *Mashiah*. For example, in one talk, after associating the birth of a girl with *kabbalat ol* and *bittul*, the Rebbe continued as follows:

> It is explained in hasidic teachings that in the future the superiority of the girl over the boy will be revealed – such that not only will "the voice of the bride" be heard (not like nowadays when "the voice of a woman is prohibited" [*kol be'isha erva*]),[32] but even more than that, "the female will encircle the male." The preparation for this is our contemporary service of *kabbalat ol*, which is the service of the girl.[33]

It is specifically the form of service that seems "lower" and secondary that has the capacity to bring *Mashiah*. Accordingly, the Rebbe enjoined his male listeners to adopt this feminine quality as part of their own trajectory of spiritual ascent.

Women and the Paradox of Malkhut

Elsewhere, the Rebbe directly connected these ideas with the paradoxical nature of the *sefira* of *malkhut*.[34] After the splitting of the Sea of Reeds, Moses led the Jewish men in a song of praise and thanksgiving. In

---

31. *Torat Menahem* 5747: 4, 309. See also *Iggerot Kodesh* 23, letter 8991.
32. Berakhot 24a.
33. *Torat Menahem* 5711: 1, 149–50. "The voice of the bride" is a phrase taken from the final blessing recited at a wedding.
34. *Likkutei Sihot* 11, Beshallah, no. 2.

addition, the Torah relates that "Miriam the prophetess, Aaron's sister,"[35] led the women in song and dance. Rashi, troubled by the identification of Miriam as specifically Aaron's sister, offers two explanations:

> When did she prophesy? When she was [known only as] "Aaron's sister," before Moses was born, she said, "My mother is destined to bear a son" [who will save Israel]. Another explanation: [It is written] "Aaron's sister" since he risked his life for her when she was afflicted with leprosy; [thus] she is called by his name.[36]

After a thorough textual analysis of the two explanations, the Rebbe noted that they seem to depict Miriam in opposite fashions. The first explanation highlights her towering status as a prophetess, while the second seems to define her in relation to her brother.

This, the Rebbe continued, is the paradox of *malkhut*:

> Miriam represents the *sefira* of *malkhut*, and in the *sefira* of *malkhut* we find two dimensions: (1) the *sefira* of *malkhut* is rooted in the Divine Essence, which is above all of the *sefirot*, and (2) the *sefira* of *malkhut* "has nothing of its own" (similar to the moon to which it is compared), only what it receives from the higher *sefirot*.[37]

Similarly, the Rebbe explained, from one perspective Miriam achieved the heights of prophecy, while simultaneously she was "subservient" to her older brother. These two extremes, while seemingly contradictory, are actually intricately intertwined:

> Because [*malkhut*] is in a complete state of *bittul* and only receives from the *sefirot* above it, therefore the energy of the Divine Essence contained in the light that is drawn to it can be felt within it, even though that energy cannot be felt in the higher

---

35. Ex. 15:20.
36. Rashi on Ex. 15:20.
37. *Likkutei Sihot* 11, Beshallah, no. 2, *se'if* 5.

> *sefirot*.... [Similarly] the superior qualities of Miriam – the *sefira* of *malkhut* – result from her effacement (*beteila*) to Aaron, the *sefirot* of *ze'eir anpin*.[38]

The Rebbe did not leave this discussion in the cosmic or biblical realm, but rather explicated the timely relevance for contemporary women:

> This is a special lesson for Jewish women and girls: Even though in many ways they are on a higher level than men (so much so that in the future, "the female will encircle the male"), still they should know that our Rabbis taught: "A worthy woman fulfills the will of her husband," and it is through this that they effectuate the revelation of the superior qualities that are found within them.... [Subsequently] she imparts these levels to her husband... until in the future the notion of "the female will encircle the male" will be revealed.[39]

It is through the feminine service of *bittul* that a woman can access the root of *malkhut* – the Divine Essence. Once achieved, her true nature and oneness with the Divine Essence is revealed, and she is transformed into a source of illumination relative to "her husband" who receives from her.[40]

In summary, the Rebbe, it seems, was fundamentally aligned with the traditional spousal relationship in which the wife is enjoined to fulfill and actualize the will of her husband (though on a practical level in matters of dispute he often exhorted husbands to follow their wives' opinions[41]). However, in line with the general inversion of intuitive

---

38. Ibid.
39. Ibid.
40. In addition to the feminine characteristic of *bittul*, the Rebbe spoke about how other traditional female traits such as pure faith and a rich emotional life also allowed women to have a more natural path to the Divine Essence. See, for example, *Likkutei Sihot* 31, *Yitro*, no. 1, *se'if* 6; *Torat Menahem* 5746: 3, 442–43; ibid., 5749: 1, 387; *Likkutei Sihot* 30, *Vayehi*, no. 1, *se'if* 4; ibid., 30, *Vayetzeh*, no. 3; *Torat Menahem* 5745: 4, 2190–91.
41. See, for example, *Iggerot Kodesh* 16, letter 5814.

hierarchies and the role of the *tahtonim* in the messianic process, it is this form of "lowly" service that has the power to access the Divine Essence. Therefore, the end of time will see a role reversal in which the wife is the "higher" and more active of the pair.

In keeping with this messianic reality, the Rebbe offered an alternative interpretation to the rabbinic statement "A proper wife performs (*osah*) the will of her husband." Instead of the literal understanding of *oseh* as "performs," it can also be construed as "makes" or "creates." In the end of time, it will be the wife who influences her husband and "creates" his will, in contrast to obeying his will.[42]

Respecting Women
In this regard it is also important to emphasize that the Rebbe admonished husbands to treat their wives with the utmost love and respect. While this obligation is codified in the Talmud and cited in later halakhic codes, the Rebbe felt that it took on greater significance nowadays. For example, he once wrote to a husband:

> When thinking about your wife, you should constantly remember that the Jewish people and each Jew in particular is referred to as the wife of the King of kings, the Holy One, blessed be He. So when you ask Him to fulfill your heart's desires...you must model the same in how you treat your own spouse [to be in consonance with what] our Sages say that one needs to "honor her more than himself" (Rambam, *Mishneh Torah, Hilkhot Ishut* 15:19), and especially upon contemplating that we stand at the end of the exile and are close to the complete redemption when "the female will encircle the male." This alone should engender feelings of honor and care toward your wife.[43]

---

42. *Likkutei Sihot* 4, Balak, *se'if* 4; *Torat Menahem* 5743: 2, 1086.
43. *Iggerot Kodesh* 6, letter 1718. For more emphatic statements regarding proper respect for women in general and one's wife in particular, see *Torat Menahem* 5726: 3, 66–67; ibid., 5749: 2, 437–38.

The true nature of women becomes increasingly revealed as we approach the Messianic Era. This basic fact should inspire men to re-intensify their honor and respect for women in general and their wives in particular.

The *Akeret HaBayit*

Another related traditional female role that the Rebbe affirmed but recontextualized was that of the wife as an *akeret habayit* – the mainstay of the home. The Rebbe followed the classical model found in rabbinic literature that the wife is the primary force in domestic matters. Many have argued that associating women with the domestic realm inevitably puts her in a secondary and supportive role. By contrast, the Rebbe consistently characterized the *akeret habayit* in very active terms and attributed great personal, cosmic, and messianic significance to all aspects of her role.

The Akeret HaBayit Spiritually Influencing Her Family

One major theme in the Rebbe's discussions of an *akeret habayit* is the recasting of the homemaking position to one of pivotal spiritual influence. The wife's task is not merely practical domesticity, but chiefly that the household, and its center of operations, the house, are permeated with an atmosphere of Torah and Judaism. The Rebbe pointed to the *akeret habayit* as a model of a person who is both materially and spiritually aiding others, a mission of immense significance in the Rebbe's worldview.

One example of this portrayal is a talk of the Rebbe to the 1982 graduating class of Beis Rivkah – a Chabad girls' high school in Crown Heights. He noted that when God informed the Jewish people at the foot of Mount Sinai about the impending gift of the Torah, He told Moses: "So shall you say to the House of Jacob and tell the sons of Israel."[44] The Midrash comments that "the House of Jacob" refers to the Jewish women, while "the sons of Israel" refers to the men. This order indicates that Jewish women have the primary role in receiving the Torah, which "very much underscores an advantage of Jewish

---

44. Ex. 19:3.

women and girls, that they precede the men in everything connected to the Giving of the Torah."[45]

As we will see, in several talks the Rebbe used this as a springboard to discuss women and Torah study. Here, however, he took this precedence of women in a different direction:

> This is the unique mission (*shelihut*) that is placed upon Jewish women and girls: to know that they are granted the privilege and the responsibility to act not only upon themselves, but upon the entire household. As an *akeret habayit*...she creates the proper atmosphere in the entire house, which influences (*mashpia*) anyone who comes through the house – the husband, children....
>
> Since the Holy One, blessed be He, bestowed this mission (*shelihut*) on Jewish women and girls, He certainly granted them the necessary abilities to practically fulfill it, and with joy and goodness of heart.[46]

God Himself highlighted the primacy of the *akeret habayit* in the preamble to the Giving of the Torah due to her crucial role as the spiritual influencer of her household.

The Akeret HaBayit's Influence on the Outside World
The *akeret habayit* does not merely influence the members of her family. Rather, the Rebbe asserted that when an *akeret habayit* creates the proper environment in the home, her household will inspire others to live similarly. Accordingly, even while spending much time within the environs of her home, the *akeret habayit* creates an abode that shines beyond its own walls and influences the greater world.

The Rebbe would often emphasize this point. For example, in an address to the Lubavitch Women's Organization, after reiterating that women have the unique capacity to create a proper Jewish home, he drew an analogy between such a home and the *Beit HaMikdash*:

---

45. *Torat Menahem* 5742: 3, 1657.
46. Ibid. See also *Torat Menahem* 5744: 1, 114; ibid., 5746: 3, 441; ibid., 5745: 4, 2088; ibid., 5748: 4, 341.

> Every Jewish home needs to be modeled upon the *Mishkan* and the *Beit HaMikdash*, in which the Holy One, blessed be He, resided, as the verse states, "I shall dwell in them," meaning that the entire home should be pure and sanctified such that God can say about it, "I shall dwell in them."[47]

As we have seen, the Rebbe did not view the *Beit HaMikdash* as an island of sanctity within a dark and secular world. Rather, the full sanctity of the *Beit HaMikdash* can be realized only when it transcends the walls of the Sanctuary and reveals the divinity of the outside world.[48] Each Jewish home has an identical mission:

> It is not only that the house itself will be holy and pure, but that the holy and pure environment of the home will influence even those outside the home – the neighbors, the area, the entire city, and the entire world. This means that the Jewish home is made into a "tower of light" that shines on the entire area with light, as "a mitzva is a candle and the Torah is light" (Prov. 6:23), following the paradigm of the *Beit HaMikdash*, from where light emanated to the entire world.[49]

Far from being passive and secondary, a woman's role as an *akeret habayit* places her at the forefront of the mission to transform the world.

The Akeret HaBayit and the Creation of a Dira BaTahtonim

Furthering this line of reasoning, the Rebbe often spoke of the unique role of the *akeret habayit* in the mission of creating a *Dira BaTahtonim*. Revealing the entire world as a home for the Divine Essence begins with the creation of a microcosmic *Dira BaTahtonim* in the form of a Jewish home through the labor of each individual *akeret habayit*. The Rebbe articulated this connection between every Jewish home and

---

47. *Torat Menahem* 5742: 4, 2268. See also *Torat Menahem* 5743: 4, 2013–14.
48. See chapter 4, section "Conquering the Mundane Spaces of the World."
49. *Torat Menahem* 5742: 4, 2268.

the global *Dira BaTahtonim* at the first International Conference of *Sheluhot*:[50]

> The mission (*shelihut*) [of each and every Jew] is included in the command "And you shall make for Me a Sanctuary"...that the house of each and every Jew should be a temple for the Holy One, blessed be He, a house of prayer and acts of kindness, and from the sanctuary of private homes the sanctity will spread to the entire world, such that the entire world will be made into a temple for God, a *Dira BaTahtonim*. This mission takes on added significance for Jewish women. Since each one is an *akeret habayit* ("the essence [*ikkar*] of the home"), meaning that the happenings of the home are dependent on her, including and especially the behaviors of her children and husband, the main responsibility of the mission to create a *Beit HaMikdash* for the Holy One, blessed be He, falls upon the *akeret habayit*.

In this manner, the Rebbe accorded women the highest mission while still focusing on the importance of their domestic responsibilities.

The Recharacterization of Household Chores
The conception of an *akeret habayit* as the creator of the *Dira BaTahtonim* has ramifications for the nature of her work. While she must expend effort to cultivate the proper interpersonal and spiritual atmosphere in her home, much of the energy of an *akeret habayit* will presumably be focused on more mundane household labors such as cooking. How can these tasks become part of the lofty mission of the *akeret habayit*?

Perhaps as a way of addressing this question, the Rebbe drew from his expansive conception of a *Dira BaTahtonim*. When the Divine Essence is finally disclosed in the lowest realm with the creation of the *Dira BaTahtonim*, we will be able to perceive God in the materiality of

---

50. Ibid., 5751: 2, 296. For more on the connection between an *akeret habayit* and the creation of a *Dira BaTahtonim*, see *Torat Menahem* 5742: 4, 2269; ibid., 5746: 3, 439–40.

this world. Similarly, the *akeret habayit* can ensure that even the material aspects of her home disclose the presence of God in the home.

The Rebbe addressed this theme in his talk to the 1990 graduates of Beis Rivkah and the counselors of Jewish summer camps. After once again reiterating the importance of the *akeret habayit* he defined the role as follows:

> The special mission of an *akeret habayit* is to transform the material elements of the home into holiness, meaning not only to ensure that the material elements do not contradict or negate sanctity, and [not only that the physical] helps strengthen matters of holiness, but [even] that the very material items themselves become holy.[51]

As a model for this perspective, the Rebbe pointed to lighting Shabbat candles, a mitzva of the home for which women have a special affinity. The essence of the mitzva is to employ a physical candle for a sanctified goal which literally and metaphorically shines light in all directions. Acting similarly in regard to all material aspects of the home can transform the materiality of the home and the entire world into a *Dira BaTahtonim*.[52]

NEW OPPORTUNITIES

In addition to recasting seemingly supportive and secondary tasks as active missions of cosmic significance, the Rebbe also broadened the scope of Chabad women's activities to include areas that were heretofore dominated by men. Two main areas of theoretical and practical note are Torah study and engagement in public outreach activities.[53] The Rebbe

---

51. *Torat Menahem* 5750: 3, 345–46.
52. See also *Torat Menahem* 5748: 4, 342; ibid., 5720: 1, 402, where the Rebbe discussed cooking and kitchen work in similar terms, for example, by ensuring that the food is *kasher*.
53. It is important to note that despite these innovations, the Rebbe never deviated from halakhic or ritual norms and customs. The one possible exception was a *yehidut* (private audience) with R. Shlomo Riskin, in which the latter relates that the Rebbe encouraged him to allow women to hold Torah scrolls during the Simhat Torah

rooted both of these innovations in the kabbalistic predictions of the eschatological rise of *malkhut*.

Torah Study
Traditional Sources of Women's Torah Study
Traditionally, Jewish women did not engage in serious Torah study in large numbers. This reality was rooted in two talmudic texts. First, the Talmud exempts women from the obligation of Torah study, interpreting the verse "And you shall teach them to your sons" to exclude one's daughters.[54]

Second, and perhaps more impactfully, the Talmud elsewhere discourages women from learning with a harsh analogy: "One who teaches his daughter Torah is considered as if he taught her promiscuity."[55] Rashi explains that the average woman does not have the necessary intellectual acumen to properly understand and apply the Torah and will instead use her newfound knowledge and "cunningness" for nefarious purposes. Faced with these sources and a general societal context that discouraged female education, Jewish communities did not institutionalize formal girls' schools.

Despite these circumstances, the twentieth century saw a major increase in women's Torah education. The Rebbe identified this as a fundamentally positive phenomenon and encouraged its development, systemization, intensity, and scope. Well aware of the innovativeness of this shift specifically within a hasidic context, the Rebbe labored textually, conceptually, and programmatically to win over the conservative elements of his own community to his vision of creating a cadre of learned women.

---

dancing. See Joseph Telushkin (2014), 221–22. However, it seems that the Rebbe sent R. Riskin a follow-up letter discouraging him from this practice. For more details and analysis, see Yosef Yitzhak Greenberg (*Emor* 5765); Boruch Oberlander (*Hukkat* 5765).
54. Kiddushin 30a.
55. Sota 21b.

The Giving of the Torah

A foundational point in the Rebbe's teachings regarding Torah study is that the entire Torah was given to all Jews, irrespective of the practical irrelevance of certain sections for specific individuals or populations.[56] Regarding women, he would often highlight this point through referencing the prominent place that women occupy in the Giving of the Torah. As noted above, at Sinai, God first addressed the women: "So shall you say to the House of Jacob," and only then addressed the men. The primacy of women underscores their essential connection to the entire Torah despite their formal exemption from studying Torah and fulfilling certain positive commandments.[57]

This essential relevance of the entire Torah to women is the subtext for the Rebbe's analysis of the halakhic issues regarding women and Torah study. While he remained completely bound by the key rabbinic sources and the rigorous methodology of halakhic inquiry, his conclusions disclose an expansionist tendency. The Rebbe carefully weighed the relevant sources regarding a variety of Torah disciplines and genres, but ultimately consistently concluded that women should be fully engaged in Torah study.

Learning Relevant Halakhot

One area of Torah that was traditionally open to women's study, at least in principle, is the halakhot that are practically relevant to them. This exemption to the general discouragement of women studying Torah has its root in medieval halakhic literature,[58] but characteristically, the Rebbe frequently referred to the Alter Rebbe's formulation. After citing the talmudic disapproval of teaching one's daughter Torah, the Alter Rebbe writes: "Nevertheless, women are also obligated to study the halakhot that are necessary for them, such as the laws of *nidda*, ritual immersion, salting meat, and the like, and all positive commandments that are not

---

56. See, for example, *Torat Menahem* 5749: 1, 84.
57. See, for example, *Torat Menahem* 5747: 1, 329. For a longer analysis of the various rabbinic sources regarding whether the entire Torah was given to women or not, see *Likkutei Sihot* 31, *Yitro*, no. 1.
58. *Sefer HaHasidim*, *siman* 313, codified by the Rema in *Shulhan Arukh, Yoreh De'ah* 246:6. For a dissenting opinion, see *Shu"t Maharil*, *siman* 199.

time bound, and all biblical and rabbinic prohibitions, in which women are commanded just like men."[59]

While this might seem like a limited regimen and a mere practical facilitator of proper halakhic observance, the Rebbe argued that this statement, in fact, justifies a robust, expansive, and direct obligation for women to study much of the Torah.

First, he noted that this category includes the majority of the halakhic system. As women are obligated in all negative commandments and are exempt from only approximately thirty (out of 248) positive commandments,[60] this statement of the Alter Rebbe obligates women to study the vast bulk of Torah. The fulfillment of this mandate requires the establishment of an extensive educational system for girls and the cultivation of a deep desire for lifelong learning.[61]

In addition to highlighting the quantity of halakhic materials that is traditionally (at least textually) in the domain of female study, the Rebbe staked a position regarding the fundamental nature of this obligation. In a 5730/1970 talk[62] dedicated to the nature of a woman's obligation to engage in Torah study, the Rebbe opened with the logical assertion that the talmudic exemption "You shall teach your sons and not your daughters" was categorical in nature, barring women from any direct obligation to study Torah. As such, the obligation of women to study the halakhot that are pertinent to them must be construed as functional in nature – they must study so they will know how to properly observe. This means that despite the vast quantity of knowledge that they must master, women have no inherent and independent obligation of study Torah.

The Rebbe, however, quickly problematized this assertion by pointing to another passage from the Alter Rebbe's halakhic code that has a different implication. In the laws of the morning blessings, the Alter Rebbe writes that women must recite the blessing over Torah study due to their obligation to study the halakhot that are relevant to

---

59. *Shulhan Arukh HaRav, Hilkhot Talmud Torah* 1:14.
60. From R. Saadia Gaon and *Ritz Gei'ut* in *Teshuvot HaGeonim* (Lik), *siman* 120.
61. *Torat Menahem* 5750: 3, 171. Similarly, see *Torat Menahem* 5728: 1, 239.
62. *Likkutei Sihot* 14, *Ekev*, no. 2.

them.[63] The Rebbe reasoned that an activity that is a mere preparatory stage in the fulfillment of a mitzva should not warrant its own blessing. If so, we are faced with a contradiction in the Alter Rebbe's halakhic code – if a woman's obligation to study relevant halakhot is simply to enable proper observance, why should she recite a separate blessing on the Torah study itself?

The Rebbe responded by pointing to a principle developed by the Rogatchover Gaon in several halakhic contexts.[64] The Rogatchover Gaon argued that even if a certain activity is initially construed as a preparatory stage leading toward a mitzva, as long as this activity is legally required, it ultimately transcends its initial purpose and is vested with an independent status. The classic example cited by the Rebbe is the status of *holakha* – the priest's walking with the blood of a sacrifice toward the altar. While this process presents as a mere connecting phase between the two main services of catching the blood (*kabbala*) and sprinkling it on the altar (*zerika*), the halakhic system treats *holakha* as an independent act of service.[65]

Similarly, irrespective of the fact that a woman's obligation to study Torah is generated by a goal external to the study itself (that is, the fulfillment of mitzvot), once such Torah study is required, it becomes vested with an independent status. At the end of the day, therefore, women's Torah study warrants a blessing as the fulfillment of a direct mitzva, no less than a man's fulfillment of the independent mitzva of Torah study.

More than just resolving a conceptual complication in the Alter Rebbe's writings, the Rebbe argued that this shift in the nature of a woman's obligation to study relevant halakhot markedly impacts the scope of such study. While a functionally motivated study might be capped with mastery of the practical curriculum, an independent obligation of Torah study has no such limitation. As the Rebbe put it:

---

63. *Shulhan Arukh HaRav, Orah Hayyim* 47:10.
64. See the references in *Likkutei Sihot* 14, *Ekev*, no. 2, note 25. For other instances where the Rebbe employed this principle, see *Likkutei Sihot* 17, *Aharei Mot*, no. 2, *se'if* 5; ibid., 17, *Kedoshim*, no. 4, *se'if* 4.
65. The halakhic expression of this construction of halakha as an independent stage is that an incorrect thought during the halakha can render the entire sacrifice invalid. See *Mishneh Torah, Hilkhot Pesulei HaMukdashin* 13:4.

Since learning the halakhot of these mitzvot becomes an independent endeavor and is an independent goal of Torah study, it is understood that such study is not limited to the times when one needs to know how to perform the mitzvot practically. Rather, even a woman who already knows the halakhot that are necessary for her and knows how to follow them still is connected to the study of Torah and therefore can make a blessing on the study of Torah.[66]

In the Rebbe's final formulation a woman has a "constant obligation" to study Torah, which lasts "the entire day."[67]

Learning Hasidism
The Rebbe also argued that the category of halakhot relevant for women includes a deep engagement with the study of hasidic teachings. He argued that the mitzvot of loving, fearing, and knowing God are paramount obligations which apply to women just as much as to men. As such, the optimal means of fulfilling such mitzvot – studying Hasidism – must be equally obligatory upon both genders. As he once put it:

> The commandments of belief in God, loving God, and fearing God are constant and ever-present obligations, and therefore women are obligated to fulfill them. And there is an explicit ruling of Rambam: "What is the path toward loving and fearing God? When a person contemplates His actions and sees His wisdom...." This is the precise content of Hasidism.[68]

This was the halakhic underpinning of the Rebbe's insistence that there be a robust curriculum of Hasidism in Chabad girls' high schools.

---

66. *Likkutei Sihot* 14, *Ekev*, no. 2, *se'if* 5.
67. Ibid., *Haazinu*, no. 2, *se'if* 6.
68. *Torat Menahem* 5746: 1, 578. See also *Torat Menahem* 5750: 3, 172, and ibid., 5748: 1, 227–28.

Talmud Study

The next stage in the Rebbe's expansion and encouragement of women's Torah study relates to two areas that were previously out of their domain. First, what of the sections of halakha that are not relevant for women? Should women be encouraged to seriously study the halakhot of tzitzit and tefillin from which they are exempt, yet constitute formidable sections of halakhic literature? Second, even in the areas of relevant halakhot that women are obligated to study, what is the mode and texture of this investigation? Are they to become engrossed in the intricate talmudic discussions that form the conceptual underpinning of the halakhot, or are they to suffice with studying the more practical aspects of halakha?

The Rebbe responded expansively to both of these questions. While admittedly working from a paucity of sources, he spoke approvingly of women being engaged in all aspects of the breadth and depth of Torah study. We will briefly outline his analysis of the earlier sources and then develop the philosophic framework that guided his innovative understanding and application of these sources.

He first noted that even if a woman is exempt from certain modes or parts of Torah study, the general concept of volunteerism is present.[69] Just as many women take the four species on Sukkot and hear the shofar on Rosh HaShana despite their technical exemption, so too, they can volunteer to study Torah. Such volunteerism is of value to one's religious development, even if the rabbinic tradition hails the superiority of fulfilling mitzvot out of a sense of commandedness.[70]

In addition, the Rebbe contended that there might be a tinge of normativity in a woman's engagement in in-depth and practically irrelevant Talmud study. The Talmud notes that women merit the World to Come by encouraging their husbands and children to study Torah.[71] This statement has been traditionally understood to mean that the wife/mother is not studying Torah herself but can partner in the studying of her male relatives by facilitating their learning. The Rebbe noted, however, that the highest level of encouragement one can offer is through

---

69. *Torat Menahem* 5750: 3, 172–73.
70. Kiddushin 31a.
71. Berakhot 17a.

active interest and engagement with the subject matter. With this in mind, he depicted the following scenario:

> When the child returns home the mother should ask her child what he learned in school, and the child will tell the mother about his studies, be it in Scripture, Mishna, or even Talmud... and the mother should, on her own, add explanations concerning these studies. Similarly, regarding her husband... when he returns home, she should ask her husband what he learned in Kollel... and not only that, but she should add on from her own thoughts. This should be underscored based on the custom in our later generations (with the endorsement and encouragement of *Gedolei Yisrael*) that women and girls study the Oral Torah in addition to the "halakhot that are necessary for them" (*Shulhan Arukh HaRav, Hilkhot Talmud Torah* 1:14).[72]

While clearly assuming that the wife is the *akeret habayit* and not the one who is studying in Kollel, he still argued that she needs the skills and proficiency to "speak in learning" with her husband. As anyone who has engaged talmudic texts is aware, even this level of facility requires serious preparatory study.

Even as the Rebbe sought to locate sources that obligated women in all sorts of study, he was cognizant that the Talmud itself seems to explicitly discourage such intellectual engagement, as it will lead a woman to "promiscuity." Does this not negate any possibility to interpret the sources in a manner that encourages such study?

The Rebbe's halakhic response was the reiteration of a halakhic-pedagogical contention raised by several prominent twentieth-century halakhic authorities. R. Yisrael Meir Kagan (1838–1933), known as the *Hafetz Hayyim* and the author of the authoritative *Mishna Berura*, wrote that the problem of promiscuity and undue cunningness[73] is relevant only in a society that bars women from other forms of education.[74] In

---

72. *Torat Menahem* 5750: 3, 227. See also *Torat Menahem* 5750: 3, 172.
73. See Rashi on Sota 21b, s.v. *ke'ilu*.
74. *Likkutei Halakhot*, Sota, ch. 3.

such contexts there is concern that a rigorous intellectual diet of deep Torah study will lead a woman astray. Today, however, with the advent of a gender-blind compulsory education, girls and women are anyway engaged in sophisticated secular studies. This educational shift in the broader world transforms in-depth Torah study from being discouraged to an obligatory enterprise. As the Rebbe explained:

> And from this [the establishment of girls' schools] it is understood that a similar shift is necessary regarding the study of the Oral Torah (in addition to the "halakhot that are necessary for them"). Since women and girls are studying various subjects and "cunningness is entering them"[75] anyway, it is not only *permitted* for them to learn the Oral Torah but...it is *obligatory* to teach them the Oral Torah...including the *reasons* behind the laws and the talmudic discussions, as it is human nature (man or woman) to *greatly enjoy* such learning. Through this, their talents and senses will develop in the spirit of our holy Torah.[76]

Thus, the Rebbe effectively opened the entire talmudic and hasidic corpus to women.[77]

A Positive Development
While each of these expansions has its own internal justification, the Rebbe also sought to create a general framework for these changes. On the one hand, he described the establishment of a formal system of girl's schools as a practical necessity to combat negative influences, hardly an idealistic vision. However, in addition to this defensive measure, the Rebbe also provided a positive conceptual formulation. This latter position is clearly articulated in a talk in 5750/1990 dedicated to women's education:

---

75. Rashi on Sota 21b.
76. *Torat Menahem* 5750: 3, 173.
77. However, at times the Rebbe also practically limited the scope of this injunction for the sake of keeping within communal norms. See the series of letters collected by Chaim Rappaport (Tamuz 5773), 151–55.

> It should be noted that this [increase in women's learning] is one of the *positive innovations* of the later generations. Even though the permissibility and the necessity of women learning the Oral Torah is due to the descent of the generations (*yeridat hadorot*)... the practical result is *positive* – that there is more studying of Torah. One can suggest that the reason that we merited this increase in Torah study specifically in the later generations... is because in the end of the exile there is an emphasis on preparing for redemption, to the extent that there is already a taste of a state similar to that of redemption: "In those days there will be an increase of knowledge and wisdom" (*Mishneh Torah, Hilkhot Teshuva* 9:2).[78]

The explosion of Torah study in the world in general, and for women in particular, contains messianic potency. Rambam describes the Messianic Era as one in which there will be an increase of Godly knowledge for all people. Therefore, as the world readies for redemption, both men and women must increase their study of Torah and knowledge of God.

In addition to this general point, the Rebbe added that the upsurge of Torah study among women is growing at an exponentially greater rate than the parallel development among men. The reason for this, he explained, is the prominent and paramount role that women will play in the Messianic Era: "It can be suggested that since in the future [the level of]...'the female will encircle the male' will be revealed, the increase of Torah study in later generations is primarily apparent among women."[79] Beyond a specific halakhic reaction to a dynamic social reality, the Rebbe saw the hand of God in "forcing" the Jewish leaders to open the gates of Torah to women. It is part of the disclosure of *malkhut*'s true nature and its reunification with the Divine Essence.

Entering the Public Sphere
The Rebbe's Conservative Perspective on Women in the Public Sphere

The Rebbe deeply believed that the first responsibility of an adult woman is toward her family as per her role as *akeret habayit*. This notion was

---

78. *Torat Menahem* 5750: 3, 174.
79. Ibid., note 42.

intertwined with the rabbinic conception of the home being the primary sphere of a women, based on the dictum "All honor [awaits] the King's daughter who is within," and the rabbinic conception of *tzeniut* or modesty.

Therefore, despite the great value the Rebbe placed on engaging and transforming the "outside" world, in many talks he emphasized that women can participate in the completion of this intergenerational mission without entering the public sphere through two mediums: (1) transforming her home into a shining beacon that will illuminate her community and ultimately the entire world, and (2) encouraging her husband's and sons' public activities. For example, in one talk, after highlighting the crucial role of the *akeret habayit* in educating her children, the Rebbe added that in this way the *akeret habayit* can aid in "conquering the world": "This can be accomplished through her educating her sons to conquer the world outside of the home, for [regarding herself], 'All honor [awaits] the King's daughter who is within.'"[80] Similarly, elsewhere, the Rebbe described that a woman can act through influencing her husband:

> And through this [positively influencing their husbands], women will also influence the world outside of their homes. Even though Jewish women do not need to be involved with outside matters, as "All honor [awaits] the King's daughter who is within," nevertheless, through the fact that they influence their husbands, they ensure that not only their homes are a dwelling place (*dira*) for God, but also the elements outside their home are a dwelling place for God.[81]

In effect, a woman can influence the world without breaching the literal and metaphorical walls of her home.

This point is sharpened by several instances where the Rebbe cautioned against women unnecessarily entering the public sphere. He spoke out against girls going to public demonstrations as a violation of the notion of *tzeniut* and "All honor [awaits] the King's daughter who is within."[82] Similarly, he expressed disappointment that single women

---

80. Ibid., 5742: 4, 2023.
81. Ibid., 5718: 1, 153.
82. *Sihot Kodesh* 5731: 2, 363.

were increasingly finding it necessary to enter the workforce prior to marriage on identical grounds.[83] Clearly, the Rebbe's echoed and applied some of the conservative and restrictive sentiments of "All honor [awaits] the King's daughter who is within."

The Need for Women in the Public Sphere
Simultaneously, though, the Rebbe animated an army of women to go out to the streets, college campuses, and far-flung places in order to bring the light of Judaism to the world at large. Fully aware of the seeming conflict between the public-facing activism that he was encouraging and his understanding of "All honor [awaits] the King's daughter who is within," the Rebbe dedicated several sections of talks to navigating this tension. As he did regarding women's Torah study, the Rebbe proposed two distinct and yet related rationales to Chabad women's religious activism – one focusing on the decadent nature of the generation and the second on the proximity to the coming of *Mashiah*. In addition, he set clear guidelines regarding the extent and nature of such activities.

On the most basic level, the Rebbe explained that sending women into the streets was an unavoidable concession to the urgent needs of the generation. For example, in one talk the Rebbe acknowledged that many people had a legitimate complaint against extending educational opportunities and mitzva campaigns to girls and women:

> There are those who come with claims: Why did [Chabad] recently begin to become so involved with girls' education, even though this was not the case in previous generations? And especially since the current form of girls' education is connected with leaving their homes and going outside to get to school... which is the opposite of "All honor [awaits] the King's daughter who is within".... And even more so, [Chabad] does not suffice with this, but even communal activism became a matter not just for men but also for women, and, on the contrary, women are more active and effective in this than men... it is impossible to be involved

---

83. *Torat Menahem* 5743: 4, 1869.

with the public without going outside, the opposite of "All honor [awaits] the King's daughter who is within."[84]

The Rebbe responded that he was merely following the precedents of recent great Torah authorities who certainly realized that they were breaking with traditional halakhic and communal norms. It must be that these authorities were relying on the dictum of "A time to do for the Lord; they have made void Your Torah,"[85] a rare talmudic allowance to violate certain prohibitions in the face of existential threats.[86] In the twentieth century, not tapping into the resource of educated Jewish women to spread the light of Torah would be tantamount to communal suicide.[87] As the Rebbe put it elsewhere: "Even though in earlier generations, women were not involved in such activities [as spreading Hasidism] due to 'All honor [awaits] the King's daughter who is within,' in our times there is a need."[88]

Dinah and a Unique Form of Feminine Outreach
Not satisfied with simply construing women's public involvement as a pragmatic allowance, the Rebbe also constructed a unique theorization of activism as a feminine value. One articulation of this teaching followed a long analysis of Dinah's kidnapping.[89] The Torah tells us: "Dinah, the daughter of Leah, whom she had borne to Jacob, went out to look about among the daughters of the land"[90] and that she was subsequently kidnapped and raped by Shechem. Rashi notes that the Torah identifies her as the daughter of Leah in order to highlight a commonality between mother and daughter: "However, because of her going out she was called the daughter of Leah, since she (Leah) too was in the habit of going out." A cursory reading of Rashi might lead one to believe that he is partially

---

84. Ibid., 5725: 2, 171–72.
85. Ps. 119:126.
86. Gittin 60a.
87. *Torat Menachem* 5725: 2, 172. See also *Torat Menachem* 5750: 3, 176, where the Rebbe invoked this idea for women's education.
88. *Torat Menachem* 5714: 2, 66.
89. *Likkutei Sihot* 35, *Vayishlah*, no. 3.
90. Gen. 34:1.

blaming the victim. Had Dinah stayed within the safe confines of her home, her tragic saga never would have unfolded.[91]

However, for a host of textual and conceptual reasons, the Rebbe rejected this approach and argued for an opposite understanding. Notwithstanding her terrible story, Dinah's desire to engage "the daughters of the land" was inherently positive and should be held up as a model for future women. As the Rebbe put it:

> [Dinah] teaches a lesson for Jewish women: Even though "All honor [awaits] the King's daughter who is within" and women are the *akeret habayit*, as their main mission is to build a Jewish home...those women who are graced with special qualities and are able to influence others "outside" should use these qualities in a modest fashion for the sake of Heaven – to bring hearts closer to the service of God and to help return the women found "outside."[92]

While acknowledging their traditional domestic role, the Rebbe used Dinah as a model for women who have similar inclinations to use their God-given talents to actively "bring hearts closer to the service of God" no matter where they be.

The Rebbe added that women's activism needed to have a specifically feminine form. This would, in some ways, circumscribe their public activity but also allow them to channel their unique talents toward greater effect:

> It is obvious that this effort needs to be as befitting a Jewish woman, in a modest fashion, such that even in the "going outside" it needs to be recognizable that "All honor [awaits] the King's daughter who is within".... And just the opposite! The nature of feminine intimacy and softness will help them succeed in bringing hearts closer to the service of God even more than the men. As is evident, when a person tries to bring a person close through ways

---

91. In fact, *Midrash Tanhuma* (*Vayishlah*, *siman* 12) cites the verse "All honor [awaits] the King's daughter who is within" as a contrast to Dinah's activities.
92. *Likkutei Sihot*, 35, *Vayishlah*, no. 3, *se'if* 6.

of peace and pleasantness there is much more success – the effect is more internal and has more permanence – than if the activity is accomplished through arguments and wars (as is the manner of men – "A man's manner is to conquer" [Rashi on Gen. 1:28]).[93]

Women have a unique contribution to make in the world of public activism and influence. Just as their softer and gentler natures allow them to optimally influence their family in a subtle fashion, so too, these same characteristics are crucial for success outside the home.

Elsewhere, the Rebbe elaborated that this gentleness and pleasantness can be a deeper meaning of the phrase "All honor [awaits] the King's daughter who is within." Even while actively engaged with the outside world, she is able to influence others in an inward manner. In contrast to men, who exert their influence in a more confrontational and "conquering" fashion, a woman can "act in an 'inner' fashion, with respect and refined character traits... such that she will have an inner effect, meaning that the one who is being influenced will willingly accept the influence."[94] Needless to say, the Rebbe felt that such a method of outreach would yield greater and more permanent changes in the outside world.[95]

A Messianic Vision

All of these aspects of womanhood make the work of Jewish women crucial for the world's redemption. Their activities, be it in the home or on the streets, are the social expression of the spiritual ascent of *malkhut* toward its root in the Divine Essence. Perhaps the most emphatic expression of this theme is from one of the Rebbe's final talks.[96] He began by highlighting R. Yosef Yitzhak's shift toward addressing Chabad women as a distinct group and sourcing this shift in the primacy that the Torah grants to women at the Giving the Torah and other key moments in Jewish history.

---

93. Ibid.
94. *Torat Menahem* 5751: 1, 243.
95. See *Torat Menahem* 5751: 1, 240–42, and especially note 99, which says that this "inner" form of influencing is associated with the *sefira* of *malkhut*.
96. *Torat Menahem* 5752: 2, 183–92.

Then, shifting lenses from the past to the present and future, the Rebbe continued:

> And nowadays the main point [that needs to be emphasized] is the unique connection between women and the redemption. The Rabbis teach us, "In the merit of the righteous women in that generation, the Jews were redeemed from Egypt" (Sota 11a), and the same is true regarding the future redemption... that it will be in the merit of the righteous women.[97]

This classic teaching had an acute practical relevance:

> And since our generation is the last generation of exile and the first generation of redemption... my father-in-law exerted effort to influence women in order to hasten the redemption in the merit of the righteous women of our generation.
>
> In addition, the advantage of Jewish women is emphasized not only in bringing the redemption, but also and mainly in the redemption itself – as is known and explained in kabbalistic and hasidic books, that in the future the superiority of the *sefira* of *malkhut* (receiver [*mekabel*], woman), whose root is above all of the *sefirot* (influencer, man), will be revealed, as the verse states: "The female will encircle the male" and "The woman of valor is a crown of her husband."

In what became a coda to his hundreds of talks on women's issues, the Rebbe unambiguously created a messianic framework. The recharacterization of traditional female roles in addition to the opening of new vistas before them are all part of the last generation's mission: bringing *Mashiah*.

CONCLUSION

The Rebbe's re-envisioning of the role of women consisted of his characteristic mix of traditionalism and innovation. While scrupulously adhering to his inherited textual tradition, the Rebbe creatively reconstrued old

---

97. Ibid., 183–84.

precedents to apply them in new ways required by the new circumstances and opportunities of his time. Even more, a deeper understanding of the nature of a redeemed world reveals that certain trends of modernity are part of the progress toward redemption.

Secondary Literature Consulted for Chapter 15, "'The Female Will Encircle the Male': The Rise of Women in the Final Generation"

Susan Handelman, "Women and the Study of Torah in the Thought of the Lubavitcher Rebbe."

Susan Handelman, "Putting Women in the Picture: The Rebbe's View on Women Today."

Yitzhak Kraus, "Dor HaGeula: Tafkidan shel Nashim BeMishnato shel HaRav Menahem Mendel Schneerson, HaAdmor MiLubavitch."

Naftali Loewenthal, "'Daughter/Wife of Hasid' or 'Hasidic Woman'?"

Naftali Loewenthal, "Spiritual Experience for Hasidic Youths and Girls in Pre-Holocaust Europe – a Confluence of Tradition and Modernity."

Naftali Loewenthal, "Women and the Dialectic of Spirituality in Hasidism."

Ada Rapoport-Albert, "From Women as Hasid to Women as 'Tsadik' in the Teachings of the Last Two Lubavitcher Rebbes."

Ada Rapoport-Albert, "The Emergence of a Female Constituency in Chabad."

Eldad Veil, "Tehilata shel Tekufat HaNashim: Nashim VeNashiyut BeMishnato shel HaRebbe MiLubavitch."

Zev Wolf, *El Neshei UVnot Yisrael: HaIsha, HaEm VehaBat HaYehudiya BiRe'iyato shel HaRebbe MiLubavitch*

Elliot Wolfson, *Open Secret*, 200–23.

Chapter 16

Between Universalism and Particularism: Non-Jews in the *Dira BaTahtonim*

One of the unique aspects of the Rebbe's leadership was his interest in non-Jewish society and the world at large. By all accounts he cared deeply about the material, moral, and spiritual life of all people, and worked for the betterment of people in many walks of life. On a personal level, he met and corresponded with global leaders and statesmen, ranging from local city councilmen to the president of the United States, advising and encouraging them about issues he saw as crucial to the moral and spiritual fabric of society. As noted in chapter 1, his efforts bore fruit and he gained American presidential and congressional recognition.

What drove the Rebbe in this direction? As we have seen, the Rebbe grounded all of his innovative interests and activities in his understanding of classical sources and how they applied to the modern era.

The Demographics of Dira BaTahtonim

The present chapter will probe the Rebbe's understanding of whether and how non-Jews can live lives of spiritual growth and sanctity. More particularly, how might they participate in the mission of transforming the physical world into God's dwelling place (*Dira BaTahtonim*)? Will they experience the messianic redemption of the world? We will also gain an understanding of how the Rebbe addressed questions concerning the nature of Jewish chosenness and the relationship between the Jewish people and the rest of humanity.

JEWISH CHOSENNESS

The Torah unequivocally states that the Jewish people are God's chosen people. This begins with Abraham, the first patriarch. God declares that "I will make you into a great nation, and I will bless you, and I will aggrandize your name, and [you shall] be a blessing. And I will bless those who bless you, and the one who curses you I will curse, and all the families of the earth shall be blessed in you."[1] Abraham's descendants, the Jewish people, are described as God's "firstborn,"[2] whom God loves.[3] Following the Exodus from Egypt, standing at the foot of Mount Sinai, the Jewish people entered a unique covenant with God, which distinguished them from all other nations. God proclaimed to them, "You shall be to Me a treasure out of all peoples...and you shall be to Me a kingdom of princes and a holy nation."[4]

Rabbinic Literature

The Sages concretized the chosen status of the Jewish people in many liturgical formulations. For example, they instituted that before studying Torah one should recite the following blessing: "Who has chosen us from all the peoples and given us His Torah. Blessed are You, Lord, Giver of the Torah."[5]

---

1. Gen. 12:2–3.
2. Ex. 4:22.
3. Deut. 7:8.
4. Ex. 19:5–6.
5. Berakhot 11b.

This chosen status is reflected in rabbinic law as well.[6] The Talmud mandates many practices and prohibitions that highlight the distinct status of the Jewish people and reinforce its integrity. For example, various measures are taken to avoid the type of fraternizing with non-Jews that could lead to intermarriage, which is regarded as a severe sin.[7] The Talmud also goes a step further and includes various statements about the moral inferiority of the nations of the world, especially in comparison with the Jewish people. For example, "all good" actions undertaken by other nations are said to be tainted by the motive of "self-glorification."[8] By contrast, Jews are assumed to be characterized by innate, inherited moral virtues that make them "merciful, bashful, and doers of kindnesses."[9] Distinctions like these are treated with such seriousness that they actually inform legal rulings.[10]

Together with negative statements about non-Jews, however, we also find positive ones emphasizing the potential that all human beings have to attain higher levels of wisdom and morality. While one sage ruled that "a gentile who engages in Torah study is liable for the death penalty," another ruled that "a gentile who engages in Torah study is like a High Priest." The Talmud reconciles the two opinions by asserting that the latter ruling allows gentiles to study only the Torah laws related to the Noahide Laws.[11] According to another rabbinic source, "there are righteous individuals among the gentiles who have a portion in the World to Come."[12]

Rambam

This brief survey demonstrates that the medieval Jewish authorities were heirs to a complex canon about non-Jews. These Jewish thinkers analyzed the different strands in biblical and rabbinic literature and began to frame the issue of Jewish chosenness in new ways. One central question

---

6. For more sources and analysis, see Sacha Stern (1994), 1–79.
7. Eiruvin 19a; Rambam, *Mishneh Torah, Hilkhot Issurei Bi'ah* 12:13.
8. Bava Batra 10b; Shabbat 33b.
9. Yevamot 79a
10. See, for example, Mishna Avoda Zara 2:1–2.
11. Sanhedrin 59a.
12. Tosefta Sanhedrin 13:2; Rambam, *Commentary to the Mishna*, Sanhedrin 10:2.

raised in medieval Jewish philosophy was whether Jews are essentially and ontologically different from non-Jews. In other words, when developing a taxonomy of beings, should Jews and non-Jews be included in the same category due to the fact that they are all humans? Or perhaps, biology notwithstanding, Jews and non-Jews are essentially different and belong to distinct categories because they are constitutively distinct in terms of their spiritual makeup.

According to many scholars, Rambam was a proponent of the first position. While he codifies many of the harsh legal rulings that stem from talmudic assumptions regarding non-Jews,[13] in his voluminous writings he does not differentiate between Jews and non-Jews regarding the essential nature of their souls.[14] Rather, the Jewish people are distinguished for their greater acquired wisdom and character traits, which make them a more complete form of human being. At the same time, Rambam lauds gentiles who dedicate themselves to gaining knowledge of God and describes the high spiritual level that they can attain.[15]

This approach climaxes in Rambam's descriptions of the Messianic Era. There, he amplifies the prophetic vision and creates a picture that includes non-Jews in the great eschatological intellectual and spiritual awakening. For example, when codifying the mission of *Mashiah*, Rambam writes:

> He will then perfect the entire world, motivating all the nations to serve God in unison, as [the verse] states: "For then I will transform the peoples to a purer language, that they will all call upon the name of God and serve Him with one purpose" (Zeph. 3:9).[16]

---

13. See, for example, *Perush HaMishnayot, Bava Kama* 4:3 where Rambam describes non-Jews as being akin to animals due to the fact that "they do not have complete 'human' characteristics." For more sources and analysis, see Yitzhak Sheilat (2010), 81–82.
14. See, for example, *Mishneh Torah, Hilkhot Yesodei HaTorah* 4:8; *Guide for the Perplexed*, III:54. For more sources and analysis, see Menahem Kellner (2016), especially 39–44; Yitzhak Sheilat (2010), 63–84.
15. *Mishneh Torah, Hilkhot Shemitta VeYovel* 13:13.
16. *Mishneh Torah, Hilkhot Melakhim UMilhemoteihem* 11:4.

Similarly, when Rambam describes the utopian existence of the messianic redemption, he employs a similar theme:

> In that era, there will be neither famine nor war, envy nor competition, for good will flow in abundance and all the delights will be [freely] available as dust. The occupation of the entire world will be solely to know God.[17]

In the Messianic Era, the entire world will "call upon the name of God" and strive to "know [Him]."[18]

Kuzari

Rambam's approach is often contrasted with that of another preeminent medieval Jewish thinker, R. Yehuda HaLevi.[19] In his work, the *Kuzari*, R. Yehuda HaLevi describes an elusive "divine matter" that was originally vested in all mankind, but due to human sin was soon limited to the Jewish forefathers and eventually the Jewish people. He argues that for this reason Jews do not fit into any of the classical categories in medieval taxonomy – inanimate objects, flora, fauna, and humans – but rather represent a fifth and more elevated category.[20] Similarly, only Jews are able to directly communicate with God through prophecy, while even the most righteous non-Jews are constitutionally incapable of this experience.[21]

While underscoring the special status of the Jewish people, the author of the *Kuzari* also portrays their relationship with the other nations of the world in terms of interdependence and mutuality. In one of his metaphors, Israel is likened to a seed that can only grow when it is nourished by the earth, to which the broader human population is likened. Along similar lines to Rambam, but perhaps more poetically, R. Yehuda HaLevi depicts the eschatological era as a time when the seed will elicit from the earth a new fruition:

---

17. Ibid., 12:5.
18. For an elaboration of this theme, see Menahem Kellner (2016), 168–200.
19. Menahem Kellner (2016), 21–30.
20. *Kuzari*, I:103.
21. Ibid., I:115. For an analysis and partial tempering of this idea, see Howard Kreisel (2001), 136–47.

> The nations serve to introduce and pave the way for the expected *Mashiah*, who is the fruition.... Then, if they acknowledge him, they will become one tree. Then they will revere the root which they formerly despised.²²

The universal redemption will see the blossoming of a positive relationship between Jews and gentiles without obliterating the fundamental distinction between them. The Jewish people are the seed, or the root, of redemption, and their special role is to lead the rest of the world to its ultimate aim.²³

Kabbalists

The kabbalistic tradition generally affirms and amplifies the essentialist approach of R. Yehuda HaLevi.²⁴ Many kabbalistic texts assert that while Jewish souls stem from God Himself, non-Jewish souls are rooted in impure cosmic forces often referred to as the "Other Side" (*Sitra Ahra*) or the "impure shells" (*kelippot hatemeot*). For example, R. Hayyim Vital describes gentiles' souls as emerging from "the bad portion that was mixed into the first man (*Adam HaRishon*)."²⁵ As such, the nations of the world and the impure forces that reside in them are in a state of constant battle with the Jewish people, who represent God in this world.

This depiction, though, needs to be tempered by two interrelated points, one theoretical and one practical. First, from a more theoretical perspective, we have seen that the kabbalistic worldview champions a doctrine of monism, according to which even the impure cosmic forces themselves are manifestations of divinity. Thus, we find descriptions in kabbalistic literature that the *Sitra Ahra* itself was created by and empowered by God to do its work.²⁶

In addition, on a practical level, many kabbalists expanded tenets of intra-Jewish moral conduct to non-Jews as well. Strikingly,

---

22. *Kuzari*, IV:13.
23. See Dov Schwartz, (2017), 43–46.
24. For sources and analysis, see Moshe Hallamish (1998), 289–311; Hanan Balk (2013), 47–61.
25. *Sefer HaGilgulim*, ch. 1.
26. *Zohar, Pekudei*, 237b.

the very same R. Hayyim Vital who wrote that non-Jews' animal souls are inhabited by the forces of impurity, also wrote, "One should love all [of God's] creations, even gentiles."[27] Arguably, this stems from the kabbalistic perspective that all creations, even the most impure, are rooted in the one God.[28]

Tanya

This tension in kabbalistic teachings regarding the moral inferiority of non-Jews and the lower spiritual source of their souls, versus their monistic inclusion within God, is also found in classic Chabad literature. Putting these different strands in conversation with one another creates a nuanced picture of the nature and role of non-Jews in early Chabad thought.

On the one hand, a cursory reading of the first chapter of *Tanya* indicates that the Alter Rebbe adopted a version of the essentialist approach. *Tanya* opens with an excursion into the inner makeup of the Jew and explains that the Jewish people are inhabited by two souls: The first, an "animal soul" that "originates in the *kelippa* and *Sitra Ahra*," is enclothed in the bloodstream, vitalizes the daily physical functioning of the body, animates its natural instincts, and gives rise to elemental emotions that are not shaped by the intellect. The second soul is called the "divine soul" and is "truly a part of God from above" (*Tanya, Likkutei Amarim*, ch. 2). This divine soul empowers its otherwise earth-bound human owner to transcend its animalistic limitations and attain elevated levels of divine perception and altruistic service of God.

The Alter Rebbe then cites R. Hayyim Vital's *Etz Hayyim*, which says that the level of *kelippa* associated with the animalistic soul of a Jew is called *noga*, which also contains some good. He briefly contrasts it with Kabbala's starker assertions about the inner makeup of the animalistic souls of the nations of the world and the Talmud's statements about their moral shortcomings:

27. *Shaarei Kedusha*, ch. 1, sec. 5.
28. For more sources and analysis, see Hallamish (1998), 305–6.

> The [animal] souls of the nations of the world, however, emanate from the other, impure *kelippot* which do not contain any good, as is written in *Etz Hayyim*... that "all the good done by the nations is done for their own benefit." As the Talmud comments on the verse "The kindness of the nations is sin" (Prov. 14:34) – "All the charity and kindness that the nations of the world do... is only for their own self-glorification" (Bava Batra 10b).[29]

The souls that vitalize the bodies and instincts of the nations of the world are associated with the impure cosmic energies of *kelippa* that inhabit our physical world and conceal Godliness, and thus constrain their owners from achieving true altruism.[30]

This difference between Jews' and non-Jews' souls, and their related moral and spiritual horizons, appears to convey a stark picture. Yet, the Chabad masters taught that *Tanya*'s passage is not exhaustive of the topic.

First, R. Hillel of Paritch, a leading disciple of the first three Chabad Rebbes, writes that from other passages in the Alter Rebbe's canon[31] it becomes clear that the founder of Chabad had certainly not intended to declare that all non-Jewish souls are inherently associated with only selfish materialism and negative forces. Rather, the souls of the "righteous of the nations" (*hasidei umot haolam*) who lead upright and spiritual lives are rooted in *kelippat noga*, and are thus capable of self-transcendence and altruistic kindness.[32] Similarly, the Alter Rebbe explains elsewhere[33] that the righteous among the nations can reach the level of angels in their comprehension and meditation of Godliness.

---

29. *Tanya, Likkutei Amarim*, ch. 1.
30. See *Sefer HaArakhim Chabad*, vol. 2, "Umot HaOlam," 293–94, for similar statements from the leaders of Chabad.
31. He cites *Seder Tefillot MiKol HaShana*, vol. 1, 287b. For other similar sources, see *Sefer HaArakhim Chabad*, vol. 2, "Umot HaOlam," 317.
32. *Likkutei Biurim* to *Kuntrus HaHitpaalut* 47b. The Rebbe cited this teaching of R. Hillel of Paritch in *Likkutei Sihot* 8, *Hosafot*, 345, and in his notes to *Lessons in Tanya, Likkutei Amarim*, ch. 1.
33. *Seder Tefillot MiKol HaShana*, 284c and 287b–288a, and 29a–b. See also *Maamarei Admor HaZaken 5564*, 90–91, and *Maamarei Admor HaZaken Al Mamarei Razal*, 40–41.

But even when speaking of non-Jews more generally, Chabad literature contains various other layers and perspectives that attenuate the seemingly categorical passage from the first chapter of *Tanya*. For example, Chabad Rebbes, beginning with the Alter Rebbe, write of another "soul" that is found in all human beings – the "intellectual soul" (*nefesh hasikhlit*).[34] This soul is associated with the term "image of God" which Rambam defines as the human being's divinely endowed capacity to make rational choices. So even as only Jews contain the "divine soul" that facilitates sublime transcendence, both Jews and non-Jews are instructed and empowered to use their rational capacity to rein in the bestial instincts of the animalistic soul and lead moral and upright lives.[35]

On a more foundational level, later Chabad Rebbes noted that even regarding the non-Jewish souls that are associated with the impure *kelippot*, the Alter Rebbe could not have possibly meant that they contain "no good whatsoever," as this contradicts perhaps the most fundamental principle of *Tanya* – the unity of all creation within God. Accordingly, just as there is a divine spark deeply embedded within every element of creation, the same certainly holds true for all humans.[36]

Following this line of reasoning, the *Tzemah Tzedek* in his glosses on *Tanya* wrote: "'The three impure *kelippot* have no good at all' – i.e., within the fabric of their own selves. However [they contain] vitality of a divine spark in exile."[37] Similarly, two generations later, the Rashab wrote: "When the Book of *Beinonim* says that the three impure *kelippot*

---

34. See, for example, *Maamarei Admor HaZaken* 5568: 1, 116; *Or HaTorah, Bamidbar*, vol. 1, *Derushei Shavuot*, "Havivin Yisrael." For the unique role that the intellectual soul has in a Jewish psyche of mediating between the divine soul and the animal soul, see *Likkutei Torah Behukotai* 47c-d.
35. *Mamarei Admor HaZaken* 5568: 1, 116. It is important to note, however, that despite the similarities between the "intellectual soul" of Jews and non-Jews, the influence of the divine soul of a Jew causes important differences between them. For an elaboration, see *Likkutei Sihot* 15, *Noah*, *siha* 4.
36. See *Torat Menahem* 5746: 4, 252, where the Rebbe infers from the Alter Rebbe's formulations in *Tanya* that all human beings were created by a direct word of God and are more closely connected with Him than other creations.
37. Printed in *Derekh Mitzvotekha, Hosafot – Kitzur Tanya*, 388.

contain no good at all, this does not mean that there is no spark at all, as it is impossible for anything to exist without a good spark."[38]

Finally, these ideas are also found in the Alter Rebbe's description of redemption. When discussing the Messianic Era in *Likkutei Amarim*, chapter 36 (which later became a central chapter in the Rebbe's teachings), the Alter Rebbe concludes that the ultimate redemption will also affect the nations of the world:

> [At] "the end of time"...the physicality of the body and of the world will be purified, and they will be able to apprehend the revealed divine light which will shine forth to Israel by means of the Torah.... And through the superabundance of the illumination upon the Jewish people, the darkness of the nations will also be lit up, as is written, "And the nations shall walk by your light" (Is. 60:3).... And as we pray [in the Rosh HaShana and Yom Kippur liturgy], "Appear in Your majestic splendor and excellence upon all the inhabitants of the world."

When the divine core of every aspect of this world will be revealed for all to see, all of humanity will be "lit up" and radiant with divinity.

THE REBBE ON JEWISH CHOSENNESS
Introduction

As we have seen, early Torah literature contains various themes including: an emphasis on Jewish chosenness and ontological uniqueness, assertions of the divine composition of all of creation, negative teachings about non-Jewish souls and behaviors, and a universalistic messianic vision. As an heir to this complex tradition, the Rebbe certainly had the textual basis and the analytical acumen to continue to develop all of these themes equally.

Strikingly, though, the Rebbe did not. He almost entirely avoided describing non-Jewish souls as stemming from the impure cosmic forces. Instead, both theoretically and practically the Rebbe consistently emphasized and expanded upon the sources that carve out space

---

38. *Beshaa SheHikdimu* 5672, 770.

Between Universalism and Particularism

for non-Jewish Godliness, goodness, and service of God. When he was asked about the meaning of the Alter Rebbe's description of non-Jews in the first chapter of *Tanya*, the Rebbe referred his questioners to the above-cited glosses of the *Tzemah Tzedek* and the Rashab, which state that everything contains a divine spark,[39] and noted that non-Jews are "certainly" capable of altruism.[40] Similarly, he spoke of Jewish chosenness in a way that created room for Jews and non-Jews to work together to create the global redemption.

Let us now discuss these themes in the Rebbe's thought and see how he conceptualized and applied them for modern times.

An Essential and Transcendent Connection to God

As an heir to three millennia of rabbinic and kabbalistic teachings, the Rebbe unapologetically understood that the Jewish people were chosen by God for a unique mission on earth and endowed with a unique transcendent divine soul to fulfill it. This transcendent divine soul inherently binds the Jewish people with the Divine Essence. In hasidic texts, this is reflected in the Jewish people's special connection to the tetragrammaton, *Hashem*, God's personal name that expresses His essence.[41]

By contrast, the created world and all its other inhabitants, including the overwhelming majority of humanity, is connected with the divine name *Elokim*, which reflects God's revelation through the boundaries of nature. This is most clearly expressed in the very first verse of the Torah, "...*Elokim* created heaven and earth." The limitations of nature conceal the full potency of God's infinitude, allowing the world to maintain its finite existence.[42]

This foundational difference is what pushes the Jewish people into an entirely different category than the nations of the world.[43] Every single

---

39. *Iggerot Kodesh* 1, letter 95. See also *Iggerot Kodesh* 1, letter 14.
40. Recorded by Yehudis Fishman, "The Atomic Energy in the Male-Female Relationship."
41. See, for example, *Tanya, Iggeret HaTeshuva* ch. 4. In the context of this book, see chapter 2, section "The Short Path"; chapter 7, section "A Jew's Choice"; chapter 10, section "Inner *Hashgaha* versus Outer *Hashgaha*."
42. For a list of sources see *Sefer HaArakhim Chabad*, vol. 2, "Umot HaOlam," 266–67, 275, 285, 294, 299–302.
43. *Torat Menahem* 5747: 3, 356–57.

Jew is inherently bound with the Divine Essence due to the transcendent divine soul that God endowed within all Jews. This is a theme that we have already encountered in the context of free will,[44] *hashgaha*,[45] and intra-Jewish love.[46]

This distinction between Jews and non-Jews is also manifest in two utterly distinct typologies of belief in God.[47] As a general rule, the world's inhabitants can apprehend God only through the finite veil of creation, using the rational faculties of their souls to appreciate how nature reveals its Creator.[48] Their recognition of God, the Rebbe explained, "is not axiomatically intuited; rather the world's existence brings them to recognition of God."[49] Such is the natural state of all created beings; they can relate to God only in accord with the limited terms of their own finitude.

However, the transcendence of the divine soul with which the Jewish people are uniquely endowed connects them inherently to the superrational perspective of *Hashem* too. In the Rebbe's words, "The faith of the Jewish people does not emanate from the world. The Jewish people are bound essentially with Godliness, therefore Godliness is axiomatically intuited by them.... In this [intuition] there are none of nature's constrictions, and they axiomatically intuit levels of Godliness that transcend nature too."[50]

As noted above, the Alter Rebbe taught that all human beings possess an "intellectual soul," by dint of which they are "in the image of God" (*betzelem Elokim*).[51] In this sense, the Rebbe explained, every human being possesses a form of divine soul. The intellectual soul that is possessed by Jews and non-Jews alike[52] is a revelation of God within

---

44. Above, chapter 7, note 48.
45. Above, chapter 10, sections "Inner *Hashgaha* versus External *Hashgaha*" and "Functional *Hashgaha* versus Inherent *Hashgaha*."
46. Above, chapter 13, section "*Ahavat Yisrael* and Love of God."
47. *Likkutei Sihot* 1, Metzora, *se'ifim* 1–5.
48. See *Sefer HaArakhim*, vol. 2, "Umot HaOlam," 272–77.
49. *Likkutei Sihot* 1, Metzora, *se'if* 2.
50. Ibid.
51. Gen. 1:26–27.
52. See, however, note 41 above.

the limits of nature and rationale (*Elokim*). However, as explained in *Tanya*, the "second soul" possessed by the Jewish people is a direct revelation of God's supernatural transcendence (*Hashem*).[53]

This is also reflected in the distinction between the commandments given to all of humanity and those given only to the Jewish people. The mitzvot given to mankind as a whole comprise matters whose merits can be appreciated even by human understanding. Whereas those given to the Jewish people include many precepts that fundamentally transcend reason and are instead fulfilled out of a sense of suprarational and essential subjugation to God.[54]

Despite this sharp delineation between the rational manifestation of *Elokim* and the superrational manifestation of *Hashem*, the Rebbe underscored that in the Messianic Era "all flesh shall see together that the mouth of *Hashem* spoke" (Is. 40:5). With the redemption of the world, all nations will experience "the name *Hashem* that transcends the nature of the world."[55]

Jewish Chosenness: Responsibility and Servitude

The Rebbe was well aware of the discomfort that the whole notion of Jewish chosenness arouses in some quarters.[56] After all, how can a sense of the special status and transcendence of the Jewish people be squared with the kind of humility that is so fundamental to serving God, and to any kind of spiritual growth? Doesn't this lead to pride, which is the very antithesis of the Hasidic ideal of *bittul* (self-effacement)?

And yet, the Rebbe noted, it is indisputable that the Jewish people's chosenness by God is fundamental to Jewish religious thought and life. This is emphasized each and every day with the liturgical blessing in which we thank God "Who has chosen us from all the nations and given us His Torah." Why must this be repeated so often, and why is it so emphasized in the Torah itself?

---

53. *Sefer HaMaamarim* 5737, 275.
54. See above, chapter 5, section "Mitzvot and the Divine Essence."
55. *Likkutei Sihot* 25, Yod-Tet Kislev, *se'if* 6.
56. See *Torat Menahem* 5744: 2, 1207.

The answer, said the Rebbe, is that chosenness is commensurate with responsibility. The point is not simply that the Jewish people are privileged, and the point is certainly not that they should therefore feel entitled. Rather, "the primary intention in emphasizing the loftiness of the Jewish people is to emphasize the immensity of the responsibility that is placed upon them."[57] Citing Rashi's commentary on the Torah,[58] the Rebbe emphasized that the Jewish people are called "a nation of priests" (Ex. 19:6) because to be a priest is to be a "servant."[59] "Their vocation," he explained, "is to 'stand before God to serve Him.'"[60] In this vein, the Rebbe cited the talmudic formulation: "Do you think I am giving you rulership!? I am giving you servitude (*avdut*)!"[61]

On one occasion, when asked by a visiting college student if he believed "that the Jews are the chosen people," the Rebbe responded: "Yes. Not because of our endeavors, but because we are given additional obligations; and additional obligations require additional powers in order to fulfill them."[62]

Moreover, the Rebbe emphasized that this chosenness and responsibility to act as God's servants are relevant not only to the particulars of Torah study and mitzva observance as prescribed for Jews. Rather, their scope is universal:

> A Jew is not permitted to forget about the world and about the existence of the other nations of the world.... His vocation is to "perfect the world under the sovereignty of the Almighty" (*letaken olam bemalkhut Shadai*). Put simply: A Jew must influence the world around him to run in a fitting manner, in accord with justice and honesty (*tzedek veyosher*).[63]

---

57. *Torat Menahem* 5744: 2, 1207.
58. See Rashi on Ex. 28:3.
59. *Torat Menahem* 5744: 2, 1207.
60. Deut. 10:8.
61. Horayot 10a–b.
62. Shmuel Lew, "The Rebbe Speaks to College Students," available at https://chabad.org/354697.
63. *Torat Menahem* 5742: 1, 179

Similarly, the Rebbe once said: "Every Jew [is not merely an individual, but] also a communal person, who has an obligation toward all Jews, and...to the entirety of creation."[64]

In the above-mentioned conversation with a college student, the Rebbe made a similar point: "In a system that is very settled and in which everything is calculated, every part must be used to the full capacity for which it was meant. If an individual – and certainly a society – has certain possibilities, it is not only their own private business, but it concerns the entire society around; and in a larger outlook, it concerns the entire universe."[65]

In summary, the Rebbe did not shy away from, or apologize for, the lofty status accorded to the Jewish people by the Torah. At the very same time, he made it clear that this should never be taken as an excuse for any sort of chauvinism, self-satisfaction, or complacency. On the contrary, a greater awareness and appreciation of their chosenness should endow each Jew with a greater awareness of the immense responsibility, and difficult vocation, that they have uniquely been tasked to perform.

Distinctions and Interdependence Between Jews and Non-Jews

On a number of occasions, the Rebbe explained that we cannot rationally understand *why* God established such distinctions between people, for "we do not know the ways of the Creator and His reasons for acting in a certain way."[66] After all, this choice is rooted in the Divine Essence, which transcends all rational thought, and is not even bound by the distinction between infinitude and finitude.[67] As the Rebbe wrote:

> For reasons best known to God Himself, He wished that there should be many nations in the world, but only one Jewish people,

---

64. Ibid., 5714: 1, 46. Also see *Torat Menahem* 5750: 2, 430.
65. Shmuel Lew, "The Rebbe Speaks to College Students."
66. *Likkutei Sihot* 6, *Hosafot*, Yitro, 317–18.
67. See *Torat Menahem* 5720: 2, 306, where the Rebbe connected the Divine Essence's choice with its ability to unite finitude with infinity. See, chapter 7, section "The Basis for the Divine Essence's Choices."

> a people who should be separated and different from all the other nations, with a destiny and function of its own. ...[68]

Once the divine choice has been made, however, the distinct responsibilities of Jews and and non-Jews are as irreplaceable and mutually dependent as they are non-interchangeable. The Rebbe compared this to the function of different organs within a single body:

> Everything and every person has its own purpose or task, and this does not make anyone any more or less important, for all are important in the totality of things, just as every limb or organ of a body is important. Indeed, if one member would wish to change his function, it would not only disturb his own personal harmony, but would also disturb the total harmony. Imagine, for a moment, what would happen if the brain would wish to do the work of the heart to pump blood; it certainly would be disastrous, for even an extra tiny drop of blood in the brain would be dangerous, whereas the heart must always have an ample supply of blood. ...[69]

The Rebbe's approach is clear. On the one hand, the Jewish people were ontologically unique and chosen for a unique set of responsibilities. Yet, the distinct missions of the Jewish people in particular and humanity as a whole are all fundamentally interdependent. They are all part of a single interconnected organism.

One of the most salient, and perhaps surprising, aspects of the Rebbe's scholarship and teachings is the extensive degree to which he examined and innovatively illuminated the Torah mission for all humanity.

THE TORAH PATH FOR ALL HUMANITY

Having discussed the transcendent status of the Jewish people, let us now turn to the Rebbe's treatment of universal religiosity and ethics.

---

68. Letter from the Rebbe, dated Hanukka 5732, available at chabad.org/1883988. A similar discussion can be found in *Likkutei Sihot 6, Hosafot*, Yitro, 317–18.
69. Letter from the Rebbe, Hanukka 5732, chabad.org/1883988.

Between Universalism and Particularism

As background, let us note the following two points. First, despite the presence of universalistic themes in earlier Chabad literature, they were not given sustained emphasis for most of the movement's history. Second, many of the Rebbe's contemporaries advised Jews to self-segregate in order to protect their communities from the negative influences of the outside world, or at least emphasized building up their own Jewish communities. Given that many of them had personally witnessed the catastrophic decimation of Jewish life in Europe, and given the increasingly powerful threat of cultural secularization, their inward-looking stance is hardly surprising.

The Rebbe, however, took a different approach. In response to a person who was troubled about how God could have allowed the Holocaust to happen, the Rebbe wrote:

> Despite the lack of satisfactory answer to the awesome and tremendous "Why?" – one can, and must, carry on a meaningful and productive life, promote justice and kindness in one's surroundings, and indeed, help create a world where there should be no room for any holocaust, or for any kind of man's inhumanity to man.[70]

In line with this sentiment, the Rebbe sought to expand the humanistic, spiritual, and religious horizons of all humanity both theoretically and practically. To this end, he charted a detailed blueprint for all humans to help create the global redemption. Drawing on biblical and rabbinic literature, he taught that the Torah provides a broad moral and ethical path that should guide the lives, not only of Jews, but of all human beings.

The Rebbe's signature project vis-à-vis the world at large was the campaign to inspire all people to observe the universal Noahide Laws that are included in the Torah. Indeed, never before had a Jewish leader initiated a program in which Jews en masse would actively raise awareness of the Noahide mitzvot among their non-Jewish neighbors.

Understanding the basis and contours of the Noahide Laws campaign will allow us also to gain deeper insight into the theoretical and

---

70. Letter from the Rebbe dated to 23 Shevat 5744, available at chabad.org/2188391.

The Demographics of Dira BaTahtonim

practical standing of non-Jews in the Rebbe's thought. It will also help us understand how this construct fits within the broader framework of his philosophy and activities.

The Noahide Laws Campaign
Halakhic Background

The Talmud teaches that all human beings are obligated to keep seven mitzvot, which are rooted in the Torah's narratives of Adam and Noah.[71]

It is important to note, however, that the Rebbe never understood these precepts as a narrow list of seven commandments, but rather as a foundational code that sets out the most basic parameters of a much broader vision. This vision goes beyond simple behavioral concerns, and extends into an array of intellectual, social, spiritual, and educational dimensions. As we will see, the Rebbe often emphasized that at the core of the Noahide Laws is the recognition of God's oneness (monotheism) and sovereignty.

Here is Rambam's codification of these mitzvot:

> Six precepts were commanded to Adam: (1) the prohibition against worship of false gods, (2) the prohibition against cursing God, (3) the prohibition against murder, (4) the prohibition against incest and adultery, (5) the prohibition against theft, and (6) the command to establish laws and courts of justice.... The prohibition against eating flesh from a living animal [the seventh mitzva] was added for Noah.[72]

While there is a suggestion in halakhic literature that these laws have been abjured,[73] the vast majority of halakhic decisors assume that they are still binding on the non-Jewish population.[74]

---

71. Sanhedrin 57a.
72. *Mishneh Torah, Hilkhot Melakhim UMilhemoteihem* 8:1.
73. See, for example, *Shu"t Penei Yehoshua, Yoreh De'a*, siman 1.
74. For sources an analysis, see Matityahu Broyde (5757–5758), 89–91.

In addition to codifying these mitzvot as obligations for all people, Rambam also notes that the Jewish people have a particular responsibility to ensure that all of humanity adheres to them:

> Moses gave the Torah and mitzvot as an inheritance only to the Jewish people.... However, someone who does not desire to accept Torah and mitzvot should not be forced to. By the same token, Moses was commanded by the Almighty to compel (*lakuf*) all the inhabitants of the world to accept the commandments given to Noah's descendants.[75]

Rambam obligates Jews to "compel" all of humanity to keep these Noahide mitzvot.

However, for the span of eight hundred years since the publication of *Mishneh Torah*, this halakha inspired negligible discussion and action. It is not quoted in *Shulhan Arukh*, giving the impression that no practical obligation exists to compel non-Jews to observe their mitzvot. In fact, to explain the Jewish people's disregard for this passage in Rambam, several halakhic authorities assert that Rambam's ruling is binding only upon a Jewish government and court. Individual Jews, however, and particularly those living in the Diaspora, have no obligation toward their non-Jewish neighbors in this regard.[76]

The Rebbe's Understanding of Rambam

The Rebbe, however, in a talk he edited for the rabbinic journal *HaPardes*, offered a very different approach.[77] Through a scholarly analysis of Rambam's rulings, he argued that the halakha categorically obligates all Jews to encourage humanity as a whole to live up to the ideals of the Noahide Laws.[78] He also reasoned that Rambam's term "*lakuf*" does not necessarily

---

75. *Mishneh Torah, Hilkhot Melakhim UMilhemoteihem* 8:10.
76. See Shaul Yisraeli, *Amud Yemini*, vol. 1, *siman* 12:1:12, and David Bleich (2011), 338.
77. "Sheva Mitzvot Benei Noah," *HaPardes* 59:9 (Sivan 5745), 7–14. For a parallel analysis, see *Likkutei Sihot* 26, *Yitro*, no. 3, *se'ifim* 1–10.
78. "Sheva Mitzvot Benei Noah," 7. See also *Torat Menahem* 5743: 2, 637; ibid., 5743: 3, 1333.

mean to coercively compel, but includes any form of influence, such as convincing and exhorting.[79]

Why Now?
While this mission toward the broader world was firmly rooted in Rambam and classical rabbinic literature, the Rebbe admitted that practically it was a massive innovation. So why had no one previously taken up the cause of the Noahide Laws?

The primary reason for this, the Rebbe argued, was due to the danger associated with such efforts in earlier times. For millennia, if a Jew had been caught speaking to his Christian neighbor about the Noahide mitzvot he would have been summarily punished for religious interference. Accordingly, it wasn't remotely applicable in practice, and therefore went unmentioned in practical works of halakha. Rambam's code, by contrast, comprehensively contains all mitzvot and is not bound by historical concerns.

In the twentieth century, Jews were granted the privilege and responsibility to actually fulfill this halakhic mandate, perhaps for the very first time. In an era when the dangerous impediments to its actualization no longer existed, Rambam's authoritative ruling reemerged as a practical obligation.[80] The Rebbe contended that in addition to providing protection from persecution, the very fabric of free societies, especially in America, granted many Jews a historic opportunity to raise awareness of the Noahide Laws.[81] Many Jews had friendly or business relationships with non-Jews, and some had reached positions of extraordinary influence, at levels unimaginable even in the recent past. As a firm believer in *hashgaha*, the Rebbe perceived these changes as providing opportunities

---

79. "Sheva Mitzvot Benei Noah," 7. See also *Torat Menahem* 5743:2, 1333.
80. *Torat Menahem* 5743: 3, 1333; ibid., 5747: 2, 616.
81. In the Rebbe's talks about non-Jews and the Noahide mitzvot, he often highlighted the uniqueness of America as a country that was founded on biblical values, and the need to influence American society to live up to its lofty founding values. See, for example, *Torat Menahem* 5743: 2, 906–8; 5744: 3, 1432–35; ibid., 5747: 2, 54–57; ibid., 5750: 2, 70–71; ibid., 5751: 2, 94; and the following recorded talk: www.chabad.org/213518. For a comprehensive analysis of the Rebbe's conceptualization of America, see Philp Wexler and Eli Rubin (2020).

that carry divine purpose and obligation, especially to share the knowledge of the Noahide mitzvot, both individually and on a global scale.[82]

As we will see later in the chapter, the Rebbe did not see this shift of non-Jewish societies to being more open as a mere technical social change. Rather, the Rebbe understood this very change in non-Jewish society and the opportunity that it afforded to influence non-Jews to live Godly lives as part of a larger movement of the world toward the ultimate messianic reality.[83]

Expanding the Noahide Laws

As mentioned above, the Rebbe did not understand the Noahide Laws in a narrow sense that restricted them to the seven mitzvot specifically codified by Rambam. Through analyzing classical sources, he delineated several categories of religious, ethical, and virtuous activity as implicit extensions of the Noahide Laws. Two related lines of reasoning can be discerned in the Rebbe's explanations of why many additional precepts of the Torah, including positive commandments, are prescriptive for all humanity, not only the Jewish people.

1. Lashevet Yetzarah and Human Civilization

The first line of reasoning lay in the fundamental rationale and spirit of the Noahide Laws, which the Rebbe consistently linked to the verse in Isaiah explaining the purpose of the world (45:18): "God, who formed the earth and made it ... did not create it to be desolate; He formed it to be settled (*lashevet yetzarah*)."

This verse is generally cited by rabbinic sources in the context of the imperative to procreate. The world should not be left barren of people, but should be settled and civilized through the optimal expansion of the human population. The Rebbe, however, regularly invoked this verse to emphasize the much broader point originally expressed by Isaiah: The purpose of the world's existence is to be realized through engaging with it and developing it into a flourishing "settled" human civilization that fulfills the moral and ethical telos set for it by its Creator. This requires

---

82. *Torat Menahem* 5743: 2, 636; ibid., 5745: 2, 849–51.
83. See, below, section "The Particular, the Universal, and the Coming of *Mashiah*."

The Demographics of Dira BaTahtonim

that human beings tame their baser instincts and act humanely toward one another, both on interpersonal and international levels.

The Rebbe considered the ethical imperative of *lashevet yetzarah* to be the underlying rationale of the Noahide Laws. Here's how he expressed this point on one occasion, in a talk to young children:

> The content of these mitzvot (and their details) is to realize the verse "He formed it to be settled," that the world should be "settled," a place that is fit to live in peacefulness and in tranquility....
>
> When the nations of the world fulfill the seven Noahide Laws, it strengthens and adds in the [realization of the promise] "I will give peace upon the land" (Lev. 26:6)...peace between one nation and another, peace between one person and another...peace (and completeness) between God and His creations, which includes all the nations, all animals, all plant-life, and even inanimate things....[84]

This passage succinctly encapsulates the Rebbe's decades of teaching that the Noahide Laws embody an all-embracing ethic that encompasses relations between one individual and another, as well as between nations. Taking it further, it also includes "peace" between humanity and the natural world. The underlying imperative of the Noahide Laws is a requirement to act in ways that ensure the wholesomeness of all of human society, and synergy between humans and the ecological system that we inhabit.

2. Natural Law and Human Civilization

The second line of reasoning appears to build on the first. From the basic notion of the imperative to foster a world that is "settled," peaceful, harmonious, and complete, the Rebbe took the further step of arguing that reason itself is a source of legal precepts that are incumbent upon humanity to follow. The Rebbe argued that God endowed the rational capacity of every person with an innate degree of moral discernment. Consequently, although the Torah is a divine text, it also recognizes and endorses a form of natural law as a source of binding obligation.

---

84. *Torat Menahem* 5747: 3, 305–6.

Between Universalism and Particularism

In a series of talks the Rebbe delivered on this topic in the spring of 1987, he pointed out that Rambam writes that the mitzva of *tzedaka* is not one of the Seven Noahide Laws.[85] Yet, the Rebbe argued, it is clear that all of humanity is obligated to help the poor. This is demonstrated by the biblical statement that the people of Sodom were punished because "they did not support the poor and the needy" (Ezek. 16:49). Given that, at least according to Rambam, the Seven Noahide Laws do not obligate non-Jews to be charitable, how could the people of Sodom be punished for such a transgression? This question, the Rebbe said, leads to the conclusion that "there are precepts that are not included in the Noahide Laws, yet they must be fulfilled by all of humanity," because they "are mandated by human reason."[86]

Based on this, the Rebbe continued, many of the Torah's mitzvot that are incumbent on the Jewish people by dint of divine authority "are also obligatory for all humanity, even though they were not directly commanded to fulfill them."

Throughout this discussion the Rebbe repeated the earlier point that the Torah's universal legislation is rooted in the principle of *lashevet yetzarah*. The central concern of natural law, as discerned through this prism, is to foster the flourishing of human civilization. As the Rebbe went on to say:

> Elements [of the Torah] that are related to the civilization of the world, for example, general conduct between one person and another in accord with justice and honesty... including not to swindle or lie, are obligatory to be fulfilled by all humanity, not as normative mitzvot, but rather as something that is mandated by human reason.[87]

Examples cited by the Rebbe include the obligation to honor one's parents and to mourn for a deceased relative. While one might have

---

85. *Mishneh Torah, Hilkhot Melakhim UMilhemoteihem* 10:10, as cited and discussed in *Torat Menahem* 5747: 3, 428.
86. *Torat Menahem* 5747: 3, 428–29.
87. Ibid., 429.

thought they were relevant only within the Jewish community, these precepts are universally applicable as they relate to proper interpersonal comportment.[88]

This notion of natural law also accounts for a seemingly hypothetical talmudic statement that even without the Torah we would learn the virtue of modest behavior from a cat. Though the Torah contains instructions about the virtue of modesty, the Rebbe explained that the Talmud's statement is highly relevant for humanity at large, who are not explicitly commanded to act in accord with those instructions. The universal obligation to act modestly is not formally commanded, but is nevertheless binding because this virtue can be observed in the natural behavior of cats, and is certainly understood by human intellect as well.[89]

Just as there are rational virtues that become obligatory by dint of natural law, so too there are vices that fall outside the bounds of direct legislation encoded in rabbinic literature, and yet they are clearly inhumane and therefore forbidden. For example, according to Jewish law one is required to provide food for one's children only up to the age of six. Beyond that age, a court of law cannot force a parent to provide food, and the parent who does not provide food transgresses no prohibition. Following the Talmud, however, Rambam declares that if parents act with such inhumanity toward their own children, they should be shamed with the public proclamation that they are "cruel" and that they are more abject than non-kosher birds who have sufficient moral instinct to feed their young.[90]

Since this is a matter of natural law rather than an explicit commandment, it applies not only to Jews but to all of humanity.[91] This gives a much broader connotation to Rambam's ruling that "any human being who is careful to observe the Noahide commandments is one of the 'righteous of the nations' who is awarded a portion in the World to Come." The Rebbe goes so far as to say that if a person, Jew or non-Jew, "acts only and exclusively in accord with the mitzvot ... and in all other

---

88. Ibid., 5746: 4, 254.
89. Ibid., 5747: 3, 429. For further discussion along the same lines, see *Likkutei Sihot* 5, *Vayishlah* no. 1, *se'ifim* 4–9; ibid., 38, *Naso* no. 2, *se'if* 3.
90. Ketubot 49b; *Mishneh Torah, Hilkhot Ishut* 12:14.
91. *Torat Menahem* 5747: 3, 431.

respects acts in a way that is the opposite of humane, it is impossible that they will have a portion in the World to Come."[92]

The Foundation of the Noahide Laws: Belief in God
The First of the Seven Laws

As we have seen, the Rebbe built up an expansive concept of the Noahide Laws that is rooted in the natural moral intuition that every human being is endowed with. Yet, he also made it absolutely clear that this intuitive morality stands on the firm foundation of divine commandment. As mentioned above, the authoritative basis for this concept is the seven mitzvot commanded by God to Adam and Noah, from whom all of humanity descends. Indeed, the very first of these seven laws is the prohibition against idol worship, which requires unwavering commitment to monotheism. In fact, the Rebbe emphasized, the very notion of a divine command assumes an axiomatic recognition of God's sovereignty:

> Accepting God's sovereignty... is the very foundation for accepting and fulfilling the commandments. This is why [Rambam] writes that we [are obligated to] compel [all humanity] "to *accept*," and not merely "to fulfill," the commandments; "acceptance" here connotes acceptance of God's sovereignty.[93]

Why is faith in the One God the very foundation of the Noahide Laws? Why is our innate moral intuition not sufficient? This question was addressed by the Rebbe in many writings and teachings. One succinct example is found in the Rebbe's notebooks that date from the pre-Holocaust era:

> Acceptance of the Seven Mitzvot due to the dictate of rationality alone will not last truly and eternally; moral logic may be refuted by immoral logic. This is why the obligation is to "*accept* the Noahide mitzvot"... i.e., as the *command* of God.[94]

---

92. Ibid., 430.
93. "Sheva Mitzvot Benei Noah," 9.
94. *Reshimot Hoveret* 167, 168.

The Demographics of Dira BaTahtonim

Human reasoning may indeed have an innate capacity of moral intuition, but it is not infallible. There will be times when the faculty of reason overcomes its moral inclination with arguments that are as clever as they are crooked. Only a divine command can place morality on a true and eternal footing.

The Rebbe elaborated this point at greater length in a letter written in 1962. While referring to the combination of belief in God and basic moral precepts in the Ten Commandments, it clearly articulates the very same idea that he expressed earlier concerning the Noahide Laws:

> Even self-evident moral precepts, if left to human judgment alone, without the binding force of Divine Authority and Sanction, can out of self-love be distorted so as to turn vice into virtue.
>
> Indeed, interpreting the moral precepts of "Thou shalt not murder" and "Thou shalt not steal," from the viewpoint of selfish gain, many a nation in the world, as well as many an individual, have legalized their abhorrent ends, not to mention that they have justified the means to those ends – as has been amply demonstrated, to our sorrow, particularly in recent years.
>
> If by rejecting the Commandments of "I am God" and "Thou shalt have no other Gods" or even by dissociating them from "Thou shalt not murder" and "Thou shalt not steal," the safeguard against bloodshed and theft, even in their most brutal forms, were removed from humanity's conscience, it is certainly hopeless to expect safeguards against "Thou shalt not murder" and "Thou shalt not steal," in more subtle ways, such as the bloodshed of character assassination, or the theft of the mind (*ganeivas da'as*) and the like....
>
> Even the simplest precepts of morality and ethics must rest on the foundation of "I am God" and "Thy shalt have no other Gods" – and only then can their compliance be assured.[95]

In addition to the possibility of "immoral logic," here the Rebbe also notes the fundamentally subjective nature of human logic, which makes

---

95. Letter from the Rebbe, dated to *Erev Shabbat Yitro* 5722. Available at chabad.org/1840498.

it susceptible to distortion and bias born of "self-love." This is true, he writes, both on the "individual" level and the "national" level, and can lead to the removal of all moral safeguards from humanity's conscience. The only true safeguard for even the "simplest precepts of morality and ethics" is the foundational commitment to the eternal God.

On other occasions, the Rebbe linked this principle explicitly to the most horrifying moral abuse of the twentieth century, namely the Holocaust:

> The only way to ensure the principal commandments which are vital for the very existence of humanity in a civilized way – for example, "Do not murder," "Do not steal," "Do not covet," and so on – is if they are founded on the knowledge that there is an "owner to this palace"[96] ...
>
> The simple proof for this is what we saw clearly in the most recent generation: The very country in which science and the philosophy of ethics flourished, from there sprang a behavior that was entirely barbaric, to the point that no one believed that human beings were capable of acting in such a way! Especially people that prided themselves on their philosophy and morality, and were prone to say that the whole world should learn morality from them!
>
> The reason for this was that their morality was not founded on the most basic foundation of everything – the awareness that there is an "owner to this palace" which created the world and conducts it ... and therefore one must follow His directives. ...[97]

Having lived in Germany in the 1930s, the Rebbe had witnessed the rise of Nazism with his own eyes, and saw it as a prime example of how the power of human reason could be heinously and violently corrupted if

---

96. Paraphrase of Genesis Rabba 39:1.
97. *Torat Menahem* 5743: 2, 900. See also *Torat Menahem* 5746: 1, 406; letter from the Rebbe dated 16 Shevat 5724, available at chabad.org/1899565; Shmuel Lew, "The Rebbe Speaks to College Students," https://chabad.org/354697.

The Demographics of Dira BaTahtonim

its moral compass wasn't irreducibly anchored in the eternal authority of God's commandments.

On still another occasion the Rebbe explained the link between God and morality as follows:

> What will make a human being a better and more decent person is an awareness that there is "an eye that sees and an ear that hears";[98] an awareness of always being in the presence of a Supreme Being – our Heavenly Father who cares how every one of His children conducts himself or herself, and before whom every one of us will have to account for our every action, word, and thought.[99]

The recognition that there is an "owner to this palace," an "eye that sees," impels human beings to reason in a way that is not morally reprehensible, but rather morally astute. As the Rebbe conceptualizes it, even the "natural law" component of the Noahide Laws is not as natural as one might think. Natural law does not emanate from human reason alone. Its ultimate foundation is acceptance of divine sovereignty, a personal awareness that we are bound to live according to the moral code that the Creator endows in nature.

In consonance with this principle, the Rebbe encouraged all people to cultivate a personal relationship with God. Below we will explore some of the practical dimensions of this.

Beginning Each Day with God

In the later years of his leadership, especially in the 1980s, some of the Rebbe public talks began to be broadcast live on satellite television. Although the Rebbe spoke in Yiddish, simultaneous translations of his talks were also made available to viewers. On these occasions the Rebbe sometimes addressed all of humankind explicitly.

In a talk delivered in 1982, he spoke of the rabbinic directive that upon awakening each morning from sleep one should contemplate the fact

---

98. Mishna Avot 2:1.
99. From a memo titled "Re U.N." dated 10/21/87, prepared by the Rebbe's secretariat and edited in his own hand.

that one is in the immediate presence of God, the King of kings.[100] This will motivate the individual to fulfill their divinely ordained "purpose and mission." While one might have thought that such contemplation was relevant only for Jews, the Rebbe broadened its application to all of humanity:

> This matter is relevant to all human beings. It is understood that the general notion that "I was created to serve my Maker"[101] is related to the principal mitzva of the Noahide Laws, which is the denial of idol worship (*avoda zara*). This includes any endeavor (*avoda*) that is foreign (*zara*) to, and in opposition to, humane conduct generally.
>
> It is accordingly understood that gentiles too should begin their day by contemplating the mission (*shelihut*) placed upon them by the Creator of the world.... This contemplation and thought will impact their conduct, speech, and action throughout the entire day.[102]

In this passage the Rebbe combines two ideas. The first is a very expansive concept of the God-given mission to humanity, as expressed in the prohibition of *avoda zara*: resist doing anything that is foreign to humane conduct. The second is a universalization of the codified Jewish practice of beginning the day by contemplating the presence of God and one's personal mission to fulfill one's God-given purpose. This combination powerfully brings the most general sense of morality, of the humane, into a formative moment of union, of deep intimacy, between the individual and God.

The Moment of Silence Campaign

All these ideas were practically applied in another campaign the Rebbe initiated and championed: instituting a moment of silence for children in the American public school system at the beginning of their school day.

While the educational system is intended to teach useful knowledge for life, the Rebbe argued that without a strong moral foundation, all this knowledge can actually be used for narcissistic purposes, leading

---

100. Cited in *Shulhan Arukh HaRav, Orah Hayyim*, 1:1.
101. Kiddushin 82b.
102. *Torat Menahem* 5742: 3, 1199.

to the destruction of humanity. Therefore, it is vital that at the beginning of every day a child should have a minute of silence dedicated to reflecting on their purpose here on earth, and the existence of a Supreme Being who takes interest in each of them and observes their individual behavior.

It is hard to change one's habits later in life, he argued, and becoming used to thinking only of personal gain and not of the betterment of the wider world (*lashevet yetzarah*) leads to the kind of moral decay that underlies so many of the challenges faced by society. Since selfish thinking is a root cause, the optimal path toward a more civilized society is through strengthening cognizance of an all-knowing God to whom we are all personally responsible. A moment of silence was the practical vehicle through which this goal could best be attained. Here is how the Rebbe put it in one talk:

> Through instituting a moment of silence, the child will know that before the day of study begins he is given time to reflect on the most important thing in his life... [i.e.,] a world view, faith in the Creator of the world and its Providential Master, per his parents' guidance....
>
> And even if the parents do not have the time to educate their children properly, they can surely explain to them that lollipops and football, or being strong enough to hurt your friend, is not what is most important in life. What *is* most important in life is being a human worthy of the name, i.e., a person who behaves according to the principles of justice and honesty (rather than acting like a beast in the jungle). And especially if the child remembers what his parents taught him about the Creator of the world and its Providential Master, "an eye that sees and an ear that hears."[103]

Education is the formative basis of society, especially in the childhood years. Therefore, to effectively ensure that people live their lives in a way that is moral and civilized, education must be grounded in the cultivation of a personal sense of responsibility to God.

---

103. *Torat Menahem* 5746: 1, 408. For more sources and analysis, see Philip Wexler and Eli Rubin (2019), 166–73.

Uniting with God, Uniting with People

The personal moment of introspection at the outset of each day also has a powerful interpersonal dimension. As the Rebbe explained:

> The advantage of thought relative to speech and action is that through thought a person can ascend beyond the borders that separate the self from all other people ... and unite with the other....[104]

While speech and action are embodied and therefore localized, thought is fundamentally spiritual and therefore transcends one's localized and individualized limitations.

The Rebbe went on to explain that by thinking about another person and their needs one can bridge interpersonal divisions. Even more broadly, a shared thought can ultimately bring *all* of humanity together as one:

> When every person sets aside, sanctifies, a portion of their time in order to contemplate and think about the ultimate purpose of the creation of the world, "to serve my Maker," by dint of everyone doing so all are united together... to engage in a single purpose and goal – to reveal divinity to all of humanity.[105]

When each individual contemplates their God-given mission, all of humanity can share a numinous experience and a unified sense of higher purpose. Thereby, each individual can "transcend the separation between themselves and the rest of humanity... in actuality, in daily life."[106]

Later in the same talk, the Rebbe cited chapter 32 of *Tanya*, which explains the highest ideal of *ahavat Yisrael*, love for one's fellow Jew. The Rebbe applied these principles more broadly to the relationship between each human being and the rest of humanity:

---

104. *Torat Menahem* 5742: 3, 1200.
105. Ibid.
106. Ibid.

> When a person connects to God, he becomes united with all other people around him. As explained in *Tanya*, chapter 32, that when one contemplates "their root and source in the God of Life" then [one appreciates that] "all of them are equal and there is one Father for all," and more so, "who knows their greatness and stature?" I.e., it is possible that God is more satisfied and happy with the conduct of the other than He is satisfied and happy with oneself.[107]

The Rebbe continued to apply this more specifically to interpersonal humility. The Torah relates that Moses was "exceedingly humble, more so than all the people on the face of the earth" (Num. 12:3). The straightforward meaning of the verse is that Moses was more humble *than* anyone else. Citing a discourse of the Alter Rebbe, the Rebbe explained it to mean that Moses felt humble in relation *to* everyone else. Moreover, "all the people on the face of the earth" should be understood in the most literal and expansive sense. Moses was able to see that every other person, whether Jewish or not, might in some way give God more satisfaction and happiness than he, Moses himself, did. The humility of Moses serves as a model for all to emulate.[108]

Earlier we saw that the Rebbe applied the Chabad model of contemplating God as a daily practice for all of humanity. Now we've also seen that the Rebbe universalized another central motif of Chabad thought: interpersonal love and humility. Moreover, connecting to God and connecting to people are fundamentally intertwined:

> When a person connects to God, he unites with all the people around him, and with all of humanity in its entirety. For our one Father in Heaven created "all the people on the face of the earth": every human being throughout the world was created from "the simple oneness of God."[109]

---

107. Ibid., 1204.
108. Ibid., 1205.
109. Ibid.

Between Universalism and Particularism

All of humanity is linked together in the service of God.

Moral Introspection, Prayer, and Teshuva
Other dimensions of universal spiritual practice, as charted by the Rebbe, include moral introspection, prayer, and repentance. These are additional ingredients in his vision for all people to transcend worldliness and materiality and live lives of holiness.

In the notebook entry discussed above, the Rebbe expressed this in very clear terms:

> It is incumbent upon every human, by virtue of being endowed with intellect and free choice, to take account of all their actions, carefully consider all that is occurring around them, and especially to consider what is happening with their own selves. And the principal question – which is the foundation of the entire span of a person's life upon the earth – is: What is the purpose of my creation?[110]

The very fact that humans were given the capacity to introspectively reflect on their lives and take account of their actions indicates that keeping a moral inventory of one's behavior and reflecting on where one stands in fulfilling one's purpose in life is an inherent responsibility for all people.

In a talk he delivered in 1985, the Rebbe spoke of prayer and spiritual return to God's embrace (*teshuva*) as practices that all people should engage in. The prophet Jonah, he pointed out, was sent by God to inspire the non-Jewish people of Nineveh to abandon their sinful ways and return to God through prayer:

> This story became part of the eternal lessons of the Torah to teach us that the people of Nineveh – the Children of Noah – are also commanded to pray to God that He shall provide their needs, as

---
110. *Reshimot, Hoveret* 167, 164.

The Demographics of Dira BaTahtonim

well as the notion of repentance (for missteps).... This is part of the commandment prohibiting idol worship.[111]

Prayer and repentance, accordingly, are integral components in the spiritual lives of all people.

Emulating the Holiness of the Levites

In a detailed talk in 1964, the Rebbe cited the following passage from Rambam's code. It follows the delineation of the unique vocation bequeathed to the tribe of Levi:

> Not only the tribe of Levi, but each and every person of all the inhabitants of the world whose spirit generously motivates him, and who understands with his wisdom to separate himself and stand before God to serve Him and minister to Him and to know God, proceeding justly as God made him, removing from his neck the yoke of the many reckonings which people seek, he is sanctified as holy of holies. And thus David declared (Ps. 16:5): "God is my chosen portion and my cup; You direct my fate."[112]

The Rebbe noted that "Maimonides makes an extraordinary point... which the commentaries do not highlight: The vocation of a Levite is not only accessible to Jews, but to 'all the inhabitants of the world.' That is, non-Jews too can reach this lofty station."[113] Simply put, all people of the world can emulate the holy vocation of the Levites, who unburdened themselves of all material concerns and dedicated themselves exclusively to the service of God.

Further analyzing Rambam's wording, the Rebbe pointed out that the inclusiveness of this statement is underscored by the preface of the words "each and every person" before the words "of all the inhabitants of the world." This is not a redundancy, explained the Rebbe. Rather,

---

111. *Torat Menahem* 5745: 5, 2722.
112. *Mishneh Torah, Hilkhot Shemitta VeYovel* 13:13.
113. *Torat Menahem* 5724: 3, 228.

Rambam wanted to make it absolutely clear that the lofty vocation of the Levites is not restricted to any class of people:

> While "all the inhabitants of the world" already includes both Jews and non-Jews, one might have thought that it is said only regarding intellectuals. Therefore, emphasis is required that this is accessible to "each and every person," whether of an intellectual bent or a practical bent, and likewise not only Jews but also "all the inhabitants of the world."

How does one take on the extraordinary vocation of the Levites?

In responding to this question, the Rebbe distinguishes between "separating" from the world and "recusal" from the world. When Rambam wrote that the aspiration of the Levite is "to separate himself and stand before God," the intention was not an utter recusal, an utter transcendence of nature; rather one can remain among "all of the inhabitants of the world" and yet establish "an axiomatic mindset that one is separated from worldly affairs, that one is not like the rest of the world, that one is not steeped in worldliness."

This, however, is only the first step. The Rebbe continued his word-by-word analysis of Rambam's exhortation to emphasize that the Levite service is distinguished by a feeling of closeness with God, achieved through intellectual and emotional work, harnessing the mind and the spirit to raise the individual out of the materialism of the physical world, ultimately becoming "sanctified as holy of holies." This, the Rebbe pointed out, refers to the very pinnacle of holiness that can be attained only by the High Priest, who alone may enter the Holy of Holies, the innermost sanctum of the Temple.[114]

In addition to arguing for an expansive scope of the Noahide Laws in all its different dimensions, the Rebbe especially emphasized the expansive scope of the laws' first commandment. Implicit in the prohibition against idol worship is an exhortation to accept the sovereign authority of the One God, and to develop a personal relationship with the One God, through contemplation, prayer, and interpersonal

---

114. Ibid., 229–32.

The Demographics of Dira BaTahtonim

harmony. Ultimately, the Rebbe taught, all people can aspire to embrace an all-encompassing holy vocation akin to that of the High Priest. Such a vocation is open not only to members of one particular nation, but to "all of the inhabitants of the world."

Just as the Rebbe analyzed classical halakhic sources to greatly expand the traditional concept of Torah's universal message for humanity, so too he charted a program of universal spiritual practice that would help all people to live in the image of God every day.

From Sinai to the World
Universal Dimensions of the Sinaitic Revelation

In the classic model of the Sinaitic revelation, God descended upon the mountain in order to give the Torah to the Jewish people. In other words, its significance is particularistic in nature, consecrating a covenantal bond between God and the Jewish people. Indeed, the Rebbe frequently referenced the rabbinic metaphor of Sinai as a wedding between the Jewish people and God.[115]

However, the Rebbe also highlighted rabbinic passages that demonstrate Sinai's universal relevance. One midrash relates that when God gave the Torah to the Jewish people there was global stillness: "The birds did not chirp and the fowl did not fly...rather, the world was silent and the voice emanated, [saying,] 'I am the Lord your God.'"[116] The Rebbe elaborated that this worldwide silence was not a mere tangential detail in the Sinaitic revelation but reflects God's broader purpose:

> It is explicit [in this midrash] that the events of Mount Sinai were not just for the sake of the Jewish people, but rather that God's kingship and dominion were revealed in the entirety of creation.[117]

The Rebbe intertwined this notion of a global revelation with his understanding of the Torah's purpose:[118] the unification of the upper and lower

---

115. *Torat Menahem* 5712: 1, 95; ibid., 5719: 1, 135; ibid., 5717: 1, 87.
116. Exodus Rabba 29:9.
117. "Sheva Mitzvot Benei Noah," 10.
118. See chapter 5, section "The Rebbe on the Significance of Sinai."

realms so that God can be revealed through every aspect of creation.[119] In this sense, the Giving of the Torah initiates the universal revelation that ultimately culminates in the Messianic Era.[120]

In a similar vein, the Rebbe noted the midrashic teaching that the great voice of God at Sinai self-divided into the seventy languages.[121] This, he said, indicates that the same voice of God that instructed the Jewish people to follow the Torah also directly instructed the Noahide mitzvot to non-Jews.[122]

Building from these midrashim, the Rebbe introduced yet another dimension into the universal Noahide Laws, namely that the Giving of the Torah actually empowers all people to connect with God more optimally than before the Giving of the Torah. In one talk, the Rebbe cited the talmudic teaching that God first offered the Torah to the nations of the world, and only when they refused to accept it, did He offer it to the Jewish people.[123] The Rebbe interpreted the very fact that the Torah was offered to the other nations as an endowment that holds enduring relevance for them, despite their subsequent refusal. "It is obvious," he said, "that when God acts, His actions have an effect."[124] By virtue of God's overture alone, He gave all the nations "the ability to fulfill their mitzvot optimally," meaning, to live in accord with the Noahide Laws *"because God commanded them in the Torah."*[125]

We have already discussed the rational dimensions ("natural law") and the theistic basis (belief in God) of the Noahide Laws. But Rambam emphasizes that these universal mitzvot should optimally be observed "because the Holy One, blessed be He, commanded them in the Torah and informed us through Moses our teacher."[126] In many talks, the Rebbe explained that this additional dimension – the Sinaitic

---

119. See, for example, *Likkutei Sihot* 36, *Yitro*, no. 3, *se'if* 2; ibid., 8, *Shavuot*, *se'if* 4; ibid., 16, *Mishpatim*, no. 1, *se'if* 7; *Torat Menahem* 5745: 3, 1409.
120. *Torat Menahem* 5747: 4, 96; ibid., 5748: 2, 247.
121. *Exodus Rabba* 28:6.
122. *Likkutei Sihot* 4, *Va'ethanan*, *se'if* 2.
123. *Avoda Zara* 2b; *Sifrei Devarim*, *piska* 343.
124. *Torat Menahem* 5747: 3, 402.
125. Ibid., citing *Mishneh Torah, Hilkhot Melakhim UMilhemoteihem* 8:11.
126. *Mishneh Torah, Hilkhot Melakhim UMilhemoteihem* 8:11.

Revelation – enables all the nations of the world to achieve a deeper relationship with God that transcends the limited bounds of nature. The Giving of the Torah at Sinai opens the way for all of humankind to enter into a relationship with God that transcends reason, so that all of humanity will ultimately serve God together, "to worship Him of one accord."[127]

God's overtures to the nations of the world revolutionized the nature of the Noahide mitzvot. These mitzvot are now included in the Torah that God gifted to the world at Sinai, and, as Rambam taught, they should optimally be kept with this consciousness.

Universal Dimensions of Torah Study

The Talmud states that Torah study is an inheritance unique to the Jewish people, and thus non-Jews are permitted and encouraged to study Torah only insofar as it informs the observance of "their seven mitzvot."[128] Ostensibly this severely narrows the corpus of Torah teachings that may be studied by non-Jews. However, building off this rabbinic ruling, the Rebbe greatly expanded, both theoretically and practically, these parameters while remaining within their bounds.

First, the Rebbe noted the comment of the Meiri, who broadens this concept to include not only "the fundamentals of the seven mitzvot" but also "their details and what stems from them," further explicating that, in fact, "the majority of the principles of the Torah are included in them."[129] That is to say, Torah study of the seven mitzvot includes also all Torah ideas that are connected to the spirit of the Noahide Laws: fundamentally, the creation of a civilized world (*lashevet yetzarah*).

Second, the Rebbe posited that all Torah ideas that are understood by the human intellect – the "image of God" in man – are to be studied by all people. The very fact that a particular Torah teaching resonates with the human understanding and experience is itself a sign that it is intended for all beings created with intellect – the image of God in all of humanity.[130]

---

127. Zeph. 3:9. See *Torat Menahem* 5750: 3, 249; *Likkutei Sihot* 21, Yitro no.1, *se'if* 12.
128. Sanhedrin 59a.
129. Meiri, Sanhedrin 59a, s.v. *ben Noah*.
130. *Torat Menahem* 5746: 4, 254–55.

As an example, the Rebbe cited the Torah's teachings with regard to death and mourning. On the practical level, there is a time set aside for intense grieving after one's loved one passes away, followed by a gradual process of return to normal life. This transition is marked by clearly demarcated periods with different levels of mourning (the first seven days, the first thirty days, the first year). Additionally, addressing the painful questions death provokes, the Torah teaches the mourner that death means one's loved one passes on for the sake of a higher ascent into the world of truth. Such teachings, the Rebbe said, are relevant to all people, as they naturally resonate with the human intellect and experience and can help all members of human society to better cope with grief in a healthy manner.[131]

Similarly, the Rebbe explained that the "inner dimension" of the Torah – especially as revealed in the teachings of Hasidism – should be studied by every human being, because its central messages can help all people to excel in their spiritual vocation. Hasidic teachings add warmth, vitality, and depth to one's relationship to God and to the fulfillment of the mitzvot in which one is obligated, by explaining them and illuminating them with a multiplicity of meanings. This applies not only to Jews but to all people.[132]

In one talk the Rebbe noted that the imperative to share the "inner dimension" of the Torah "includes efforts to publicize among the nations of the world the belief in the unity of God, as it flows from the tetragrammaton (*Hashem*), as expansively explained by the Alter Rebbe in Part Two of the holy *Tanya, Shaar HaYihud VehaEmuna*."[133] Study of Hasidism's explanations of the unity of God, in particular, will strengthen and deepen the ability of all people to live in accordance with the Noahide Laws, which is underpinned by belief in God.[134]

The Rebbe further noted the comment made by the Tosafists, that the Talmud considers a non-Jew who studies Torah related to the Noahide Laws to be "like a High Priest," due to a linguistic connection

---

131. Ibid.
132. *Iggerot Kodesh* 23, letter 8682.
133. *Likkutei Sihot* 25, Yod-Tet Kislev, *se'if* 8.
134. See also *Torat Menahem* 5744: 4, 267 note 54.

between the Torah which is "more precious than pearls (*peninim*)," and the High Priest who serves in the innermost Temple chamber (*lifnim*). From this the Rebbe deduced that this study is not simply a technical requisite in order to know how to act, but rather is valued as Torah study for the sake of Torah study in its own right.[135]

Citing the statement in the *Sifrei* that "the crown of Torah is available for all who populate the world,"[136] the Rebbe concluded that in addition to the obligation to act in accord with the Noahide Laws, all of humankind is commanded to study Torah as an end in itself, and not only as a preparation for practice.[137] This, he argues, is also reflected in Rambam's description of the Messianic Era, when "the occupation of the entire world will be solely to know God,"[138] i.e., to study Torah.[139]

The Particular, the Universal, and the Coming of *Mashiah*
Lashevet Yetzarah and Dira BaTahtonim

This chapter began with the questions of whether and how non-Jews might participate in transforming the physical world into God's dwelling place (*Dira BaTahtonim*), and whether and how they will experience the messianic redemption.

By now the answer to both is beginning to come into focus. We've seen that the Rebbe affirmed the principle that God formed the world "to be settled" (*lashevet yetzarah*) as the underlying rationale and spirit of the Noahide Laws. This actually expresses the connection between these laws and the ultimate telos of *Dira BaTahtonim*:

> The most vital and encompassing mission (*shelihut*) of the nations of the world is to make the world a fitting place to be settled by humankind, *lashevet yetzarah*. And through the world becoming

---

135. Likkutei Sihot 14, Ekev, no. 2, *se'if* 3; ibid., 27, Hadran al HaRambam, *se'if* 13.
136. Sifrei, Korah, piska 119.
137. Likkutei Sihot 27, Hadran al HaRambam, *se'if* 13.
138. Mishneh Torah, Hilkhot Melakhim UMilhemoteihem 12:5.
139. Likkutei Sihot, 27, Hadran al HaRambam, *se'if* 13.

a settlement (*yishuv*) and a dwelling (*dira*) for man below, it will ultimately also become a dwelling for "Supernal Man" [God].[140]

Creating a fitting dwelling place for God below, the *Dira BaTahtonim* – which is the messianic telos of the world – is fundamentally dependent on humanity's mission to turn this world into a fitting dwelling place for humankind, a place in which human civilization flourishes in the most optimal way (*lashevet yetzarah*).[141]

In a different talk, the Rebbe spoke of how observance of the Noahide Laws can actually be the culminating action that brings the entire world into the Messianic Era. In this context, he cited the ruling of Rambam that "every person shall see themselves...and likewise the entire world as half meritorious, etc. If he will do a single mitzva he will sway the entire world to the side of merit, and cause salvation and redemption to himself and to them."[142] This, the Rebbe emphasized, applies both to Jews and non-Jews:

> By means of a single action...that fulfills the will of God – i.e., the Noahide Laws for all the people of the world, and the six hundred and thirteen mitzvot for Jews – one can change the entire world for the better...including the ultimate salvation and redemption, the true and complete redemption through our righteous *Mashiah*.[143]

Even a single act in fulfillment of God's will, by a single individual, be they a Jew or a non-Jew, can usher in the Messianic Era for the entire world.

---

140. *Torat Menahem* 5750:1, 396. For elaborations on the relationship between *lashevet yetzara* and *Dira BaTahtonim*, see *Likkutei Sihot* 5, *Vayishlah* no. 1, *se'if* 8; ibid., 20, *Vayetzeh* no. 3; ibid.,. 25, *Noah* 7 *MarHeshvan*, *se'if* 10.
141. For an early articulation of the connection between the spread of ethical monotheism and the Messianic Era, see *Torat Menahem* 5711: 1, 155.
142. *Mishneh Torah, Hilkhot Teshuva* 3:4.
143. *Torat Menahem* 5746: 2, 457–58.

The Noahide Laws and the Hastening of Redemption

This connection between non-Jewish observance of the Noahide Laws and redemption brings a new dimension to the Noahide Laws campaign. Earlier in the chapter we noted the Rebbe's discernment that non-Jewish society had developed a more open stance toward Jews. This renewed the halakhic force of the obligation to motivate non-Jewish observance of the seven mitzvot. In addition to this pragmatic reason, the Rebbe also spoke about the Noahide Laws campaign as part of the generational responsibility to refine and elevate every element of the world to hasten the coming of *Mashiah*.

The Rebbe once emphatically articulated this connection between the Noahide Laws campaign and the coming of *Mashiah* in response to the unease some expressed about the campaign. After noting that some Jews were surprised and perturbed by the call to disseminate monotheism and the Noahide Laws beyond the Jewish community, the Rebbe responded:

> This... flows from a fundamental misunderstanding regarding *the very belief* in the coming of *Mashiah*. It seems that the Jew who asked this question thinks that the coming of *Mashiah* means that *Mashiah* will take *him* out of exile and then *he* can live a good and peaceful life....
>
> The truth is, however, that not only will the coming of *Mashiah* redeem the Jewish people, but the *entire world* will experience redemption – the existence of the entire world will be "perfect[ed]... under the sovereignty of the Almighty."[144]

Along with critiquing the parochialism of the naysayers, the Rebbe reprimanded them for not appreciating the historic mission with which they had been entrusted:

> Since we are situated at the end of the exile and we are nearing the time of redemption, we should place particular emphasis on things that prepare for and hasten the future redemption....

---

144. Ibid., 2, 938.

> The Jewish people's responsibility... includes influencing the nations of the world to observe the seven Noahide mitzvot, *lashevet yetzarah* ... through which the world becomes fit and prepared for the ultimate destiny of "perfect[ing] the world under the sovereignty of God" (*Aleinu* prayer).[145]

A true understanding of *Mashiah* requires the Jewish people to look beyond their own aspirations and realize that the entire world will participate in and experience the redemptive process.

Moreover, the Rebbe explained, the universality of the messianic redemption is hardly peripheral to the main event. Rather, "it is one of the fundamental foundations of belief in the coming of the *Mashiah*, as explained in many biblical verses and statements of the sages."[146]

On another occasion, the Rebbe spoke of the Jewish people's mission to create a *Dira BaTahtonim* as generating a sense of universal responsibility:

> Included in the charge to create a *Dira BaTahtonim* is also the Jewish people's effort to perfect the entire world through influencing the nations of the world to observe the seven Noahide mitzvot.... For, simply put, to make a *dira* for God in the *tahtonim* means that the entire world is to become a *dira* for God.
>
> This is the essential meaning of the prophecy, "And the glory of the Lord shall be revealed, and *all flesh* together" – i.e., the entire creation – "will see that the mouth of the Lord spoke" (Is. 40:5). As Rambam ruled, King *Mashiah* will "perfect *the entire world* to serve God together...." From all this it is understood that the Jewish people must also act [now] to perfect the entire world.[147]

In the next talk he delivered at that same *farbrengen*, the Rebbe expounded on this theme:

---

145. Ibid., 937.
146. Similarly, see *Torat Menahem* 5747: 2, 613–18; ibid., 5745: 3, 1718–19.
147. *Torat Menahem* 5743: 3, 1206.

The Demographics of Dira BaTahtonim

> Every person should do everything possible to spread goodness and righteousness among all nations of the world...to inspire a deeper awareness of the "eye that sees and the ear that hears"... This, in turn, should lead to additional action...to observe the seven Noahide Laws.
>
> ...Doing this in accord with Torah and through the path of Torah "whose paths are pleasant, and all her ways are peaceful" brings people closer together, including causing closeness of heart between Jew and gentile. This new closeness between people will bring peace to the world – and all concerns and worries about the world shaking and trembling, and about war brewing between nations, they all dissolve, and peace and harmony prevails in the world.
>
> With this peace and harmony we taste the harmony of the seventh millennium, the harmony of body and soul (i.e., the Messianic Era).[148]

Clearly, the Rebbe saw the observance of the Noahide mitzvot as part of "perfecting the entire world" and bringing about the Messianic Era.

The Redemptive Illumination of the Kelippot

The universal redemption that the Rebbe saw as quickly approaching included not only all people but, indeed, all reality. In the Messianic Era, the Rebbe argued, even the basest elements of the spiritual and terrestrial worlds will become illuminated with divine light. Accordingly, the Rebbe spoke of a progressive process in which the concealed and exiled divine spark would emerge and shine increasingly more brightly, as the time for global redemption neared. This process of positive transformation seems to provide additional context for the Rebbe's general push to bring Godliness to the entire world, including through the Noahide Laws campaign.

An example of this transformational approach is found in the Rebbe's teachings about the power of the Hanukka menora.[149] The Talmud teaches that the timeframe for the menora to be lit extends "until foot

---

148. Ibid., 1215–16.
149. See *maamar* "Lehavin Inyan Nerot Hanukka 5726" (*Sefer HaMaamarim Melukat*, vol. 2, 131–41); *maamar* "Tanu Rabbanan Mitzvat Ner Hanukka 5738" (*Sefer*

traffic in the marketplace ceases" (*ad shetikhleh regel min hashuk*) which is further identified as the time when "the foot traffic of the people of Tarmod ceases" (*ad dekalya rigla deTarmuda'ei*).[150] Rashi identifies the *Tarmuda'ei* as a nation of woodchoppers who were always last to leave the public market.

Fusing talmudic commentary and kabbalistic-hasidic hermeneutic, the Rebbe posited that this seemingly technical halakhic description encodes also the essential potency and purpose of the Hanukka lights. The letters of *Tarmuda'ei* can be rearranged to spell *moredet*, the rebels, referring to those who rebel against God[151] and are entrenched in the dark "marketplace," a realm characterized by multiplicity and impure forces. The word *shetikhleh*, which literally means "to finish," can also be translated as "yearning." Thus, this talmudic teaching can be read to mean that the Hanukka lights thoroughly transform even those who rebel against God, to the point that they will experience a deep yearning and desire for Godliness.

Applying this to the larger sweep of history and the process of messianic redemption, the Rebbe taught that it is specifically in these final moments of exile (*ikveta deMeshiha*) that "the darkness of exile" is "doubly thick."[152] Yet, like the Hanukka menora, the emerging light of the Divine Essence will extend even to the *Tarmuda'ei* – those who previously rebelled against God will now experience mystical yearning for God's embrace. The Rebbe explicitly noted that all people, even "those among the non-Jews who rebel against God," will be transformed and "connected with the light of Hanukka."[153]

The Rebbe expressed a similar sentiment in a 1959 Yod-Tet Kislev talk on the importance of spreading Hasidism. He noted that the final passage of the entire book of *Tanya* consists of the biblical words, *zeh*

      HaMaamarim Melukat, vol. 2, 162–69). In addition, see *Torat Menahem* 5744: 2, 688–92; ibid., 5748: 2, 122–32.
150. Ibid.
151. The Rebbe cited this teaching from R. Naftali Hertz Bacharach, an early Lurianic kabbalist, recorded in his book *Emek HaMelekh* 108a.
152. *Maamar "Tanu Rabbanan Mitzvat Ner Hanukka"* 5738, *se'if* 9.
153. *Torat Menahem* 5750: 2, 45.

The Demographics of Dira BaTahtonim

leumat zeh, "this corresponding to that."[154] In that particular context, the Alter Rebbe uses the phrase to indicate a symmetry between the inner secrets of the Torah and the outer halakha. The Rebbe noted, however, that this phrase certainly contains also its more straightforward application – as used elsewhere in *Tanya* by the Alter Rebbe himself[155] – to the positive and negative forces of the world that are pitted against each other. The fact that *Tanya* concludes with an allusion to these negative forces, the Rebbe reasoned, is significant:

> The conclusion of *Iggeret HaKodesh* and *Kuntres Aharon* [the final section of *Tanya*] with the words *zeh leumat zeh* alludes to the ultimate goal of Hasidism.
>
> *Zeh leumat zeh* refers to the three completely impure *kelippot*, and the goal is to elevate them from the lowest depths to the highest point. Similar to the halakhic concept that repentance can transform "sins to become like merits" (Yoma 86b), the ultimate purpose of the inner part of Torah is…that *all things*, even those alluded to by the lower meaning of *zeh leumat zeh*, are to be transformed and elevated to a state of complete good.[156]

In other words, Hasidism will not only reach the outer extremities of the mundane and secular but even transform evil itself.

Concluding the talk with his customary citing of relevant prophetic passages, the Rebbe connected the dissemination of Hasidism with the ultimate transformation of the Messianic Era:

> The ultimate "spreading of the wellsprings outside" is to reach even the three completely impure *kelippot*. As the verses state: "I will remove the spirit of contamination from the earth" (Zech.

---

154. This phrase originates in Eccl. 7:14.
155. See, for example, *Likkutei Amarim*, ch. 6.
156. *Torat Menahem* 5720: 1, 194. For the notion that repentance, which is connected with the power of the Divine Essence and the Messianic Era, has the ability to uplift the three impure *kelippot*, see *Likkutei Sihot* 9, Va'ethanan, no. 3, *se'if* 7.

Between Universalism and Particularism

13:2) and "I will transform all the nations to a purer language... to serve Him with one accord" (Zeph. 3:9).[157]

The spread of the redemptive teachings of Hasidism, the inner part of Torah, will engender a spiritual redemption of the three impure *kelippot*. This is a cosmic transformation. As a result, even those who previously rebelled against God – be they Jewish or not – will proclaim God's Oneness in unison and fulfill their own roles in creating a *Dira BaTahtonim*.

Discussions such as these can perhaps deepen our understanding of how and why the Rebbe so extensively expounded on the Torah's universal path for humankind, and initiated the Noahide Laws campaign.[158] Given that the imminent messianic redemption would transform and illuminate all reality – including elements that previously lay outside the realm of holiness – the practical work of accelerating the coming of *Mashiah* included a universal dimension, namely, to disseminate the philosophy and observance of monotheism and the Noahide Laws to the entire world.

Ethical Monotheism and the Process of Illumination
In fact, on certain occasions the Rebbe spoke of this positive transformation as a process that was already underway, thus indicating the imminence of *Mashiah*'s arrival. In this regard, the Rebbe spoke of the receptivity among non-Jews to the Noahide Laws as a positive change in the world that was a sign that redemption was near.

On Purim 5747, the Rebbe addressed at length why he felt that the world was on the cusp of redemption.[159] Among other changes in the world, the Rebbe spoke positively about the transformation in non-Jewish society vis-à-vis the idea of the Noahide Laws.

> [The receptivity of non-Jews to the seven mitzvot] demonstrates that a change has occurred in the world – and in this case, a change for the better...regarding this matter, the situation has

---
157. *Torat Menahem* 5720:1, 195.
158. This final point is most explicit in *Torat Menahem* 5750: 2, 44–52.
159. For a longer analysis of this and other similar talks, see chapter 20, section "Redemption's Imminence."

> become more illuminated even to the point that the nations of the world feel that the Noahide Laws are beneficial to them, and they are graciously receptive and helpful to those who speak with them about it.[160]

The Rebbe went on to highlight that even leaders of nations proclaim its foundational significance to society.[161]

While this transformation indicates that the world is on the cusp of redemption, it will ultimately take human effort to pass the threshold and make redemption a reality. Therefore, the Rebbe argued, now is the time to redouble efforts in spreading ethical monotheism and the Noahide Laws globally in order to hasten redemption:

> It is understandable that specifically now [on the cusp of redemption] is the time to constantly speak about the redemption... similarly regarding the topic of the Noahide Laws: Since we stand in the era that is close to the redemption... it is understood that now is the most fitting time to ready the entire world for redemption, when its ultimate purpose of "He formed it to be settled" (*lashevet yetzarah*) will be realized.[162]

That is, non-Jewish society is becoming more purified as redemption approaches. Spreading awareness of the seven mitzvot among an already receptive non-Jewish society will hasten the culmination of this process.

How Will the Nations Experience the Messianic Redemption?

Now that we have established that the Rebbe's vision of redemption includes the entire global population, the question arises: How did he harmonize this with the kabbalistic teachings about the Jewish soul's inherent chosenness, the Jewish people's unique responsibility in creating a *Dira BaTahtonim*, and common descriptions of redemption as the particularistic enterprise of redeeming the Jewish people from exile?

---

160. *Torat Menahem* 5747: 2, 617.
161. Ibid., 618.
162. Ibid., 626.

Between Universalism and Particularism

While not contradictory, the confluence of these themes appears to create a tension. In what way, if any, do the differences between Jews and non-Jews impact their experience of the global redemption?

The Rebbe returned to these questions on several occasions and provided a range of approaches.[163] The common denominator of the Rebbe's talks on this topic is that he consistently emphasized both of the above elements, namely the universal nature of redemption and yet the unique experience and role of the Jewish people.

In one talk,[164] drawing from some of the biblical prophecies and Maimonidean laws that he often referred to, the Rebbe elaborated on the universal nature of God's revelation in the Messianic Era. On the other hand, the Rebbe pointed out that there are other passages where the messianic purpose of the world seems to be associated specifically with the Jewish people. One midrashic interpretation of the very first word of the Torah is cited at the beginning of Rashi's commentary on the Torah:

> [God created the world] for the sake of the Torah, which is called "the beginning of His way" (Prov. 8:22), and for the sake of the Jewish people, who are called "the first of His grain" (Jer. 2:3).

This midrash indicates that creation is for the sake of the Jewish people.[165]

Elaborating the sources' differing implications about the nature of the ultimate redemption, the Rebbe outlined two possible approaches to how non-Jews will experience the ultimate redemption:

> (1) The nations of the world will experience redemption [only] as a detail within the redemption of the Jewish people.
> (2) They will experience their redemption also as a substantive matter in its own right. I.e., the entirety of the world – every

---

163. See, for example, *Likkutei Sihot* 24, *Ki Tavo*, no. 1; ibid., 32, *Tazria*, no. 1, *se'if* 6; ibid., 30, *Lekh Lekha*, no. 2, *se'if* 9; ibid., *Likkutei Sihot* 20, *Vayetzeh*, no. 3; *Torat Menahem* 5742: 3, 1697–98.
164. *Likkutei Sihot* 23, *Balak*, no. 2.
165. The Rebbe often cited this midrash. See, for example, *Likkutei Sihot* 5, *Vayishlah*, *se'if* 8; ibid., 36, *Va'era*, no. 2, *se'if* 4; *Torat Menahem* 5716: 2, 305; ibid., 5726: 3, 88; ibid., 5745: 1, 503; ibid., 5729: 1, 114; ibid., 5751: 4, 285.

> detail within it – will feel inherently that the Supernal intent in their creation and redemption is (also) *their own [independent]* refinement and elevation. For they are also the creation of the Holy One, blessed be He.[166]

The first possibility is that redemption will be primarily an experience for the Jewish people, and non-Jews will experience it too by virtue of their support for and participation in the Jewish people's long-awaited emancipation.

The second alternative, however, maintains that non-Jews have an inherent and independent role and purpose in the entirety of Creation and in its ultimate Redemption; they will personally and inherently experience the Godly transformation and elevation of *Mashiah*, in and of their own right.

After outlining these options, the Rebbe marshaled Maimonidean formulations in support of the expansive approach. In Rambam's halakhically definitive description of the Messianic Era there is no indication that non-Jews will be privy to the Divine Revelation only through their proximity to the Jewish people. Rather, non-Jews will have their own independent redemption and relationship with God.

Through a careful reading of the Alter Rebbe's lengthy elaboration in *Tanya* concerning the Messianic Era, cited earlier in this chapter, the Rebbe deduced that this universal approach was shared by the Alter Rebbe: all people of the world will be inherently transformed and will shine with their own inherent light.

However, even if all the nations will independently experience the messianic revelation, there will be a qualitative difference between the experience of Jews and non-Jews in the ultimate redemption:

> In the future, upon the revelation of the Godly truth – the revelation of "God is One" in the world in the most comprehensive possible manner – the entirety of creation, including the nations of the world, will feel inherently that "they exist only from the truth of His existence" and that without the Holy One, blessed

---

166. *Likkutei Sihot* 23, Balak, no. 2, *se'if* 7.

be He, "nothing else can exist" (Rambam, *Mishneh Torah, Hilkhot Yesodei HaTorah* 1:1)....

In regard to the Jewish people, however, the revelation will be that the essence of their existence is the Divine Essence, so to speak, i.e., that "the Jewish people and the Holy One, blessed be He, are one."[167]

This distinction flows from the aforementioned distinction between all the nations of the world and the Jewish people. While the rest of humanity encounters divinity as it engages through the medium of created reality, the Jewish soul has an axiomatic and unmediated relationship with divinity itself.[168] Thus, in the Messianic Era – when all beings will be raised to their loftiest stature – the nations of the world will experience that their existence is an expression of "the truth of His existence," while the Jewish people will fully and acutely experience their axiomatic oneness with God's essential self.

All Flesh Shall See the Glory of Hashem

In another talk,[169] the Rebbe further elaborated on the transformative transcendence that all people will experience in the Messianic Era.

Earlier in this chapter we noted that the Jewish people are endowed with a special connection with *Hashem*, God's personal name that expresses His essence. The other nations, by contrast, connect with the divine name *Elokim*, which reflects God's constricted revelation through the limited boundaries of nature.

Drawing on earlier sources, the Rebbe explained that the "innovation" of the messianic redemption will be characterized by a revolutionary overcoming of the binary between *Elokim* and *Hashem*, which will "have a global impact on all nations of the world." The Rebbe noted that "this is explicit in many scriptural verses and messianic prophecies," and went on to quote Rambam's halakhic code:

---

167. Ibid., *se'if* 11.
168. See, above, section "The Rebbe on Jewish Chosenness."
169. *Likkutei Sihot* 25, Yod-Tet Kislev, *se'ifim* 6–9.

> The entire world will be perfected... as it says, "Then I shall transform the nations to a purer language, that *all of them will invoke the name of Hashem* and worship Him of one accord" (Zeph. 3:9).[170]

The Rebbe further emphasized that

> this foretelling regarding the nations of the world, is not merely an incidental addition that we will enjoy upon the arrival of our righteous *Mashiah*. Rather, this is connected to the very essence of the redemption: When the *Shekhina* will emerge from exile, the truth of *Hashem* will thereby be revealed, i.e., that "all the beings of the heavens, the earth, and what is between them came into existence only from *the truth of His being*,"[171] referring to the name of *Hashem* which transcends the (nature of the) world.[172]

The redemption of the *Shekhina* means that the natural world will no longer inhibit the revelation of the truth of *Hashem*. Hence the nations of the world, too, will "invoke the name of *Hashem*...that transcends the (nature of the) world." This isn't merely incidental, but an essential expression of the messianic innovation.

The Rebbe went on to apply this to the pre-messianic mission: "Disseminating the belief in the world's unity with God – as that unity flows from *Hashem* – among all the nations," and especially in the manner that this [higher unity] is explained in the second part of the Alter Rebbe's *Tanya*, "is a preparation for the universal and complete redemption, that the Oneness of God...shall shine and become well known among the nations of the world."[173]

The study of Hasidism by all of humanity will significantly expand and deepen the scope of the very anchor of the Noahide Laws – belief in God – and provide a foretaste of the divine knowledge

---

170. *Mishneh Torah, Hilkhot Melakhim UMilhemoteihem* 11:4.
171. *Mishneh Torah, Hilkhot Yesodei HaTorah* 1:1. See chapter 4, section "The Material World in the Thought of the Rebbe."
172. *Likkutei Sihot* 25, Yod-Tet Kislev, *se'if* 6.
173. Ibid., *se'if* 8.

to which humanity will be privy in the Messianic Era. As such it will also "hasten" the ultimate messianic advent, which is characterized by the unmediated experience of God's transcendence (*Hashem*) by all nations and people.

CONCLUSION

Drawing from the full breadth of the rabbinic corpus, including philosophical, halakhic, and hasidic traditions, the Rebbe linked the role and mission of non-Jews to their participation in the Messianic Era. He also took note of the unique opportunity of living in an open society, and argued that for the first time Jewish people could act on the imperative codified by Rambam to persuade the other nations of the world to act in accord with the Noahide Laws. His analysis of classical sources greatly expanded the scope of these laws, and articulated a vision that would extend great significance to all humanity.

Secondary Literature Consulted for Chapter 16, "Between Particularism and Universalism: Non-Jews in the *Dira BaTahtonim*"

Alon Dahan, *Goel Aharon*, 535–85.

Yitzhak Kraus, *HaShevi'i*, 224–49.

Loewenthal, Naftali, *Hasidism Beyond Modernity*, 79-126.

Chaim Miller, *Turning Judaism Outward*, 319–37.

Eli Rubin, "Divine Zeitgeist: The Rebbe's Appreciative Critique of Modernity."

Eli Rubin, "Universal Responsibility: Faith, Education, and Humanity."

Elliot Wolfson, *Open Secret*, 224–64.

Chapter 17

The *Nasi* and the People

The Rebbe's vision of creating a *Dira BaTahtonim* encompassed every single individual, from all demographics, each understood to be endowed by God with his or her own unique role in achieving this common goal. One question that arises is the role of leadership in this framework. Does the fact that all Jews share an essential identity and all are working toward a single goal undermine the conceptual basis for one of the key social elements of Hasidism, namely the unique place of the spiritual leaders, the *Tzaddikim*?

Throughout his tenure, the Rebbe dedicated dozens of teachings to exploring the contours of an ideal Jewish leader. These studies draw on classical Jewish literature to create a nuanced picture of the qualities and role of such a person, one that highlights the leader's unique qualities and responsibilities while still maintaining the fundamental construct of seeing all Jews as a single entity.[1] After reviewing aspects of the relevant material in the Rebbe's teachings, we will attempt to close the gaps between theory and practice and examine how the Rebbe might have applied this leadership model to his own life and leadership.

---

1. See chapter 13, section *"Ahdut Yisrael."*

MODELS OF LEADERSHIP

Jewish tradition contains various models of religious leadership. Each model comprises two related parts: (1) the qualities that set the leader apart from the masses, and (2) the manner and spheres in which the leader influences the people.

Leadership in the Talmud

In talmudic literature, the dominant model of religious leadership is the scholar-teacher. These elite individuals spent their days and nights immersed in Torah study and perceived their main role as teachers of Torah to the people.[2] This prevailing paradigm is so pervasive that the Sages often retroject it onto biblical figures, transforming, for example, King David from a warrior king to a sage who studied and taught Torah.[3]

However, even as the formal study of Torah was the main occupation of the sages and their students, other elements also were perceived as vital to their leadership role. First, the ideal Torah scholars also embodied exemplary character traits, and students were supposed to learn from their life practices as well as from the formal knowledge that they transmitted. As the Talmud states: "If the teacher is similar to an angel of the Lord, then seek Torah from his mouth, and if not, do not seek Torah from his mouth."[4]

Also, certain sages functioned as miracle workers, aiding their followers with their metaphysical prowess. For example, the Talmud transmits the following teaching in the name of Rabbi Pinhas bar Hama: "Anyone who has a sick person in his home should go to a sage and ask for mercy on his behalf, as it is stated: 'The wrath of a king is as messengers of death; but a wise man will pacify it' (Prov. 16:14)."[5] Here we see that even if the Divine King had ordained death, the sage had the ability to intercede and bring about healing and salvation. Likewise, Rabbi Ami teaches that "in a generation when the heavens corrode like copper [which prevents them] from bringing down dew and rain... go to

---

2. Ephraim Urbach (1968).
3. Yitzhak Heinemann (1970), 36–37.
4. Moed Katan 17a.
5. Bava Batra 116a.

the most pious individual of the generation, and he will profusely pray for it."[6] In several places we find variations on the later dictum: "What the *Tzaddik* decrees, God upholds."[7]

Even more strikingly, several passages indicate that certain uniquely righteous individuals hold a crucial place in the cosmic scheme. For example, the Talmud records the following tradition: "The earth rests on one pillar and *Tzaddik* is its name, as it is stated: 'But a righteous person is the foundation of the world (*tzaddik yesod olam*)' (Prov. 10:25)."[8] While arguably ambiguous, this passage suggests that the righteous individual upholds the entire world in a manner that transcends his other roles.

These different aspects of leadership can be brought to bear on a celebrated passage regarding the value of "cleaving" to a Torah scholar. Commenting on the verse that enjoins the Jewish people to "cleave to God," the Talmud comments:

> But is it possible to cleave to the Divine Presence? Isn't it written: "For the Lord your God is a devouring fire" (Deut. 4:24)? Rather, this verse teaches that anyone who marries his daughter to a Torah scholar, and one who conducts business on behalf of Torah scholars, by investing their money, and one who utilizes his wealth to benefit Torah scholars with his property in some other way, the verse ascribes him credit as though he is cleaving to the Divine Presence.[9]

This passage describes cleaving to a Torah scholar as the means by which to fulfill the biblical mandate to cleave to God. Indeed, Rambam codifies the imperative to cleave to Torah scholars as one of 248 positive commandments of the Torah. The rationale behind the correlation between God and Torah scholars, though, is left ambiguous. Which aspect of the Torah scholar justifies this radical theological assertion?

---

6. Taanit 8a.
7. See, for example, Avoda Zara 19a, Ketubot 103b, Deuteronomy Rabba 10:3.
8. Hagiga 12b.
9. Ketubot 111b.

Rambam understands the imperative to cleave to Torah scholars as being rooted in the student's need to learn from his teacher. As Rambam writes:

> It is a positive commandment to cleave unto the wise and their disciples in order to learn from their deeds, as it states: "And you will cling to Him." …Therefore, one should try to marry the daughter of a Torah Sage and marry his daughter to a Torah Sage.… Similarly, our Sages have directed [us], saying: "Sit in the dust of their feet and drink in their words thirstily."[10]

In other words, "cleaving" to a Torah scholar is a means of studying his ways and words, which are modeled after God's attributes and "conduct." In *Sefer HaMitzvot* Rambam adds that this also brings you "to believe the truths."[11]

Leadership in Kabbala

Even as kabbalistic sources highlight the Torah prowess of the Torah scholar, they amplify the more mystical talmudic passages regarding righteous individuals. Accordingly, the *Tzaddik* in kabbalistic literature is not only a Torah scholar, teacher, and role model, but is also the site of a unique and intense divine revelation.

This idea emerges clearly from a celebrated passage in the Zohar. The Torah obligates male Jews to make a pilgrimage to the *Beit HaMikdash* on holidays with the following words: "Three times during the year shall all your male[s] appear directly before the face of the Master, the Lord, the God of the Jewish people."[12] While the simple import of the verse is that the people should be seen by God, the Zohar comments: "Who is the face of the Master? It is R. Shimon bar Yohai."[13] Thus, the Zohar audaciously refers to the *Tzaddik* as the countenance of God.

---

10. *Mishneh Torah, Hilkhot Deot* 6:2.
11. *Sefer HaMitzvot, Mitzvat Aseh* no. 6.
12. Ex. 34:23.
13. Zohar, *Bo*, 38a.

The portrayal of R. Shimon bar Yohai as the countenance of God is also related to the portrayal of Moses as the ultimate teacher of Torah and the ultimate conduit of divine revelation. Elsewhere in the Zohar we read that at the gathering of sages known as the *idra rabba*, R. Shimon proclaimed: "Today I see what no one has seen since the day Moses ascended Mount Sinai the second time.... Moreover, I know that my face is radiant, and Moses did not know that his face was radiant. Thus it is written, 'And Moses did not know that the skin of his face was radiant' (Ex. 34:29)."[14]

It is in this context that kabbalistic and hasidic sources understand the talmudic passages, cited at the beginning of this chapter, regarding the unique role and status of the *Tzaddik*. He is an individual whose very person is a conduit for the radiance of God in the world, as well as being a teacher who transmits new Torah illumination. While the Zohar singles out the figure of R. Shimon bar Yohai, it also states elsewhere that "the extension of Moses is in each and every generation, and in each and every *Tzaddik*" as well as "in each scholar who toils in Torah."[15]

According to the Zohar, another important dimension of leadership, and especially that of Moses, is that he is called "the faithful shepherd"[16] or "the shepherd of faith" (*raaya mehemna*). This idea is so central that a large part of the Zohar – the sections in which Moses reveals the mystical meaning of the mitzvot to R. Shimon bar Yohai – actually bears the title *Raaya Mehemna*. In one oft-cited passage, R. Shimon quotes the verse "Trust in the Lord and do good; dwell in the land and be nourished by faith,"[17] and says of Moses: "That supernal faith shall be fed and nourished from Him, through you."[18] Thus we see that a Jewish leader, according to the Zohar, is like a shepherd who feeds and nourishes his sheep, instilling within them a deep faith in God.

---

14. Zohar III, *Naso*, 132:2.
15. *Tikkunei Zohar* 112a.
16. This description of Moshe also appears in Esther Rabba 7:13.
17. Ps. 37:3.
18. Zohar III, *Pinhas*, 225b.

The Hasidic *Tzaddik*

With this brief background we can begin to understand the centrality of the *Tzaddik* in both the teachings and the social dimensions of hasidic life. In this context, the transparency, or *bittul*, of the *Tzaddik* to God leads to an intensification of the rabbinic imperative to cleave to Torah scholars. Instead of focusing *solely* on learning from their ways or on acquiring knowledge of God, as per Rambam, Hasidism embraces the kabbalistic idea that on a more essential level the *Tzaddik*, because of his righteousness and *bittul* to God, is the central conduit of divine revelation in the world, and therefore fundamental to religious life.

R. Yaakov Yosef Polnoye formulates the principle as follows:

> The *Tzaddik* is called "the temple of God" in which God dwells.... Now when a man attaches himself to the Torah scholar in whom the *Shekhina* dwells, he is *ipso facto* attached to God in actuality.[19]

The *Tzaddik*'s closeness to God and the resultant revelation of Godliness inside him explains the talmudic assertion that cleaving to him is itself a form of cleaving to God.[20]

This idea is often linked to a kabbalistic reading of the Talmud's statement that the *Tzaddik* is "the foundation (*yesod*) of the world," according to which the *Tzaddik* is seen as the "channel" (*tzinor*) through which all divine bounty flows to reach earth.[21] Because the *Tzaddik* is so deeply connected to God, the benefits of cleaving to a *Tzaddik* extend to all areas of spiritual and material welfare.[22]

The importance of connecting to a *Tzaddik* is reinforced by the Lurianic notion of interconnected souls. Arizal taught that Adam and Moses were "general souls" that included all other souls within

---

19. *Tzafenat Paane'ah, Bo*. Translation from Norman Lamm (1999), 307.
20. For an elaboration of this point, see Ada Rapaport-Albert (May 1979), 296–325.
21. See, for example, *Meor Einayim, Yitro*, p. 109. For more sources and discussion, see Moshe Idel (1995), 189–207.
22. For further sources and discussion of this point, see Rivka Schatz-Uffenheimer (1960), 373–75.

The Demographics of Dira BaTahtonim

themselves.[23] Early hasidic thinkers extended this idea to the *Tzaddik*, asserting that every *Tzaddik* bears a general soul that includes the roots of his followers' souls within it. This soul connection enables the *Tzaddik* to properly guide and even metaphysically elevate each of those connected to him.[24]

Leadership in the Alter Rebbe's Thought

The Alter Rebbe's description of the *Tzaddik* in *Tanya* can be divided into two interrelated parts: the *Tzaddik* as an individual, and the *Tzaddik* in his role as the center of the community. As we have seen,[25] most of the discussion of the *Tzaddik* in *Tanya* relates to the nature of his unique soul and service of God. The Alter Rebbe describes that the soul of the *Tzaddik* does not contain evil, and he is therefore naturally drawn to the punctilious performance of the mitzvot and naturally experiences intense love and awe of God. In these chapters of *Tanya*, the *Tzaddik* is mostly used as a foil against which to describe the ordinary person and his quest to become a true *Beinoni*. In this sense, the *Tzaddik* is ostensibly to be seen as a person to admire rather than to be closely emulated by the ordinary person, who must strenuously work to grow spiritually.

Tanya, though, is ultimately a practical guide to the service of God, and therefore in two places the Alter Rebbe elaborates on the relevance of the *Tzaddik* for the ordinary person. In chapter 2 of *Tanya*, the Alter Rebbe introduces the idea of the Jewish person's "divine soul" which is "truly a part of God." He notes that on the one hand, the divine soul of every Jew has an identical source and makeup, i.e., God. Despite this uniformity, though, the soul manifests differently in each person depending on how concealed it is within the external layers of one's personality. For the *Tzaddik*, the divine soul is fully revealed. For the rest of the Jewish people, however, the divine soul undergoes more contractions and is more concealed.

---

23. For a brief discussion and sources of this idea in Lurianic sources, see Arthur Green (1977), 336–37.
24. See, for example, *Toledot Aharon, Likkutim*, 46c (Jerusalem, 5726). For more sources and discussion, see Norman Lamm (1999), 266–67; Mendel Piekarz (1999), 39.
25. Chapter 2, section "For It Is Exceedingly Near to You."

The Nasi and the People

As we saw in earlier chapters, much of *Tanya* is spent outlining a range of strategies for a person to employ to disclose the divine soul and make it more manifest in the daily life of the aspiring *Beinoni*. Even before embarking on that journey, the Alter Rebbe prefaces that in addition to the work of the individual, connecting to a *Tzaddik* is a necessary ingredient for this soul revelation:

> The nurture and vitality of the life, spirit, and soul of the masses is drawn from the life, spirit, and soul of the *Tzaddikim* and sages, the heads of the Jewish people in their generation. This explains the saying of our Sages on the verse "And cleave to Him" (Deut. 30:20) that "anyone who cleaves to a Torah scholar is deemed by the biblical verse as if attached to the Divine Presence itself."[26] For, through attachment to the scholars, the *nefesh*, *ruah*, and *neshama* of the masses are bound up and united with their original essence and their root in [God].[27]

The *Tzaddik*'s and the non-*Tzaddik*'s divine souls are of the same "essence" and therefore bound together. This connection allows for the divine vitality to flow from God through the *Tzaddik* to the people. Concurrently, when a person "cleaves" to the revealed divine soul of the *Tzaddik*, he becomes united with his own soul's "original essence," which is God.

Similar lines appear later in *Tanya*.[28] There, the Alter Rebbe cites a teaching from the Zohar that every Jewish person contains "an aspect" (*behina*) of Moses's soul, through which they are empowered to know God and be inspired with awe of God, which according to the Talmud is but "a small thing" for Moses.[29] The aspect of Moses within each individual, the Alter Rebbe explains, is activated by the leaders of each generation:

> Sparks from the soul of our teacher Moses...clothe themselves in the body and soul of the sages of the generation, "the eyes of

---

26. Ketubot 111b.
27. *Tanya, Likkutei Amarim*, ch. 2.
28. Ibid., ch. 42.
29. Ibid.; Berakhot 33b.

the congregation,"³⁰ to impart knowledge to the people, that they may know the greatness of God and [thereby] serve Him with heart and soul. For the service of the heart is according to [one's degree of Godly] knowledge, as is written: "Know the God of your father, and serve Him with all your heart and with a longing soul" (I Chr. 28:9).³¹

The leaders of the generation contain "sparks" of Moses's soul and they empower the people to know God and serve God.

A close reading of the chapter in *Tanya* demonstrates that the *Tzaddik* provides for his followers on two distinct but connected planes. First, the *Tzaddik* teaches his students about the greatness of God, which according to the earlier sections in *Tanya* enables the student to cultivate love and fear of God.³² On a deeper level, the *Tzaddik*'s soul connection with his students is the conduit through which the Moses within each of their souls is brought to the fore. In other words, the mentorship and soul connection of the *Tzaddik* enables them to access a higher form of divine worship than they could attain unaided.

In several of his oral discourses the Alter Rebbe more clearly articulates the impact of the *Tzaddik* on the soul of the disciple. As we have seen, the process of self-effacement (*bittul*) is a key method through which a person can pierce through the outer layers of one's personality that conceals the divine soul and reveal the *yehida*, or the essence of the soul, within.³³ Using this terminology, the Alter Rebbe teaches that through connecting with the *Tzaddik* – the site of a unique form of divine revelation – one can raise one's perspective to see the true all-encompassing unity of God and achieve a more profound consciousness

---

30. Language drawn from Taanit 24a and Rashi on Numbers 15:24.
31. *Tanya, Likkutei Amarim*, ch. 42.
32. See, for example, Moshe Hallamish (1980), 79–92; Roman Foxbrunner (1993), 125–26, who argue that amongst the early hasidic leaders, the Alter Rebbe uniquely emphasized the pedagogical aspects of his role.
33. Chapter 7, section "*Mesirut Nefesh* and the *Yehida*"; Chapter 11, section "The Mechanism of *Bittahon*"; Chapter 12, section "*Simha* and *Bittul*"; Chapter 13, section "*Bittul* as Eliciting the *Yehida*"; Chapter 14, section "Method of Achieving Unity"; Chapter 15, section "Women, *Bittul*, and the Divine Essence."

of *bittul*.³⁴ This, in turn, allows for the revelation of the student's latent divine soul which will become manifestly connected to God.

Importantly, the Alter Rebbe repeatedly warned that this process is not automatic. While the *Tzaddik* can teach, enable, empower, and facilitate, it is ultimately up to the Hasid to use these tools and experiences to rise in his own service of God.

THE ROLE OF THE *TZADDIK* IN THE THOUGHT OF THE REBBE

Understanding the Rebbe's approach to the role of a *Tzaddik* is aided by looking at two sets of sources. First, on several occasions the Rebbe synopsized the role of a Rebbe to non-Hasidim who were unfamiliar with kabbalistic teachings or the hasidic parlance. These English-language elucidations provide us with unique glimpses of the Rebbe's perspective on the *Tzaddik*'s role. After looking at these sources we will broaden the scope of inquiry to some of the Rebbe's many extensive teachings on the role of the *Tzaddik*, and particularly, the leader of Chabad. As we will see, the Rebbe drew from the models of leadership discussed above but developed the picture of an ideal religious leader in unique ways that are consonant with the general framework of his own thought.

When non-Hasidim asked the Rebbe about the role of a hasidic Rebbe, he described it without hasidic terminology. He did not skirt the issue by feigning that it was identical to that of a pulpit rabbi or teacher of Torah. On several occasions, the Rebbe candidly articulated the soul connection that exists between a Rebbe and those connected with him, which transcends the connection between an "ordinary" Torah teacher and his students.

---

34. *Torah Or* 28a–c. For an analysis of this discourse and an explanation of its centrality to the development of the Alter Rebbe as Hasid and then as hasidic leader, see Eli Rubin, "The Second Refinement and the Role of the Tzaddik: How Rabbi Schneur Zalman of Liadi Discovered a New Way to Serve G-d." In this regard, see Nahum Greenwald (2011), 37–50, who argues that achieving a consciousness of *bittul* is the ultimate goal of connecting to a *Tzaddik* in Chabad thought.

The Demographics of Dira BaTahtonim

The Soul Connection

Once, when asked in 1952 "What is a Rebbe?" the Rebbe began his response as follows:

> A Rebbe does not consider himself superior to his Hasidim. He merely contains those parts of the souls of his Hasidim that are connected with him. When a Hasid comes to the Rebbe with a problem, he tries to find in the Rebbe the part of his own soul which is included in the Rebbe's and connect it with his soul – and thus be connected with the Rebbe's soul. It is through this connection that the Hasid receives his material and spiritual life and needs.[35]

The Rebbe highlighted the *Tzaddik*'s role in helping those connected to him find resolution to what ails them, through a soul connection that exists between them and through which material and spiritual good flow.

The Rebbe elucidated this point with an analogy to electricity:

> For example, let us take the electric bulb which produces light. The bulb itself is incapable of producing light, however there are electrical power plants stationed in some distant part of the city which generate the necessary power to produce light. There must be a channel through which the power can pass and reach each individual bulb – in addition to the constitution of the bulb which enables it to receive the power from the power plant. The channel is a wire which connects the power station to the bulb, and when this connection is opened by turning on the switch the bulb receives the power and will then function.
>
> The same applies to a Rebbe and Hasidim. The Rebbe is the power plant which produces the needed strength and power to fulfill the commandments and obligations (spiritual) and also conveys the material. The greater the Rebbe is, the more light he will produce.... The channel through which the Hasid can receive these necessities is his soul, which is connected to the soul of the Rebbe.[36]

---

35. Recorded by Nissan Mindel; available at www.chabad.org/664336.
36. Ibid.

The Rebbe produces the "energy" that flows into the Hasid, who was not able to fully shine on his own. This flow of energy from the Rebbe enables the Hasid to live a richer spiritual and material life.[37]

The Hasid Must Work
Though the Rebbe did not elaborate on this point in this particular exchange, the power-plant analogy places a great deal of responsibility on the Hasid. The raw energy provided by a Rebbe is independently useless, unable to brighten a room. It is the Hasid who, like the bulb, must have the "constitution" to receive it and the presence of mind to employ it properly. The Rebbe foregrounded this aspect of the Rebbe-Hasid relationship on another occasion:

> I cannot speak about myself; but I can tell you about my own Rebbe. For me, my Rebbe was the geologist of the soul. You see, there are so many treasures in the earth. There is gold, there is silver, and there are diamonds. But if you don't know where to dig, you'll only find dirt and rocks and mud. The Rebbe can tell you where to dig, and what to dig for, but the digging you must do yourself.[38]

The soul connection between the *Tzaddik* and his followers enables the *Tzaddik* to look into a person's soul and guide them on their proper path. The person, however, must then work to actually implement this guidance.[39]

---

37. At other occasions the Rebbe employed the parable of electric power differently, with God as the power source, the Jew as the lamp, and the Rebbe's role to help the Jew find his connecting wire or switch, to help activate the connection between the two. (See "The Rebbe Speaks to Hillel Students," available at www.chabad.org/392177.)
38. Zalman Schachter Shalomi (2015), preface. Compare with www.chabad.org/114878.
39. Similarly, see the Rebbe's English-language description to Herbet Weiner of the mechanics of a "blessing" in Hasidism: "It is possible for the *Tzaddik*, the Rebbe, to awaken powers slumbering within a man. It is also possible to bring him into contact with a higher level of powers outside his own soul. A person lives on one floor of a building and needs help from the floor above; if he can't walk up himself, someone else must help him get that help" (from Herbert Weiner, "Alone with Moses").

The *Tzaddik*'s Dedication

In addition to teaching about this soul connection, the Rebbe also highlighted another key aspect of hasidic leadership: the *Tzaddik*'s complete dedication to those connected to him. After elaborating on the power-plant analogy, the Rebbe explained that this soul connection functions as a channel only if the *Tzaddik*'s bond with his followers is the defining feature of his life:

> The sole duty of the Rebbe is to deliver the above-mentioned necessities, spiritual and material, to his Hasidim. Although the Rebbe is also required to fulfill his own bodily functions, that is not his purpose or true function; it is only because his soul is bound with an earthly body which cannot exist without these functions. If one comes to a rabbi complaining of a headache and the rabbi gives him an aspirin, we surely won't say that this is the function of a rabbi. The same is with a Rebbe when he must carry out the necessary functions of his body.[40]

Similarly, on another occasion the Rebbe explained that this process of helping others necessitates the *Tzaddik*'s *bittul* to the one seeking his help:

> When a man comes [to a Rebbe] with a problem, there are only two alternatives – either send him away, or try to help him. A man knows his own problem best, so [the Rebbe] must try to unite oneself with him and become *batel*, as dissociated as possible from one's own ego. Then, in concert with the other person, one tries to understand the rule of divine providence in this particular case.[41]

A true *Tzaddik* must rid himself of all ego to facilitate his connection to those seeking his counsel.

---

40. Recorded by Nissan Mindel; retrieved from www.chabad.org/664336.
41. Herbert Weiner, "Alone with Moses."

The Nasi and the People

In summary, when the Rebbe summarized the role of a hasidic leader, he spoke of the soul connection and interdependence of the *Tzaddik* and his followers. The *Tzaddik* must be entirely dedicated to those who turn to him, enabling him to serve as a conduit for spiritual and material energy. On the other end, the Hasid must have the presence of mind to recognize his dependence, receive the divine bounty from the *Tzaddik*, and then use this energy and invest independent effort to achieve greater heights in his own service of God. As we will see, these themes are amplified and elaborated in the Rebbe's more in-depth and source-based talks about the nature and role of the *Tzaddik*.

THE *NASI* OF THE GENERATION

A Single Leader

Early hasidic thinkers differed on how to conceptualize the coexistence of multiple *Tzaddikim* within a single generation. While some embraced the notion of a plurality of parallel *Tzaddikim*,[42] others argued that every generation contains also a solitary figure who stands above others as the *Tzaddik hador* – the primary *Tzaddik* of the generation.[43] While each second-tier *Tzaddik* might have a soul connection to a specific congregation, the *Tzaddik hador* serves this function for the entire world. His soul is the vehicle through which God connects with every aspect of the world.

The Rebbe emphatically embraced the latter approach. Characteristically preferring to derive his opinion from the Talmud and other parts of the corpus of the revealed part of the Torah in addition to Kabbala and Hasidism, the Rebbe cited the following talmudic anecdote as a source for the notion of a single *Tzaddik hador*.

The Talmud records a tradition that even as Moses ensured that after his passing Joshua would be assisted by the Elders, nonetheless, Moses still emphasized: "There must be one clear leader for the generation (*dabar ehad lador*), not two or more leaders for the generation."[44] Citing this passage as the standard-bearer, the Rebbe highlighted: "The *nasi* of the generation is one [person], 'one clear leader

---

42. See, for example, the sources cited in Norman Lamm (1999), 266–67.
43. See, for example, *Likkutei Moharan* 56:1.
44. *Sanhedrin* 8a.

for the generation.'"[45] Elsewhere the Rebbe deduced from other rabbinic teachings that, similar to Moses, King David, and *Mashiah*, this leader – referred to by the Rebbe as the *nasi* – is supposed to be the single joint Torah and political leader of the entire Jewish people.[46]

The Expansion of Moses

Conceptually, the existence of a single principal *Tzaddik* per generation is reinforced by Zoharic references to an elite cadre of *Tzaddikim* who are "the expansion of Moses in each generation."[47] It is clear that Moses was unique in his generation, categorically greater than the rest of the people.[48] According to the Rebbe, the Zohar's identification of certain people as "the Moses of their generation" underscores their singularity. Just as Moses was the single leader of his generation, his "expansion" in each generation takes on the same role.

For the Rebbe, this single leader of the generation is not just Moses's heir. Rather, the leader of each generation contains the very essence of Moses's soul, albeit garbed in a different body. Accordingly, throughout all of history there is but a single soul of Moses that in each generation dons new bodily clothing.

This idea emerges, among many other places, from the Rebbe's analysis[49] of rabbinic statements that associate Moses with eternity. For example, the Talmud teaches that the *Mishkan* that Moses constructed was never destroyed and will exist forever.[50] What is the basis for this eternality? The Rebbe explained that it is Moses's connection to the trait of truth.

The midrash describes Moses as a man of truth who delivered the Torah of truth to the Jewish people.[51] One of the key qualities of truth

---

45. *Torat Menahem* 5744: 2, 890.
46. See *Likkutei Sihot* 23, *Pinhas*, no. 2, *se'ifim* 4–9; ibid., 25, *Vayigash*, no. 2, *se'if* 1; ibid., 31, *Beshallah*, no. 1, *se'if* 6.
47. *Tikkunei Zohar*, *tikkun* 69. In addition, the Rebbe would cite the midrashic passage in Genesis Rabba (56:7) that "there is no generation that does not contain [a person] like Moses."
48. The Rebbe's language from *Likkutei Sihot* 4, *Korah*, *se'if* 3.
49. *Likkutei Sihot* 26, *Shemot*, no. 1.
50. *Sota* 9a.
51. *Midrash Tanhuma*, *Shemot*, *siman* 26. See also *Bava Batra* 74a. The Rebbe emphasized the connection between Moses and the attribute of truth in various contexts; see

is its eternality, as per the verse in Psalms: "The truth of God is eternal."[52] Moses's activities, too, whether gifting the Torah to the Jewish people or bringing the *Shekhina* into the world through the *Mishkan*, are thus endowed with the eternality of God's truth.[53]

This, explained the Rebbe, is the subtext for a most surprising talmudic statement. Despite the Torah clearly stating, "And Moses died there,"[54] the Talmud records a tradition that "Moses did not actually die... but he still stands and serves God."[55] The Rebbe noted that this cannot merely refer to Moses's life force eternally existing in the spiritual realm, as this is true for all righteous individuals. Rather, it must mean that Moses, as the man of truth, continues to exist somehow in the physical world.[56]

But how can Moses live in this world if the Torah itself states that he died on Mount Nevo? The Rebbe asserted that the Torah merely recounts the demise of Moses's body. Since, however, as the Alter Rebbe wrote, "the life of a *Tzaddik* is spiritual and not physical," Moses's real self was his unique soul, and it is this essence of Moses that transcends death and always remains present in our world:

> The essential life of Moses was not the physical life of his body, but the spiritual life of his soul. This spiritual life remains eternally within our material world by being enclothed within the body of the *nasi* of the generation, in each and every generation.[57]

Notwithstanding appearances, the essential soul of Moses is present within the primary leader of the generation.[58]

---

52. *Likkutei Sihot* 26, *Shemot*, no. 1, *se'if* 6; ibid., 26, *Hosafot*, 302; *Torat Menahem* 5746: 2, 335. Ps. 117:2.
53. *Likkutei Sihot* 26, *Shemot*, no. 1, *se'if* 5. See also *Torat Menahem* 5751: 2, 435–36.
54. Deut. 34:5.
55. Sota 13b.
56. *Likkutei Sihot* 26, *Shemot*, no. 1, *se'if* 7.
57. Ibid.
58. See *Torat Menahem* 5711: 1, 273, where the Rebbe took pains to emphasize that even though one might think that the "expansion of Moses" indicates a dilution of sorts, nonetheless the entire essence of Moses's soul lives within each generation's *nasi*.

The Demographics of Dira BaTahtonim

This identification of the *nasi* of the generation with Moses became the basis for much of the Rebbe's teachings regarding a *nasi*. The Rebbe analyzed many aspects of Moses's personality, piety, and leadership, and asserted that all "expansions of Moses" manifest an identical array of qualities.

THE QUALITIES AND ROLE OF THE *NASI*
Bittul

One defining characteristic of Moses was his ultimate *bittul* to God. Described in the Torah as "the humblest of all people,"[59] Moses removed his ego until he was like a servant whose "entire existence was the existence of his Master."[60] The Rebbe connected this to the halakhic principle: "What is acquired by a servant is acquired by his master,"[61] and further noted that according to the interpretation of Rashi this means that the servant does not first make the acquisition and then transfer ownership to the master. Rather, the object is directly acquired by the master when the servant obtains it; the servant is simply regarded as an extension of the master's own self.[62]

According to the Rebbe, this degree of effacement is the import of the midrashic description of Moses's role at Sinai: "The *Shekhina* spoke through the mouth of Moses."[63] In other words, Moses's very throat and physical body existed for him only as a "chariot" and a vehicle for the Divine Essence that spoke through him.[64] Moses the person achieved such a degree of *bittul* that he was totally transparent to the Divine Essence, which shined unencumbered through him. Similarly, the Rebbe explained that this ultimate effacement to God also undergirded the above-mentioned point of Moses's eternality. Since Moses

---

59. Num. 12:3.
60. *Likkutei Sihot* 16, Pekudei, no. 2, *se'if* 6. For more discussions regarding Moses's degree of *bittul*, see *Torat Menahem* 5729: 4, 5; ibid., 5743: 4, 2060.
61. Pesahim 88b.
62. *Likkutei Sihot* 16, Pekudei, no. 2, *se'if* 6.
63. Exodus Rabba, *siman* 3.
64. See, *Torat Menahem* 5718: 1, 26–27, 317; ibid., 5723: 3, 103, note 19; ibid., 5724: 1, 344; *Likkutei Sihot* 3, Behukkotai, *se'if* 2.

himself and all his handiwork radiated "God's truth," both Moses and the items he fashioned at God's behest last for eternity.[65]

This complete *bittul* to God is a defining characteristic of every *nasi* throughout history. For example, David, the *nasi* of his generation, is also described as a "servant"[66] of God, a term that exemplifies this state of total *bittul*. Therefore, like Moses, David is also eternal via his dynasty and capital city, which are everlasting institutions.[67]

Applying this concept to events even thousands of years later, the Rebbe applied this confluence of complete *bittul* and transcending the limitations of time to a later *nasi* – the Baal Shem Tov. While relating a story in which the Baal Shem Tov was able to foretell events in the future, the Rebbe explained that this power stemmed from the fact that "*Tzaddikim* are not independent entities unto themselves; their entire beings are Godliness." Since God transcends time, this automatically becomes the reality as well of the *nasi*, who reaches the epitome of *bittul* to God.[68]

Complete Dedication to the People

Just as the *nasi* practices *bittul* to God, he has a similar posture of complete dedication toward the Jewish people. All his activities are for their benefit and he does not perceive himself as being an entity independent from them. This absolute identification with the people manifests itself in the *nasi's* willingness to sacrifice everything about his material and spiritual well-being for the sake of the people.

In one talk, the Rebbe highlighted this trait by exploring the Zohar's contrast of the approaches of Abraham and Moses toward the sinners in their generation. On one level, Abraham is the paradigm of self-sacrifice, spending his life nomadically traversing the Middle East in an attempt to spread the word of God to the idolatrous populace. However, his prayers for the city of Sodom reveal a limitation to his efforts: his argument to save the city was predicated on the righteousness of its

---

65. *Likkutei Sihot* 26, *Shemot*, no. 1, *se'if* 9.
66. Ezek. 37:24.
67. *Likkutei Sihot* 16, *Pekudei*, no. 2, *se'if* 7; ibid., 25, *Vayigash*, no. 2, *se'if* 9.
68. *Torat Menahem* 5711: 1, 55.

The Demographics of Dira BaTahtonim

inhabitants. Once God informed him that there was not a group of righteous people, Abraham abandoned his efforts to entreat God.

Moses, however, was different:

> But the leadership of Moses, the faithful shepherd, was different. When the Jewish people sinned, Moses demanded that God forgive *all* of them, even the wicked ones.... Moses said, "If You do not [forgive them] erase me from Your book!" (Ex. 32:32)... He endangered himself for the Jewish people. Even though based on reason and logic, there was no justification to pray for someone who wantonly sinned with the Golden Calf, Moses endangered himself for them with an immutable determination and self-sacrifice that transcended logic.[69]

Moses was willing to give up *everything* he held dear and for which he had toiled and sacrificed, to save *idolators* who were wantonly and publicly repudiating everything they had just heard directly from God. This form of self-sacrificial leadership was a defining feature of Moses's life.[70]

The Rebbe emphasized that this form of self-sacrificial dedication for the *entire* generation is definitional for every subsequent *nasi*: "The same applies to the 'expansion of Moses' [i.e., the *nasi*] of the generation... that he sacrifices himself for all of the Jewish people."[71] This complete dedication causes the *nasi* to be attentive to *all* of the needs of *all* of the people. The Rebbe reiterated the extent of this devotion:

> Even though based on reason and rationality it is possible to make a calculation that someone else could carry out a certain matter and [the *nasi*] is therefore not obligated to do it himself; and, similarly, it is possible to make a calculation that according to the *Shulhan Arukh*... one does not have to sacrifice his life for

---

69. *Torat Menahem* 5715: 2, 158.
70. See *Likkutei Sihot* 34, *Vezot Haberakha*, no. 1, *se'if* 5, where the Rebbe discussed why the Torah concludes its eulogy of Moses with a reference to his breaking of the tablets. See also *Likkutei Sihot* 34, *Ekev*, no. 1, *se'ifim* 8–9.
71. *Torat Menahem* 5715: 2, 160.

certain needs of others – which then prohibits sacrificing one's life for them – nevertheless, the behavior of the *nesi'im* is not to enter into any calculations whatsoever. Since they are dedicated in absolute totality to the Jewish people, to the point of "If You do not [forgive them] erase me from Your book!" what room is there for any calculations?[72]

Explicitly drawing on the model of Moses, the Rebbe argued that the *nasi* is infinitely dedicated to the Jewish people, entering even halakhically questionable territory for their sake.[73]

It is important to note that even as the *nasi* cares for all the generation, he simultaneously never loses sight of each individual. Rather, a true *nasi* "immerses himself into the situation of [each] individual"[74] and from that vantage point helps the person with what is best for him. The *nasi* never dispenses directives to an individual person solely based on the general mission of the collective, but each lesson is tailored for the ultimate benefit of the person with whom he is speaking.[75]

Bridging Heaven and Earth

The *nasi*'s complete *bittul* to God on the one hand, and his simultaneous total self-sacrifice toward the people and their realities on the other, enables him to serve as a bridge to connect them. This is alluded to in Moses's declaration: "I stand between God and [the people]" (Deut. 5:5).

Already in his opening *Bati LeGani* discourse, the Rebbe underscored that it was specifically Moses who succeeded in bringing the *Shekhina* down to earth. In his teachings about the nature of Moses and his successors throughout history, the Rebbe attributed this capacity to Moses's ultimate *bittul* to God while simultaneously living as a human being among the people.

---

72. Ibid.
73. See also *Torat Menahem* 5713: 1, 337, which says that the *nasi*'s "whole essence is his role as the shepherd of the Jewish people."
74. *Likkutei Sihot* 33, *Masei*, no. 1, *se'if* 7.
75. Ibid. See also *Likkutei Sihot* 33, *Korah*, no. 1, *se'ifim* 6–7.

On one occasion[76] the Rebbe developed the association between Moses's *bittul* and his bridging of the worlds through the lens of Psalms, chapter 90. This chapter begins with the phrase "A prayer of Moses, the man of God" and relates to God's seeming absence from this world. The chapter concludes with the following prayer: "And may the pleasantness of *Hashem* our God be upon us, and the work of our hands establish for us, and the work of our hands establish it." The Midrash teaches that this prayer was recited by Moses at the dedication of the *Mishkan*.

The Rebbe argued that the end of the chapter harkens back to its beginning. The reason that Moses successfully built the *Mishkan* and overcame God's concealment in the world, to which the end of the chapter alludes, was that he was "Moses, the man of God."

The Midrash hones in on the inherent paradox of this description, "man of God," which hyperliterally can be rendered "God-man": "If 'God,' why does it say 'man,' and if 'man,' why does it say 'God'? Rather, his bottom half was a man while his top half was God."[77]

This is not a heterodox statement of dualism that places Moses as an equal to God. Rather, the Rebbe explained the midrash to mean that Moses embodied both complete *bittul* to God, making his "top" half entirely transparent to the Divine Essence, while still living in a physical body as a "regular" part of the lowest and most material realm.[78] It was this capacity of Moses to both transcend this world but also be of this world that allowed him to be the conduit through which divinity is brought to the people.

In this regard, the Rebbe often employed the language of the Rebbe Rashab and described Moses as a "connective intermediary" (*memutza hamehaber*).[79] The Rashab presented an analogy of two diametrically different entities which are fused together by a third that contains elements of each of the others. So, too, it is Moses, who is totally transparent to and one with God but also totally of and dedicated to

---

76. *Torat Menachem* 5751: 2, 430–38.
77. *Midrash Tehillim*, ch. 90.
78. See *Torat Menachem* 5751: 2, 433–34.
79. Ibid., 5751: 2, 433.

the people, who "stands between God and [the people]"⁸⁰ to bring God to the people and create the reality of "face-to-face God spoke to you."⁸¹

It goes almost without saying that Moses and his successors did not merely channel a lower level of divinity, but rather the Divine Essence itself. Through bringing down Torah from Mount Sinai and building a home for God in the form of the *Mishkan*, Moses served as the bridge to reunite the Divine Essence with the lowest realm. As history progresses, each *nasi* must continue the work of Moses to further disclose the Divine Essence in the world. In the Rebbe's words: "The role of the *nasi*...is to effect the revelation of the Divine Essence in the entirety of creation."⁸² Each *nasi* furthers the process that the original Moses began, incrementally bringing the Divine Essence back to the lowest levels.

THE *NASI* AND THE PEOPLE

The Importance of *Hitkashrut*

The understanding that Moses (and, by extension, his successors) "stands between God and [the people]" as the "connective intermediary" has immense ramifications for the rest of the population. If the *nasi* is utterly transparent to the Divine Essence and is thus the "connective intermediary" through which divinity is channeled to the people, it follows that connecting to the *nasi* helps access the Divine Essence itself. Thus, the notion of *hitkashrut*, or connecting oneself to the *nasi* – in the spirit of the biblical command of *dveikut*, or cleaving, to the righteous – becomes an important element in the service of the ordinary Jew.

Once again, the Rebbe drew lessons from Moses to contemporary manifestations of this idea. After elaborating on Moses's role as the "connective intermediary" for his generation, the Rebbe added:

> Just like this is true for the generation that entered the Land of Israel...so too in every generation, in order to receive the divine light the people need a "connective intermediary," the "expansion

---

80. Deut. 5:5.
81. Ibid. 5:4.
82. *Torat Menahem* 5752: 1, 70.

of Moses in each generation." This is the reason that Hasidim attribute so much importance to connecting (*hitkashrut*) to the Rebbe.[83]

Our discussion of *hitkashrut* will relate to three interrelated issues: (1) What is lacking in the service of the ordinary Jew without *hitkashrut* to a *Tzaddik*? (2) What must the Hasid do and feel to cultivate *hitkashrut*? (3) How did the Rebbe conceptualize *hitkashrut* such that the state of being connected to a *Tzaddik* achieves its goal? As we will see, ultimately the Rebbe saw the *nasi* and the people as being two sides of a unified entity, each intimately bound and dependent upon the other.

The Goals of *Hitkashrut*

As we have seen in several contexts, the Rebbe taught that one's service of God should ideally emanate from the essence of the soul – the *yehida* – meaning, with a sense of identification and oneness with God.[84] On occasion, though, the Rebbe noted that demanding this form of service from every Jew is inherently problematic. Only the *Tzaddik*, who contains no evil inclination and is totally effaced before God, can achieve this level of oneness with God. Everyone else, though, no matter how sincere and righteous, still contains some element of ego and self-interest which serves as a barrier between the person and God. How, then, can the Torah expect the impossible from the vast majority of Jews?

The Rebbe often answered that *hitkashrut* to the *nasi* assists the ordinary Jew in overcoming this challenge. As he once formulated it:

> A person cannot connect and become one with the Divine Light using his own limited faculties alone. Therefore, there needs to be a connection to a "connective intermediary."[85]

Or, on a different occasion:

---

83. Ibid., 5712: 1, 282.
84. See, for example, chapter 6, section "Know Him in All of Your Ways," and chapter 12, section "Suprarational *Simha*."
85. *Torat Menahem* 5712: 1, 282.

The Nasi and the People

> One can seemingly ask: How can one's service be from the essence of the soul...? The answer is that this occurs through *hitkashrut* to the Rebbe.[86]

In short, "connecting" with someone who is effaced before God assists a person in achieving the desired *bittul* with the accompanying revelation of the *yehida* and feeling oneness with God.[87]

While these statements explain the motivation and goals of *hitkashrut*, to be fully understood it requires more analysis. How does "connecting" with the *nasi* allow one to reveal their *yehida*, to be transparent to the Divine Essence? With this in mind, we will now turn to the second of the questions above and explore what *hitkashrut* practically requires of the Hasid. Then, we will be better equipped to understand the conceptual underpinnings of *hitkashrut* and how connecting to a *Tzaddik* helps a person achieve oneness with God.

Means of *Hitkashrut*

What does it mean for the ordinary person to connect with the *nasi*? When the Rebbe was asked this very question, he consistently responded that *hitkashrut* consists of studying the *nasi*'s Torah teachings, emulating his ways, and acting in accordance with his directives.

For example, in a public letter penned during the year of mourning for his father-in-law, the Rebbe cited his predecessor that

> *hitkashrut* is through studying [the *nasi*'s] Torah and following the "straight path that he has taught us from his ways, and we will walk in his paths."[88]

---

86. Ibid., 5711: 2, 297.
87. In this regard, see also *Likkutei Sihot* 4, *Korah*, *se'if* 6, for a more specific and detailed explanation for what is lacking in the mitzvot of the ordinary Jew without the assistance of the *nasi*.
88. *Torat Menahem* 5710, 222. The final clause is a paraphrase from *Tanya, Iggeret HaKodesh*, letter 27.

The Rebbe repeated this sentiment dozens of times, even including it in his ethical calendar, *HaYom Yom*.[89]

On the most basic level, the Rebbe spoke of these elements as a fulfillment of the mitzva of "cleaving to Torah scholars," which, as we have seen, Rambam defines as studying their Torah and learning from their ways.[90] In addition, though, the Rebbe spoke of each of these elements as engendering a spiritual process which intensifies the soul connection that exists between the *nasi* and the people of the generation.

The first item in the Rebbe's practical formula of *hitkashrut* is studying the *nasi*'s Torah teachings. In addition to the value of the Torah itself, the Rebbe emphasized that studying the *nasi*'s Torah allows for an existential connection between the person and the *nasi*. Just as God expressed His essence through the Torah, a parallel phenomenon exists with each *nasi*:

> "*Tzaddikim* are similar to their Creator" (Ruth Rabba 4:3). Just as God, the Giver of the Torah, said, "I have written and given Myself," and through the learning of Torah [God says,] "You have taken Me" (Leviticus Rabba 30:13), this is also true regarding *hitkashrut* to *Tzaddikim* through the learning of their Torah.[91]

Learning the Torah of a *Tzaddik* connects one with the essence of that *Tzaddik*. This is true whether or not the *Tzaddik* currently occupies a physical form, as his Torah teachings express his eternal soul. Therefore, the Rebbe stressed that learning the Torah of a deceased *Tzaddik* is a form of summoning that *Tzaddik*'s soul and connecting with him.[92]

The second element that the Rebbe mentioned is behavioral: emulating the *nasi* and following his directives. The Rebbe spoke about this category in two complementary ways. In some instances, the Rebbe describes this behavioral element as a natural outgrowth of studying the

---

89. For a small sampling, see *Torat Menahem* 5710, 10; ibid., 5711: 1, 125; *Iggerot Kodesh* 19, letter 7412.
90. *Torat Menahem* 5721: 2, 67.
91. Ibid., 5722: 3, 261–62. See also *Torat Menahem* 5747: 2, 283.
92. *Torat Menahem* 5713: 2, 219. See also *Likkutei Sihot* 32, Nisan, *se'if* 5; *Iggerot Kodesh* 3, letter 556.

nasi's Torah. The more one understands the ideas and mission that vivify the *Tzaddik*, the more inspired one will be to emulate him and follow the practical directives that emerge from these teachings.

For example, in an early letter, the Rebbe described that, based on the classic Chabad paradigm, *hitkashrut* begins with using one's intellect to study the *nasi*'s teachings. This will then have an impact on the character traits and behaviors of the one studying that unique Torah:

> Since the intention of the one who taught the Torah [i.e., the *nasi*] is to draw one's intellect into one's character traits and to thereby transform one's character traits...this necessitates *hitkashrut* through following his path and his directives regarding character traits and thoughts, speech and action.[93]

The cerebral study of the *nasi*'s Torah will naturally lead to a transformation of the studier's character traits and behaviors.

Taking this a step further, the Rebbe explained that a higher level of *hitkashrut* includes developing a deep understanding of the *nasi*'s mission and practically dedicating oneself to that mission. Even bereft of direct instruction from the *nasi*, a person who is "dedicated and connected [to the *nasi*]" should be able to intuit what activities are important to the *nasi* after studying the *nasi*'s behaviors and teachings. Once these activities are identified, the Hasid will naturally fully embrace these projects. Similar to studying the Torah of the *nasi*, the Rebbe argued that such behavioral dedication is not merely a proper life path but also constitutes a form of "'taking' of the essence [of the *nasi*]."[94]

In addition to dedicating oneself to the *nasi*'s mission and desiring to practically fulfill it, the Rebbe spoke of another element regarding the importance of following the *nasi*'s directives. Even if a person does not understand or identify with the *nasi*'s directives, proper *hitkashrut* involves complete obedience to these instructions.[95]

---

93. *Likkutei Sihot* 34, *Hosafot*, 266.
94. *Torat Menahem* 5721: 1, 277.
95. Ibid., 5710, 163–64; ibid., 5716: 1, 139–40; ibid., 5751: 4, 202.

On one level the Rebbe spoke about obeying the directives of a *nasi* as stemming from the general rabbinic notion of recognizing the superior wisdom and Torah knowledge of one's Rebbe.[96] However, the Rebbe added a deeper dimension as well, connecting obedience with the notion of *hitkashrut*. As the *nasi* is completely transparent to God and His Torah, his word reflects God's will and should therefore be obeyed immediately and without questioning, similar to soldiers who set aside any intellectual reservations or hesitations and blindly follow the general's commands.

A biblical model of this behavior is the tribe of Levi, who, upon Moses's charge, immediately took up arms and killed those who worshipped the Golden Calf, including their own relatives. Asking how they reconciled this with the Torah's command to honor one's father and mother, the Rebbe explained:

> It was due to their dedication to Moses, the first recipient of the Torah; they did not engage in any calculations. They knew a single thing – that they must follow the directive of Moses! They knew that every word of Moses was in accordance with the commands of the Torah.[97]

Their complete trust in Moses caused them to efface their own intellect before the command of Moses.[98]

Once again, the Rebbe argued that this utter obedience is not the sole province of the original Moses, but applies equally to those in future generations who bear his essence:

> The same applies in every generation, when one hears a directive from the *nasi* of the generation – "the expansion of Moses in each generation" – there is no place for [waiting until] the matter settles in one's mind, for looking into books and so forth. Rather, one must fulfill the directive.[99]

---

96. Ibid., 5718: 2, 292.
97. Ibid., 5718: 2, 293.
98. See *Torat Menahem* 5752: 2, 120, where the Rebbe spoke of *bittul* to a Rebbe.
99. *Torat Menahem* 5718: 2, 294.

Any hesitation indicates a lack of proper *hitkashrut*.

As indicated above, part of the background and motivation for a person to follow the *nasi*'s directives is an understanding of the greatness of the *nasi* and that he is a reliable conveyor of God's word.[100] An additional element is a belief that the *nasi* is entirely dedicated to his people and has everyone's best interests at heart. This is true regarding the generation as a whole, and also regarding the personalized guidance that the *nasi* can give each individual based on the latter's own life situation and spiritual level.

These directives can assist the Hasid in every aspect of his life,[101] ranging from his spiritual life of studying of Torah, fulfilling mitzvot, repenting for sins, and acting more selflessly toward others, to "material" matters such as "children, health, and livelihood."[102] Ultimately, these personalized directives are for the benefit of the individual Hasid and help him fulfill his own mission in this world.[103]

A Consciousness of Interdependence

The relationship between an ordinary person and the *nasi*, though, goes beyond studying the nasi's teachings and following his directives. Rather, the Rebbe described that all the material and spiritual good that people receive is channeled by God through the *nasi*.

The Rebbe strongly articulated this point in a public letter to Hasidim a few months after his father-in-law's passing (before he himself became the Rebbe). After describing the qualities of a *nasi*, the Rebbe writes that Hasidim should contemplate that

> from him and through him are directed all material and spiritual benefactions; and by being connected [*hahitkashrut*] to him (in his letters he has taught us how this is accomplished) we are

---

100. See also *Torat Menahem* 5729: 4, 302–3.
101. *Torat Menahem* 5710, 23–24.
102. Moed Katan 28a. The Talmud teaches that these three items depend on "fate" and not one's "merit."
103. For other mentions of the *nasi*'s reliability regarding his role in aiding each individual's material and spiritual state, see *Likkutei Sihot* 11, *Hosafot*, 212; *Torat Menahem* 5746: 1, 350–51.

> bound and united with the spiritual root, and with the ultimate supernal spiritual root.[104]

A Hasid should contemplate that everything he has in this world is channeled through the *nasi*. This further underscores the importance of *hitkashrut* through studying his Torah and following his directives. Thereby, the Hasid can become connected with the "ultimate supernal spiritual root."

The Rebbe focused on this theme in a later talk about the role of Moses. One might have thought that Moses's mission is exhausted by his teaching of Torah to the Jewish people. The Talmud,[105] however, relates that in addition to spiritual sustenance in the form of Torah, Moses also provides for the Jewish people's physical sustenance and well-being in the form of the miraculous manna, water, and clouds of glory. The Rebbe explained that this is due to the fact that

> Moses is the shepherd of the Jewish people. He guides them that they should behave properly and *through him all of their needs are bestowed upon them....*[106]

Or, as the Rebbe said a little later in the talk: "He is concerned and provides for the Jewish people everything that they need in both materiality and spirituality."[107]

But this bestowment is not entirely automatic. While the *nasi* provides for all his people, in order to optimally "receive the benefactions" of Moses, the people must

> stand in *bittul* and *hitkashrut* to him. They need to be given over to him like sheep to a shepherd, sheep that have no will of their own, but they go to where the shepherd leads them. When they do not have any personal desires, both material and spiritual,

---

104. *Iggerot Kodesh* 3, letter 635. Translation is adapted from www.chabad.org/2278234.
105. Taanit 9a.
106. *Torat Menahem* 5718: 1, 91.
107. Ibid. See also *Iggerot Kodesh* 6, 1767, and *Torat Menahem* 5745: 5, 2961–62, where the Rebbe used Moses caring for the Jewish people's material needs as a model for the fact that even "material benefactions" are channeled through the *nasi*.

The Nasi and the People

rather they are given over entirely to Moses, then they become a vessel to receive the blessing...."[108]

Fulfilling the various means of *hitkashrut* allows for the pathways that connect the *nasi* with the people to be completely "open."[109] This facilitates an optimal flowing of the benefactions from God through the *nasi* to the people.

Just as the people are dependent on the *nasi*, so too the *nasi* is dependent on the people. Using the analogy of a human body, the Rebbe often compared the *nasi* to the "head"[110] and the "heart"[111] of the generation. On one level this means that, similar to these central organs, the *nasi* provides material and spiritual energies to the rest of the body. However, the Rebbe extended this analogy by noting that there is a symbiotic relationship between the head and the heart and the rest of the limbs of the body. Just as the limbs cannot function independent of the head and the heart, similarly, the head and the heart cannot properly fulfill their function or reach their potential without the hands and the feet.

One way that the Rebbe spoke about this was regarding the practical realization of the *nasi*'s mission which, as we have seen, is to reveal divinity in our world. The Rebbe emphasized throughout his teachings that this objective requires much hands-on work all throughout the globe. Even as great as the *nasi* is, he is unable practically to accomplish this great mission alone. Accordingly, each and every person who is connected to the *nasi* becomes his *shaliah* (emissary) to practically do the work.[112] Or, as the Rebbe once put it, the *nasi* needs "hands and feet and other limbs to spread Torah."[113]

---

108. *Torat Menahem* 5718: 1, 92. See also ibid., 5711: 1, 48, note 8; ibid., 5714: 2, 59.
109. See, *Iggerot Kodesh* 3, letter 745.
110. This is based on *Tanya, Likkutei Amarim*, ch. 2, cited above. For an example relevant to the point at hand, see *maamar* s.v. "*VeAta Tetzaveh* 5741" (published in *Torat Menahem* 5752: 2, 330–40), *se'if* 2.
111. This is based on Rambam's (*Hilkhot Melakhim UMilhemoteihem* 3:6) description of the king of the Jewish people as "heart of the congregation of the Jewish people." For an example relevant to the point at hand, see *Torat Menahem* 5748: 2, 494–98.
112. See, for example, *Torat Menahem* 5748: 4, 154–56.
113. *Torat Menahem* 5745: 3, 1695.

This practical realization of the *nasi*'s mission in turn provides renewed energy and an elevation in the status of the *nasi*. Employing an analogy of the body's cyclical cardiovascular system, the Rebbe explained that even as the heart pumps the blood to the rest of the body, providing it with sustenance and energy, the blood then returns to the heart and provides it with energy to continue to beat. This will then "increase with greater strength and greater vigor"[114] the spiritual level of the *nasi* and his ability to provide for and assist the people of his generation.

A Consciousness of Identity

Now that we have seen some of what *hitkashrut* entails and the interdependence of the people and the *nasi*, let us turn to the Rebbe's conceptual understanding of their relationship. Ultimately, the *nasi* and the people are two manifestations of the same unified entity.

In one talk,[115] the Rebbe developed this unified identity through the lens of a comment of Rashi in his commentary on the Torah. There is a discrepancy between the Torah's two accounts of the messengers sent from the Jewish people's camp to King Sihon. In the book of Numbers, the Torah says the Jewish people sent the messengers: "The Jewish people sent messengers to Sihon."[116] However, in the book of Deuteronomy, when Moses retells the story, he says that he himself sent them: "I sent messengers from the desert of Kedemoth to Sihon."[117] Rashi notes this contradiction and offers the following solution:

> These verses supplement each other.... Moses is the Jewish people, and the Jewish people are Moses – to teach you that the leader of the generation is equal to the entire generation, because the leader is everyone (*hanasi hu hakol*).[118]

---

114. Ibid., 5748: 4, 155–56.
115. *Likkutei Sihot* 33, *Hukkat*, no. 2.
116. Num. 21:21.
117. Deut. 2:26.
118. Rashi on Deut. 2:26.

The Nasi and the People

In a characteristically itemized interpretation, the Rebbe explained that Rashi's comment contains two distinct but interrelated statements about the relationship between Moses and the people.

"Moses is the Jewish people" is a statement about the nature of Moses. As a true leader, he is not a "private person" who acts on behalf of the Jewish people, but rather, "he is a public person in the essence of his being." Despite being "exalted and elevated over the people," he simultaneously has no distinct identity outside of his role as the *nasi*. His very essence is created by the people as per the rabbinic statement "There is no king without a people."[119] The fact that Moses as the *nasi* is one with the people means that whatever action Moses takes is itself considered an action taken by the entire nation.

The inverse of this equation is that the Jewish people are entirely identified with Moses. As Rashi articulates it: "The Jewish people are Moses." In addition to the people being *dependent* on Moses as noted earlier, the Rebbe understood this to be a statement of identity. The people become enfolded within the collective identity of the *nasi*.[120]

The Rebbe once expressed this unity of identity when speaking about the spiritual effect of immersing oneself in the Alter Rebbe's Torah teachings:

> This will cause not only *hitkashrut* (connection [between two separate things]) but actual cleaving and [even] oneness, to the point that the student transcends his individual identity and there remains only the reality of the Rebbe, the *nasi*.[121]

The ultimate expression of *hitkashrut* is that the *nasi* and the people see themselves as part of the same entity.

Conceptualizing the *nasi* and the people as a single entity comprised of different parts explains how *hitkashrut* accomplishes its goal of allowing each Jew to access the *yehida*, which is intricately bound

---

119. *Torat Menachem* 5747: 1, 504. For an elaborate analysis of what the people provide the *nasi*, see *Torat Menachem* 5748: 2, 497–98; ibid., 5752: 2, 338–40.
120. See, for example, *Torat Menachem* 5744: 5, 2492; *Likkutei Sihot* 4, *Hosafot*, 1321–22.
121. *Torat Menachem* 5722: 3, 262.

with the Divine Essence. As noted above, it is unreasonable to expect the ordinary Jew to reveal the essence of his soul, due to the natural and built-in propensity of ego and self-interest. However, the unity of the *nasi* and the people means that the extraordinary level of service of the *nasi* becomes accessible to the people, despite their own inherent limitations. Just as the *nasi* achieves total *bittul* and is simply a vehicle for the will of God, so too, the people, due to their oneness with the *nasi* are empowered to reach this unity with God as well.

In one example of how the Rebbe applied this idea, he related that the Rebbe Rashab was naturally attuned to the halakhic system:

> [He] accustomed his body to conduct itself according to *Shulhan Arukh*, by nature.... Just as the nature of a stone is that it falls from an elevated station to a lower one...not due to knowing intellectually that this is a law of nature, but because such is its [inherent] nature. And the conduct of a person in accord with Torah and its commandments must be in the same manner – that whatever is the will of the Creator is done by his body automatically, as if such is its nature.[122]

The Rebbe went on to rhetorically ask how ordinary people can be expected to act in accord with such a high degree of attunement to the will of God on an ordinary day of the year. The answer to this question, he explained, lies in appreciating the Torah as a singular collective unit, and especially though unity with the *nasi*:

> Through uniting with "the heads of the Jewish people whose souls are the head and the mind" (as is written in *Tanya*) – and being that he is a "servant" of the head and the mind – a modicum of the worship of the head and the mind is drawn to him as well (even though on his own part he has no relationship to this).[123]

---

122. Ibid., 5721: 2, 141.
123. Ibid., 142.

Here we see that the extraordinary spiritual and devotional gifts of the *nasi*, including their complete attunement with the will of God, are not simply held up as unreachable ideals to be admired from afar. Rather the identification of the *nasi* as the "head and mind" of the people means that they are a single entity, like one body, and the special qualities of the leader flow down from the head to all the other limbs of the body that are united with it, so that they can participate even in the loftiest of ideals, such as becoming a natural vehicle for the will of God.[124]

God, the *Nasi*, and the People

In one early talk the Rebbe brought together many of the above strands. Weaving together the *nasi*'s degree of *bittul* to God and the unity that is created between the *nasi* and the people through *hitkashrut*, the Rebbe reached an admittedly far-reaching conclusion.

He began the talk by noting that people go to their Rebbe to ask for assistance regarding both spiritual and material matters. After a small elaboration, the Rebbe directly challenged this entire practice:

> Some people ask: How can one ask things from a Rebbe? Is this not a problem of having an "intermediary"?[125]

While the Rebbe did not elucidate the question, he was presumably referring to Rambam's fifth principle of faith, which states that the sole object of worship should be God Himself, thereby disallowing even "using intermediaries to reach God."[126] How, then, can one ask a *Tzaddik* to improve one's spiritual or material life?

The Rebbe responded as follows:

> "The Jewish people, the Torah, and God are one." This does not mean that the Jewish people connect with Torah, which in turn is connected to God, but rather that they are literally one (*had mamash*). Similarly, the connection (*hitkashrut*) between

---

124. See also *Torat Menahem* 5745: 2, 1100; ibid., 5750: 1, 16, for similar formulations.
125. *Torat Menahem* 5710, 23–27.
126. Rambam, *Commentary to the Mishna*, Introduction to *Perek Helek*.

> Hasidim and a Rebbe is not as if there are two elements that are united, but they are all made literally as one. A Rebbe is not "an intermediary that separates" but rather "an intermediary that connects." Therefore, from the perspective of the Hasid, he, the Rebbe, and God are all one....
>
> Therefore, there is no room for questions regarding an "intermediary," since this is the Divine Essence itself as it placed itself in a body. This is related to the statement in the Zohar: "Who is the face of God? It is R. Shimon bar Yohai."[127]

Citing the Zoharic passage that in some way identifies a *Tzaddik* as the "face of God," the Rebbe, based on his reading of earlier texts, reached an extreme but logical conclusion. As we have seen, the *bittul* of a *Tzaddik* is so great that even in his physical form he is fully transparent to the Divine Essence, or in the Rebbe's terminology, "the Divine Essence itself as it is placed in a body."[128] At the same time, through *hitkashrut*, the *Tzaddik* and the people are seen as a single entity. Thus, due to a combination of the *bittul* of the *Tzaddik* to God and the *hitkashrut* of the person to the *Tzaddik*, which allows for the revelation of the person's *yehida*, the ordinary person is able to unite with God. Accordingly, once the relationship between God, the *Tzaddik*, and the person is so conceptualized, there is no problem of an intermediary.

The Revelation of the *Yehida* and Jewish Unity

The unity of the *nasi* with the people and his ability to elicit their *yehida* leads to another capacity of the *nasi* – his ability to unite the Jewish people. As we have seen, when a person transcends his limited self-perception and accesses his innermost essence, he can see the Jewish people as a single soul diffused into different bodies.[129] As such, the people can become united through their connection to the *nasi*.

---

127. *Torat Menahem* 5710, 25–26.
128. The Rebbe's assertion that the *nasi* is the "Divine Essence as it placed itself in a body" was accused as being heretical by various parties. See David Berger (2001), 159–74, and the sources cited in Alon Dahan (2014), 385, note 168. For a Chabad response, see R. Zalman I. Posner (Fall 2002).
129. See chapter 13, section "*Ahdut Yisrael* Perspective No. 1: Indivisible Unity."

The Nasi and the People

The Rebbe once spoke of the *nasi*'s role in facilitating Jewish unity based on the Talmud's description of the Jewish people's celebratory song at the banks of the Sea of Reeds.[130] The Torah states: "Then Moses and the Jewish people sang,"[131] demonstrating that everyone participated in the song. Why, then, does the Torah highlight that Moses sang? R. Nehemya[132] offered the following interpretation: Moses began the song alone but was soon joined by the rest of the Jewish people, who sang together in a state of prophetic inspiration.

While R. Nehemya's explanation deftly accounts for the verse's formulation, a conceptual question remains. If the Jewish people were able to sing such a complex song in unison, why was there a need for Moses to begin the song? Why could they all not start the song together?

The Rebbe explained that without Moses's opening, the Jewish people would never have achieved the requisite unity to prophesy together:

> For this form of absolute unity, in which the entirety of the Jewish people was as a single person … can only occur through Moses our teacher. And the explanation is that Moses was the head of the generation and the *nasi* of the generation; therefore, he included the entire generation as one, as Rashi says: "Moses is the Jewish people … the *nasi* is everything." This unity of the Jewish people (as they are included within Moses) is above division.[133]

The Rebbe elaborated that the people's connection to Moses as the *nasi* allowed each of them to access and reveal his own *yehida*. Once revealed, it became apparent that all Jews were parts of a single, indivisible soul, enabling them to share the same prophecy and sing together. Thus, the fact that "the *nasi* is everything" is intertwined with the *nasi*'s ability to help the people access their *yehida* and become completely unified.

---

130. *Likkutei Sihot* 31, Beshallah, no. 1.
131. Ex. 15:1.
132. Sota 30b.
133. *Likkutei Sihot* 31, Beshallah, se'if 2.

The *Yehida HaKelalit*

The *nasi*'s capacity to empower each person to access his own *yehida* justifies a unique title that Hasidism grants the *nasi*. As the Rebbe once wrote, "In the language of Hasidism, the *nasi* of the entire generation is referred to as the 'Collective *Yehida*' (*Yehida HaKelalit*) of the generation, as he reveals the *yehida* within each and every Jew."[134] More than a mere title, the Rebbe argued that defining the *nasi* as the *Yehida HaKelalit* has important ramifications. In his seminal talk "On the Essence of Hasidism," the Rebbe developed the connection between the *yehida* of the soul and the *yehida* of Torah, i.e., Hasidism. Both represent the innermost essence of the subject at hand and both are intimately bound with the Divine Essence itself.[135]

Therefore, as the *Yehida HaKelalit* of his generation, the *nasi* is connected not only with the *yehida* of each person, but also with teaching and disseminating Hasidism. The Rebbe clearly articulated this position in a footnote to the above-mentioned talk: "The heads of the Jewish people in each generation – the *nesi'im* who revealed Hasidism – they are the *Yehida HaKelalit* of the Jewish people."[136] Thus, the *nasi* of the generation, in addition to his complete *bittul* to God and dedication to the people, is a teacher of the *yehida* of the Torah, or Hasidism.

The *Mashiah* of the Generation

The fact that the *nasi* is the *Yehida HaKelalit* who teaches Hasidism is linked to yet another concept that the Rebbe associated with the *nasi*. A classic rabbinic tradition teaches that each generation contains a righteous person whom God can choose to be the *Mashiah* if the generation is worthy.[137] Throughout his talks, the Rebbe referred to this potential *Mashiah* as the "*Mashiah* of the generation."

In his talk "On the Essence of Hasidism," the Rebbe taught that *Mashiah*'s ultimate mission is to reveal the inner essence (*yehida*) of everything – the world, each person, and Torah – thereby demonstrating

---

134. Ibid., note 52.
135. See chapter 9, section "The Unifying Essence of Torah."
136. *Kuntres Inyana shel Torat HaHasidut*, note 43.
137. See, for example, *Shu"t Hatam Sofer*, vol. 6, *siman* 98.

The Nasi and the People

that all of creation constitutes varied expressions of the same singular Divine Essence. Accordingly, the *nasi* of the generation, who empowers the people to access their *yehida* and reveals the *yehida* of Torah in the form of Hasidism, is also the potential *Mashiah* of the generation. As the Rebbe once said:

> The *nasi* of the generation is also the *Mashiah* (the redeemer of the Jewish people) of the generation, just as [was true regarding] Moses our teacher (the first *nasi*) – "the first redeemer is also the final redeemer" (Exodus Rabba 2:4). As it is known, in every generation there is a person who is fitting based on his righteousness to be the redeemer, and when the time arrives God will reveal Himself and send him. It is logical that this [*Mashiah* of the generation] is the *nasi* of the generation.[138]

The Rebbe elaborated that Hasidism identifies the *yehida* of each person as "a spark of *Mashiah*" that is contained within each Jew. Through *hitkashrut* to the *nasi*, the *nasi* empowers each person to access and reveal their *yehida*, which discloses one more spark of *Mashiah* in this world. Therefore, the *nasi*'s role of revealing the *yehida* of each person is bit by bit creating the messianic reality in this world. The *nasi*, as the Yehida HaKelalit, is truly the potential *Mashiah* of the generation.[139]

We are now equipped to answer the opening question of this chapter as to whether the Rebbe's teachings regarding the essential unity of all Jews undermines the unique status and role of the leader. On the one hand, the *nasi* stands above the people, transcendent and lofty. But, ultimately, the goal of the *nasi* is to transcend his transcendence and empower the people to reveal their own *yehida* and the utter unity of the Jewish people. On the other hand, the people should realize the utter transcendence of the *nasi* and their dependence on him. They must connect themselves to him by studying his Torah, following his directives, and making his mission their mission. Ultimately, then, they as well will become totally transparent to the Divine Essence.

---

138. *Kuntres Beit Rabbenu SheBeVavel, se'if* 5.
139. See also *Torat Menahem* 5746:1, 342–43; ibid., 5747:1, 266.

The Demographics of Dira BaTahtonim

WHO IS THE *NASI*?

Having arrived at a description of the *nasi*, we must ask if it is possible to positively identify such a person. Regarding past generations, the Rebbe considered Moses, David, R. Yehuda HaNasi, R. Shimon bar Yohai, and Arizal as the *nesi'im* of their respective generations. More recent centuries seem to lack such singular luminaries. Who in recent history was the extension of Moses?

The President of Israel Is Not the "*Nasi*"

We know from a letter the Rebbe wrote to Yitzhak Ben-Zvi, the second president of the State of Israel, that the Rebbe did not use the term *nasi* freely. While the standard Hebrew title for the Israeli president is "*hanasi*," the Rebbe refrained from using this word and instead addressed the letter to *Mr.* Ben-Zvi. At the end of the letter, the Rebbe apologized for this possible slight and explained his rationale:

> Since my *heder* (kindergarten) days, and even before then, I have envisioned the future redemption, the redemption of the Jewish people from their final exile, such a redemption as would justify the suffering, decrees, and massacres of the Diaspora. Part of that glorious future and part of that redemption will be the *nasi* as king – not the *nasi* of one tribe, but one over whom there is no one but God his Lord (Horayot 11a). ... Therefore, it is so difficult for me to use this term with regard to the Jewish people at a time when…"the Jewish people are persecuted, oppressed, despised, harassed, and overcome by affliction" (Yevamot 47b). I could have used the word insincerely, but since I have heard that his honor is truthful, I did not want to be false (paraphrase of Yoma 69b), and his honor is forgiving.[140]

While not thrusting upon the president of Israel a long discourse on Hasidism, the basic contours of the Rebbe's letter match his doctrine of the *nasi*. The *nasi* is a messianic leader of the entire Jewish people who is directly connected to God.

---

140. *Iggerot Kodesh* 12, letter 4226.

The Nasi and the People

Based on the language of the letter, one might have concluded that the Rebbe did not think the title "*nasi*" was applicable at all during a time of "persecution and oppression." However, the Rebbe believed that in every generation there must be a bearer of the soul of Moses with all of the above qualities. Can these people be identified?

The Rebbes of Chabad

The Rebbe emphatically answered yes. In the two centuries preceding his tenure, the individuals who most exemplified the traits of the *nasi* were the Baal Shem Tov, the Maggid of Mezritch, the Alter Rebbe, and all the leaders of Chabad up to and including R. Yosef Yitzhak Schneersohn. They were leaders who completely banished their own egos, achieved absolute *bittul* to God, worked tirelessly and with self-sacrifice for the entirety of the Jewish people, and studied and spread the *yehida* of Torah – Hasidism. As such, the Rebbe regularly referred to all his predecessors as the *nasi* and the expansion of Moses in their generation.[141]

One clear articulation of this identification, with all its cosmic ramifications, appears in a talk about proper protocol at a Chabad wedding. The Rebbe urged future grooms to recite a specific *maamar* chosen by R. Yosef Yitzhak as a means of summoning and connecting with the souls of the previous leaders of Chabad. The Rebbe then said:

> One should add that this is relevant not only for members of our community but for all types of Jews … that also at their weddings they should recite the *maamar* entitled *Lekha Dodi*.… Because the life vitality of all the Jewish people, whoever they are, is drawn through the *nesi'im* … even those people who opposed them also receive their vitality through the *nesi'im*.[142]

---

141. See, for example, *Inyana shel Torat HaHasidut*, note 43, *Torat Menahem* 5750: 2, 183; ibid., 5744: 3, 1873; ibid., 5716: 2, 41; ibid., 5751: 4, 355; ibid., 5752: 1, 24–30; *Iggerot Kodesh* 3, letter 635; *Likkutei Sihot* 2, Behaalotekha, *se'if* 1.
142. *Torat Menahem* 5713: 2, 220.

The Rebbe continued that this was why the Alter Rebbe wanted Hasidism to be studied by all Jews and not just one specific group. The leaders of Chabad and their teachings are necessary channels for spiritual vitality for every Jew. The Rebbe concluded that in the end of time the wish of the Alter Rebbe will be fulfilled and all Jews will study Hasidism.

R. Yosef Yitzhak

The Rebbe mainly described this phenomenon in relation to his father-in-law, whom he referred to dozens of times as "the expansion of Moses of the generation." R. Yosef Yitzhak worked tirelessly on behalf of all Jews on issues as diverse as spreading Hasidism to providing material assistance for the needy.[143] His boundless love for Jews caused him to sacrifice his spiritual and material well-being to help them in whatever way possible, resulting in his being arrested by the Russian authorities for these efforts.[144]

Since R. Yosef Yitzhak was the *nasi* of his generation, his actions and life story take on national and even cosmic importance. For example, the Rebbe attributed tremendous significance to R. Yosef Yitzhak's arrest and subsequent release:

> The decree and imprisonment and the exile in 5687 endangered the continued observance of Judaism, Heaven forbid, as this was a concealment of the observance and spreading of Torah of the *nasi* of the generation and therefore of the entire Jewish people (for the "*nasi* is everything"), which upon this [the continued observance of Judaism] the existence of the Jewish people is dependent.[145]

The *nasi*'s imprisonment was not a private affair but rather endangered the continuity of Torah observance for the entire Jewish people. Accordingly, his release from the Russian prison also ignited and "released from

---

143. *Likkutei Sihot* 33, *Hukkat*, no. 2, *se'if* 7; *Torat Menahem* 5714: 2, 16–17.
144. *Likkutei Sihot* 2, *Hosafot*, 494; ibid., 33, *Korah*, no. 1, *se'if* 7.
145. *Torat Menahem* 5748: 3, 560.

prison" every Jew's inherent connection with God and serves as a precursor for the ultimate redemption.[146]

The Rebbe consistently applied this form of interpretation to the events of R. Yosef Yitzhak's life. He paralleled R. Yosef Yitzhak's intra-European and ultimately transatlantic sojourns with the ten exiles of the high court during the time of Roman persecution.[147] R. Yosef Yitzhak's establishment of 770 Eastern Parkway as his home and synagogue made it into the primary and central exilic synagogue, investing the walls of the building with a sanctity similar to that of the future *Beit HaMikdash*.[148] The Rebbe even connected the establishment of the United Nations in New York City to R. Yosef Yitzhak's efforts, while residing in New York, to purify the world.[149]

WHO IS THE *NASI* OF THE SEVENTH GENERATION?

If this was the Rebbe's view of his predecessor, one would presume that by accepting the mantle of Chabad leadership, the Rebbe himself became the generation's *nasi*. However, his talks from 1950 until his stroke in 1992 indicate a different self-perception. In his own rhetoric, the Rebbe himself hardly existed as a subject, while he constantly and consistently refers to R. Yosef Yitzhak as the current *nasi* of the generation, even decades after his passing.

R. Yosef Yitzhak's Continued Leadership

This curious state of affairs began in the year between R. Yosef Yitzhak's passing and R. Menahem Mendel Schneerson's official acceptance of the position of Rebbe. Channeling the kabbalistic and Chabad teachings regarding the eternality of a *Tzaddik*, the major thrust of the Rebbe's talks during this uncertain year was that his father-in-law's death had changed nothing fundamental about the leadership of Chabad or of the world. As the Rebbe said less than a month after his father-in-law's passing:

---

146. Ibid., 563.
147. *Kuntres Beit Rabbenu ShebeVavel*, *se'if* 6.
148. Ibid.
149. *Torat Menahem* 5752: 2, 270, note 26.

The Demographics of Dira BaTahtonim

> Those who knew the Rebbe [R. Yosef Yitzhak] during the thirty years of his leadership [*nesiuto*] know that the Rebbe will not abandon his Hasidim... the only difference is from our perspective: that in the past someone could have thought that when he entered into the Rebbe's presence to discuss his personal affairs he could hide certain things as he wanted. Now, however, it is clear that the Rebbe knows even the hidden matters, since in the past the Rebbe was enclothed in a physical body, as opposed to now when he transcends the limitations of the body and he is entirely spiritual.
>
> On the other hand, since "a *Tzaddik* who passes away is more present in all of the worlds than when he was alive,"[150] which means that "even in this world of action he is more present,"[151] it is certain that *the Rebbe still leads the entire world*, and the community of Hasidim in particular.[152] [Emphasis added.]

Even after his passing, R. Yosef Yitzhak was still present in this world and still led the generation. The Rebbe instructed the Hasidim to strengthen their *hitkashrut* with his father-in-law through a consciousness of connection,[153] studying his Torah[154] and following his past instructions with an emphasis on acting selflessly toward others.[155]

Even after the Rebbe's explicit acceptance of his own role as leader, he still referred to his father-in-law as the single *nasi* of the generation. The Hasidim still needed to have *hitkashrut*[156] and *bittul*[157] to R. Yosef Yitzhak through studying his Torah and fulfilling his directives of spreading Torah and acting selflessly toward others. All of Chabad's emissaries around the globe were, in fact, emissaries of R. Yosef Yitzhak.[158] And,

---

150. *Tanya, Iggeret HaKodesh*, section 27, based on the Zohar.
151. Ibid.
152. *Torat Menahem* 5710, 16.
153. See, for example, *Torat Menahem* 5710, 94.
154. *Torat Menahem* 5710, 13; *Iggerot Kodesh*, 3, letter 561.
155. *Torat Menahem* 5710, 62.
156. Ibid., 5716: 1, 139; ibid., 5717: 3, 131.
157. Ibid., 5750: 2, 183.
158. Ibid., 5748: 4, 154–56.

perhaps most importantly, it was R. Yosef Yitzhak who empowered each person to access their *yehida* and do the work necessary for the generation to bring *Mashiah*.[159]

Therefore, even as late as 1992, forty-two years after his father-in-law's passing, the Rebbe still emphasized:

> Each person needs to resolve to increase, with vigor and strength, the enterprises, Torah, and service of... my teacher, my father-in-law, the *nasi* of our generation... and in particular through *bittul* and *hitkashrut* to his eminence, my teacher and father-in-law, the *nasi* of our generation... who is inside each of us... whose main mission was "to bring the days of *Mashiah*," really and literally.[160]

Thus, in the Rebbe's rhetoric – and presumably consciousness – R. Yosef Yitzhak was a constant presence and the major force behind Chabad's growth and activities. By contrast, in his talks, the Rebbe did not carve out an independent space for himself. Yet, from a practical standpoint, it was clearly the Rebbe and not his father-in-law who was leading Chabad, and presumably, world Jewry, as the *nasi* of the generation.

A Unified Persona?

What is the meaning of this strange situation? While the Rebbe never explicitly addressed this issue, on a few rare occasions he hinted at an approach. It seems that the Rebbe viewed himself entirely as an extension of his father-in-law. For example, just one month after assuming the leadership of Chabad, the Rebbe echoed something his father-in-law had said about his own father and predecessor, the Rashab:

> After the Rashab passed away, his eminence, my teacher and father-in-law, once said that he did not want to say about his father that "his soul is in *Eden* (paradise)," as "why should I say that his soul is in *Eden* if it is easier to say that his soul is in me?"

---

159. Ibid., 5752: 2, 339–40.
160. Ibid., 5752: 2, 120.

[The Rebbe concluded regarding his father-in-law,] similarly, I do not say, "His soul is in *Eden*," but rather that his soul is in me.[161]

It seems that the Rebbe viewed himself as completely *batel* to his own Rebbe – his father-in-law – to the extent that the latter literally continued to live through his son-in-law and successor.[162]

The Rebbes and the *Sefirot*

A deeper understanding of the mechanics of this unification of the sixth and seventh Rebbes requires further background to the Rebbe's understanding of the previous six leaders of Chabad. While they all functioned as the *nasi* of their generation and were completely effaced before the Divine Essence, each Rebbe still had his own distinct style. On several occasions, the Rebbe cited a tradition from his father-in-law that each of the previous leaders of Chabad represents a different *sefira* that was associated with his particular mode of service.[163]

While the exact alignment of Rebbes and *sefirot* varies from citation to citation, the Rebbe was convinced that his father-in-law represented the sixth of the lower *sefirot*: *yesod* (foundation).[164] This *sefira* is associated with the biblical figure of Yosef (the first name of his

---

161. Ibid., 5711: 1, 326.
162. Another possible statement of the Rebbe in this direction is found in *Torat Menahem* 5713: 1, 264. There, it is recorded that the Rebbe told a Hasid: "It is the same Rebbe with the same behaviors, but he is enclothed in different clothing – brighter clothing...therefore what does it matter to you? The main thing is that it is the same Rebbe." It is possible to interpret this statement as entirely referring to R. Yosef Yitzhak, and the "brighter clothing" that R. Yosef Yitzhak now has being the spiritual clothing that replaced his physical body upon his passing. Accordingly, the Rebbe was simply affirming the continuity of his father-in-law's leadership, which he did dozens of times. However, the Rebbe's reference to "the same behaviors" seems to indicate that he was referring to a person living within a physical body. If this is correct then the import of the Rebbe's statement was that R. Yosef Yitzhak continued to be the Rebbe, though now enclothed within a new physical body – that of the Rebbe.
163. *Torat Menahem* 5711:1, 106; ibid., 5712: 1, 33–35; ibid., 5729: 1, 163.
164. Ibid., 5729:1, 163–64; ibid., 5718: 1, 124–25; ibid., 5750: 2, 261, note 124.

The Nasi and the People

father-in-law), who was the *Tzaddik* that served as the foundation of the world (*tzaddik yesod olam*).

In the cosmic order, *yesod* is gendered masculine and is supposed to actively inject the divine flow into *malkhut* – the seventh and lowest of the lower *sefirot*.[165] This unification of *yesod* and *malkhut* brings the full breadth of the divine light into the lowest level, triggering the ultimate rectification.

Based on this structure, it would make sense that the Rebbe, as the leader of the seventh generation, should personify the *sefira* of *malkhut*. In fact, despite the Rebbe's silence on this matter, many of his Hasidim did make this identification and considered him to embody the *sefira* of *malkhut*.[166] As we have seen, the role of *malkhut* is to receive, reveal, and practicalize the flow from the higher *sefirot*, similar to the Rebbe, who practically implemented Chabad teachings in heretofore unimaginable proportions.

Chabad teachings emphasize that the only way that *malkhut* can properly receive and actualize the divine flow is through *bittul* – total effacement to the *sefirot* that precede it.[167] If we are to apply this theme to the seventh Rebbe as well, perhaps we have an approach to understand the paradoxical nature of the Rebbe's stance toward his own leadership.

Presumably, the Rebbe recognized that he was the leader of the generation and, in consonance with the *sefira* of *malkhut*, he focused his leadership on practical implementation. In his own self-perception, however, his leadership was suffused with a sense of complete effacement before and unification with the previous six Rebbes, and with his father-in-law, *yesod*, in particular. Despite appearances, due to the Rebbe's level of *bittul*, his father-in-law still functioned as the *nasi* of the seventh generation.[168]

---

165. Aryeh Kaplan (1990), 67.
166. See, for example, Levi Yitzhak Ginsberg, "HaRebbe Raayatz Sefirat HaYesod Mehaber Shamayim VaAretz"; Chaim Dalfin (1998), 132–33.
167. See chapter 15, section "Philosophic Background: The Paradox of *Malkhut*."
168. The Rebbe was very circumspect about his own self-perception. However, on several occasions he arguably indicated a belief in his own extraordinary powers. See, for example, Herbert Weiner, "Alone with Moses," www.chabad.org/574972.

The Generation of *Malkhut*

There is one more important element to add in this context. Despite the fact that the Rebbe did not identify himself as the personification of the *sefira* of *malkhut*, he did grant this title to the entirety of the seventh generation.

In a talk marking the fiftieth anniversary of his own arrival to America, the Rebbe noted that R. Yosef Yitzhak lived for seventy years and settled in the last decade of his life at 770 Eastern Parkway. This confluence of "full sevens" in the life of R. Yosef Yitzhak is important, as "he gives strength to the seventh generation which comes after him (and which corresponds to the *sefira* of *malkhut*)."[169] The seventh generation receives the necessary strength for its unique mission from R. Yosef Yitzhak. The Rebbe continued that "it was known" that his father-in-law corresponded to the *sefira* of *yesod* and "our entire generation – all of the men, women, and children – are the *sefira* of *malkhut*."[170] Accordingly, the seventh generation (*malkhut*) receives its vitality from R. Yosef Yitzhak (*yesod*), giving each of them the strength to fulfill their individual and collective mission.

This democratization of the seventh generation's mission is a hallmark of the Rebbe's management style. While he certainly wanted his instructions to be implemented, he mostly refrained from appointing specific people to specific missions. Rather, he would speak of the need and urgency of a specific project and then leave it up to anyone who would rise from the ranks to take initiative.

The Rebbe's favoring empowerment rather than dependency was so crucial to the seventh generation that he highlighted it on his first night as the leader of Chabad. Immediately after delivering his first *maamar*, the Rebbe said:

> Listen, Jews! The leaders of Chabad demanded that Hasidim must achieve things themselves on their own and not rely on the Rebbe. This is the difference between the approach of Polish Hasidism and the approach of Chabad. The Polish approach was based

---

169. *Torat Menahem* 5751: 3, 382.
170. Ibid., note 73.

on the verse "And the righteous will live by his faith" (*vetzaddik be'emunato yihyeh*) (Hab. 2:4), which can also be read as "The *tzaddik* will give life through faith in him" (*vetzaddik be'emunato yehayeh*). Therefore, we all need to work, with our 248 limbs and the 365 sinews of the body and the soul....

I do not, Heaven forbid, recuse myself from helping as much as I am able.... It is obvious that the fashioning of a Dira BaTahtonim requires the participation of all of us, of every Jew. Each person needs to work in order to fulfill his mission.[171]

As we will see, the theme of personal responsibility intensified both theoretically and practically in the Rebbe's later years.[172]

In summary, as the leader of the seventh generation, which is parallel to the *sefira* of *malkhut*, the Rebbe's leadership embodied the seemingly conflicting postures of this *sefira*. On the one hand, practically, he served as the "king," directing a global operation and expecting his directives to be fulfilled. Simultaneously, though, he practiced the *bittul* of *malkhut*, both toward his father-in-law and toward the people of his own generation, creating no space for himself in the constructs of his own talks.

CONCLUSION

The Rebbe depicted the ideal Jewish leader as embodying what seems to be a paradox. On the one hand, the *nasi* is the clear and unequivocal leader of the generation. The people need to follow him, and they achieve an optimal relationship with God and their own true selves only through a connection with him. Simultaneously, though, the *nasi* must epitomize *bittul* and the empowerment of others. He is a vehicle through which each and every person individually and the generation collectively can come face-to-face with the Divine Essence. It seems that this was the type of leadership that the Rebbe sought to implement.

---

171. *Yemei Bereshit* (1993), 386–87.
172. See chapter 20, section "Personal Redemption."

Secondary Literature Consulted for Chapter 17, "The *Nasi* and the People"

Alon Dahan, *Goel Aharon*, 382–90.

Nahum Greenwald, "Deveikut VeHitkashrut LeTzaddik lefi Shittat HaHasidut."

Yitzhak Kraus, *HaShevi'i*, 41–44.

Yosef Yitzhak Meislish, *HaTekufa VehaGeula BeMishnato shel HaRebbe MiLubavitch*, 46–59.

Jacob Immanuel Schochet, *Chasidic Dimensions*, 81–124.

Part 5

Contemporary Issues

Chapter 18

The Secularization and Spiritualization of Science

While the friction between Torah and science has existed for many centuries, modernity elevated these conflicts to unprecedented levels. With the advent of the scientific method, a new caste of confident scientists systematically brought human knowledge to new horizons. Many of their findings about issues ranging from the age of the universe to the origin of rodents seemed to contradict the assumptions of the biblical and talmudic systems. Understandably, these direct points of discord caused much confusion in the observant Jewish community.

Progress in scientific theory was accompanied by a technological revolution that radically changed the texture of modern life. Electricity lit up the dark night. Telephones and radios allowed for instant global communication. The atom bomb decimated a city in a moment. These inventions created a public image of science as an all-powerful force while religion seemed to be archaic, not only unable to generate these advancements but even impotent to provide perspective on the meaning of these wide-ranging shifts.

As one who studied science in Berlin and Paris with several of the world's leading scientific theoreticians, the Rebbe felt that he had a particular responsibility to clarify the relationship between science and Torah. He vociferously and prolifically defended Torah against the popular conception that modern science could in any way displace the authority of Torah. In addition, he created a Torah-based lens that endowed advancements in theoretical and applied science with religious significance. His approach to both sides of the relationship between Torah and science can be seen to stem from the same foundational principles that we have seen at work in his thought more broadly.

BACKGROUND: ORTHODOX APPROACHES TO CONFLICTS BETWEEN TORAH AND SCIENCE

Mapping the Options

To appreciate the range of Orthodox Jewish responses to contradictions between science and Torah we will hone in on one of the major flashpoints – the age of the universe and the related theory of evolution. While a traditional understanding of the opening chapter of Genesis and its rabbinic commentaries is that the world was created less than six thousand years ago over the span of six days, the overwhelming consensus of the scientific community is that the universe is billions of years old and that life on earth evolved over millions of years. How is an Orthodox Jewish thinker to respond to this conflict?

There were three basic responses in the Orthodox Jewish community: rejection, synthesis, and the splitting of the realms.[1] Some rabbis contended that a scientific claim that contradicts the Torah must perforce be incorrect. R. Moshe Feinstein, for example, without relating to the science itself, refers to textbooks that portray the scientific community's approach to cosmology as "books of heresy from which it is forbidden to learn."[2]

By contrast, some rabbis were convinced by the claims of the scientific community and attempted to demonstrate that these conclusions

---

1. For broad surveys of this topic, see Natan Slifkin (2006), 136–234, and Ira Robinson (2006), 163–224.
2. *Iggerot Moshe, Yoreh De'ah* 3:73.

were in consonance with the biblical and rabbinic tradition. As one might expect, this enterprise often entails a reinterpretation of biblical verses and/or reliance on obscure midrashic passages. An advocate of this approach was R. Yisrael Lipshitz (1782–1860), who attributed the existence of dinosaur fossils to the midrash that "God built worlds and destroyed them"[3] before creating our current world.[4] Similarly, R. Eli Munk (1910–1981) argued that the word "day" in the Torah's creation story can refer to eons of time.[5]

A third approach, championed by R. Avraham Yitzhak Kook (1865–1935), sought to separate science and Torah. According to R. Kook, God did not intend the Torah to be a science textbook but rather to convey spiritual and moral truths. Therefore, it is possible that when God wrote the Torah, He "sacrificed" scientific accuracy for the sake of an optimal articulation of the Torah's ultimate spiritual message.[6]

Situating the Rebbe

The Rebbe was an enthusiast of the scientific method and the advancements of modern science, yet he firmly believed that the conclusions of scientists should never lead to the reinterpretation of a verse or a halakha out of its simple meaning. He perceived the other approaches as being rooted in a "fear"[7] of science that is based on mistaken assumptions about science's ability to conclusively establish absolute truth. Accordingly, in instances when the conclusions of scientists conflicted with the simple understanding of a statement of the Torah, the Rebbe fully adopted the Torah and rejected the consensus of the scientific community.

The Rebbe's affirmation of the Torah's truth over the consensus of the scientific community stems from two interrelated points: (1) his philosophical understanding of the nature of God, the Torah, and the world, and (2) his scientific education, which led him to appreciate the

---

3. Ecclesiastes Rabba 3:11.
4. *Derush Or HaHayyim*, printed in *Tiferet Yisrael* following Tractate Sanhedrin.
5. Eli Munk (1974), 49–50.
6. *Iggerot HaRe'iya* 1, 105; *Eder HaYakar*, 37–38; *Maamarei HaRe'iya*, 10–11.
7. *Iggerot Kodesh* 15, letter 5449.

THE NATURE OF TORAH AND THE WORLD
An Unnecessary Order

scientific method's tremendous potential but also recognize its inherent limitations.

The Rebbe was a firm believer in the order of the spiritual and physical worlds. As an heir to the Chabad tradition, he fully affirmed the complex kabbalistic system of internal laws and logic that govern the interactions of cosmic spiritual forces. Similarly, as a student of the sciences, he embraced the scientific order of the universe.

However, a foundational axiom in the Rebbe's thought is that nothing about the spiritual or physical order is an absolute necessity. On various occasions, the Rebbe cited earlier authorities that describe God as "the impossibility of impossibilities" (*nimna hanimnaot*), meaning that God is completely unbounded by any structure or rules. Referring particularly to the Divine Essence that completely transcends any description, the Rebbe once said:

> Since all of the rules of logic were created by Him, may He be blessed, it is understood that He who created all of these definitions is not bound by them, Heaven forbid, as the Rashba wrote in his well-known responsa (*siman* 418) that God is "the impossibility of impossibilities," meaning to say that for the Divine Essence there is nothing that is impossible.[8]

This tenet shatters the theoretical grounding of the basic axioms of human, Jewish, and Chabad worldviews. God could have made fish that fly or a triangle with four sides.[9] In addition, despite the compelling nature of Rambam's logic, God could have made a world that was not contingent on Him,[10] or have constricted Himself to a bodily form.[11]

---

8. *Likkutei Sihot* 27, *Hosafot*, 252.
9. See *Guide for the Perplexed* 3:15 that God cannot construct a square whose diagonal is shorter than its side.
10. *Likkutei Sihot* 27, *Hosafot*, 253–54.
11. See *Likkutei Sihot* 15, *Lekh Lekha*, no. 2, note 33. This is part of the Rebbe's defense for the "great ones" cited by Raavad (*Mishneh Torah*, *Hilkhot Teshuva* 3:7) who

The Secularization and Spiritualization of Science

Similarly, He could have avoided manifesting Himself through the ten *sefirot*[12] or have totally abandoned the created worlds (*tzimtzum kifshuto*),[13] despite the Alter Rebbe's vigorous logical proofs against this approach.[14]

If so, why do intellectual disciplines – secular and religious alike – strive to uncover the inner logic and rules of the cosmic systems? And more problematically, how do they succeed in their endeavors? The only answer is that God willed that the cosmos should function in a manner that can be rationally analyzed and understood. As the Rebbe once said about the kabbalistic system:

> Since God is omnipotent, it is obvious that creation could have occurred in many completely different ways. And God chose (or, in a different formulation – God *desired*); in the language of our Rebbes: "God's will arose that this world should be in the way that it is now" (*Likkutei Torah Torat Shmuel* 5731: 1, 302) and "It is His will that anything that can be in accordance with [human] logic should be logical" (*Sefer HaMaamarim* 5658, 120).[15]

Similar to God's initial decision to create the world, the spiritual and physical laws that govern the universe are simply the manner in which God *chose* to manifest Himself.[16] It is part of the same inscrutable will of God that motivated creation.

The Torah as the Tool for Creation

The notion that all the laws of spirituality and science are the result of God's inscrutable will forms the foundation of the Rebbe's argument that

---

believed in God's corporeality.
12. *Torat Menahem* 5748: 1, 551–54.
13. *Iggerot Kodesh* 20, letter 7465; *Likkutei Sihot* 15, Lekh Lekha, no. 2, note 33; *HaMelekh BiMesibo*, vol. 2, 217–22.
14. *Tanya, Shaar HaYihud VehaEmuna*, ch. 7. Similarly, see *Torat Menahem* 5751: 3, 398, note 48, which says that God could have established a world without the need for perpetual recreation (elucidated in *Tanya, Shaar HaYihud VehaEmuna*, ch. 2).
15. *Torat Menahem* 5748: 1, 552.
16. See chapter 7, section "The Basis for the Divine Essence's Choices."

the Torah is the ultimate source of truth regarding all aspects of reality. This is further grounded in the midrashic teaching that God "used" the Torah to create the world:

> The Torah says, "I was the artisan's tool of God" (Prov. 8:30). In the way of the world, a king of flesh and blood who builds a castle does not do so from his own knowledge, but rather from the knowledge of an architect, and the architect does not build it from his own knowledge, but rather he has scrolls and books in order to know how to make rooms and doorways. So too, God gazed into the Torah and created the world.[17]

While much Chabad ink was spilled in precisely interpreting this midrash,[18] its basic import is clear. When God's internal desire arose to create the world, He "found" the blueprint for this creation in the Torah. Torah is thus the primary expression of God's will which forms the basis of the created worlds with all their structure. Therefore, the Torah is the ultimate source from which the laws of nature flow, and it can be read as the ultimate authoritative account of nature itself.

An All-Comprehensive Torah

This conception of Torah as the primary expression of God's will which created all of reality immediately disqualifies the third approach above, which limits Torah to providing moral and spiritual truths but not scientific ones. As the basis of creation, Torah is definitionally the most authoritative source of information for all aspects of the created worlds.

The Rebbe once forcefully expressed this idea of the all-encompassing nature of Torah in a conversation with a group of scientists. One scientist asked the Rebbe for his opinion on the "mutual influence" of Torah and science. The Rebbe's response was an unequivocal rejection of the questioner's assumptions:

---

17. Genesis Rabba 1:1.
18. See the references in Nahum Greenwald (Nisan 5770), 27–28.

The Secularization and Spiritualization of Science

Monotheism is a concept that does not tolerate mutual influences, as God is present in every place and every item in the world, and "there is no place bereft of Him".... In truth, this [mutual] influence can never occur, as all the true sciences are included in the Torah and flow from it.[19]

Torah and science are not two distinct disciplines that run parallel to each other with specific points of interaction and influence. Rather, Torah is the primary and all-encompassing body of divine knowledge from which all the facts and rules of created reality emerge, including those discovered through empirical investigation by scientific researchers. Similarly, the Rebbe repudiated the assertion that the Torah is not a source of scientific facts. Without calling him out by name, he termed such a proclamation by Professor Yeshayahu Leibowitz[20] a "doubly thick darkness"[21] and a complete misunderstanding of Torah's fundamental nature.

The Rebbe pointed to a talmudic story as a proof that traditional rabbinic literature assumes that all knowledge is sourced in the Torah:

> Caesar said to R. Yehoshua: "After how long a gestation does a snake bear young?" He answered: "After seven years." [Caesar countered:] "But the sages of Athens have mated snakes and they give birth after three years! [R. Yehosha answered:] "Those snakes were already pregnant for four years.[22]

Clearly, R. Yehoshua felt that it was within his purview to argue with the elders of Athens on issues of science. From the continuation of the passage it is clear that R. Yehoshua derived his number from biblical exegesis and not from external sources.

Here are the Rebbe's comments on this passage:

---

19. *Emuna UMadda: Iggerot Kodesh MiKevod Kedushat Admor Shelita MiLubavitch* (1977), 139.
20. Characteristically, the Rebbe did not refer to Yeshayahu Leibowitz by name. However, see Yirmiyahu Branover (2000), 102, note 4, who makes this identification.
21. *Sihot Kodesh* 5732: 2, 439.
22. Bekhorot 8b.

It is not merely a story from ancient history; it is a part of Torah. Ravina and R. Ashi, compilers of the Talmud, chose to include this anecdote as a portion of the Oral Torah. Thus it became a part of Torah, which derives from the word *horaa*, directive. One of the directives that may be derived... is a more general lesson: Torah has insight and information about everything in our world, as there is no entity without its source in Torah.[23]

This reinforces the more general point: Torah is the basis of all reality and therefore an authoritative source of information about the natural world as well.[24]

THE TRUTH OF TORAH AND OF SCIENCE

As Torah expresses the divine will which created the universal order, it is perforce the gold standard of absolute truth. By contrast, the findings of science reflect the attempt of the limited human mind to reconstruct aspects of that order. While these attempts are valiant and valuable, there will always be aspects of reality that are definitionally beyond the grasp of scientific inquiry or which are yet to be fully understood. As time goes on, after all, scientists continue to discover more and more about the natural world, and it is quite clear that the picture is far from complete. Accordingly, it is obvious that on points of conflict one should prefer the Torah's account to that of the scientific community.

In particular, the Rebbe highlighted two areas that even scientists concede are beyond their field of examination: foundational axioms and absolute conclusions.

The Axioms of Science

The Rebbe elaborated on the nature of scientific axioms in an early letter. Focusing on the rabbinic dictum "If anyone tells you there is knowledge

---

23. *Sihot Kodesh* 5732, 440. Translation adapted from www.chabad.org/112693.
24. For similar sentiments based on the principle that God gazed into the Torah to create the world, see *Torat Menahem* 5744: 1, 95–98; ibid., 5748: 4, 175–77.

among non-Jews, you may believe it... but if one tells you there is Torah among them, do not believe it,"[25] the Rebbe commented:

> This terse statement contains an indication of the radical difference between general science and the Jewish religion....
>
> The cardinal difference is this: Science, in general, has two weak points: First, it is based on certain postulates which science cannot substantiate or prove satisfactorily and which consequently may be accepted, rejected, or substituted by contrary postulates. In other words, the entire structure of science rests, at bottom, on unscientific principles, or, better, on premises which cannot be scientifically substantiated.[26]

As philosophers of science note, modern science is built on axioms that remain unproven. For example, scientific inquiry assumes the existence of an objective reality that is shared by all rational observers. While this assertion is reasonable and useful, it is not objectively provable. The Rebbe felt that this "weakness" is rooted in the limitations of the human mind.[27]

The Torah, however, suffers from no such weakness:

> Inasmuch as the Torah is not the product of man, but is divinely revealed at Sinai... being given by God the Absolute, its foundations are likewise absolute truths, not mere suppositions.... That is why the Torah is called *Toras Emes* – the Law of Truth – for its teachings are absolute and its foundations are not postulates, but absolute truths.[28]

---

25. Lamentations Rabba 2:13.
26. Letter dated 10 Sivan 5712 (1952), published at www.lchaimweekly.org/lchaim/5770/1121.htm, cited in Chaim Miller (2007), 366.
27. Similarly, see *Torat Menahem* 5746: 3, 289, where the Rebbe noted that even as scientists discover the rules of nature they will never be able to fathom *why* the rules exist as they do.
28. Continuation of letter dated 10 Sivan 5712, cited above.

Instead of resting on unverified axioms, the Torah itself is the absolute bedrock foundation of truth.

The Conclusions of Science

The Rebbe felt that just as science suffers from a lack of absoluteness regarding its foundational axioms, it similarly cannot reach definite conclusions. Until the early twentieth century, scientists perceived their findings as absolute laws of nature. However, as the Rebbe frequently reminded his interlocutors, the discoveries in theoretical physics of the early twentieth century (which he witnessed firsthand while studying under Erwin Schrödinger at the University of Berlin) humbled scientists, preventing them from making claims of absolute certainty.

Once, when writing to a group of Orthodox scientists, the Rebbe cited this internal check on modern science as a reason to avoid reinterpreting the Torah in instances of conflict with science:

> What is even more surprising – and as yet I have not received any answer from those with whom I had occasion to speak on the matter – is that the said apologetic attitude [of some Orthodox Jews toward the Torah in relation to science] is completely out of harmony with the view of contemporary science. If a century ago, when scientists still spoke in terms of absolute truths, it was understandable why a person who wished to adhere to his faith might have been embarrassed to challenge "scientific" claims, this is no longer the case in our day and age. Contemporary science no longer lays claim to absolutes; the principle of probability now reigns supreme, even in practical science as applied in common daily experiences.[29]

The Rebbe traced this contemporary attitude of modern scientists to the findings of Werner Heisenberg:

---

29. From the Rebbe's letter to the Association of Orthodox Jewish Scientists, retrieved from www.chabad.org/112235.

The Secularization and Spiritualization of Science

> Need one remind our Orthodox Jewish scientists, who still feel embarrassed about some "old-fashioned" Torah truths, in the face of scientific hypotheses, that Heisenberg's "principle of indeterminacy" has finally done away with the traditional scientific notion that cause and effect are mechanically linked, so that it is now quite unscientific to hold that one event is an inevitable consequence of another, but only most probable? The nineteenth-century dogmatic, mechanistic, and deterministic attitude of science is gone. The modern scientist no longer expects to find Truth in science. The current and universally accepted view of science itself is that science must reconcile itself to the idea that whatever progress it makes, it will always deal with probabilities; not with certainties or absolutes.[30]

Similarly, the Rebbe once wrote to Dr. Cyril Domb, an Orthodox professor of theoretical physics, about contradictions between Torah and science:

> As a matter of fact, the whole problem is based on a popular misconception as to what science is. Where there is a true understanding of what science really is, there is no room for such confusion. For, as it is well known but too often overlooked, the sciences, even the so-called exact sciences, are at bottom nothing more than assumptions, work hypotheses, and theories which are only "probable," as indeed you pointed out in your article, but all too briefly.[31]

Once again, this is to be contrasted with Torah, which, as a divine body of knowledge, provides absolute facts: "On the other hand, religious truths are definitive and categorical."[32]

---

30. See also *Iggerot Kodesh* 13, letter 4414, where the Rebbe references Heisenberg's principle in a letter to R. Yitzhak Herzog, the first chief rabbi of Israel, who held a doctorate in chemistry.
31. Retrieved from www.chabad.org/664344.
32. Ibid.

Rejecting Apologetic Reinterpretation

In light of these fundamental differences between Torah and science, the Rebbe rejected reinterpreting the Torah to reconcile it with science. Such a method would be called for if we were faced with two equally valid but seemingly contradictory truths. Here, however, the certainty of the Torah's truths far outweighs the findings of science. In this context, the Rebbe frequently employed the talmudic formula *bari veshema bari adif*, "When there is a certain claim and an uncertain claim, the certain claim prevails,"[33] fully affirming the absolute truth of the Torah over scientific findings.[34]

One extreme illustration of the Rebbe's non-apologetic approach was his response to the issue of spontaneous generation. In various contexts, rabbinic literature seems to confirm the prevalent pre-modern notion that certain insects and rodents are produced from non-living matter. When someone asked the Rebbe about the claim that "there is a consensus in biology that [spontaneous generation] is not true," he responded: "[Spontaneous generation] is the approach of the Torah … and is the basis of several halakhot … all consensuses are speculative."[35]

Elsewhere,[36] the Rebbe elaborated that scientists have no method of proving beyond a shadow of a doubt that a specific egg emerged from a living parent insect and not from non-living matter. Since the scientific consensus glosses over a gap in the relevant information, there is no reason to disavow the Torah's account of spontaneously generating insects and rodents.

Irresponsible Scientists

Beyond the inherent limitations of modern scientific inquiry, the Rebbe felt that certain scientific consensuses were based on clearly irresponsible

---

33. See, for example, Ketubot 12b.
34. See, for example, the above letter to Professor Domb; *Iggerot Kodesh* 15, letter 5378; ibid., letter 5449.
35. *Iggerot Kodesh* 19, letter 7242*.
36. *Emuna UMadda*, appendix no. 2, 131–32. See also a letter that is available at crownheights.info/letter-and-spirit/511076/letter-spirit-genetic-mutations-4/. For a longer analysis that contextualizes the Rebbe's approach within a survey of approaches to this issue, see Chaim Rapoport (11 Nisan 5764).

speculation. One conspicuous example was the issue of the age of the universe. When relating to this issue, the Rebbe would first refer to the general notion that scientific consensus cannot be conceived of as absolute truth. Then he would challenge science's ability to even reach a conclusion with a high level of probability when it comes to an event that took place in the deepest past, given that it does not have any way to assess these events empirically, in real time.

For example, the Rebbe once outlined two methods of inference that scientists employ:

> (1) The method of interpolation (as distinguished from extrapolation), whereby, knowing the reaction under two extremes, we attempt to infer what the reaction might be at any point between the two; and
> (2) The method of extrapolation, whereby inferences are made beyond a known range, on the basis of certain variables within the known range. For example, suppose we know the variables of a certain element within a temperature range of 0 to 100, and on the basis of this we estimate what the reaction might be at 101, 200, or 2000.
> Of the two methods, the second (extrapolation) is clearly the more uncertain. Moreover, the uncertainty increases with the distance away from the known range and with the decrease of this range. Thus, if the known range is between 0 and 100, our inference at 101 has a greater probability than at 1001.[37]

Since no scientists witnessed the cosmological events they profess to describe with factual certainty, but arrive at their hypotheses through extrapolation, their conclusions cannot be considered definitive: "Let us note at once that all speculation regarding the origin and age of the world comes within the second and weaker method, that of extrapolation." As a proof to this, he would further note that the various schools

---

37. Letter retrieved from www.chabad.org/112083. This letter was published in *Challenge: Torah Views on Science and Its Problems*, ed. Aryeh Carmell and Cyril Domb (New York: Feldheim, 1976), 142–49.

of science (astronomy, geology, archaeology, and so on) reach widely differing conclusions, based on "conclusive" proofs, regarding the age of the universe.

An additional weakness that the Rebbe would point to regarding the conclusion of scientists about the age of the universe was its inability to explain the origins of matter itself.

> Consider, for example, the so-called evolutionary theory of the origin of the world, which is based on the assumption that the universe evolved out of existing atomic and subatomic particles which, by an evolutionary process, combined to form the physical universe and our planet, on which organic life somehow developed also by an evolutionary process, until Homo sapiens emerged. It is hard to understand why one should readily accept the creation of atomic and subatomic particles in a state which is admittedly unknowable and inconceivable, yet should be reluctant to accept the creation of planets, or organisms, or a human being, as we know these to exist.[38]

In other words, while scientists developed elaborate theories of how the universe developed and became more complex over the course of billions of years, these scientists admit that there is much uncertainty about the original formation of atoms.

Based on the above weaknesses in the scientific account of the age of the universe, the Rebbe concluded that it is obvious that the biblical account, which is stamped with the certainty of divine authority, should be preferred.[39]

The Truth of Torah
According to the Rebbe, since the Torah is absolute truth it (1) has a normative, or prescriptive, weight, and (2) is eternally true and applicable.

---

38. Letter published at www.chabad.org/112083.
39. For similar letters, see *Iggerot Kodesh* 13, letter 4414; ibid., 7, letter 1996; ibid., 15, letter 5449.

The Rebbe directly contrasted each of these elements with the findings of science.

The Normativity of Torah

The Rebbe felt that the contingent nature of scientific axioms prevents science from generating normative obligations. Since the axioms themselves are unproven, a person can theoretically choose to accept them or not. Moreover, even if a person accepts the axioms, science definitionally reports only on relationships between different factors ("cause A" will generate "result B") but can never tell a person if the result is desirable. In the Rebbe's words:

> There are two points here: (1) It is the person's prerogative whether to accept the axioms or not, and (2) also in the case that he does accept them, there is nothing to compel him to act in a manner that is consistent with the results of the particular method. For all the method says is, "If you act this way, the result will be such and such." But if the person is willing to accept the adverse consequences, there is nothing that compels him not to act in any way he desires. In other words, science does not instruct life, but only narrates – as a sort of fortune teller – a sequence of events, maintaining that according to past experience, and based upon certain axioms which we fancy to accept as true, things will unfold in such and such a manner.[40]

Science's limited scope of discovering the natural order of cause and effect cannot morally obligate a person.

The Rebbe concluded the above letter by contrasting the descriptive nature of science with the prescriptive nature of Torah:

---

40. *Iggerot Kodesh* 6, 1662. Translation is adapted from www.chabad.org/435115. For an early articulation of some of these ideas, see *Reshimot, hoveret* 3, 45–47 (adapted at chabad.org/1211029), where the Rebbe recorded notes for a lecture he delivered at a mathematics conference.

> Utterly different is our holy Torah. As the wisdom of the Absolute Existence – the Almighty – it is absolute. Its axioms, as well as the rules that dictate the manner in which laws are to be derived from these axioms, are utterly true. And since this is the wisdom of the Creator of the entire world, man included, it is self-understood that these laws obligate a person to act in concurrence with them, and in no other way.[41]

The truths of the Torah are not simply descriptions of the world as seen and analyzed from the limited perspective of humankind, but rest on the axiomatic foundation of the Absolute. And since the Torah is the blueprint for the world, which was created with a divine purpose, every aspect of Torah generates an obligation to conform with the divine purpose that it reveals. It is the Torah's rootedness in God, that engenders its ability to legislate practical action in the world that God created.

The Eternality of Torah

The Torah's divine nature also leads to the eternality of its truths and norms. The Rebbe explained that this flows from a basic axiom regarding the nature of Torah: "Just as it is impossible that there be a change in the 'self' of God, Heaven forbid, similarly it is impossible for there to be a change in Torah and mitzvot."[42] Torah, as the expression of the Divine Essence, cannot change.

What is included in the term "Torah"? Basing himself on talmudic and hasidic teachings that describe the entirety of rabbinic literature as being rooted in the Sinaitic revelation, the Rebbe established an expansive definition of "Torah." In his view, all of talmudic literature represents the absolute and unswerving truths of God.[43]

This doctrine, however, is challenged by the sheer diversity of talmudic literature. The Talmud contains not only analyses of halakha

---

41. For a similar contrasting of Torah and science regarding their respective ability to create obligatory laws to follow, see *Likkutei Sihot* 2, *Hosafot*, Shavuot, *se'if* 3; *Torat Menahem* 5748: 4, 175, note 10.
42. *Likkutei Sihot* 23, Shavuot, no. 3, *se'if* 1. The Rebbe sourced this phrase in *Mabit's Beit Elokim, Sha'ar HaYesodot*, chapter 34.
43. Ibid., *se'if* 2.

The Secularization and Spiritualization of Science

and biblical verses, but also seems to function as a repository of folk wisdom and medical advice. The Talmud, for example, records that an earache should be treated with the fat of a large beetle, and gum pain should be soothed with the fat of a goose.[44] What is the contemporary status of such medical advice?[45]

It is needless to say that the medical community has long abandoned these practices of Late Antiquity and has adopted treatments of greater efficacy. Even within the Jewish tradition, halakhic authorities as early as the pre-medieval *Geonim* rule that talmudic medicine should no longer be employed.[46] Some even went as far as to assert that the Talmud's medicine is rooted in a rabbinic adoption of ancient Persian best practice.[47]

All of this posed a challenge for the Rebbe's expansive perspective that the entirety of rabbinic literature is an expression of divinity. The Rebbe firmly believed that all such medical advice was rooted in the divine Revelation at Sinai. This conviction was so strong that the Rebbe even suggested that the *Geonim* who wrote otherwise were not expressing their true opinion: "These words were written only to ease the minds of the questioners even though they [the *Geonim*] themselves did not agree."[48] Not being convinced by this argument, the Rebbe later suggested that even if the *Geonim* recorded their actual belief, their opinion was later rendered incorrect by virtue of Rambam's ruling (in the Rebbe's understanding)[49] that all of the Oral Torah stems from Sinai.[50]

The Rebbe admitted, however, that practically speaking, post-talmudic halakhic authorities did not advocate following these medical instructions. He himself consistently recommended that ailing people see the most current specialists and kept abreast of new developments

---

44. Avoda Zara 29a.
45. For a comprehensive review of talmudic medicine's reception in the post-talmudic era, see Mordechai Halpern (2011), 469–82.
46. See, for example, *Yam shel Shlomo* on Hullin 8:12, which says that the earlier authorities created a prohibition (*herem*) against following the practices of talmudic medicine.
47. See, for example, *Shu"t R. Sherira Gaon*, cited in *Otzar HaGeonim*, Gittin 68b.
48. *Torat Menahem* 5743: 3, 1571.
49. See *Mishneh Torah, Hilkhot Teshuva* 3:8, and the Rebbe's interpretation of it in *Torat Menahem* 5743: 3, 1571.
50. *Torat Menahem* 5743: 3, 1573–74.

discussed in professional medical literature.⁵¹ If talmudic medicine is just as divine as the rest of the halakhic system, why would it have fallen out of Jewish practice?

Citing medieval Torah authorities,⁵² the Rebbe responded that it is not the Torah that changed, but the constitution of people:

> The change in the nature of the body and the constitution of humans in our period, which causes some of the talmudic medicines to no longer be effective…does not change the fact that this matter or halakha in the Talmud…is an eternal instruction, part of the eternal Torah – for the instruction is eternal. However, the object of the command…is changed; it is no longer the same body that existed as in the time of the command.⁵³

The medical information in the Talmud is an eternal part of the Torah, but it is geared to a specific bodily makeup. The Talmud's instructions are always theoretically binding, but as the makeup of the body changes over history they no longer have practical relevance.

While this solves the conceptual contradiction between the eternality of the entire Torah and our lack of adherence to these talmudic passages, the Rebbe was still not satisfied. The Talmud provides no indication that these instructions will be invalidated later in history, implying that they are still applicable. But, once again, this is refuted by the consensus of Jewish historical practice that long ago abandoned these talmudic cures.

The Rebbe's final formulation in this particular talk returns us to the theme of the Torah's transcendence. In his view, Torah is the source of *all* of the created world, material and spiritual aspects alike. As such, each mitzva has a multitude of disparate but related meanings, each corresponding to a different plane of existence. For example, the mitzva of tefillin has a distinct meaning in our material world: to place leather

---

51. See the letters compiled at www.chabad.org/2306909.
52. See, for example, *Tosafot*, Moed Katan 11a, s.v. *kivra*.
53. *Likkutei Sihot* 23, Shavuot, no. 3, *se'if* 4.

boxes on our head and arm. In each of the spiritual worlds, though, the same mitzva refers to a specific form of spiritualized service.

After establishing this principle, the Rebbe returned to talmudic medicines. While the properties of our material bodies might change over the course of history, rendering the terrestrial meaning of these instructions obsolete, this is impossible for the spiritual meaning of the instruction. As the Rebbe said: "The spiritual content is eternal…and their [spiritual] therapeutic effectiveness exists forever."[54] Therefore, even today, these medical instructions are relevant and applicable on a spiritual plane, albeit not for the current human physique.

In summary, the Rebbe felt that every line of Torah is an expression of the Divine Essence and therefore eternally true and relevant. He did not retreat from this approach even when faced with an abundance of evidence that swaths of talmudic literature were obsolete and possibly adopted from external sources. Instead, he developed a conception of the relationship between the wisdom of God and earthly realities that allowed him to hold these two principles together: talmudic medical advice is eternally true and relevant, even if often inapplicable to contemporary medical problems.

The Reversibility of Science

The Rebbe contrasted Torah's eternality with the reversibility of scientific "truths." In the above-cited letter to Professor Domb, the Rebbe connected the historical changes in the scientific consensus with the inherent limitations of the scientific method:

> In other words, science cannot, *a priori*, challenge religion, especially our religion, for science can never speak in terms of absolute truth. The best proof for this, as you also mention in passing, is that many scientific theories of the past which had been accepted as ultimate have been swept away "absolutely" and categorically, to the extent that science can be "absolute."[55]

---

54. *Likkutei Sihot* 23, Shavuot, no. 3, *se'if* 6.
55. Retrieved from www.chabad.org/664329.

The Rebbe highlighted the scientific community's shifts regarding the structure of the solar system as an example of the transitory nature of scientific theories. The Torah seems to accept a geocentric model, in which the earth is stationary and the sun revolves around the earth. In the sixteenth century, Nicolaus Copernicus's observations and formulas led him to introduce the heliocentric model, where the earth revolves around the sun. Once this model became accepted by the scientific community, many rabbis took a defensive posture and violently reinterpreted the Torah to conform with the heliocentric model.

All of this, argued the Rebbe, was unnecessary. As he wrote to Professor Domb:

> A glaring example is provided by the question of the geocentricity (of our global earth) in the planetary system, and better still the universe, which had been such a bone of contention between scientists and theologians, and when Copernicus's theory was accepted, many theologians hastily began their apologetics by attempting to reinterpret biblical passages in the light of the new scientific "truth," but not very convincingly so. Now, according to the theory of relativity, it is held that from the scientific point of view, either theory could be accepted.[56]

As the Rebbe elaborated in other letters,[57] one of the innovative conclusions of Einstein's theory of relativity was that it is impossible to determine the precise relationship between two moving objects. Therefore, there was currently no reason to favor the Copernican model over the older geocentric model that a literal rendering of the Torah espouses.[58] The Rebbe pointed to this shift from scientific certitude to doubt as a

---

56. Retrieved from www.chabad.org/664344.
57. *Iggerot Kodesh* 7, letter 1996; ibid., 15, letter 5449; *Emuna UMadda*, 143.
58. Yirmiyahu Branover (2000), 429–37, notes that this Einsteinian undercutting of Copernican science was already formulated by Professor Hans Reichenbach, a prominent student of Einstein (who held positions at the University of Berlin and later at the University of California, Los Angeles), in a 1928 paper called "The Philosophy of Time and Space."

glaring warning for those who put too much stock in the eternality of scientific "truths."

Summary
In instances of conflict between Torah and the conclusions of the scientific community, the Rebbe insisted on favoring Torah. He based this approach on a hasidic model of the Torah's relationship to the world and his personal understanding of modern science's own admitted limitations.

THE DANGERS OF SCIENCE
Let us now broaden our horizons from the Rebbe's treatment of specific contradictions between Torah and science to his conception of science and its advancements more generally. In line with traditional Chabad teachings, the Rebbe developed a nuanced approach toward the study and application of science. For the unprepared or uninitiated, engaging science on the intellectual or technological levels can be a perilous endeavor. With the proper preparations and framework, however, engaging in theoretical and applied science has great spiritual potential and even messianic potency.

Tanya on Science
Tanya teaches that the permitted (non-obligatory and non-prohibited) actions and items of this world are part of the realm of *kelippat noga*, characterized by a mixture of good and evil potential. This creates a limbo state for these actions and items. Their ultimate trajectory depends on the intent of the human agent who engages them. If, for example, a person eats permitted food solely to satiate his hunger, the food, due to the person's purely physically oriented intentions when consuming it, remains unredeemed and therefore stays in the domain of the *kelippot*. If, however, a person eats "in order to broaden his mind for the service of God and for His Torah," the carnal act of eating elevates the essence of the food: "Then the vitality of the meat and the wine which originated in *kelippat noga* is extracted from the evil and ascends to God like a burnt offering."[59]

---

59. *Likkutei Amarim*, ch. 7.

The Alter Rebbe explained that studying science is not fundamentally different from partaking in permitted food. If a person studies science gratuitously, the unredeemed knowledge "clothes and defiles his divine soul's faculties of Chabad [i.e., the qualities of *hokhma, bina*, and *daat* that constitute the intellect] with the impurity of the *kelippat noga* contained in those sciences." This will not occur, however, if a person contextualizes their study within one's service of God and

> employs them (these sciences) as a useful instrument, namely, as a means of earning a more affluent livelihood with which to be able to serve God, or if he knows how to apply them (the sciences) in the service of God or to his better understanding of His Torah. This is the reason why Maimonides and Nahmanides, of blessed memory, and their adherents, engaged in them.[60]

According to the Alter Rebbe, this was the reason that Rambam and Ramban studied the natural sciences.

Practically, the Alter Rebbe's dire warnings became the dominant strain in Chabad lore and life.[61] In particular, the later Chabad Rebbes – Rashab and R. Yosef Yitzhak – actively discouraged secular studies with few exceptions (most notably, of course, was the Rebbe himself).

The Rebbe's Warnings About Secular Science

The Rebbe forcefully affirmed the Alter Rebbe's reservations about studying science without a proper spiritual framework.[62] For example, he once noted that the Alter Rebbe did not speak of secular studies as a *prohibited* activity but rather one that insidiously *contaminates*:

---

60. Ibid., ch. 8.
61. There were exceptions to this general approach. For example, see *Iggerot Kodesh* 18, letter 6777, where the Rebbe records and brings evidence that the Maharash was familiar with contemporary medical writings and even wrote prescriptions in Latin "in the style of doctors."
62. See *Iggerot Kodesh* 11, letter 3784, where the Rebbe adamantly affirmed that the Alter Rebbe's warning applies to even natural sciences and not just philosophy.

It is similar to regular, halakhic, impurity – that even though one does not discern any difference in the contaminated object... nonetheless, through a single touch with an item that contaminates, the Torah declares that it too is contaminated and cannot enter sanctified space...based on this we can understand the stringency of studying "outside knowledge," as the Alter Rebbe did not use a language of prohibition or unfitness...but of contamination, which is more stringent.[63]

Even the most minimal contact with secular studies under improper conditions can have an extremely detrimental effect. Elsewhere, the Rebbe explained that outside of the realm of Torah study, intellectual activities such as secular studies naturally nourish a person's ego, which is the antithesis of the Chabad ideal of *bittul*, which is actually *cultivated* by Torah study.[64]

Should One Study in a University?

The Rebbe's position regarding university studies was informed by these same views. Drawing on his own experience of close to a decade in university settings, he generally discouraged young Jews from enrolling in college.[65] In his talks and letters on the topic, the Rebbe carefully located the problem in the prevailing attitudes and environment of college campuses which were fundamentally secular, making it nearly impossible to study scientific subjects with a consciousness of divine service or within a Torah-based intellectual framework.

For example, in the middle of one of the Rebbe's most science-positive talks, he added that in no manner should his positive rhetoric be construed as an approval of attending college:

---

63. *Torat Menahem* 5742: 4, 1837–38.
64. Ibid., 5721: 3, 224. On a practical level, due to these dangers and other factors, the Rebbe passionately advocated for elementary school education with minimal or no secular studies. A relatively early treatment of this issue appears in *Torat Menahem* 5715: 1, 73–75.
65. See, for example, the letter published at www.chabad.org/2391356.

Contemporary Issues

> It should be clarified, even though it is obvious, that this talk does not relate to the problems of studying in a university, which is a serious prohibition and danger... as the entire environment and philosophy is permeated with heresy of God's detailed *hashgaha*... and in most campuses there is no concept of shame or modesty and they ridicule all who take these concepts into account.[66]

Similarly, in a letter to parents who wanted their son to receive a college education, the Rebbe wrote:

> I am aware, of course, that there are boys who together with their yeshiva education attend college. I have occasion to meet with them, and I can assure you that very few come out unscathed from the tremendous conflicts involved. Even those who on the surface appear to be wholesome have no peace of mind, and very, very few indeed of those who mixed yeshiva with college have remained completely wholesome inwardly as well as outwardly.[67]

The intellectual and social environments of college studies and campus life are so thoroughly secularized that it is nearly impossible for the average religious young man or woman to maintain their Jewish life practices and faith without a sense of confusion and painful inner conflict.[68]

THE TORAH'S POSITIVE TAKE ON SCIENCE
Halakha Trusts Scientists

Despite these stark warnings, the Rebbe saw tremendous potential in the study and application of science after a person develops the proper

---

66. *Likkutei Sihot* 15, Noah, no. 2, *se'if* 3.
67. Retrieved from www.chabad.org/1877091.
68. More sources and anecdotes are collected in the following magazine: *A Chasidisher Derher* (Sivan 5777): 38–51, retrieved from derher.org/wp-content/uploads/2017/10/Derher-Sivan-5777.pdf. Also, see Shmuli Zalmanov (2016), 210–25.

spiritual framework.⁶⁹ On a fundamental level, he perceived that the Torah had a healthy respect for scientists and a positive orientation to science. For example, in one letter, after rejecting the cosmological account adopted by modern scientists, the Rebbe added the following remark:

> It should be self-evident that my letter did not imply a negation or rejection of science or of the scientific method. In fact, I stated so explicitly toward the end of my said letter. I hope that I will not be suspected of trying to belittle the accomplishments of science, especially as in certain areas the Torah view accords science even more credit than science itself claims; hence many laws in halakha are geared to scientific conclusions (e.g., as in medicine), assigning to them the validity of objective reality.⁷⁰

The Torah itself trusts doctors to accurately assess a patient and determine proper treatment, even to allow him to eat on Yom Kippur.⁷¹ This trust points to the high regard that the Torah has for science, despite its limitations and dangers.

The Method of *Bittul*

How does one ensure that his study of the sciences will be with a consciousness of divine service and not an act of self-contamination? Characteristic of his approach to other aspects of the material world, the Rebbe saw *bittul* as a key prerequisite for this enterprise. Only by striving to overcome self-interest can a person properly study and apply secular studies without it leading toward contamination and the amplification of the ego.

This, the Rebbe argued, was the lesson of the Hanukka story. The *Hashmona'im* did not wage a war against Greek wisdom per se, but against the fact that the Greeks desired to weaponize such wisdom and

---

69. In this context it is important to note that in a letter (*Likkutei Sihot* 12, *Hosafot*, 197–99) enumerating the permissible reasons for engaging in secular studies, the Rebbe added that even if there is no present benefit but one plans on using the knowledge for a positive purpose in the future the study is permissible.
70. Retrieved from www.chabad.org/112083. See also *Torat Menahem* 5726: 1, 314.
71. *Shulhan Arukh, Orah Hayyim, siman* 618:1.

Contemporary Issues

make the Jewish people "forget your Torah," that is, the divine nature of the Torah.[72] But if a person engages in secular wisdom without self-interest but with a fundamental sense of *bittul*, it can be a positive experience: "One's study [of secular studies] can only be proper… if a person turns away from and abandons all his own matters and desires, effacing his own being."[73] Such an individual can study secular wisdom for the sake of Heaven, similar to Rambam and Ramban.[74]

The Upper and Lower Waters

If the halakhic system trusts science, Kabbala goes farther and imbues great mystical significance to the proper engagement with the sciences. The Rebbe elicited this idea from a passage in the Zohar to *Parashat Noah*.[75] The Torah describes the commencement of the great flood in the following fashion: "In the six hundredth year of Noah's life, in the second month, on the seventeenth day of the month, on this day, all the springs of the great deep were split, and the windows of the heavens opened up."[76] The Torah identifies two sources of water – the springs of the deep and the windows of the heavens.

Building upon the rabbinic symbolism of water as Torah, the Zohar understands that this verse refers to a great outpouring of wisdom that will flood the world:

> And six hundred years into the sixth millennium the gates of wisdom from above and the fountains of wisdom from below will open, and the world will be corrected as a preparation for its elevation in the seventh [millennium].[77]

---

72. Liturgy of Hanukka.
73. *Torat Menahem* 5726: 1, 313–14.
74. See also *Torat Menahem* 5729: 3, 359–61.
75. Most of this section is based on a seminal talk published in *Likkutei Sihot* 15, *Noah*, no. 2, which analyzes the spiritual potential of science. For several other occasions where the Rebbe spoke about this passage in the Zohar and its connections to science, see *Likkutei Sihot* 7, *Hosafot*, 206; ibid., 35, *Hosafot*, 241, note 10; *Torat Menahem* 5746: 2, 40; ibid., 5748: 4, 178. note 32.
76. Gen. 7:11.
77. Zohar, *Vayera*, 117a.

The Secularization and Spiritualization of Science

Based on the age of Noah at the time of the flood, the Zohar predicts that the world will be doubly flooded with wisdom during the sixth century of the sixth millennium (1740–1840 CE). The outpouring of upper and lower wisdom will help prepare the world for the messianic seventh millennium.

What are these forms of wisdom that will rush into the world with messianic potency? The Rebbe explained that the "wisdom from above" refers to the secrets of the Torah. This prediction accurately unfolded as Hasidism, the deepest of such secrets, was revealed and disseminated during that century.[78]

If wisdom from "above" refers to the secrets of the Torah, the Rebbe reasoned that wisdom from "below" signifies "knowledge of the world," i.e., science. This interpretation is corroborated by the great advancements in science that occurred in the late eighteenth and early nineteenth centuries that changed the face of society.

According to this approach, the Zohar cast the parallel explosions of Hasidism and science as a prelude to the coming of *Mashiah*. The first half of the statement perfectly melds with the Rebbe's broader philosophy, as he often articulated a direct causal link between the dissemination of hasidic teachings and *Mashiah*.[79] The Rebbe noted, though, that the relevance of science for this messianic enterprise is harder to explain:

> We can understand how the revelation of the inner dimension of Torah is a preparation for the world's "elevation in the seventh"… The question is, however, what relationship is there between the progress and discoveries of science and the era of *Mashiah*?[80]

The Rebbe responded that science, when properly applied and contextualized, could aid the messianic process in three ways: (1) as a model for heretofore unimaginable messianic realities, (2) as a tool for disseminating Torah, and (3) as part of a more fundamental and more universal intellectual shift toward a messianic understanding of reality.

---

78. *Likkutei Sihot* 15, Noah, no. 2, *se'if* 1.
79. See, for example, chapter 8, section "Hasidism and *Mashiah*."
80. *Likkutei Sihot* 15, Noah, no. 2, *se'if* 1.

Science as a Model

The prophet Isaiah predicted that in the Messianic Era humans will be able to viscerally experience God: "And the glory of God shall be revealed, and all flesh together shall see that the mouth of God spoke" (Is. 40:5). The Rebbe noted that Isaiah does not focus on an intellectual or disembodied spiritual experience but rather on a bodily and tangible connection to God: "That even our physical flesh will see that 'the mouth of God has spoken.'"[81] What does this mean? How can we conceive such experience and strive to actualize it in our present reality?

Modern science, the Rebbe explained, gives us the tools to envision such a phenomenon. To illustrate this point, he pointed to the mishna in Avot that instructs people to imagine God as "an Eye that sees and an Ear that hears"[82] everything. For most of human history, this task was exceedingly difficult, as visual and auditory experiences were limited to one's immediate surroundings. One had to envisage God in terms that did not exist in the world.

Now, however, the situation is different. Speaking in 1977, the Rebbe highlighted that the relatively recent inventions of the telephone, radio, and television shattered previous boundaries of human perception. It is now possible to instantaneously hear or see something that occurs on the other side of the globe or even in space. This newfound ability must impact our conception of "an Eye that sees and an Ear that hears":

> When a person has such a tangible example for this concept, his meditation about the concept that "behold God stands over him ... and looks at him, and searches his [mind] and heart to see if he is serving Him in a fitting manner"[83] will be not merely in a manner of abstract analysis, which does not always have a full effect on a person. Rather, it will be in a manner much closer to the person's physical senses and feelings, and therefore have a

---

81. Ibid., *se'if* 4.
82. Mishna Avot 2:1.
83. *Tanya, Likkutei Amarim*, ch. 41.

The Secularization and Spiritualization of Science

greater effect on his emotions, and subsequently on his thought, speech, and action.[84]

Properly internalizing the lessons of new communications technology can help make God more of a tangible and real presence in our lives. Applying this model to the prophet Isaiah's description of our future palpable connection to God can also assist in our understanding and striving toward this complete experience of God.[85]

Science as an Instrument of Dissemination
A second element of the messianic potency of science helps close the gap between the upper and lower realms of wisdom. While utilizing science as a means of making God more of a "tangible reality" is certainly positive, the Rebbe noted that the Zohar indicates a more intimate relationship between science and Hasidism. In fact, the Rebbe posits that this connection is the divine purpose of the entire scientific revolution:

> The Zohar's tying of secular wisdom's development with the revelation of (the inner dimension of) Torah and not [merely with an eventual] "elevation in the seventh [millennium]" is proof that this is the entire intent and true essence of this development. (The fact that the benefits of this advancement can be used for other areas is only so that man should have free will.)[86]

Just as the Midrash teaches that the sole reason for gold's creation was for the purpose of the *Mishkan*, the House of God,[87] similarly, the essential purpose for which science, the "gold" of earthly knowledge, was

---

84. *Likkutei Sihot* 15, Noah, no. 2, *se'if* 4.
85. The Rebbe frequently used new findings or inventions in science as models for the proper service of God. See, for example, *Sihot Kodesh* 5735: 2, 211, where he pointed to the computer as a model for performing mitzvot quickly even without independent understanding, and *Iggerot Kodesh* 13, letter 4575, where he employed the example of the atom bomb as a model for the immense power contained within each individual item or person.
86. *Likkutei Sihot* 15, Noah, no. 2, *se'if* 6.
87. Exodus Rabba 35:1.

Contemporary Issues

created, is to be used for Torah and mitzvot, particularly in relation to the revelation and dissemination of the teachings of Hasidism.[88] Therefore, the Rebbe was not satisfied with the first approach alone of merely utilizing specific results of scientific advancements as a parable to enhance one's service of God. Rather, he sought more direct connections between science and Torah with a particular focus on the revelation and dissemination of hasidic teachings.

The Rebbe suggested that one primary and practical connection between science and Hasidism is in the crucial area of dissemination. As we have seen, the Rebbe frequently reflected on Rambam's description of the messianic globalization of knowledge.[89] The recent advancements in communication technology supply the means through which all of Torah, but Hasidism in particular, can be spread globally in a heretofore unprecedented fashion.[90]

During much of the Rebbe's tenure, the primary new avenue for disseminating Hasidism was the radio. Beginning in 1960, Chabad launched a radio program dedicated to *Tanya* lectures, and the Rebbe himself took an active role in editing the in-depth classes. Subsequently, he began to speak periodically of the significance of spreading Torah on the radio.[91]

In the Rebbe's first talk on the topic in 1960, he noted that until this moment, the two main forms of spreading Hasidism were oral and written communication. While these mediums are effective, they suffer from the limitations of time and place. Human speech can be heard only within a certain radius, and a printed book takes time to spread to the corners of the globe. Now, however, the Rebbe argued that a new era of dissemination was beginning:

---

88. The Rebbe returned to this connection between the gold of the midrash and modern technology several times. See, for example, *Torat Menahem* 5720: 2, 147–48; ibid., 5722: 2, 118.
89. Rambam, *Mishneh Torah, Hilkhot Melakhim UMilhemoteihem* 12:5. See chapter 16, sections "Rambam" and "Why Now?"
90. *Likkutei Sihot* 15, *Noah*, no. 2, *se'if* 7.
91. See, for example, *Likkutei Sihot* 23, *Hosafot*, 482–83; *Torat Menahem* 5721: 2, 173–74; ibid., 5722: 2, 118–19. For a more comprehensive list of sources, see Yirmiyahu Branover (2000), 174.

The Secularization and Spiritualization of Science

> But there is another means of dissemination – speaking on the radio – that has two advantages: [The speaker's voice] does not weaken.... Instead, the same energy with which the person spoke it [in one end of the world] can be heard at the other end of the world.... And it does not take a long time to spread... similar to the speed of light.[92]

The Rebbe spoke of the radio's invention as a divinely orchestrated event to facilitate a more optimal form of disseminating God's Torah, and especially its inner dimension as expressed in Hasidism. God granted the world a tool that had qualities similar to light to spread the "light" of Hasidism in heretofore unprecedented ways.

From the Rebbe's talks about this radio program, it is apparent that he faced internal and external opposition. Some of the conservative elements in the Orthodox community considered it improper to use a modern invention that was symbolic of modern culture and materialism for Torah lectures. For example, two years after the radio lectures began, the Rebbe mentioned that "at the beginning there were those who opposed this program and some of them have not yet tired... and they even clothe [their complaints] in the mantle of 'fear of Heaven.'"[93]

The Rebbe's response was to expound upon the above themes. Everything in the world exists for the sake of serving God, and, as the midrash underscores regarding gold, this is especially true for items that have unique properties. Applying this mandate to the radio, the Rebbe argued that it is wasteful not to harness this potential for the service of God and of Hasidism in particular.

In an impassioned later talk, the Rebbe cited those who thought that the radio was rooted in the *Sitra Ahra* (evil force) and therefore not suitable to spread Torah. His response was classic: "Heaven forbid that the *Sitra Ahra* has the power to create something! Heaven forbid! This is the exact opposite of the Torah and [the basics of Jewish] faith."[94]

---

92. *Torat Menahem* 5720: 2, 146.
93. Ibid., 5722: 2, 118.
94. Ibid., 5742: 2, 1041–42.

The Rebbe asserted that only God has the capacity to create, and therefore every created item is imbued with a specific divine purpose. This is equally true regarding new inventions. While the average person does not realize the divine purpose of the radio and may use it frivolously, Jews have an obligation to employ the radio for the "goal and objective of its creation," which is to disseminate Torah.[95]

Scientific Developments and the Messianic Consciousness

Despite the propriety of using the "lower wisdom" to disseminate Hasidism, the Rebbe did not consider this application as exhausting the Zohar's parallelism between Hasidism and science. Spreading Torah on the radio still only *utilizes* science as an *instrument* to further a Torah goal. This supportive role is not the ultimate perspective on the partnership between science and Torah: "The true fusion of secular wisdom with Torah is when one can discern in the secular wisdom itself concepts of the Torah's inner dimension."[96] Science itself discloses and teaches the wisdom of Hasidism. What does this mean?

The Rebbe explained that the essence of hasidic teachings is that there is an all-encompassing divine unity:

> The inner dimension of Torah reveals the ultimate unity of God in the world. That despite the existence of myriad creations, the myriad does not contradict God's essential oneness, since the very existence of the many [separate entities] is derived from the essential oneness of God, as is explained in various sources.[97]

As this singular divinity encompasses and permeates every aspect of creation, it follows that the notion of oneness should be apparent in the world itself.

---

95. In addition to practical dissemination, the Rebbe highlighted another advantage of spreading Hasidism on the radio. See *Likkutei Sihot* 15, Noah, no. 2, *se'if* 7, where the Rebbe mentioned that the very fact that the radio waves broadcasting Hasidism permeate the entire world has a purifying effect.
96. *Likkutei Sihot* 15, Noah, no. 2, *se'if* 8.
97. Ibid.

It is exactly this point that new scientific developments are uncovering: "This idea – the oneness of the world (which in its innermost essence is the oneness of God) – is becoming ever more apparent with the further development of scientific knowledge." In the past, people based their worldviews on their observations of the world's diversity. Each natural force was considered to be entirely separate from the others. Items with disparate appearances were considered to be comprised of fundamentally different elements.

Now, however, the Rebbe continued, the situation has changed dramatically. Science is continuously whittling away at this conception of substantive diversity and is instead disclosing the uniformity that exists at the substratum of the material world:

> However, the more science advances and develops, the more it reaches a recognition that the diversity and disparity among the various elements is only an external factor – [i.e.,] the way in which the components fuse, the degree of contraction or expansion, etc. Science is instead continually decreasing the number of elements' fundamental components, recognizing that the fundamental existence of the world consists of the *unification* of the two aspects of quantity and quality (matter in which energy is contained, and the energy itself).[98]

The entire world with all its dizzying diversity is composed of the same subatomic building blocks. Even matter and energy are no longer considered essentially distinct entities.[99]

This revelation of the material oneness of creation is the ultimate way that science prepares the world for the coming of *Mashiah*. As the Rebbe concluded:

> The revelation of the inner dimension of Torah automatically causes the development of worldly wisdom, since through this

---

98. Ibid.
99. See *Emuna UMadda*, 140, where the Rebbe explicitly mentions Einstein in this regard.

a "taste" of the Torah of *Mashiach* (which reveals God's oneness in the world) exists in a manner which is (at least) a "taste" of "all flesh [together] shall see [that the mouth of God has spoken]" (Is. 40:5).[100]

The disclosure of the oneness of the material world provides a taste of the Messianic Era. When the ultimate Messianic Era will be ushered in it will become clear and apparant that the *substance* of this unity is none other than Godliness itself:

> The world itself [will] become a "vessel" for the oneness of God.... When we see this, we truly realize that this unity is not something separate from the simple unity of Godliness (which is revealed in Hasidism). Through this, the "world is corrected to be elevated in the seventh [millennium]" (*Zohar, Vayera*, 117a) very soon.[101]

When Hasidism permeates the entire world and the Messianic Era arrives, it will be clear to all that the unity of the material world is "essentially, the unity of God."[102]

A Historical Shift

The Rebbe used this developmental construct to explain *Tanya*'s negative rhetoric on science. For example, in one talk the Rebbe underscored the material unity that science discloses and how this can lead a person to believe in a single creator and see the unity within creation. After developing this positive usage of science, the Rebbe asked:

---

100. *Likkutei Sihot* 15, *Noah*, no. 2, *se'if* 8.
101. Ibid.
102. See also *Torat Menahem* 5746: 3, 290–91, where the Rebbe pointed to the constancy of scientific laws (such as gravity) as they apply to matter regardless of the latter's size and shape as an example of unity in nature. In *Torat Menahem* 5726: 1, 318, the Rebbe claimed that this notion of unity in nature is a fundamentally Jewish idea and non-Jewish scientists received it from the Jewish people, similar to the story (mentioned in Abarbanel's commentary to Jer. 1:6) of Plato hearing wisdom from Jeremiah.

> If through the wisdom of the non-Jews one can reach the matter of "unity," why is it stated in *Tanya* that [the wisdom of the non-Jews] "clothes and defiles his divine soul's faculties of Chabad [i.e., the qualities of *hokhma*, *bina*, and *daat*] with the impurity"?[103]

The Rebbe responded that *Tanya* was correctly reacting to the pernicious dangers of unredeemed secular wisdom that existed in the Alter Rebbe's time. Before the full dissemination of Hasidism, secular science remained in the realm of emphasizing the disparity of different elements which led a person away from recognizing the principle of unity.

Nowadays, however, two shifts occurred. First, science itself began inching toward discovering the interconnectedness and unity of the natural world. Second, the advent of Hasidism helps a person be mentally and spiritually prepared for seeing this unity of nature as an expression of the oneness of God:

> And this matter began to arrive in the world in recent years, as is explained by the *Zohar*... meaning that not only was there the beginning of the revelation of secrets of the Torah, such that even young children can learn them, but similarly, regarding worldly knowledge, [scientists] began to discover that every item is not independent but is rather connected with something broader, and they are discovering the common denominators between all elements in nature. Until one reaches the recognition that the point which unites all items of this world is divinity.[104]

The confluence of the Rebbe's understanding of Chabad philosophy, the nature of scientific study, and the progression toward a unified redemptive consciousness undergirded his more robust endorsement of the sciences.

---

103. *Torat Menahem* 5729: 3, 359.
104. Ibid., 362–63.

Contemporary Issues

CONCLUSION

The Rebbe's perspective on modern science reflects many foundational ideas. On the one hand, he was unapologetic when it came to upholding the Torah's truth, ready to challenge what he saw as the overconfidence and overreach of the scientific consensus. However, he simultaneously celebrated the trend of modern science toward the discovery of ever deeper levels of inherent unity that he felt was reflective of the unity of God. In addition, he spoke of technological advances as creating divinely ordained opportunities (and therefore imperatives) to integrate science into the generation's divine service.

Secondary Literature Consulted for Chapter 18, "The Secularization and Spiritualization of Science"

Yirmiyahu (Herman) Branover and R. Yosef Ginzberg, *Ma Rabbu Maasekha Hashem: HaMadda VehaTekhnologya BeMishnato shel HaRebbe MiLubavitch.*

Menahem Bronfman, "Gishat HaRebbe MiLubavitch LeMadda VeTekhnologya: Le'ametz, akh Lehakir BaMigbalot."

Meir Klein, *BeHippus ahar Merkaz HaIggul: HaRetorika shel Madda VeTekhnologya etzel HaRav Menahem Mendel Schneerson.*

Chaim Miller, "Science and Technology in the Works of the Lubavitcher Rebbe," in *The Thirteen Principles of Faith: Principles 8 and 9; The Torah*, 363–96.

Eli Rubin, "Torah on the Radio: Using Technology for Positive Purpose."

Elliot Wolfson, *Open Secret*, 301, note 3.

Chapter 19

The Land of Israel and the State of Israel

The Rebbe was a great lover of the Land of Israel. Complete volumes have been filled with his teachings about the land, its centrality, and the importance of the events that were occurring therein.[1] These talks conveyed a deep and visceral emotional connection to the land, the security and flourishing of its inhabitants, and the success of its society and government. He believed that the Land of Israel is a key component of national and individual Jewish identity and therefore cultivating a conscious connection with the land has immense religious significance. He often concluded talks with a desire that the Jewish people return to the Land of Israel and to Jerusalem in particular.

Despite the clear positive connection to the land itself that permeated the Rebbe's thought, he had a more nuanced approach to some of the ideologies and movements that swirled around the land and the state in modern times. In fact, the Rebbe's teachings regarding these issues are fraught with tensions and seeming contradictions.

---

1. See, for example, note 107 below.

On the one hand, the Rebbe strongly critiqued the standard ideology of Religious Zionism, which sees the State of Israel as the beginning of redemption. He saw aspects of the State of Israel and the rhetoric around it as actually delaying the coming of *Mashiah*. He did not call for a mass immigration to the land and sought to strengthen Jewish communities in the Diaspora.

Simultaneously, though, he saw the establishment of the state as the means through which God, in His kindness, saved the lives of millions of Jews. He sought to materially and spiritually strengthen the citizens of Israel, lauded members of the IDF, and frequently hosted Israel's prime ministers, generals, and cultural leaders, who respected his advice.

While these tendencies might seem contradictory, the Rebbe viewed his overall perspective as holistic. As with every other topic he dealt with, the Rebbe's perspective emerged from his understanding of Torah and Chabad teachings as they relate to the historical moment. In this chapter we will first discuss the Rebbe's thoughts on the relationship between the Land of Israel and the Diaspora and then demonstrate how this approach impacted his posture toward Zionism and the State of Israel.

BACKGROUND

Jewish thinkers during the exile developed a complex relationship with the Land of Israel. While Jewish liturgy and law affirms the Jewish people's eschatological desire to once again dwell in the embrace of the land, thought leaders were challenged to consider the land's relevance in their present exilic state of existence. This is a vast topic, but an outline of a few of the general trends is necessary to properly contextualize the Rebbe's approach.

Medieval Jewish Thought

Scholars note the emergence of conflicting trends regarding the Land of Israel in medieval Jewish thought. Many thinkers, most notably R. Yehuda HaLevi, speak of the land as the spiritually and materially ideal location and therefore as the object of intense desire.[2] Some medieval

---

2. See, for example, *Kuzari*, I:95, II:14. For further development and analysis, see Yitzhak Sheilat (2010), 158–61; Yohanan Sillman (1991), 79–89.

rabbis, including R. Yehuda HaLevi and Ramban, acted on this longing and moved to the land.

Simultaneously, though, other thinkers developed a streak of trepidation alongside this desire. In their view, the land is so holy that the very prospect of day-to-day living there was terrifying and mostly relegated to a messianic dream to be realized when the Jewish people would be spiritually worthy. In their current reality, only the most pious should have the audacity to contemplate relocating to the land.

R. Meir of Rothenberg exemplified this mindset. Despite his own attempted emigration, he offered a stern warning to anyone daring to consider such a move:

> A person [who moves to the Land of Israel] must become an ascetic and be careful to avoid committing any sins and keep all the agricultural mitzvot. For if a person sins in the Land of Israel he will be punished more than he would if he sinned in the Diaspora ... as there is no comparison between rebelling in the king's palace and rebelling outside of the palace, and this is the meaning of the verse "And it is a land that consumes its inhabitants."[3]

This factor was more than a theoretical consideration and practically dissuaded people from immigrating to the Land of Israel.[4]

Early Kabbala

Early kabbalists developed their own approach to the land's relevance. Characteristic of their general methods of interpretation, these kabbalists often understood references to the Land of Israel as symbolically signifying a specific spiritual plane. On one level, this symbolic interpretation makes the land eternally relevant. Simultaneously, though, understanding the land as a metaphor for a specific spiritual quality can diminish the centrality of the actual geographic place.

This allegorical approach is expressed in a remarkable statement of R. Ezra of Gerona, a contemporary of Ramban. In a poem about

---

3. Cited by his student, *Tashbetz Katan*, siman 559.
4. For more sources and analysis of this perspective, see Aviezer Ravitzky (1998), 1–41.

the Land of Israel, he employed kabbalistic language to describe the proximity of the Land of Israel to God. This divine immanence allows a person who lives within the confines of the land to receive atonement for his sins. R. Ezra then continues that this immanence and atonement, which characterize the land, can be attained in the Diaspora as well. In fact, he wrote that when Jews "suffer for the love of God in exile" they are elevated to the spiritual level of those who reside in the Land of Israel and are therefore "exempt from the obligation to live in the Land of Israel."[5] The Land of Israel is a relevant category in his thought despite his living in the Diaspora, expressly due to the fact that aspects of the spiritual life of the land can be accessed outside of its specific geographic borders.

Early Hasidism
Early Hasidism continued these themes. Hasidic leaders certainly invested much time and mental energy elaborating on the spiritual uniqueness of the land and fostering a sense of its desirability in their followers. In 1777, a group of Hasidim, led by R. Menahem Mendel Vitebsk, a primary disciple of the Maggid of Mezritch, took these descriptions as a practical program and took leave of their European homes to settle in the land.

Simultaneously, though, Hasidism further developed the earlier kabbalistic tendency to allegorize the Land of Israel. Two notable trends must be noted in this regard. First, in consonance with Hasidism's general tendency to psychologize earlier kabbalistic categories,[6] many hasidic thinkers spoke of a "Land of Israel consciousness" that allows a person, and particularly a *Tzaddik*, to access aspects of the spiritual uniqueness of the land wherever one might be.[7] Conversely, "exile" refers not only to physically being in the Diaspora, but also to the fact that "the divine soul is clothed ... with the foreign desires of the animal soul."[8]

---

5. Cited in Gershom Scholem (1998), 34. For more sources and analysis, see Havivah Pedayah (1991), 233–89 (this passage is cited on pp. 243–44).
6. See chapter 8, section "Early Hasidism."
7. See, for example, *Likkutei Moharan Tinyana*, *siman* 71. See also ibid., *siman* 40.
8. Mittler Rebbe, *Shaarei Teshuva* 2, 62c.

The Land of Israel and the State of Israel

A second factor that impacted the allegorization of the land was Hasidism's adoption of the Lurianic notion of *birur hanetzotzot*, the mission to raise divine sparks that are hidden in the material world. With this approach, exile not only is a punishment for the Jewish people's sins, but also represents a divinely ordained mission to free the sacred sparks that are trapped among the nations and lands of the world. From this perspective, living in the Diaspora presents the Jewish community with a unique opportunity and responsibility.[9]

These trends appear as well in early Chabad thought. The Alter Rebbe was both a theoretical and practical lover of the Land of Israel. According to Chabad tradition, he actually embarked on the journey to immigrate to the land until his senior colleague, R. Menahem Mendel of Vitebsk, convinced him to return to Russia to lead the masses who remained there. After his dream of immigration did not materialize, he exerted great effort to raise funds for the hasidic community in Tiberias and even attributed his release from the Russian prison to the merit of the Jews in the Land of Israel.[10] At the same time, the Alter Rebbe and his heirs employed the Land of Israel as an allegory for specific spiritual qualities.[11]

The Rebbe's teachings regarding the Land of Israel are suffused with the above tensions. As we will see, the Rebbe put these ideas into conversation with two historical factors: (1) The Rebbe's understanding of the mission to create a *Dirah BaTahtonim* and its application to modern times, and (2) the founding of the State of Israel.

THE UNIQUENESS OF THE LAND OF ISRAEL IN THE THOUGHT OF THE REBBE

The Rebbe often spoke about the spiritual uniqueness of the Land of Israel. In these talks, the Rebbe highlighted that many of the ideals and

---

9. See, for example, *Torah Or*, 6a. For more sources and analysis, see Moshe Idel (1998); Yoram Jacobson (2014), 212–16.
10. From a letter the Alter Rebbe wrote to R. Levi Yitzhak of Berditchev, cited in *Beit Rebbe*, vol. 1, 70.
11. See, however, Moshe Hallamish (1998), 242–43, who notes that this form of allegorization of the land is actually less prevalent in the Alter Rebbe's thought when compared to his peers.

Contemporary Issues

ideas that were close to his heart could be optimally realized only within the confines of the land.

The Fusion of the Spiritual and the Physical

One frequent theme in the Rebbe's talks about the land is its special capacity to fuse the spiritual and the physical. For example, he once said the following:

> The content of the superiority of the Land of Israel is expressed in the verse "A land the Lord, your God, looks after; the eyes of the Lord your God are always upon it" (Deut. 11:12), meaning to say that God's *hashgaha* is there in a deeper and revealed fashion (more than in other lands). This means that in the Land of Israel, even in the physicality of the land ... divinity is felt in a more revealed fashion.[12]

The verse speaks of God's attention and providence being more focused on the land. After citing this verse, the Rebbe immediately transitioned from the general theme of *hashgaha* to the ability to sense divinity in the land itself.[13] As we have seen, this merging of materiality into divinity is a leitmotif in the Rebbe's thought.

Continuing this theme, the Rebbe located the root of the biblical spies' catastrophic report in their lack of appreciation for this very point. The spies preferred their spiritualized existence in the desert, where their physical needs were cared for by God. God, however, desired that the Jewish people serve Him through the *tahtonim* – all of the mundane aspects of everyday living that they would need to engage in upon entering the land. In this sense, material Jewish existence in the Land of Israel exemplifies the lowly yet lofty service of "working in the matters of the world, physical matters"[14] – a descent for the purpose of creating a *Dira BaTahtonim*.[15]

---

12. *Likkutei Sihot* 13, Shelah, no. 1, *se'if* 4.
13. See also *Torat Menahem* 5730: 3, 469–70.
14. *Likkutei Sihot* 13, Shelah, no. 1, *se'if* 4.
15. See also *Torat Menahem* 5745: 1, 549–52; ibid., 5722: 1, 282–83.

The Rebbe also spoke of the clear Godly nature of the materiality of the Land of Israel in other contexts. He contended that in the Land of Israel it is "visible and apparent" that all of one's material livelihood stems directly from God, while in the Diaspora one is more prone to mistakenly conceive of the natural order as having an independent existence.[16] Similarly, the Rebbe associated exilic life with a more ascetic lifestyle replete with fasting and the avoidance of anything but the basic material necessities. By contrast, a person who lives in the Land of Israel, which "bridges heaven and earth,"[17] is able to properly engage and harness the physicality of the body.[18]

The Land and the Divine Essence
In other talks, the Rebbe went further and associated the Land of Israel with the Divine Essence itself. For example, the Rebbe once wondered about Moses's strong desire to enter into the Land of Israel. Had Moses not literally ascended to heaven itself? What more could he possibly anticipate on the western side of the Jordan?

The Rebbe responded that Moses understood that the physical Land of Israel surpassed even the highest heavens:

> All of the worlds, even the worlds that transcend *Atzilut* [the first worlds to emanate from *Ein Sof*], are referred to as "worlds," meaning to say that they are a reality that is an additional item to the Infinite (*Ein Sof*). This is not the case regarding the physical Land of Israel, whose content is the Divine Essence itself (*Atzmut mamash*).[19]

---

16. *Likkutei Sihot* 39, *Ki Tavo, se'if* 4.
17. *Torat Menahem* 5718:1, 228.
18. Ibid., 5718:1, 227–29. For a technical description of the difference between the nature of divinity in the Land of Israel and the Diaspora that uses hasidic terminology (*derekh maavar* versus *derekh hitlabshut*), see *Torat Menahem* 5718: 1, 282; ibid., 5715: 2, 281–84.
19. *Torat Menahem* 5718: 1, 29.

Contemporary Issues

As a proof text, the Rebbe cited the Alter Rebbe's letter[20] that only the Divine Essence has the capacity to create physicality. While the original letter relates to the entire material plane of existence, in this talk the Rebbe highlighted its unique relevance to the Land of Israel.

The Land and the People

In addition to the unique qualities of the land, the Rebbe underscored the eternal and essential connection that exists between the Land of Israel and the Jewish people. In one classic talk, the Rebbe developed this theme through analyzing the opening words of Rashi's commentary on the Torah. Rashi famously asked why the Torah does not begin with the first mitzva given to the Jewish people and instead begins with cosmology and stories of the ancestors of the Jewish people:

> "In the beginning" (Gen. 1:1): Said R. Yitzhak: It was not necessary to begin the Torah except from "This month is to you" (Ex. 12:2), which is the first commandment.... Now for what reason did He commence with "In the beginning"? Because of [the verse] "The strength of His works He related to His people, to give them the inheritance of the nations." For if the nations of the world should say to Israel, "You are robbers, for you conquered by force the lands of the seven nations [of Canaan]," they will reply, "The entire earth belongs to the Holy One, blessed be He; He created it (this we learn from the story of Creation) and gave it to whomever He deemed proper. When He wished (*birtzono*) He gave it to them, and when He wished (*birtzono*), He took it away from them and gave it to us."

The Rebbe returned to these words dozens of times, but for our purposes we will focus on one question that he asked regarding the claim of the nations of the world that the Jewish people stole the land from the seven Canaanite nations.

---

20. *Tanya, Iggeret HaKodesh*, sec. 20. See chapter 3, section "*Atzmut* and the Lowest Realm," and chapter 4, section "'The Humble Soul' and 'This World of Falsehood.'"

A cursory reading of Rashi indicates that the nations of the world felt that the Jews had no rights to the land, since they conquered it by force from the Canaanites. This, the Rebbe said, does not seem to align with accepted international norms of the ancient world, which often saw nations invading neighboring lands. Why would the nations of the world focus their ire on the Jewish people's conquest of the land as opposed to any other nation's act of invasion and occupation?

The Rebbe responded that the nations of the world understood the fundamental uniqueness of the Jewish people's connection to their land. In the words of the Rebbe:

> Generally, when an item is transferred from a person to another through any form of acquisition – sale, gift, conquering in a war – the item's essence does not change. The item's ownership by one person or another does not express itself in the item itself.... But the Jewish people's conquering of the land is different, for once they conquered the "land of the seven nations," a change occurred in the very essence of the land... that it is now the land of the Jewish people in all of its essence forever, such that it can never again be associated with another nation.[21]

Even after Jewish people were exiled from the land, the Rebbe continued, they still refer to it as "our land."[22] It was this form of essential bonding of people and land that the nations of the world protested.

What, then, is God's response to their objection? According to Rashi, it is simply that God created the world and "gave it to whomever He deemed proper when He wished." The Rebbe explained that Rashi's choice of the word "*birtzono*" signifies that God's gifting of the Land of Israel to the Jewish people stemmed from a deep and elemental desire within God.[23] As we have seen, God's *choice* of the Jewish people reflects His innermost essence, as indescribable and inscrutable as that

---

21. *Likkutei Sihot* 5, Bereshit, no, 1, *se'if* 7.
22. See also *Sihot Kodesh* 5736: 2, 473–74, which says that a Jew always feels at home in the Land of Israel.
23. See *Torat Menahem* 5752: 1, 193–94.

is.[24] Similarly, God's pairing of the Land of Israel with the Jewish people is part of this divine choice.

THE LAND OF ISRAEL AND THE DIASPORA

These deep-seated beliefs in the uniqueness of the Land of Israel and its profound connection to the Jewish people could theoretically have motivated the Rebbe to categorically encourage people to immigrate to the Holy Land. This, however, was not the case. The Rebbe never called for a mass migration to the Holy Land and in many cases discouraged individuals from emigrating. A survey of the Rebbe's talks and letters on this topic demonstrates that three distinct points served as the basis for this lukewarm attitude toward moving to the land: (1) the demanding nature of living in the land, (2) the detrimental impact that immigration can have on those individuals left behind, and (3) his understanding of exile, redemption, and the mission of creating a *Dirah BaTahtonim*.

The Demands of the Land

In an early talk, the Rebbe directly addressed those Jews who seemed to sincerely desire to flee exile to "a land the Lord, your God, looks after."[25] The Rebbe was not enthusiastic about this enterprise and proceeded to systematically dismantle possible motivations to move to the land.[26]

Among other factors, the Rebbe related to the fact that a hypothetical Hasid might claim that there is a mitzva to live in the Land of Israel. The Rebbe responded that many authorities assume that living in the Land of Israel is not a bona fide obligation but rather a praiseworthy achievement that goes beyond what is required. Moreover, he cited the opinion of R. Meir of Rothenberg (noted above) that the Land of Israel is for only the religious elite. If a person cannot commit to upholding an exemplary pious standard, it is better to remain in the Diaspora and not risk angering God within His palace.

Similarly, when the Rebbe wrote to people who were planning to visit or move to the land, he often exhorted them about this point. For

---

24. See chapter 7, section "The Basis for the Divine Essence's Choices."
25. Deut. 11:12.
26. *Likkutei Sihot* 2, *Hosafot, Re'eh*.

The Land of Israel and the State of Israel

example, in one letter he described that before entering the palace of a human king, a visitor will first change into his finest garments. As the "garments" (*levushim*) of a person's soul are his thoughts, speech, and actions, anyone who visits the Land of Israel must be sure to elevate these "garments" for the duration of his stay.[27]

The Overall Impact of Immigration

While the higher religious standards demanded by living in a sanctified spot is a serious factor, independently it might not have accounted for the Rebbe's misgivings about immigration. Rather the Rebbe would often highlight the pragmatic negative impact that immigration can have on the Jewish communities and individuals around the globe.

For example, when an active community member would consult with the Rebbe regarding immigration to the land, the Rebbe would ask him to reflect upon how his immigration would impact the community. If the person's absence would leave a gaping hole in the spiritual or material fabric of the community, the Rebbe would discourage immigration.

In this vein, let us look at a particularly telling episode. The Rebbe was once asked by an active member of the South African Jewish community about his view on immigrating to Israel. In response, the Rebbe discouraged him from immigrating and drew from the historical example of the Jewish communities in Morocco as a model:

> A classic example is the emigration from Morocco. The *aliya* campaign was concentrated on the group of least resistance – the spiritual leaders – despite my warnings, behind the scenes, of the disastrous consequences of despoiling the local communities of their leadership. The basic argument was that "the leaders must show the way; the flock will follow." What happened was that the leaders did, by and large, make *aliya*, but the local communities became largely demoralized. In the end, hundreds of thousands of Moroccan Jews emigrated, not to the Land

---

27. *Iggerot Kodesh* 7, letter 2060. See also *Iggerot Kodesh* 17, letter 6194; ibid., 19, letter 7061; *Torat Menahem* 5744: 2, 798; ibid., 5744: 4, 2559.

of Israel, but to France, to be exposed to forces of assimilation they had not met before.[28]

The Rebbe's approach was clear. Immigrating to the Land of Israel could not be at the expense of Jews being served in the Diaspora. In one interview with an Israeli journalist about the topic, the Rebbe insisted that he supported immigration for the average person but told educators and leaders that they should take the example of "a captain of a ship in a stormy sea who must always be the last one to leave the boat."[29]

Inner and Outer Exile

In addition to this pragmatic approach, the Rebbe simultaneously developed a complex perspective on the nature of the Land of Israel, exile, redemption, and the mission of creating a *Dirah BaTahtonim*. The Rebbe constantly spoke about the uniqueness of the geographic Land of Israel, constantly referring to it as "a land the Lord, your God, looks after; the eyes of the Lord your God are always upon it" (Deut. 11:12). But at the same time, he firmly believed that certain qualities of the Land of Israel transcend geographic borders and should be accessed throughout the globe.

The Rebbe differentiated between two levels of exile: the "external" exile of physically being banished from the Land of Israel, and the "internal" exile of being distant from God. Of these two forms of exile, the Rebbe insisted that inner distance from God is the central defining category of Diaspora and exile. As such, living in the land does not necessarily change a person's fundamental exilic existence.

In a relatively early talk, the Rebbe clearly articulated this blurring of clear geographic borders for the state of being in exile. Speaking about the effects of the destruction of the *Beit HaMikdash*, the Rebbe said:

> Once the *Beit HaMikdash* was destroyed, and "because of our sins we were exiled from the land" (from the holiday liturgy), as "children who have been exiled from the table of their father"

---

28. www.chabad.org/2387581.
29. Cited in Moshe Ishon (1980), 209. See also Yona Cohen (1980), 163–64.

The Land of Israel and the State of Israel

(Berakhot 3a), the Land of Israel itself entered an exile, since exile does not have to necessarily be at a geographic distance. Rather, a person could be situated in a location of closeness, but "they turned their backs to Me and not their faces" (Jer. 2:27), and this is the greatest exile, "and I will hide My face on that day" (Deut. 31:18).[30]

The state of exile is endemic and pervasive, persisting irrespective of geographic location. Exiting the exile and entering the land is less dependent on a geographic migration and more on repairing the individual's and world's relationship with God.[31]

The Rebbe straightforwardly applied this model to those who desired to immigrate to the Land of Israel, thinking that by this very act they would extricate themselves from exile. Using strong and even harsh formulations, he contended that when a person moves from the Diaspora to the Land of Israel, "he does not flee from the Diaspora to the Land of Israel, but rather he takes with him the 'air' of the Diaspora to the Land of Israel, and there he lives embedded in the air of the Diaspora."[32] Unless a person repents and repairs the sins that were the reason for the exile – "because of our sins we were exiled from our land" – he transplants his exilic life to the Holy Land, which is an affront to the land's sanctity.

Exile as *Hashgaha*

If one can live in the Land of Israel and still be in exile, what then is the call of the hour? The Rebbe emphatically argued that the roots of redemption lie in realizing that everything, including exile, is orchestrated by God to provide the Jewish people with opportunities to create a *Dira BaTahtonim*. Accordingly, the fact that the majority of Jews are born in the Diaspora speaks volumes about the divinely mandated national mission. Similarly, the fact that a specific Jew finds himself in the Diaspora should be perceived as setting the stage for his individual mission.

---

30. *Torat Menahem* 5718: 1, 228.
31. See also *Likkutei Sihot* 35, *Hosafot*, 262.
32. *Likkutei Sihot* 2, *Hosafot, Re'eh, se'if* 4.

The Rebbe once emphatically emphasized this Diaspora-oriented mindset:

> The main service today is in the Diaspora. This is evident from the fact that the majority of the Jewish people – both quantitatively and qualitatively – live specifically in the Diaspora. Similarly, regarding the Torah, once the exile intensified with the passing of Rabbenu HaKadosh (R. Yehuda HaNasi), [the Torah] was revealed specifically in the Diaspora.... Similarly, regarding the revelation of the inner secrets of the Torah, this mainly occurred in the Diaspora... and similarly, regarding the revelation of Hasidism, which is the main revelation of the secrets of the Torah, the two great luminaries – the Baal Shem Tov and the Alter Rebbe – both wanted to travel to the Land of Israel but due to divine providence remained in the Diaspora. The main service today is in the Diaspora.[33]

The very fact that most of recent Jewish history has unfolded and continues to unfold in the Diaspora is not something to rebel against but is a divine message about where the Jewish people need to be to complete the mission of creating a *Dirah BaTahtonim*.

Once again, the Rebbe directly used this perceived *hashgaha* as an argument against moving to the Land of Israel:

> We should say to such a person [who wants to immigrate to the Land of Israel]: "You are not in exile based on your desire, and you will not leave exile simply based on your desire. This is a matter for God. And since exile is a divinely ordained phenomenon, you do not need to flee from here, as wherever you are, you are by the table of God (paraphrase of Hullin 139a)."[34]

Those who are born in the Land of Israel or need to flee their homes in the Diaspora for the safety of the land are selected by God to merit

---

33. Ibid., 9, *Hosafot*, 341.
34. Ibid., 2, *Hosafot*, *Re'eh*, *se'if* 4.

The Land of Israel and the State of Israel

actually living in the land.[35] There are even some Jews who are born in the Diaspora but whose true mission lies within the borders of the land.[36] The majority of Jews who are born into the Diaspora, however, need to realize that they have a specific mission to fulfill beyond the geographic borders of the land. This is particularly true for those who are positively impacting their Diaspora community.[37]

Make, Here, the Land of Israel
The Rebbe's identification of the Diaspora as the central setting for the divine service in contemporary times immediately begets another question: What is the nature of this service? What does God expect the Jewish people to accomplish in the Diaspora?

As a response, the Rebbe frequently cited a statement of the *Tzemah Tzedek* that was later recorded in a letter penned by R. Yosef Yitzhak. R. Yosef Yitzhak related that when a Hasid told the *Tzemah Tzedek* of his strong desire to immigrate to the Holy Land, the *Tzemah Tzedek* responded as follows:

> R. Hillel of Paritch [a leading Hasid of the first three Chabad Rebbes] did not miss the Land of Israel, and you want the Land of Israel? We need the Land of Israel here. Make, here, the Land of Israel.[38]

R. Yosef Yitzhak explained that the purpose of life is to "enlighten the darkness of this world with the light of Torah and the paths of service." The means toward enlightening the darkness of the exile is encoded in a midrashic understanding of the term *Eretz Yisrael* (the Land of Israel):[39] "Why is it called *Eretz*? Because it desires (*ratzta*) to perform the will (*ratzon*) of its Creator." As R. Yosef Yitzhak explained:

---

35. *Torat Menahem* 5730: 2, 103.
36. *Sihot Kodesh* 5736: 1, 444–45.
37. See, for example, *Sihot Kodesh* 5736: 1, 444, and the letter to an active member of the South African Jewish community, cited above in note 28.
38. *Iggerot Kodesh Admor Moharaayatz* 1, letter 274.
39. *Genesis Rabba* 5:8.

> *Eretz* is *ratzon* (will), and the Land of Israel [represents] the essential will that exists in every soul. Living in the Land of Israel means that in every place where Jews live until the time of redemption, they must reveal their essential will through the *mesirut nefesh* of the service of *birurim* [i.e., extracting sparks of sanctity]. And the tool for this is Torah.[40]

The Land of Israel symbolizes the inner desire of Jews, and really all of creation, to align itself with the will of its Creator. "Make, here, the Land of Israel" refers to the service of enlightening the exile by revealing this inner desire in oneself and one's surroundings no matter where one might be.

The force of this transformative mission was a major part of the Rebbe's misgivings about leaving the Diaspora. As the Rebbe once cited from his father-in-law:

> When a Jew who is situated in the Diaspora wants to immigrate to the Land of Israel, he must contemplate whether he already accomplished all of the things that he needed to accomplish in the Diaspora… if he wants to merit his portion in the Land of Israel he must work in the place where he is situated to transform [that place] into the Land of Israel.[41]

As this mission will be completed only with the coming of *Mashiah*, the Rebbe contended that until that point Diaspora Jews should, by and large, remain in the Diaspora.

TRANSFORMING THE WORLD INTO THE LAND OF ISRAEL

The Rebbe often cited and applied the mandate of "Make, here, the Land of Israel." In his teachings, this statement implies an expansion of certain qualities of the land to the entire globe. When discussing "Make, here, the Land of Israel," the Rebbe took some of the unique characteristics

---

40. *Iggerot Kodesh Admor Moharaayatz* 1, letter 274.
41. *Torat Menahem* 5730: 2, 102–4. See also *Likkutei Sihot* 9, *Hosafot*, 340.

The Land of Israel and the State of Israel

of the land and charged his followers to create that selfsame spiritual reality in the Diaspora.

Transforming the Materiality of the Diaspora

As noted above, one of the main features of the Land of Israel in the Rebbe's thought is its fusion of divinity with the material world. Accordingly, the Rebbe understood the mandate "Make, here, the Land of Israel" as a charge to enlighten even the coarse materiality of the Diaspora by revealing its inner divine nature.

In one talk, the Rebbe spoke of the similarities shared by the Jewish people and the Land of Israel. Instead of using this association to limit the Jewish people's potency to the confines of the land, the Rebbe argued that this connection allows them to expand the land's borders:

> Since the Jewish people are similar to the Land of Israel, it is within their ability to make the entire world into the Land of Israel, meaning that they can transform all of the material items in their environment into vessels for divinity, a place for His dwelling. This is the significance of the Land of Israel from a spiritual perspective.[42]

The historic mission of the Jewish people is the purification of the terrestrial realm through the disclosure of its inherent divinity. This messianic task can be accomplished only through diligent and self-sacrificial work in the Diaspora itself (the *tahtonim*).

Elsewhere, the Rebbe used this idea to expand R. Yosef Yitzhak's original formulation regarding "Make, here, the Land of Israel." In his letter, R. Yosef Yitzhak wrote of the need to do *birurim* – to extract the sparks of sanctity – from the Diaspora. The Rebbe, however, was not satisfied with focusing on only the sparks themselves, instead advocating a more comprehensive and ambitious project:

> Through descending into exile...in addition to extracting the sparks of sanctity that are scattered in the world, much more can

---

42. *Torat Menahem* 5714: 1, 115.

occur. Even the place where the sparks are found – the entire world – will be transformed into sanctity, meaning to say that the entire world will become the Land of Israel.[43]

It is not enough to find the few holy sparks and souls in the Diaspora and extract them from their material encasing. Rather, the fusion of divinity and materiality that characterizes the Land of Israel must permeate the entire globe, and in that sense transform the world into the Land of Israel. As the Rebbe emphasized, this requires a direct and prolonged engagement with every part of the globe.[44]

The Diaspora and the Divine Essence

Earlier in this chapter we saw that the Rebbe associated the materiality of the Land of Israel with the Divine Essence. In light of the partial porousness of the land's borders and the all-encompassing nature of the Divine Essence, it is no surprise that in several talks the Rebbe contended that the Divine Essence is present and must be disclosed in the Diaspora as well. Understandably, this impacts upon the nature of diasporic service.

In one talk,[45] the Rebbe went so far as to describe the location of Jewish communities throughout the globe as stemming from a *choice* of the Divine Essence. He explicated that, similar to God's choice of the Land of Israel, this choice of locations in the Diaspora stems from God's innermost essence.

The Rebbe developed this theme from Rambam's description of the meritoriousness of living in the Land of Israel:

> At all times, a person should dwell in the Land of Israel, even in a city whose population is primarily gentile, rather than dwell in the Diaspora, even in a city whose population is primarily Jewish. This applies because whoever leaves the Land of Israel for the Diaspora is considered as if he worships idols.[46]

---

43. *Likkutei Sihot* 30, *Vayehi*, no. 3, *se'if* 6.
44. See also *Torat Menahem* 5743: 1, 161–62.
45. *Likkutei Sihot* 18, *Masei*, no. 2.
46. *Mishneh Torah, Hilkhot Melakhim UMilhemoteihem* 5:12.

The Land of Israel and the State of Israel

Surprisingly, Rambam, based on the Talmud, continues that Babylonia attained a similar status: "Just as it is forbidden to leave the chosen land for the Diaspora, it is also forbidden to leave Babylonia for other lands."[47] What is the basis of this prohibition against leaving Babylonia? In what way is it comparable to the Land of Israel?

Through a scrupulous textual analysis that requires its own study, the Rebbe concluded that the Land of Israel is imbued with two forms of uniqueness:

> There are two general items that differentiate the Land of Israel from other lands: (1) as the midrash stated, "Beloved is the Land of Israel that the Holy One, blessed be He, *chose* it";[48] and (2) the fact that the Land of Israel is sanctified.[49]

These two levels are parallel to the Rebbe's analysis regarding the uniqueness of the Jewish people. In that discussion, the Rebbe made it clear that while the Jewish people's sanctity is an important attribute, this sacredness was not the true basis for God's love of the Jewish people. Rather, even where "Esau is a brother to Jacob"[50] and no distinction exists between Jews and non-Jews, nonetheless, the Divine Essence *chose* the Jewish people due to their embeddedness in the most basic strata of the Divine Essence.[51] Similarly, the Rebbe argued that God's choice of the land transcends the land's special sanctity and is instead rooted in God's most elemental will.

With this background, we can appreciate the radical nature of the Rebbe's next statement. He interpreted Rambam to mean that even as Babylonia cannot rival the Land of Israel regarding its *sanctity*, nonetheless, the very fact that Jews were exiled there indicates that God *chose* it to be the current home for the Jews:

---

47. Ibid.
48. *Midrash Tanhuma, Re'eh,* siman 8.
49. *Likkutei Sihot* 18, Masei, no. 2, *se'if* 5.
50. Mal. 1:2.
51. See chapter 7, section "The Basis for the Divine Essence's Choices."

> Just as God chose the Land of Israel as the place of the Jewish people's freedom and redemption from the Egyptian exile, and also afterward when the Jewish people behaved properly [and were redeemed], similarly, God chose Babylonia as the place of the Jewish people's exile during the time of their exile.

It was this choice of God that grants Babylonia its elevated status, albeit temporarily.

In this talk, the Rebbe still carefully singled out the Land of Israel as God's *eternal* choice. Nonetheless, the fact that the Rebbe used the same term, "choice," in reference to a diasporic location is highly significant. The other objects of God's choice – the Jewish people and the Torah – remain indisputably unique. By contrast, locations in the Diaspora can become the temporary objects of God's *choice* as the places where the Divine Essence *desires* the Jewish people to live and to transform at a given time.

Similarly, the Rebbe connected the Divine Essence with the Jewish people's service in the Diaspora to demonstrate the Diaspora's significance in its own right. While certain rabbinic passages refer to mitzvot performed in the Diaspora as merely paving the way for a return to the land,[52] the Rebbe explained that while true on a certain level, this understanding does not exhaust the value of these mitzvot:

> Since the One God has a single goal of having a *Dira BaTahtonim*, and everything was created with the power of the Divine Essence…every matter of this world (even the supporting details and means) contains the potency of the Divine Essence, which transforms it into…the bearer of an independent goal…. Even though "here" is not the Land of Israel, and the service in the Diaspora and in exile is a preparation for the perfect service of the ultimate redemption in the Land of Israel (for which the Jewish people pray daily), since it is certainly not a coincidence that we are in exile but rather due to *hashgaha*…there is an inherent purpose in this place itself…which is to make a *Dira BaTahtonim*

---

52. *Sifrei Devarim, piska* 43.

and, in the language of the *Tzemah Tzedek*, "Make, here, the Land of Israel," meaning to make it into a land (*Eretz*) where Judaism (*Yisrael*) is revealed.[53]

The Divine Essence's desire for a global *Dira BaTahtonim* invests intrinsic meaning in the Jews' performance of mitzvot all over the globe.

A Global Mission

The Rebbe spoke of the mandate "Make, here, the Land of Israel" as applying on both the individual and collective levels. On an individual plane, each person needs to purify his own part of the world. For example, in one talk the Rebbe said:

> The statement of the *Tzemah Tzedek* is well known: "Make, here, the Land of Israel," meaning to say that wherever a Jew is, it is his duty to transform [that place] into the Land of Israel. This can be understood based on the fact that the term *eretz* stems from the word *ratzon* (will).... When a Jew acts in a manner that enables his [inner *ratzon*] to be revealed in his household, then through this he transforms his home into the Land of Israel. And when he acts in this manner toward all of those in his environment (his portion of the world), then through this he transforms all of his surroundings into the Land of Israel.[54]

This expansion of the Land of Israel begins with small steps, each person influencing his own immediate family and surroundings.

If each Jew acts in this fashion, then the Jewish people collectively will transform the entire world. The Rebbe interpreted the dispersion of Jews to the remote corners of the world in the twentieth century as part of the divine plan to spread certain qualities of the Land of Israel over the whole globe.[55] In this context, the Rebbe often cited the following midrash: "In the future, Jerusalem will expand throughout all of

---

53. *Torat Menahem* 5751: 4, 58–59.
54. Ibid., 5743: 1, 847–48.
55. Ibid., 5749:1, 305.

the Land of Israel, and the Land of Israel will expand in all of the lands."[56] While this midrash still affirms the uniqueness of the Land of Israel, it predicts a messianic revolution in the Diaspora's status. Characteristically, the Rebbe understood this forecast as a practical and urgent obligation.[57]

The Place of the *Nasi*

This partial flexibility regarding the location of God's *choice* is most apparent in the Rebbe's discussions of his father-in-law's gravesite. In an early talk[58] the Rebbe described that Moses, on his own merits, could have entered the Land of Israel immediately following the sin of the spies. Nonetheless, the *nasi* of the generation was completely dedicated to the people and would not abandon his flock in pursuit of greater closeness to God. Moses therefore stayed in the desert to continue shepherding that doomed generation. Similarly, R. Yosef Yitzhak remained in the Diaspora and was buried in New York City, enabling him to continue to help the Jewish people living in the Diaspora – in that when Jews come to pray at his grave, "their *yehida* becomes bound with the *yahid* (the Singular One, i.e., God)," which assists them in their divine service.

The Rebbe elaborated on the uniqueness of the gravesite of a *Tzaddik* in the Diaspora by explaining that a dimension of the Land of Israel shines there. The Talmud explains that during the Revival of the Dead, there will be tunnels that connect the gravesites of the righteous with the Land of Israel.[59] This will allow these righteous individuals to roll subterraneously to the Land of Israel from where they will arise.

The Rebbe noted that there is a halakhic principle that the status of the inside of a tunnel is governed by its opening. This means that a tunnel which opens in the *Beit HaMikdash* but whose expanse extends beyond the borders of the building is still considered entirely sanctified.[60] Similarly, the gravesite of a *Tzaddik*, even in the Diaspora, attains aspects

---

56. *Yalkut Shimoni Yeshayahu, remez* 503.
57. See, for example, *Likkutei Sihot* 30, *Vayehi*, no. 3, *se'if* 6.
58. *Torat Menahem* 5714: 2, 27–33.
59. Ketubot 111a.
60. Pesahim 86a.

of the sanctified status of the Land of Israel due to the fact that there will be tunnels connecting them with the Land of Israel.[61]

The Rebbe then took this idea a step further. While the Land of Israel is certainly associated with the Divine Essence, this identity became nearly imperceptible after the destruction of the *Beit HaMikdash*. As the Rebbe put it, "It requires great effort and toil for this [essential connection between the Land of Israel and God] to be drawn out and revealed within one's practical daily existence."[62] This limitation, though, does not exist when it comes to the gravesite of a *Tzaddik* who is connected by tunnels with the redeemed Land of Israel:

> Since regarding a *Tzaddik* there is no concept of destruction, for him the essential specialness of the Land of Israel is openly revealed, meaning to say that in the place where he is resting, even in the Diaspora, it has the status of the Land of Israel due to the tunnels that open in a place of sanctity. Therefore, [the place where he is resting] has an advantage over the Land of Israel after the destruction of the *Beit HaMikdash*.[63]

Prayer at the grave of R. Yosef Yitzhak has the unique potency of prayers that were offered during the time when the *Beit HaMikdash* stood. This gives such prayers an advantage, from a certain perspective, over prayers recited in the current geographic Land of Israel.

In summary, the Rebbe firmly believed in the uniqueness of the geographic Land of Israel and constantly expressed his yearning for the entire Jewish people to return to it immediately with *Mashiah*. Simultaneously, though, he called for expanding aspects of the land's qualities to the world as a whole. This was directly linked to his understanding of the nature of redemption as the creation of a universal *Dira BaTahtonim* and the all-encompassing nature of the Divine Essence.

---

61. Even though these tunnels do not yet exist, the Rebbe noted that regarding the laws of the spread of ritual impurity of a corpse, the Mishna (Ohalot 7:3) treats a future passageway as one that already exists.
62. *Torat Menahem* 5714: 2, 34.
63. Ibid., 34–35.

Contemporary Issues

ZIONISM

This discussion about the nature of the Land of Israel and the Diaspora provides crucial background for understanding the Rebbe's approach to the modern State of Israel.

On the most elemental level, the Rebbe saw the founding of the State of Israel as a fundamentally positive phenomenon. This was due to the fact that the state serves as a source of "salvation" for Jews. Having their own sovereign state helps ensure the Jewish people's physical safety as they are now disassociated from their enemies and have the means to protect themselves.[64] In addition, an autonomous Jewish state is a safe haven for Jews to immigrate to if there are persecutions in other areas of the world. The Rebbe emphasized that this is particularly true

---

64. One of the main rabbinic arguments against the establishment of the State of Israel stems from "the three oaths." The Talmud (Ketubot 111a) records that when the Jews were exiled, God made them take three oaths, one of which was that "the Jews should not ascend to *Eretz Yisrael* as a wall, but little by little," which was understood to mean that the Jewish people should not seize the Land of Israel by force before the coming of *Mashiah*. The Rebbe had a nuanced perspective regarding these oaths. On the one hand, it is clear from his letters and talks that he believed that the oaths were still relevant and that they reflected the notion that "the amount of time that the Jewish people are in exile is not dependent on them," meaning that, in theory, the Jewish people are prohibited from waging an offensive military campaign to conquer the Land of Israel. See, for example, *Torat Menahem* 5717: 1, 66; ibid., 5729: 1, 300; *Iggerot Kodesh* 7, letter 2138; ibid., 22, letter 8398. However, the Rebbe did not employ this talmudic passage as an argument against the establishment of the State of Israel. It seems that he felt that once Jews had slowly immigrated to Israel without waging a war, these Jewish inhabitants of the land had the right to self-defense and self-governance, and therefore the establishment of the state and its early wars were not violations of the oaths. This understanding of the Rebbe's opinion appears in Wolpo (1981), 144, 228–29, which is a book written about the Land of Israel based on talks and letters of the Rebbe, which the Rebbe himself would give people to read. In line with this understanding of the Rebbe's approach to the three oaths, it bears mentioning that in his talks against land for peace, the Rebbe raised the theoretical possibility that holding onto the conquered territories was a violation of "ascend[ing] as a wall." However, he rejected the practical relevance of the oath in this regard due to the fact that the territories were conquered miraculously in defensive wars. See, for example, *Torat Menahem* 5742: 1, 499; ibid., 5742: 2, 839, and also ibid., 5730: 2, 111–12.

The Land of Israel and the State of Israel

in a post-Holocaust world in which one can clearly see the results of Jews not having had a safe haven to flee to.[65]

However, notwithstanding seeing the positive value of the State of Israel, the Rebbe was ideologically opposed to seeing the establishment of the state as fundamentally changing individual or national Jewish identity. In particular, he expressed trenchant critique of the Religious Zionist ideology that saw the state through a messianic lens. Many learned adherents of this approach declared that they were living in the "beginning of the redemption" due to two intertwined factors: (1) the return of Jewish masses to the Land of Israel was a fulfillment of the ancient prophecies of the ingathering of the exiles (*kibbutz galuyot*), and (2) the establishment of the State of Israel represented a messianic return of Jewish sovereignty.

While the Rebbe was convinced that *Mashiah*'s arrival was imminent, he emphatically repudiated characterizing the era as the "beginning of the redemption." Accordingly, the Rebbe dissociated the facts on the ground from messianic prophecies and highlighted the many problematic elements in the modern State of Israel. At the same time, as we will see,[66] the Rebbe would often reference the biblical verses promising the Land of Israel to the Jewish people as a support for the modern Jewish state's sovereignty over the land,

Rambam's Description of Redemption

One of the Rebbe's basic retorts to the claim of the "beginning of the redemption" was that it contradicted Rambam's description of the messianic process:

> There are those who claim that we are currently in the "beginning of the redemption." May God save us from those who say this!... This approach is against an explicit ruling of Rambam...that redemption will come via *Mashiah*, and the sequence is explicit in Rambam: "If a king will arise from the House of David who diligently contemplates the Torah and observes its mitzvot as

---

65. Yehuda Feldi (1980), 120; Shalom Dov Wolpo (1981), 23–24; Wolpo (2005), 23–27.
66. See, later in this chapter, section "No Legal Right."

prescribed by the Written Law and the Oral Law, as did David, his ancestor, and [this king] will compel all of Israel to walk in (the way of the Torah) and rectify the breaches in its observance, and fight the wars of God, we may, with assurance, consider him *Mashiah*. If he succeeds in the above, builds the Temple in its place, and gathers the dispersed of Israel, he is definitely the *Mashiah*."[67]

Rambam explicates that the "gathering of the dispersed of the Jewish people" will be orchestrated by *Mashiah* after he fights the wars of God and rebuilds the *Beit HaMikdash*. In other words, the redemption will "begin and end through *Mashiah*." The Rebbe argued that halakhic sources carry more practical authority than other aspects of Torah, and therefore other biblical or midrashic statements which indicate that *kibbutz galuyot* can occur before *Mashiah* pale in comparison to the explicit halakhic ruling of Rambam.[68]

The State of Israel and *Malkhut Yisrael*

In addition, the Rebbe did not attribute sweeping religious significance to the regaining of Jewish political sovereignty per se. By contrast, many Religious Zionist rabbis assert that the return of Jewish sovereignty, even before the coming of *Mashiah*, constitutes a fulfillment of the mitzva of appointing a king.[69] R. Tzvi Yehuda Kook, a leading thinker in the Religious Zionist community, famously assigned cosmic importance to the State of Israel and declared: "This is the state that the prophets foresaw."[70] The Rebbe, however, adamantly asserted that the State of Israel was "not a Jewish kingdom and certainly not the dynasty of the House of David."[71]

For the Rebbe, if the State of Israel is not messianic and does not even constitute the fulfillment of a mitzva of appointing a king, then its establishment did not fundamentally change the Jewish people or their relationship with the land. The land belonged to the Jewish people

---

67. *Torat Menahem* 5743: 1, 509.
68. Ibid., 5727: 3, 197–98.
69. R. Shaul Yisraeli, *Amud HaYemini, siman* 7; R. Hershel Schachter, *BeIkvei HaTzon, siman* 32.
70. "Mizmor Yod-Tet LeMedinat Yisrael," available at www.yeshiva.org.il/midrash/2022.
71. *Torat Menahem* 5749: 1, 355.

from the time of Joshua. This elemental fact was neither bolstered nor actualized by the vote of the United Nations or the Zionist Congress.

The historical ownership of the Jewish people of the Land of Israel made the Rebbe reticent to use the term "the State of Israel." As he once wrote in a letter:

> It is (slightly) surprising that you are astonished that many circles, including myself, did not accept nor use the term *Medinat Yisrael* [State of Israel]. The reason for this is obvious: The land of Canaan was given as an inheritance to the Jewish people from the time of Abraham, and instead of "land of Canaan" the name was established as the "Land of Israel." This has been established for several thousand years, established in the Torah, and even engrained in the mouth of all the Jewish people from old to young. This is not determined by a vote or a majority which might change from time to time.[72]

In another letter, the Rebbe extended this argument and wrote that he would be comfortable using the term "State of Israel" if it was clear that the Jewish people's rights to the land stem from a divine gift. Since, however, the founders and leaders of the State of Israel saw their rights to the land as stemming from the Balfour Declaration and the United Nations, he was reticent to use the term.[73]

The Dangers of Saying "The Beginning of the Redemption"
If the Rebbe had felt that characterizing the State of Israel as "the beginning of the redemption" was simply another mistaken ideology, he probably would not have devoted as much time and attention to critiquing it. In his view, however, the messianic component of Religious Zionist ideology was no mere neutral error. Rather, it was a pernicious perspective that was delaying the coming of *Mashiah* and could sow confusion in the spiritual lives of countless Jews.

---

72. *Likkutei Sihot* 39, *Hosafot*, 268.
73. Ibid., 35, *Hosafot*, 259.

False Complacency

One of the Rebbe's main critiques against referring to "the beginning of redemption" was that it fostered a false sense of complacency and weakened people's resolve from what is necessary to bring about true redemption.[74] Citing the prophet Jeremiah, who in a different context warned against complacency, the Rebbe continued:

> When one says, "Peace, peace!" (Jer. 8:11) in a time when this is not [a description of] the true reality, it causes people to think that they can sleep soundly and not act. Regarding our issue, if this is not the beginning of the redemption, and yet we allow people to think that it is... we cause people to not engage in the activities that are necessary to generate the actual beginning of the redemption, which prolongs the exile... of the Jewish people and of the *Shekhina* itself![75]

Religious leaders must instruct their constituents that despite the miracles performed around the State of Israel, the last moments of exile consist of a "doubly thick darkness" that can be pierced only by enlightening the world with Torah and mitzvot. Declaring that we are living in the beginning of the redemption jeopardizes the performance of the generation's actual tasks necessary to bring *Mashiah*.

Inner Exile

Similarly, the Rebbe was concerned that identifying "the beginning of redemption" with the State of Israel could weaken people's connection to authentic Torah and mitzvot. The reason for this is that the Rebbe saw many aspects of the state and its leaders as deeply sunk within an "inner exile."[76] As such, declaring the state to be the beginning of the

---

74. The Rebbe once suggested (*Torat Menahem* 5729: 4, 238–39) that some leaders presumably realize the mistakenness of the "beginning of redemption" position and that their true goal was to valiantly but falsely give Jews a "good feeling."
75. *Torat Menahem* 5727: 3, 195.
76. See, for example, *Torat Menahem* 5743: 1, 512.

redemption would create confusion among the people by misleading them to identify "darkness as light."

This "inner exile" of the early Zionist leaders was apparent in their very motivation to create a state. Instead of desiring a "Jewish state," they wanted a "state for the Jews,"[77] in order that "the House of Yehuda should be as all of the nations."[78] The Rebbe argued that this approach was responsible for the spiritual deterioration of thousands of Jews.[79] Fundamentally, he saw this approach as incorrectly trying to forge a new national identity around land, language, and culture as opposed to Torah and mitzvot, which truly express the Jewish people's national essence.[80]

According to the Rebbe, this orientation toward "non-Jewishness" continued into the state itself, which he felt instituted policies that actively hurt Torah observance. Most infamously, in the early years of the state, the government coerced many pious *Mizrahi* immigrants to send their children to secular schools.[81] Similarly, the Israeli government declared, in the Rebbe's words, that "each person has the right to behave in accordance with his beliefs and it is not humane to coerce a person to act otherwise,"[82] which essentially prescribes personal freedom over halakhic observance into the fabric of Israeli society. As the Rebbe put it: "When Torah is put up for a vote, Heaven forfend,"[83] it is clear that we are hardly at the beginning of the redemption.

The Rebbe argued that this endemic infatuation with "non-Jewishness" was also apparent in the Israeli government's "attitude of submissiveness" to the non-Jews of the world.[84] As noted above, instead of declaring that the Land of Israel was divinely gifted to the Jewish people as an eternal inheritance, the Zionist leaders cited the Balfour Declaration and the United Nation's vote.[85] Similarly, instead of staunchly

---

77. *Torat Menahem* 5720: 1, 398.
78. Ibid., 5711: 2, 91.
79. *Likkutei Sihot* 39, *Hosafot*, 269.
80. *Iggerot Melekh* 1, letter 9.
81. *Torat Menahem* 5711: 2, 85–90.
82. Ibid., 5715: 2, 164–65.
83. Ibid., 165.
84. Ibid., 5743: 1, 118, 242, 395; ibid., 5743: 2, 638–39.
85. *Likkutei Sihot* 39, *Hosafot*, 268; ibid., 35, *Hosafot*, 259.

defeating the Arab enemies that attack Israel, they were always concerned with the question "What will they say in Washington?" and were never resolute enough in proactive and reactive self-defense, leading to the loss of Jewish life.[86] As this deference and submissiveness was a direct outgrowth of the collective inner exile of the State of Israel, it was both delusional and dangerous to describe the state as "the beginning of the redemption."

The Rebbe and the State of Israel

Despite the Rebbe's critique of certain aspects of the State of Israel and Religious Zionism, the Rebbe recognized the importance of the state's contributions to Jewish life.

As noted above, on a basic level, the Rebbe saw the State of Israel as contributing to the "salvation" of Jewish lives. This salvation occurs on two interrelated planes. On the micro level, he spoke of Israel's early military victories as saving the lives of the Jews who were living in the Land of Israel. Engaging in these defensive wars was a mitzva and the outcomes were miracles wrought by God and executed through the selflessness of the Israeli army.

He wholeheartedly encouraged his followers to thank God for the War of Independence and the Six-Day War, even characterizing those who were silent as "not properly fighting against their evil inclination and therefore fell under its sway... and are ungrateful in a most astonishing manner."[87] Characteristically, the Rebbe emphatically emphasized that these miracles were an expression of God's love for the Jewish people, which must be reciprocated by the Jewish people renewing their commitment to Torah and mitzvot.[88]

Furthermore, on a more macro plane, the Rebbe felt that Jewish self-governance had the advantage of limiting Jewish dependence on the nations of the world. On one level, as noted above, the independence

---

86. *Likkutei Sihot* 35, 260–61; ibid., 25, *Hosafot*, 438–42; *Iggerot Kodesh* 26, letter 9613 (addressed to R. Shlomo Yosef Zevin).
87. *Iggerot Kodesh* 11, letter 3469. See also *Iggerot Kodesh* 10, letter 3104; ibid., 24, letter 9778; *Torat Menahem* 5712: 2, 154; ibid., 5727: 3, 195.
88. *Torat Menahem* 5727: 3, 91–92; ibid., 5728: 1, 214–15. See also Shmuel Kraus (1999), 500–501.

of Jews from non-Jews aids Jewish security. And even beyond directly saving Jewish lives, the Rebbe highlighted that Jewish self-governance militates against non-Jewish interference into the affairs of the Jewish people, which in the long run can protect the physical and spiritual well-being of many Jews.[89]

The Rebbe explicitly noted that this cluster of "salvations" through self-governance in theory could have been accomplished by creating an autonomous Jewish community in Uganda or anywhere else in the world. He even drew comparisons to earlier semi-autonomous Jewish communities during the time of exile, such as those that existed under the Eastern European Council of the Four Lands in the early modern period. However, the Rebbe argued that it was a unique expression of God's kindness that He set events into motion that enabled this form of an autonomous Jewish community to come into being in the Land of Israel.[90]

Moving from the theoretical to the practical, even as the Rebbe did not attribute religious status to the state and its institutions, in practice he integrated the Israeli Chabad community into them. In contrast to several other hasidic leaders, he instructed his Hasidim to scrupulously pay taxes,[91] vote[92] (while still remaining detached from any particular political party),[93] and ensured that Chabad schools were part of the governmental school systems.

Characteristically, the Rebbe also he invested great efforts in the material and spiritual advancement of the state and its inhabitants.[94] He encouraged the development of industries[95] and educational institutions. He had a warm relationship with many high-profile Israeli

---

89. Yehuda Feldi (1980), 120; Shalom Dov Wolpo (1981), 23–24; Wolpo (2005), 23–27.
90. Yehuda Feldi (1980), 120.
91. *Sihot Kodesh* 5729: 1, 486.
92. *Iggerot Kodesh* 11, letter 3559.
93. See the sources compiled by Mordechai Menashe Laufer (28 Iyar 5756).
94. For brief overviews of Chabad's activities in the State of Israel, see "Al Pe'ilut Chabad BeEretz Yisrael," he.chabad.org/469739; Chaim Miller (2014), 272–74.
95. One example of this was the Rebbe's encouragement of Efraim Ilin to establish the first car assembly plant in Israel. For a first-person description of the events, see Efraim Ilin, "Investing in Israel."

politicians from across the spectrum, including Zalman Shazar, Ariel Sharon, Yitzhak Rabin, and Menachem Begin, who regularly visited him on their trips to America. According to interviews with Israeli journalists, these military and political leaders were impressed with the Rebbe's intimate familiarity with the social intricacies of Israeli society, its complex security concerns, and the keen advice he offered, despite never having visited.[96]

The Rebbe had a particular affinity for the IDF. Many Chabad Hasidim served in the army, and the Rebbe gave the highest accolades to all soldiers who defended the people and the Land of Israel.[97] He showed great honor for injured soldiers[98] and established a fund and programs for the widows and orphans of fallen soldiers.[99] In addition, from the earliest years of the state, he sent his Hasidim to army bases to assist soldiers with their material and spiritual needs.

Paving the Way Toward Redemption
While the Rebbe generally avoided associating the return of the Jewish people to the Land of Israel with the imminent coming of *Mashiah*, at times he did argue that aspects of this return were aiding in the messianic process. Perhaps most directly, in private conversations during the early days of the state, the Rebbe referred to God's gift of Jewish self-governance as a form of a trial run before the coming of *Mashiah*. God wanted to "test" the Jewish people and see if without the interference of non-Jews, they would be able to establish a society that as much as possible reflected the Torah's ideal vision within the context and confines of

---

96. See Shalom Yerushami, Yosi Elituv, Aryeh Ehrlich (2017) for an in-depth exploration of the Rebbe's relationship with high-profile Israeli leaders. A brief description was presented by Yehuda Avner, "The Rebbe: His Moral Vision as Statesman and Diplomat," www.oxfordchabad.org/851894.
97. *Iggerot Kodesh* 29, letters 11,008, 11,025. For other sources, see "8 Devarim SheAmar HaRebbe al Hayyalei Tzahal," available at he.chabad.org/3320334.
98. For a video of speeches that the Rebbe delivered to injured Israeli soldiers, see he.chabad.org/3320488 and he.chabad.org/3320489.
99. For brief descriptions of the Rebbe's instructions and Chabad's activities for the families of fallen soldiers, see "HaIma shel Mishpahat HaGibborim," available at www.col.org.il/show_news.rtx?artID=29413; "Yomam HaGadol shel HaYetomim," available at he.chabad.org/517614.

The Land of Israel and the State of Israel

an exilic reality. It is needless to state that the Rebbe felt that on many levels the actual government of Israel was failing the test spectacularly.[100]

However, the Rebbe did identify several aspects of the revival of Jewish life in the Holy Land under a Jewish government as paving the way toward *Mashiah*. For example, he once addressed his father-in-law's motivation for instructing a group of Russian Hasidim displaced by World War II to establish an agricultural community – Kefar Chabad – in the Land of Israel. The Rebbe explained that in addition to finding these refugees a safe haven, R. Yosef Yitzhak had a deeper mission in mind:

> The innovations of the [R. Yosef Yitzhak] concern matters which indicate that we are in the *ikveta deMeshiha*, which are associated with redemption. Settling the Land of Israel through the founding of Kefar Chabad is a preparation for the reality that will be revealed with the coming of *Mashiah* in all of the Land of Israel. Then, there will be agricultural work ... as is detailed by the prophet Isaiah.[101]

The prophets describe the great bounty that the Land of Israel will produce at the end of time, which the Rebbe understood will be fulfilled literally.[102] Accordingly, the Rebbe felt that the establishment of a Torah-oriented agricultural community would help accelerate the actualization of the prophecy.[103] Even as the Rebbe did not see the flourishing of agriculture in the Land of Israel as the beginning of redemption itself, he still considered it to be an important "preparation" for the times of *Mashiah*.

Similarly, despite his trenchant opposition to political Zionism, the Rebbe saw some form of redemptive value in messianic rhetoric surrounding the State of Israel. In one talk, he noted that despite R. Yosef

---

100. Yehuda Feldi (1980), 120; Shalom Dov Wolpo (1981), 23–24; Wolpo (2005), 23–27.
101. *Torat Menahem* 5728: 2, 80.
102. See *Torat Menahem* 5718: 2, 248.
103. As the community from which Hasidism was supposed to spread to the entirety of the Land of Israel, the Rebbe spoke of Kefar Chabad as being a central and capital city. See *Torat Menahem* 5728: 2, 80; ibid., 5726: 2, 187–90.

Yitzhak's opposition to such talk, his father-in-law did not wage a public battle against it.[104]

The Rebbe explained that his father-in-law's silence on the matter was based on a certain degree of benefit that the messianism surrounding the state offered. As a model, he cited Rambam's comments regarding Christianity and Islam. While Rambam adamantly believed that these are false faiths, he contended that God allowed them to proliferate in order to "prepare the way for *Mashiah*'s coming" through spreading the world with "mention of *Mashiah*, Torah, and mitzvot." This way, when the true *Mashiah* arrives, the nations of the world will be ready to receive him.

Similarly, the Rebbe suggested, even though the messianic rhetoric surrounding the state was "not true," nonetheless it is part of the divine plan: "[The people who connect the establishment of the State of Israel with redemption] prepare the way for *Mashiah*'s coming, since in the meantime everyone is talking about redemption, even though this is not the true redemption." In other words, even though speaking of the State of Israel as the beginning of redemption is false, this sort of rhetoric helps develop the messianic consciousness that is a necessary precursor to the Messianic Era.

Finally, in his later years, the Rebbe spoke about the massive immigration of Russian Jews after the fall of the Iron Curtain as a "taste" of the ingathering of the exiles.[105]

LAND FOR PEACE

Generally, the Rebbe was not vocal about political issues and did not instruct his Hasidim to vote for specific political parties. Nonetheless, there were specific issues that the Rebbe felt were halakhic and not political in nature, which others had overlooked, regarding which he led public campaigns. Perhaps the most ubiquitous and prominent of these issues was his opposition to the concept of land for peace.[106] From the

---

104. *Torat Menahem* 5712: 2, 153–54.
105. See chapter 20, section "The Fall of the Soviet Union."
106. The Rebbe's other very public campaign was to modify Israel's Law of Return to conform with the halakhic definition of Jewishness. In 1958, Prime Minister David Ben-Gurion sent letters to fifty leading Jewish scholars, including the Rebbe, requesting their definition of who should be considered Jewish from the

The Land of Israel and the State of Israel

days immediately following the Six-Day War until his debilitating stroke more than twenty-five years later, the Rebbe constantly and consistently spoke out against returning the conquered territories to Arab control.[107]

What was the basis for the Rebbe's objections to territorial concessions for the sake of peace? He made it clear dozens of times that he did not see eye to eye with the Religious Zionist stance that such concessions would be a reversal of the redemptive process. Rather, the Rebbe based his opposition on a combination of security and halakhic concerns, his understanding of Jewish ownership over the land, and a sense of realpolitik.

Halakhic and Security Considerations

When discussing land for peace, the Rebbe would often cite the following halakha codified in *Shulhan Arukh*:

> When there is a [Jewish] city close to the border, then, even if [enemies mount an attack, although they] come only for the purpose of [taking] straw and stubble, we should [take up arms] and desecrate the Shabbat because of them. For [if we do not prevent their coming] they may conquer the city, and from there the [rest of the] land will be easy for them to conquer.[108]

The Rebbe felt that this halakha was directly applicable to the post-1967 security situation in Israel. Speaking in 1977, the Rebbe said:

> Now the situation is such that the entirety of the Land of Israel is not far from the border. Therefore, every city is defined as a border city.... From this it is understood that it is forbidden to

---

government's perspective. The Rebbe's response (recorded in *Iggerot Kodesh* 18, letter 6714) launched his decades-long campaign to have the law correspond with the halakhic tradition. See Chaim Miller (2014), 284–90, for a description of the Rebbe's talks and activities in this regard.

107. These speeches and letters comprise more than seven hundred pages and are collected in the book *Karati VeEin Oneh*, ed. Levi Yitzhak Groner and Moshe Leib Krishveski (Jerusalem, 2004).

108. *Shulhan Arukh, Orah Hayyim* 329:6. Translation adapted from www.chabad.org/72559.

> transfer any territory of the Land of Israel to non-Jews, since this is a clear and codified halakha. Since [all of Israel] is a border city, it is incumbent on every Jew to do all that is necessary so that there be sufficient guns (not because we want to demonstrate "my strength and the power of my hand," but rather), since this is a command of God that is rooted in the security of many Jews... and has the authority of a ruling of *Shulhan Arukh*.[109]

The Rebbe also underscored that Israeli military experts affirmed the above halakha and warned that Israeli territorial concessions would endanger lives. As the Rebbe wrote in a letter, "I repeat: All of the military professionals and experts (that I know), without exception all responded that any relinquishment of Yehuda and Shomron and the Golan will certainly endanger lives."[110] Once this is so, the Rebbe argued that all talk of long-term benefits from a peace treaty were too speculative to carry any security or halakhic weight. Common sense and halakha give more credence to the immediate endangerment of life than to the possibility of a future long-term peace.

In addition, the Rebbe simply did not trust the Arab nations. While we have seen his high regard for aspects of Western society,[111] he thought it was extremely naive to make concessions based on promises from Arab governments. As he once said:

> It is impossible to trust the promises of non-Jews – their promises have no standing, as it is clear that they will not keep them.... In addition, it is explicit in the Torah: "Esau hates Jacob" (Rashi on Gen. 33:4).... [Israeli politicians] trust the promises of the Arabs despite the fact that they see how they "kept" their promises in the past – that within twenty-four hours of a promise they broke it.[112]

---

109. *Karati VeEin Oneh*, vol. 1, 224, from Asara BeTevet 5738.
110. *Likkutei Sihot* 15, *Hosafot*, 489.
111. See chapter 16, note 43.
112. *Karati VeEin Oneh*, vol. 1, 113–14, from Simhat Torah 5736.

The Land of Israel and the State of Israel

Similarly, the Rebbe argued that trusting in the United Nations or the United States to enforce a peace treaty was a fool's dream.[113]

No Legal Right

In consonance with these halakhic and security concerns, the Rebbe emphasized that the Israeli government did not have the legal authority to return the captured territories. The Land of Israel belongs to the Jewish people no matter which state controls the land. This being the case, if God, in His kindness, finally returned the land to Jewish control, no government has the right to uproot Jewish settlements and return the land to non-Jews.

Therefore, while still disavowing the notion of "the beginning of the redemption" and highlighting the significance of the Jewish Diaspora, the Rebbe remarked:

> We should go out and strongly proclaim that the Land of Israel is owned by the Jewish people, and our authority in this regard is that "we call out in the name of God" – since "the Holy One, blessed be He, gave it to us." The detailed calculations of how many years the non-Jews lived in the land versus how many years the Jews lived there do not matter. [All that matters is] that the Holy One, blessed be He, gave it to us, and anyone who wants to take it from the Jewish people are "robbers" from God and from the Jewish people.[114]

Similarly, on a different occasion, after expounding on the Jewish people's ownership over the entire land, the Rebbe remarked:

> From this it is obvious that no one can change this fact [the Jewish people's ownership of the land], and therefore regarding these people who give parts of the Land of Israel to the non-Jews – this

---

113. Ibid., 320, *siha* from *Parashat Re'eh* 5738.
114. *Torat Menahem* 5729: 1, 299.

has no importance or significance, because "the word of our God will stand eternally."[115]

The Rebbe emphasized that this was not a violation of the three oaths, which prohibit forcing the redemption, as all of the land was conquered in a *defensive* war and miraculously given to the Jewish people. This was a clear divine message for the Jewish people to annex and resettle what is rightfully theirs.[116]

A Plan of Action

So what, then, did the Rebbe suggest the State of Israel do regarding the conquered territories? First, as noted above, Israeli leaders need to replace their feelings of submissiveness to non-Jews with the resolve to stand before the world and proudly proclaim their divine right to all the land within the biblical borders of Israel and their willingness to fight to retain it. Only then will the Arabs and international community realize the futility of their military and diplomatic avenues and eventually accept the new reality.[117]

In tandem with these proclamations, the Rebbe advocated that Israel quietly build settlements and put facts on the ground. This will both fortify the border and simultaneously show Israel's determination to retain the land by making it increasingly difficult for concessions to be made. As the Rebbe said on several occasions, "Action is the main thing," a general theme of his thought that was also true regarding the settling of the land.[118]

CONCLUSION

The Rebbe's extended discussions of the nature of the Land of Israel and the State of Israel demonstrate some of the unique elements of his leadership. While most of the Jewish world divided itself into Zionist

---

115. Ibid., 5742: 1, 499.
116. Ibid.
117. See, for example, *Karati VeEin Oneh*, vol. 1, 293, from Lag BaOmer 5738.
118. *Karati VeEin Oneh*, vol. 1, 317, *Erev Shabbat, Parashat Va'ethanan* 5738; ibid., 383–84, *Parashat Vayetzeh* 5739.

The Land of Israel and the State of Israel

and non-Zionist camps, the Rebbe was unique in his approach to the issues. He plumbed the depths of Torah and Chabad teachings to see what was necessary in order to bring *Mashiah* and attempted to practically apply his conclusions.

Secondary Literature Consulted for Chapter 19, "The Land of Israel and the State of Israel"

Alon Dahan, *Goel Aharon*, 462–525.

Alon Dahan, "Yahaso shel R. Menahem Mendel Schneerson LaTziyonut, LeEretz Yisrael ULeMedinat Yisrael," 301–23.

Yehiel Harari, *Sodo shel HaRebbe*, 227–52.

Jonathan Garb, *The Chosen Will Become Herds: Studies in Twentieth-Century Kabbalah* 64–69.

Aviezer Ravitzky, *Messianism, Zionism, and Jewish Religious Radicalism*, 193–206.

Eli Rubin, "Integrity and Peace: The Torah, the People, and the Land."

Shalom Dovber Wolf, *Bein Or LeHoshekh: Medinat Yisrael – At'halta DiGeula o Hoshekh Kaful UMekhupal*.

Part 6

The True and Complete Redemption

Chapter 20

"Until When?" The Rebbe's Push for *Mashiah*

From his earliest days, the Rebbe was enchanted and challenged by a vision of redemption.[1] His vivid depictions of a world in which God would eradicate human suffering[2] and a clear consciousness of the work necessary to create it accompanied him throughout his life.[3] As we have seen, every aspect of his theoretical philosophy and practical programming was in some way oriented toward the ultimate healing of the world.

This chapter will analyze three interrelated questions regarding the Rebbe's efforts for achieving redemption: (1) What was the Rebbe's conception of a redeemed world? (2) Why did the Rebbe speak of the realization of this goal as imminent? (3) What implications, other than

1. *Iggerot Kodesh* 12, letter 4226, to Yitzhak Ben-Tzvi, the president of Israel. See chapter 17, section "The President of Israel Is Not the *Nasi*."
2. See *Iggerot Kodesh*, ibid.
3. For indications that redemption was on the Rebbe's mind in his pre-leadership years, see *Reshimot Hoveret* 11, 321–22, and Eli Rubin, "Lisbon, 1941: The Messiah, the Invalid and the Fish."

the ones outlined in the previous chapters, should living at this pivotal moment have for the members of the last generation of exile?

Our study of the Rebbe's drive toward redemption will mainly draw from the Rebbe's final decade of teaching (5742–52/1982–92). During his first three decades at the helm of Chabad, the Rebbe treated messianism as a theme among a broad constellation of interconnected concepts. In his final decade, however, the nature of redemption, its imminence, and the need to do the final work to create a redeemed world slowly became ever more dominant themes in his talks. This culminated in his final two years (1991–92/5751–52), when nearly every talk highlighted the need to practically bring *Mashiah* and usher in the Messianic Era.[4]

BACKGROUND

Unequivocally, belief that there will be a Messianic Era led by a human redeemer referred to as "the *Mashiah*" is a mainstay of rabbinic Judaism. This conformity, though, belies a variety of approaches to how central this idea should be in the consciousness of a Jew in exile. More specifically, various approaches exist regarding how much the exilic Jew should consciously strive to create the messianic reality. Some strands of Jewish thought, often stemming from Maimonidean rational philosophy, downplay the significance of redemption as a motivating factor in daily Jewish life.[5] According to this approach, a person should focus on his own obligations toward God without thinking about the promised reward of the Messianic Era.

Messianism in the Jewish Mystical Tradition

By contrast, Jewish mysticism, at least from the time of Arizal, was suffused with a messianic mindset.[6] Central to Arizal's teachings was the

---

4. The Rebbe himself acknowledged this shift; see, for example, *Torat Menahem* 5747: 2, 613. See also Aryeh Solomon (2000), who surveyed the frequency of various themes in the Rebbe's talks. A comparison of his charts from different decades of the Rebbe's leadership (Solomon, 50–51, 116–17, 168–70) demonstrates the rise of redemption as a theme in the Rebbe's later years.
5. See, for example, David Berger (2011), 278–88; David Shatz (2015), 274–315.
6. For the classic studies of Gershom Scholem in this regard, see Scholem (1954), 240–44, 281–84; Scholem (1971), 43–48, 59–77. More recent scholars have demonstrated

notion that the world is in some way "broken" from its inception and the Jewish people are charged with the mission of repairing this spiritual, cosmic rupture. Each mitzva, especially if performed with the correct mystical intention, mends a small section of the cosmos and advances the world toward its state of ultimate perfection for which it was created.

In conjunction with ritual performances that repair the spiritual substructure of reality as a whole, Jewish mystics also spoke of a personal redemption in the form of a "redeemed" or messianic consciousness.[7] Through intense spiritual work these mystics sought to achieve personal perfection via a consciousness of complete unification with God. Each individual's state of "redemption" plays an integral role in the ultimate collective redemption of the entire world.

Messianism in Early Chabad

These themes of personal and collective redemption were interwoven into Chabad thought from its inception.[8] On a cosmic scale, the Alter Rebbe described the messianic reality as the full disclosure of the divine light within the confines of the material world.[9] Building from Arizal's conception of the purpose of a mitzva, the Alter Rebbe added that each mitzva literally creates part of the messianic reality by drawing down the highest recesses of divinity into our world.[10] Moving from the cosmic/collective to the personal, the Alter Rebbe relates to the emergence of "the innermost point" of the Jewish soul – a consciousness that is above

---

that the same drive toward redemption, albeit in a different form, also permeated early Kabbala. See, for example, Moshe Idel (1998).

7. See, for example, Moshe Idel (1998), 61–79.
8. Scholars have long debated if Hasidism was a messianic movement that was actively trying to bring *Mashiah* or if it neutralized this messianic focus with a shift toward personal redemption. Gershom Scholem (1971), 176–202, argues for the latter position, while Isaac Tishby (1967), 1–45, takes the former approach. Naftali Loewenthal (1996) argues that Chabad intertwines the concepts of personal and collective redemption, such that the focus of Hasidism is not on one at the expense of the other, but rather that personal redemption helps create the reality of collective redemption.
9. *Tanya, Likkutei Amarim*, ch. 36.
10. Ibid., chs. 36–37.

the intellect – as a messianic event.[11] As we will see, the Rebbe drew heavily from these themes when formulating his approach to redemption.

A REDEEMED WORLD

Before launching into the Rebbe's urgent message of redemption's imminence and his view of the work necessary to actualize redemption, it is necessary to briefly outline his more theoretical discussions on the characteristics of the Messianic Era. These discussions provide important context for understanding the rationale and nature of his time-sensitive and mission-focused talks.

As with every aspect of his thought, the Rebbe drew from two primary sets of sources to build a picture of a redeemed world: halakhic sources, with a particular focus on Rambam, and Hasidism. While these two sets of work seem to depict disparate visions of the future, the Rebbe contended that they are actually different layers of the same reality.

Rambam's Halakhic Definition of Redemption

The classical source for an authoritative Jewish account of the Messianic Era is the final chapters of *Mishneh Torah*. There, Rambam describes various aspects of the Messianic Era: the return of Jewish sovereignty under the Davidic dynasty, the rebuilding of the *Beit HaMikdash*, the ingathering of the exiles, world peace, physical bounty, and a great desire for knowledge of God. What is the relationship between these distinct details? Is there an overarching single definition that runs through these beautiful manifold descriptions?

In several characteristically detailed textual analyses, the Rebbe honed in on the beginning of Rambam's treatment of the laws of *Mashiah*:

> In the future, the messianic king will arise and renew the Davidic dynasty, restoring it to its initial sovereignty. He will build the Temple and gather the dispersed of Israel. Then, in his days, the observances of all the statutes will return to their previous state.

---

11. *Tanya, Iggeret HaKodesh*, sec. 4. Similarly, see *Likkutei Torah, Vayikra*, 2a.

We will offer sacrifices, and observe the Sabbatical and Jubilee years according to all their particulars as described in the Torah.[12]

The Rebbe noted that according to Rambam's basic description, *Mashiah*'s activities ("In the future...the dispersed of Israel") segues into the restoration of the complete halakhic system ("the observance of all the statutes will return to their previous state"). *Mashiah*'s mission will be to enable and ensure the complete fulfillment of all mitzvot. As the Rebbe explained:

> What is lacking in our fulfillment of Torah and mitzvot due to the fact that the Jewish people and the *Beit HaMikdash* are not complete (which is the general meaning of exile) will be completed by *Mashiah*. This is the mission of *Mashiah*: that he restore "the Davidic dynasty," and "the observance of all the statutes will return to their previous state," meaning that he will restore perfection to the halakhot and mitzvot of the Torah.[13]

The Rebbe argued that the complete fulfillment and expression of Torah and mitzvot is the essential characteristic of the Messianic Era. Therefore, the idea that *Mashiah* will redeem the Jewish people from foreign control but will not restore the complete halakhic system is entirely outside normative Jewish dogma.[14]

The Rebbe placed other aspects of Rambam's description of the Messianic Era as well under the heading of "perfection of Torah and mitzvot." For example, in the final halakha of *Mishneh Torah*, Rambam writes:

> The occupation of the entire world will be solely to know God. Therefore, the Jews will be great sages and know the hidden matters, grasping the knowledge of their Creator according to the full extent

---

12. *Mishneh Torah, Hilkhot Melakhim UMilhemoteihem* 11:1.
13. *Likkutei Sihot* 18, Balak, no. 2, *se'if* 9. See also *Torat Menahem: Hadranim al HaRambam, Hadran al HaRambam* 5746, 101–2.
14. See also *Likkutei Sihot* 34, Shofetim, no. 3, where the Rebbe argued based on Rambam that belief in *Mashiah* is intertwined with belief in eternality of Torah and mitzvot.

of human potential. As it states: "The world will be filled with the knowledge of God as the waters cover the ocean bed" (Is. 11:9).[15]

The Rebbe noted that in addition to being a vision of inspiration and beauty, this presentation by Rambam is actually describing the optimal fulfillment of a mitzva: knowing God.[16] Rambam opens *Mishneh Torah* with a detailed description of the central mitzva of "I am the Lord your God," which generates the obligation to understand as much about God as humanly possible. At the end of *Mishneh Torah*, Rambam returns to this theme and explains that the Messianic Era will usher in a more perfect fulfillment of this mitzva – and together with it all other mitzvot – than is currently possible. Rambam's words are both inspirational and also a technical description of the ultimate fulfillment of this mitzva.[17]

Similarly, the Rebbe understood Rambam's description of humanity living in peace and fraternity as a manifestation of the complete expression of Torah and mitzvot. Non-Jews engaging in their seven mitzvot while also entirely occupied with their form of Torah study and pursuit of knowledge of God will cultivate a mass integration of the divine values of peace and brotherhood. Therefore, from this perspective, world peace is also the fulfillment of the ultimate expression of Torah and mitzvot.[18]

Hasidism's Definition of Redemption

The Rebbe saw the hasidic descriptions of the Messianic Era as a deeper understanding of Rambam's halakhic definition. Hasidism teaches that Torah and mitzvot are rooted in the Divine Essence itself.[19] Hence, the full expression of Torah and mitzvot is identical with the revelation of the

---

15. *Mishneh Torah, Hilkhot Melakhim UMilhemoteihem* 12:5.
16. *Torat Menahem: Hadranim al HaRambam, Hadran al HaRambam* 5746, 101–12.
17. See *Likkutei Sihot* 27, *Hosafot*, 239–40, which says that this is also the highest form of Torah study.
18. *Sihot Kodesh* 5733: 2, 106–7; *Likkutei Sihot* 23, Balak, no. 2, *se'ifim* 9–10. See also *Torat Menahem: Hadranim al HaRambam*, 65–66, where the Rebbe argues that even physical bounty is a manifestation of the complete disclosure of Torah and mitzvot.
19. *Inyana shel Torat HaHasidut, se'if* 3.

"Until When?" The Rebbe's Push for Mashiah

Divine Essence in the material world (which is the only plane of existence where Torah and mitzvot can be practically fulfilled).[20] This revelation of the Divine Essence in the lowest plane is called a *Dira BaTahtonim*, the ultimate reason for God's engagement with creation in the first place.[21]

At the apex of history, the *yehida* of the world will be disclosed, and every aspect of the world – from humanity to inanimate objects – will be clearly perceived as an expression of the Divine Essence.[22] Wherever one "looks" one will see God shining through each nook and cranny of the material world. The Rebbe saw an expression of this vision in the final lines of Rambam's *Mishneh Torah*: "The world will be filled with the knowledge of God as the waters cover the ocean bed." In the Rebbe's words:

> The revelation of the Divine Essence will be constant, and it will permeate the boundaries of the world, meaning to say that the reality of the [material] world will remain ... but in a fashion that is entirely permeated with "knowledge of God," similar to the creatures of the water that appear as part of the water – that their entire existence is encompassed by the water of the ocean.[23]

The world will be revealed as entirely submerged in the unifying "sea" of God. Each mitzva brings the world closer to this reality.

REDEMPTION'S IMMINENCE

Introduction

The Rebbe declared in his first discourse that "we are at the end of this period [of *ikveta deMeshiha* (the footsteps of *Mashiah*)]," and that the generational mission was to draw the Divine Essence into the lowest realm. In line with this, in his later years, the Rebbe often referred to

---

20. See, for example, *Torat Menahem: Hadranim al HaRambam, Hadran al HaRambam* 5748, 146, which states that "Torah is absolutely one with His Essence" and which explores the implications of this concept for the complete revelation of Torah at the end of history.
21. See, for example, *Likkutei Sihot* 17, *Shemini*, no. 1, *se'ifim* 8–10.
22. *Inyana shel Torat HaHasidut, se'ifim* 5, 21.
23. *Torat Menahem: Hadranim al HaRambam, Hadran al HaRambam* 5748, 151.

the generation as "the last generation of exile,"[24] even at times adding "and it follows, the first generation of redemption."[25] From where did he derive such a far-reaching conclusion?

In general, this identification of the era was rooted in an unprecedented confluence of both extremely positive and negative phenomena in Jewish society and the world at large.[26] Seeing these sorts of events and trends as indicative of *ikveta deMeshiha* flows directly from the Rebbe's conception of redemption that was outlined above. On the one hand, the term *Dira BaTahtonim* indicates that redemption must come in the context of *tahtonim* – the lowest and darkest moments of history. Conversely, the Rebbe read and reread Rambam's halakhic description of the Messianic Era and analyzed each detail and term. He understood that society as a whole was moving toward the realization of that vision, and that these positive phenomena indicated proximity to redemption. With this background, let us turn to the sources and phenomena that the Rebbe cited when discussing redemption's imminence.

Negative Phenomena

In a letter he wrote in 1968, the Rebbe briefly responded to a questioner who appears to have asked him about his declarations of redemption's imminence. The Rebbe tersely responded as follows:

> You ask for an explanation of a statement in one of the general messages, a statement to the effect that we are living in the era of *ikveta deMeshiha*. This is based on many statements of my father-in-law. See also the signs of this era as indicated by the Rabbis (see the end of Sota). It is not difficult to see these signs in our present generation.[27]

---

24. See, for example, *Torat Menahem* 5745: 1, 671; ibid., 5746: 1, 317; ibid., 5748: 2, 272; ibid., 5748: 3, 511; ibid., 5749: 2, 220; ibid., 5749: 4, 235; ibid., 5750: 3, 24; ibid., 5751: 3, 160.
25. See, for example, *Torat Menahem* 5743: 2, 875; ibid., 5748: 3, 493; ibid., 5749: 1, 22, 391; ibid., 5749: 2, 386; ibid., 5750: 2, 447; ibid., 5750: 3, 24; ibid., 5751: 3, 248; ibid., 5752: 2, 39, 46, 89, 180, 353; *Iggerot Kodesh* 15, letter 5467.
26. *Torat Menahem* 5747: 2, 627.
27. Retrieved from www.chabad.org/2189968.

"Until When?" The Rebbe's Push for Mashiah

The Rebbe pointed to two items as support for his interpretation of the contemporaneous historical moment: (1) R. Yosef Yitzhak's statements and (2) the signs provided in rabbinic literature indicating the end of time. In many talks and letters the Rebbe elaborated upon these two points.

R. Yosef Yitzhak's Wartime Statements

The Rebbe saw his messianism as a direct continuation of his father-in-law's understanding of his own era. In 1939, R. Yosef Yitzhak fled Nazi-occupied Poland for America, where he quickly directed his energies toward strengthening the remnants of Lubavitch and, more generally, Jewish life in America. Among his other programs and projects, he launched a monthly journal called *HaKeria VehaKedusha*, which was to be a platform for his wartime messages to a dangerously complacent American and world Jewry.[28]

This journal, printed intermittently from 1940 to 1945, showcased articles from R. Yosef Yitzhak that highlighted the need for repentance by contextualizing World War II and the decimation of European Jewry within a distinctly messianic framework. He most passionately expressed this line of thinking in a series of four public letters (*kol korei*),[29] published in *HaKeria VehaKedusha* and elsewhere, in which he urgently called on all Jews to recognize the war as the final "birth pangs of *Mashiah*."[30] The following is an excerpt from the second public letter:

> "Immediately to redemption!" Be prepared for imminent redemption! It is coming with quick steps even if you do not recognize it. It is "standing behind the wall" (Song. 2:9). The righteous redeemer is behind the wall, and the time to prepare to greet him is very short![31]

---

28. For sources and details about this journal, see Naftali Loewenthal (1996), 61–69.
29. The letters were republished by Vaad Hayyalei Beit David, and are available under the title "Le'alter LiGeula" at drive.google.com/drive/u/0/folders/0B2k04CfIO mXwU2JwdlQzcmcydW8?tid=0B4mWfMamtZnjMUlKY3lMZEVZY1U.
30. See Sanhedrin 98b.
31. Excerpt from R. Yosef Yitzhak's second public letter (from 16 Sivan 5701 [1941]).

The True and Complete Redemption

According to R. Yosef Yitzhak, the only way to prepare for the arrival of *Mashiah* was complete repentance, leading him to coin the charge "Immediately to repentance, immediately to redemption!" Similarly, on a different occasion he declared that the Jewish people had nearly completed their exilic service and now needed only to "polish their buttons" to bring *Mashiah*.[32]

The year 1945 saw the conclusion of the war but not the redemption of the world. Soon after the war's end, R. Yosef Yitzhak suspended the journal and also toned down the messianic rhetoric from his talks and letters.

R. Yosef Yitzhak's wartime declarations made an indelible impression on his son-in-law. As a devoted Hasid of his father-in-law, during much of the 1940s the Rebbe concluded hundreds of letters with the phrase "Immediately to repentance, immediately to redemption" and continued this practice for two years after the war's end.[33]

The Rebbe's focus on his father-in-law's messianic pronouncements continued even after R. Yosef Yitzhak's passing. For example, on 20 Av 5710 (1950), six months after his father-in-law's death, the Rebbe referred to his father-in-law's letters as "the general assurance with which [R. Yosef Yitzhak] assured the Jewish people"[34] and exhorted the Hasidim to follow the instructions of their departed Rebbe in order to merit its actualization. Particularly in the Rebbe's later years, as we will see, he referenced his father-in-law's pronouncements dozens of times.

Signs from Rabbinic Literature
In addition to his father-in-law's pronouncements, the Rebbe drew his understanding of this historical moment from the rabbinic descriptions of *ikveta deMeshiha*. The concluding mishna of Tractate Sota is the most prominent of these passages:

---

32. *Sefer HaSihot* 5688–91, Simhat Torah 5689, 42. See there, note 51, for references to dozens of places where the Rebbe cited and elaborated upon this metaphor.
33. See many of the letters published in *Iggerot Kodesh*, vols. 1–2. Naftali Loewenthal (1996), note 18, demonstrates that the Rebbe continued signing his letters this way until 1947, two years after R. Yosef Yitzhak ceased this practice.
34. *Torat Menahem* 5710, 173.

> In the times of the approach of the *Mashiah*, impudence will increase and high costs will pile up. Although the vine shall bring forth its fruit, wine will nevertheless be expensive. And the monarchy shall turn to heresy, and there will be no one to give reproof about this....
>
> And the wisdom of scribes will putrefy, and people who fear sin will be held in disgust, and the truth will be absent. The youth will shame the face of elders; elders will stand before minors. Normal family relations will be ruined: A son will disgrace a father.... The face of the generation will be like the face of a dog; a son will no longer be ashamed before his father. And what is there for us to rely on? Only upon our Father in heaven.[35]

In several talks and conversations, the Rebbe expressed his opinion that the events foretold in this mishna aptly describe the current state of society. For example, in 5744 (1984), during a talk about spreading Hasidism, the Rebbe said:

> Since we are standing in the "end of time" (*aharit hayamim*), and according to all the signs that are explained in the end of Tractate Sota we are literally close to the arrival of Elijah[36]... we need to increase the revelation of the inner aspect of the Torah in every place, limitlessly.[37]

In particular, the Rebbe emphasized that "impudence" is a hallmark of the current generation,[38] even once humorously remarking to Israeli

---

35. Sota 49b.
36. The heralder of *Mashiah*. See, for example, Eiruvin 43b.
37. *Torat Menahem* 5744: 1, 452.
38. Characteristically, the Rebbe at times spoke of the positive elements embedded in this impudence and how it must be channeled toward the service of God. See, for example, *Torat Menahem* 5713: 1, 212; ibid., 5746: 2, 832; ibid., 5748: 4, 269, note 71.

Chief Rabbi Mordechai Eliyahu that this sign has been fulfilled in "exemplary fashion."³⁹

In addition to the descriptions from the above mishna, the Rebbe focused on a midrashic statement that associates international wars with *Mashiah*'s impending arrival: "R. Eliezer b. Avina said, 'If you see kingdoms at war with each other, look forward to the feet of *Mashiah*.'" In the 1980s the Rebbe began applying this passage to the Cold War and the proxy wars that were flaring all around the globe.⁴⁰ In his view, the existence of two rival superpowers with the ability to destroy civilization was the ultimate state of "kingdoms at war."

Positive Phenomena

Concurrent with these negative indicators of proximity to the Messianic Era, the Rebbe also identified and frequently highlighted heretofore inconceivable positive shifts that were "tastes"⁴¹ of an imminently redeemed world. We have already touched upon several of them: the revelation and spread of the wellsprings of Hasidism,⁴² the presence of Jewish communities in all corners of the globe,⁴³ the shift of Western society and America in particular toward embracing ethical monotheism,⁴⁴ the return of assimilated younger Jews to Jewish identity and observance,⁴⁵ the rise of the feminist movement,⁴⁶ the innovative Torah of the

---

39. *Torat Menahem* 5745: 5, 3090–91. For more instances where the Rebbe argued that the generation fulfilled the rabbinic criteria for the final generation, see *Torat Menahem* 5742: 1, 454; ibid., 5747: 2, 624, 628; ibid., 5750: 4, 179; ibid., 5751: 3, 320; ibid., 5751: 4, 38.
40. *Torat Menahem* 5747: 2, 628. See also *Torat Menahem* 5743: 4, 1740–41; *Torat Menahem* 5744: 2, 1243.
41. See chapter 14, section "Tasting Serenity."
42. See chapter 8, section "Hasidism and *Mashiah*."
43. See chapter 4, section "Ramifications of the Denial of Secular Space," and chapter 18, section "University Studies."
44. See *Torat Menahem* 5751: 2, 94; ibid., 5751: 3, 188–89.
45. See, for example, *Torat Menahem* 5717: 1, 63–66; maamar "VeHaya BaYom HaHu 5728," se'if 8 (*Sefer HaMaamarim Melukat*, vol. 1, 16, and note 61); *Torat Menahem* 5728: 1, 214–16.
46. See chapter 15, section "A Messianic Vision."

Rogatchover,[47] various events in the Land of Israel including the State of Israel's miraculous military victories,[48] and scientific advancements.[49] These unprecedented positive phenomena expressed a world nearing its ultimate perfection as the Rebbe understood it – the complete expression of Torah, mitzvot, and, most crucially, the Divine Essence itself.

In addition to these trends, the Rebbe interpreted various major international events as signs of the world's progress toward redemption, most notably the Gulf War and the fall of the Soviet Union.

The Gulf War
During the summer of 1990 Iraqi forces invaded Kuwait, triggering the formation of an American-led international coalition to confront Iraq. In January 1991, the coalition forces launched an offensive against Iraqi troops in Kuwait, eventually leading to the coalition's occupation of Iraq.

In response to this offensive, Iraq launched scud missiles at Israel, an American ally not involved in the fighting. Against the predictions of experts, who foretold extensive casualties, the Scud missiles that Iraq shot into Israel resulted in only a handful of civilian deaths.

The Rebbe interpreted every aspect of this war through a distinctively messianic lens. From the war's inception, he repeatedly connected the events of the war to the following midrash found in *Yalkut Shimoni*:

> R. Yitzhak said: "In the year that the king *Mashiah* is revealed, the king of Persia will attack an Arab king, and the Arab king will go and consult with them [the nations of the world]. And all the nations of the world will be stormy and startled and will fall on their faces and be pained like the pains of a woman in labor, and the Jewish people will be stormy and startled and will say, "Where should we go, where should we go?" And he says to them: "My children, do not fear. All that I have done I have done for your sake. Do not fear. The time of your redemption has arrived."[50]

---

47. See chapter 9, section "The Rogatchover."
48. See, for example, *Torat Menahem* 5728: 1, 215.
49. See chapter 18, section "Scientific Developments and the Messianic Consciousness."
50. *Yalkut Shimoni, Yeshayahu, remez* 499.

According to the Rebbe, this midrash perfectly matched the sequence of the war.[51] Modern Iraq is included in the domain of ancient Persia, allowing the opening line of the midrash to refer to Sadaam Hussein's invasion of Kuwait. Kuwait's consultation with the "nations of the world" refers to the forming of an international coalition against the ruler of Iraq (Persia). Meanwhile, the midrash describes the Jewish people as being terrified and directionless despite their neutrality, as they were in the months of the Gulf War.[52]

As he did before each of Israel's previous wars,[53] in the time leading up to the Gulf War the Rebbe exhorted the Jews of Israel to have *bittahon* (trust in God) that no harm would befall them. Citing biblical descriptions of the land, he assured a worried populace that Israel was the safest place in the world as "God's eyes are upon it"[54] and even encouraged people to travel to the country. In this context, he cited this midrash to buttress his message. For example, here is the first such occasion:

> May it be God's will that we will immediately merit to see the third *Beit HaMikdash* ... and particularly since all of the rabbinic signs regarding the time of the end of the exile and the time of redemption have been fulfilled, including the sign of the *Yalkut Shimoni* (which has been publicized recently): "R. Yitzhak said: In the year.... The time of your redemption has arrived:" So may it be for us, that from the start there is nothing from which to be startled, for we already have an assurance of "Do not fear. The time of your redemption has arrived."[55]

---

51. See, for example, *Torat Menahem* 5750: 4, 179, 288; ibid., 5751: 1, 137, 189, 202; ibid., 5751: 2, 122, 140, 189, 264, 385, 443; ibid., 5751: 3, 321.
52. It is important to note that the Rebbe, who assiduously avoided negative formulations, did not focus on this line of the midrash.
53. See, for example, *Torat Menahem* 5727: 2, 414–15; Eli Rubin, "Integrity and Peace: The Torah, the People and the Land," for links to texts of telegrams and messages that the Rebbe sent to the residents of Israel before the Six-Day War.
54. *Torat Menahem* 5751: 2, 189.
55. Ibid., 5750: 4, 180.

The Rebbe used this midrash as part of an assurance that no harm would come to the Jewish people.

When the war concluded with a decisive coalition victory and minimal loss of life, which the Rebbe defined as miraculous, he continued to cite the midrash, emphasizing its concluding assurance of redemption. For example, a few months after the war's conclusion, the Rebbe spoke of the significance of the year 5751/1990–91, during which the bulk of the Gulf War occurred:

> In addition to the fact that we are in real proximity to the true and complete redemption...this is the year that the promise of "As in the days of your exodus from the land of Egypt, I will show him wonders" (Mic. 7:15) should be fulfilled. And we have already seen wonders in actuality that testify that this is the "year that the king *Mashiah* is revealed," which means that we are already on the cusp of the beginning of the days of *Mashiah*, on the cusp of redemption, and immediately [we should experience] redemption drawn down and its completion.[56]

In the Rebbe's eyes, the miracles of the Gulf War indicated proximity to the miracles of the ultimate redemption.[57]

The Fall of the Soviet Union

The Rebbe interpreted the fall of the Soviet Union similarly. Like most members of the free world, the Rebbe saw the Soviet Union as the evil superpower, a threat to both world peace and its own citizens. As a Jew, this image was sharpened for the Rebbe by the fact that millions of Jews were trapped behind the Iron Curtain.[58] And for the better part of a century, Communist Russia had been Chabad's ultimate antagonist,

---

56. Ibid., 5751: 4, 39.
57. See, for example, the public letter written by the Rebbe before Passover 5751, published in *Likkutei Sihot* 37, *Hosafot*, 164–68.
58. Throughout his years of leadership, the Rebbe quietly worked to aid the Jews trapped behind the Iron Curtain both spiritually and materially. For a description of these operations and the Rebbe's opposition to the public demonstrations, see Joseph Telushkin (2014), 293–306, and Chaim Miller (2014), 288–90.

highlighted by the regime's imprisonment of R. Yosef Yitzhak for his religious leadership. The quick and nearly bloodless fall of the Soviet Union and the transformation of Russia into a free and Jewishly tolerant society were understood by the Rebbe as being exemplars of God's miracles and "tastes" of the ultimate redemption. The Rebbe highlighted several aspects of this change.

In the winter of 5750 (1990), the Rebbe called attention to the seismic shift in the lives of Russia's millions of citizens. He mentioned that there were those who were still skeptical that the world was progressing in a remarkably positive direction that would culminate in the imminent arrival of *Mashiah*, claiming instead that "the world was functioning normally." The Rebbe felt that this was ignoring overt facts:

> In recent years...there are extreme revolutions occurring, and in the kindness of God they are occurring peacefully, without wars and bloodshed...and so seamlessly so as to appear as if all is ordinary in the world. [This is happening] starting with Russia (the country from which the *nasi* of our generation came), which, after a period of seventy years under a fearful and violent regime that spread its dread over all of citizens of the country...suddenly and in a very small amount of time underwent a drastic change by its own leaders in the form of government.[59]

The Rebbe described this revolution, in conjunction with similar drastic revolutions that were simultaneously occurring in China and India, as signs that "we are standing in the final moments of *ikveta deMeshiha*."[60]

Elsewhere, the Rebbe spoke about another previously inconceivable ramification of the Soviet Union's dissolution: the complete turnaround in the treatment of millions of Jews. The emigration of millions of Russian Jews who were previously trapped behind the Iron Curtain was a "taste of the 'ingathering of the exiles'" as foretold by the prophets.[61]

---

59. *Torat Menahem* 5750: 1, 420–21. See also *Torat Menahem* 5751: 1, 202.
60. *Torat Menahem* 5750: 1, 422.
61. See *Torat Menahem* 5751: 1, 29; ibid., 5752: 2, 371.

"Until When?" The Rebbe's Push for Mashiah

Even more surprisingly, this ingathering was not due to people fleeing persecution, but rather actually assisted by the Russian government. Similarly, the Rebbe saw the ability for new *sheluhim* (emissaries) to work unfettered in the same cities that persecuted Chabad as nothing less than a "wonder," which "emphasizes that immediately we should see the greatest wonder – the true and complete redemption."[62]

In summary, the Rebbe saw a world that although spiritually deficient was simultaneously experiencing trends and events that were "tastes" of redemption. This image matched what the sources – both halakhic and mystical – taught about the nature of the unfolding process of global perfection.

THE OBLIGATIONS OF THE LAST GENERATION
A Flurry of Activity

Having outlined the Rebbe's basis for his statements about *Mashiah*'s imminent arrival, we must now turn to the next question: What was the Rebbe's goal in speaking so constantly and emphatically about this point? What was he trying to accomplish?

In a 5746 (1986) talk, the Rebbe directly addressed this issue. After once again describing the proximity to *Mashiah*, he raised the possibility that with this knowledge some people might simply sit back and rest on their laurels, confident in the inexorability of redemption:

> Based on what we said, that we are in a time period whose entire essence is "for everyone to stand ready" for the building of the third *Beit HaMikdash* and the complete and true redemption, a person might think that in this situation there is no need for more toil but rather only to "pack one's bags" and wait for the coming of *Mashiah*.[63]

Characteristically, the Rebbe categorically rejected this passive posture. Rather, in his view, proximity to redemption demanded the exact

---

62. *Torat Menahem* 5751: 4, 135–36.
63. Ibid., 5747: 2, 205.

opposite: an increase and intensification of one's service – "above measure and limitation."[64]

When analyzing the Rebbe's dozens of pronouncements about *Mashiah*'s imminence in the context of the complete talks, it becomes clear that his overwhelming objective was to spur people toward greater religious heights, which would bring *Mashiah* "in actuality." Consistently, whenever the Rebbe spoke about the proximity to *Mashiah*, he soon transitioned to the unique *obligations* that this creates. The final surge toward *Mashiah* depended entirely on an increase in Torah and mitzvot, with the particular approach that the Rebbe developed.

This response to *Mashiah*'s proximity flows directly from the Rebbe's understanding of the long arc of history toward redemption. Since Sinai, each mitzva drew down the Divine Essence one more level toward the lowest level of the material world. Now, within tantalizing grasp of actualizing the entire purpose of creation, the world needed one final surge of mitzvot and goodness to finally reunify the Divine Essence with its original abode.

Why Did R. Yosef Yitzhak's Statements Remain Unactualized?

For the Rebbe, the increased obligation clarified a glaring issue: the seeming inaccuracy of his father-in-law's assurances of an imminent redemption. By the time of the Rebbe's above-cited talks, decades had already passed since R. Yosef Yitzhak's wartime declarations, and redemption had still not arrived. On various occasions the Rebbe explicitly addressed this issue and always concluded with variations of the same response: some element of the mission to transform the world had yet to be accomplished.

For example, in a 5745 talk, the Rebbe cited those who assumed that R. Yosef Yitzhak must have been exaggerating regarding the immediacy of *Mashiah*'s arrival considering that forty years later the world still stood unredeemed. The Rebbe forcefully rejected this interpretation:

> This claim is the claim of "the old and foolish king" [i.e., the evil inclination] (Eccl. 4:13).... "Immediately to redemption" means literally

---

64. Ibid., 206.

immediately, and it is obvious that this was the intention of the *nasi* of our generation ... but due to our great sins we did not merit it.[65]

According to the Rebbe, his father-in-law was highlighting a unique opportunity for the world to achieve immediate redemption, as opposed to offering a definitive prediction of when that redemption will take place. While "immediately to redemption" does connote extreme temporal proximity, redemption is contingent on the Jewish people concluding the final elements of their mission.

Calculating the End-Time

The Rebbe contextualized R. Yosef Yitzhak's adoption of an action-oriented assurance of redemption within a long tradition of Jewish authorities. While the Talmud curses those who attempt to calculate the date of *Mashiah*'s arrival (*ketz*),[66] the Rebbe noted that a long list of eminent authorities, including R. Saadia Gaon, Rashi, Rambam, Ibn Ezra, Ramban, Abarbanel, R. Hayyim ibn Attar, the Vilna Gaon, the Alter Rebbe, and Malbim all offered dates for the end of the exile.[67] What allowed these halakhic authorities to contravene this prohibition?

In one talk, the Rebbe focused on the Talmud's rationale for the prohibition. Here is the relevant passage:

> R. Shmuel bar Nahmani says that R. Yonatan says: May those who calculate the end of time be cursed, as [people][68] would

---

65. *Torat Menahem* 5745: 5, 2622. Regarding the quotation from the verse in Ecclesiastes, see Ecclesiastes Rabba 4:13, which says that this refers to the evil inclination.
66. Sanhedrin 97b.
67. *Likkutei Sihot* 29, *Devarim-Hazon*, *se'if* 9. In an unpublished note available at drive. google.com/open?id=0B1b-ppeGd_P0RTYzVFAwMjRtM2M5Mkh2Z1FWLUFx MXNscHRZ the Rebbe wrote about a person who was uncomfortable with R. Yosef Yitzhak's messianic rhetoric and therefore distanced himself from Chabad. The Rebbe's response was that this person would presumably also have to stop associating with the list of earlier Torah authorities mentioned above, as they all provided dates for the *ketz*.
68. This translation follows Rambam in *Mishneh Torah, Hilkhot Melakhim UMilhemoteihem* 12:2. Rashi, however, interprets this line as referring to the very individuals who are engaging in the calculations.

say once their calculated end-time arrived and the *Mashiah* did not come that he will no longer come at all. Rather, the proper behavior is to continue to wait for his coming.[69]

The Talmud thus makes clear that the ban emanates from the Sages' concern that an unrealized messianic expectation can engender despair and a general religious weakening.

The Rebbe contended that the aforementioned authorities intended to combat that very phenomenon by offering their dates for the *ketz*. On a psychological level, the Rebbe cited Rambam's justification for R. Saadia Gaon's publication of a date on the grounds that it was a calculated strategy to strengthen a despondent people's hope in the coming of *Mashiah*. On a deeper level, the Alter Rebbe taught that the messianic reality is created through "our actions and service" during the exilic period.[70] Spiritual giants have the capacity to perceive this incrementally aggregating development and the extent of the remaining work. In addition, they can be granted a vision that the messianic reality could be fully formed by a specific date if the Jewish people accelerate their amassment of mitzvot and make an additional push toward redemption.

Armed with this knowledge, these authorities revealed the *ketz* to their generations with these goals in mind:

> The revelation of the *ketz*... [by these righteous leaders] serves as an inspiration for increasing service of Torah and mitzvot... and it grants strength for this service. Therefore, it is obvious that this is not included in the prohibition against calculating the *ketz*.... On the contrary, because it is serves as an inspiration and grants strength for this service, they need to reveal it.[71]

A *Tzaddik*'s revelation of a *ketz* generates an *increase* in religious activity in addition to lending spiritual support for such a push. Thus, the Rebbe

---

69. Sanhedrin 97b.
70. *Likkutei Sihot* 29, *Devarim-Hazon, se'if* 9. The Rebbe emphasized that this buildup began at the moment that the *Beit HaMikdash* was destroyed.
71. Ibid.

explained, R. Yosef Yitzhak's push toward *Mashiah* needs to be understood within the context of this tradition of obligation-generating and action-inducing messianic prediction. The Rebbe's own statements of redemption's imminence had a similar normative nature, as they regularly led to his outlining the obligation to intensify one's service of God.

THE UNIQUENESS OF THE LAST GENERATION

While the Rebbe certainly understood Chabad's push toward redemption within the context of the long tradition of offering a *ketz*, he also marked his father-in-law's pronouncements as unique within the annals of Jewish history. As the Rebbe said in 5748 (1988):

> Throughout all the generations of exile, the Jewish people anticipated and prayed daily for the coming of *Mashiah*, and certainly this is true regarding the *Tzaddikim* and *nesi'im* of the Jewish people… and several of them sacrificed everything to hasten the *ketz*.…
>
> Nonetheless, this does not compare to the "storm" about bringing *Mashiah* that was started by his eminence, my father-in-law, the *nasi* of our generation, through his… published declaration in *HaKeria VehaKedusha*: "Immediately to repentance, immediately to redemption!" Immediately is specific, [meaning] actually immediately.[72]

The Rebbe felt that the unprecedented urgency of R. Yosef Yitzhak's declarations reflected a new era of pushing for redemption.

As we have seen, this new era of messianic urgency had broad practical ramifications for the Rebbe. Over the course of his tenure, when speaking of his signature initiatives, he would often highlight their role in finishing the global transformation to the utopian world described by Rambam and mystical texts. In his later years, the Rebbe intensified and expanded the scope of the unique service of the times in several significant ways.

---

72. *Torat Menahem* 5748: 4, 266. See also *Torat Menahem* 5714: 2, 161.

The True and Complete Redemption

Personal Redemption
The Democratization of the Mission
One major theme of the Rebbe's later talks was the democratization of the messianic mission. While we have seen that the Rebbe's inclusive picture of a *Dira BaTahtonim* was a guiding light throughout his tenure, in his later years he constantly emphasized that the conclusion of the exilic mission needed to be accomplished by each and every person. As the Rebbe said in 5751 (1991):

> Each Jew – man, woman, and even child – has the responsibility to increase their service to bring *Mashiah* in actuality… there is no option to rely on other people rather than do the work oneself. This is the mission of each and every individual.[73]

The Rebbe repeated this message of responsibility and empowerment dozens of times in his later years, often reflecting on the words of Rambam that a single action of an individual person has the power to "tip the balance of the entire world to merit and save it."[74]

This message reached its crescendo in two impassioned speeches about the collective nature of the messianic mission. On Purim 5747 (1987) the Rebbe lengthily articulated his anguish and astonishment about the passing of all the various dates given for *Mashiah*'s arrival, including his father-in-law's pronouncements, without the arrival of the final redemption.

In a rare statement, the Rebbe said that he "toiled in his search" for a satisfactory answer. After much mental energy, he arrived at the following:

> I searched for an explanation, and the explanation that I found is that now the issue [of bringing *Mashiah*] has been transferred from "the *nasi* is everyone" to "everyone," meaning, to each and

---

73. *Torat Menahem* 5751: 3, 132.
74. *Mishneh Torah, Hilkhot Teshuva* 3:4. See, for example, *Torat Menahem* 5747: 1, 213; ibid., 5747: 2, 167, 207; ibid., 5750: 4, 33.

"Until When?" The Rebbe's Push for Mashiah

every Jew... now the focus to hasten redemption has become the individual responsibility of each man and woman.[75]

In earlier generations, the cosmic struggle for redemption was mainly placed on the generation's *Tzaddikim* and *nasi*. Accordingly, the average person's intentional participation in this process was through his *hitkashrut* (connection) to these elite figures. Now, however, "the matter has been transferred to each and every Jew," meaning that the final surge toward redemption depends directly on the people. In the Rebbe's words, "The statement of Rambam [that a single action can bring redemption] is now the personal issue of each individual."

This democratization of the mission to bring *Mashiah* reached its zenith on 28 Nisan 5751/1991. Identified in some Chabad circles as "the known talk" (*hasiha hayedua*) this cataclysmic talk sent shock waves through the community.

Like he did with so many other days on the calendar, he began the talk by describing how the date – 28 Nisan 5751 – was pregnant with messianic potential. Soon, though, he transitioned to an already familiar question: "Because of the unique emphasis on the redemption in this time, an astonishing question arises: How is it possible that despite all these factors, *Mashiah* has not yet come? This is beyond all possible comprehension."[76] The Rebbe's response was uncharacteristically stark:

> It is also beyond comprehension that when ten (and many times ten) Jews gather together at a time that is appropriate for the redemption to come, they do not raise a clamor great enough to cause *Mashiah* to come immediately. They are, Heaven forbid, able to accept the possibility that *Mashiah* will not arrive tonight, and even that he will not arrive tomorrow, or on the day after tomorrow, Heaven forbid....
>
> If they had sincere intent and earnest desire, and cried out with true intent, *Mashiah* would surely have come already.

---

75. *Torat Menahem* 5747: 2, 620–22. Regarding the phrase "the *nasi* is everyone," see chapter 17, section "A Consciousness of Identity."
76. *Torat Menahem* 5751: 3, 118–19. Translation adapted from www.chabad.org/2487406.

The True and Complete Redemption

What more can I to do to motivate the entire Jewish people to clamor and cry out, and thus actually bring about the coming of *Mashiah*? All that has been done until now has been to no avail. For we are still in exile; moreover, we are in an inner exile with regard to our own service of God.

All that I can possibly do is to give the matter over to you. Now, do everything you can to bring *Mashiah*, here and now, immediately....

May it be God's will that ultimately ten Jews will be found who are stubborn enough to resolve to secure God's consent to actually bring about the true and ultimate redemption, here and now immediately. Their stubborn resolve will surely evoke God's favor....

I have done whatever I can; from now on, you must do whatever you can. May it be God's will that there will be one, two, or three among you who will appreciate what needs to be done and how it needs to be done, and may you actually be successful and bring about the true and complete redemption. May this take place immediately, in a spirit of happiness and with gladness of heart.[77]

This is a unique window into the anguished mind and heart of the eighty-nine-year-old Rebbe. In this talk, his persistent optimism and positive messaging was replaced with intimations of frustration and futility. While he clearly enjoyed a lifetime of many achievements, the Rebbe expressed feelings of failure over ultimately not being able to see the fulfillment of his life's dream of seeing the complete removal of exilic suffering.

The Rebbe's reaction to these feelings is also noteworthy. Where his own efforts had not borne the ultimate fruits, he charged the people to individually and collectively intensify the work of their own personal redemption. This, in turn, would "bring about the true and complete redemption" for the world.[78]

---

77. Ibid.
78. There is a video clip available at chabad.info/moshiach/48789/ in which a woman asked the Rebbe what to do to bring *Mashiah*. The Rebbe responded, "I do not

This democratization of the messianic mission should not be construed as a desperate final grasping at straws on the part of the aged Rebbe who saw his life's objective eluding him. Rather, the Rebbe saw this elevation of the average person's role as a natural and integral part of creating the very messianic reality that he so sought and had outlined from the very beginning.

As we described in earlier chapters, the Rebbe firmly believed in the hasidic doctrine that each Jew contains a "spark of *Mashiah*" as the root of his soul.[79] Accordingly, each person can gain personal redemption by accessing and revealing their own *yehida*/spark of *Mashiah* and elevating their portion of the world assigned uniquely to them from Creation. The aggregate of a multitude of personal redemptions reveals the oneness of the Divine Essence with all people and beings, ushering in the messianic reality at large.[80] While the *nasi* can assist each person in this most formidable task, it is ultimately the individual's mission to actualize his own latent messianic potential.

Revealing the Inner Tzaddik
The need for each individual to reveal his own *yehida*, or spark of *Mashiah*, explains another anomaly of the Rebbe's later talks: the ability and responsibility of every Jew to become a *Tzaddik*. In earlier hasidic literature, there is a clear differentiation between the average person and the *Tzaddik* regarding the nature of their souls and the type of service expected of them. Increasingly over the years, and especially during his final push for *Mashiah*, the Rebbe systematically took verses, references, and forms of service that were previously uniquely assigned to the *Tzaddik*, or even to *Mashiah* himself, and applied them to each Jew.[81]

---

know. I already wrote in a letter that I do not know what to answer you." When she pressed him for a response, he responded that the way to bring *Mashiah* is by learning Torah and doing mitzvot.

79. See chapter 17, section "The *Mashiah* of the Generation."
80. See, for example, *Likkutei Sihot* 29, *Hosafot*, Simhat Torah 5746, *se'ifim* 4–5, where the Rebbe describes collective redemption as being slowly built through a multitude of personal redemptions.
81. See, for example, *Torat Menahem* 5748: 3, 151; ibid., 5749: 3, 57; ibid., 5752: 1, 273–74, 312.

The Rebbe explicitly articulated this shift in a 5751 (1991) talk about the nature of the messianic reality as "the revelation of the Divine Essence in the created reality." This existence, he argued, can be triggered only when each person becomes fully transparent to the Divine Essence – a *Tzaddik* in Chabad parlance. While the Rebbe admitted that in the past this lofty goal was unattainable for most people, he argued that times had changed:

> After all the cleansing and purification that the Jewish people underwent throughout the generations, it is possible now for each Jew to reach the level of a *Tzaddik*…the revelation of the verse "And your nation are all righteous" (Is. 60:21), as will be completely revealed with the true and complete redemption.[82]

The transformation of each Jew into a *Tzaddik* literally creates the messianic reality.

The Centrality of Messianism

The need for each person to access the *yehida*/spark of *Mashiah* of his soul and reveal himself as a *Tzaddik* is intertwined with another of the Rebbe's later themes: the elevation of messianism to the core organizing principle of a Jewish person's being and service. At the cusp of redemption, every part of a person – cognitions, emotions, speech, and actions – must be suffused with the idea of redemption and be geared to its actualization. This total dedication to striving toward redemption is both a means of accessing one's inner *yehida*/spark of *Mashiah* and the result of this inner spark's revelation and blossoming. Furthering the teachings of the Alter Rebbe highlighted at the beginning of this chapter, the Rebbe taught that this messianic mindset enables a person to achieve personal redemption and experience aspects of the global messianic reality – "to live with *Mashiah*" – even before the actual advent of the Messianic Era.

---

82. *Torat Menahem* 5751: 3, 227–28. See also, for example, *Torat Menahem* 5751: 2, 325, 443; ibid., 5751: 3, 42, 323; ibid., 5752: 1, 139; 273 note 68.

"Until When?" The Rebbe's Push for Mashiah

Thinking Messianically
In classic Chabad form, the formation of messianic consciousness and practice must begin with harnessing and transforming one's cognitions. The Rebbe taught that one's mental spaces must be suffused with a vision of the redeemed world. To this end, he enjoined people to intensely study the parts of Torah that discuss the Messianic Era, from Rambam's detailed laws of the Temple to Hasidism's descriptions of the revelation of the Divine Essence.[83] Such cognitive engagement can situate one's consciousness in the Messianic Era and help a person attain personal redemption.

Ultimately, such study and cognition will influence the rest of one's being, enabling a person to interface with the messianic reality with all of one's faculties. As the Rebbe once said:

> Regarding the special increase in learning about redemption and *Mashiah*, it is... primarily in order to begin to live with the matters of *Mashiah* and redemption. [This occurs] through the fact that one's mind becomes filled and suffused with understanding and the concepts of redemption and *Mashiah* from the Torah. From the mind it spreads and permeates even the emotions of the heart, all the way to practical speech and actions, so that they will befit this unique time when we are standing on the edge of redemption and can point with a finger and say that "behold, King *Mashiah* is here."[84]

The objective of achieving personal redemption through expanding one's consciousness even in the present – "living with *Mashiah*" – is attainable through a deep engagement with what the Torah tells us about *Mashiah*.

Feeling Messianism
Elsewhere, the Rebbe focused on the emotional aspect of this increased messianic consciousness. Every Jew's core (the *yehida*/spark of *Mashiah*) contains an elemental desire for the revelation of the Divine Essence.

---

83. See, for example, *Torat Menahem* 5749: 4, 11–12; 5751: 3, 164.
84. *Torat Menahem* 5751: 4, 41.

The True and Complete Redemption

Understanding and thinking about this redemptive revelation will elicit this latent desire and generate a conscious, burning longing for redemption.

For the Rebbe, creating and maintaining such a yearning is important for several intertwined reasons. First and foremost, Rambam rules that such a longing is an integral part of believing in *Mashiah*, one of the thirteen principles of faith.[85] In addition, the longing helps fuel the incessant activities that are necessary to bring redemption.[86] Perhaps most fundamentally, though, the Rebbe saw the very desire for *Mashiah* as positively generating the messianic reality: "Hope and anticipation for redemption hastens and causes redemption."[87] As a fervent desire for redemption stems from the spark of *Mashiah* within a person, consciously keeping this longing in the foreground helps fan and reveal this spark.[88]

Demanding Redemption

This longing for *Mashiah* links to another striking feature of the Rebbe's messianism – his posture vis-à-vis God. While much of traditional prayer is expressed in a humble and penitential manner, the Rebbe advocated "stormily" demanding redemption from God. Beginning in the early 1980s, the Rebbe adopted a grassroots children's song with the lyrics "We want *Mashiah* now!" and spoke of the need to cry out from the depths of the heart: *Ad matai*, "Until when will the Jewish people remain in exile?"

In several talks, the Rebbe carefully demonstrated that this form of demanding redemption from God is rooted in classical sources. The phrase *ad matai* itself appears in Scripture as a demand of God to save the Jewish people,[89] as well as in various prayers.[90] Similarly, the

---

85. Ibid., 5748: 4, 33, based on *Mishneh Torah, Hilkhot Melakhim UMilhemoteihem* 11:1. See also *Likkutei Sihot* 28, Hukkat, no. 1.
86. See, for example, *Torat Menahem* 5751: 3, 132.
87. *Torat Menahem* 5746: 1, 157. The Rebbe cited this idea from the Hida (*Midbar Kedemot, maarekhet* 100, *siman* 16) and Radak to II Sam. 24:25.
88. *Torat Menahem* 5751: 4, 185–86.
89. Ps. 74:10. See, for example, *Torat Menahem* 5744: 2, 987–90.
90. The Rebbe pointed to the text of *tikkun hatzot* and the fifteenth blessing in *Shemoneh Esreh*. See, for example, *Torat Menahem* 5744: 3, 1686.

Rebbe marshaled a variety of rabbinic passages where rabbis brazenly demanded that God respond to their prayers.[91]

Despite the sources for demanding redemption from God, the Rebbe admitted that this mode of prayer seems irreverent [92] and was not the dominant mode of Jewish prayer for generations.[93] Why, then, did the Rebbe prominently encourage people to "storm" the heavens?

A key element of the Rebbe's rationale was, once again, the unique historical moment in which he lived. At the end of history, the length and darkness of the exile and the proximity to redemption should arouse within the Jewish people such a deep revulsion for the former and desire for the latter that they should simply no longer be able to tolerate an imperfect world. As the Rebbe said about the declaration of *ad matai*, "We are not questioning [God], but declaring that we cannot tolerate the pain of the exile.... 'Woe to the children who were exiled from their parents!' (Berakhot 3a)."[94]

The Rebbe so firmly saw these demands for redemption as a natural expression of the desire for redemption that he characterized those who were hesitant to use such language as too complacent with their exilic existence.[95] Demanding redemption is a manifestation of actively anticipating redemption, and, therefore, hesitating to adopt this posture "prevents redemption." [96]

Messianic Action
Messianism, as the core of a person's soul, cannot permeate just a person's thoughts and feelings. Rather, even the aspect that is at the farthest periphery from the soul – a person's physical actions – must be animated and permeated by the spark of *Mashiah*.[97]

---

91. Most famously, perhaps, is the talmudic story of Honi HaMe'agel. For a list of sources, see *Torat Menahem* 5744: 3, 1680–88; ibid., 5747: 2, 165 note 75.
92. *Torat Menahem* 5746: 3, 464.
93. Ibid., 5747: 2, 165. See also the talk from 19 Nisan 5748, recorded at hageula.com/vid/malkeinu/15288.htm.
94. *Torat Menahem* 5746: 1, 96.
95. Ibid., 5744: 2, 987.
96. Ibid., 5747: 2, 165.
97. Ibid., 5751: 4; ibid., 5752: 1, 312.

For the Rebbe, this begins first and foremost with the consistent performance of mitzvot. In a talk outlining the general intentions one should have when performing mitzvot, the Rebbe highlighted the importance of a messianic orientation. Building from the formulation of the Alter Rebbe that the messianic revelation of the Divine Essence in the material world "is dependent on our actions and [divine] service throughout the period of exile," the Rebbe argued:

> The service of a Jew in the time of exile needs to be suffused with constant anticipation and aspiration for redemption...that he feels that through his fulfillment of Torah and mitzvot his service will bring and hasten redemption...and not only that it will bring redemption, but that redemption is a single matter with (*inyan ehad*) the essence of his spiritual service.[98]

While this mindset was sublimated for most Jews during the exilic period, it was particularly crucial for the time "when the Jewish people feel that *Mashiah* 'stands behind the wall' (Song. 2:9)" to adopt this stance.[99]

CONCLUSION

The Rebbe's understanding of the cosmic historical process, the nature of redemption, and current events led him to believe that *Mashiah*'s arrival was imminent. Living in redemption's shadow imbued each person with greater responsibility and a sense of urgency to actualize this potential for redemption. The totality of each person should become suffused with the push for *Mashiah*. This total dedication to the messianic idea enables each person to access his or her own *yehida*/spark of *Mashiah* and achieve personal redemption, which, in turn, helps create the long-awaited collective redemption.

---

98. *Likkutei Sihot* 22, Tazria-Metzora, *se'ifim* 9–10.
99. Ibid., *se'if* 13.

Secondary Literature Consulted for Chapter 20, "'Until When?' The Rebbe's Push for *Mashiah*"

Alon Dahan, *Goel Aharon*, 586–609.

Rahel Elior, "Tehiyat HaMeshihiyut BaHasidut Chabad BaMe'a HaEsrim: HaReka HaHistori VehaMisti, 1939–1996," in *Chabad: Historya, Hagut VeDimmui*, 267–300.

Naftali Loewenthal, "The Neutralisation of Messianism and the Apocalypse," *Mehkerei Yerushalayim BeMahshevet Yisrael*, 59–73.

Yosef Yitzhak Meislish, *HaTekufa VehaGeula BeMishnato shel HaRebbe MiLubavitch*.

Aviezer Ravitzky, *Messianism, Zionism, and Jewish Religious Radicalism*, 193–206.

Eli Rubin, "The Idealistic Realism of Jewish Messianism."

Dov Schwartz, *Mahshevet Chabad MiReshit Ve'ad Aharit*, 286–318.

Elliot Wolfson, *Open Secret*, 265–300.

Chapter 21

Redemption Is Here?

The previous chapter outlined the Rebbe's understanding of the generation's unique historical moment and the method that he conceived to work toward creating a redeemed reality. While some of the Rebbe's formulations about *Mashiah*'s imminence may seem stark and jarring, they were always tempered by a call to action. In his last years, however, the Rebbe at times seemed to speak not only of *Mashiah*'s imminent future arrival, but about the current unfolding of redemption before the world's eyes. It is to these expressions that we turn in this chapter.

METHODOLOGICAL INTRODUCTION

At the outset, it is important to note several methodological considerations regarding the Rebbe's later talks. While these points were applicable at various times during the entire course of his tenure, for many Hasidim they are crucial prisms through which to understand many, if not all, of these later talks.

Scholars have noted a strong affinity between classical Midrash and hasidic discourses.[1] Both at their core employ similar hermeneuti-

---

1. For the exegetical affinity between Chabad teachings and classical Midrash, see Naftali Loewenthal (2013), 429–55; Eli Rubin "Intimacy in the Place of Otherness."

Redemption Is Here?

cal tools to interpret a Torah text. As opposed to focusing on the simple meaning of the passage at hand, Midrash and hasidic teachings utilize symbolism, wordplay, and a range of other non-linear methods to arrive at heretofore hidden meanings, often relating to issues of existential and religious significance. This sort of exegesis naturally gives rise to the non-literal nature of midrashic and hasidic rhetoric, already noted, respectively, by Rambam[2] and scholars of Hasidism.[3]

In the context of the current chapter, I will briefly outline three of the most relevant forms of non-literal, hasidic-midrashic rhetorical devices that the Rebbe employed at various points in his tenure.

Torah as Prayer

On several occasions, the Rebbe described how Torah study can function as a form of prayer. One of his primary sources was a story from the Zohar that during a severe drought R. Shimon bar Yohai generated a rainstorm through teaching Torah to his students.[4] The Rebbe explained that generally, prayer, which pierces the Divine Essence itself, is the most potent force to engender a change in the world. Torah study, however, engages with God's revealed wisdom (*hokhma*) and is therefore less powerful. The Torah of R. Shimon, however, was different. Since he revealed the essence of Torah, his teachings pierced the Divine Essence and, therefore, similar to prayer, had the capacity to change the very fabric of reality and bring rain during a time of drought.[5]

It was clear to Hasidim that the Rebbe was not just speaking abstractly but that, in the tradition of hasidic Rebbes, the Rebbe himself

---

For a broader perspective that incorporates teachings from a wide array of hasidic masters, see Ora Wiskind-Elper (2018) and especially her methodological introduction. For the relationship between the teachings of R. Nahman of Breslov and Midrash, see Shaul Magid (2001), 15–66.

2. Rambam, *Commentary to the Mishna*, introduction to *Perek Helek*.
3. See, for example, Moshe Idel (2006); Elliot Wolfson (2002); Susan Handelman (1991), 89–92; Levi Brackman, "The Kabbalah of Deconstruction," in Sanford L. Drob (2009), 180–204.
4. See, for example, *Torat Menahem* 5727: 2, 416–24; ibid., 5742: 3, 1416–18; ibid., 5750: 3, 185–90.
5. *Torat Menahem* 5750: 3, 188.

would on occasion harness Torah study to positively affect the world.[6] For example, one of the instances when the Rebbe underscored the generative powers of Torah was at a *farbrengen* on the eve of the Six-Day War. In that talk, he emphasized that every Jew's Torah study can change reality and that a *farbrengen* where there is unity among Jews is a particularly auspicious time to positively affect the world.[7]

Immediately following this talk, the Rebbe transitioned into an analysis of the various classifications of wars in halakha and Hasidism. In his teaching, the Rebbe underscored that the "highest" form of war is when God is so present and active that He obviates entirely the need for actual fighting.[8] While the Rebbe's examination of the categories of war stands as an objective engagement in Torah study, the tense historical context and the framework created by the Rebbe himself made it clear that that he was engaging in a prayer couched as Torah.

In addition to the above, in the Rebbe's later years many Hasidim detected an actual shift in the Rebbe's tone of voice, style, and delivery that engendered a different experience in a listener. Despite the Rebbe's physical proximity to them, it seemed to these Hasidim that their Rebbe, who in these years often spoke with eyes closed, was, at times, engaged in a personal dialogue with God to which they were privy but which they did not fully understand. In their mind's eye, the Rebbe's mode of speaking conjured an image of a biblical prophet suspended between heaven and earth, simultaneously arguing with God to redeem the world and with his people to do what was necessary to create the messianic reality.[9]

The Power of Positive Words

A theme related to the generative powers of Torah is the potency of *bittahon* in thought and speech.[10] As outlined earlier, the Rebbe deeply

---

6. See, for example, Hillel Zaltzman, "The Miracle of Stalin's Death," where he describes the events of the *farbrengen* of Purim 5713 and their connection to Stalin's death.
7. *Torat Menahem* 5727: 2, 416–24.
8. Ibid., 427–31.
9. Chaim Rapoport (2011), 124. He writes that this was not only his impression but that it was shared by others.
10. See chapter 11, section "Optimism."

felt that thought and speech were endowed by God with the capacity to change reality – both for good and for "the opposite of good." For this reason, the Rebbe strenuously avoided using negative formulations in his speaking and even articulating negative eventualities.[11] In particular, when speaking about the Jewish people, the Rebbe assiduously applied to them the most positive and lofty of descriptions.[12] Many Hasidim see the power of positive language as a critical lens through which to understand the Rebbe's messianic rhetoric.

Hyperbole

Another important methodological point is the Rebbe's use of hyperbole. The Talmud already notes that God Himself employed exaggerated language in Scripture, such as describing the Canaanite cities as having "fortified walls up to the heavens."[13] Rashi explains that God mimicked human beings, who use hyperbole as a literary technique to forcefully emphasize a point.[14]

The Rebbe highlighted[15] another layer of meaning of the Torah's use of hyperbole based on the teachings of the Italian kabbalist R. Azarya of Fano,[16] who argued that even as the Torah's language might be imprecise from our human perspective, the word of God always signifies a literal truth on a spiritual plane.[17] For example, even if the Canaanite cities did not have physical walls that reached the sky, the verse expresses a real spiritual truth: the Land of Israel has spiritual walls that rise to the heavens and forbid entry to the angels of non-Jewish nations.

Many Hasidim felt that over the years the Rebbe occasionally spoke in hyperbole in precisely this manner. As spiritual guide to thousands of people, the Rebbe employed exaggerated language to inspire them to greater heights. Also, since the Rebbe possessed deep spiritual

11. See Joseph Telushkin (2014), 109–17.
12. See chapter 13, note 100.
13. Deut. 1:28.
14. Tamid 29a.
15. *Torat Menahem* 5713: 2, 107; ibid., 5728: 3, 282; ibid., 5742: 1, 234.
16. *Shu"t Rema MiFano*, siman 73.
17. As a parallel, see *Tanya, Likkutei Amarim*, ch. 13, which says that "true" service is subjectively defined.

The True and Complete Redemption

perception, these Hasidim felt that his words were at times referring to spiritual planes of existence that are beyond the perception of the average human being.

One clear example of this form of rhetoric was the Rebbe's frequent citation of R. Levi Yitzhak of Berditchev's statement that on *Shabbat Hazon* (the Shabbat before Tisha BeAv) God shows a vision (*hazon*) of the third *Beit HaMikdash* to each and every Jew. The Rebbe spent much time analyzing the impact of this vision, comparing and contrasting it with a range of experiences, such as that of a pilgrim traveling to the *Beit HaMikdash*,[18] and a person who hears one of the various types of voices that emerge from heaven.[19]

After reading the very vivid, nearly "tangible" language employed in some of these talks, one might think that the Rebbe literally thought that on *Shabbat Hazon* every Jew actually saw a physical structure with their naked eyes.[20] However, this is not the case. On several occasions the Rebbe explicated that many Jews do not actually *see* the *Beit HaMikdash* with their eyes, but rather, on a deeper plane, their *soul* sees a spiritual vision which positively affects them and challenges them to "bring down" this vision into the physical world.[21] Though the Rebbe used language referring to actual sight, he was not referring to a physical reality. Once again, for many Hasidim, the Rebbe increasingly spoke in this mode during his later years.

The Internal Debate

With this background, we can begin to appreciate that learned and loyal Chabad Hasidim debate the proper prism through which to understand certain passages from the Rebbe's later talks. One group favors literal reads of these passages, contending that the Rebbe believed that redemption had begun; the live, flesh-and-blood *Mashiah* had been at

---

18. *Torat Menahem* 5747: 4, 167.
19. *Likkutei Sihot* 9, *Devarim*, no. 3, *se'if* 4.
20. See, for example, *Likkutei Sihot* 39, *Shabbat Hazon*, where a literal read of the talk would leave a person with the impression that the Rebbe thought each Jew literally saw the *Beit HaMikdash*.
21. See, for example, *Likkutei Sihot* 29, *Shabbat Hazon*, *se'ifim* 1–2; *Torat Menahem* 5747: 4, 165–68; ibid., 5749: 4, 100.

least partially revealed and that he would imminently finish the redemption process. Another group, though, based on various contextual cues, favors non-literal interpretations of these selfsame words. The reasons for this type of interpretation include the general methodological techniques employed by the Rebbe that were outlined above, in addition to the internal evidence from the specific talks themselves.

In this chapter, I will first present some of the key passages from the Rebbe's talks with as few explanatory comments as possible. After outlining the passages themselves, I will return to this debate and further develop the arguments for the two camps.

REDEMPTION UNFOLDING?

The Return of Prophecy

As noted in the previous chapter, the Rebbe cited his father-in-law's declaration "Immediately to repentance, immediately to redemption" on dozens of occasions. Based on the majority of his talks, it would seem that the Rebbe simply saw these assurances as the latest calculation of the end-time (*ketz*), which has a long history in Jewish sources. However, some Hasidim feel that on one occasion near the end of his life the Rebbe went further and imbued R. Yosef Yitzhak's pronouncement with greater authority.

On *Shabbat Parashat Shofetim* 5751/1991,[22] the Rebbe reflected on the halakhot of prophets and prophecy. He noted that Rambam codifies the obligation to listen to a prophet as one of the foundational tenets of Judaism and an ever-present mitzva. This categorical presentation, the Rebbe explained, meant that obeying prophets "is a halakha for all generations,"[23] as some form of divine inspiration and prophecy exists in all eras.[24]

The Rebbe contended that the practicality of this point intensifies as the world readies for redemption. In a letter, Rambam wrote that prophecy would return to the Jewish people prior to the arrival of

---

22. *Torat Menahem* 5751: 4, 190–205.
23. Ibid., 198.
24. Ibid., 198, and 199, where the Rebbe used the qualifier of *me'ein* ("similar to").

The True and Complete Redemption

Mashiah as "a prelude" to the ultimate redemption.[25] Due to the indications of *Mashiah*'s proximity, the Rebbe applied Rambam's statement to the previous Rebbes of Chabad – "our teachers, our *nesi'im*" – who functioned as "the extension of Moses" in their respective generations.[26] They experienced "the beginning of and something similar to" prophecy and were therefore able to reveal the word of God in their hasidic teachings.[27]

Until this point, there is nothing particularly surprising in this talk. The Rebbe had previously identified the leaders of Chabad as the "Moses of their generation," and the connection between Hasidism and prophecy was well established.[28] At this point, however, when the Rebbe shifted to the practical takeaway of this phenomenon, he said the following regarding R. Yosef Yitzhak:

> One should publicize to himself and to others with whom he has contact that they must accept upon themselves the instructions and advice of "your judges...and advisors"(Is. 1:26)...including, particularly, the *nasi* of our generation...the judge of our generation, the advisor of our generation *and the prophet of our generation*, as the Torah commanded, "I will set up a prophet for them from among their brothers like you, and I will put My words into his mouth" (Deut. 18:18) and "to him you shall listen" (18:15), and as Rambam codified, when a person has the merits and individual perfection required of a prophet, and he performs signs and wonders – as we saw and see continually in the fulfillment of the blessings of the leader of our generation, the Rebbe [R. Yosef Yitzhak] – "we do not believe in him only because of the sign [he performed]...but because of the commandment which Moses gave in the Torah" (*Mishneh Torah, Hilkhot Yesodei HaTorah* 10:1).[29] [Emphasis added.]

---

25. *Iggeret Teiman*, ch. 3.
26. See chapter 17, section "The Rebbes of Chabad."
27. *Torat Menahem* 5751: 4, 199.
28. See, for example, *Likkutei Sihot* 2, Balak, *se'if* 2.
29. *Torat Menahem* 5751: 4, 201.

The Rebbe applied to his father-in-law classical descriptions of prophets and prophecy drawn from the Torah and Rambam.

The Rebbe continued to reiterate the practical ramification of R. Yosef Yitzhak's status:

> We need to publicize to all the people of the generation that we merited that the Holy One, blessed be He, chose and appointed a human being with free will, who is in his own right immeasurably greater than the generation to be your judge, your advisor, *and the prophet of the generation*. That he shall give instructions and advice regarding the service of the Jewish people in this generation and all people in this generation in all matters of Torah and mitzvot, and with regard to conduct in general day-to-day life, including "in all your ways (know Him)" and "all you deeds (shall be for the sake of Heaven)"... culminating in the main prophecy – the prophecy of "Immediately to repentance, immediately to redemption" – and immediately "behold, *Mashiah* comes" (Song of Songs Rabba to Song. 2:8).[30] [Emphasis added.]

Read alone these specific words would indicate that R. Yosef Yitzhak's messianic proclamations had at least a partial status of prophecy, lending greater authority to these declarations than similar statements of earlier authorities. It is important to note, though, that the Rebbe went on to enjoin the people to engage in specific forms of divine service for the "prophecy" to be actualized.

The Work Is Done

Hasidic thought has always asserted that Jews remain in exile in order to complete their collective exilic mission. Therefore, even when R. Yosef Yitzhak spoke of the imminence of *Mashiah*'s arrival during World War II, he still emphasized that the last stages of the Jewish people's mission lay before them. His proclamation "Immediately to repentance, immediately to redemption" assumes that the age-old precondition of repentance had not yet been fully met.

---

30. Ibid., 202.

The True and Complete Redemption

On several occasions in the 1980s the Rebbe confirmed this understanding of R. Yosef Yitzhak's statement and embraced repentance as a requirement of redemption. For example, the Rebbe felt a need to clarify that despite the seemingly insurmountable nature of this challenge to achieve complete repentance, *Mashiah* could still arrive at any moment, as the Zohar and Rambam explain that repentance can be accomplished in a "single moment."[31]

In the middle of 5751/1991, however, the Rebbe seemed to shift emphasis. Interspersed with his rhetoric of an imminent but future redemption, he at times seemed to intimate that the Jewish people had already repented and thereby fulfilled this precondition for redemption. For example, on the fast of Asara BeTevet of that year, in the midst of a talk focused on the importance of defending the Jewish people, the Rebbe listed several reasons why *Mashiah* should come immediately:

> Since through the thirteen attributes of mercy, sins (which are the cause of exile) are nullified...immediately and without delay comes the true and complete redemption...and certainly after "all of the appointed times have passed" (Sanhedrin 97b) and they already repented [beginning with a thought of repentance]... most certainly "they are immediately redeemed" (*Mishneh Torah, Hilkhot Teshuva* 7:5).[32]

In this passage, the Rebbe referred to repentance as a condition for redemption that the Jewish people had already fulfilled. The Rebbe repeated this sentiment in several talks over the course of the next year and a half.[33]

A similar shift seemed to occur regarding the "polishing of the buttons" that R. Yosef Yitzhak referred to as standing between the Jewish people and redemption.[34] Throughout most of his tenure, the Rebbe

---

31. Ibid., 5745: 5, 2622–23; ibid., 5746: 2, 554.
32. Ibid., 5751: 2, 106–7.
33. Arguably, this begins before 1991. See, for example, *Torat Menahem* 5743: 3, 1232; ibid., 5749: 3, 256. See also *Torat Menahem* 5751: 2, 65, 119, 125, 133; ibid., 5751: 4, 39; ibid., 5752: 1, 222, 241; ibid., 5752: 2, 89.
34. See chapter 20, section "Positive Phenomena."

cited this metaphor as a goal yet to be accomplished. In his final years, however, he said that this too had been completed:

> Based on all of the signs that are in rabbinic literature about the end of time...our generation is the last generation of exile and the first generation of redemption, as my father-in-law testified... that in his own day the Jewish people had already completed the matters of service and only needed to "polish the buttons" and to stand ready for *Mashiah*...*most certainly after spreading Torah, Judaism, and the wellsprings outward...they have even finished "to polish the buttons,"* and we are standing ready to greet our righteous *Mashiah*.[35] [Emphasis added.]

In the fifty years since the beginning of World War II, the Jewish people completed the service of "polishing the buttons" and were now ready for *Mashiah*.[36]

The Rebbe had similar reflections about the totality of the Jewish people's mission in exile. Reflecting in 5751 on the Lurianic notion of elevating the divine sparks that are embedded in the contaminated realms, the Rebbe said: "The exilic work of gathering the sparks (for which God sent the Jewish people into exile) in the entire world has already been completed."[37] As such, the Jewish people should intensify all aspects of their divine service, thus bringing about the immediate arrival of *Mashiah*.[38]

Mashiah and Nuclear Disarmament

In addition to describing the completion of the exilic service, the Rebbe also spoke of the spirit of *Mashiah* as beginning to tangibly impact the world. On *Shabbat Parashat Mishpatim* 5752 (1992), the Rebbe dedicated

---

35. *Torat Menahem* 5751: 3, 320–21.
36. See also *Torat Menahem* 5750: 2, 109, 418; ibid., 5750: 3, 24, 411; ibid., 5750: 4, 206; ibid., 5751: 1, 117, 249, 319; ibid., 5751: 2, 133, 335, 376; ibid., 5751: 3, 320–21, 346; ibid., 5751: 4, 47, 170, 190, 211, 322; ibid., 5752: 1, 122, 157, 222, 286, 365; ibid., 5752: 2, 106, 256.
37. *Torat Menahem* 5751: 2, 20.
38. Ibid., 22–23.

The True and Complete Redemption

a talk to the treaty signed by American president George H. Bush and Russian president Mikhail Gorbachev to drastically reduce their countries' respective nuclear armaments. The Rebbe highlighted that Isaiah's well-known prophecy describes disarmament as a messianic goal: "And He shall judge between the nations and reprove many peoples, and they shall beat their swords into plowshares and their spears into pruning hooks."[39] For the Rebbe, this 1991 treaty was "the beginning of the fulfillment of this goal."[40]

The Rebbe continued by noting that the above verse does not speak about disarmament as merely an aspect of the overall messianic reality, but rather as a direct result of *Mashiah*'s impact on the nations. As such, the US-Russian treaty was attributable to the effect of *Mashiah* himself:

> Since we are at the "peak time" for the coming of *Mashiah* – "Behold, *Mashiah* comes"[41] – we already see something similar to and the beginning of the effect of King *Mashiah* on the nations... through God instilling in the hearts of the kings of the nations to decide and proclaim together that they shall beat their swords.[42]

Even before the revelation of *Mashiah*'s identity, the Rebbe saw *Mashiah*'s influence upon the nations through his orchestration of the beginnings of world peace.

Greeting *Mashiah*

In line with the above passages regarding the completion of the exilic service and the nascent influence of "*Mashiah*," in 5752/1992 the Rebbe seemed to identify a new mission for the generation – to ready oneself to actually greet King *Mashiah*.

This sentiment was first expressed during a talk on *Parashat Hayei Sara* 5752, during the annual *sheluhim* convention. The Rebbe began his

---

39. Is. 2:4.
40. *Torat Menahem* 5752: 2, 268.
41. Song of Songs Rabba to Song. 2:8.
42. *Torat Menahem* 5752: 2, 268.

talk with a review of the reasons that *Mashiah*'s arrival was imminent and made the following remark:

> As we have already spoken about many times (and particularly in the last few months and weeks), that based on the pronouncement of the Sages that "all of the appointed times have passed [and now the matter solely depends on repentance]" (Sanhedrin 97b), and based on the pronouncement of his eminence, my father-in-law, the *nasi* of our generation, that the Jewish people have also already repented, until they have completed all of their service (including "polishing the buttons") and are standing ready to greet our righteous *Mashiah*, therefore, the service and the mission is now to be practically prepared to actually greet the righteous *Mashiah*.[43]

Later in the talk, the Rebbe emphasized that even the mission of spreading the wellsprings of Torah and Hasidism was already completed[44] and now "the only matter that remains in the service of the *sheluhim* is to actually greet *Mashiah*."[45]

What does this practically entail? The Rebbe continued by explaining that preparing to "actually greet *Mashiah*" means ensuring that all the work in spreading Jewish practice and learning should be permeated with a messianic consciousness, to teach people about the meaning of *Mashiah*, i.e., to become sensitized to the world's inherent divinity.[46] The Rebbe concluded with a prayer that this should bring about the actual arrival of *Mashiah*.[47] Even as he argued that all the work was done, he called for the work to continue with an even greater intensity, fueled by a heightened degree of anticipation.

---

43. Ibid., 286.
44. Ibid., 297.
45. Ibid., 298. See also ibid., 277.
46. Ibid., 298.
47. Ibid., 299.

The True and Complete Redemption

Perhaps the Rebbe's most extreme formulation came on the eve of 20 Kislev 5752. The Rebbe offered a prayer for the realization of the messianic unification of people with God and then said the following:

> And particularly in these days – *the days of Mashiah*, and this is where we are currently found – we need only to open our eyes, and then we will see that the true and complete redemption is already present and that the entirety of the Jewish people...is prepared...to approach and sit by the table, a table that is set with all of the delicacies and all of the good...and most primarily [they are prepared] to "know God" (*Mishneh Torah, Hilkhot Melakhim UMilhemoteihem* 12:5) [as it says]: "The world will be filled with the knowledge of God as the waters cover the ocean bed" (Is. 11:9).[48] [Emphasis added.]

The Rebbe continued with a prayer that this should continue to unfold.

DID THE REBBE SEE REDEMPTION?
The Literalists

With this sketch of the Rebbe's themes and statements from his final years, we can now present the two primary schools of thought among Hasidim as to their Rebbe's intent.[49] A literal rendering of the above citations leads to the conclusion that the Rebbe had a firm conviction that (1) the Jewish people had already repented, (2) they had completed their exilic missions as outlined in classical hasidic thought, (3) the messianic process was already partially realized, and (4) it was guaranteed that the messianic process would be imminently completed.

---

48. Ibid., 5752: 1, 393–94. Similarly, see *Torat Menahem* 5752: 1, 354–55, 367; ibid., 5752: 2, 106.
49. The rest of this chapter and the next chapter will outline the current debate in Chabad about the meaning of certain passages in the Rebbe's later talks. Many of the proofs marshaled by the messianist side start appearing in books and pamphlets after the Rebbe's passing in 1994. As I have no direct evidence that the messianist/non-messianist debates occurred in 1991–1992 when the talks were first delivered and published, I refrained from using the past tense. Instead, I focused on the debate that still exists now about these passages.

These sentiments appear to be buttressed by the Rebbe's relating to R. Yosef Yitzhak's messianic proclamations as a "prophecy" that needed to be publicized. While the Rebbe underscored in that very talk that the Jewish people needed to intensify their divine service in order to bring *Mashiah*, still he spoke of engaging in these activities "out of anticipation and complete certainty that immediately we will see with our own physical eyes that 'behold, *Mashiah* comes.'"⁵⁰ One group of Hasidim interprets the Rebbe's words in this literal fashion and are convinced that they are living in a semi-redeemed world and that *Mashiah* will reveal himself imminently.⁵¹

The Non-Literalists
In marked contrast, others counter that the above citations need to be contextualized within the framework of the Rebbe's longstanding rhetorical styles,⁵² that employ a range of non-linear devices to convey meaning and messages. Accordingly, the Rebbe's statements about the Jewish people having already completed their exilic mission should be understood in context of his pronouncements about an imminent redemption that were discussed in the previous chapter. In other words, they are some combination of a prayer to God, a description of spiritual realities and opportunities, and a means of inspiring the people to

---

50. *Torat Menahem* 5751: 4, 188.
51. For two Chabad monographs that analyze these later talks and take the literalist position, see Yosef Yitzhak Meislish (2005); Shalom Dovber Wolf (2016). This latter book is the latest and most comprehensive work of this sort. For his treatment of the sources and themes of this chapter, see Shalom Dovber Wolf (2016), 319–63; 481–596. This is also the conclusion of Alon Dahan (2014), 587. It is also important to note that in 1993 (when the Rebbe was alive but incapacitated due to his stroke), R. Yoel Kahn, the chief transcriber of the Rebbe's talks, who had been with the Rebbe since 1951, took a literalist position regarding these talks. See the following articles in the Chabad magazine *Kefar Chabad*: Yoel Kahn (21 Tevet 5753), 11–13; Yoel Kahn (6 Shevat 5753), 13–16. After the Rebbe passed away, however, R. Yoel (14 Tamuz 5754), 22–25, retracted and admitted that due to the rush of emotions of the time period he made methodological mistakes in his approach to these talks. However, in that same article, (p. 25), R. Yoel still referred to the Rebbe's statements about *Mashiah* coming as being said "in the style of prophecy."
52. See section "Methodological Introduction."

greater heights. These Hasidim argue that to render these selections of the Rebbe's words literally, necessarily leads to incorrect interpretation.

In addition to these general points, there are at least four related internal reasons marshaled to support this interpretive approach:

Contradictory Assertions
One support for non-literal interpretations of the Rebbe's words is that many of these passages, if interpreted literally, are contradicted by other lines in the same talk. For example, as noted above, on 10 Tevet 5751/1991 the Rebbe declared that the Jewish people had already fulfilled the precondition of repentance and hence were deserving of redemption. However, according to a recording of the talk,[53] a few minutes later, the Rebbe said that "even if they are not deserving," redemption should still occur immediately. This shift in language indicates that the Rebbe's first statement that the Jewish people had already sufficiently repented should not be understood literally, but rather as a form of prayer and positive talk to create the spiritual reality of which he spoke. Similarly, much of the Rebbe's "redemption is here" rhetoric was coupled with assurances and passionate prayers for the future redemption.

Continuity of Regular Service in a Regular World
A literal understanding of the Rebbe's words regarding the completion of the exilic service can similarly be considered problematic, due to the lack of ramifications. One would expect that if the Rebbe believed that the Jewish people had fully repented, completed their entire exilic service, and now only needed "to greet *Mashiah*," he would have called for a fundamental revamping of the Jewish people's mission.

In reality, though, he never instructed any sort of slackening of the "regular" work that he encouraged throughout his tenure. Rather, as we have seen, the Rebbe accompanied every seemingly definitive statement about the immediacy of *Mashiah*'s arrival with a call to intensify the normative aspects of Jewish service according to the classical Chabad understanding. This continuity of "regular" work was apparent on other

---

53. Available at www.chabad.org/therebbe/sichoskodesh_cdo/year/5751/month/10/day/10/cat//x/41/y/26, at 6 minutes, 30 seconds.

Redemption Is Here?

fronts as well. For example, in 5752, together with his pronouncements that the world had been purified and *Mashiah* was present, the Rebbe still worked on a political level against peace talks with the Palestinians, even telling Israeli cabinet minister Moshe Katzav that he would work to topple the government if the talks continued.[54]

According to the non-literalist camp, this continuity of "regular" service and work militates against a literal understanding of the Rebbe's statements about living in a purified world. Instead, they argue that the Rebbe's statements about the end of exilic service are a supplication to God,[55] or perhaps his vision of a spiritual realm,[56] or both. Accordingly, our material world, including all its inhabitants, still consists of a mixture of good and evil and still requires further purification as has been the case throughout human history. This point is buttressed by the simple, observable fact that evil still exists globally and in the heart of every human, something that the Rebbe himself acknowledged.[57]

Expressions of Futility and Bewilderment

Another factor that points to the non-literal nature of the Rebbe's messianic expressions was that he also publicly questioned the value of his activities, expressed feelings of deep dejection, and declared that he did not know the path forward.[58] The most famous of these talks is "the known *siha*" of 28 Nisan 5751 (excerpted above),[59] in which the Rebbe declared that his efforts were unsuccessful in bringing *Mashiah* and charged the people to continue the work necessary to reveal the Divine Essence in the physical world. This passage exudes a sense of failure on

---

54. *Torat Menahem* 5752: 2, 376–79. This point is emphasized by Aviezer Ravitzky (1996), 202. For more on the Rebbe's trenchant opposition to land-for-peace initiatives, see chapter 19, section "Land for Peace."
55. Chaim Rapoport (2011), 124–25; Yehezkel Sofer (2012), 248–50.
56. Menahem Mendel Kaplan (1997), 48–50.
57. For an interesting approach of R. Simon Jacobson (one of the primary draft writers of the Rebbe's talks during this period) on how to understand the Rebbe's statements about a purified world in light of the continued existence of evil, see www.shturem.net/uploadfile/mp3/jacobson_simon_770_13iyar.mp3.
58. Yehoshua Mundshine, "Nevua, Hakhrazot, Pirsumim, VeOd"; Chaim Rapoport (2011), 125.
59. See chapter 20, section "Personal Redemption."

the part of the Rebbe, and reading it gives one the impression that he felt that he himself would not see the "true and complete redemption."

The Rebbe expressed even darker sentiments nearly a year later, less than a month before his debilitating stroke. In the beginning of Adar 5752/1992, a young mother in Crown Heights was murdered in her home. The Rebbe was deeply affected by this event and dedicated a painful talk to the significance of sanctifying God's name in life and death.

In one section of the talk, the Rebbe spoke of the inexplicable situation of yet more Jewish blood being spilled in a time when *Mashiah* should have already arrived:

> It is completely incomprehensible what occurred here. And there is no one to ask, as everyone that is present here does not know, just as I do not know... and meanwhile, the Holy One, blessed be He, impedes the complete and true redemption – Heaven forbid, it should not be, for even another moment![60]

The Rebbe lamented the fact that the orphaned children would carry the trauma of their mother's murder for "many long years."

The Rebbe then broadened his talk and broached the topic of his push for *Mashiah* more generally:

> What is to be gained if we give another reason [why *Mashiah* should come] and another reason – until we no longer know what there is left to do? They tried through the path of joy of the sixty days of Adar... they tried all the paths and he still has not come. The true and complete redemption has still not arrived! And what is there to be gained if I say this again and again, and afterward they review it and write it down? We still do not have the true and complete redemption in actuality.
>
> What is there to gain from all the claims and reasons if the Holy One, blessed be He, as if...

---

60. Translated from the transcription of this talk, in Binyamin Lipkin (2000), 195–96. The edited version, *Torat Menahem* 5752: 2, 310–13, does not convey the same sense of despondency.

Here, the Rebbe was silent for a few long moments. He then continued, "We should not speak regarding the Holy One, blessed be He, for He does not need anyone to make recommendations for Him or to come to His defense. He will manage on His own."[61]

This talk, one of the last that the Rebbe delivered, expresses the antithesis of a redeemed world or of certainty in *Mashiah*'s immediate arrival. The non-literalists assert that these sentiments must be taken into account when interpreting the Rebbe's messianic pronouncements, leading them to the conclusion that the Rebbe did not see himself as living in a partially redeemed reality. It is important to note, though, that by his next talk, this dark tone was absent and was once again replaced by the Rebbe's more usual optimistic messianic rhetoric.

Chabad Messianic Rhetoric

A final point is also highly significant. While the intensity and frequency of the Rebbe's messianic pronouncements are unique, the Chabad oral and textual tradition contains similar formulations from the previous two generations. For example, a decade prior to World War II, R. Yosef Yitzhak declared, "The era of the elevation of the sparks has been completed, and now a new era is beginning in our lives...to prepare ourselves to greet *Mashiah*...to literally greet *Mashiah*."[62] Similarly, already from the early 1900s, the Rashab declared to his Hasidim that they were living in the "last generation" and that "without a doubt" they would greet *Mashiah*.[63]

The Rebbe was well versed in his predecessors' talks and was clearly familiar with these statements. Yet despite the literal falsity of the Rashab's and R. Yosef Yitzhak's messianic declarations, the Rebbe repeated these statements almost verbatim to the Hasidim of the seventh generation. It is fair to assume that the Rebbe did not consider his

---

61. Ibid.
62. *Sefer HaSihot* 5687, 121–22.
63. *Torat Shalom* 5667, 73–74.

predecessors to be false prophets and therefore presumably understood their definitive pronouncements in a non-literal way.[64]

Unfortunately, we do not have direct evidence regarding the Rebbe's precise understanding of his predecessors' statements. Perhaps he felt that these predictions were contingent on the Jewish people's "actions and service," and were even, perhaps, a means of inspiring the people to greater religious heights, as described in the previous chapter.[65] Or perhaps the Rashab and R. Yosef Yitzhak were simply following the Chabad formula of *bittahon* – "Think good and it will be good" – according to which a person must believe and profess that the "visible and manifest good" will occur and that this belief aids in creating that ideal reality.[66] Or were they prayerful statements addressed to God? Or a combination of all of the above factors? The single point that seems clear is that the Rebbe understood his predecessors' statements in a non-literal fashion. That being so, this group of Hasidim argued that the Rebbe's own comparable words must be similarly viewed.

CONCLUSION

During his final years, the Rebbe intensified his messianic rhetoric by speaking of redemption as currently and inexorably unfolding. While some Hasidim think that the Rebbe was speaking literally and definitively, others simply heard their Rebbe using the time-honored rhetorical techniques of a hasidic Rebbe. Until today the precise meaning of the Rebbe's words remains shrouded in mystery.

Secondary Literature Consulted for Chapter 21, "Redemption Is Here?"

Alon Dahan, *Goel Aharon*, 586–609.

---

64. See Yehoshua Mundshine, "Nevua, Hakhrazot, Pirsumim, VeOd"; Shlomo Dovber Levin (5 Tevet 5758), 23–31; Chaim Rapoport (2011), 122–23. These statements were also collected by Aviezer Ravitzky (1996), 199.
65. See chapter 20, section "The Obligations of the Last Generation."
66. See Aviezer Ravitzky (1996), 195.

Rahel Elior, "Tehiyat HaMeshihiyut BaHasidut Chabad BaMe'a HaEsrim: HaReka HaHistori VehaMisti, 1939–1996," in *Chabad: Historya, Hagut, VeDimmui*, 267–300.

Yosef Yitzhak Meislish, *HaTekufa VehaGeula BeMishnato shel HaRebbe MiLubavitch*.

Yehoshua Mundshine, *Iggeret LeYedid*.

Yehoshua Mundshine, "Nevua, Hakhrazot, Pirsumim, VeOd."

Aviezer Ravitzky, *Messianism, Zionism, and Jewish Religious Radicalism*, 193–206.

Eli Rubin, "The Idealistic Realism of Jewish Messianism," available at www.chabad.org/2766417.

Dov Schwartz, *Mahshevet Chabad MiReshit VeAd Aharit*, 286–318.

Yehezkel Sofer, *BeMai KaMiflegei: HaPulmus HaMeshihi BiTenuat Chabad*.

Shalom Dovber Wolf, *Inyano shel Mashiah*, 319–63; 481–596.

Elliot Wolfson, *Open Secret*, 265–300.

Chapter 22

The Rebbe and the *Mashiah*

Perhaps the most sensitive and contentious issue that arises when exploring the Rebbe's thought is his self-perception. As we have seen, despite thousands of public talks, the Rebbe was circumspect about himself and for the most part assiduously avoided speaking in the first person.[1] While this practice continued for his entire tenure, nonetheless, a group of Hasidim, which we will refer to as the messianists, believe that in his later years the Rebbe effectively proclaimed himself to be King *Mashiah* through a series of allusions and half statements. Others, however, vociferously reject these assertions. They argue that the messianists' interpretation of these statements are decontextualized and therefore incorrect. In addition, this second group of Hasidim calls attention to a series of unique talks and activities in which the Rebbe seemed to be preparing himself and his Hasidim for his passing.

---

1. See chapter 17, section "Who Is the *Nasi* of the Seventh Generation?"

Two points are important to state from the outset. First, the Rebbe never declared himself to be the *Mashiah* in any explicit form. Simultaneously, though, despite being cognizant of this belief among Hasidim, he never publicly denied that he was *Mashiah*.[2] Second, the differing orientations to the Rebbe's personal messianic aspirations or identity are deeply enmeshed with the debate described in the previous chapter. Those who believe that when the Rebbe spoke of a completely purified world and the presence of *Mashiah* in the world he meant that it is already so in literal actuality, also tend to interpret selections of the Rebbe's remarks as proclamations that he himself is the final redeemer. Conversely, those who understand the Rebbe's words about redemption being already underway as non-literal and prayerful, also contend that the proper interpretive lens for the Rebbe's remarks that are cited by the messianists demonstrates that these conclusions are baseless.

THE CONTEXT

The *Nasi* of the Generation

The conviction among Hasidim that the Rebbe would be *Mashiah* long predated these later talks and was instead rooted in classical Chabad philosophy. As we have seen, Chabad texts refer to the *nasi* of the generation as the "*Mashiah* of the generation," since the *nasi*'s primary responsibility is to disclose the Divine Essence within the material realm, the ultimate purpose of creation. In addition, this "*Mashiah* of the generation" is the person whom God will select to be the actual redeemer of the world if the generation completes its exilic mission.[3] For generations, Chabad Hasidim always assumed that their Rebbe, be it the Rashab, R. Yosef Yitzhak, or the Rebbe himself, was the *nasi hador* and therefore had the potential to be the final redeemer.[4]

---

2. Binyamin Lipkin (2000), 186. However, see Chaim Rapoport (2011), 125, where he describes seeing a Jewish Educational Media (JEM) video clip in which the Rebbe emphatically told an Israeli journalist that he was not *Mashiah*.
3. See chapter 17, section "The *Mashiah* of the Generation."
4. See *Torat Menahem* 5747: 1, 266, which says that the Rebbe himself mentioned this part of Chabad life and lore. For this idea from the perspective of a Hasid, see Yoel Kahn, *Kefar Chabad* (6 Shevat 5753), 13–16.

The True and Complete Redemption

Early Attempts

This idea, coupled with a firm belief in the imminence of *Mashiah*'s arrival, led some Hasidim to fervently believe from the earliest moments of Rebbe's leadership that he would be *Mashiah*. In 5725/1965, R. Avraham Paris, an elderly and leading Israeli Chabad Hasid, acted upon this belief and distributed thousands of copies of a letter that he wrote declaring the Rebbe to be King *Mashiah*. When the Rebbe heard about R. Paris's activities he immediately sent a sharply worded message to him to cease distribution at once and to retrieve every letter to remove them from circulation. As a loyal Hasid, R. Paris followed the Rebbe's instructions.[5]

A more public version of these events repeated itself nearly twenty years later. Hasidim had recently begun singing a song that referred to the Rebbe as the ultimate redeemer: "Soldiers of our master, our teacher, soldiers of our righteous *Mashiah*, he will lead us with 'tanks' to our land... he will redeem us." The Rebbe's response was unusually harsh:

> Here is an opportunity to mention an improper practice that requires fixing... there are those who are "*shpitz* [overzealous] Chabad," who think that they know what needs to be done and how to behave. And while everyone around them tries to warn them that their behavior is improper, it does not have any impact, as they think that no one can rebuke them because no one reaches their level, since they are "*shpitz* Chabad."[6]
>
> These words are intended for those who as a result of their speeches, publications, or songs have caused thousands of Jews to distance themselves from the Baal Shem Tov and from

---

5. See Eliyahu Wolf (2001), 98–100; Yehoshua Mundshine, *Iggeret LeYedid*.
6. In this context it is also important to note that it is possible that the Rebbe never publicly denied that he was *Mashiah* because he realized that the messianists would not be dissuaded from their beliefs and would actually use the Rebbe's denial as further motivation to publicly insist that he was King *Mashiah*. The Rebbe articulated some of this rationale on *Shabbat Parashat Noah* 5752/1992. Then, some Hasidim also sang a song that likewise referred to the Rebbe as *Mashiah*. The Rebbe reacted sharply saying that he should really leave the room in protest but he nonetheless stayed for two reasons: "It will anyway not help, and it will cause a disruption in '[how good and how pleasant it is for] brothers also to dwell together,' since if I leave, then others will leave as well."

learning and practicing Hasidism.... If you want to sing a hasidic song – there are many songs!... Go in the path that our masters, our *nesi'im*, have charted for us. No one needs new practices whose only impact will be to cause a new fight against the Baal Shem Tov and the Alter Rebbe, God forbid.[7]

The Rebbe's impassioned critique quelled these declarations for some time.[8]

THE REBBE PREPARING FOR HIS PASSING

In addition to rebuffing these proclamations, another indication that the Rebbe did not see himself as the actual *Mashiah* was in the practical steps that he took to prepare for his passing.

Writing a Will

On 22 Shevat 5748/February 10, 1988, the Rebbe's wife, Haya Mushka, passed away. In the midst of his grief, the Rebbe (through his secretary R. Yehuda Krinsky) asked a lawyer to draft a legally binding will for himself. By the end of the seven-day mourning period, the Rebbe had signed a will that bequeathed his own assets to Chabad's central organization, Agudat Hasidei Chabad.[9]

In addition to ensuring the future transfer of his personal assets, the Rebbe took similar action regarding the leadership of Chabad institutions. Soon after his wife's passing, the Rebbe asked R. Hodakov and R. Mindel, two senior members of his secretariat, to draft a document that delineated his wishes for the major Chabad organizations for a

---

7. *Torat Menahem* 5745: 1, 465. The translation of the term *shpitz* in the talk is from Chaim Miller (2014), 405.
8. It is important to note that the Rebbe based his critique on the detrimental impact of the song as opposed to the actual content of the claim. Some Hasidim contend from this that the passage of time and development of events allowed their public proclamations that the Rebbe was Mashiah. Most prominently, see R. Yoel Kahn's interview in *Kefar Chabad* 558 (Shevat 5753), 15. For a rejoinder, see Yehoshua Mundshine, *Iggeret LeYedid*.
9. Binyamin Lipkin (2000), 47–53. For a copy of the will, see Lipkin, 61–64.

time "after one hundred and twenty."[10] Several months later, the Rebbe requested that the main Chabad organizations update their boards of directors and to ensure that their legal paperwork was in perfect order.[11]

Decentralizing Chabad

These initiatives on the part of the Rebbe, as important as they are, were conducted behind closed doors and were known to only a privileged few. By contrast, at around the same time, the Rebbe publicly conducted a parallel initiative – one that sent shock waves through the community of Hasidim. For the first thirty-seven years of his leadership, the Rebbe constantly gave personalized blessings and advice to individual petitioners. Even though following his heart attack in 1978 the Rebbe, following his doctors' orders, gradually reduced and then ceased to see people in *yehidut* (private meetings), nonetheless, he continued to respond to thousands of inquiries that were delivered via the mail or his secretariat. In the winter of 5748/1988, however, the Rebbe publicly asked people to refrain from asking him for individualized blessings or personal advice.

The first intimation of this shift was the Rebbe's talk on 11 Shevat 5748. The Rebbe discussed the fact that the previous decade saw private meetings replaced with events in which he would deliver a general blessing to an entire group of visitors together (*yehidut kelalit*). While this approach would seem generic and less effective, the Rebbe contended that the collective unity of the people in the room gave his blessings more potency than ever before.

The Rebbe added that the same principle applied to advice. His "general advice" to the entire group would guide them just as reliably as the personalized counsel his visitors used to receive in private meetings. Here, the Rebbe defined his "general response" to the entire group:

> For medical matters one should follow the advice of an expert doctor (and it is better if there are two experts); for livelihood and financial issues one should follow the advice of colleagues and friends who are proficient in these issues; regarding the service

---

10. Ibid., 67–77. An unsigned draft of the document appears in Lipkin, 78–84.
11. Ibid., 97–103.

of God one should follow the dictum of the Mishna, "Make for yourself a teacher" (Avot 1:6) ... for these matters and similar ones (to exclude exceptional circumstances, etc.), there is no need for each person to ask individually and to wait for an individual response, but rather [each one] should act in accordance with the general response that is based on the instructions of the Torah.[12]

In other words, the Rebbe instructed those who would normally be asking him for advice to seek and follow the counsel of the experts in whatever area of life they felt they were lacking, instead of addressing their questions to him.[13]

The Rebbe offered two rationales for this change, one technical and one fundamental. On a basic level, he emphasized that as the volume of requests increased, there was not enough time to respond to each person's individual requests. In addition, and more importantly for our purposes, the Rebbe spoke of this shift as a natural outgrowth of the people's maturation and growth:

> In our days, after the people have achieved great things in the spreading of Torah, Judaism, and the wellsprings [of Hasidism], accompanied with the potency and mission of my father-in-law, the *nasi* of the generation, each individual person has been given the capabilities to succeed and reach the truth, especially if he learns and toils in the Torah of the *nasi* of the generation.[14]

As we noted earlier,[15] in his later talks the Rebbe transferred the responsibility to bring *Mashiah* from the *nasi* to the people, arguing that the

---

12. *Torat Menahem* 5748: 2, 308.
13. The Rebbe spoke of the need to "make for yourself a teacher" many times in the previous year. See, for example, *Torat Menahem* 5746: 4, 173–74; ibid., 5747: 1, 206–12, 470–74; ibid., 5747: 2, 339, 488–89, 632–35; ibid., 5747: 3, 61–64, 196–205; ibid., 5747: 4, 122–23, 212–13; ibid., 5748: 1, 511–12. However, the talk excerpted above marks the first time the Rebbe said to refrain from asking him for advice.
14. *Torat Menahem* 5748: 2, 308.
15. Chapter 17, section "The Generation of Malkhut," and chapter 20, section "Personal Redemption."

time had come for each person to access and reveal their inner *Tzaddik*. Similarly, the Rebbe highlighted the inner strength of each individual and instructed them to navigate their life issues without him.

The Rebbe continued this theme in his next talk. A mere five days after recusing himself from personal questions, he once again emphasized that after so many decades of following the path of R. Yosef Yitzhak, the Hasidim had been given "the necessary strength to follow the straight path that he taught us...until the point that the senses of the student become identical to the senses of the Rebbe."[16] The Rebbe once again recommended that when in doubt, a person should consult with a teacher to find the proper path.[17]

One week after this talk, the Rebbe's wife passed away. Immediately following the seven-day mourning period, the Rebbe once again returned to this theme of decentralization, though this time interweaving darker premonitions of his own passing. This talk turned on the talmudic call to "calculate the calculation of the world,"[18] a metaphor for taking a proper accounting of one's actions so that one will merit the World to Come.

The Rebbe cited a story he heard from his father-in-law, that as the *Tzemah Tzedek* aged Hasidim approached him and asked him to "calculate the calculation of the world," by which they meant that he should give them instructions as how to act after his passing.

As usual, the Rebbe took the fact that he heard this story from his father-in-law as a personal mandate: "The very fact that this story was shared with us indicates that we need [to follow King Solomon's advice that] 'The living should take to heart' (Eccl. 7:2), to 'calculate the calculation of the world.'"[19] The Rebbe then reiterated his earlier call to consult with medical experts and those with financial acumen regarding questions in these areas. In addition, the Rebbe called for each person and each Chabad community to appoint a committee of three Chabad rabbis to adjudicate personal and local communal issues. This

---

16. *Torat Menahem* 5748: 2, 325.
17. Ibid.
18. Bava Batra 78b.
19. Binyamin Lipkin (2000), 54–55, transcribed from the recording.

committee/court would be the representatives of the Rebbe, as the Rebbe stated: "We transfer [responsibility for deciding on communal and personal concerns] to the minds of these three people, and they receive the position and the authority to deliver a ruling in their location."[20] The Rebbe expressed hope that this would create clarity for how to act "for many good years."[21]

It seems that the Hasidim reacted to this talk with a mixture of anguish and disbelief. While the decentralization of Chabad was a difficult but understandable concept, many Hasidim simply did not know how to handle the Rebbe addressing his own passing. As such, this talk was not committed to writing despite the Rebbe's repeated requests that he be given a draft of the talk to edit. It was eventually published at a later date.[22]

DID THE REBBE EVER SAY HE WAS *MASHIAH*?

Setting the Stage

These activities indicate that the Rebbe spent at least the last four years before his stroke in 1992 preparing himself and his Hasidim for his passing. This, of course, militates against the notion that the Rebbe believed himself to be *Mashiah*, since, as the Rebbe underscored on several occasions, *Mashiah* would usher in an era of immortality.[23] Why, then, do the messianists proclaim the Rebbe to be "King *Mashiah*," who is the "final redeemer" of the Jewish people?[24]

---

20. Ibid., 56.
21. Ibid.
22. For the editorial history of this talk, see Binyamin Lipkin (2000), 56. A censored version of the talk was published in *Torat Menahem* 5748: 4, 397–407 (in the back of the book at the end of the entire year's talks as opposed to its proper place in the calendar year).
23. See, for example, *Torat Menahem* 5748: 4, 112.
24. This is the language of the first *pesak din* (halakhic ruling) that the Rebbe was *Mashiah*. See *Teshura MiSimhat HaNisuin shel Yosef Yitzhak VeHaya Mushka Taub* (22 Adar 5769), 7, available at old2.ih.chabad.info/images/notimage/45333_he_1.pdf.

The True and Complete Redemption

These Hasidim (the messianists) point to a combination of factors and sources as proof of their position.[25] We have already outlined how the Rebbe was the clear "*Mashiah* of the generation" in the eyes of his Hasidim.[26] Add to that the Rebbe's declaration in his opening *maamar*, that the seventh generation of Chabad was charged to create the utopian reality by drawing down the *Shekhina* into this lowly world. The messianists claim that it stands to reason that if this generation would be the "last generation of exile and the first generation of redemption,"[27] then the *nasi* of the generation, who is the potential *Mashiah* of the generation, would be the final redeemer. Moreover, as we have seen, the Rebbe often spoke about the generation's proximity to the Messianic Era. Thus, according to the messianists, when in his later years, the Rebbe said that the Jewish people's mission in exile had been completed (which they read literally), it follows that the Rebbe himself – the *Mashiah* of the generation – was revealed as the ultimate redeemer.

It is within this context that the messianists highlight certain passages from the Rebbe's talks during 5751 and 5752 and interpret them to mean that (1) the final redeemer had become revealed in the world, and (2) that person was the Rebbe himself.

This whole approach is fiercely debated by other Hasidim (the non-messianists), who wage a two-pronged battle. First, they dispute the former group's interpretations of specific passages, contending that the messianists are simply misrepresenting them by lifting them from the broader context of their respective talks and conjuring hidden meanings where none exist. More broadly, the non-messianists also challenge the entire methodology of the messianists by asserting that the Rebbe's words need to be understood through a wider lens of spiritual, inspirational, and especially prayerful meaning as per the Rebbe's longstanding rhetorical style, rather than literally.

At the outset, it is important to emphasize that the passages that will be quoted are not representative of the bulk of the Rebbe's talks even

---

25. The rest of this chapter will outline the current debate in Chabad about the meaning of certain passages in the Rebbe's later talks.
26. See chapter 17, section "The *Mashiah* of the Generation."
27. See chapter 20, section "Redemption's Imminence."

during these later years. Rather, as described in the previous chapters, the Rebbe spent these years emphasizing the need for each person to work tirelessly to reveal the Divine Essence within themselves and within the material realm more broadly. However, in several instances, the Rebbe said a sentence or two in the middle of a talk that the messianists argue signals to his own messianic aspiration or identity. It is to some of these disputed passages that we now turn our attention.

BeHezkat Mashiah

In the previous chapter we saw that the Rebbe explained that *Mashiah's* influence spurred nuclear disarmament. On several occasions the Rebbe further developed the notion of *Mashiah's* current existence by citing Rambam's codified words about the messianic process. Rambam describes that *Mashiah* will emerge via the following sequence of events:

> If a king will arise from the House of David who diligently contemplates the Torah and observes its mitzvot as prescribed by the Written Law and the Oral Law, like David, his ancestor, and will compel all of Israel to walk in (the way of the Torah) and rectify the breaches in its observance and fight the wars of God, we may presume him to be *Mashiah* (*behezkat shehu Mashiah*).
>
> If he succeeds in the above, builds the Temple in its place, and gathers the dispersed of the Jewish people, he is definitely *Mashiah* (*Mashiah bevaddai*).[28]

Rambam outlines a two-stage revelation of *Mashiah*. If a righteous leader of the Davidic line increases religious observance among the Jewish people and fights the wars of God, then he gains the presumptive status of *Mashiah*. Building the *Beit HaMikdash* and gathering the dispersed Jews transforms this presumption into a certainty.[29]

---

28. *Mishneh Torah, Hilkhot Melakhim UMilhemoteihem* 11:4.
29. In his analyses of Rambam's laws of *Mashiah*, the Rebbe carefully differentiated between these two stages. See, for example, *Torat Menahem* 5749: 3, 197–98; ibid., 5750: 2, 110.

The Rebbe was of course aware that the *Beit HaMikdash* remained unbuilt and there was certainly no *Mashiah bevaddai*. However, according to the messianists, he indicated that there was a living person who was *behezkat Mashiah*. For example, on 21 Tevet 5752/1992, one day after the anniversary of Rambam's passing, the Rebbe reflected on Rambam's groundbreaking contribution of organizing and codifying the laws of *Mashiah* in the same fashion as every other area of halakha. After once again imploring people to study these halakhot in depth, the Rebbe concluded his talk with a prayer:

> May it be God's will that due to the very resolution [to study Rambam], they should immediately be rewarded with the actualization of Rambam's words at the end of his book, that *after there already is* [fulfillment of Rambam's words]: "A king will arise from the House of David who diligently contemplates the Torah and observes its mitzvot as prescribed by the Written Law and the Oral Law, like David, his ancestor, and will compel all of Israel to walk in (the way of the Torah) and rectify the breaches in its observance and fight the wars of God" – in which case he is *behezkat Mashiah* – *there should already immediately be Mashiah bevaddai*.[30] [Emphasis added.]

On the one hand, the entire paragraph is expressed prayerfully ("May it be God's will that..."), indicating that all the subsequent sentences are wishful and not descriptive, in the same vein as the Rebbe's conclusion to thousands of other talks.[31] However, the messianists highlight that the Rebbe seemed to change from present to future tense in the middle of the paragraph. According to this reading, the Rebbe was stating that "there already is" a person who is *behezkat Mashiah*, and then he prayed that this person should emerge immediately as *Mashiah bevaddai*.[32]

Those who claim that in the above prayer the Rebbe affirmed the existence of a presumptive *Mashiah* seem to be at a disadvantage. One

---

30. *Torat Menahem* 5752: 2, 107.
31. See Yaakov Leib Altein (*Korah* 5757), 8–9.
32. Shalom Dovber Wolf (2016), 452–53.

of Rambam's criteria for such a designation is a leader[33] who "fights the wars of God." Which Jewish person during the Rebbe's lifetime led a successful military campaign against the Jewish people's enemies such that the Rebbe could say that there was a person who was *behezkat Mashiah*?

The messianists assert that the Rebbe addressed this issue a few months earlier. At the end of his talk at the *sheluhim* convention of 5752, the Rebbe once again listed reasons that redemption should come immediately. After reviewing some of the global events of the previous year, the Rebbe said, "And we see in actuality (*befo'al*) how 'he fights the wars of God' has occurred and he has been victorious in many, many matters – and especially through wars of peace."[34] Here, the Rebbe cited Rambam's language about the military success of the person who is *behezkat Mashiah* and applied this description to an unidentified "he" who was victorious through "wars of peace." The messianists interpret this sentence in light of the talk cited in the previous chapter in which the Rebbe attributed the peaceful fall and disarmament of the Soviet Union to the influence of *Mashiah* himself.[35] According to this weaving together of the different passages, the Rebbe publicized that a certain unnamed figure who was instrumental in the downfall of the Jewish people's enemies was the person who "fought the wars of God" and was therefore *behezkat Mashiah*.[36]

The non-messianists counter that this is a perversion of the Rebbe's intent.[37] On a contextual level, they highlight that even after the above talks, the Rebbe continued to pray for the *future* coming of *Mashiah* indicating that *Mashiah* had not yet arrived in any form. Then,

---

33. In a much earlier letter from 5727/1967, published in *Likkutei Sihot 8, Hosafot*, 361, the Rebbe inferred from Rambam's formulation that there is no requirement for having the formal status of a halakhic king in order to attain the status of *behezkat Mashiah*; rather, Rambam refers to a national Jewish leader. For a more detailed analysis of an argument for how the Rebbe fulfilled all of Rambam's requirements to be *behezkat Mashiah*, see Shalom Dovber Wolf (2016), 364–74, and especially 448–66.
34. *Torat Menahem* 5752: 1, 297.
35. See chapter 21, section "*Mashiah* and Nuclear Disarmament."
36. Shalom Dovber Wolf (2016), 457–60.
37. Chaim Rapoport (2011), 120–21, note 312; Yehezkel Sofer (2012), 207–23.

regarding the specifics of the messianist argument, the non-messianists counter that while the Rebbe employed Rambam's formulation of "he fights the wars of God," this can hardly be regarded as evidence that the Rebbe felt that there existed an actual human who had already satisfied the halakhic criteria to be *behezkat Mashiah*. On the contrary, they cite numerous passages from throughout the Rebbe's tenure where he argued that as a halakhic text, Rambam's *Mishneh Torah*, including the laws of *Mashiah*, must be analyzed and applied in accordance with the rigorous methodology of halakhic rulings.[38] In fact, the Rebbe frequently argued against messianic Zionism on the grounds that it does not conform with the precise legal import of this very halakha in *Mishneh Torah*.

Accordingly, these Hasidim argue that the Rebbe would never have considered a person to legally be *behezkat Mashiah* unless that person matched Rambam's criteria in an observable manner that matches the rigorous halakhic standards of evidence. Rather, in the above passage, the Rebbe was employing a standard hasidic literary device of midrashically appropriating Rambam's language to speak about a spiritual reality or to reflect on the messianic significance of recent events or another non-literal meaning. This is a far cry from actually expressing a legal opinion that a real live person was actually *behezkat Mashiah*.

The Existence of *Mashiah* and the Revelation of *Mashiah*

Thus, Hasidim sharply debate whether the Rebbe stated that there was an actual living person who was *behezkat Mashiah*. For the messianists, who insisted that he did, the next natural question was, did the Rebbe ever identify or even hint at the identity of such a person?

Their answer is a resounding yes. In their perception, on several occasions the Rebbe referred to the current *nasi* of the generation – which in his rhetoric was always his father-in-law, but in the eyes

---

38. See, for example, *Likkutei Sihot* 5, *Vayetzeh*, no. 2, note 51. For a dozen other examples, see Chaim Rapoport (2011), 120–21. However, see also *Torat Menahem* 5743: 1, 71, where the Rebbe used the language of Rambam and spoke of *Mashiah* waging a peaceful and pleasant spiritual "battle" to "conquer" the parts of the Land of Israel that were still in Arab hands.

The Rebbe and the Mashiah

of the Hasidim was him – as the one who had begun to be revealed as the final *Mashiah*.

One talk highlighted by the messianists was delivered on *Shabbat Parashat Vayera* 5752. Toward the end of this talk, the Rebbe repeated that in every generation there is a person who is righteous enough "to be the redeemer, and when the time comes, God will appear to him and send him." He then continued:

> And based on the teachings of my father-in-law, the *nasi* of the generation, the *Mashiah* of the generation, all the work has been completed and we stand ready to greet *Mashiah*, and in these days all of the impediments and blockages have been nullified. *Since this is the case, there is* (not just the reality of *Mashiah*, metziut deMashiah, but) *also the revelation of Mashiah*, and now we just need to greet our righteous *Mashiah* in actuality.[39] [Emphasis added.]

The Rebbe then implored his listeners to further intensify their messianic consciousness, as discussed earlier.[40]

The fact that the Rebbe referred to R. Yosef Yitzhak as "the *Mashiah* of the generation" is not at all surprising. This title simply identifies R. Yosef Yitzhak as the single *nasi* of the generation who was worthy of redeeming the Jewish people, something that the Rebbe had elaborated upon as part of his general teachings about the role of the *nasi*.[41]

According to the messianists, the next part of the passage enters new territory. Taken all together, the literal import of the Rebbe's words is that this potential *Mashiah* ("*Mashiah* of the generation"), who was the *nasi* of the generation and had always existed in a concealed fashion (*metziut deMashiah*), had now become revealed. Thus, according to the beginning of the passage, this latent potential redeemer was none other

---

39. *Torat Menahem* 5752: 1, 277.
40. See chapter 20, sections "The Obligations of the Last Generation" and "The Uniqueness of the Last Generation."
41. See, for example, *Torat Menahem* 5746: 1, 342–43, and chapter 17, section "Who Is the *Nasi* of the Seventh Generation?"

The True and Complete Redemption

than R. Yosef Yitzhak, the *nasi* of the generation, who had now become revealed as the final redeemer.[42]

The messianists support their interpretation of this passage by highlighting the general context of the talk. A few minutes earlier, the Rebbe had spoken of the students of Chabad's central yeshiva, Tomkhei Temimim, as charged with preparing the path toward global redemption. This mission was assigned to them by the Rashab, the yeshiva's founder, who referred to his students as "the soldiers of David."

Continuing this theme, the Rebbe added:

> This is more accentuated in our generation, the third generation to our master (the Rashab)…in which the mission of the "soldiers of David" to bring *Mashiah* is completed…and in our generation we are already in the ninetieth year (*shenat hatzaddik*)…and we begin the era that is associated with Psalms, chapter 90 (*Tzaddik*), which concludes with "And may the pleasantness of the Lord our God be upon us, and the work of our hands establish for us, and the work of our hands establish it," which refers to the future *Beit HaMikdash*.[43]

These words require analysis. While the "ninetieth year" is identified as the "year of the *Tzaddik*" due to the fact that the numerical value of the Hebrew letter *tzadi* is ninety, the general meaning of the above passage remains opaque. In what way is 5752/1992 the ninetieth year? And what is the connection between the "ninetieth year" and the messianically themed ninetieth chapter of Psalms?

There is a longstanding Chabad custom for each person to recite daily the chapter of Psalms that corresponds to one's age.[44] In addition, many Hasidim recite the chapter that corresponds to the age of the Rebbe.[45] The Rebbe turned eighty-nine on the 11 Nisan 5751, locating this talk

---

42. Shalom Dovber Wolf (2016), 422–23.
43. *Torat Menahem* 5752: 1, 275.
44. *Iggerot Kodesh Admor Moharaayatz* 10, letter 3355. For an explanation of the custom, see *Torat Menahem* 5721: 1, 269.
45. The Rebbe recommended that Hasidim continue to say the chapter that corresponded to R. Yosef Yitzhak's age. See *Likkutei Sihot* 2, *Hosafot*, 10 Shevat, *se'if* 4;

The Rebbe and the Mashiah

in the middle of his ninetieth year. Accordingly, it seems that the Rebbe was emphasizing that his ninetieth year – the year of the *Tzaddik* – was a ripe time for the rebuilding of the third *Beit HaMikdash*, which is a theme of the ninetieth chapter of Psalms.[46]

In the progression of the Rebbe's talk, this indication of proximity to redemption based on his own age flows into his comment that R. Yosef Yitzhak was the "*Mashiah* of the generation" and that there already was a "revelation of *Mashiah*." The messianists contend that the juxtaposition of these themes indicates that the *Mashiah*, who not only existed (*metziut deMashiah*) but was also "revealed," was the Rebbe himself.[47]

Once again, the non-messianists counter that the messianists were approaching this talk through the wrong interpretive lens. The very paragraph under scrutiny (cited above in this section, beginning with the words "And based on the teachings of my father-in-law") opens with a statement that the Jewish people have already completed their exilic service. As we have seen, the non-messianists offer several reasons to favor a non-literal interpretation of this statement, most notably by highlighting the simple fact that humans were still plagued by the evil inclination. Accordingly, just as the Rebbe did not literally mean that the world had been completely purified, he similarly did not intend the statement of *Mashiah* having revealed himself to be understood as a literal, real-world event. Rather, the Rebbe was speaking prayerfully, and/or about a spiritual reality that he perceived but was imperceptible to the regular human eye.

Similarly, the non-messianists argue that the Rebbe's reference to the "year of the *Tzaddik*" is best understood within the context of his usual rhetorical techniques. The Rebbe would regularly interpret the date of a talk and other items of current events to demonstrate the messianic potential of the moment.[48] For example, in this very talk,

---

Iggerot Kodesh 3, letters 658, 670.
46. The Rebbe had already noted the significance of this year on other occasions. See *Torat Menahem* 5751: 3, 29, note 11; 190, note 124; ibid., 5752: 1, 145. See also *Torat Menahem* 5752: 2, 179, note 134; 296, note 85; 315.
47. Shalom Dovber Wolf (2016), 444–47.
48. Due to his firm belief in *hashgaha*, the Rebbe often attributed significance to the specific day on which he was speaking (see, for example, *Torat Menahem* 5744: 4, 2646; ibid., 5745: 5, 2927–28) or at least to the *parasha* of the week. This practice

the Rebbe highlighted how the confluence of 18 Heshvan, the date when the talk was delivered, and *Parashat Vayera*, which was to be read on the upcoming Shabbat, was an opportune time for the coming of *Mashiah*.[49]

These Hasidim argue that the frequency and shifting nature of these homilies indicate that the Rebbe was simply using all relevant information to raise the messianic consciousness of his listeners. As noted above, the Hasidim had been reciting Psalms, chapter 90, since 11 Nisan 5751, and therefore that chapter and its content was on their minds. Accordingly, the non-messianists argue that the Rebbe's interweaving of this chapter into his messianic rhetoric should be understood as part of his general technique of employing all possible factors to inspire the Hasidim to greater heights.

The Mission of R. Yosef Yitzhak

The Rebbe's talk one week later at the *sheluhim* convention of 5752 contains a similar construct and is similarly debated. In this talk the Rebbe declared that the *sheluhim* had completed their mission and now needed only to "greet *Mashiah*."[50] At one point, though, the messianists claim that the Rebbe went further and hinted at the identity of the *Mashiah* that the *sheluhim* were to greet.

One of the central sources in this talk was a midrash that identifies *Mashiah* as the ultimate *shaliah*. When God tells Moses to go and redeem the Jewish people from Egypt, Moses attempts to deflect the mission onto another person: "Send now [Your message] with whom You would send."[51] The midrash explains that Moses was telling God:

---

dates back to the Alter Rebbe, who referred to studying the *parasha* of the week as "living with the times." For sources regarding the content and context of the Alter Rebbe's statement, see Eli Rubin, "Living with the Times: Rabbi Shneur Zalman of Liadi's Oral Teachings." For the Rebbe's usage of this phrase, see *Likkutei Sihot* 1, 10 Shevat, *se'if* 18; ibid., 2, *Lekh Lekha*, *se'if* 1; *Torat Menahem* 5713: 3, 73, among dozens of other instances.

49. *Torat Menahem* 5725: 1, 267, 272–73.
50. See chapter 21, section "Greeting *Mashiah*."
51. Ex. 4:13.

"Master of the World: Send now Your message with whom You would send, in the hands of *Mashiah*, who will be revealed in the future."[52]

Employing this reference, the Rebbe spoke of the need to "greet *Mashiah*":

> It is known that in every generation a scion of the House of David is born who is fitting to be *Mashiah*..." and based on the teachings of my father-in-law, the *nasi* of our generation, the single *shaliah* of our generation, and the single *Mashiah* of our generation, which has finished all of the work, it is understood that *the "send now* [Your message] *with whom You would send" is beginning to be fulfilled* – *the shelihut of his eminence, my father-in-law, our Rebbe.* And from this it is understood that the single item that remains in the service of *shelihut* is to greet our righteous *Mashiah* in actuality so that he can fulfill his *shelihut* in actuality to take the Jewish people out of exile![53] [Emphasis added.]

In this passage, the final service of "greeting *Mashiah*" is completely intertwined with the person and mission of R. Yosef Yitzhak. The Rebbe used the verse "send...with whom You would send," which the midrash associates with the final redeemer, as a reference to the mission of R. Yosef Yitzhak. Moreover, this mission was "beginning to be fulfilled," indicating that *Mashiah*/R. Yosef Yitzhak had already begun to be revealed and positively affect the world. Also, once again, immediately prior to these words the Rebbe mentioned the significance of "the year of the *Tzaddik*."[54]

The non-messianists respond as expected. The fact that R. Yosef Yitzhak was "the single *Mashiah* of our generation" simply identifies him as the generation's *nasi* who is working toward redemption and worthy of becoming the actual redeemer. Similarly, they argue that the Rebbe's charge to "greet *Mashiah*" was not meant as a charge to literally and practically meet the physical person of *Mashiah*, as evidenced by

---

52. *Midrash Lekah Tov* to Ex. 4:13.
53. *Torat Menahem* 5752: 1, 298.
54. Ibid., 297.

the Rebbe's constant calls to increase one's classical study of Torah and performance of mitzvot (indicating that the exilic work had not yet been completed) and the other factors outlined above. As such, they contend the whole notion of the Rebbe referring to his father-in-law or himself as the literal and practical *Mashiah* that the Hasidim had to greet is a gross misinterpretation of the Rebbe's words.

The Significance of 770 Eastern Parkway

Another flash point for this debate is a pamphlet of compiled talks, edited by the Rebbe and published in Heshvan 5752, entitled "The House of Our Teacher in Bavel,"[55] which is dedicated to the significance of the central Chabad synagogue and *beit midrash* at 770 Eastern Parkway. The pamphlet opens by citing the Talmud's interpretation of the verse "I have become for them a minor sanctuary (*mikdash me'at*) in the lands [of exile]"[56] as a reference to "the house of our teacher in Bavel."[57] Rashi explains that this refers to the house of Rav, the leader of Babylonian Jewry.

Through a characteristically detailed textual analysis, the Rebbe concluded that in every generation there is a single central house of study and prayer that is the spiritual home of the *nasi* of the generation and the exilic home of the Divine Presence.[58] The Rebbe laced this central home with messianic significance. It was there that the Divine Presence resided in a manner reminiscent of the *Beit HaMikdash*.[59] It was there that the *Mashiah* of the generation resided, waiting for the call to redeem the Jewish people.[60] And the Rebbe raised the possibility that this *Beit HaMikdash* of the Diaspora would be the location from which *Mashiah* would reveal himself to the Jewish people and inform them of their redemption.[61]

---

55. Ibid., 414–25.
56. Ezek. 11:16.
57. Megilla 29a.
58. *Torat Menahem* 5752: 1, 419–20.
59. Ibid. The Rebbe cited this idea from Maharsha, *Hiddushei Aggadot*, Megilla 29a, s.v. *atidim*, in addition to other sources.
60. Ibid.
61. Ibid., note 38.

Moving from the talmudic period to the present, the Rebbe identified 770 Eastern Parkway, the synagogue and *beit midrash* of R. Yosef Yitzhak, as this central exilic location.[62] In a much-cited allusion, the Rebbe noted that the numerical value of *beit Mashiah* (the house of *Mashiah*) is 770.[63]

For the non-messianists, all this essay does is elaborate on the significance of the spiritual home of R. Yosef Yitzhak, the *nasi* of the generation. For the messianists, though, this pamphlet adds fuel their fire. They view the fact that the Rebbe identified his own spiritual home as *Beit Mashiah* and even raised the possibility of the actual *Mashiah* announcing redemption from there as further steps in the Rebbe's slow march toward fully revealing himself as the final redeemer.

Mashiah (Menahem Is His Name)

Until now we have seen messianist arguments that focus on passages about R. Yosef Yitzhak, which the messianists assume were really self-referential on the part of the Rebbe. Going further, they also point to several acronyms that pepper some of the Rebbe's final talks that they contend refer directly to the Rebbe's own personal messianic identity or aspirations.

On many occasions, the Rebbe repeated Rambam's formulation that if the Jewish people repent, they will be redeemed immediately (*miyad hen nigalin*).[64] On 20 Shevat 5752, the Rebbe suggested that the letters of *miyad* (immediately) – *mem*, *yod*, and *dalet* – are an acronym for **M**oshe, **Y**israel (Baal Shem Tov), and **D**avid (representing *Mashiah*).[65]

The Rebbe explained that these three figures are intertwined in the messianic process. Moses, the first redeemer of the Jewish people, is transformed into the final redeemer (David/*Mashiah*)[66] through the revelation of the teachings of the Baal Shem Tov. While they lived in

---

62. Ibid., 421–24.
63. Ibid., note 91.
64. *Mishneh Torah, Hilkhot Teshuva* 7:5. See, for example, *Torat Menahem* 5715: 1, 14; ibid., 5748: 1, 403.
65. *Torat Menahem* 5752: 2, 221.
66. This is based on Exodus Rabba 2:4, which states, "Moses is the first redeemer; he is the final redeemer."

different millennia, this triad forms a single unit, and the final generation merits the revelation of all three of these figures together. This temporal unity is alluded to in another acronym of *miyad* – **M**oshe, **Y**ehoshua, *d*oram (their generation) – meaning that despite the fact that Moses (Moshe) and Joshua (Yehoshua) lived and led in different generations, on a spiritual plane they transcend time, are united as one, and appear in the same generation.

The Rebbe continued that this spiritual and temporal unification of discrete figures was uniquely relevant:

> In our generation there is a revelation of the three of them: *mem* (the first letter of *Mashiah*), *yod* (the first letter of the two names of his eminence, my father-in-law [Yosef Yitzhak]), and *dalet* (*doram*) ..."the first redeemer is the final redeemer," David, King *Mashiah*.[67]

The Rebbe seems to be saying that just as Moses and Joshua were spiritually and temporally united (*doram*), so too, *Mashiah* and R. Yosef Yitzhak are of the same "generation" (*doram*) despite the fact that R. Yosef Yitzhak died before *Mashiah* arrived. What does this mean?

This enigmatic statement is thrown into relief by the gloss that appears as a footnote to the word *Mashiah* in the above quote: "Note (*leha'ir*) that Menahem is his name (Sanhedrin 98b)." This refers to a talmudic passage where the rabbis offer different suggestions for the future redeemer's name. The final opinion cited in the passage is that *Mashiah*'s name will be Menahem.

While the Rebbe did not explicitly speak of himself, the messianists argue that this is a highly suggestive gloss. The Rebbe was speaking of the spiritual unification of R. Yosef Yitzhak with the final redeemer and in this charged context noted that the name of the final redeemer is Menahem, which is the Rebbe's first name. The messianists understand that the Rebbe was speaking of his own messianic identity and unification with R. Yosef Yitzhak and Moses.

---

67. *Torat Menahem* 5752: 2, 221.

A similar comment appears in a talk from one week later. The Rebbe concluded his talk with a prayer that *Mashiah* come *miyad* (immediately) and then added: "With all of the interpretations that are in *miyad* (including the acronym of the generations of **M**oshe, **Y**israel Baal Shem Tov, and **D**avid, King *Mashiah*)."[68] The footnote there adds the following:

> And more particularly for our generation, the acronym of *miyad* hints to the three eras of his eminence, my father-in-law, the *nasi* of our generation (see the pamphlet from the talk of *Parashat Va'era* of this year...), in accordance with their proximity to us – *Mashiah* (**M**enahem is his name), **Y**osef **Y**itzhak, **D**ovber (the second name of [Yosef Yitzhak's] father).

To understand this comment, we need to follow the Rebbe's reference to his speech from a few months earlier on *Shabbat Parashat Va'era* 5752. There, the Rebbe spoke of R. Yosef Yitzhak's life as being divided into three periods, each representing a broadening and intensification of his work to spread Torah and Hasidism.[69]

The first period stretches from R. Yosef Yitzhak's birth in 5640/1880 until 5680/1920, when his father, the Rashab (Shalom Dovber) passed away. This era saw both the opening of Yeshivat Tomkhei Temimim, which laid the groundwork for all future Chabad activities, and the beginning of R. Yosef Yitzhak's activities under the tutelage of his father. R. Yosef Yitzhak's ascent to leadership in 5680 commenced the second era of his life, in which he worked tirelessly to spread Torah despite Russian persecution. This era ended with R. Yosef Yitzhak's passing in 5710/1950. Then, a third era began: "the continuation of his being the *nasi* after his passing." During these forty-plus years the wellsprings spread around the globe until "the work has been completed and everything is already prepared for the future meal – the days of *Mashiah*."

Now the meaning of the Rebbe's comments about the acronym of *miyad* comes into focus. The letters of *miyad* refer to these three eras in R. Yosef Yitzhak's "life." Working backward, the *dalet* refers to R. Yosef

---

68. Ibid., 282.
69. Ibid., 119.

The True and Complete Redemption

Yitzhak's father, the Rashab, whose second name was **D**ovber. The *yod* refers to R. **Y**osef Yitzhak himself, **Y**osef Yitzhak. We are left with the *mem*, which the Rebbe said refers to "*Mashiah* (**M**enahem is his name)."

The messianists take this as an allusion to the Rebbe's identity as or aspiration to be *Mashiah*. The logic goes as follows. According to the Rebbe's earlier talk, the third era of R. Yosef Yitzhak's "life" refers to the years of the Rebbe's own leadership. Then a few months later, on 27 Shevat, the Rebbe described the same years with the words "*Mashiah* (Menahem is his name)." This comment seems to define this era as being the time of Menahem (the Rebbe's name), who is *Mashiah*.[70]

The non-messianists argue that a cursory look at the Rebbe's corpus reveals his wide-ranging use of such acronyms and allusions that connect various figures and events to *Mashiah*. For example, when speaking about the *Tzemah Tzedek*, whose first name was also Menahem, the Rebbe on several occasions noted that Menahem is the name of *Mashiah*.[71] Similarly, on the first anniversary of the passing of his brother-in-law, R. Shmaryahu Gurary, the Rebbe reflected on R. Shmaryahu Gurary's role as the director of Yeshivat Tomkhei Temimim and the yeshiva's significance in hastening the redemption. The Rebbe noted that his brother-in-law's name, Shmaryahu, alludes to the final redemption. After demonstrating that the letters of Shmaryahu allude to various verses that relate to redemption, the Rebbe noted that Shmaryahu's father's name was Menahem, which is the name of *Mashiah*.[72]

It is clear that the Rebbe did not think that the *Tzemah Tzedek*, R. Shmaryahu Gurary, R. Shmaryahu's father, or many other people who were

---

70. Similarly, on one occasion the Rebbe prayed that the true and complete redemption should come immediately, without delay, in actuality (*tekhef umiyad mamash*) and then said, "with all of the acronyms of *miyad* and all of the acronyms of *mamash*." This is available at 1:30 of the following clip (but not in the published remarks), chabad.info/video/rebbe/dailyvideo/35367/.

    See Shalom Dovber Wolf (2016), 411, note 74, who understood that the "acronyms of *mamash*" refer to the Rebbe's own name – **M**enahem **M**endel **Sch**neerson. This is distinct from the times the Rebbe employed the more usual formulation of "all of the interpretations of *mamash*," which is less likely to be self-referential, as per the analysis of Chaim Rapoport (2011), 117–19.

71. *Torat Menahem* 5725: 4, 270; ibid., 5749: 4, 349.
72. Ibid., 5750: 2, 337.

alluded to over the years in discussions of the *Mashiah*, were actually the final redeemer. Rather, the Rebbe presumably had at least two intentions when speaking of these allusions: (1) to employ them as a rhetorical device that would inspire the listeners to think about their own role in furthering redemption, and (2) to note that these individuals furthered the redemptive process. As such, the non-messianists feel that the Rebbe's association of his own name with the talmudic name of *Mashiah* fit squarely within an established and clearly non-literal, rhetorical technique.

Summary

In summary, the Rebbe never explicitly declared that he was *Mashiah*.[73] However, the messianists argue that the above passages, coupled with the Rebbe's general messianic rhetoric and his descriptions of the seventh generation, create a compelling picture of the Rebbe's own messianic identity. Conversely, another group of Hasidim strongly reject what they see as a distorted understanding of the Rebbe's speaking style and the elevation of decontextualized and cryptic sentences as harbingers of a new cosmic era. Instead, they see his democratization of the mission and emphasis on each person revealing their own inner *Tzaddik*/spark of *Mashiah* as the key motif of the Rebbe's later years. This theme was most intensely expressed in the Rebbe's impromptu talk from 28 Nisan 5751 (excerpted above), where he painfully expressed failure in the mission of bringing *Mashiah* and passed the baton to the people. Accordingly, the main legacy of the Rebbe's focus on *Mashiah* and redemption is the need for each person to elevate their consciousness and practical service to "live with *Mashiah*."

No matter what the Rebbe actually meant, the rise in both his rhetoric and age generated a parallel rise in the tension, anticipations, and emotions among his followers. All of this came to a crashing halt on 27 Adar 5752, when the Rebbe suffered a debilitating stroke while

---

73. In addition to the debates outlined above regarding the meaning of the later talks, the messianists and non-messianists have different narratives regarding the Rebbe's reaction when various people publicly and privately referred to him as *Mashiah* in his presence. For some such instances see Binyamin Lipkin (2000), 185–90; Chaim Rapoport (2011), 125; Joseph Telushkin (2014), 425–28; Dovid Nah'shon, *Teshura MiSimhat HaNisuin shel Yosef Yitzhak VeHaya Mushka Taub* (22 Adar 5769).

The True and Complete Redemption

praying at his father-in-law's gravesite. Even though he lived for over two years after the stroke, he was unable to speak, effectively bringing his Torah teachings to an end.

A PERSONAL REFLECTION

As outlined above, the Rebbe left a trail of conflicting evidence regarding his own messianic aspirations, leading many Hasidim and academics[74] to fervently assert or deny that he thought he was *Mashiah*. While it is impossible to be certain, my understanding of the sources lies between these two poles. To my mind, when one considers his teachings regarding the nature of the generation, the role of the *nasi*, together with his later formulations, it would seem highly unlikely that he never entertained the possibility that he would become the *Mashiah*.[75]

However, the countering evidence indicates that these thoughts remained no more than that – a possibility. It would seem to me that he must have viewed himself as a candidate, even a likely candidate, for messiahship, such that if he and his generation fulfilled their mission then he could very well become the redeemer of the Jewish people.

This understanding of the conflicting evidence is buttressed by an unconfirmed anecdote related by R. Yehudah Groner, a member of the Rebbe's secretariat. One day during his later years, the Rebbe asked him: "Why do people say that I am *Mashiah*?" A bewildered R. Groner responded that the Hasidim felt that the Rebbe fulfilled the requirements delineated by Rambam. According to R. Groner, the Rebbe responded as follows: "The person who is *Mashiah* – it needs to be

---

74. Tomer Presco (2009); Alon Dahan (2014), 587; Dahan (September 2014); Yitzhak Kraus [cited in Gay Kantur (2013), 184–85] conclude that the Rebbe thought he was *Mashiah*. See Samuel Heilman and Menachem Friedman (2010), 231, who strongly imply this as well. By contrast, Elliot Wolfson (2009), 272–300, contends that the real secret of the Rebbe was a call to overcome the need for a *Mashiah* figure through each individual shifting to a messianic consciousness. Similarly, two of the Rebbe's recent biographers dismiss the claim that the Rebbe thought he was *Mashiah*. See Chaim Miller (2014), 398–407; Joseph Telushkin (2014), 418–31. Others, such as Yehiel Harari (2013), 266–70 and David Berger (2014), argue that it is impossible to definitively determine the Rebbe's true intention.
75. This is also the approach of Rabbi Adin Even-Israel Steinsaltz (2014), 197–98.

revealed to him from above. At the current time (*le'et atta*), it has not been revealed to me."[76]

If this anecdote is accurate, it seems that the Rebbe might have been waiting for such a revelation, or at least considered it a possibility. That message from heaven, however, never came, and the Rebbe died in an unredeemed world.

This leads us to a final point which was mentioned earlier but deserves to be underscored in this context. Even if the Rebbe considered himself a candidate to be *Mashiah*, this never became a major topic in his talks. The allusions to his father-in-law or to possibly to himself as the ultimate redeemer – which I feel are not to be glossed over – are a negligible percentage of his output even in the later years. Similarly, the possibility of the Rebbe's conception of his own candidacy to be *Mashiah* did not lead him to public expressions of self-aggrandizement or even to portray himself as beyond self-doubt. His status or lack thereof as the redeemer of the Jewish people did not greatly occupy his public declarations. This is borne out by a short note he wrote right before his stroke: "There is no obligation to search for the identity of *Mashiah*."[77] Instead, he focused his efforts on what he considered to be the ultimate imperative – creating the messianic reality. As he emphasized, this mission required each person to do their own service of accessing their own *yehida* and revealing the Divine Essence in their own portion of the material world.[78]

---

76. Binyamin Lipkin (2000), 188. There is reason, however, to be skeptical of the accuracy of this telling. On a different occasion, R. Groner told the story differently; see chabadinfo.com/news/rabbi-groner-testifies-the-rebbe-affirmed-title-melech-hamoshiach/. See also Yehoshua Mundshine, "Kavim LiDemuto shel Shakran," where he raises serious issues about the accuracy of many of R. Groner's stories.

77. Binyamin Lipkin (2000), 186 (at the end of the chapter the author inserted a copy of the actual note). Non-messianists, such as Yehoshua Mundshine ("Nevuot Hakhrazot Pirsumin VeOd"), have marshaled this note as important evidence. For a messianist rejoinder, see Shalom Dovber Wolf (2016), 413–14.

78. Elliot Wolfson, in his lecture "Chabad Messianism and the Present Future" (available at www.youtube.com/watch?v=dM-yQeuLS3w), at 18:20 notes that it is ironic that scholars analyzing the Rebbe's later years and rhetoric tend to focus only on the issue of personal messiahship while the Rebbe's whole description of the Messianic Era delineates revelation of the *yehida*/Divine Essence that demonstrates the ability to expand beyond individual consciousness and experience the unity of all being.

The True and Complete Redemption

While not completely analogous, this understanding of the Rebbe's focus dovetails nicely with a story he told earlier in his tenure. In 5720/1960 the Rebbe related that when his father-in-law had issued his public letters during World War II proclaiming *Mashiah*'s imminent arrival, R. Yosef Yitzhak was aware that some of his Hasidim assumed that he himself would be the *Mashiah*. When word spread that Chabad Hasidim were engaging in messianic speculation about their Rebbe, other communities reacted negatively. The Rebbe related that one Polish hasidic Rebbe offered the following defense of Chabad:

> Let us think. We believe in and wait for *Mashiah* "every day that he should come." Some people recite this daily...some have thoughts that *Mashiah* is present. Once this is the case, since you know that you are not *Mashiah* and I know that I am not *Mashiah* but somebody must be the *Mashiah*, what difference does it make that they say that he is the one?[79]

While one might argue that this approach is irresponsible, according to this story, R. Yosef Yitzhak felt that the detrimental effects of unrealized hope in an individual *Mashiah* paled in comparison to the benefit of having people truly thinking about and striving for the ultimate redemption.

In contrast to R. Yosef Yitzhak, who quieted his messianic rhetoric with the end of the war, the Rebbe kept speaking about *Mashiah* and redemption until his sudden aphasic stroke became the point of no return. While we can never know a person's inner thoughts, it seems that whether or not he felt that he was destined to be the *Mashiah* was an issue of secondary importance to his life's work. The Rebbe's main mission, however, as represented by the bulk of his output and efforts, was to encourage people to create redemption by disclosing the Divine Essence within all aspects of reality – themselves, others, and the material world at large.

I hope that this book helped illuminate a crucial aspect of this general mission, namely the Rebbe's project to reveal and refract the essence of Torah in all of its multifarious dimensions. As the Rebbe expressed it in his landmark essay "On the Essence of Hasidism," the

---

79. *Torat Menahem* 5720: 2, 129–30.

messianic ideal is realized – both within the world that is each individual and within the world at large – through revealing a "new" and "essential" vitality within the Torah.[80]

Secondary Literature Consulted for Chapter 22, "The Rebbe and the *Mashiah*"

Alon Dahan, *Goel Aharon*, 586–609.

Rahel Elior, "Tehiyat HaMeshihiyut BaHasidut Chabad BaMe'a HaEsrim: HaReka HaHistori VehaMisti, 1939–1996," in *Chabad: Historya, Hagut VeDimmui*, 267–300.

Yisrael Greenberg and Yisrael Kaufman, *Besuras HaGeula*.

Yehiel Harari, *Sodo shel HaRebbe*, 253–73.

Samuel Heilman and Menahem Friedman, *The Rebbe: The Life and Afterlife of Menachem Mendel Schneerson*, 228–38.

Menahem Mendel Kaplan, "Zihui Nasi HaDor im Mashiah SheBaDor."

Binyamin Lipkin, *Heshbono shel Olam*.

Yosef Yitzhak Meislish, *HaTekufa VehaGeula BeMishnato shel HaRebbe MiLubavitch*.

Chaim Miller, *Turning Judaism Outward*, 398–410.

Tomer Presco, "HaMashiah HaAvud shel Chabad," *Tekhelet* 36.

Chaim Rapoport, "Chabad's Messianism" *Tekhelet* 41.

Chaim Rapoport, *The Afterlife of Scholarship*.

Yehezkel Sofer, "Mikhtav LeYedid SheHihmitz."

Yehezkel Sofer, *BeMai KaMiflegei*.

Joseph Telushkin, *Rebbe*, 415–35.

Shalom Dovber Wolf, *Inyano shel Mashiah*.

Elliot Wolfson, *Open Secret*, 265–300.

---

80. *Inyana shel Torat HaHasidut*, se'ifim 6–8.

Bibliography of Secondary Literature

Altein, Yaakov Leib. "BeHezkat Mashiah." *Kovetz Mashiah UGeula* 3 (*Parashat Korah* 5757).
———. *Hassidut Mevueret* Volume 1. Brooklyn: Heichal Menachem, 2003.
Altman, Alexander. "Saadya's Conception of the Law." *Bulletin of the John Rylands Library* 28:2 (1944).
Ariel, Shemuel. "Ha'im Kol Irua Mekhuvan MiShamayim." *Tzohar* 28 (5767).
Avner, Yehuda. "The Rebbe: His Moral Vision as Statesman and Diplomat." Retrieved from www.oxfordchabad.org/851894.
Avtzon, Yonah, and Eliyahu Touger. *Led By G-d's Hand: The Ba'al Shem Tov's Conception of Hashgacha Peratis – Based on the Works of the Lubavitcher Rebbe, Rabbi Menachem M. Schneerson*. Brooklyn: Sichos in English, 1998.
Balk, Hanan. "The Soul of a Jew and the Soul of a Non-Jew: An Inconvenient Truth and the Search for an Alternative." *Hakirah* 16 (2013).
Berger, David. "Miracles and the Natural Order in Nahmanides." In *Rabbi Moses Nahmanides: Explorations in His Religious and Literary Virtuosity*. Edited by Isadore Twersky. Cambridge, MA: Harvard University Press, 1983.
———. "Some Ironic Consequences of Maimonides' Rationalist Approach to the Messianic Age." In *Cultures in Collision and Conversation*. Boston: Academic Studies Press, 2011.

———. *The Rebbe, the Messiah and the Scandal of Orthodox Indifference.* London: The Littman Library of Jewish Civilization, 2001.

———. "Did the Rebbe Identify Himself as the Messiah – and What Do His Hasidim Believe Today?" (July 2014). Retrieved from www.tabletmag.com/jewish-news-and-politics/179435/berger-rebbe-messiah.

Bergstein, Avraham. "Shittat HaRashba BeNimna HaNimnaot." *Kovetz He'arot UVe'urim* 919 (*Behar-Behukkotai*, 5766).

Bilu, Yoram, "Samuel Heilman and Menachem Friedman, *The Rebbe: The Life and Afterlife of Menachem Mendel Schneerson*" *AJS Review* 35:2 (November 2011): 449–54.

Blau, Yitzchak. *Fresh Fruit and Vintage Wine.* Jersey City: Ktav Publishing House, 2009.

Bleich, J. David. *Contemporary Halakhic Problems.* Volume 2. New York: Ktav Publishing House, 2011.

Blidstein, Yaakov. "HaSimha BeMishnato HaRuhanit shel HaRambam." *Eshel Be'er Sheva* 2 (1980).

Brackman, Levi. "The Kabbalah of Deconstruction." Retrieved from www.chabad.org/330018.

Branover, Yirmiyahu, and Yosef Ginzberg. *Mah Rabu Maasekha Hashem: HaMadda VehaTekhnologya BeMishnato shel HaRebbe MiLubavitch.* Jerusalem: Shamir, 2000.

Brody, Baruch. "Jewish Reflections on the Resurrection of the Dead." *The Torah u-Madda Journal* 17 (2016–2017).

Bronfman, Menahem. "Te'ima MiTorato shel HaRebbe." Retrieved from he.chabad.org/2977072.

———. Hamishah Me'afyenim LeDarko HaToranit HaYehudit shel HaRebbe MiLubavitch. Retrieved from www.alysefer.com/the-rebbe-tora/.

———. "Gishat HaRebbe MiLubavitch LeMadda VeTekhnologya: Le'ametz, akh Lehakir BaMigbalot." Retrieved from www.alysefer.com/science-and-technology-teachings-of-the-lubavitcher-rebbe/.

———. "Madua HaRebbe MiLubavitch Koh Hibbev et Torat HaGaon HaRogatchover?" Retrieved from www.alysefer.com/rogatshuver/.

Bronstein, Yosef. "Pre-Messianic Modifications in the Thought of Rav Kook and the Lubavitcher Rebbe." *Hakirah* 23 (2017).

Broyde, Matityahu. "Hovatam shel Yehudim Le'oded Shemirat Mitzvot Benei Noah al yedei Nokhrim." *Dinei Yisrael* 19 (5757–5758).

Buber, Martin. *The Origin and Meaning of Hasidism*. New York: Horizon Press, 1960.

Cohen, Shaye. *From the Maccabees to the Mishna*. Louisville, KY: Westminster John Knox Press, 2014.

Cohen, Yona. "Parashat Mihu Yehudi Garma LeKera BaAm" in *HaRebbe: Sheloshim Shenot Nesiut*. Edited by Hanoch Glitzenstein and Adin Steinsaltz. Jerusalem: Defus Monson, 1980.

Dahan, Alon. *Goel Aharon: Mishnato HaMeshihit shel R. Menahem Mendel Schneerson HaRebbe MiLubavitch*. Tel Aviv: Contento de Semrick, 2014.

———. "Yahaso shel R. Menahem Mendel Schneerson LaTziyonut, LeEretz Yisrael ULeMedinat Yisrael." In *Chabad: Historya, Hagut VeDimmui*. Edited by Jonathan Meir and Gadi Sagiv. Jerusalem: The Zalman Shazar Center, 2016.

———. "Pashut Lomar et HaEmet." *Makor Rishon* (September 2014).

Dalfin, Chaim. *The Seven Chabad-Lubavitch Rebbes*. Northvale, NJ: Jason Aronson, 1998.

Dauber, Jonathan. "The Baal Shem Tov and the Messiah: A Reappraisal of the Baal Shem Tov's Letter to R. Gershon of Kutov." *Jewish Studies Quarterly* 16:2 (2009).

Deutsch, Shaul. *Larger than Life: The Life and Times of the Lubavitcher Rebbe Rabbi Menachem Mendel Schneerson*. New York: Chasidic Historical Productions, 1995.

Dienstag, Israel. "Maimonides on Providence – Bibliography." *Daat* 20 (Winter 1988).

Drob, Sanford. *Kabbalah and Postmodernism: A Dialogue*. New York: Peter Lang, 2009.

Dubov, Nissan Dovid. *To Love A Fellow Jew: The Mitzva of Ahavas Yisrael in Chasidic Thought*. Brooklyn: Sichos in English, 1999. Retrieved from www.chabad.org/2312259.

———. "The Sefirot." Retrieved from www.chabad.org/361885.

Ehrlich, Avrum. *The Messiah of Brooklyn: Understanding Lubavitch Hasidism Past and Present*. Jersey City: Ktav Publishing House, 2004.

Elior, Rachel. *The Paradoxical Ascent to God: The Kabbalistic Theosophy of Chabad Hasidism*. Translated by Jefferey Green. Albany, NY: SUNY Press, 1993.

———. "Messianic Expectations and Spiritualization of Religious Life in the Sixteenth Century." *Revue des Etudes Juives. CXLV,* 1986

———. "Tehiyat HaMeshihiyut BaHasidut Chabad BaMe'a HaEsrim: HaReka HaHistori VehaMisti, 1939–1996." In *Chabad: Historya, Hagut VeDimmui*. Edited by Jonathan Meir and Gadi Sagiv. Jerusalem: The Zalman Shazar Center, 2016.

Elituv, Eliyahu Meir. *Mishnato shel HaRebbe MiLubavitch*. Beitar Ilit, Israel: Meir Elituv, 2012.

Etkes, Immanuel. *The Besht: Magician, Mystic, and Leader*. Translated by Saadya Sternberg. Waltham, MA: Brandeis University Press, 2005.

———. *Rabbi Shneur Zalman of Liady: The Origins of Chabad Hasidism*. Translated by Jefferey M. Green. Waltham, MA: Brandeis University Press, 2015.

Feldi, Yehuda. "Nisayon VeHazara Kelalit Lirot Im Zakhinu," in *HaRebbe: Sheloshim Shenot Nesiut*. Edited by Hanoch Glitzenstein and Adin Steinsaltz. Jerusalem: Defus Monson, 1980.

Feldman, Daniel. *The Right and the Good: Halakha and Human Relations*. Brooklyn: Yashar Books, 2005.

Feldman, Jonathan. *The Power of the Soul over the Body: Corporeal Transformations and Attitudes Towards the Body in the Thought of Nahmanides*. Dissertation. New York: New York University, 1999.

Fox, Marvin. *Interpreting Maimonides*. Chicago: University of Chicago Press, 1990.

Foxbrunner, Roman. *Chabad: The Hasidism of R. Shneur Zalman of Lyady*. Northvale, NJ: Jason Aronson, 1993.

Freeman, Tzvi. "Are All Believers Insane?" Retrieved from www.chabad.org/2539704.

Garb, Jonathan. *The Chosen Will Become Herds: Studies in Twentieth-Century Kabbalah*. Translated by Yaffa Berkovitz-Murciano. New Haven, CT: Yale University Press, 2009.

Gellman, Jerome. "Zion and Jerusalem." In *Rabbi Abraham Isaac Kook and Jewish Spirituality*. Edited by Lawrence Kaplan and David Shatz. New York: New York University Press, 1995.

———. "The Denial of Free Will in Hasidic Thought." In *Freedom and Moral Responsibility: General and Jewish Perspectives*. Edited by C. H. Manekin and M. M. Kellner. Bethesda, MD: University of Maryland Press, 1997.

———. "Hasidic Mysticism as an Activism." *Religious Studies* 42 (2006).

Ginzberg, Levi Yitzhak. "HaRebbe Raayatz Sefirat HaYesod Mehaber Shamayim VaAretz." Retrieved from abc770.org/article_node_1680/.

Glitzenstein, Hanokh. *HaRebbe: Sheloshim Shenot Nesiut*. 1980.

Goldberg, Avraham. *Bittahon Ish: Biurim, Iyunim, VeHe'arot BeSugyat Mitzvat HaBittahon*. Jerusalem: Goldberg, 2002.

Gopin, Shneur Zalman. "Yesh: Shiflut o Bitui LeAtzmut Hashem." *Maayanotekha* 29 (Sivan 5771): 18–23. Retrieved from www.toratchabad.com/Content/Images/uploaded/maynotechPDF/29.pdf.

———. "Mitzvat Ahdut Hashem." *Maayanotekha* 25 (Sivan 5770): 10–17. Retrieved from www.toratchabad.com/Content/Images/uploaded/maynotechPDF/25.pdf.

Gottlieb, Yaakov. *Sekhaltanut BiLevush Hasidi: Demuto shel HaRambam BaHasidut Chabad*. Ramat Gan, Israel: Bar-Ilan University Press, 2009.

———. "HaRebbe VehaRambam." In *HaShevi'i: HaRebbe MiLubavitch Rebbe Menahem Mendel Schneerson*. Jerusalem: Torat Chabad LiVnei HaYeshivot, 2013.

Green, Arthur. "The *Tzaddik* as *Axis Mundi* in Later Judaism." *JAAR* 48 (1977).

Green, Yekutiel. "*Derishot HaRebbe BeAvodat Hashem Gedolot Mishel Admor HaZaken*." Retrieved from www.col.org.il/show_news.rtx?fromAdmin=yes&artID=76283.

Greenberg, Yosef Yitzhak. "*Hakkafot Nashim*." In *Kovetz He'arot UViurim* 899 (Emor 5765). Retrieved from www.haoros.com/Archive/index.asp?kovetz=899&cat=11&haoro=3.

Greenberg, Yisrael, and Yisrael Kaufman. *Besuras HaGeula: The Announcement of the Redemption*. Brooklyn: Vaad L'Hafotzas Sichos, 1998.

Greenwald, Nahum. "Al Kabbalat Mahari Serug BeTorat HaHasidut: 'Reshimu,' 'Malbush,' VehaTzimtzum Shelifnei HaTzimtzum HaRishon BeHasidut Chabad." *Heikhal HaBesht* 31 (Nisan 5771).

———. "Mashma'uta VeGidra shel 'Malkhut' – HaSefira HaAharona." *Heikhal HaBesht* 21 (Kislev 5768).

———. "Mahuta VeGidra shel 'Malkhut' – HaSefira HaAharona." *Heikhal HaBesht* 23 (Tamuz 5769).

———. "Adam Kadmon lefi HaHasidut." *Heikhal HaBesht* 29 (Nisan 5770).

———. "Deveikut VeHitkashrut LeTzaddik lefi Shittat HaHasidut." *Heikhal HaBesht* 30 (Tishrei 5771).

———. "Hashgaha Peratit al pi Shittat HaBesht." *Maayanotekha* 23 (Kislev 5770). Retrieved from www.toratchabad.com/Content/Images/uploaded/maynotechPDF/23.pdf

Gutel, Nerya. "Behira Hofshit: Metziut Retzuya o Mesima Meuletzet." *Hagut BaHinnukh HaYehudi* 3–4 (2002).

Halbertal, Moshe. *Concealment and Revelation: Esotericism in Jewish Thought and Its Philosophical Implications*. Translated by Jackie Feldman. Princeton, NJ: Princeton University Press, 2007.

Hallamish, Moshe. *Mishnato HaIyunit shel R. Shneur Zalman MiLiadi*. Dissertation. Jerusalem: The Hebrew University, 1976.

———. *An Introduction to Kabbalah*. Translated by Ruth Bar-Ilan and Ora Wiskind-Elper. Albany, NY: SUNY Press, 1990.

———. "HaYahas LeUmot HaOlam BeOlamam shel HaMekubalim." *Mehkerei Yerushalayim BeMahshevet Yisrael* 14 (1998).

———. "Yahasei Tzaddik VeEida BeMishnat Rebbe Shneur Zalman MiLiadi." In *Hevra VeHistorya*. Edited by Yehezkel Cohen. Jerusalem: Misrad HaHinnukh VehaTarbut, 1980.

Halpern, Mordechai. "Madda URefua BaTalmud: Shitot Geonim, Rishonim, VeAharonim." In *Refua, Metziut, VeHalakha*. Jerusalem: HaMakhon al Shem Dr. Falk Shlezinger LeHeker HaRefua al pi HaTorah, 2011. Retrieved from www.medethics.org.il/website/index.php/he/research/2012-02-29-11-36-06/2012-03-05-10-08-21/135-assiabook14/1381-science-and-medicine-talmud#ftn22.

Handelman, Susan. "Women and the Study of Torah in the Thought of the Lubavitcher Rebbe." In *Jewish Legal Writings by Women*. Edited by Micha D. Halpern and Chana Safrai. Jerusalem: Urim Publications, 1998.

———. "Putting Women in the Picture: The Rebbe's View on Women Today." Retrieved from www.chabad.org/161694.

———. *Fragments of Redemption: Jewish Thought and Literary Theory in Benjamin, Scholem, and Levinas*. Bloomington, IN: Indiana University Press, 1991.

Harari, Yehiel. *Sodo shel HaRebbe*. Tel Aviv: Yedioth Ahronoth, 2013.

Harvey, Warren. "Peirush HaRambam LeBereshit 3:22." *Daat* 12 (1984).

Heilman, Samuel, and Menachem Friedman. *The Rebbe: The Life and Afterlife of Menachem Mendel Schneerson*. Princeton, NJ: Princeton University Press, 2010.

Heinemann, Yitzhak. *Darkhei HaAggada*. Jerusalem: Magnes Press, 1970.

Ives, Yosef. *Seder HaHishtalshelut: Mavo LeTorat Hishtalshelut HaOlamot VehaSefirot al pi Mishnat Hasidut Chabad*. Brooklyn: Heichal Menachem, 2010.

Idel, Moshe. "The Parable of the Son of the King and the Imaginary Walls in Early Hassidism." In *Judaism: Topics, Fragments, Faces, and Identities in Honor of Rivka*. Edited by Haviva Pedaya and Ephraim Meir. Beersheba: Ben-Gurion University of the Negev Press, 2007.

———. "White Letters: From R. Levi Isaac of Berditchev's Views to Postmodern Hermeneutics." *Modern Judaism* 26 (2006): 169–92.

———. "We Have No Kabbalistic Tradition on This." In *Rabbi Moses Nahmanides (Ramban): Explorations in His Religious and Literary Virtuosity*. Cambridge MA: Harvard University Press, 1983, 31–81.

———. *Kabbalah: New Perspectives*. New Haven, CT: Yale University Press, 1988.

———. *Hassidism: Between Ecstasy and Magic*. Albany, NY: SUNY Press, 1995.

———. "Eretz Yisrael Hi Hiyut MehaBorei: Al Mekoma shel Eretz Yisrael BaHasidut." In *Eretz Yisrael BaHagut HaYehudit BaEt HaHadasha*. Edited by Aviezer Ravitzky. Jerusalem: Yad Yitzhak Ben-Tzvi, 1998.

———. *Messianic Mystics*. New Haven, CT: Yale University Press, 1998.

Illin, Ephraim. "Investing in Israel." Retrieved from www.chabad.org/2336308.

Ish HaYarei. "BeInyan Mashiah min HaHayyim." *Kovetz Mashiah UGeula* 1 (5757): 8–14.

Ishon, Moshe. "HaMatkal shel Chabad" in *HaRebbe: Sheloshim Shenot Nesiut*. Edited by Hanoch Glitzenstein and Adin Steinsaltz. Jerusalem: Defus Monson, 1980.

Jacobson, Simon. *Toward a Meaningful Life: The Wisdom of the Sages.* New York: William Morrow, 2002.

Jacobson, Yoram. "The Land of Israel and Canaan: A Case Study of the Spiritual World of Gur Hasidim." In *The Gift of the Land and the Fate of the Canaanites in Jewish Thought.* Edited by Katell Berthelot, Joseph E. David, and Marc Hirshman. New York: Oxford University Press, 2014.

Jacobson-Maisels, James. "Embodied Epistemology: Knowing through the Body in Late Hasidism." *The Journal of Religion* 96:2 (April 2016).

Kahn, Yoel. *Sugyot BaHasidut: Musagei Yesod BeMishnat Chabad.* Jerusalem: Torat Chabad LiVnei HaYeshivot, 2012.

———. "Mahutam shel Yisrael." *Maayanotekha* 15 (Kislev 5768): 3–10. Retrieved from www.toratchabad.com/Content/Images/uploaded/maynotechPDF/15.pdf.

———. "Afsut HaBeria kelapei HaBorei – Shetei Dargot." *Maayanotekha* 1 (Nisan 5764): 2–8. Retrieved from www.toratchabad.com/Content/Images/uploaded/maynotechPDF/01.pdf.

———. "Matzui VeEino Matzui" (23 Shevat 5772). Retrieved from www.toratchabad.com/מצוי-ואינו-מצוי.

———. "Hasidut UMashiah Hainu Hakh." *Kovetz Mashiah UGeula.* Volume 2 (5757): 3–21.

———. *Gidran shel Mitzvot, Hukkim, UMishpatim BeMishnato shel HaRebbe.* Brooklyn: Kehot Publication Society, 1994.

———. *Mahutam shel Yisrael BeMishnat HaHasidut.* Brooklyn: Heichal Menachem, 2001.

———. "HaHiddush HaMahapkhani Shenithollel BeMatan Torah." *Maayanotekha* 6 (5765): 2–11. Retrieved from www.toratchabad.com/Content/Images/uploaded/maynotechPDF/06.pdf.

———. "Moshe Rabbenu, David HaMelekh, VehaBaal Shem Tov." *Maayanotekha* 25 (5770): 2–7. Retrieved from www.toratchabad.com/Content/Images/uploaded/maynotechPDF/25.pdf.

———. "She'eilat HaBen HeHakham." *Maayanotekha* 24 (5770): 2–9. Retrieved from www.toratchabad.com/Content/Images/uploaded/maynotechPDF/25.pdf.

———. "Ad Delo Yada: Lemaala MeihaYedia." (13 Heshvan 5779). Retrieved from www.toratchabad.com/עד-דלא-ידע-למעלה-מהידיעה.

———. "HaYaad Hasofi shel HaTeshuva." *Maayanotekha* 7 (Elul 5765): 6–15. Retrieved from www.toratchabad.com/Content/Images/uploaded/maynotechPDF/07.pdf.

———. "Bein Yada LeLo Yada." *Maayanotekha* 16 (Adar 5768): 3–12. Retrieved from www.toratchabad.com/Content/Images/uploaded/maynotechPDF/16.pdf

———. "Hu Tziva VeNivrau." *Maayanotekha* 27 (Kislev 5771): 6–11. Retrieved from toratchabad.com/הוא-ציוה-ונבראו.

———. "Sidrat Raayonot Meyuhadim im HaRav Yoel Kahn Shlita." *Kefar Chabad* 556 (21 Tevet 5753).

———. "Sidrat Raayonot Meyuhadim im HaRav Yoel Kahn Shlita." *Kefar Chabad* 558 (6 Shevat 5753).

———. "Eikh Mit'hazkim BeEmuna BeShaa Kol Kakh Hashukha?" *Kefar Chabad* 623 (14 Tamuz 5754). Retrieved from col.org.il/news/29982#full.

Kalmenson, Mendel. *A Time to Heal: The Lubavitcher Rebbe's Response to Loss and Tragedy*. Brooklyn: Ezra Press, 2015.

Kantur, Gay. *HaAkademiya Mekabelet Penei Mashiah* (Israel), 2013.

Kaplan, Aryeh. *Inner Space: Introduction to Kabbalah, Meditation, and Prophecy*. Jerusalem: Moznaim, 1990.

Kaplan, Menahem Mendel. "LeMashma'utam shel Bituyim Setumim BeSihot Horef 5752," *Pardes Chabad* 2 (1997): 43–50.

———. "Zihui Nasi HaDor im Mashiah SheBaDor," *Pardes Chabad* 8 (2002): 139–44.

Kaploun, Uri, and Eliyahu Touger. *As a Father Loves His Only Son: Talks of the Lubavitcher Rebbe on Bitachon*. Brooklyn: Sichos in English, 2010.

———. *In Good Hands: 100 Letters and Talks of the Lubavitcher Rebbe, Rabbi Menachem M. Schneerson, On Bitachon, Trusting G-d*. Brooklyn: Sichos in English, 2005.

Kasher, Hanna. "'Olamkha Tireh BeHayekha' al Hatramato shel HaOlam HaBa LeHayyim Alei Adamot." In *Mehkerei Yerushalayim BeMahshevet Yisrael 21: Kerakh Sefer Zikkaron LeGershom Shalom BiMelot Esrim VeHamesh Shanim LiFetirato* (5767), 415–54.

Kasher, Menahem. *Mefanei'ah Tzefunot*. Jerusalem: Mekhon Tzafnat Panei'ah, 1976.

Kauffman, Tsippi. *BeKhol Derakhekha Dei'eihu: Tefisat HaElokut VehaAvoda BeGashmiyut BeReshit HaHasidut.* Ramat Gan, Israel: Bar-Ilan University Press, 2009.

———. "Hasidic Women: Beyond Egalitarianist Discourse," *BeRon Yahad: Studies in Jewish Thought and Theology in Honor of Nehemia Polen.* Edited by Ariel Even Mayse and Avraham Yizhak Green. Boston: Academic Studies Press (2019), 223–57.

Kellner, Menahem. *Science in the Bet Midrash: Studies in Maimonides.* Brighton, MA: Academic Studies Press, 2009.

———. *Gam Hem Keru'im Adam: HaNokhri BeEinei HaRambam.* Ramat Gan: Israel, Bar-Ilan University Press, 2016.

———. "Maimonides' 'True Religion': For Jews or All Humanity." In *Menahem M. Kellner: Jewish Universalism.* Edited by Hava Tirosh-Samuelson and Aaron Hughes. Boston: Brill, 2015.

Klausner, Yisachar Dov. "LeOlam Yehei Adam Tokho KeVaro," *Torat Nahalat Har Chabad* 79 (Elul 5764).

Klein, Meir. *BeHippus ahar Merkaz HaIggul: HaRetorika shel Madda VeTekhnologya etzel HaRav Menahem Mendel Schneerson.* Master's thesis, Bar-Ilan University Press, 2014.

Kohanzad, Max Ariel. *The Messianic Doctrine of the Lubavitcher Rebbe, Rabbi Menachem Mendel Schneerson.* Dissertation. University of Manchester, 2006.

Koskoff, Ellen. *Music in Lubavitcher Life.* Chicago: University of Illinois Press, 2001.

Koss, Andrew. "War Within, War Without: Russian Refugee Rabbis during World War I." *AJS Review* 34:2 (November 2010).

Kraus, Shmuel. *Nasi VeHasid: Kishrei Rabbotenu Nesi'enu UViMeyuhad shel HaRebbe im Shneur Zalman Shazar UMishpahto.* Kefar Chabad, Israel: Agudat Hasidei Chabad BeEretz HaKodesh, 1999.

Kraus, Yitzhak. *HaShevi'i: Meshihiyut BaDor HaShevi'i shel Chabad.* Tel Aviv: Yedioth Ahronoth, 2007.

———. "Dor HaGeula: Tafkidan shel Nashim BeMishnato shel HaRav Menahem Mendel Schneerson, HaAdmor MiLubavitch." In *Isha, Hava, Adam: Nashiyut Yehudit bein Hitpat'hut LeMesoret.* Edited by Aviva Sharvat. Jerusalem: Rubin Mass, 2008. 145–63.

Kreisel, Howard. "Asceticism in the Thought of R. Bahya Ibn Paquda and Maimonides." *Daat* 21 (1988).

———. *Prophecy: The History of an Idea in Medieval Jewish Philosophy.* Dordrecht, Netherlands: Kluwer Academic Publishers, 2001.

Lamm, Norman. *Torah Lishmah: Torah for Torah's Sake in the Works of Rabbi Hayyim of Volozhin and His Contemporaries.* Hoboken, NJ: Ktav Publishing House, 1989.

———. *The Religious Thought of Hasidism: Text and Commentary.* Hoboken, NJ: Ktav Publishing House, 1999.

———. *The Shema: Spirituality and Law in Judaism.* Philadelphia, PA: Jewish Publication Society, 1998.

———. *Seventy Faces: Articles of Faith.* Hoboken, NJ: Ktav Publishing House, 2002.

Laufer, Mordechai Menashe. "Hineh BaOhel." *Hitkashrut* 205 (*Parashat Korah*, 5758): 10–14. Retrieved from chabad-il.org/hit/hit205.htm.

———. "Mayim SheEin Bahem Sof." *Hitkashrut* 1003 (7 Heshvan 5774). Retrieved from www.chabad.org.il/Magazines/Article.asp?ArticleID=9965&CategoryID=1786.

———. "Adam al HaYare'ah." *Hitkashrut* 191 (22 Adar 5758). Retrieved from chabad-il.org/hit/hit191.htm.

———. "HaBehirot BeYisrael." *Hitkashrut* 95 (28 Iyar 5756). Retrieved from www.chabad.org.il/Articles/Article.asp?ArticleID=1245&CategoryID=786.

———. "HaGra Mehayev Limmud Penimiyut HaTorah." *Hitkashrut* 822 (9 Iyar 5770). Retrieved from www.chabad.org.il/Magazines/Article.asp?ArticleID=6763&CategoryID=1389.

———. *Kelalei Rambam al pi Sihot UMikhtevei Menahem Mendel Schneerson.* Kefar Chabad, Israel: Kehot Publication Society, 1990.

Leibowitz, Aryeh. *Hashgacha Pratis: An Exploration of Divine Providence and Free Will.* Southfield, MI: Targum Press, 2009.

Levin, Feital. *Heaven on Earth: Reflections on the Theology of Rabbi Menachem M. Schneerson, the Lubavitcher Rebbe.* Brooklyn: Kehot Publication Society, 2002.

Levin, Shlomo Dovber. *Toledot Chabad BeRusya HaTzarit.* Brooklyn: Kehot Publication Society, 2010.

———. "HaNevua Le'alter LiGeula." *Kovetz Mashiah UGeula* 7 (5 Tevet 5758).

Lichtenstein, Aharon. "In Clarification of the Trait of *Bittahon*." *De'ot* (1976).

———. *By His Light: Character and Values in the Service of God*. Edited by Reuven Ziegler. Hoboken, NJ: Ktav Publishing House, 2003.

Lipkin, Binyamin. *Heshbono shel Olam*. Lod, Israel: Makhon HaSefer, 2000.

Loewenthal, Naftali. "The Apotheosis of Action in Early Chabad." *Daat* 18 (1987): v–xix.

———. "Midrash in Chabad Hasidism." In *Midrash Unbound: Transformations and Innovations*. Edited by Michael Fishbane and Joanne Weinberg. Oxford, England: The Littman Library of Jewish Civilization, 2013.

———. *Communicating the Infinite: The Emergence of the Chabad School*. Chicago: University of Chicago Press, 1990.

———. "The Baal Shem Tov's *Iggeret HaKodesh* and Contemporary Chabad 'Outreach.'" In *Let the Old Make Way for the New: Studies in the Social and Cultural History of Eastern European Jewry, Presented to Immanuel Etkes*. Edited by David Assaf and Ada Rappoport-Albert. Jerusalem: The Zalman Shazar Center for Jewish History, 2009.

———. "The Neutralisation of Messianism and the Apocalypse." *Jerusalem Studies in Jewish Thought*. Volume 13 (1996).

———. "'Daughter/Wife of Hasid' or 'Hasidic Woman'?" *Jewish Studies* 40 (2000): 21–28.

———. "Spiritual Experience for Hasidic Youths and Girls in Pre-Holocaust Europe – A Confluence of Tradition and Modernity." In *Jewish Spirituality and Divine Law: The Orthodox Forum Series*. Edited by Adam Mintz and Lawrence Schiffman. Jersey City: Ktav Publishing House, 2005, 407–54.

———. "Women and the Dialectic of Spirituality in Hasidism." In *Within Hasidic Circles*. Edited by Emmanuel Etkes, David Assaf, Israel Bartal, Elchanan Reiner (pp. 36–59). Jerusalem: The Bialik Institute, 1999.

———. *Hasidism Beyond Modernity: Essays in Chabad Thought and History*. Liverpool, England: Littman Library of Jewish Civilization, 2020.

Lorberbaum, Yair. *Tzelem Elohim: Halakha VeAggada*. Jerusalem: Schocken Books, 2004.

———. "Reflections on the Halakhic Status of Aggada." *Dinei Yisrael* 24 (2007).

Magid, Shaul. "Associative Midrash: Reflections on Hermeneutical Theory in Rabbi Nahman of Bratslav's *Likkutei Moharan*." In *God's Voice from the Void*. Edited by Shaul Magid. Albany, NY: SUNY Press, 2002.

———. *Hasidism on the Margin: Reconciliation, Antinomianism, and Messianism in Izbica and Radzin Hasidism*. Madison, WI: University of Wisconsin Press, 2003.

Majesky, Shlomo. *The Chassidic Approach to Joy*. Brooklyn: Sichos in English, 1995.

Margoliyot, Ron. *Mikdash Adam: HaHafnama HaDatit VeIzuv Hayei HaDat HaPenimiyim BeReshit HaHasidut*. Jerusalem: Magnes Press, 2004.

Matt, Daniel. "Ayin: The Concept of Nothingness in Jewish Mysticism." In *Essential Papers on Kabbalah*. Edited by Lawrence Fine. New York: New York University Press, 1995.

———. *Zohar: The Book of Enlightenment*. New York: Paulist Press, 1983.

Mayse, Ariel-Evan. "The Sacred Writ of Hasidism: Tanya and the Spiritual Vision of Rabbi Shneur Zalman of Liady." In *Books of the People*. Jerusalem: Straus Center for Torah and Western Thought and Maggid Books, 2017.

Meislish, Yosef Yitzhak. *HaTekufa VehaGeula BeMishnato shel HaRebbe MiLubavitch*. Kefar Chabad, Israel: Agudat Hasidei Chabad, 2005.

Meitles, Yisrael. "HaLamdanut HaFilosophit shel Rebbe Yosef Rozen BiDerashotav shel Rebbe Menahem Mendel Schneerson." Master's thesis. Ramat Gan, Israel: Bar-Ilan department of Jewish philosophy, 2013.

———. *Hakirot VeHitbonenut Hasidiyot BaHiddushim shel HaGaon HaRogotchivi*. Israel, 2016. Retrieved from shorturl.at/dmFKN.

Mendele. "Kevod Kedushat Gisi Admor Shlita" (11 Shevat 5776). Retrieved from chabad.info/magazine/120404/.

Miller, Chaim. *The Thirteen Principles of Faith: Principles 8 and 9: The Torah*. Brooklyn: Kol Menachem, 2007.

———. *Turning Judaism Outward: A Biography of the Rebbe, Menachem Mendel Schneerson*. Brooklyn: Kol Menachem, 2014.

Mindel, Nissan. *Rabbi Schneur Zalman*. Brooklyn: Chabad Research Center and Kehot Publication Society, 1969–73.

———. *Rabbi Schneur Zalman Volume 2: The Philosophy of Chabad*. Brooklyn: Chabad Research Center and Kehot Publication Society, 1974.

Mundshine, Yehoshua. "HaTo'ar Shlita Ahar Histalkut." *Kovetz Mashiah UGeula* 4 (5757).

———. "Nevua, Hakhrazot, Pirsumim, VeOd." Retrieved from web.archive.org/web/20180710163736/shturem.net/index.php?section=blog_new&article_id=160.

———. *Iggeret LeYedid*. Retrieved from web.archive.org/web/20210228092833/www.shturem.net/index.php?section=blog_new&article_id=127.

———. "Kavim LeDemuto shel Shakran." Retrieved from www.docdroid.net/mhbI7uU/document.

Munk, Eli. *The Seven Days of the Beginning*. Jerusalem: Feldheim, 1974.

Nir, Elhanan. "Ezrat HaGufim Ein BeYadeinu: Yahas R. Shneur Zalman MiLiadi LeMezukot Parnassa VeInyenei Olam HaZeh." *Asif* 1 (5774): 190–205.

Oberlander, Boruch. "Hakafot shel Simhat Torah LeNashim." In *Kovetz He'arot UViurim* 902 (*Hukkat* 5765). Retrieved from www.haoros.com/Archive/index.asp?cat=11&haoro=7&kovetz=902.

Oberlander, Boruch, and Elkanah Shmotkin. *Early Years: The Formative Years of the Rebbe, Rabbi Menachem M. Schneerson, as told by documents and archival data*. Brooklyn: Jewish Educational Media and Kehot Publication Society, 2016.

Pedaya, Haviva. "Eretz shel Ruah, VeEretz Mamash." In *Eretz Yisrael BeHagut HaYehudim BiYemei HaBeinayim*. Edited by Moshe Hallamish, Aviezer Ravitzky. Jerusalem: Yad Yitzhak Ben-Tzvi, 1991.

Piekarz, Mendel. *HaHanhaga HaHasidit: Samhut VeEmunat Tzaddikim BeAspaklaryat Sifruta shel HaHasidut*. Jerusalem: The Bialik Institute, 1999.

Pilma, Shlomo. *Shalmei Todah: Sukkot*. Bnei Brak, 5766.

Polen, Nehemia. Review of *The Rebbe: The Life and Afterlife of Menachem Mendel Schneerson*, by Samuel C. Heilman and Menachem M. Friedman. *Modern Judaism* 34:1 (February 2014).

———. "Miriam's Dance: Radical Egalitarianism in Hasidic Thought." *Modern Judaism* 12:1 (1992).

Polter, Dovid Shraga. *Listening to Life's Messages: Adapted from the Works of the Lubavitcher Rebbe*. Brooklyn: Sichos in English, 1997. Retrieved from www.chabad.org/81776.

———. *Learning Something From Everything*. Brooklyn: Sichos in English, 2015. Retrieved from www.chabad.org/2980121.

Posner, Zalman. "The Splintering of Chabad," *Jewish Action* (Fall 2002). Retrieved from s3.amazonaws.com/ou.org/publications/ja/5763/5763fall/JUSTBETW.PDF.

Preiss, Avraham Aharon. "Kuntres VeAhavta LeRe'akha Kamokha." In *Torat HaAdam LeAdam: Kovetz Torani BeMitzvot shebein Adam LeHavero*. Vol. 4 (5762).

Presco, Tomer. "HaMashiah HaAvud shel Chabad." *Tekhelet* 36 (summer 2009). Retrieved from tchelet.org.il/article.php?id=448.

Rapoport-Albert, Ada. "God and the Zaddik as the Two Focal Points of Hasidic Worship." *History of Religions* 18:4 (May 1979).

———. "On Women in Hasidism: S. A. Horodetsky and the Maid of Ludmir Tradition." In *Hasidic Studies: Essays in History and Gender* (pp. 318–67). Liverpool: The Littman Library of Jewish Civilization, 2018.

———. "The Emergence of a Female Constituency in Chabad." In *Hasidic Studies: Essays in History and Gender* (pp. 368–426). Liverpool: The Littman Library of Jewish Civilization, 2018.

———. "From Women as Hasid to Women as 'Tsadik' in the Teachings of the Last Two Lubavitcher Rebbes." In *Hasidic Studies: Essays in History and Gender* (pp. 427–70). Liverpool: The Littman Library of Jewish Civilization, 2018.

Rapoport, Chaim. *The Afterlife of Scholarship: A Critical Review of "The Rebbe" by Samuel Heilman and Menachem Friedman*. Oporto Press, 2011.

———. "Limmud Gemara LeNashim." In *Kovetz He'arot UViurim* 1056 (Tamuz 5773).

———. "Shittat Rabbenu *zy"a* BiDvar Harigat Kinnim BeShabbat BaZeman HaZeh." *He'arot UViurim* 878 (11 Nisan 5764).

———. "Chabad's Messianism." *Tekhelet* 41 (summer 2010). Retrieved from azure.org.il/include/print.php?id=549.

Ravitzky, Aviezer. "Eretz Hemda VeHarada: HaYahas HaDu'erkhi LeEretz Yisrael BeMekorot Yisrael." In *Eretz Yisrael BaHagut HaYehudit BaEt HaHadasha*. Edited by Aviezer Ravitzky. Jerusalem: Yad Yitzhak Ben-Tzvi, 1998.

———. *Messianism, Zionism, and Jewish Religious Radicalism*. Translated by Michael Swirsky and Jonathan Chipman. Chicago: Chicago University Press, 1996.

Reitzes, Menahem Mendel. "LeShitateih BeMishnato." *HaShevi'i: HaRebbe MiLubavitch Rebbe Menahem Mendel Schneerson*. Jerusalem: Torat Chabad LiVnei HaYeshivot, 2013.

Robinson, Ira. "'Practically I am a Fundamentalist': Twentieth-Century Orthodox Jews Contend with Evolution and Its Implications." In *Jewish Tradition and the Challenge of Darwinism*. Edited by Geoffrey Cantor and Marc Swetliz. Chicago: Chicago University Press, 2006.

Ross, Tamar. "Mussag HaElokut shel HaRav Kook." *Daat* 8 (1982): 109–28.

Roth, Areil. *Keitzad Likro et Sifrut Chabad*. Ramat Gan, Israel: Bar-Ilan University Press, 2017.

Rozen, Yitzhak. "HaHalal BeMishnato shel HaRebbe MiLubavitch." *Yodei Bina* 2 (5764). Retrieved from archive.li/Ux34c#selection-217.0-217.3.

Rubin, Eli. "Immanent Transcendence: Chassidim, *Mitnagdim*, and the Debate about *Tzimtzum*." Retrieved from www.chabad.org/2306809.

———. "Everywhere Revealed How Everyone, Children Included, Can Apprehend the Unknowable Essence of G-d." Retrieved from www.chabad.org/2788328.

———. "Absent Presence: The Revelatory Trace (*Reshimu*) of Divine Withdrawal." Retrieved from www.chabad.org/3004920.

———. "Covert Luminosity: The *Reshimu*, the *Kav*, and the Concretization of Creativity." Retrieved from www.chabad.org/3201311.

――. "Intimacy in the Place of Otherness: How Rationalism and Mysticism Collaboratively Communicate the Midrashic Core of Cosmic Purpose." Retrieved from www.chabad.org/2893106.

――. "Beyond Borders: International Jewish Renaissance." Retrieved from www.chabad.org/2619814.

――. "A Bridge Across Infinity: How the Revelation at Sinai Changed the Cosmic Map." Retrieved from www.chabad.org/2122647.

――. "The Rebbe: An In-Depth Biography of a Scholar, Visionary, and Leader." Retrieved from www.chabad.org/2619397.

――. "Do Chabad Teachings Say Anything About the Mind-Body Problem?" Retrieved from www.chabad.org/3432275.

――. "Emancipation, Multiculturalism, and the Perpetual Passover: Rabbi Menachem M. Schneerson's Vision of Modern Progress as Religious Opportunity." Retrieved from www.chabad.org1816231.

――. "Education, Postmodernism, and the Challenge of Tradition: Reflections on the Enduring Relevance of Rabbi Menachem M. Schneerson's Religious Thought." Retrieved from www.chabad.org/1885173.

――. "Making Chasidism Accessible." Retrieved from www.chabad.org/2080148.

――. "The Essence of Chassidism: A Message Beyond the Medium." Retrieved from www.chabad.org/2619816.

――. "On the Eternal Unfolding of the Transcendent Torah: Torah Hermeneutics in the Thought of R. Menachem M. Schneerson." Retrieved from www.chabad.org/1723583.

――. "Living with the Times: Rabbi Schneur Zalman of Liadi's Oral Teachings." Retrieved from www.chabad.org/2087776.

――. "Integrity and Peace: The Torah, the People, and the Land." Retrieved from www.chabad.org/2619817.

――. "Divine Zeitgeist: The Rebbe's Appreciative Critique of Modernity." Retrieved from www.chabad.org/2973252.

――. "Universal Responsibility: Faith, Education, and Humanity." Retrieved from www.chabad.org/2619821.

――. "The Second Refinement and the Role of the Tzaddik." Retrieved from www.chabad.org/3041292.

———. "Torah on the Radio: Using Technology for Positive Purpose." Retrieved from www.chabad.org/2619815.

———. "Lisbon, 1941: The Messiah, the Invalid, and the Fish." Retrieved from www.chabad.org/2236391.

———. "The Idealistic Realism of Jewish Messianism." Retrieved from www.chabad.org/2766417.

Saiman, Chaim. "Legal Theology: The Turn to Conceptualism in Nineteenth-Century Jewish Law." *Journal of Law and Religion* 21 (2006).

Schatz-Uffenheimer, Rivka. *Hasidism as Mysticism: Quietistic Elements in Eighteenth-Century Hasidic Thought*. Translated by Jonathan Chipman. Princeton, NJ: Princeton University Press, 1993.

———. "Anti-Spiritualizm BaHasidut: Iyunim BeMishnat R. Shneur Zalman MiLiadi." *Molad* 20 (1963).

———. "LeMahuto shel HaTzaddik BaHasidut: Iyunim BeTorat HaTzaddik shel R. Elimelekh." *Molad* 18 (1960).

Segel, Yosef Yitzhak. *Osher VeOsher: Idud HaYeluda BeMishnat HaRebbe Melekh HaMashiah* (Petah Tikva, Israel: Makhon Mamash, 5775). Retrieved from shorturl.at/kmnC3.

Schochet, Jacob Immanuel. "The Philosophy of Lubavitch Activism." *Tradition* 13:1 (Summer 1972).

———. *Chasidic Dimensions*. Brooklyn: Kehot Publication Society, 1990.

Scholem, Gershom. *Major Trends in Jewish Mysticism*. New York: Schocken Books, 1954.

———. *Origins of the Kabbalah*. Translated by Allan Arkush. Princeton, NJ: Princeton University Press, 1987.

———. *The Messianic Idea in Judaism*. New York: Schocken Books, 1971.

———. *On the Kabbala and Its Symbolism*. New York: Schocken Books, 1965.

———. "Teuda Hadasha LeToldot Reshit HaKabbala," *Mehkerei Ha-Kabbala* 1 (1998).

Schreiber, Daniel. "Asymptotically Approaching God: 'Kedusha' in the Thought of Ramban." *Tradition* 44:1 (2011).

Seeskin, Keeneth. *Searching for a Distant God: The Legacy of Maimonides*. New York: Oxford University Press, 2000.

Shapira, Yehuda Leib. "BaDerekh el HaTamtzit." In *HaShevi'i: HaRebbe MiLubavitch Rebbe Menahem Mendel Schneerson*. Jerusalem: Torat Chabad LiVnei HaYeshivot, 2013.

Shatz, David. "A Framework for Reading *Ish ha-Halakha*." In *Turim: Studies in Jewish History and Literature Presented to Dr. Bernard Lander*. New York: Touro College Press, 2007.

———. "The Muted Messiah: The Aversion to Messianic Forms of Zionism in Modern Orthodox Thought." In *Rethinking the Messianic Idea in Judaism*. Edited by Michael Morgan and Steven Weitzman. Bloomington, IN: Indiana University Press, 2015.

Sheilat, Yitzhak. *Bein HaKuzari LeRambam: Limmud Mashveh*. Maaleh Adumim, Israel: Hotzaat Sheilat, 2010.

———. "Segulat Yisrael: Shitot HaKuzari VehaRambam," *Ma'aliyot* 20 (5759).

Shochet, Azriel. "Al HaSimha BaHasidut." *Tziyon* 16 (1951).

Shohat, Refael. *Olam Nistar BeMamadei HaZeman: Torat HaGeula shel HaGra MiVilna, Mekorotehah, VeHashpaatah LeDorot*. Ramat Gan, Israel: Bar-Ilan University Press, 2008.

Shwartz, Dov. *Mahshevet Chabad: MiReshit Ve'ad Aharit*. Ramat Gan, Israel: Bar-Ilan University Press, 2010.

Sillman, Yohanan. "Artziyutah shel Eretz Yisrael BeSefer HaKuzari." In *Eretz Yisrael BeHagut HaYehudim BiYemei HaBeinayim*. Edited by Moshe Hallamish and Aviezer Ravitzky. Jerusalem: Yad Yitzhak Ben-Tzvi, 1991.

Slifkin, Natan. *The Challenge of Creation: Judaism's Encounter with Science, Cosmology, and Evolution*. Ramat Beit Shemesh, Israel: Zoo Torah, 2006.

Socher, Abraham, "The Chabad Paradox," *The Jewish Review of Books* (Fall 2010). Retrieved from jewishreviewofbooks.com/articles/233/the-chabad-paradox/.

Sofer, Yehezkel. *BeMai KaMiflegei: HaPulmus HaMeshihi BiTenuat Chabad*. Israel: Yehezkel Sofer, 2012.

———. "Mikhtav LeYedid Shehihmitz." Retrieved from old2.ih.chabad.info/#!g=1&url=article&id=47066.

Sokol, Moshe. "Maimonides on Freedom of the Will and Moral Responsibility." *Harvard Theological Review* 91:1 (1998): 25–39.

———. "Attitudes Toward Pleasure in Jewish Thought: A Typological Proposal." In *Judaism Examined*. New York: Touro College Press, 2013.

Solomon, Aryeh. *The Educational Teachings of Rabbi Menachem M. Schneerson*. Northvale, NJ: Jason Aronson, 2000.

Soloveitchik, Joseph. *And from There You Shall Seek*. Translated by Naomi Goldblum. Jersey City: Ktav Publishing House, 2008.

———. *The Lonely Man of Faith*. Jerusalem: Maggid Books and OU Press. 2012.

Stein, Daniel. "The Limits of Religious Optimism: The Hazon Ish and the Alter of Novardok on *Bittahon*," *Tradition* 43:2 (2010).

Steinsaltz, Adin Even-Israel. *My Rebbe*. Jerusalem: Maggid Books, 2014.

Stern, Aryeh. "Segulat Yisrael LeDaat HaRambam." *Tzohar* 25 (5766).

Stern, Sacha. *Jewish Identity in Early Rabbinic Writings*. Leiden; New York: Brill, 1994.

Tauber, Yanki. "Love According to the Rebbe." Retrieved from www.chabad.org/2756.

———. "The Divine and the Human in Torah." Retrieved from www.chabad.org/2625316.

Telushkin, Joseph. *Rebbe: The Life and Teachings of Rabbi Menachem Mendel Schneerson, The Most Influential Rabbi in Modern History*. New York: Harperwave, 2014.

Tishby, Isaiah. "The Messianic Idea and Messianic Trends in the Growth of Hasidism." *Tziyon* 32 (1967).

Tzuriel, Moshe. "Halakha o Aggada." *HaMa'ayan* 18:1 (Tishrei 5738).

———. "Halakha o Aggada – Hemshekh." *HaMa'ayan* 18:2 (Tevet 5738).

Urbach, Ephraim. *Hazal: Pirkei Emunot VeDeot*. Jerusalem: Magnes Press, 1975.

———. "The Talmudic Sage: Character and Authority." *Journal of World History* 11 (1968): 116–47.

Veil, Eldad. "Tehilatah shel Tekufat HaNashim: Nashim VeNashiyut BeMishnato shel HaRebbe MiLubavitch." *Akadamot* 22 (Nisan 5769): 61–85.

Weiner, Herbert. "Farewell, My Rebbe: Thoughts on Leadership." *New Jersey Jewish News*, June 2, 1994. Retrieved from www.chabad.org/66879.

———. "Alone with Moses." Retrieved from www.chabad.org/524749.

Weiss, Yosef. "Torat HaDeterminizm LeRav Yosef Mordekhai Lerner MeIshbitz." In *Sefer Yovel LeYitzhak Be'er*. Edited by S. Ettinger,

Sh. Baron, B. Z. Dinur, I Halpern. Jerusalem: HaHevra HaHistorit HaYisraelit, 1960.

Wexler, Philip, and Rubin, Eli. "'The Lower Half of the Globe': Kabbalah and Social Analysis in the Lubavitcher Rebbe's Vision for Judaism's American Era." In *Kabbalah in America: Ancient Lore in the New World.* Edited by Brian Ogren (Leiden; Boston: Brill, 2020), 292–315.

Wiederblank, Netanel. *Illuminating Jewish Thought: Explorations of Free Will, the Afterlife, and the Messianic Era.* Jerusalem: Maggid Books, 2018.

Wineberg, Shalom. *Healthy in Body, Mind, and Spirit, Based on the Teachings of the Lubavitcher Rebbe.* Brooklyn: Sichos in English, 2005.

Wineberg, Yosef. *Lessons in Tanya* (5 volumes). Translated by Levy Wineberg. Brooklyn: Kehot Publication Society, 1987.

Wiskind-Elper, Ora. *Hasidic Commentary on the Torah.* London: The Littman Library of Jewish Civilization, 2018.

Wodzinski, Marcin. "Women and Hasidism: A 'Non-Sectarian' Perspective." *Jewish History* 27 (2013).

Wolf, Eliyahu. *Ehad Haya Avraham: Avraham Pariz, Sippuro shel Hasid UMekushar.* Kefar Chabad, Israel: Sifriyat Eishel, 2001.

Wolf, Shalom Dovber. *Inyano shel Mashiah: Likkut Sikum VeSiddur Ikkarei Torato shel Kevod Kedushato Admor Melekh HaMashiah Shlita Odot Inyano shel Mashiah VeHaGeula HaSheleima.* Tel Aviv: Agudat Talmidei 770, 2016.

Wolf, Zev. *El Neshei UVnot Yisrael: HaIsha, HaEm VehaBat HaYehudiya BiRe'iyato shel HaRebbe MiLubavitch.* Brooklyn: Kehot Publication Society, 2001.

Wolfson, Elliot. *Open Secret: Postmessianic Messianism and the Mystical Revision of Menahem Mendel Schneerson.* New York: Columbia University Press, 2009.

———. *Circle in the Square: Studies in the Use of Gender in Kabbalistic Symbolism.* Albany, NY: SUNY Press, 1995.

———. "By Way of Truth: Aspects of Nahmanides' Kabbalistic Hermeneutic." *AJS Review* 14:2 (1989).

———. "Achronic Time, Messianic Expectation, and the Secret of the Leap in Chabad." In *Chabad Hassidism: History, Thought, Image.*

Edited by Jonathan Meir and Gadi Sagiv (pp. 45–86). Jerusalem: The Zalman Shazar Center, 2016.

———. "Assaulting the Border: Kabbalistic Traces in the Margins of Derrida." *Journal of the American Academy of Religion* 70:3 (September 2002): 475–514.

———. "Chabad Messianism and the Present Future." Retrieved from www.youtube.com/watch?v=dM-yQeuLS3w.

Wolpo, Shalom Dov. *Daat Torah BeInyenei HaMatzav BeEretz HaKodesh.* Kiryat Gat, Israel: 1981.

———. *Bein Or LeHoshekh: Medinat Yisrael – At'halta DiGeula o Hoshekh Kaful UMekhupal.* Kiryat Gat, Israel: 2005.

Yaakovson, Yaakov. "BiMevuhei HaAyin VehaYesh: Iyun BeSifrah shel Rahel Elior, 'Torat Ahdut HaHafakhim.'" *Kiryat Sefer* 68 (5758).

———. "Torat HaBeria shel R. Shneur Zalman MiLiadi." *Eishel Be'er Sheva* 1 (5736): 307–68.

Yerushalmi, Shalom, Yossi Elituv, and Aryeh Ehrlich. *BeRega HaEmet: HaRebbe MiLubavitch VehaDialog HaBit'honi HaMedini im Mekablei HaHahlatot BeYisrael.* Hevel Modi'in, Israel: Kinneret, Zemorah Bitan, 2017.

Zalmanov, Shmuli. *The Rebbe's Children.* CreateSpace Independent Publishing, 2016.

Zaltzman, Hillel. "The Miracle of Stalin's Death." Retrieved from www.chabad.org/2995717.

The fonts used in this book are from the Arno family

Maggid Books
The best of contemporary Jewish thought
from Koren Jerusalem